Books to Help Children Cope with Separation and Loss

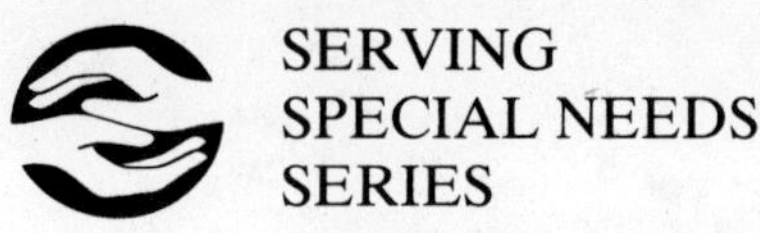

SERVING SPECIAL NEEDS SERIES

ACCEPT ME AS I AM
Best Books of Juvenile Nonfiction on Impairments and Disabilities
by Joan Brest Friedberg, June B. Mullins, and Adelaide Weir Sukiennik

BOOKS FOR THE GIFTED CHILD
by Barbara H. Baskin and Karen H. Harris

BOOKS FOR THE GIFTED CHILD, Volume 2
by Paula Hauser and Gail A. Nelson

BOOKS TO HELP CHILDREN COPE WITH SEPARATION AND LOSS, 2nd Edition
by Joanne E. Bernstein

BOOKS TO HELP CHILDREN COPE WITH SEPARATION AND LOSS, Volume 3
An Annotated Bibliography
by Joanne E. Bernstein and Masha Kabakow Rudman

CHALLENGING THE GIFTED
Curriculum Enrichment and Acceleration Models
by Corinne P. Clendening and Ruth Ann Davies

CREATING PROGRAMS FOR THE GIFTED
A Guide for Teachers, Librarians, and Students
by Corinne P. Clendening and Ruth Ann Davies

HEALTH, ILLNESS, AND DISABILITY
A Guide to Books for Children and Young Adults
by Pat Azarnoff

HIGH/LOW HANDBOOK
Books, Materials, and Services for the Problem Reader
by Ellen V. LiBretto

MORE NOTES FROM A DIFFERENT DRUMMER
A Guide to Juvenile Fiction Portraying the Disabled
by Barbara H. Baskin and Karen H. Harris

NOTES FROM A DIFFERENT DRUMMER
A Guide to Juvenile Fiction Portraying the Handicapped
by Barbara H. Baskin and Karen H. Harris

PARENTING THE GIFTED
Developing the Promise
by Sheila C. Perino and Joseph Perino

SERVING THE OLDER ADULT
A Guide to Library Programs and Information Sources
by Betty J. Turock

Books to Help Children Cope with Separation and Loss

An Annotated Bibliography

VOLUME 3

Joanne E. Bernstein
and
Masha Kabakow Rudman

R. R. BOWKER
New York

Published by R. R. Bowker Company,
a division of Reed Publishing (USA) Inc.

Printed and bound in the United States of America

Library of Congress Cataloging-in-Publication Data

Bernstein, Joanne E.
Books to help children cope with separation and loss / Joanne E. Bernstein and Masha Kabakow Rudman.
p. cm.
Includes indexes.
ISBN 0-8352-2510-0 (v. 3)
1. Separation (Psychology)—Juvenile literature—Bibliography.
2. Loss (Psychology)—Juvenile literature—Bibliography.
3. Bereavement—Psychological aspects—Juvenile literature—Bibliography. 4. Bibliotherapy for children. I. Rudman, Masha Kabakow.
Z7204.S45B47 1989
[BF575.G7]
016.1559'3—dc19 88-7591
CIP

ISBN 0-8352-2510-0

For Florence and Leonard Bernstein,
wonderful in-laws
J.E.B.

For my husband, Sy, whose steadfast support
and rational perspective enable me to survive
M.K.R.

Contents

Preface

Life is a series of losses, large and small.

Loss is the complex set of reactions with which we respond to the changes and separations we meet through the years.

Loss never ceases to challenge us, for with every change—even those we have elected—and, indeed, in every manifestation of growth, there are adjustments to be made.

For each of us life begins with a major loss experience as we are thrust from the warmth of our mothers' wombs. Soon thereafter, we are likely to be confronted with another loss situation, when a new sibling enters the family and we no longer occupy center stage.

And the loss cycle continues. As youngsters, we endure separation from our parents when a baby-sitter comes; we suffer loss when we go off to school, leaving the family circle for new horizons.

Among the most shocking of loss experiences are those that alter the structure and functioning of family life. Responses to the tragic separations caused by death, divorce, desertion, illness, and war are of lasting impact. Experiences that are often a response to the initial separation—living with stepparents, adjusting to foster care or adoption, and sometimes shifting for oneself—also carry with them the elements of separation and loss.

These and related topics are among the subjects treated in the books for young people annotated in this, the third volume of *Books to Help Children Cope with Separation and Loss.* This book, like the previous volumes, is a bibliographic guide to fiction and nonfiction books for young people, ages 3 to 16, on the themes of separation and loss. It is designed to provide adult guides—those parents, librarians, teachers, and counselors who have the opportunity to influence the lives of children—with as much information as they need to choose books suitable for the children they serve. Increasingly, these adults are aware of the burgeoning supply of books dealing with loss situations and they want to know more about them—where to find them, how they can be used to help young people handle their problems, which ones deal with the particular problems that they are interested in, and which ones are good literature. *Books to Help Children Cope with Separation and Loss,* Volume 3, is offered in response to this continuing need.

Following the format of the first two volumes, the book is divided into three parts. Part I contains two essays from the 1983 volume that have been updated, as well as two new essays that are intended to aid the adult guide in helping children cope with their feelings of loss. Chapter 1, "Separation and Loss," discusses the significance and manifestations of separation and loss in child development, elucidating children's concepts and reactions, and summarizing recent theories and research in the field. Information and ideas on how to use children's books for therapeutic value are provided in Chapter 2, "Bibliotherapy: A Means of Helping Young People Cope with Separation and Loss." This chapter is devoted to the principles and practices of bibliotherapy, with specific reference to the use of bibliotherapy in dealing with problems of loss. It includes a review of research findings and a discussion of the limitations of bibliotherapy, a topic of continuing interest and debate in professional literature. Chapter 3, "Strategies and Applications of Bibliotherapy," by Patricia A. Edwards, Center for the Study of Reading, University of Illinois at Urbana-Champaign, demonstrates further how the principles of bibliotherapy can be applied in practice. The primary audience is teachers, but the ideas and procedures can be used and adapted for use by librarians, psychologists, and others. Chapter 4, "Writing about Loss: Notable Authors Discuss Their Work," by the authors and Marie Louise Sorensen, provides in-depth interviews with noted writers of children's literature whose works frequently have loss themes. How do these writers choose their subjects for fiction or nonfiction works? In what manner do they approach the material? How do they envision their audiences? These and the other questions in the interviews result in a varied, rich look behind the scenes of children's literature.

Part II, the major portion of the book, is an annotated bibliography of 606 books (none of which were discussed in the 1977 or 1983 volumes) for young people relating to the experiences of separation and loss. Entries are arranged in thematic categories, such as death, divorce, serious illness, and adoption, and each entry includes a descriptive, evaluative annotation, noting the book's strengths and weaknesses both as literature and as a bibliotherapeutic medium. Users of this book are urged to read the Introduction for a detailed description of book selection criteria and notes on the arrangement of annotations.

For those who wish further guidance in the study of separation and loss and bibliotherapy, an extensive series of revised and updated bibliographies citing selected references for adult guides is included in Part III. The "Appendix: Directory of Organizations" lists names and addresses of organizations providing services or literature to adult guides and children coping with problems of separation and loss. These organizations include a variety of self-help groups, as well as professional and voluntary organizations. As an aid to users, five separate indexes are included providing access to the text by author, title, subject, interest level, and reading level.

Acknowledgments

A work of this magnitude requires many resources and many helpers. Our thanks go to:

The notable authors who kindly agreed to be interviewed about their opinions regarding loss and separation. Patricia A. Edwards who contributed Chapter 3. All the publishers who generously contributed their books so that this volume could be as complete as it is. Students in our courses, especially Megan Jasper and Margarita Bonifaz, for their perceptive comments and for bringing a number of books to our attention. Marie Louise Sorensen who helped locate information, organized strategies, and provided constant professional acumen. Irene Taafaki for her sensitive and analytical reading. Rudi Dornemann for his research, countless hours of work at the computer, and his unfailing sense of humor. Dee McWilliams, JanetLee Beswick, Jean Scott, and Mary Ann Ryan for their solid and reliable work. Nancy Boland for her research skills, good humor, and quick and competent assistance. Marie Cora for her patience in transcribing tapes and her general availability. And Rich Lussier and Eric Heller for saving Masha's life several times when the computer failed.

A special thanks is also given to the staff at the Jones Library, Amherst, and the University of Massachusetts Reference Room for their amiable and professional assistance. Also, the staff at the Brooklyn College Library and the Children's Book Council, New York.

Finally, we thank our families, especially Masha's grandson Sam for providing inspiration.

Introduction

In the years since the publication of the 1977 and 1983 volumes of *Books to Help Children Cope with Separation and Loss,* publishers' lists have brought a virtual torrent of books on loss subjects. The body of literature produced for children and young adults has included thousands of titles on topics such as war, death, divorce, stepsiblings, adoption, desertion, and family alienation. A variety of criteria and considerations were applied in selecting titles for inclusion in this volume.

Criteria for Book Selection

The initial step in preparing this bibliography was an exhaustive search of such notable book review media as *School Library Journal, Publishers Weekly, Kirkus, The Horn Book, Bulletin of the Center for Children's Books,* and *The New York Times Book Review* for titles of books published from 1983 to 1988 that appeared suitable for inclusion. Each "candidate" for inclusion in this bibliography was carefully read and critically examined in light of the following questions:

What is the book's scope and nature?

Are all the statements within the book accurate?

If not, is the misinformation or objectionable attitude one that an adult might wish to clarify or correct?

What is the book's emotional impact?

How is religion handled if at all?

Is the book worthwhile from a literary viewpoint, satisfying readers on the verbal and emotional levels and, possibly, on the spiritual level?

Does the book appear to be straight fiction or nonfiction based on fact—or is it heavily biased?

The 606 books included here were chosen because they have lasting value, are good literature, and continue to circulate widely among children. Over 90 percent of the books in this third volume cover the years 1983 to 1988. The second volume, originally published in 1983, covers the years 1955 to 1982 and is still in print.

In each case, primary emphasis was placed on the utilization of literary criteria. These criteria include excellence of character, worthiness of theme, beauty of style, and appropriateness of plot.

Underlying all criteria are the compilers' firm conviction that books selected for any bibliography for children should serve to connect people with all other people, reinforcing the universality of the human condition in all its aspects. Only then can there follow interaction between reader and printed word. And only if there is involvement will the world of the reader enlarge with the insight that others have shared the same problems and found a variety of solutions.

Other Considerations

As in any process of selection some exceptions were made to the accepted rule. Adult guides who select books for particular youngsters should have adequate information about those books that contain damaging misinformation or may lead to false hopes on the part of a child, as well as those that are concerned with controversial subject matter or are biased. Thus, certain recent books that enjoy considerable popularity and wide circulation have been included, even though, in the opinion of the compilers, they are poorly written and may be of questionable therapeutic value. In such cases, the compilers have taken care to point out pertinent strengths or weaknesses in the annotations.

Other books have been listed even though they have not been reviewed in any of the aforementioned sources. Since many loss experiences are avoided as subjects for discussion in our culture, these books either were not welcomed in the reviewing media or were dismissed as inappropriate or lacking in interest for young people. Other times, the books were not reviewed widely because they were products of small, specialized presses (for example, those dealing primarily with feminist, ethnic, or family issues). Consequently, such books are often not generally available to the public, even though they may be of considerable value in helping young people accept separation and loss. Therefore, one of the purposes of this bibliography has been to locate such books, many of which were published before the time was ripe, and to give them new light.

The adult guide may find it useful to consider some additional factors that entered into selecting titles. The explosion of realistic books for children during the last decade has brought to the fore a multitude of books that deal with hushed-up topics; it is in these books that the themes of loss are confronted in terms and settings that are actually met by children today. The child who is groping toward an understanding of his or her own feelings of loss will most clearly identify with the characters in such books, and thus a major goal of bibliotherapy will have been met.

The emphasis in selection has been on current books published between 1983 and 1988. A major purpose has been to sift through the current surfeit of these realistic books and to identify those that are of surface or momentary value and those that, because of their universality of theme and superior literary treatment, are likely to be sought after by young readers. In addition some high-quality books by small and large publishers appearing prior to 1983 are now included.

In order to create a unified reference work and one that is manageable in terms of size, this volume has, for the most part, confined its scope to realistic works. It includes only a sampling of fantasy, history, and biography and a few folktales, even though separation and loss are recurring themes in many of these works. Similarly, short stories and poetry have usually been omitted.

In general, more books have been selected for the younger age groups. This is partly because readers between the ages of 12 and 16 usually read adult fare in addition to works written primarily for young people. For the younger readers especially, works that approach loss through the symbolic world are plentiful. Many books in which animals reflect the emotions of human beings gain response from small children.

The works of certain authors are seen repeatedly in the bibliography, not because of any particular bias toward these authors but because certain writers seem to be frequently drawn to themes of loss and the challenge of change as it affects the human condition. Some of these authors have been interviewed and their points of view about their work appear in Chapter 4.

It will be noticed that the number of books listed within each category varies considerably. Some groups boast more than 100 books, while others contain fewer. Also, the distribution of books for each age group in the several categories is rather skewed. These reflect the overabundance of books in some areas and the dearth in others. In both cases, careful selection was necessary.

It will also be noted that since the first volume (1977), when death exploration was a predominant theme, the focus of publishers' lists seems to have shifted. Besides death, the topics highlighted in their catalogs today are stepparents, stepsiblings, child abuse, and serious illnesses, such as AIDS and anorexia nervosa. Also, realistic books for young people have become more specialized. Having adequately investigated the usual aspects of birth, death, and divorce many times over, authors and publishers are now attending to special needs. Thus, we have books related to specific deaths, such as the death of a friend or the death of a relative, and we have books about specific illnesses, such as cancer and diabetes, including books written or adapted from the writings of children under ten years of age. Some books are guides for seeking professional help with family problems. Often, these specialized books have been published by small publishing houses, but increasingly the larger publishers are issuing titles designed to meet specific interests and needs in a heterogeneous society.

Another noteworthy trend includes the recent publication of many nonfiction books about loss subjects. These range from discussion of drugs and drug abuse to coping with death and divorce.

In addition, there is a gray area in publishing today. Some books seem to straddle the fence between fiction and nonfiction. Clearly written with the primary aim of informing and helping, these books, nonetheless, in format resemble fiction. The reader is asked to follow along with the life problems of imaginary characters. In compiling the bibliography, it was often difficult to classify such books. At times, the compilers used the classification systems that the publishers of the books used. Other times, it became more a matter of the compilers' reactions to the tone of the book. How much did the book focus on one character, thereby more closely resembling fiction? What portion of the book, regardless of the presence of a character, consisted of instructions to the reader and his or her parent?

Arrangement of Annotations

The annotations are arranged in a number of categories in accordance with the loss experience that is the focus of attention. In fiction, for instance, this would be the key loss faced by the protagonist. When a book includes more than one important loss experience, the additional loss experiences as well as the primary category are given in the Subject Index. Within each category, books have been alphabetically arranged by the author's surname.

Each annotation includes current bibliographic data—author, title, illustrator, city of publication, publisher, publication date, number of pages, and availability in hardbound or paperback editions—and a classification of the book as fiction or nonfiction. Because prices change so rapidly, book prices are not given. Users are advised to see the latest edition of *Books in Print* for price information.

An interest level has been established for each book by taking into account three factors: various studies of children's interests, the publishers' own assessments, and the evaluation of the compilers. Each book has also been assigned a reading level, arrived at with the use of the Fry Readability Graph. (See Edward Fry, "A Readability Formula That Saves Time," *Journal of Reading* 11 [April 1968]: 513–516, 575–578; and Edward Fry,

"Fry's Readability Graph: Clarifications, Validity, and Extension to Level 17," *Journal of Reading* 21 [December 1977]: 242–252.) This graph, developed by Edward Fry of the Rutgers University Reading Center, makes it possible to estimate the readability of a children's book simply and quickly, with accuracy within a grade level. These guidelines have been followed: Where sample passages have indicated that readability is reasonably consistent throughout the book tested, a single grade has been used to denote the readability level. Where sample passages have indicated that readability varies considerably throughout the book, a range of grades denotes the variation in difficulty.

Readability level descriptions are but one guideline for selection and should be viewed in terms of their limitations as well as their usefulness. On the one hand, because readability formulas such as Fry's are based on word and sentence length, they do not take into account a book's ideas, which may be expressed in very simple language but actually involve very sophisticated concepts demanding larger life experience for understanding. On the other hand, children will read complex material on subjects that interests them or in which they have a good background. They can often display remarkable ability to decode and comprehend long words and complicated passages. Also, if the subject does not interest them, or if they lack experience with it, easier material may sometimes become insurmountable. For these reasons, it is wise to think of readability levels as loose, rough estimates, to be used with flexibility and active judgment.

It is hoped that, taken in combination, the information on interest and reading levels will be useful to the adult guide in choosing the appropriate book for each child. It should be noted that some books with an interest level appropriate for young children have a much higher reading level because they are meant to be read aloud. By the same token, some books with a high interest level and a low reading level are appropriate for older children with limited reading ability and for younger children with a wide range of interests. As a further aid to adult guides, separate indexes grouping books by interest level and reading level are included.

PART I

Using Books to Help Children Cope with Separation and Loss

1

Separation and Loss

It is incumbent on each of us to learn about separation and loss simply because, whether we will it or not, so much of life is given over to coping with these crises. The way in which we, as adult guides, handle loss is one indicator of the way in which we handle all aspects of life. If we ignore feelings of loss, it is not because we haven't handled them. We have merely falsely implied that they will take care of themselves. Rabbi Earl Grollman, a noted expert on divorce, death, and other separations, has said, "Mental health is not the denial of tragedy but a frank acknowledgement of it. Better to say to child or adult, 'I could cry, too' rather than, 'There, there, you mustn't cry.' "[1] For both adults and children, there is no genuine protection from trauma.

At the same time, to help children cope with their losses adequately, adult guides need information. They need clarification of children's concepts of separation, for they differ from those of adults. Such information will yield insights into children's behavior. They also need to know about the range of possible reactions to separation so that they can determine if the youngsters are mourning appropriately or, in repressing mourning, are planting seeds that may lead to increased trouble and even continued problems in adulthood. Finally, adult guides need to determine ways to aid youngsters actively through periods of loss.

The separations mentioned within these pages are stressful for adults. Imagine how much more stressful they are for children, who live in an environment vastly different from that of their adult guides—in years, in intellectual growth, in psychological insight, and in ability to cope emotionally. For many years, youngsters are dependent on others for their practical needs. Magical thoughts and imagination are some of the means they use to explain the complex world they live in. Without the life experience with which adults develop resources for coping with crises, they are more vulnerable when loss strikes. They ask their questions with greater fear of the unknown. Why is this happening to me? Why am I different from other children? Why must I hurt this way? When will it end?

Children's Concepts of Separation

Children's ideas about temporary and permanent separation develop slowly, on a par somewhat similar to their ideas concerning time. Those who have dealt with children in any capacity recognize that until about the age of nine, youngsters do not properly estimate durations of time. Nor do they firmly grasp what being old or young truly means.

The Beginnings

The concept of temporary separation begins with awareness of alternate states of wakefulness and sleeping. Infants in cribs begin to see a pattern—they will be alone for a period and then a comforting figure will return. The next development for babies is their playful investigation of this curious phenomenon of absence and presence. Games of "peek-a-boo, I see you" are evidence of children's desire to master this concept. Other youthful experiments include the common act of throwing toys from cribs and high chairs. For as long as other family members will participate in the game, babies do not tire of it.

Next, the young investigators take on the concept of permanent separation. They have noticed that some things do *not* reappear, ever. "How amazing," they reflect, as they fiddle with the functions of trash can pedals and toilet flush systems. Actually, they ponder a phenomenon instinctively called "all-gone" by parents for generations. And when allowed safe opportunity to examine temporary and permanent separation in a context of games, youngsters pave the way toward a healthy concept of that most shocking of permanent separations, death.

A Difference of Degree

Children's concepts of death are integrally related to their ideas about all other permanent separations, for the bereavement felt in related loss situations, such as divorce, desertion, and other instances, is of the same kind suffered after the death of someone close. The difference is one of degree, not kind. To understand this, think of the way people react on losing a treasured piece of jewelry. A low feeling, perhaps resembling psychosomatic sickness, may linger for a day or two, reappearing with renewed intensity at the next appropriate time to wear the jewelry. This is bereavement. After death or divorce, somatic symptoms such as fatigue and listlessness and emotional manifestations such as depression and sadness last much longer. They are far more intense and may be somewhat more complex, but the difference remains primarily of degree, not kind. The ways in which individuals cope with all types of permanent separation are tied to their concepts of death.

Before Age Five

The person who is probably best known for research concerning children's concepts of death is Maria Nagy,[2] whose investigations involved groups of Hungarian children. Her findings reveal that children under five years of age (an approximation) usually do not see death as irreversible. Unable to separate death from life, they see life in death. They often view the dead as living in some limited state, either within the grave or in another place. The psychological reason behind such perceptions is that young children know that they themselves are alive. Viewing the entire world through egocentric glasses, they cannot imagine anything so totally unlike themselves. For this reason, very young children will defend the idea that mountains are alive. Those children under five who are able to assimilate the idea of physical death may think that to be dead is to be asleep or on a journey. At this age death is likely to be viewed as temporary, gradual, and/or reversible. We never completely overcome this immature concept of death. Adults bear remnants of this attitude when using the term "rest in peace." Perhaps this is a comforting example of retaining the concepts of a child. But at other times, bearing remnants of years gone by is not so comforting, as indicated when those bereaved by death become enveloped in turmoil if it rains on the grave weeks after a burial.

Ages Five through Nine

Between the approximate ages of five and nine, children begin to see death as a permanent state. In Nagy's study, children in this age group were likely to personify death, perhaps seeing it as an angel or as an old man. Children often feel that they cannot see the "death man," but that the person carried off sees him for a brief moment. In this stage, the existence of death is accepted, but it must be externalized so that one may escape the grasp of the death carrier. The externalization of death can be readily seen in children who hide under the bed after hearing of a death. What they express is a need for protection from the rampage of death; perhaps it is contagious.

Gerald Koocher, an American investigator, has examined children's concepts of death in the United States.[3] His findings agree with those of Nagy, with one interesting twist. In the five to nine age range, none of the American children mentioned either a "death man" or "death angel."

Instead, they wanted to know all they could about procedures regarding survival, death, and burial. Koocher feels that this is akin to the idea of protection. His subjects are saying, "Perhaps my knowledge will keep me safe. If not, I will go through the experience with the support of my own background and skill. It will be as painless as possible because I have prepared."

Ages Nine and Up

Finally, at age nine or thereafter, children acknowledge freely that death is permanent and universal. They now know that one cannot escape the "death man," for there is no such being. Death is a natural part of life, governed by laws. Although the concepts of children age nine and over regarding permanent separation parallel those of adults, their emotional reactions are not those of adults.

Young People's Reaction to Separation

Separation is a universal, necessary part of life. Without separation, it is impossible to develop individual personality, make choices, or mature. Still, throughout life there remains an important drive for attachment, interdependency, and contact.

A crucial task of the first two years of life is to develop strong enough bonds with a parent (or parent figure) so that separation can succeed in the toddler period and beyond. How to separate and still maintain the connection is one of the main issues for young children, indeed for the rest of our years. In going off to a baby-sitter, grandparent, or teacher, young children unconsciously ask themselves if they will be any less significant if they allow these other individuals into their circle. Do they have enough identity to carry on through this separation?

If, in their bonding, children find a way to carry a consistent internal picture and memory of the loved parent within themselves (this phenomenon is called object constancy), they will be better able to bridge the separation. At times, failure to adapt to a normal separation experience, such as going away to camp or college, really is an echo of earlier inadequate or overindulged bonding and earlier failures to separate. One of life's central struggles is to maintain an appropriate balance between attachment and self-actualization, between dependence and independence, and between connectedness and the establishment of identity. This seesaw between closeness and distance continues to challenge every human being.

In recent years, aspects of grief and mourning have become subjects for study by psychiatrists, doctors, the clergy, hospital staffs, psychologists, educators, and others. In exploring this new field, called thanatology, investigators have found that reactions to separation are fairly predictable, involving a range of emotions that are reported time and again. The following is an overview of these reactions. If children do not react in all the ways listed, do not be overly concerned. Some people do not respond in the "usual order of things." In fact a usual order of things may not truly exist. For example, some children may respond to a loss by becoming quiet or wanting to be alone; others may become silly. Some may cry a lot, others hardly or not at all. No one response is the correct one. What's more, there is no timetable for grief, after which people should be able to put the event "behind them."

What is of essence after a major loss experience is that there be *some* change in habits or response—that is, youngsters not ignore the impact of the experience but react to it in some way. The loss experience is not just an event taking place in one moment in time. It is an ongoing experience that must be grappled with for years or even a lifetime.

Shock

When first confronted with a significant separation, many people respond with a dazed feeling. "Oh, no," a young girl may wail, after a parent announces plans to remarry. "You can't do this to me!" In the days that follow, nothing has meaning; daily chores and responsibilities are barely carried out; if done at all, they are accomplished while her mind is concentrated elsewhere.

Somatic Symptoms

Acute grief is often accompanied by bodily symptoms. Common manifestations of bereavement are shallowness of breath, fatigue accompanied by inability to sleep, and lack of appetite. There are many other possibilities. Sudden physiological changes can be explained to children, so that they will realize that these changes are a normal part of life.

Denial

Childhood mourning has been described by Gilbert Kliman.[4] The first step in the mourning process is testing and accepting the reality of the loss. Until children meet the irreversibility of the separation numerous times, they will not be convinced of its finality. For example, one child instinctively runs up to the bedroom, expecting to find the father who has left the mother. Another absentmindedly sets a place at dinner, only to be reminded once again about a death or separation. A third child sets up a bargaining scheme in her head: "If I do all my homework and never argue with Mommy, maybe you'll come back." The parent doesn't return no matter what the child does, and so the bargain is eventually proven false.

Underlying both children's and adults' denial is intense wishing, also magical thinking. In our wish to control the event, our minds impose a new, more satisfying set of circumstances so things will go our way. Denial fades as the loss sets in, however, it may not disappear completely and can be accepted as such. Like many emotions surrounding our deepest experiences, denial can suddenly appear, an unexpected guest, long after the loss has ostensibly been integrated. For example, a young woman whose father died when she was an adolescent finds at her wedding, eight years later, that she is feeling dazedly incomplete. She discovers that she is absentmindedly "looking" for her father that day, for in her heart he should be there.

Anger, Guilt, and Depression

Separation is often followed by reactions of anger. It is a justifiable response and quite normal. Young people may rail against other family members or berate bystanders, simply because they haven't gone through the same loss. For example, one youngster deliberately picked a fight with her best friend, severing the relationship, because she could no longer bear visiting a house where there were two parents.

Sometimes anger is an attempt to do the past over, thereby changing it. Thus a child might do everything within imagination to try to get thrown out of a foster placement, repeating the abandonment trauma in hopes that this time the emotions will be mastered.

Anger may also be directed at self, in the form of guilt. "Why did I always say fresh things? Why was I always so nasty?" Youngsters, even more than adults, blame themselves for what befalls them. It may be difficult to convince them that a grandfather died because he was old, not because unpleasant things were said. Nor will youngsters easily accept the intervention of bad luck or fate in their lives, being unable to fully imagine events without a reason. And, they think, the reason *must* concern them. Thus, the truck didn't simply careen down the block, suddenly killing their dog. *They* must have done something careless. Guilt is sometimes greater in accidents. We do not feel we can control disease, but accidents may be viewed as preventable.

Youngsters often do not recognize that mean thoughts exert no influence on actual happenings. For them, a teenage uncle may have joined the army and gone far away because the child wished he would drop dead—that wish made long ago, when the uncle was teasing one ill-equipped to answer back.

For many people, anger is foisted upon God. "What did I do? Why is God doing this to me?" The cruel, unwanted twists of life are difficult to fathom; wrath against the Supreme Being is a common, normal response.

Fantasies of reunion or return to old situations are especially intense if children feel guilty about circumstances before the change. Even love can be a source of guilt, as exemplified by the parent who remarries. When the child responds to the stepparent with warmth, he or she might feel pangs of disloyalty to the absent biological parent. Sometimes, in reaction to conflict, not knowing which side to identify with, a child may withdraw or become hostile. Actually this is a response to the pain of depriving oneself of needed attachments.

Being egocentric, youngsters may see an event as the manifestation of an adult's wish to abandon. They ask themselves if they were loved. If they were, how could they be deserted in this unnatural way, they ponder. In reaction to their own emotional development, they hold onto daydreams of reunion longer than they might. At the very least, this lengthens the period of denial. If carried farther, perhaps youngsters act on their desires. In the extreme, guilt and longing may appear as suicidal tendencies.

Depression has been termed anger turned inward. Youngsters coming to terms with the finality of change often feel depressed. A lackluster dullness may seem to pervade for a while. Some children feel helpless, even hopeless, as they are drained of emotion. It is difficult for them to realize that they are not alone in their emptiness, and the depression may intensify.

Embarrassment

For many children separation is a source of embarrassment—and a difficult one at that. They know they've done nothing wrong—it's not their fault that their parents are divorced, or that their mother died. Yet they feel awkward when asked about it, or speak of it only when they must, or are humiliated every time it comes up. They wonder why this is so and react with additional guilt.

Fear

It is natural that youngsters who confront a loss experience should fear further such experiences. If one relative dies, will another? If a school year has been marked by one teacher leaving after another, can security be found in the teacher presently in the classroom? If the natural parents gave up their child for adoption, might the adoptive parents decide to do the same?

Some children react with action instead of talk. Some may pick themselves up bodily and run away from their anxieties. Others, in attempts to master the trauma, may need to play out the scenes repeatedly, trying to understand through dramatic play. Still others may respond with a crisis of lost self-esteem and identity; fearing deprivation of their love object endangers their integrity and they may fall apart.

Underlying most of these fears is the basic question, "Who will take care of me?" As loss is mastered in stages, it is a good idea to allow children to touch base with the important adults in their lives in times of need. A call from the child to the parent at work, a drop-in visit from the child to a favorite teacher from days gone by, a note in the child's lunch box—these ways to keep in touch help allay anxieties.

Curiosity and Need to Master

Children are curious about death and other loss experiences. Both those who have been directly affected and those who have not are highly interested. They do not shy away until they are taught that the sad aspects of existence, particularly death, are considered by many adults to be improper subjects for discussion and investigation.

Children's dramatic play may reflect death and other loss themes. Whenever one group of six-year-olds got together, their play seemed inevitably to get around to acting out a traumatic event in one of the youngster's lives, the imprisonment of a brother. Day after day the scenario was acted out. The role-play was an effort to come to terms with the pain of loss.

Other youngsters have great interest in looking at and touching dead birds and animals. They may kill insects. Such play, instead of being morbid preoccupation, is also a way to master feelings of loss, in this case, the permanence and irreversibility of death.

Children need to confront their losses and that confrontation will help them toward mastery of the event. As we are aware, children often master the environment through actions and making something concrete rather than through words. We can help them by allowing them their dramatic representation for as long as it is necessary and by facilitating that play by providing materials—paints, puppets, blocks, games, dolls, and so forth. Even teenagers may need concrete ways to explore emotional events, and their card games and sports activities may serve as a way to reenact the troublesome situation. Adult guides need to reflect on reasonable bounds as well. Children need the dramatic play and concrete learning opportunities. However, if a child keeps playing out the same scenario day after day, week after week and the action does not change, or if a child has an inordinate interest in killing animals to see what happens, perhaps this child is not working out the behavior through play. A professional consultation should be considered.

Sadness

Along with the other feelings and reactions described, it is common for youngsters to feel sad after a separation—to cry and let it out. But children's sadness is often not like that of those more mature. This difference, called the "short-sadness span" by Martha Wolfenstein,[5] is often a source of consternation to the adults who observe it without understanding. When youngsters experience loss, they feel deeply unhappy for a while, but then they quickly replace their distress with industrious, joyous pursuits. The adult is often shocked at the behavior, which resembles lack of feeling. Actually, according to Wolfenstein, the child becomes preoccupied with normal living only because the sadness is so huge that it would be overwhelming and intolerable to continue to experience it. One child in Wolfenstein's study group said the following would occur if children allowed their full feelings to surface:

> They would cry and cry. They could cry for a month and not forget it. They could cry every night when they went to bed and dream about and dream about and the tears roll down their eyes and they won't know it and they were thinking about it and tears just running down their eyes at night while they are dreaming.[6]

It is understandable that youngsters would hesitate to relinquish control. After all, they have spent all their years in quest for control—in toilet training, diminished outbursts, and the development of conscience. It is hard now to let go, no matter what the provocation might be.

Absent or Delayed Mourning

When children do not react at all to a significant separation, they often displace their feelings onto another event. One might be surprised to see sudden and bitter tears over a death on a television show. Mourning may be delayed if the significant adults in children's lives consciously or unconsciously indicate that loss is shameful and that mourning must be limited.

If mourning continues to be delayed, or seems absent altogether, it constitutes a danger signal for the family and others. Those who suffer in silence plant seeds for future, continued pain. It is in the expression of grief that the pain is exorcised. Without its expression, it remains—a nagging, inexplicable depression against which battle must continually be waged.

In youngsters, unexpressed grief may surface in many possible manifestations, ranging from academic failure to juvenile delinquency, from sullen withdrawal to promiscuity, from fear of being alone to unwillingness to make friends.

If, in the face of trauma, mourning remains absent or delayed throughout childhood, it can interfere with normal adult life. Those children who will not allow their emotions direct expression are in effect saying, "This event has hurt me so much I can never again let anything touch me." Remaining fearful of rejection and abandonment, those who cannot mourn may shy away from the fulfillment of love relationships. Coming to grips with the inevitability of loss and expressing reactions to those losses when they come enable human beings to survive them. Only then do they become fully available to risk going on with the joys of living.

Helping Children Cope

One must ask why, if loss experiences are so inevitable and universal, they are ignored in almost all school curricula. Few adults living today have had formal training with which to meet whatever changes life will hold. There are several reasons.

Until recently, little was known about loss experiences. As the major and most significant loss area, death was taboo, and so research focused neither on death nor on related loss subjects. Another reason is that today's youth has been falsely called a deathless generation. Most youngsters have two parents throughout childhood. Separated from their grandparents by hundreds of miles, the deaths of older relatives can appear as remote incidents, without emotional effect. And if there should be a death within the immediate family, technical advances are such that the person rarely dies at home. Children are deliberately and specifically excluded from hospitals. In addition, today's children live in megalopolises, unable to see the natural life and death cycle of a farm.

American society has been one of great promise. In our culture, death and other separations have come to be looked on as unnatural events, perhaps even sins. In a system that can send people to the moon, why can't we master disease, old age, and the final mystery of death? We're embarrassed, but to pretend we're not, we hide those who remind us, the ill and aged, in segregated facilities, hesitating to answer questions about them.

But we cannot fool ourselves. We are not without death, and we are not without loss. About 1 in 20 young people loses a parent through death by age 18. Approximately one out of three marriages ends in divorce. And one family in five moves yearly. News of losses of this magnitude cannot be kept from youngsters. If they do not undergo these traumas themselves, surely they hear of the losses of neighbors and schoolmates.

Honesty about Loss Experiences

Children look to adults for guidance. Those adults aid youngsters best if they are honest—honest about the fact that along with life's ecstasies go life's agonies, and honest about the nature of those agonies.

Children want to know. They want to know about divorce: Who decides whom the children stay with? Will they get a stepparent? Will it constitute disloyalty to the natural parent if they love their stepparent? They want to know about cemeteries: what they are, why we need them, and what happens there. Honest information about these and other loss situations helps youngsters to master the facts of their existence.

Children deserve honesty without euphemism or unnecessary complication. If told a dead person went to sleep, many youngsters fear going to sleep. Likewise, if parents unnecessarily make a baby-sitting separation into a trauma by sneaking out on children, fear is the result. Finally, it is unjust to make children angry or fearful of God, as often happens when youngsters are told God "took" someone in death. "What kind of God is this?" they ask. "And who will He take next?" Some religious groups, however, focus positively on the love of God, which is with people both in life and in death.

It takes years for youngsters to master concepts of permanent separation. If children are not told anything about a loss situation, they are left with only their own fantasies, which can be worse than the reality. The message becomes "This topic is too dreadful to talk about at all." To sabotage children's efforts to understand seems unfair, whether by omission or euphemism. Likewise, children deserve explanations of the confusing aspects of the media. In cartoons, animals and people may be electrocuted or thrown from cliffs, yet they get up to do battle once more, seemingly unscarred. The number of losses in newscasts also presents a dilemma—in their enormity, the tragedies depicted may become meaningless. Adult guides can play a role in keeping children's concepts of reality on keel by being on hand to discuss issues as they arise.

Aware of death, divorce, and other separations, children are naturally fearful. They may ask if they will be abandoned. Honest replies are called for. Many children have been left distraught, after being boldly reassured that their parents would never die or divorce, only to have it happen. Life has no pat assurances.

Explanations to children need not be lengthy and should be couched in terms geared to their ability to understand. Children are more concerned with how events affect them than causes, but it is important to establish an atmosphere of openness early. Even bearing in mind children's needs to make everything "all better," false hopes are diminished by open discussion.

Bruce Danto, psychiatrist and head of Detroit's Suicide Prevention Center, has said about response to suicide:

> Kids are the most lied-to group of people next to the Internal Revenue Service. . . . Rather than grieving and working out the problems as a family, they are generally shunted away and almost never told the truth.[7]

Although these remarks refer to suicide, they could easily refer to other losses—divorce, adoption, and so forth—perhaps in lesser degree.

When approaching an impending or a current change, children benefit from being prepared. They should be told in advance. They need to be given an idea of how their routines and living style will be restructured with the change. Most of all, they need reassurances of family affection. Sometimes parents and other adult guides must explain the change repeatedly, cognizant that difficult emotional material may not be absorbed or may be distorted. Besides honesty, no matter how cruel, the best gift children can be given in times of stress is personal time.

Grief Must Be Expressed

Each time children are allowed to express feelings of loss, their mastery over the irreversibility of permanent separation becomes more complete. For adult guides to enable this to happen, they must not deny youngsters' grief or protect them from hurt. It is unwise to brush over the feelings, trying to thrust the experience ever so quickly into the past. It is better to acknowledge children's feelings by reflecting them back to them, for example, "I know you are (scared, worried, angry, hurting, and so on)." When adults quickly remove a dead pet from view, they keep an experience in mastery away from children. Looking at it, perhaps touching it, will create a lasting impression of death's finality. If they go the next step and swiftly replace the pet, they announce that loved ones are quickly replaceable, almost interchangeable. Again, children are cheated of opportunities to express and master feelings. In addition, young people sense and assimilate the dismay and shame of their guides.

Youngsters need help as they go through the process of mourning. Kliman elucidates three stages.[8] In the first, testing and accepting the reality of loss, youngsters need to be allowed to have the painful experiences. Each time they look for the absent person, they are reminded. Willingness to discuss the experience will enable youngsters to bring it out in the open. This can be achieved when adults talk about feelings they've had.

The second stage is working over and coming to terms with memories related to the loss. For example, one youngster wants to look at photographs of his beloved aunt who has moved across the country. Another wants to hear and rehear stories about the times shared with a deceased grandmother. In sharing memories with children, adults state that it is permissible to talk about loss. If they make sure to bring up some of the bad times along with the good, youngsters are prevented from developing idealized pictures of people gone by. Those times gain perspective.

The third stage, according to Kliman, involves the cultivation of substitute object relationships. For example, a child who has lost a mother begins to gravitate to a particular aunt at family functions or enjoys warm rapport with a teacher at school.

Adults often wonder if children should attend funerals. A funeral service has several functions: It is a way of saying good-bye. It is also a way of reinforcing the reality of permanent separation. At funeral services participants also share and release feelings among family, friends, and members of the community. Psychologists feel that funeral attendance is far more beneficial than protection, for fantasies are often worse than the real thing. If children experience vivid reality, subsequent fantasies of reunion will be less intense. The funeral also takes place early in the mourning process and sets the tone of sharing for subsequent stages of bereavement. The difference between deliberate exclusion and an invitation to share in family sorrow can mean the difference between children who hide grief and those who are able to talk about feelings. In sharing feelings with another person, children gain release. They also realize they are not alone in their problems.

Children of any age can safely be permitted to attend funerals of immediate family members if they want to go, and it is recommended that children age seven or more be encouraged to attend the funerals of close relatives so that they can set the stage for later sharing. Children should be given an overview of what they can expect to experience before the funeral itself—the room can be described, the likely content of the service, if and how the body will be viewed. It is further recommended that a relative or friend who is well known to each child but not one of the primary grievers be assigned to care for the child. That person's assignment is to follow the child's lead, letting him sleep at the service if that is what he must do, getting up and leaving with her if that is what she must do.

Children need to know that it is permissible to feel unhappy. They also need to know that even in their grief they can enjoy themselves—this, too, is permissible. They need to see the nature of mourning: At one moment, one family member may need comforting, while another seems unscathed and becomes the source of comfort. Then the seesaw shifts and the comforter may need to be comforted.

In seeing and being part of the mourning process, children find out one of life's truths: While part of a group, each of us is alone—sadly, inevitably, alone—separate. In keeping with this idea, it is unfair to expect children to play a role, acting out an adult's world view. Thus, if the adult's philosophy implies being courageous in the face of loss, that approach shouldn't be imposed on others. Each person must find his or her own approach and philosophy.

Adult guides can help children express emotions by allowing youngsters to follow their own bent, by allowing them to act age-appropriate (instead of parentifying them), and by maintaining as much order and consistency as possible amid disruption.

Awareness

Adult guides will be helpful if they are aware—aware of their own pain, rejection, and isolation; aware of differences between themselves and children; aware when outside help is needed; and aware of avenues for obtaining help.

Several significant differences exist between the responses of adults and children to separation. Children lack adult means for resolving crisis in every sphere—economic, emotional, and social. Youngsters cannot themselves make the decision to leave an unbearable situation, electing to change schools, move, or live with a new family. Adults are more apt to make these choices for them, choices that all too often result in the continuation of the loss cycle for children, as they move into new and unfamiliar situations, while at the same time attempting to cope with the original bereavement.

Children do not have the experiential perspective with which to evaluate, subjectively and objectively, what happens to them. As noted earlier, youngsters lack the notion of chance. What is more, the number and variety of relationships that adults build over the years is unavailable to children. For adults, these become avenues for problem resolution. Couched within the confines of a singular, insulated, nuclear family, youngsters can rarely take advantage of wider horizons.

Youngsters are also more likely to be deficient in using the language of emotion. Unable to say, "I am in pain," children are more likely to act out in puzzling ways or to develop somatic symptoms of distress. Finally, children often do not realize that help is available if pain is expressed. They imagine they must suffer in silence.

Some adult guides have found the following ideas beneficial: (1) talking about troubling behavior at a calm time, not when it is occurring; (2) helping children find the words for their pain by giving their emotions names, while at the same time trying not to intimidate, for example, a divorced woman discussing her boyfriend with her son: "You seem to pout when I go out with Tom. I could be wrong, but I wonder if you pout because you feel left out"; (3) encouraging outside adults to be involved with the loss situation as it affects the child, for example, sending condolence cards, sharing memories, visiting; and (4) setting up a time at appropriate intervals (daily, weekly, whatever) to discuss the situation. At such times family members could work toward honest discussion that neither goes out of control nor bottles up emotion.

It is the obligation of adult guides to recognize signs that bereavement presents a crisis worthy of outside intervention. Adults should consider professional help if:

a youngster has pretended absolutely nothing has happened

schoolwork takes a dramatic decline or a youngster develops a phobic fear of school

news of a death or other significant loss was kept from a youngster for a long time or if that youngster was told lies

a youngster threatens suicide

a youngster panics frequently

a child frequently physically assaults others

a youngster could not get along with the family member who is gone or gets along poorly with the family members who remain

suicide is a cause of death

a youngster becomes deeply involved with drugs

a child begins committing serious socially delinquent acts

a youngster is totally unwilling or unable to socialize with other children

any family member is depressed for a lengthy period

there is physical assault, uncontrollable anger, or incapacitating fear in the family

the family seems overwhelmed by the event/problem

Psychotherapy can be beneficial. The goals of therapy will likely include some or all of the following: finding ways to express feelings about the loss situation, clarifying fantasies and their meanings and diminishing distortions, minimizing self-destructive behavior and fears, enriching communication patterns in central relationships, and finally healing wounds and gaining a perspective for the future that is hopeful.

The choices in treatment today are varied and rich. Therapy can be either short term, usually revolving around resolution of a crisis, or it can be long term, aiming at clearing up deeper, long-standing problems. People can seek individual, group, or family therapy. Each mode has its own benefits, individual therapy affording the client time and a new, neutral but supportive relationship for only the client, for example. In the so-called human laboratory of a group, adults or children can learn how they interact and use what they learn to improve their outside relationships. And in family therapy, the entire system of functioning can be examined and strengthened.

As there are many choices for mode of treatment, therapists have different training. An effective therapist can be a psychiatrist, psychologist, clinical social worker, pastoral counselor, psychiatric nurse practitioner, family therapist, and so forth. Their outlooks can differ, too. Some may stress cognitive therapy, looking at present behavior patterns first, then attitude. Others may stress psychodynamics, looking at how past life events have shaped thought and behavior patterns, aiming for insight that can lead to behavioral change. Still others may look at family systems, investigating how several generations may contribute to the present balance of family roles and how those roles might change for improved functioning.

In choosing a therapist, it is important to ask what formal training the person has and what approach will be taken to the problem. What is equally important as the training or the outlook, however, is a good relationship with the therapist. It has been shown that all the methods can lead to an improvement if two factors are present: The client feels understood and the client feels the therapist cares.

In the past decade an important source of comfort has come onto the scene, supplementing psychotherapy or being sought instead. This is the self-help group, which could also be called the "shared help" group, for the thrust is one of helping oneself through an environment in which others are helped by one's presence. Frank Reissman, founder of the National Self-Help Clearinghouse, estimates that 5,000,000 Americans are presently involved in 500,000 such groups across the nation.

The self-help movement has spread for many reasons. One is the diminution of government services for social and emotional crises. Another is the decline of the family, place of worship, and neighborhood as sources for succor and support. A third reason is the trend in mental health care in this country toward deinstitutionalization. But perhaps the most important reason is this: "Who can better help heal the wound of another, as one who has felt the same wound."

Self-help groups may take many forms. Some are bridge groups, to which people turn in distress so they can cope with their crises on an emergency basis. When they no longer need the group's support, they leave, and others come in. Other groups, also addressing a predicament, are sought for more long-term support. Some groups offer direct services to members; others focus on research, education, information, and referral. Many of the groups function superbly because their focus is one that requires only minimal professional caretaking (such as a chronic disorder), but is helped by large doses of human concern.

The very strength of the self-help movement is testament to the disillusionment of citizens over the government's provision of human and social services. There is a concomitant fear, however, that if government officials see organizations performing admirably, often on no more than a volunteer basis, government will continue to diminish services and relieve itself of responsibility. Problems notwithstanding, self-help is a sweeping movement capturing the energies of thousands. The University of Texas–

Arlington Graduate School of Social Work now offers an organized curriculum in self-help—the first professional school to do so. Thus, the self-help movement serves to revitalize professionals.

What does a self-help group do for individual members? Whatever their plight—be it divorce, anorexia nervosa, bereavement, child abuse, starting a stepfamily—people can start to see themselves as sources of strength; their experiences, no matter how terrible, can provide information and emotional comfort to others. With the realization comes change in self-perception and also change in public perception. In concentrating on abilities rather than disabilities, self-help groups can provide objectivity, an exchange of ideas, fellowship, new friends, and encouragement during bleak times. The group may offer a lifeline where none existed before. By participating in discussion meetings or through reading the materials published or disseminated by the group, members may find a way to cope with stigma, maintain independence, and release feelings that have been sources of shame. The shared condition members rally around can itself help them deal with the outside world that seems to exclude them. Members can often confide to the group feelings they can't share at home. Another benefit is that by being part of a self-help chain, members save money that might have been spent for professional care.

In seeking a self-help group, potential members should examine the group carefully. Is it part of a national affiliate? If so, what has the group accomplished on a national level? Does the group publish or provide reading materials? Does the group meet the specific needs of your problem? What resources does it have for children's growth? Is it likely to continue to focus on the needs you have now? How is the group structured? Is there adequate leadership so that your needs can be met? Is there leadership training? Is the atmosphere helpful from the start? Does everyone's opinion garner respect, or is there a cliquishness? Depending on individual need, the answers to some of these questions may be important.

A list of some self-help groups that may be of interest to readers appears in the Appendix of this volume.

A Final Word

Young people look to adult guides for direction in forming their lives. It is from adults that they will learn their behavior patterns for the future: whether grieving is normal and permissible or whether it is forbidden and wrong and a source of discomfort. Perhaps the most important aspect of helping young people cope with loss is the willingness of adult guides to expose their own grief while at the same time encouraging children to express theirs. For the way in which adults handle trauma determines youngsters' ability to survive their own difficulties. And only if they survive, physically and mentally, can they come forth from crisis strong and ready once again to celebrate life.

Notes

1. Earl Grollman, ed., *Explaining Death to Children* (Boston: Beacon, 1967), p. ix.
2. Maria Nagy, "The Child's View of Death," in *Meaning of Death,* ed. Herman Feifel (New York: McGraw-Hill, 1959), pp. 79–98.
3. Gerald Koocher, "Childhood, Death, and Cognitive Development," *Developmental Psychology* 9, no. 3 (1973): 369–375.
4. Gilbert Kliman, *Psychological Emergencies of Childhood* (New York: Grune & Stratton, 1968), pp. 86–88.
5. Martha Wolfenstein and Gilbert Kliman, eds., *Children and the Death of a President* (Garden City, N.Y.: Doubleday, 1965), pp. 239–240.
6. Ibid.
7. Harriet Sarnoff Schiff, *The Bereaved Parent* (New York: Crown, 1977), p. 42.
8. Kliman, *Psychological Emergencies.*

2

Bibliotherapy

A Means of Helping Young People Cope with Separation and Loss

Adult guides who wish to help children come to terms with loss have a good ally in books, for books have been tools for preventing and solving psychological problems for as long as both books and problems have existed. As far back as ancient Grecian times, the door of the library at Thebes bore the inscription "healing place of the soul." The idea it expressed is both very old and very new.

Definitions

The term "bibliotherapy," most simply defined, means helping with books. The Greek roots of the word are *biblion* (book) and *therapeia* (healing). Most practitioners of bibliotherapy have spoken of the communication that takes place between the reader and the material, but some have further delineated concepts of bibliotherapy. Caroline Shrodes, a pioneer in the field, states that interaction is "between the personality of the reader and imaginative literature," going on to state that it "may engage his emotions and free them for conscious and productive use."[1] Shrodes's definition would seem to restrict bibliotherapy primarily to fiction and poetry. Karl Menninger does not limit his definition of bibliotherapy to one form of reading or another but points to "designating carefully selected books on mental hygiene for therapeutic purposes."[2]

A definition from the *Dictionary of Education* states that bibliotherapy is the "use of books to influence total development, a process of interaction between the reader and literature which is used for personality assessment, adjustment, growth, clinical and mental hygiene purposes; a concept that ideas inherent in selected reading material can have a therapeutic effect upon the mental or physical ills of the reader."[3]

Webster's Third New International Dictionary also refers to selection of materials in its definition of bibliotherapy: "The use of selected reading materials as therapeutic adjuvants in medicine and psychiatry; *also,* guidance in the solution of personal problems through directed reading."[4] First published in 1961, this definition was officially accepted by the American Library Association in 1966.[5] It is important to note that the definition does not suggest that bibliotherapy offers a complete solution to any problem; rather, it is an "adjuvant" or facilitator of treatment. The definition also implies some additional professional or nonprofessional input other than the selection of reading matter.

Within the context of library services, Margaret Monroe views bibliotherapy as an extension of reference services and reading guidance. All three are sought for informational, instructional, or guidance needs. According to Monroe, reference services are primarily objective, informational, and of short duration. Reading guidance is more subjective and geared toward education. Bibliotherapy functions as a long-term service approach with a therapeutic goal. Bibliotherapy, as one arm of readers' services, is espoused by Margaret Hannigan as well, who claims a bibliotherapist brings "a refined application of [the] normal librarian's function as readers' advisor."[6]

Rhea Rubin, author of the *Bibliotherapy Sourcebook* and *Using Bibliotherapy: A Guide to Theory and Practice,* defines bibliotherapy as "a program of activity based on the interactive processes of media and the people who experience it. Print or non-print material, either imaginative or informational, is experienced and discussed with the aid of a facilitator." The goal is "either insight into normal development or changes in disturbed behavior." "Clients" are categorized in three broad groups: patients and prisoners, individuals with behavioral or emotional problems, and normal persons in times of crisis.[7]

An investigation of bibliotherapy in the *Australian School Librarian* uncovered two opposing schools of thought. One group viewed bibliotherapy as "a highly specialized process for treating specific disorders of emotional or nervous origin, to be used only by skilled practitioners." The other conceived of bibliotherapy as "a guidance tool which may be used by virtually anyone interested in books, reading, and other people's problems."[8] No wonder author Ruth Churchyard titled her article "Bibliotherapy: What's That?" Despite the continuing lack of consensus, it is important and useful to be aware of the stated definitions and their appropriateness in certain cases.

In addition, the premise of this book tends to contrast with some aspects of the stated definitions. The premise of this book is that everyone can be helped through reading. One might not necessarily be faced with a problem, one might not be in therapy, and one might not be directed to the reading material. The authors feel, bibliotherapy is a process in which every literate person participates at one time or another. Bibliotherapy is seen as the self-examination and insights gained from reading, no matter what the source. The source can be fiction or nonfiction; the reading can be directed (in settings ranging from reading guidance to formal therapy), self-directed, or accidental. The reader might begin reading when actively looking for insights, or the insights might come unexpectedly. In any case, the insight is utilized to create a richer and healthier life. Salient factors must be present: The author must communicate with readers in either aesthetic form or discourse with readers; the readers must, in turn, understand and respond, hopefully with conscious awareness, leading to attitudinal and/or behavioral changes. Such changes can be brought about with the help of an outsider or can be self-induced.

Evalene P. Jackson, another early advocate of bibliotherapy, recognizes this view, distinguishing between two kinds of bibliotherapy, calling one explicit and the other implicit. The first is conducted by a trained therapist with a hospital librarian as a partner in the team. Implicit bibliotherapy is called "a resource of the culture, present under some circumstances for those who can find and make use of it. The reader's advisor may provide guidance in the implicit sense."[9] This distinction allows for the inclusion of happy accidents that help individuals and also allows guides other than medical staff to take part. Explicit bibliotherapy might be compared to bibliotherapy as a science, whereas implicit bibliotherapy might be compared to bibliotherapy as an art. The latter might also be termed bibliotherapeutic rather than therapy itself.

Thus we see that definitions of bibliotherapy vary, from the inclusion of very formalized programs administered by physicians in cooperation with librarians for the benefit of seriously disturbed patients[10] to the very informal activity that is within the grasp of every adult guide who gains familiarity with literature and respectful awareness of possible beneficial or deleterious effects of literature on young people.[11]

History and Research

One of the early advocates of bibliotherapy as a helping agent for mental patients was Benjamin Rush, who as early as 1812 recommended novels to patients.[12] John Minson Galt II seems to have been the first American to write about the benefits of literature in treating the mentally ill, starting his work in the early 1800s. His best-known work is an essay titled "On Reading, Recreation, and Amusements for the Insane," published in 1853. Galt thought of the library as a place in which remedies for emotional difficulties could be found, emphasizing medical supervision and guidance. One of the first to use the word "bibliotherapy" was Samuel McChord Crothers, in an article in the *Atlantic Monthly* in 1916.[13]

In the 1930s there was a new interest in the field, which still saw itself aligned formally with mental institutions and medical staff and which viewed books as a pharmacy for the mind. One noteworthy study of this period was done by Elizabeth Pomeroy, when an attempt to study the field from an empirical base resulted in "Bibliotherapy—A Study in Results of Hospital Library Service."[14] In the paper, 1,538 case reports were studied, a sample that is hardly matched today.

The most important figure of that period, however, is William Menninger, who in 1937 read a paper before the American Psychiatric Association on the subject. Along with his brother, Karl Menninger, he utilized his ideas at the famed Menninger Clinic. The two believed that physicians should assign readings, with the physician approving purchases and responsible for the shape and growth of the library collection. The librarian was a technical member of the team, but the doctor was in charge.

In the 1940s, additional articles and papers on the subject appeared, examining the psychological validity of the field. In one, Salomon Gagnon, a psychiatrist, stated a guiding principle that "of all the remedies to the sick man, reading is the only one he accepts naturally."[15] During the 1950s, some of the seminal thinking in the field was done by Caroline Shrodes and others who examined the state of the art, influencing the field greatly from a philosophical point of view.

In 1962, Artemisia J. Junier, then a librarian at a Veterans Administration hospital, expressed the thoughts of the times in asking how bibliotherapy could be made into a more acceptable science. The arguments over definitions of the term were already known (and continue until this day), and Junier asked that work be done toward standardization.[16] The hopeful movement toward consensus was an important theme in a history-making 1962 issue of *Library Trends* devoted to bibliotherapy.[17] The fact that an entire issue, edited by Ruth Tews, was concerned with the field was in itself impressive; the articles explored the problems of bibliotherapy without conclusion. In a historical overview, W. K. Beatty expressed the thought that standardized practices and philosophical agreement in bibliotherapy were unlikely.[18] Also significant that year was the inclusion of a "Bibliotherapy Clearinghouse" in the *Association of Hospital and Institution Libraries Quarterly*.

During the 1960s, further on-site research was reported. In 1963 a pilot bibliotherapy program began in New York under the guidance of Margaret Hannigan and William Henderson, who were working with young drug addicts close to parole. Case studies indicated the success of bibliotherapy.[19]

Although many people have struggled to define bibliotherapy, few institutions formally structure their services to include ongoing bibliotherapeutic services. A few psychiatric hospitals in Finland have literary circles that operate in ways similar to bibliotherapy groups.[20] There are programs at St. Elizabeth's Hospital in Washington, D.C., and the Santa Clara Free Library in San Jose, California, sponsors a program. But most other programs fall into the category of the short-term experiment.

Rhea Rubin is hopeful for more societal utilization of bibliotherapy. Reflecting on current trends that would make this more likely, she points to a public interested in psychological causes for events, a populace obsessed with self-actualization, and a society in which many of those who would previously have been institutionalized (mental patients and offenders) are now released. The result, according to Rubin, is that public and private agencies are forced to provide services to meet the needs of these groups and to examine the training necessary for the provision of these services. "Bibliotherapy is one means to satisfy public interest in self-actualization. It promotes self-growth based on shared experience and discussion of literature."[21]

Rubin points to the interdisciplinary nature of bibliotherapeutic possibilities, citing recent literature in which 35 percent of the articles on this subject appeared in library journals and 65 percent were found in the journals of other fields, such as psychology, education, nursing, and occupational therapy. Rubin feels this is because bibliotherapy is usually practiced in a group setting and inherits its thrust from group psychology and adult education programs such as the Great Books program.[22]

In her articles and books about bibliotherapy, Rubin divides today's bibliotherapy into three categories: institutional, clinical, and developmental. The first takes place in institutions such as hospitals and prisons, using informational and insight-oriented literature. Clinical bibliotherapy is used with groups of clients with emotional or behavioral problems and can take place either in an institution or within the larger community. The goals can be either insight or behavioral change, and the materials are likely to be imaginative literature. The facilitator is either a librarian or a doctor, with one acting as consultant for the other in most cases. Developmental bibliotherapy is likely to include both imaginative and informational literature and is used with the average, normal populace. The goal is to promote and maintain mental health and to foster self-actualization. This is the approach most often used in public libraries and schools. Rubin makes particular note of the role schools have taken, pointing out that schools "have been obvious sites for bibliotherapy because it is compatible with the goals of contemporary education, which include fostering development of a whole, adjusted personality able to deal with today's world. Students are already in an atmosphere conducive to reading and discussion, a library is usually available, the students are gathered five days a week, and curriculums are often varied and flexible."[23]

Rubin foresees greater community use of bibliotherapy in the future, with local institutions in the vanguard. Halfway houses, addiction centers, nursing homes, and outpatient centers are some of the obvious locations. The National Council on the Aging has started a reading and discussion program aimed at fostering self-esteem and human potential, and it is offering the service to senior citizen centers and nursing homes.[24]

At present, although model training programs for bibliotherapists have been described by Rubin, Margaret Kinney, and others, few ongoing, established bibliotherapy services exist, and little formal training is available. The first course in bibliotherapy for college credit was offered in 1980, by the Villanova University Graduate School of Library Science. In that same year the New School for Social Research offered the first college course in poetry therapy. The first comprehensive program for training was begun in 1973 at St. Elizabeth's Hospital. A two-year program, it includes a minimum of 448 training hours. The end result is a certificate as a poetry therapist given by the Association for Poetry Therapy.

Currently there is no bibliotherapy certification procedure. Rubin calls for guidelines for certification as interest in this field grows. She suggests a multilevel certification system that distinguishes among the types of bibliotherapy and whether the person will be working alone or as part of a team. All of her recommendations call for background knowledge of the literature of both mental health and librarianship.[25]

Other studies of note include the following: J. Webster managed to diminish fear of the dark and fear of dogs in first graders by reading stories that demonstrated the positive side of the feared phenomena, and following up with discussion.[26] Interviews three months after the stories were completed indicated that of 35 children fearful of the dark, 21 were less fearful, and all five children afraid of dogs were less frightened. It is not known, however, if change in attitude was accompanied by changes in behavior. In another study concerning fear of the dark, William L. Mikulas and his associates conducted four experiments using a children's story and related games designed to help children overcome their fear. The materials incorporated behavior modification of fear reduction, including modeling, counterconditioning, and shaping. Overall, the story and games were found therapeutic, cost-effective, and enjoyable.[27] A third study about fear was conducted by Robert C. Newhouse. He attempted to determine the effectiveness of bibliotherapy to reduce generalized fear in 30 second-grade students. Results supported the hypothesis that fear would be reduced through bibliotherapy, but Newhouse warns that measures should be taken to ensure a good research design and maximization of the treatment over an extended period.[28]

Researchers have tried to use books to change perceptions and behavior about family situations. One example is the work of John Sheridan and his associates. In their study, 48 seventh to ninth graders from changing families (as a result of divorce, separation, death, military service, remarriage, or other causes of parental absence) were assigned to one of two treatment groups: structured group counseling or explicit bibliotherapy, or a wait-control group that received standard individual counseling. Subjects were administered the Piers-Harris Children's Self-Concept Scale pre- and post-treatment; they also completed an attitudinal survey of the help they received. Subjects in the group counseling and bibliotherapy groups rated the help they received higher than subjects in individual counseling.[29] On a smaller scale, Terry Connor and associates undertook to prepare a nine-year-old boy for family placement through the use of the creation of a life storybook. Life storybooks are designed to answer the what, where, and why questions about a child's life experiences and to allow the child to express feelings about these events.[30] Through the creation of his own book, the boy began to unravel his confusion and discard some of his negative emotions.

Researchers have also found that attitudes toward sociological and anthropological groups can be altered by reading. The effect of reading material upon second- and seventh-grade students concerning attitudes toward blacks has been investigated by E. P. Jackson[31] and John Litcher and David W. Johnson.[32] Attitudes toward Eskimos have been investigated in a bibliotherapeutic framework by R. H. Tauron,[33] who worked with third graders; American Indians were the group considered by F. L. Fisher, who worked with fifth graders.[34] All four investigating researchers believed that attitudinal changes could be effected toward other minorities as well. All four reported changes of significance. When minority characters were given favorable presentation, readers were likely to respond in a positive direction.[35] When minority group characters were portrayed in an unfavorable light, the attitudes of readers were negative.[36] Again, in these studies, the findings reflect paper-and-pencil tests or students' stated opinions, suggesting identification with literary characters. They do not reflect subsequent behavior.

Means of doing bibliotherapeutic work must come under discussion when evaluating the success. One study that yielded interesting results is Fisher's, mentioned above. Three groups of fifth-grade students took part, each being treated differently. One group consisted of middle-class whites; the second was lower-class blacks; the third, racially mixed, middle-class youngsters. Within each group, three different procedures took place. In one subgroup, children read stories. In the second, they read stories and participated in discussions led by the classroom teacher. In the third subgroup, there was no story reading. All subgroups took attitudinal and information tests regarding American Indians. As expected, reading the stories produced positive attitudinal changes, but when stories and discussion took place, the attitudinal changes were even more significant. Discussion also led to greater information gain on the posttest. Attitudinal change took place most frequently in the middle-class, racially mixed group; and the attitudes of blacks toward American Indians showed greater change than those of whites. Once again, it is suggested that identification with the characters yields this result.

Another study emphasizing group discussion after reading is that of D. W. Biskin and K. Hoskisson, in which a group of fourth and fifth graders who both read and talked about moral conflicts encountered by fictional characters gained considerably in moral maturity over the group that merely read the stories.[37]

Time spent in discussion was also important in a study conducted by Dorrie Prouty, in which fourth graders read story and information books about death.[38] Students were helped toward clarifying which books of those they had read meant most to them and then they met and wrote to the authors of these books. Both actions released some of their feelings and fears regarding the subject.

It is also important to investigate behavioral changes brought about by bibliotherapy. At present, few studies do this effectively. Few studies also demonstrate the permanence of attitudinal changes. One study that does give evidence of behavioral change is that of David Gerald Jarmon, in which the effectiveness of rational-emotive therapy, bibliotherapy, and attention-placebos was examined in the treatment of speech anxiety.[39] Perhaps Jarmon tells us something of great importance when indicating that although of the three treatments used, bibliotherapy was the most effective, the gains were not maintained in a follow-up investigation. Jarmon's hypothesis that this might be due to the "brief nature of the treatment" is one that must be investigated in future studies.

A survey of 50 Australian primary school teacher-librarians revealed that most felt there was a strong connection between children's level of ability and the influence of books on their intellectual development, the link being more marked for those of above-average ability. However, the majority considered that books could not influence personal behavior or moral and ethical values. Most of the respondents practiced a form of bibliotherapy that they called reader guidance.[40]

In contrast to this study, in which the above-average learner stands a better chance to benefit from books, Barbara Lenkowsky and Ronald Lenkowsky presented a case study in which they claim that there is little evidence that bibliotherapy helps the normal child to cope better, but that reading about problems and their resolutions may enable the learning-disabled adolescent to live a more fulfilling life. Unfortunately, this study does not present findings for many adolescent subjects over a long period.[41]

A word of warning is given by Lucy Warner in an article in *School Library Journal.* Recent research has "called into question whether exposure to vicarious experiences really purges intense emotions or merely stirs them up."[42] This assertion is corroborated by Anne Marrelli's dissertation, in which school anxiety was treated through reading. The children became more anxious than before.[43]

Warner reviewed 28 doctoral theses in the bibliotherapy field since 1969. All used control groups. In 10, bibliotherapy was found unsuccessful. Among the studies in which bibliotherapy was deemed successful, almost all qualified their conclusions. In four studies, short-term gains, when followed up, were not maintained. In two studies, improvement in theory did not translate into behavioral change. Four studies produced positive results only with subjects who had already acknowledged their problem and expressed desire to change. Four studies revealed other techniques to be more successful than bibliotherapy, but two of these made positive claims for it in conjunction with other techniques. Only two studies gave unqualified endorsement to bibliotherapy![44]

In the 1980s, interest and investigation in both the art and science of bibliotherapy have continued, with publications growing rapidly in number. Those who wish to practice bibliotherapy and those who wish to study its effects will continue to learn as the field advances.

Reading Can Help Children Cope

Books can help children cope with many of life's vicissitudes. Because loss is a recurring problem throughout all stages of life, it would logically follow that loss would be a common theme in children's books and that such books would be very popular, sought after as sources of information. Books that concern moving and the advent of a new sibling are available in multitudes, but it is only in recent years that numerous books about death, divorce, and other separations have become available for children.

Reading Offers an Opportunity to Identify with Others

In psychology, people are said to identify when they behave or imagine themselves behaving as though they were actually other individuals, individuals with whom they have an emotional connection. In reading, identification takes place when the readers see themselves as aligned with characters, groups, settings, or ideas presented in the material.

Identification serves several purposes. First, readers can discover their own problems when they perceive the problems of others. Reading about the grief of others can create sudden pangs of identification, as problems that heretofore had not been consciously or completely recognized are allowed to surface. In fact, reading may actually be better than life, for it is sometimes easier to accept an unfortunate aspect of ourselves from the distance literature offers.

The fact that the reading process is a private one is an advantage to children with problems—to everyone, in fact. Most readers have had the experience of hiding a book because it is an identification they wish to keep secret. Books fit well into the human need for solitude, for reading is a private experience that allows our inner resources to grow while no one is looking. In the privacy of the home, readers may cry, pound pillows, pray, think deeply, even scream if they are so provoked. Alone, readers have time to contemplate the wonders of daily existence—the beauty of a flower, the complexity of time passing, the magnificence of the human body, the artistry of literature.

Certain subjects are kept secret by youngsters, such as being molested by a family member or being cruelly abandoned. Embarrassment caused by the problem is minimized because readers are allowed to reflect on characters and themselves within the chambers of the mind. If in reading such books as *Gillyflower,* by Ellen Howard, young people recognize that allying themselves with a sole stable adult can be the path out of an imprisoning situation, they have then found value in the literary form.

If readers wish to rehearse solutions to their dilemmas, they can do so without observation or interference. The identification process often evokes thought about solutions when readers realize that a character has coped with a situation. It is then important to examine the fictional adjustment in terms of a personal parallel, to weigh alternate proposals, and to progress toward individual solutions. At times readers then become more amenable to translating their thoughts into action and to making decisions that had formerly been repressed, set aside, postponed, or thought impossible.

In some instances, after reading about a character who has a problem, readers may want to talk about their difficulties. The literary character or the information a book provides can create the shield necessary for those unable to address such topics directly. They can then speak about the character instead of about themselves, while releasing information and revealing their feelings both to themselves and others.

Reading Helps Children Realize They Are Not Alone

According to Abraham Maslow, human beings have certain basic needs that must be met if they are to function. After physiological and safety needs, Maslow ranks the needs for belonging and love as next in importance.[45]

Reading is one way to enhance feelings of belonging. Through identification with characters and situations, readers are helped to feel less isolated. Children who are separated from a parent because of death or other reasons realize that others share their plight. This causes them to reason that they might, after all, be within the range of normality. Or, if they do conclude that they are *not* normal, it is then a relief to know that others suffer as they do. When children feel less isolated, they lose some of their embarrassment about their family situations.

The stages of mourning are readily seen, even in books for younger readers. As elucidated by Gilbert Kliman,[46] children first test and retest reality, eventually convincing themselves of the awful thing that has happened. For example, in Deborah Gould's book *Grandpa's Slide Show,* young Douglas poignantly tries to grab his grandfather's image from the screen, hoping to recapture him although he has died.

The second stage, going over the powerful memories, can be seen in Paul Fleischman's *Rear-View Mirrors.* In this book, the protagonist, Olivia, takes a symbolic bicycle ride to commune with her now-dead father, a man who had neglected her most of her life. Recounting the good and the bad puts these matters in perspective.

Kliman's third stage of mourning is the establishment of a substitute object relationship. As is the case with the previous stages, this one is portrayed in many books for youngsters. And, happily, in most books it is not portrayed in a Pollyanna, easy-does-it style, but with honesty. One such book is Joan Drescher's *My Mother's Getting Married,* in which a young girl has mixed emotions at the possibility of having a stepfather—"Everything will change," Katy says. Dinner won't be flexible anymore, and how can she possibly let Ben see her in her pajamas? In short, Katy thinks "it stinks."

Other themes of bereavement are seen in books and offer reassurance. The physical symptoms of grief are often portrayed. One example is Constance C. Greene's *Beat the Turtle Drum.* In the grief that Kate experiences after her sister Joss is killed in an accident, she remarks, "My bones feel hollow with loneliness." The short sadness span is also depicted. In Candy Dawson Boyd's *Circle of Gold,* the character Mattie Benson tries to get back into the swim of things after loss by baby-sitting, entering a writing contest, and occupying her time in various other ways.

If the reading material is sufficiently effective and succeeds in enhancing feelings of normalcy and belonging, it can, in turn, act as an agent for increasing self-esteem. As the chain continues, after self-image is bolstered, readers may show a new readiness to search for adjustment to their problems.

Reading Can Extend Horizons

Reading offers avenues to broadened interests and adventure. Books provide opportunities to be something or someone new. When readers extend their horizons and empathize with characters unlike themselves, they open themselves to several types of enrichment.

Perhaps they will grow to understand the motivations, goals, and feelings of members of another group. For example, what is it like to wait for a parent to return from prison? What are the economic, social, and emotional pressures suffered by a child such as the one in Inez Maury's *My Mother and I Are Growing Strong*. Through the eyes of a youngster whose father has been imprisoned, children may perceive, possibly for the first time, the nature of the interactions that take place between the new group and the group with which they affiliate. Through reading children may begin to see how some relationships work, economically and socially, between the children of incarcerated parents and other children. How does such a child feel and behave in school? How does he or she affect the others? Why? These are questions that can be illuminated through reading. Children who have never had to cope with a loss situation can imagine it, rehearse a solution, and remember, however vaguely, their literary experiences when a real-life situation comes about. This is particularly true of books about death and general separation, events that eventually befall all of us.

Reading about new people and situations can lead to the development of new interests. On a minimal level, the new interest can serve as a means to point children in the direction of thinking about something other than themselves. For many troubled individuals, both children and adults, this is a significant accomplishment. Once people are able to place focus away from themselves, they may become eager to gain new knowledge or hobbies. There is an added benefit: In the pursuit of information about a new area of concentration, children and adults often demonstrate increased interest in reading. For reluctant readers, material that extends horizons and contains high-interest but low-vocabulary levels can serve as an ego booster. Patricia MacLachlan's *Sarah, Plain and Tall* is such a book, written on a third-grade reading level but appealing to older readers. There can be an expansion of previous reading habits to include new forms—reference works, magazines, and so forth. Finally, there can be an increase in the difficulty of the material, which readers can effectively perceive in all its implications.

One important aim of education is establishing the ability to think critically and then using that ability to evaluate difficult, thought-provoking material and ideas. Through books, youngsters can become aware of their own value systems, considering what is important to them and examining what is important to others. They can look over those objects and goals that are treasured by each character, evaluate conflicts between value systems, and weigh solutions to the problems these conflicts present. The answers youngsters give are self-revealing. When brought to a conscious level, either in reading or in the discussion that follows, young people are offered the opportunity either to strengthen the patterns developing or to alter those patterns.

As an example of value theory in action, the book *I Never Asked You to Understand Me,* by Barthe DeClements, demonstrates conflicting life patterns. The protagonist, Didi, becomes truant during her mother's terminal illness, terrified at being left with a distant father and a great-grandmother who sees illness as something we will on ourselves. The action revolves around Didi's struggle to see her own truth and find her own ideas on how responsible each of us is for our destiny.

Reading Can Aid the Catharsis Process

The discharge of repressed emotions is a valuable aspect of a therapy program, indeed of good mental hygiene. Through involvement, readers vicariously experience the difficulties and feelings of characters, leading to catharsis. This "may provide a release of tension through symbolic gratification of socially unacceptable urges or substituting gratification of socially approved motives."[47] The purging of fear, anger, grief, and other emotions can come about in many ways. Reading is one way, as books can act as the agents that bring about tears (shed in private or shared) and evoke discussion of previously hidden feelings. Ventilation is helpful, but its benefits are usually temporary. In order for symptoms of distress to be alleviated, more is usually needed. The development of insight and an ability to work through the problems causing distress are usually components in the true resolution of difficulties.

Reading Can Lead to Insight

When tensions are partly relieved by catharsis, the emotions are freed, clearing the mind to develop insight. The ability to perceive part or most of whatever can be known of the true or underlying nature of an experience is most helpful in evaluating that experience. Without such perception or insight, it is difficult, if not impossible, to see one's motivations and those of others. Reading can help to facilitate insight: In reading about a loss experience, it is possible to relive prior loss occasions while being aware of common ground held with the literary character and material. It is indeed possible, when armed with this awareness, to come to new self-discoveries—to experience the "aha phenomenon," as it is known in psychiatric circles.

Reading provides at least one advantage over shared discussion. In reading, the discoveries, sometimes of personal shortcomings, can be faced privately without disclosure to others until readers choose to do so. Caroline Shrodes has explained: "Literature, being at once a fantasy and yet a realistic portrayal of human behavior, permits the reader, paradoxically, both an illusion of psychic distance and immediacy of experience."[48]

Nonfiction books have a special place in the process leading to insight. Books such as Eda LeShan's *When a Parent Is Very Sick* perform the same functions as adult self-help books and are valuable in solving problems. They enable children to look at themselves in relation to what is considered "normal." They can then see, with clearer vision, their strengths and weaknesses, their assets and liabilities. A clearer vision helps in the identification of motivations and in the formulation of realistic goals for the future.

Reading Can Facilitate the Sharing of Problems

Beyond insight and other processes of bibliotherapy, there is an additional desirable avenue for working through sources of difficulty: the sharing of problems. Through reading, children come to realize that the characters are imperfect, as they are. What is more, they recognize that it is permissible to be imperfect, even acceptable to admit to another (or others) that they are imperfect. Once the step of admission has been taken, the listeners are likely to reciprocate and consider their own imperfections in discussion. The overall benefit is that other people become less idealized.

This is especially important in relation to the second stage of mourning. In families where death has occurred, there is an unfortunate tendency for the deceased to be remembered automatically as perfect in every way. In divorce, however, the absent parent's weaknesses are often exaggerated and strengths overlooked by the parent who has the primary responsibility for the children. In the children's eyes, the absent parent becomes something of a villain. The children realize that they have inherited a part of the genetic makeup of the parent removed by death or divorce. The image of this parent as either angel or villain is likely to result in a loss of the child's self-esteem, for humans can never hope to match the behavior of an angel and they do not want to be thought of as inheriting the characteristics of a villain. In contrast, open discussion based on an honest appraisal of the absent person results in greater self-acceptance by the child.

Bibliotherapy can give young people the language with which to communicate their pain. Often, difficulties are felt, but people of many ages suffer in silence, not realizing help is available. A book can offer the ideas and avenues for getting that help. For example, in *Shira: A Legacy of Courage,* by Sharon Grollman, the protagonist aids herself by keeping a journal and writing poems. She pours the anger and other emotions arising from her severe diabetes into her writing. In the same book, visits to therapists are discussed, which might lead youngsters toward that path.

In discussion, readers review the material. They respond to one another about what they have read. They compare their experiences in terms of the actions and feelings of the characters and find areas of both agreement and disagreement. They investigate the consequences of the characters' actions, and in doing so reflect aloud on their own. It is natural that the sharing of problems also gives readers opportunities to find new solutions and/or modes of action to follow. If one person talks with one other person, at least two approaches to one problem are likely to be considered; in discussion, more than two personal approaches will undoubtedly be included, as each person gets to know the others, with their unique backgrounds and solutions. If more than two are present, even more solutions are available for consideration. Adult guides might wish either to group together people with the same experiences or to mix the types of problems within a group. Either position has valid support.

When readers share their problems, they also make themselves ready and receptive, as a preliminary step, for formal therapy if it is indicated. In *Bibliotherapy: Methods and Materials,* Ruthanna Penny is quoted as suggesting steps for getting readers to share their thoughts.[49] At first, readers read nonfictional material aloud, without dialogue. This teaches them to speak without fear. In the second step, readers react to questions of fact. No opinions are asked for. Finally, in the third step, readers are asked about their personal convictions.

Another technique is having young people retell the story and then examine the way one of the characters behaved and felt. This often leads to instances in which youngsters tell of similar incidents in their own lives, opening up avenues for further discussion.

Doris Robinson has related bibliotherapy to an integrated curriculum for special education students, devising specific discussion topics for particular books. For example, using *The Terrible Thing That Happened at Our House,* Marge Blaine's book about the trauma of one's mother going off to join the working force, Robinson brings up this question with her class: "Can you change a bad thing? If so, how?" Thus, the limited subject of one book becomes grist for a larger mill. Robinson also informs readers that everything in her bibliotherapy program seemed to go in slow motion, with children lingering for long periods over one idea.[50] This is echoed by H. Elser, who recently began a patient library program centered around bibliotherapy with selected materials at Danvers State Hospital in Massachusetts, perhaps the only bibliotherapy program in the country funded in part by the federal government. Elser found that the attention span of her groups, be they schizophrenic, geriatric, or adolescent, was very short, and she had to develop her own resource materials of short poems and literary passages.[51]

Discussion of materials can range from the most informal, as would be the case in a popular classroom activity called a poetry cycle, to a highly structured series of steps, as might be found in some bibliotherapy groups. In a poetry cycle, children are asked to select three poems on a topic of their choice. The classroom library boasts many poetry anthologies from which to choose. When the children share their discoveries, the teacher might ask what makes a particular child interested in poems about colors, why blue is his favorite color, how blue makes him feel, and so on.

On a more formal side of the continuum is the set of recommended steps proposed by J. Bodart:

> (1) retelling of the material, highlighting feelings, characters, and situations relevant to the problem being discussed; (2) probing into what happened in the material, to facilitate a shift in feeling and relationship, making identification more easy and vivid; (3) stimulation for the group to identify similar situations in real life or from other books to lend validity to the idea that books can extend actual experience; (4) opportunity for the group to explore the consequences of certain behavior or feelings and recapitulate what happened as a result of these feelings or actions; (5) opportunity for the group to draw conclusions or generalizations as to whether specific actions in certain situations had positive or negative effects; (6) opportunity for the group to determine the desirability or effectiveness of several actions in the specific situation.[52]

These steps, Bodart feels, whether handled in a group or with an individual, can help an individual see that he or she is not alone, that there is more than one solution to a problem, and get basic understanding of others when planning one's own solution.

Successful Bibliotherapy

Bibliotherapy is not yet at a stage where it has been fully accepted and established as a means of therapy. While its tenets are informally accepted, it is akin to, but somewhat behind, poetry and art therapy in its use in formal programs. The materials of bibliotherapy are known: fiction, nonfiction information books, biographies, science books, mythology, and more. Yet exhaustive studies of the effectiveness of bibliotherapy have not been undertaken; even if they were, results would be nearly impossible to quantify. Bibliotherapists will probably have to be satisfied (at least for the time being) that bibliotherapy exists as a tool within the many spheres of therapy. As stated earlier, it is called on as an adjuvant in many types of mental hygiene programs. Bibliotherapy can help. According to Margaret Hannigan, it is therapeutic rather than therapy.[53] It would seem unwise to look toward bibliotherapy as a cure. Just as giving children books about the facts of life does not constitute adequate sex education and can actually be a way to sidestep obligation, so it is that the offering of books about dying, moving, or divorce cannot be considered adequate education or preparation for loss. Such is the case for the use of all books in the curing of social or emotional ills.

Some feel that bibliotherapy should only be undertaken by those well versed in psychodynamics, neurosis, and psychotherapy. Others, such as ourselves, feel that it can be and is safely undertaken by those with less sophisticated expertise in human nature: teachers, librarians, doctors, lawyers, parents, and others. Bibliotherapy is often undertaken by children on their own. Perhaps, since it is the case that books are indeed consulted by people of every age in search of answers to problems *without* the presence of a formal therapeutic setting, adults who find themselves in guiding positions need not and should not feel embarrassed by their inadequate backgrounds in psychology. Perhaps, instead, adult guides should try to meet other obligations. These include the obligations of knowing how and when to introduce the materials, being sufficiently familiar with the materials, and knowing each child's particular situation.

Timing

Timing is important in utilizing literature as a tool for happier living. Preparation and planning are of the essence. Books about death and other forms of loss can be included in a school or home literature collection, along with less emotion-provoking material. Doctors can leave such books in their waiting rooms, intermingled with other reading material. The principle is the same as in a public library: The materials are readily and obviously available, but the choice is left to the individual. Range in tastes is great. The larger the collection is, the more choices there are. Some practitioners of bibliotherapy believe that books should be chosen by adults and given to children. On the other hand, Patricia Cianciolo's study concluded that, while in therapy, children preferred to select their own books rather than having them offered by the therapist.[54] The suggestion of the book by its presence in a collection, rather than by its prescription, gives children the central role. The book is not forced on children with the implication "It's good for you." Instead, children are self-motivated.

While the adult keeps books on loss available, it is often a long and patient wait until children are ready to make use of the books. Often, bereaved children will ignore these books within the collection and seek out less threatening fare. At the peak of their grief, people of all ages often cannot face mirrors of their emotions. They know their problems all too well and need other relief. This is another reason for making the books available instead of prescribing them.

The possibility of intensifying difficulties or raising defenses is avoided if guessing about timing is eliminated. Tensions within readers may prevent books from influencing their attitudes or behavior. Perhaps, when identification with character is strongest, if that character reminds readers of the very weaknesses they hate in themselves, they will respond with intense venom toward the literary figure, missing, in fact, any positive resolution of the problem found in the book.

Also, the problems of readers may prevent them from seeing what really is relevant to them. Distorted reactions, differing from those adult guides had hoped for, are indeed possible. The fears, guilts, and depression of readers may actually be intensified by reading. For some mentally ill individuals, the worlds of their own creation can be magnified and given new "reality," additionally aggravating adjustment.

When children make their own selections, there is no guessing to be done. By allowing the children to choose, the adult, aware of the children's general background, diminishes possibilities of offending children or their parents on emotional, religious, moral, or other grounds.

Adult guides can facilitate self-selection by providing means to attract youngsters to such books. This might mean decorating bulletin boards to include books about loss and compiling booklists on loss topics and placing them discreetly on racks or librarians' desks. It might mean giving book talks before groups or placing on exhibit actual copies of such books.

In developing book displays and other means to attract readership, it is additionally helpful to be on the lookout for books in which loss or other problem areas are side issues. Not as likely to frighten the timorous, sometimes these books have deep impact, as characters within a literary context struggle with bereavement. Youngsters pluck out the minor themes, seeing them in relation to the more major themes and also in relation to themselves. In many ways, such books are greater mirrors of life than those that focus strongly and continually on one loss event. In actual life, the major themes probably include growing, using one's capacities, survival itself. Although change and growth are major determinants of loss and loss is a continuing theme in life, usually one trauma is not *the* theme of one's life. Thus, adult guides should keep in mind aspects of life depicted in books besides the loss events. Are all the events authentic, and not merely those that depict loss?

Obligations Concerning Discussions of the Book

The skilled adult understands a long waiting period and is ready for the moment when children begin to read books concerning their problems; the adult is equally sensitive to definite, overt, clearly stated signs that children are amenable to having such books given to them. Under such circumstances, the offering of a book by the adult guide is acceptable.

After a book has been read by or with children, in most circumstances it is advisable that the adult be available for discussion. Although children and adults can gain some insight from reading alone, openness to discussion is a factor as important as the literature itself. However, just as the adult did not force the children to use the books, so the adult does not intrude with unwanted discussion.

The American Library Association volume entitled *Bibliotherapy: Methods and Materials* shows three factors present in the dynamic interactions that take place in successful bibliotherapy. These include the author's communication with the reader, the reader's ability to understand and respond to the material, and the therapist's ability to perceive alterations in attitude and to bring those changes to a level of awareness in the reader.[55]

Whether the adult guide is therapist, teacher, parent, librarian, or other concerned person, certain things can be done in order to help children have the optimal growth experience after reading. Perhaps most important is that the adult listen. Instead of pushing forth inquiry into the reasons for choosing the book or an analysis of it, the adult can learn how to proceed by listening instead of talking.

In listening, it is useful to appreciate the differences between sympathy and empathy in order to offer maximum help. Norman Paul has made a clear distinction.

> In sympathy . . . the subject is principally absorbed in his own feelings as projected on the object's special, separate experience. In sympathy, the subject is likely to use his own feelings as standards against which to measure the object's feelings and behavior. Sympathy, then, bypasses real understanding of the other person. . . . The empathic relationship is generous; the empathizer does not use the object as a means for gratifying his own sense of importance, but is himself principally concerned with encouraging the other person to sustain and express his feelings and fantasies.[56]

There are no feelings that one *should* feel and no guilt when they are not felt.

Listening with empathy offers children maximum opportunity for expression. It allows for the development of trust. It also provides cues that attitudinal change may have taken place. When the adult listens skillfully, it is then possible to react to the individual, receiving the necessary inspiration for ways to continue. Only after listening can the adult take the threads of conversation that children have begun and develop a more accurate conception of areas and possibilities for further discussion, as well as areas of investigation to be avoided. Only after listening does the adult know which concepts might be worth expanding and/or reinforcing and which reading material might be effective in accomplishing expansion or reinforcement. The adult will also then be a better judge of other media and techniques to use, such as films and dramatic role-play.

Other Obligations of the Adult Guide

Before beginning bibliotherapy or including a particular book that may be used therapeutically in a collection, the adult guide has several additional obligations besides good timing and skillful listening. The first, which seems most obvious, is to read the book before including it in a collection or bibliotherapy program.

The adult guide will then apply many of the same criteria utilized in selecting books for this bibliography. What is the book's scope? Is it accurate, or does it contain information that should be clarified or corrected? What is its moral or religious viewpoint? Is it worthwhile as literature? These criteria are given in the Introduction.

After examining the book, it is then necessary to reflect on the intended audience, an audience that must be thoroughly understood before the adult guide can respond to the following questions: Is the book appropriate for the age, interests, and reading level of the audience? Will the book's length, format, or level of difficulty impede any possible gains? Is the book's content in keeping with the reader's general developmental life tasks, such as the teenager's need to develop independence from parents?

The adult guide's understanding of the young people using the books should include a knowledge of their reading levels and any unusual features in their backgrounds, such as physical handicaps, that require special materials. This would include the visually handicapped, who might need recordings or large-print books. Of course, those guides who know which books for young people are available in these forms and which have high interest–low vocabulary for problem readers are ahead of the game in making proper selections.

Beyond these questions, which pertain to all types of bibliotherapy, many areas of controversy pertain to the use of books that deal with loss, particularly with those that treat death, America's last taboo. Many people ask: "Should books about death and other forms of loss be included among possible selections for children who have never themselves experienced loss? Shouldn't children be protected from pain as long as possible?" Children who have not experienced grief through death, divorce, or other separations can benefit from exposure to books on these themes. Although they are young and have not been bereaved themselves, in today's world it is probable that they have had contact with others—in school, around the neighborhood, or at home—who *have* had these experiences. Such children may have unspoken concerns and questions; reading books on themes of loss declares that it is acceptable to think about and discuss these matters. In addition, the inclusion of such books as possibilities for selection by anyone and everyone diminishes the mythical concept that children who have been bereaved may be abnormal. Instead, the inclusion reinforces a concept that is more true to life, that there are many styles of normal living that children experience on their way to maturity. Furthermore, the inclusion of books on themes of loss provides a framework for facing the problems, if necessary, at a future date. Children can look back on a vicarious experience and apply the material remembered to the reality that must now be faced.

Many other questions arise concerning books that deal with loss. It is incumbent on adults to include such books in a collection *only* after they have answered these questions with satisfaction.

Successful bibliotherapy is usually accomplished when guides themselves have a fairly good emotional adjustment to life. In keeping with their understanding of the difference between sympathy and empathy, such individuals are generally tolerant of other people's wishes, weaknesses, behavior patterns, and needs. When maximally effective, they usually also ask themselves questions about their own needs, ascertaining if they are genuinely motivated to help others or if they are acting from other less beneficial needs of their own. If guides respond to youngsters because of their own needs for power or because they themselves need emotional involvement with young people, the results are not likely to be successful. Success is more likely if guides care about people, can communicate that caring, and can read other people's communications, both verbal and nonverbal.

The most important question to ask is one that is asked of oneself. That is, have I come to reasonable terms with my own fears, distastes, and past experiences with loss? It is difficult to offer guidance unless one can examine one's own attitudes toward death and loss. One highly recommended way to bring about a confrontation with one's own predispositions is to arrange for small-group workshop discussions among adults who have like interests in using books to help children cope with loss. Reading some of the books proposed for a collection can provide the necessary spark for reflecting, questioning, and arguing until the adults in the group themselves come to terms with their own attitudes and values.

When adults participate in workshop discussions, a principle evolves that is crucial for the work with children that follows. That principle states that what is right for one person in one setting is not necessarily proper for another. Each person within the workshop offers unique and very individual responses to the hard-core issues that surface, and these responses must be respected. Some of the questions that might come up in a workshop include the following:

Is this book really most fit for the home and inappropriate for the school or library?

Might an adult guide using this book cause more problems than will be solved?

Might the book offend the childrens' families on religious or moral grounds? If so, what should be done?

Should a book on death and other forms of loss ever be read with a group, such as a class?

Could children who have not encountered loss be frightened by the book? Should they be protected from such insecurities?

On the contrary, should those who have encountered loss be protected from the book?

Should books on loss be graphic, as exemplified by a description of rigor mortis?

Whether adult guides reflect on these and other sticky questions alone or with the support of a workshop environment, if they can come out with confidence about the acceptability and appropriateness of their own responses, then individual growth can take place. It is this type of growth that can extend itself to help children.

Limitations of Bibliotherapy

As an art, bibliotherapy has many limitations. Many individuals are not inveterate readers. The help that those who don't approach books even occasionally might derive is, of course, minimal. Second, although many people are deeply affected by what they do read, there is little or no evidence indicating that all individuals are so swayed by reading material. Thus, possibilities for an imagined alliance with literary characters is greatly diminished.

In selecting materials for bibliotherapy, it is clear that personal tastes vary widely. In 1948, N. B. Smith conducted a study with children in which they were asked to name titles of books, stories, and poems that had influenced their lives.[57] Although two-thirds indicated alterations in attitude as a result of reading and one in ten felt that changes in behavior had taken place, with only one exception the books named by the children were totally diverse. This points up the fact that satisfaction and growth are indeed individual.

It becomes even more complex to select books when one realizes that it is a natural inclination for adult guides to inject their own tastes into what is made available. Often adult guides come from a different social class, professional role, and outlook from those of the readers they serve. As a result, a host of situations are seen from different eyes. The way in which adult guides view the world is likely to influence selection. At times, this is appropriate and desirable, for all of us tend to read material that reflects the nuances of our own lives. Reading that which we already are, we simply interpret the pages of the material with the background of our own experiences. Although we do seek out and become more involved in material related to our own personal experience, readers often ascribe values to characters that are actually not contained in the story, filling in with their own background.[58] In fact, when readers feel intensely about the material, the likelihood is greater that an inaccurate interpretation of the author's intent will occur. Thus, it is the case that we bring to reading material certain attitudes, and we utilize these to process the print. All too often the words can become what we want them to be.

It is dangerous to rely on books too much. Reading cannot solve all problems, and at times it can reinforce fears, add to defenses, and foster rationalization in place of action. Instead, it may be wiser to enjoy books merely for their own sake. Lucy Warner explains: "By expecting too much of books, bibliotherapists may paradoxically be diminishing their importance. Books can provide pleasure and emotional release, bring about insights, and foster new understandings, but they are not a bad influence if they stir up violent feelings. They do not fail if they cannot change a person's score on a psychological test or change his or her behavior. In fact, it is a credit to the human spirit that it resists such flagrant propagandizing."[59]

If attitudes and behavior are molded in part by reading material, then it can at times be beneficial for adult guides to bring varying viewpoints to readers, thus providing material that might counter and broaden already established opinions. But it is incumbent on the guides to be aware that readers may become less involved and may even shun the material that would serve to broaden them. Guides should also realize that such children are merely doing what human beings of all ages everywhere tend to do, even the guides themselves. When one adds to this that behavioral changes are not always easily seen by observers and attitudinal alterations are not easily or accurately measured by use of standard measurement techniques, it is evident that the selection and success of bibliotherapy are often matters of chance.

After problems of self-examination, book selection, timing, discussion and limitations are acknowledged and taken into account, the adult guide must meet one final obligation. That is maintaining the conviction that bibliotherapy is merely one component of a mental hygiene program. It is of utmost importance to keep a vigilant reminder of that fact, so that neither adults nor children begin to believe, even for a moment, that reading will magically solve problems or that insight gained from reading and discussion will replace the active work that is necessary to overcome personal difficulties.

Notes

1. Mildred Moody and Hilda Limper, Association of Hospital and Institutional Libraries, *Bibliotherapy: Methods and Materials* (Chicago: American Library Association, 1971), p. 7.
2. Sister Miriam Schultheis, *A Guidebook for Bibliotherapy* (Glenview, Ill.: Psychotechnics, 1972), p. 6.
3. Carter Good, *Dictionary of Education* (New York: McGraw-Hill, 1969), p. 58.
4. *Webster's Third New International Dictionary* (Springfield, Mass.: Merriam, 1966), p. 212.
5. Rhea Rubin, "Uses of Bibliotherapy in Response to the 1970s," *Library Trends* 28 (Fall 1979): 242.
6. Ibid., p. 241.
7. Ibid.
8. Ruth Churchyard, "Bibliotherapy: What's That?" *Australian School Librarian* 15 (Autumn 1978): 9.
9. Evalene P. Jackson, "Reading Guidance: A Tentative Approach to Theory," *Library Trends* 11 (October 1962): 99.
10. Ruth Tews, "Bibliotherapy," *Library Trends* 2 (October 1962): 97–105.
11. David Russell and Caroline Shrodes, "Contributions of Research in Bibliotherapy to the Language Arts Program," *The School Review* 58 (September 1950): 335–347.
12. Philip J. Weimerskirsh, "Benjamin Rush and John Minson Galt II, Pioneers of Bibliotherapy in America," *Bulletin of the Medical Library Association* 53 (October 1965): 510–513.
13. Samuel McChord Crothers, "A Literary Clinic," *Atlantic Monthly* (August 1916): 291.
14. Elizabeth Pomeroy, "Bibliotherapy—A Study in Results of Hospital Library Service," *Medical Bulletin of the Veterans Administration* 13 (April 1937): 360–364.
15. Salomon Gagnon, "Is Reading Therapy?" *Diseases of the Nervous System* 3 (July 1942).
16. Artemisia J. Junier, "Bibliotherapy: Projects and Studies with the Mentally Ill Patient," *Library Trends* 2 (October 1962): 136–146.
17. Ruth Tews, ed., *Library Trends* 2 (October 1962).
18. W. K. Beatty, "A Historical Review of Bibliotherapy," *Library Trends* 2 (October 1962): 106–117.
19. Margaret Hannigan and William Henderson, "Narcotics Addicts Take Up Reading," *The Bookmark* 22 (July 1963): 281–284.
20. Leena Sippola, "Parantavakirja" (A Healing Book), *Kirjastolenti* 71 (1978): 330–334.
21. Rubin, "Uses of Bibliotherapy," pp. 239–240.
22. Ibid., p. 242.
23. Ibid., pp. 243–245.
24. Ibid.
25. Ibid., p. 248.
26. J. Webster, "Using Books to Reduce Fears of First Grade Children," *The Reading Teacher* 14 (January 1961): 159–162.
27. William L. Mikulas and others, "Behavioral Bibliotherapy and Games for Testing Fear of the Dark," *Child and Family Behavior Therapy* 7 (Fall 1985): 1–7.
28. Robert C. Newhouse, "Generalized Fear Reduction in Second-Grade Children," *Psychology in the Schools* 24 (January 1987): 48–50.
29. John Sheridan, Stanley Baker, and Vladimir de Lissovoy, "Structured Group Counseling and Explicit Bibliotherapy as In-School Strategies for Preventing Problems in Youth of Changing Families," *School Counselor* 32 (November 1984): 134–141.
30. Terry Connor and others, "Making a Life Story Book," *Adoption and Fostering* 9 (2): 32–35; 46.

31. E. P. Jackson, "Effects of Reading upon Attitudes toward the Negro Race," *Library Quarterly* 14 (1944): 47–54.
32. John Litcher and David W. Johnson, "Changes in Attitudes toward Negroes of White Elementary School Students after Use of Multi-ethnic Readers," *Journal of Educational Pyschology* 60 (April 1969): 148–152.
33. R. H. Tauron, "The Influences of Reading on the Attitudes of Third Graders toward Eskimos" (Ph.D. diss., University of Maryland, 1967).
34. F. L. Fisher, "The Influences of Reading and Discussion on the Attitudes of Fifth Graders toward American Indians" (Ph.D. diss., University of California, Berkeley, 1965).
35. Jackson, "Effects of Reading"; Litcher and Johnson, "Changes in Attitudes"; Tauron, "The Influences of Reading on the Attitudes of Third Graders"; Fisher, "The Influences of Reading and Discussion on the Attitudes of Fifth Graders."
36. Tauron, "The Influences of Reading on the Attitudes of Third Graders."
37. D. W. Biskin and K. Hoskisson, "An Experimental Test of the Effects of Structured Discussions of Moral Dilemmas Found in Children's Literature on Moral Reasoning" (paper presented at the annual meeting of the American Educational Research Association, Washington, D.C., 1975).
38. Dorrie Prouty, "Read about Death? Not Me!" *Language Arts* 53 (September 1976): 679–682.
39. David Gerald Jarmon, "Differential Effectiveness of Rational-Emotive Therapy, Bibliotherapy, and Attention-Placebo in the Treatment of Speech Anxiety" (Ph.D. diss., Southern Illinois University, 1972).
40. Churchyard, "Bibliotherapy," pp. 12–13.
41. Barbara Lenkowsky and Ronald Lenkowsky, "Bibliotherapy for the LD Adolescent," *Academic Therapy* 14 (November 1978): 179–185.
42. Lucy Warner, "The Myth of Bibliotherapy," *School Library Journal* 27 (October 1980): 108.
43. Anne Marrelli, "Bibliotherapy and School Anxiety in Young Children" (Ph.D. diss., University of Southern California, 1979).
44. Warner, "The Myth of Bibliotherapy," pp. 107–110.
45. Abraham Maslow, "A Theory of Human Motivation," *Psychological Review* 50 (July 1943): 370–396.
46. Gilbert Kliman, *The Psychological Emergencies of Childhood* (New York: Grune & Stratton, 1968).
47. Russell and Shrodes, "Contributions of Research in Bibliotherapy."
48. Rubin, "Uses of Bibliotherapy," p. 250.
49. Moody and Limper, *Bibliotherapy: Methods and Materials,* pp. 15–16.
50. Doris Robinson, "A Bibliotherapy Program with Special Education Students," *Top of the News* 36 (Winter 1980): 189–193.
51. H. Elser, "Bibliotherapy in Practice," *Library Trends* 30 (Spring 1982): 647–659.
52. J. Bodart, "Bibliotherapy: The Right Book for the Right Person at the Right Time—and More," *Top of the News* 36 (Winter 1980): 183. Reprinted with permission of the American Library Association; copyright © 1980 by ALA.
53. Margaret Hannigan, "Counseling and Bibliotherapy for the General Reader," in *Reading Guidance and Bibliotherapy in Public Hospital and Institution Libraries,* ed. Margaret Monroe (Madison: Library School, University of Wisconsin, 1971), pp. 45–50.
54. Patricia Cianciolo, "Children's Literature Can Affect Coping Behavior," *Personnel and Guidance Journal* 43 (May 1965): 897–903.
55. Moody and Limper, *Bibliotherapy: Methods and Materials,* p. 18.
56. Norman Paul, "Psychiatry, Its Role in the Resolution of Grief," in *Death and Bereavement,* ed. Austin Kutscher (Springfield, Ill.: Charles C. Thomas, 1969), p. 187. Reprinted with the permission of the publisher.

57. N. B. Smith, "Personal and Social Values of Reading," *Elementary English* 25 (December 1948): 490–500.
58. A. C. Purves and R. Beach, *Literature and the Reader,* final report to the National Endowment for the Humanities (Urbana, Ill.: National Council of Teachers of English, 1972).
59. Warner, "The Myth of Bibliotherapy," p. 110.

3

Strategies and Applications of Bibliotherapy

PATRICIA A. EDWARDS

The term "bibliotherapy" has been in the professional literature for more than 50 years and most researchers agree with the idea that books can provide comfort, support, and development of character (Griffin, 1984; Jalongo, "Bibliotherapy," 1983; Jalongo, "Using Crisis-Oriented Books," 1983; Brown, 1975; Russell and Shrodes, 1950). Aristotle believed that literature had healing effects, and the ancient Romans also recognized that there is some relationship between medicine and reading. Even Shakespeare in *Titus Adronicus* (Act IV, Sc. 1, 1.34) attested to the therapeutic value of reading books when he wrote:

> Come, and take choice of
> all my library,
> And so beguile thy sorrow.

Although it is not difficult to analyze the word "bibliotherapy" and come up with the meaning "therapy using books," what is meant by therapeutic value of books has been more difficult to analyze, and some critics question the efficacy of the process. Evidence indicates that carefully selected reading, timed appropriately and used with receptive readers, does have therapeutic value. At least the practice warrants further research. Rudman (1984) supports this view and argues that "the practice of bibliotherapy—the use of books to help children solve their personal problems and become aware of societal concerns—has become accepted as an important part of teaching" (p. 3). Moreover, Lundsteen (1972) contends that in an educational context "bibliotherapy should be used to get children together with books that reveal ethical values and to promote identification with characters faced with problems similar to their own and to encourage evaluation of the character's solution" (p. 512). According to Salup and

Salup (1978), "Some of the school situations in which bibliotherapy may be found useful are: membership in a library club or group; discussion groups utilizing fiction and biography to demonstrate how one might overcome a personal habit or deficiency, and reading about various racial or ethnic groups to help understand problems or prejudice and hostility" (p. 7). Additionally, Salup and Salup point out that "bibliotherapy in the school context may be used in conjunction with educational and career planning, familial relations [and] teacher-pupil cooperation" (p. 8). In 1968, Zaccaria and Moses boasted that not a single study in a substantial body of research found bibliotherapy to be ineffective in a school situation. In recent years, however, this finding has been challenged (Newhouse and Loker, 1982; Beardsley, 1981).

Even though it is acceptable to practice bibliotherapy in an educational setting, Chadbourne (1976) has cautioned that bibliotherapy for emotionally or physically handicapped children has no place in schools even if a librarian, teacher, or counselor is the presenter. An attempt to satisfy social and developmental needs of children and adolescents should not be called bibliotherapy, however, it should play such an important role in the entire educational program that "it needs no separate 'name' " (p. 24).

Chadbourne contends that a primary objective of librarians and teachers is to instill a desire and love of reading in their students. She fears that if a great deal is concentrated on the therapeutic and literary value of what is being read, the enjoyment of reading could be destroyed. However, she believes that if the material presented to the students is available and attractive the students will select and fill their own reading needs. She suggests that "a good library service instead of 'bibliotherapy' is the answer" (p. 24).

Rather than engaging in a debate over what bibliotherapy is, is not, or should be, Olsen (1975) suggests that it is imperative for educators to recognize and deal with stressful situations in children's lives because of the considerable effects these problems may have on children's personal development, socialization, and education. Rudman further corroborates Olsen's disposition when she states:

> As educators we have within our power the means to inculcate values, develop skills, influence attitudes, and affect the physical, social, emotional, intellectual, and moral development of today's youth and tomorrow's adults. We accept this responsibility when we become parents, teachers, counselors, librarians, or take any position in which we influence children. (p. 1)

Supporting the positions of both Olsen (1975) and Rudman (1984), this chapter has as its intent to highlight how classroom teachers can incorporate bibliotherapy into their classrooms using "good" literature, and how librarians can support and reinforce their efforts to do so.

According to a number of proponents, the bibliotherapeutic process consists of four distinct phases: identification, projection, catharsis, and insight and integration (Zaccaria and Moses, p. 12). McInnis (1982) provides a detailed description of the four phases. She sees identification as the phase in which a character evokes an emotional response in the child and in which the child has opinions about the character's thoughts and actions. Projection follows as the child discerns character motives and evaluates intercharacter relationships. At this phase, the child also infers what the author's point may be, finding meanings or morals in the story. These two phases bring the child to the third, catharsis. For a child to experience this catharsis he or she "must experience an emotion that may be expressed verbally or nonverbally," according to McInnis. On reaching the fourth phase, insight and integration, the child can see himself or herself and other persons in his or her life in the story's characters. The moral found by the child in the story may be incorporated into the child's view of his or her own situation, and may help suggest ways in which problems can be solved (pp. 155–156).

In order to facilitate the effectiveness of the bibliotherapeutic process, classroom teachers and librarians must become partners. For example, if a classroom teacher uses a book to address a specific issue one year, there is no guarantee that that same book will be appropriate with an individual student or group of students the following year. Therefore, it becomes inherent that classroom teachers collaborate with librarians to continuously update their knowledge of what is generally available in children's books (Rudman).

There is no question that librarians' role is crucial to the book selection process, but they can also play other key roles. Librarians can establish a library club or discussion groups for students at the same grade level or for students from a variety of grade levels. This view is supported by Salup and Salup. Additionally, librarians should assume the role of familiarizing teachers, counselors, and parents with excellent books, book lists, and books of summaries, such as Bernstein's *Books to Help Children Cope with Separation and Loss,* Dreyer's *The Bookfinder: A Guide to Children's Literature about the Needs and Problems of Youth Aged 2–15,* and Munson's *Adventuring with Books: A Booklist for Prekindergarten to Grade 8.* Other excellent sources are books and bibliographies such as Larrick's *A Parent's Guide to Children's Reading;* Rudman's *Children's Literature: An Issues Approach;* and Spache's *Good Reading for the Disadvantaged Reader.*

As noted in Social, Education Research and Development, Inc.'s *Insti-*

tutional Library Services: A Plan for the State of Illinois (1970), the librarian must be a resource and support to the faculty. Librarians should actively assist in developing curricular materials, set up of student discussion groups, and be a force in the remotivation of these student readers. Librarians can help groups therapeutically, and can function as team members in all educational programs (p.49).

Monroe (1978) also maintains the importance of librarians' knowledge of books in their bibliotherapeutic model for library service. Monroe states, in order for the librarian to implement this model effectively, the librarian must have a good idea of how easily clients can handle print, film, tapes, and other forms of materials. Librarians must also be adept at matching materials to clients' needs and abilities, and should be capable of responding to and extending their clients' capacity for reflection and response (p. 263).

Yet another important responsibility librarians are encouraged to assume has been highlighted by Noyce (1979) and Nauman (1987). Noyce foresees that "librarians can play a vital role in increasing children's understanding of cultural/ethnic groups in their country by identifying writers who consistently present an authentic portrayal of a certain group and recommending their books for the classroom" (p. 443). Nauman observes: "School librarians today, especially those in the southern and western portions of the United States, are discovering that there have been radical changes in the ethnic backgrounds of the students using their facilities and materials [and] it is not always easy to find books that meet these children's special cultural needs" (p. 201). However, Nauman argues:

> Teachers and librarians must confront [their] responsibilities head on. . . . [They] must develop an acute awareness of the needs of children whose faces, languages, and beliefs may be radically different from [their] own. . . . [They] must help them develop and retain a healthy respect for and great pride in their uniqueness while, at the same time, helping them to adjust to a very different culture and environments. . . . [Teachers], too, can learn from these children. They may very well be [teachers and librarians] "windows on the world." (pp. 204–205)

Rudman further argues: "Members of a particular group should be able to see themselves mirrored in literature with as many facets of their heritage as possible presented and developed. This can occur only if the shelves of a classroom, home, or library contain many books about many heritages" (p. 162). In order to help teachers, librarians as well as parents should increase the number of books available to the children on ethnic minorities. Nauman urges that we provide them with criteria for book selection including such concepts as the following:

> 1. Authentic cultural perspective.
> 2. Reflection of differences in life-style, socioeconomic level, interests, and abilities.
> 3. Characters which represent positions in society apart from and uninfluenced by their ethnic heritage.
> 4. Variety in geographic location of minority groups.
> 5. Language which reflects the linguistic richness of the culture portrayed, with dialect used only as a positive differentiating mechanism, and not in any way demeaning or insulting to the characters who use it.
> 6. History accurately depicted with differing viewpoints made available for discussion and comparison.
> 7. Perspective and experienced authors with good credentials.
> 8. And last, but far from least, accurate illustrations which truthfully depict the ethnic qualities of the characters and ones which avoid stereotypes, tokenism, and demeaning implications. (p. 204)

In addition to encouraging librarians to provide ethnic literature, it is not surprising that sports literature is also an untapped resource to mend, mold, and motivate students. Heitzmann and Heitzmann (1976) point out: "Sports literature can provide the spark, develop the skills and promote the self-concept, no more could be asked of any field of writing" (p. 211). They further point out: "Sports writing can make a contribution to the field of bibliotherapy . . . [as well as] open the world of books and provide a wonderful opportunity for youngsters and even stimulate some to the point of involvement in sports" (pp. 211–212). Heitzmann and Heitzmann are also optimistic that

> students [who] become involved in sports literature or athletics will become more interested in school and develop personally as well as physically. Sports literature can play a special role in "turning on" the apathetic student possibly resulting in a healthier, happier view of herself/himself, school and the world. The library can serve as the facilitator in this regard. (p. 213)

Successful Programs Developed by Librarians and Classroom Teachers

In order to help teachers reap more benefits from the time they spend reading to children, Boothroy and Donham (1981) developed an all-school oral literature program. The oral literature program was designed as an integral part of the school's total plan for reading instruction. Boothroy and Donham appropriately concluded:

> As children grow in their sensitivity to and appreciation of language and literature, they are better able to understand and evaluate the reading we require of them in the classroom as well as their personal reading. [However, in order for books to be used therapeutically, children must learn to read critically and thoughtfully.] (p. 773)

The Boothroy and Donham all-school oral literature program is an excellent example of group bibliotherapy. Children who are coping with divorce, separation and loss, feelings of insecurity, and just plain fear can find support and comfort from their peers, classroom teacher, teachers other than their homeroom teacher, and the library media specialist.

According to Boothroy and Donham, one major requirement of an all-school program is commitment of the total staff. It also means that teachers must communicate with each other about the programs, and the library media specialist must spend time implementing the program. To ensure the successfulness of the program, they suggest the following steps. First, central themes for the entire school should be selected in order to provide continuity for the program. The teaching staff selects the themes around which the units will be planned. Then the staff discusses the theme to ensure that all are defining it similarly. (Note that student input is considered during this process.) Second, a time period for each unit is set. Meeting for two 25-minute periods per week for nine weeks is reasonable (that is, four thematic units per year). Third, the library media specialist prepares lists of books appropriate for reading aloud for the selected themes. Fourth, the teachers write blurbs describing the books they will read. These are shared in the homeroom, where children make first, second, and third choices. Fifth, the library media specialist then uses the children's choices to formulate groups, attempting to keep the groups similar in size and to match each child with an appropriate book from among those the child chose. Finally, at oral literature time, children move to the room of the teacher whose literature group they will be a part of for the nine-week period.

Sides (1982) describes a similar program called the Literature and Teaching (L.I.T.) program. Classroom teachers and library media specialists developed this literature program for primary grade students. The L.I.T. program is organized in three levels for kindergarten, first grade, and second grade. For each level, 20 children's books are selected. The literature program provides an instructional manual, a three-ring notebook divided into seven units corresponding to a variety of genres. Each unit has: Introduction and Teaching Guides—one for each book in the unit; Student Response Sheets—one for each book in the unit; and a bibliography. A typical instructional sequence requires a week. After having presented the story or poem orally, the teacher leads a brief discussion using questions suggested in the manual. Later in the week the teacher rereads the story or poem or an interesting part of it. Sides observes that the second reading serves two functions: (1) Students become better acquainted with the language of literature and with the stories themselves; and (2) the second interaction with the story helps develop literary insights by sending the student back into the story actively.

Increasingly, classroom teachers and librarians are faced with the harsh reality that young children are having to cope with a series of personal, emotional, and social pressures. The program designed by Sides is an attempt to address these youngsters' concerns as early as the kindergarten age. The program also gives these youngsters the support and strength they need to tackle life's difficult encounters.

In 1983, Sherman (1986) organized a Story Lunch program at an elementary school in Leonia, New Jersey. She planned a series of 12 sessions, 3 for each grade level attending school for a full day. The sessions ran three weeks (first grade ran for two weeks). Fliers for the program and lists of books to be read were sent out in early September; appended was a form for parents to sign and to specify which sessions their child was to attend. Children were limited to two sessions each. The student response was gratifying; about 20 to 25 students enrolled in each session. For a half hour, from noon to 12:30 P.M., four days a week, children sat on a plastic drop cloth and ate lunch while Sherman read to them. At the end of the half hour, the children went out to recess with the other children, or in bad weather, chose an indoor recess option.

The following year, Sherman accepted a children's librarian position at the Leonia Public Library. As the elementary school did not continue Story Lunch, she decided to try it in the public library. She feared children would not want to walk to the library or give up most of their recess time. So, she scheduled the sessions for 12:10 to 12:40 P.M. to allow time for the children to get there. The group was limited to 25, but the response was so overwhelming that she had to disappoint many children.

After a few years of serving as a children's librarian at the public library, Sherman returned to the elementary school. She reinstated the Story Lunch program and expanded it with the help of volunteers. Ten three-week sessions were offered to all grade levels. She found that four sessions a week works best, giving both children and readers a day off. This enables children to maintain friendships with others that do not participate in the program. An average of 90 children attended each session. Remarks from parents ranged from "He doesn't want to go to school if there's no Story Lunch" to "It's the high point of her day" (Sherman, p. 121).

According to Sherman, "The Story Lunch program has not been problem-free. Finding a number of rooms in which to hold the sessions can be difficult. Volunteers are hard to find and they haven't always liked the books I've chosen, or they have trouble keeping the interest of the audience" (p. 121). Also, she points out, "Recordkeeping is time-consuming, as are the confirmations or rejections sent home with the child" (p. 121). The positives, however, far outweigh the negatives. Some volunteers were so enthusiastic that they signed up for another session. The principal and other volunteers, including members of the Board of Education and the school superintendent, participated in the Story Lunch program. Spin-offs from the Story Lunch program occurred. For example, although Sherman invited mainstreamed special education students to enroll, two special education aides, working with multiple-handicapped youngsters, decided to hold their own story lunch sessions in their classrooms instead of sitting with their charges in the lunchroom.

Madison (1977) observed that her school was grim and not at all inviting. Consequently, she and other teachers wanted to make their school a more appealing place that would tell children that they were involved in things that interested them. As a result, they built a center in the school's front hall that would be seen by everyone who entered. The center, called the Read and Rock, held all of the fun kinds of things to read that are not generally found in media centers or the average classroom (for example, prefabricated fireplace, several rocking chairs, and bookshelves with comics such as *Spiderman,* Sunday comics, and Snoopy books). It was a place to visit between, during, before, and after class—anytime someone felt like reading and rocking. The materials in the center were quickly exhausted and expensive to substitute or replace; therefore, the teachers decided to ask the children to write short stories, books, poetry, or plays on interesting subjects and place them in the center. The ego building self-confidence that came with authorship and recognition led to the development of Happy Grams, which were sent home to the students' parents. Also, an opportunity for role-playing was provided as children were free to characterize themselves during the creation of stories, poems, and plays.

The most powerful and positive characteristics of both the Sherman (1986) and Madison (1977) approaches to helping children cope with life's difficulties was the fact that children could share their feelings privately or in a group. The Sherman Story Lunch program provides children, as it does adults, the opportunity to share their personal feelings with a friend or group of friends over lunch. The Madison approach gives children a private time for thought and reflection. They can simply rock and read and interact with the text in their own private and personal way. Brown (1975) summarized the need for group as well as individual bibliotherapy when she said:

> The student who is too inhibited or too shy to discuss personal problems directly with a teacher, counselor, or librarian, regardless of how much he may like or respect him or her, can often project his own

> problems in a much more impersonal manner through classroom discussion of book characters with [whom] he has identified. In such a discussion, [the student] feels that he is not giving himself away. [As] the class members react to his explanation of the actions and attitudes of a hero or heroine, he secretly applies such reactions to his own attitudes and conduct; or he may discuss a problem character with friends or acquaintances outside class with a similar effect. (p. 183)

Strategies for Utilizing Bibliotherapy in the Classroom

Teachers began to practice bibliotherapy in the 1940s. It was important then and it is even more important now that classroom teachers utilize bibliotherapy, because as Brown (1975) puts it, "So many young people are groping for answers" (p. 181). Rudman points out, "Children walk into the classroom with their minds crowded with issues. Teachers, who next to parents spend the most time with young people, need the competence to handle children's questions and concerns" (p. 3). However, before teachers can match the student with the right book it is crucial that they become familiar with the child and his or her situation. Brown (1975) has outlined four methods of discovering a student's problem:

> Consulting school records, conferring with other teachers or school staff members who have contact with him [or her], talking in friendly fashion with the student himself [or herself], and talking with his [or her] friends and acquaintances. Others may include: observation of behavior in the classroom, the halls, the library, the media center, the playground, or the cafeteria; talking with the student's parents; knowing the student through sponsorship of extra-curricular activities such as sports, clubs, journalism, music, or dramatic activities. (p. 183)

Although it is important that teachers address students' questions/concerns and attempt to recommend appropriate books to children at the right time, Appleberry (1986) warns:

> The approach must be subtle, in order to avoid hurting the youngster's feelings. . . . [Teachers should n]ever be too direct with children about suggesting books they "should" read, but use some of these tricks: Pull the desired book forward slightly on the shelf; most youngsters can't resist anything that sticks out. Place several difficult and dull books on the table along with the one you hope the child will take, and allow a choice from the display on the table. All teachers probably use the technique of baiting children to read books by reading [some] part[s] aloud, giving a brief summary, showing some interesting illustrations, and then asking, "Who would like to have this book first so you can find out how it ends?" [Suggest that a best friend read] the book first and then recommend it to the child who needs it. (p. 2)

A number of researchers have outlined a list of bibliotherapeutic book strategies/techniques that classroom teachers and librarians can employ in a school setting (Rudman, 1984; Criscuolo, 1977; Brown, 1975; Johns and Lunt, 1975). Rudman (pp. 403–407) suggests numerous activities for children to help them gain the full benefit from the books they are reading, as well as to share with other children what they have learned from these books.

Brown (1975) suggests 61 ways to exchange information on a book. Some examples of these are:

> Hold a panel discussion when several students have read the same book or a group of similar ones. . . .
> Appoint a committee of pupils who are avid readers to conduct peer discussions and seminars about books. . . .
> Hold a mock trial permitting the defendant to tell the story of a book of his choosing. The class renders decision on its merits. . . .
> Reproduce artist's interpretations of important scenes on slides for the whole class to enjoy. . . .
> Compose a telegram, trying to give the essence of a book in 15 words. Then expand it into a 100-word "overnight telegram." (pp. 207–210)

Finally, Johns and Lunt list activities that can assist classroom teachers and librarians in motivating children to read, as well as developing an in-depth understanding of the literature. Some of them are:

> Try the "transmitter-receiver" idea. A child reads a book and "transmits" his enthusiasm to others. In his turn he also "receives."
> Let the students "sell" books to each other. Require children to select the most interesting parts of the book, and to persuade someone else to read it.
> Make a reading railroad. Each student makes a box from hard paper and staples it to the bulletin board to represent a railroad car. You'll have a train with a car for each student. When a student reads a book, he fills out a three by five inch card and deposits it in his car.
> A chart listing books may be posted. The children can choose whatever book they want to read. When they have finished, they put a smile or a frown sticker on the chart next to the book depending on whether they liked it or not.
> Make mobiles by choosing important incidents from a character's life. (pp. 617–619)

Audiovisiotherapy/Nonprint Media

Bibliotherapy appears to be most effective with children who are in the habit of reading and who have above-average intellectual ability. Unfortunately, Axelrod and Teti (1976) point out, "Due to the inability or unwillingness of large numbers of children with learning problems to engage in reading with any degree of consistency, the idea behind bibliotherapy has been eliminated as an operable alternative" (p. 37). Feinberg (1977) maintains, "Mass media have singularly shaped and molded this generation of students" (p. 78). For this reason, Rutstein (1972) suggests, "Teachers [librarians and parents] should learn to appreciate how TV [and other forms of nonprint media] shapes these students' views of themselves, of their friends, of school and of the world" (p. 137). Axelrod and Teti conclude: "The most powerful influence affecting children [is] the screen" (p. 37).

Stewart (1982) and Weinstein (1977, 1978) agree that nonprint media can be used to supplement books as well as provide the "nonreader" or "poor reader" with an alternative resolution for profiting from the bibliotherapeutic process. Weinstein (1978), along with Davison (1983), outlines the steps teachers should follow when using media in the classroom:

1. It is essential that the teacher be well acquainted with filmstrips, slides/tapes, motion pictures, records, tapes, and other forms of nonprint media.
2. "In addition to being knowledgeable in the field of children's literature, a teacher implementing a program using nonprint media must also be knowledgeable of the students themselves as individuals" (Davison, p. 105).
3. "After establishing mutual trust and rapport, the teacher can suggest an assortment of carefully selected [films and other nonprint media] to an individual, to a small group with a common problem, or to an entire class" (Davison, p. 105).
4. Discussion following the showing of a film or other nonprint media is important and essential.
5. Teachers should never insist that children react orally to the film or nonprint media. Lundsteen (1976) notes that a sensitive teacher instinctively knows "to value the child's silent thought" (p. 218).

A study by Stewart illustrates the effectiveness of audiovisiotherapy and nonprint media. In observing a group of Navajo children, Stewart feared that "simply translating the code into a recently attained language such as English may not be sufficient for them to understand and appreciate an author's intended meaning" (p. 218). In an attempt to rectify this situation, Stewart allowed students to listen to an audiovisual presentation of a story. The media forms of filmstrips, slides, photographs, and posters were used, in variations of the activity, to illustrate the story. Commercially available or teacher-produced cassette tapes were used to present the narration of each story. The verbatim text of each story was also made available for the children to follow during the audiovisual presentation. Once the "show" was completed, students were directed to read the written text of that same presentation. Stewart noticed a dramatic change in the Navajo children's reading behavior and concluded that audiovisual media may be an effective tool for increasing comprehension. First, the visual presentation of the story gave children a clear representation of characters as well as actions and ideas that were in the text. Second, hearing and seeing a story prior to reading enabled the students to read the same story later with a greater feel for the language of a particular story. Third, a helpful function of the presentation was that children saw and heard stories, and their plots and characters, in one setting. Fourth, a factor that may have contributed to the positive changes in the children's behavior was that the children were not required to perform their unpolished reading skills before others in the classroom. Also, it was not necessary for the teachers or the aides to supervise each facet of the activity constantly. Once the students could operate the equipment and complete the other tasks assigned to them, they were capable of working on their own (pp. 220–221).

Audiovisiotherapy appears to be a viable alternative to bibliotherapy for students who have below-average intellectual ability. Students can profit from the bibliotherapeutic process via filmstrips, videotapes, motion pictures, records, slide-tape programs, and other forms of nonprint media. The study by Stewart demonstrates the effectiveness of audiovisiotherapy. Stewart's approach can be generalized to other populations of students who are coping with personal or emotional problems.

Another strategy for helping children with reading problems become acquainted with literature is through the use of videotapes. Shachter (1975) developed a series of 23 half-hour black-and-white videotaped interviews with outstanding authors, illustrators, and editors for children and young adults. Shachter concludes:

> What books cannot do, videotapes accomplish in mirroring a guest's speech patterns, mannerisms, facial expressions, unrestrained, deep-seated laughter, and also the way he answers unexpected questions from participants. In short, the videotape is the nearest thing to seeing and hearing a guest in person and may endure beyond the life span of the featured individual. (p. 774)

Tape recording parts or all of books is yet another technique for helping students reading below grade level. Carbo (1978) states:

> Teaching reading with talking books appears to be particularly effective with youngsters who have memory problems and/or difficulty learning to read through the phonics approach, and for older students who, after repeated failure, have been turned off to reading. Talking books enable older students with some reading skills to read material on their language comprehension level, and help them to integrate the rate, rhythm, and natural flow of language necessary for good compre-

> hension. In addition, with talking books, students make fewer reading errors and the possibility of forming incorrect reading patterns is diminished. (pp. 267–268)

Three recording techniques for using the Talking Book Method were devised by Carbo (1978): cuing the listener, phrase reading, and tactual reinforcement. Carbo (1981) outlines step-by-step instructions to enable teachers to cross-reference their tapes and books so they could build a permanent library of recorded books that their students could use and enjoy repeatedly. According to Carbo, in addition to being cost-effective, teacher-made tapes are better than commercially made tapes for the following reasons: (1) greater selection of materials, (2) better pacing, (3) faster and better accumulation of materials, (4) better cues, and (5) greater variety of materials (p. 187). Carbo suggests before organizing and tape recording the books, teachers need 20 high-interest books, a battery-operated tape player with headphones, and 10 blank cassette tapes. Each cassette tape should have at least 30 minutes of running time on each side.

Dramatic Activities

Role-playing, puppetry, and storytelling as therapy are dramatic activities that can be used to help stimulate the identification, catharsis, and insight Russell and Shrodes describe as essential to the effectiveness of the bibliotherapeutic process. According to Borden (1970) and Way (1967), role-playing helps develop the "whole" child, as a social-empathic person, without diminishing the uniqueness of the individual. Kukla (1987) states: "Role play lets the children become other people in other places; it allows them to participate in the events of the story and explore situations different from their own lives; it deepens their identification with the fictitious situation through the power of imagination" (pp. 74–75). Miccinati and Phelps (1980) state:

> Dramatic play can be an outlet, both physical and verbal, for students who might otherwise have no way to express their understanding or feeling about what they have read or heard. These kids can *show* what they mean. Dramatization gives children a chance to express their reactions to a story. It encourages them to read and reread to understand the story. It allows them to sharpen their sense of how a story "works," how the elements of character, plot, action, and setting work together. (p. 270)

Ross and Roe (1977) point out that drama requires the same language abilities and thinking skills that are fundamental to reading. Carlton and Moore (1968) also believe that dramatization supports the teaching of reading. They developed a technique for helping children find reasons to read, which they termed "self-directive dramatization," in which children direct themselves in acting out characters in stories they have read. The groups do not rehearse; when the decisions are made about characters, the group is ready to respond spontaneously. No props or costumes are used except those improvised on the spot. While everyone is learning what to do, the teacher sits with the rest of the children to observe. The teacher does not give any direction. Initially the teacher finds the stories in the books, but eventually the children begin to take more responsibility with story searches and selections (Vawter and Vancil, 1980).

Synchronized Movement, Pantomiming, Improvisation, and Puppetry

Synchronized movement, pantomiming, improvisation, and puppetry are other ways to involve children in a story they have just read. Miccinati and Phelps suggest: "When children are able to act out stories which they have read, they are demonstrating for themselves that reading is something more than word calling. It allows them to make of their reading something lively, something enjoyable, something with meaning for them and for others" (p. 270).

Improvisation begins with a premise and builds on it. Miccinati and Phelps describe a process where children "agree on certain story elements and then act them out, changing and adapting the story as the game progresses" (p. 271). Miller and Mason (1983) suggest: "Before improvising a story, the students should identify the characters, the story problem, the conflict, and the resolution" (p. 130). They further suggest that short stories can be played out in one improvisation. For longer stories, the children can improvise scenes in small groups. Children should be free to add characterizations and actions that can be logically inferred. Stories can be improvised repeatedly as long as new insights are being added.

Children who feel self-conscious when displaying emotion often feel comfortable projecting those feelings onto a puppet. Puppetry techniques, when combined with bibliotherapy, can guide young children through socially awkward situations and also help them gain an appreciation of good children's literature, gain knowledge about story structure, increase oral language fluency, and increase vocabulary (Clarke, 1985).

Storytelling as Therapy

Another activity for incorporating drama into the bibliotherapeutic process is storytelling as therapy. O'Bruba, Camplese, and Sanford (1984) define this as "a technique in which the teacher attempts to solve a child's problem by bringing the class a similar experience vicariously through stories retold from appropriate books" (p. 158). Unlike bibliotherapy, this practice "allows the teacher to select books or stories beyond the vocabulary and comprehension levels of students" (p. 159). Pickert and Chase (1978) suggest that story retelling "assesses a student's ability to comprehend, organize, and express language" (p. 529). O'Bruba, Camplese, and Sanford state that the focus is threefold: awareness, understanding, and finally acceptance.

They suggest that the teacher first select a story that corresponds to the emotional needs of his or her students. Second, the teacher should retell the story to meet the developmental and emotional needs of the students. And finally, after the teacher has selected an appropriate story and retells it to the class, he or she should then assign students to role-play story characters. O'Bruba, Camplese, and Sanford believe "as children actively engage in the story, understanding and positive peer acceptance are both likely to increase" (p. 159).

Research Involving Dramatics Activities

Although research involving dramatics as a means to enhance the reading process is rather limited, Miller and Mason contend that the research that has been completed indicates that dramatics is a promising instructional method.

Galda (1982) and Pellegrini and Galda (1982) found in a study of 108 children (54 boys and 54 girls) from kindergarten and first and second grades that dramatics (thematic-fantasy play) may be better than discussion and drawing for developing story comprehension. The experimenters read the children the story "Little Red Cap." At the end of the story, the children were engaged in either the thematic-fantasy play, discussion, or drawing. The children in the thematic-fantasy play group acted out the roles of the major characters. Discussion group members discussed the story in a typical classroom manner. Children in the drawing group drew the story's events. Pellegrini and Galda found that the thematic-fantasy play was the best for developing comprehension and improved the children's understanding of story language because it required more active involvement with the stories the children heard.

Dramatics activities afford children the opportunity to express their private feelings in a personal way. Furthermore, for children who wish to remain silent and to just let their actions express their feelings, dramatics activities can serve as a powerful vehicle.

Written Expression

Skill-focused bibliotherapy, journal writing, and poetry writing are three strategies classroom teachers can use to encourage children to express their feelings. Fox and Collier (1983) state that skill-focused bibliotherapy combines bibliotherapy and language experience in lesson sequences that focus on developing specific comprehension abilities. In order to use skill-focused bibliotherapy, Fox and Collier suggest teachers make the following preparations:

> 1. Select a combination of an affective theme for bibliotherapy appropriate for the needs of your children, and a comprehension skill your children could profit from having.
> 2. Select books which relate to the affective theme you have identified. Select learning activities for comprehension appropriate to the developmental level and needs of your children. (pp. 5–6)

They also encourage teachers to follow the instructional sequence below:

> 1. Read and discuss a story
> 2. Write a group story
> 3. Reread the group story
> 4. Follow-up activities [Write individual stories, play games, role-play, etc.] (pp. 6–8)

Journals

Journals are an additional opportunity for students to express their feelings and interpretations of literature. When reading a series of short books or stories, the student can write a brief reaction to each book. When reading a longer selection, the student can comment after reading a segment of the story. Students can write their free responses or can be encouraged to follow specific guidelines as they write. Kintisch (1986) states, "The most outstanding development during a 4-year study of journal writing in an elementary school in Philadelphia, Pennsylvania [was] the abundance of eager authors" (p. 172). She further states that students "take risks with paper and pencil because they have years of experience in building confidence. They are fearless and imaginative when it comes to written communication" (p. 172). Stephens (1981) suggests that the following questions can be used to help guide children's thoughts and feelings about a story they have read.

> 1. What was the story about?
> 2. How did the story make you feel?
> 3. Who was the main character?
> 4. What problem did the main character encounter?
> 5. How did the main character solve his problem?
> 6. If you had a similar problem, what would you have done? (p. 15)

Four other questioning strategies have proved successful in helping students understand the content of a story. Eberle (1972) used a method called SCAMPER to provide a set of guidelines for writing creative questions. The letters in SCAMPER stand for the type of creative responses elicited when asking questions. Martin, Cramond, and Safter (1982) applied the SCAMPER technique to reading "Little Red Riding Hood."

EXAMPLE

S	Substitute:	What do you think would have happened if there had been an elephant in Granny's bed instead of a wolf?
C	Combine:	How do you think the story may have changed if the Wolf had the same personality as Granny?
A	Adapt:	How do you think the Wolf would adapt his plan if the Hunter had walked in with Little Red Riding Hood?
M	Modify:	How can you rewrite the story to save the Wolf?
	Magnify:	How would the story be changed if Little Red Riding Hood had been much larger than the Wolf?
P	Put to Use:	How could Little Red Riding Hood have used her hood to help her?
E	Eliminate:	Rewrite the story without the Hunter.
R	Rearrange:	What would have happened if Little Red Riding Hood had arrived at her Granny's house before the Wolf arrived?
	Reverse:	Rewrite the story placing the Wolf in Little Red Riding Hood's character and Little Red Riding Hood in the Wolf's. (p. 569)

They concluded: "Teachers can use children's responses to these questions to lead into writing language experience stories. Children can share their answers and stories and discuss how events in the story led them to their conclusions" (p. 569).

Martin, Cramond, and Safter also describe another strategy called CPS (creative problem solving). The goal of CPS is to develop students who can read to discover problems and then creatively find workable solutions. They outline five steps that Torrance (1979) used to employ this technique.

1. Fact finding: Reading to get information.
2. Problem finding: Deciding what is the real problem. It is not always what it appears to be at first glance.
3. Idea finding: Brainstorming possible solutions to the problem. Evaluation of ideas does not take place at this step. Wild ideas and novel solutions should be encouraged.
4. Solution finding: Deciding from all possible solutions which is best. Two ideas might be combined to form a best solution.

5. Acceptance finding: Selling the solution. Though a solution may be "found," others must be convinced of its value. (p. 570)

According to Martin, Cramond, and Safter, the above activity starts by having students read the beginning of a story. The teacher stops the children at the point where a question or decision looms. The children are then asked to think of as many possible solutions as they can. After brainstorming a list of possible solutions and writing them on the chalkboard, the students evaluate the solutions. They are evaluated according to criteria developed by the students. Finally, students read the remainder of the story to compare their solution with the author's solution. The group's varied solutions can be compared before reading the solution.

In addition to describing strategies used by Eberle (1972) and Torrance, Martin, Cramond, and Safter describe questioning strategies that they themselves developed—ambiguous stories and branched endings. To use ambiguous stories as a questioning strategy they suggest that teachers begin by telling their students that they are going to read a story in which they will have to use their imaginations. While reading, they should try to think of as many explanations as they can for what is happening. They should try to make their explanations fit the events of the story. Children may then share their interpretations with the entire class or in smaller groups, explaining why they made certain decisions. Other questions that are useful with ambiguous stories include: What would be good titles for the story? What could have caused what happened in the story? What questions could you ask to help you decide what the story is about? What might happen next? Teachers can create ambiguous stories of their own or use parts of stories that are already written. If they choose to write their own, several points should be kept in mind. The passage should tell a story, yet leave much to the reader's imagination. The details that are included should grab the reader's interest and elicit vivid images. Finally, the ending of the story should be open for the reader to fantasize. To use stories that are already written, the teacher should seek passages with the characteristics described earlier.

Another strategy described by Martin, Cramond, and Safter is branched endings. The objective is to create many possible story endings from the same beginning. Students are placed into small groups (four to eight children per group is best). They then read, or the teacher reads to them, the beginning of a short story that places its characters in a dilemma with two possible choices. Half of the group members select one of the choices and form a subgroup while the remaining members take the other choice. The two subgroups discuss independently what they feel will happen next as a result of their decision to resolve the dilemma. One member of each subgroup acts as scribe and records their continuation of the story. This part of the story is ended by creating a new dilemma for the character to resolve in one of two ways. The groups continue the process, dividing in half at each dilemma, or branch, until each child is writing alone. At this point the child writes an ending to the story. Having completed the process, students will have as many endings as they had members in the groups. The group can reassemble and see what others wrote and why they made certain choices. The group's work can be completed to form a complete story whose readers will have to make decisions at each dilemma. Depending on their choice, readers will be directed to certain pages to continue reading, where they will soon have to make another choice. This continues until readers reach one of the endings. They may then go back in the story to explore where other decisions would have led them. As with ambiguous stories, teachers have the option of creating their own story beginnings or using ones that are already written.

Providing students with the opportunity to express their feelings in writing is an excellent way to help them to benefit from the bibliotherapeutic process. They can identify their problem(s), experience catharsis, and gain insight, all by expressing in writing their deep thoughts and feelings. No one has to read what they wrote, and students can revise their written expressions concerning a personal or emotional situation at any time they see fit and no one has to ever know.

Poetry Therapy

Poetry therapy as defined by Evans (1974) is the method of therapy based on the principle that a poem is a special medium for expressing emotions and this expression can have psychotherapeutic value. Peck (1979) suggests, "Poetry can do many things for youngsters. It can offer pleasure, familiar language, memories, the comfort of a security blanket, amusement, joy, a sense of relaxation and adventure" (p. 95). Harms and Lettow (1986) link the "intense, emotional nature" of poetry to children's reactions to their environment. They see poetry as encouraging repeated readings and listenings, as provoking consideration of language and of the human condition. Further, poetry encourages participation, empathy, and the gaining of new insights.

Painter (1980) contends: "A poem in itself carries the thought of the poet, but, in trying to understand the author's concepts, the reader reads into it a meaning based on his own experiences. The poem is; it exists for the reader to interpret on his own, to see therein himself or his experiences or his thoughts" (p. 5). According to Burke (1986), "The teacher [and librarian] is confronted with problems not of security but of profusion in poetry. The wealth of poetry available is rich and divergent in form, content, rhythm, rhyme, and mood" (p. 85). Burke goes on to say that answering the following questions can help teachers make a decision.

Does the poem sound good?
Is the rhythm of the poem pronounced?
Are there brief and simple images in the poems?
Does the poem have substance?
Is the poetry rhymed?
Does the poetry have some humor?

In addition, poems for children should be *brief*. Burke points out: "If the answer to the preceding six questions is 'yes' young children will attend to a lengthy poem. They will want the story told and the mood sustained" (pp. 85–86).

Evans recommends that the classroom be a forum in which the sharing of deep personal insights through poetic expression counteracts the growing alienation in our society. He recommends a number of ways poetry can be used as a therapeutic strategy: (1) provide poetry selections to which children read and respond, (2) provide students with poems of a similar mood or topic, and (3) have students share their poems and react to each other's work.

Lucille Clifton's *Everett Anderson's Goodbye* (Holt, 1983); Eloise Greenfield's *Honey, I Love: And Other Love Poems* (Crowell, 1978); and Mel Glenn's *Class Dismissed! High School Poems* (Houghton Mifflin, 1982) are examples of poetic works that lend themselves admirably to bibliotherapy.

Story Schema as an Aid in the Bibliotherapeutic Process

Although strategies like role-playing, puppetry, and journal writing have been around for a number of years, terms like "story schema," "story grammar," "story frames," "semantic mapping," and "semantic webbing" have surfaced only recently as strategies to help increase children's story comprehension and recall (Johnson, Pittelman, and Heimlich, 1986; Stahl and Vancil, 1986; Gordon and Braun, 1983; Moldofsky, 1983). A schema can be thought of as a framework of abstract knowledge that is both general and reflective of an individual's experiences (Stein and Trabasso, 1981). Furthermore, it is a powerful approach to helping students experience catharsis and gain insight. Moldofsky observes that schemata change as an individual processes a new experience. Tierney and Pearson (1981) state that it is assumed that each schema has "slots" that are waiting to be filled as an individual fits new ideas into existing frameworks. Collins and

Smith (1980) point out that schema theory goes beyond the surface level and focuses on both the content and the process of reading. Moldofsky recommends the following steps be used to introduce the strategy so it ties in with already existing schemata:

1. *Activating schemata.* Remind students of problems and solutions they have experienced or have inferred from previous stories.
2. *Organize schemata.* Categorize ideas. The types of problems that emerge are related to wanting or needing, feelings, thinking the "wrong" thing or thinking something different. These clues can be pointed out directly or can develop as students read more stories and are focused to expand upon currently held ideas.
3. *Modeling the process.* To clarify the process of determining the central story problem, give examples, e.g., "Who is the main character?," "What does he or she want, need, feel, or think?" "Check: Does this fit all the important things that happen in the story?" "Statement: The central story problem is that [who]_____ [pick one:] wants/needs/feels/thinks [What?] [pick one:] but/because _____." (pp. 741–742)

The Tenth Good Thing about Barney by Judith Viorst (Macmillan, 1971) is an excellent book to illustrate the steps introduced by Moldofsky. In terms of activating schemata, teachers could ask students if they ever had a cat die and what their feelings were. Then they could ask students to compare what they did to what the boy in the book did, which is step 2 (organize schemata). In modeling the process (step 3) the teacher could ask students to determine the story problem, describe the main character, and tell what the boy wanted, needed, felt, or thought. Also, the teacher could ask them to compare their feelings about their own pet (if they had lost one) to the boy's feelings about his pet.

Story Grammar

Researchers are also finding story grammar a useful tool in studying reading comprehension and in experiencing catharsis and insight. Whaley (1981) states, "Story grammar is a set of rules that will define both a text's structure and an individual's mental representation of story structure" (p. 763). Gordon and Braun point out, "These rules specify stories' component parts, the types of information that occur at various locations, and the relationships among the parts" (p. 116). They continue that by combining the story grammars developed by Stein and Glenn (1979) and Thorndyke (1977), the major story elements that come up are: setting, theme, plot, and resolution. The plot consists of five divisions: starter event, inner response, action, what happens, and reaction (p. 116).

Olson (1984) perceives that Stein and Glenn's grammar describes a story as consisting of two parts: the setting plus one or more episodes. However, she contends that five categories are subsumed under the term episode. The "initiating event" sets the story in motion, causing the main character to respond in some manner (the cat sees a bird). The "internal response" is the reaction of the character to the initiating event; it results in some feeling, thought, or goal that motivates subsequent behavior (the cat wants to eat the bird). The "attempt" is an overt action or series of actions carried out to attain the goal (the cat creeps out on the limb to reach the bird). The "consequence" is the event or action that notes attainment of the goal or failure (the limb breaks, the cat falls from the tree, failing to catch the bird). Finally, the "reaction" is an internal response that describes the character's feelings about the outcome of his or her actions. The reaction may include broader or long-term consequences resulting from reaching or not reaching the goal (the cat is unhappy and wishes she had been more careful) (p. 459).

Gordon and Braun (1983) contend that if teachers wish to increase their awareness of story grammar, the following steps should be utilized.

> *Story selection.* The teacher should choose well-formed stories because the analysis is complex. Good models often have repetitive elements.
> *Story modification.* Stories may require some rewriting for story grammar instruction. Many primary grade fables use the phrase "he said." The meaning is clearly "he said to himself," and so the phrase can be changed to "he thought" so that the internal response is clearly identifiable by the children.
> *Story analysis, parsing, and diagramming.* Teachers need to practice analyzing even well-structured stories. Once the story has been parsed into categories, diagram it for classroom use. This helps keep the structure elements constant and provides students with a visual image of the story parts and the relationships.
> *Asking questions.* All questions should be keyed to the story's structure. Derived from the story, they help the children develop expectations about its content. First, questions related to the story schema can be asked. Later story-specific questions based on the schema questions should be given. Once the story diagram is complete and the children have a summary of the text, inferential questions should be asked. (pp. 118–119)

Whaley also highlights a number of instructional tasks teachers can use to enhance children's knowledge of story structures. She adds, for younger children or poor readers these instructional tasks can become listening tasks.

> *Prediction task.* Students read incomplete stories and tell aloud or in writing what they think comes next.

> *Macro-cloze task.* This task is similar to a traditional cloze activity [where the reader tries to supply omitted words] except that instead of deleting single words, a whole story category (Setting, Beginning, Reaction, etc.) is deleted. Lines are drawn in the printed story to show where material is omitted.
>
> *Scrambled stories.* For this activity, a story can be separated into story grammar categories and jumbled. Students then read the scrambled story and reorder it to make an "effective/logical story." Discussion would center on rationales for different orders and on the functions of various story parts.
>
> *Sorting task.* Students read a brief story and then the teacher gives them sentence strips of all the sentences in the story. The children are asked to sort the sentences into piles to show which ones "go together." When this activity is first introduced, the teacher may direct the children to make a certain number of piles.
>
> *Retelling stories.* Allowing students to retell simple stories may develop or heighten their awareness of common story structures. A good way to get retelling started is for the teacher to tell a story that was read the day before and allow the children to point out any inaccuracies. After each child reads through his or her version of the story silently, they take turns retelling their version to the whole class. The class has to guess which version is the original. Reasons are discussed for accepting or rejecting certain alterations. (pp. 769–770)

That students are allowed to participate in the instructional tasks highlighted by Whaley will help them develop a better perspective of dealing more successfully with emotional issues.

Other suggestions and variations for using story grammar have been provided by Marshall (1983), Sadow (1982), McGee and Tompkins (1981), and Noyce and Christie (1981). Sadow states: "Story grammar offers a means of deriving questions that, taken as a whole, reflect the story as a whole" (p. 518). She further states: "The purpose of asking questions based on story grammar is to foster the development of a story schema. The questions should recapitulate the logical progression of events in the main story line. They thus focus attention on the internal logic and consistency of stories and provide children with systematic experiences (in addition to the actual reading of stories) from which they might derive a generalized framework for processing story information" (p. 519). Marshall found: "Question frames allow the teacher to ask questions well beyond the literal level" (p. 617). She also recognizes: "At times teachers might not wish to ask questions about a story. [This is because] questions do not give clues to the answers or help identify the kind of information the teacher thinks important" (p. 619). To solve this problem, Marshall suggests that teachers "have students retell stories after reading. Students then have to organize the information that they think important and the teacher can evaluate the completeness of the recall. . . . Effective evaluation requires a standard set of criteria to evaluate the completeness of the retelling and the opportunity to evaluate each student's retelling individually" (p. 619). Marshall's checklist looks for the theme, setting, goal or problem, attempts, resolution, and students' reactions.

In this checklist, the teacher lists the students in the left column. There are boxes for recording student retellings four times during the year. After completing a story, a student retells it and the teacher records this individual's performance on the checklist immediately. After the retelling, other students can participate by answering questions or adding information to the retelling. If a different student does the retelling each time, the evaluation takes no additional teacher time, and the teacher has a check on student comprehension ability that can be used for evaluation. Thus, a reading grade can be based on concrete evidence that comprehension has occurred during instruction rather than just during formal assessment (pp. 619–620).

Story Rule Format

McGee and Tompkins (1982) adapted Stein and Glenn's story elements to a story rule format. An example of one of their rules is: Stories have themes, which describe a problem/conflict that the main character encounters. A problem can be between someone and nature, between people or animals, or within someone. The following are examples of activities that were adapted.

1. Have children complete a chart that includes separate columns for problems with nature, between people or animals, and within characters. Children can color a picture of a character from a book that fits each category.

2. Have children make a problem book. Each child draws a picture of a problem that the character has. Then each child draws a picture of a problem that he or she has and dictates a sentence for each problem. All problem pictures are put in a book.

3. Have children act out the problem. (Stories have plots, which tell what the main character does to try to solve the problem. The ways that characters try to solve their problems are by being someone leaving home, someone meeting danger or a monster, someone finding happiness, and someone wise meeting someone foolish.)

4. Teachers can prepare pictures of ways characters try to solve the problem and children can cut and paste the pictures in order. Also, have the children use spoon or paper bag puppets to act out how the problem was solved.

Story Frames

Another strategy for helping children develop comprehension skills is through the use of story frames. Fowler (1982) points out: "A story frame is a sequence of spaces hooked together by key language elements [;] in most cases these language elements are transition words and they often reflect a specific line of thought or argument" (p. 176). Nichols (1980) says: "The intent of the frame is to provide a structure for organizing a student's written responses to a variety of content material" (p. 229). Fowler contends: "Frequent use of the story frames is particularly helpful for children who have trouble keeping to the point of a question or who write conversationally rather than in the style of written language" (p. 177). An example of a story grammar developed by Fowler focusing on the "setting" of a story is:

SETTING

This story takes place ______________. I know this because the author uses the words "______________." Other clues that show when the story takes place are ______________. (p. 177)

According to Fowler, story frames are easy to construct and can be used to help children deal with a variety of ideas, concepts, and information. Four steps are involved in their construction.

1. Read a passage or story and identify the problem on which you want children to focus. It may concern the plot or setting of a story, the facts in a passage, and so on.
2. Sketch out a paragraph that addresses the problem.
3. Take the completed paragraph and delete all words, phrases, and sentences except those needed to sustain the purpose of the paragraph. You will probably need to make a notation under certain spaces so that children will be able to follow the frame more easily.
4. Try the frame with other passages or stories that are similar in theme to the one for which the frame was intended. Modify the frame so it can be used in several situations. (p. 179)

Semantic Mapping and Semantic Webbing

Yet another set of techniques that can be used by teachers for improving children's comprehension of a story's content is through the use of semantic mapping and semantic webbing. Semantic webbing, which is similar to semantic mapping (Pearson and Johnson, 1978), is a process for organizing and integrating information. Semantic webbing, as defined by Freedman and Reynolds (1980), is "a process for constructing visual displays of categories and their relationships" (p. 677). Similarly, Johnson and

Pearson (1984) point out: "Semantic mapping is a categorical structuring of information in graphic form [and it] requires students to relate new words to their own experiences and prior knowledge" (p. 37). Johnson, Pittelman, and Heimlich believe: "The procedure of mapping provides students with a means for both activating and enhancing their knowledge bases regarding the specific topics and words discussed" (p. 780).

Cleland (1981) found that "reading teachers report that their students 'miss the issue' while enjoying the book" (p. 642), because as Adams (1977) puts it children often experience difficulties in organizing cognitively what they hear or read. However, Cleland believes that "teacher-directed semantic webbing [or mapping] can help [children] to see relationships between ideas and characters in a story" (p. 642).

Freedman and Reynolds state that the basic model for constructing a web consists of the web's core question, the web strands, the strand supports, and the strand ties. The "core question" is the focus of the web and the purpose of the inquiry; it is chosen by the teacher. All information and ideas generated for the web by the students are related in some way to the core question. "Web strands" are the answers that the students give to the core question. "Strand supports" are facts, inferences, and generalizations that students take from the story to give clarity and validity to the strands and to differentiate one strand from another. "Strand ties" are the relationships strands have with each other. To implement this strategy, teachers should follow the following basic steps:

1. Set a purpose for reading which encourages students to use a specific reading-thinking strategy. Also decide what part of the story they will read. To set the stage for webbing, students must know the purpose for which they are reading [i.e., getting the main idea, making generalizations, predicting events, etc.]. Additionally, they must know what part of the story they are to read.
2. Formulate a core question for the web based on the reading-thinking strategy and reading unit chosen. [The reading-thinking strategy involves focusing the children's attention on getting the main idea, drawing conclusions, identifying the author's purpose. Whereas the reading unit leads the children to look for certain words, sentences or paragraphs in order to answer the core question.]
3. Elicit from students possible answers to the core question. All responses should be accepted and written on the board in a list separate from the web. Then, by consensus students accept, combine, or reject the answers to the core question.
4. Build student support for the web strands. To provide the supports for a strand, students may need to reread a passage, perhaps orally. The process of justification and clarification leads to further critical, purposeful reading. On the basis of the strand supports they

offer, students may decide that one or more of the chosen strands should be rejected because they are unsupportable.

5. Guide students in relating the strands. When drawing strand ties to display strand interrelationships, the teacher should be careful not to produce a confusing mass of lines and labels.
6. Apply the web. There are at least three ways a teacher may apply a story web. A teacher may use a web to set purposes for further reading the same story. A web may also be a model for constructing other webs for the same story or for other stories. And a web can also be "brought to life" through art, drama, role playing, and other activities that relate the web concepts to students' other knowledge and experiences. (pp. 678–682)

Johnson and Pearson provide teachers a similar but slightly different instructional sequence for using semantic mapping. The sequence involves the following steps: (1) a word important to the topic is selected; (2) the word is written on the chalkboard, a chart tablet, or on a transparency; (3) the class is encouraged to think of words related to the key word, the words are then categorized; (4) the students are asked to work individually and to think of words related to the topic and to categorize their words on a sheet of paper; (5) the students share their lists with the class "and add their words to the class map in categories" (p. 39); (6) the labels for the categories are suggested by the students and put on the semantic map; and (7) the entries on the semantic map are discussed—encourage students to become aware of the new words, gather new meanings from old words, and draw relationships among the new and old words (p. 41).

Some current spin-offs from semantic mapping and semantic webbing have been developed by a number of researchers (Bergenske, 1987; McGinley and Denner, 1987; Gemake, 1984; Smith and Bean, 1983). Bergenske advises: "Before mapping stories children need help in defining elements," (p. 333), which is the missing link. Her Narrative Story Guide is helpful as a transition between finding story elements and creating stories that contain the elements of story maps. The four steps in her Narrative Story Guide are:

Step I—Explain some necessary elements of a narrative story.

1. Title—Name of story.
2. Setting—Where and when the story takes place.
3. Characters—Who is in the story.
4. Problem—Why "what characters want to happen" isn't happening, or difficulty that needs to be overcome in the story.
5. Goal—What the characters want to happen.
6. Episodes—Things that happen.

7. Resolution—How the problem was solved (how the goal was made to happen).

Step II—Analyze stories for story elements.

1. Select stories which lend themselves to this kind of analysis (one major plot, one major goal, clearly defined episodes, one major solution), e.g., "Three Billy Goats Gruff," "Cinderella," teacher composed stories, etc.
2. Reproduce some stories so students can underline elements.
3. Find, pull out, and list elements from stories in books.
4. Design story map-a-pedes. Different kinds of diagrams and pictures may be created.

Step III—Use the Narrative Story Guide (the missing link).

1. Children fill in the blanks to create their own stories.
2. Read these stories aloud.
3. Children rewrite the entire story (if desired).

Step IV—Create stories using the necessary elements.

1. Children analyze their own stories for the elements.
2. They may critique each other's stories for necessary story elements.
3. Students may list the elements, create answers for each one, and then compose a story using the items they've created.
   Example—Title: "The Rabbit's Problem." Setting: one night in spring. Characters: a crazy chicken and a confused rabbit.
4. General Story Map may be used here. [This includes the title, setting, characters, problem, goal, episodes resolution.]. . .[This] may be completed before or after the story is written. (pp. 333–335)

Story Impressions

Story impressions are story fragments in the form of clue words and phrases, which, when assembled, enable the reader to form an overall impression of how characters and events interact in the story (McGinley and Denner, p. 249). According to McGinley and Denner, "They differ from other kinds of previews in that they do not give away large amounts of story content in order to improve comprehension. Using only key words, they aid readers in building anticipatory models of the text prior to reading" (pp. 248–249). Story impressions can be used successfully by teachers if they adhere to the following sequence. McGinley and Denner suggest beginning with an introduction that lets the students know that they can invent a story based on clues that they are given, which are based on a published story. The students can brainstorm ideas for connecting the clues, and the teacher can write their ideas on a chalkboard or overhead projector. After they have finished their story, they compare it to the one that is already in print, commenting on similarities and differences between their version and the original author's. How closely the two match is not important. "The only important thing is to write a logical story based on the clues given" (pp. 251–252).

Interactive Reading

Interactive reading is a method to help children respond meaningfully to text by drawing and by writing ideas that extend and complement the story (Gemake, p. 462). Gemake recommends 11 steps that can help teachers create their own interactive reading materials. She warns that teachers need to be aware of the independent reading levels of their students, and the words and sentences they can decode.

1. Begin by pretending that you are telling your class a fairy tale. Use vocabulary and sentences that suit your students' independent level. Write down your narrative.
2. Break your story into several segments. Stop at points where feelings are aroused, characters are introduced, or action changes course. Think "Where can students step into this story and interact with the setting, characters, and plot at a literal, inferential, critical, and creative level?" Mark those spots with red pencil.
3. Decide how you wish your students to interact with the material. They can illustrate story scenes, draw details, write opinions, supply dialogue with talking balloons, predict outcomes, record feelings—the list of interactions is limited only by your objectives and inventiveness.
4. Type your narrative. Each time you reach a red mark, skip several spaces and type a solid line across the page to mark the interaction. (The lines help students focus on their task.) Then, type the directions. Be specific! Use verbs directing students to draw, write, color. For example, instruct them to "Write some sentences. . . ."; or "List three words. . . ."; or "Draw a picture of. . . ."
5. Compose and type a summary page on which students can react to story characters and plot developments. They can write about favorite characters and story parts, evaluate characters' actions, and write different endings. Finally, they can write and extend the story by composing a new adventure for the hero or changing events.
6. When your interactive story is complete, go back and box in your interactions with heavy lines so they stand out.
7. Print your story, collate your pages, and staple them together.
8. Introduce the concept to the class. You might want to complete a

story yourself to demonstrate the process. Start with short selections of just one or two pages, and move into longer narratives.

9. Provide the necessary motivation, background, vocabulary identification, and concept development for the story.
10. Give the students a reasonable amount of time to complete their assignments. This is an ongoing activity, which can take many days to finish. Students use colored markers, pencils, or crayons to create their books.
11. Set aside time for sharing the completed stories. Have the students design covers for their pieces and place them on the library shelf. Students will want to look through each other's work. (pp. 464–465)

Story Patterns, Circle Stories, and Story Maker

Smith and Bean describe three strategies that help primary grade children comprehend story events and causes. They contend, "Through these strategies, children acquire the ability to predict events and outcomes in a variety of stories and to guide the construction of their own, original stories" (p. 294).

Story Patterns. The story pattern strategy combines reading, writing, listening, and speaking with a visual diagram that helps children comprehend stories and ultimately invent their own. Moreover, it provides a common language for reading and discussing future stories in terms of cause-effect relationships, which become readily apparent when they are treated visually. A very short picture book with a simple theme, such as Esphyr Slobodkina's *The Wonderful Feast* (Hale, 1967), is a good story to illustrate the story pattern concept. As the children discover the pattern by recalling the story, the teacher helps them visualize the story structure by sketching the story animals on the board in a vertical sequence with the horse at the top and the tiny ant at the bottom. During and after this process, the story is read and retold until the idea pattern is firmly established. The next step in this lesson is for the children to create a new story using the same pattern. The teacher, by suggesting how easily the class can make a similar story, might begin with the idea of a family dinner, accompanied by a stick figure sketch. It requires only a little teacher monitoring for the children to be able to call out other people and animals to share the leftovers, making decisions as to the next smallest in size down to the very smallest, perhaps the flea on the dog, as one class suggested.

Circle Stories. Circle stories also capitalize on a visual diagram to guide students' comprehension, discussion, and writing of their own stories (Jett-Simpson, 1981). This strategy follows a predictable pattern that children can learn to identify and duplicate. The main character starts at one location and, after a series of adventures, returns to the starting point to live happily ever after.

To teach this strategy, the teacher draws a large circle on the board or butcher paper and divides it into as many pie-shaped parts as there are adventures in the chosen story. At the top of the circle, a house is drawn to represent the beginning and ending of the character's journey, whether that place is home, the cabin of the journey cake, or Mother Rabbit's lap.

After the teacher reads the story aloud, the class recalls the story to decide the sequence of events that needs to be pictured in the circle diagram. The circle story strategy can be extended for small group work. Each group is given a story to diagram on large paper. Each child in every group is given a portion to illustrate in order to complete the whole diagram. Using large paper for this process allows children in each group to draw pictures simultaneously, an activity that motivates a great deal of oral language. Some children will want to label pictures while others may write descriptive sentences or even include written quotations for their character as the activity progresses. Of course, sharing the finished products increases opportunities for language, reinforces the story pattern, and above all adds to the children's repertoire of ways to appreciate and understand stories.

Story Maker. Rubin (1980) states that the Story Maker, a more complex diagram using story structure, develops in the form of a tree. Smith and Bean contend that the Story Maker was devised primarily to improve writing skills. It develops the child's sense of story best when presented in a series of lessons. Using the Story Maker for the first time, the teacher may choose to present a prepared tree. The teacher explains each level, models its elements, and shows how a variety of stories may be developed. The actual Story Maker can be on the chalkboard, a pegboard, or in any format that lends itself easily to manipulation of the various story parts.

A second lesson may find the teacher again using prepared story contents, but this time they would not be placed in correct position on the Story Maker. Instead, the children would help determine the correct placement of each.

Summary

Olsen points out: "Any child with unrelieved stresses or unfulfilled needs who has the potential to work through his problems can benefit from bibliotherapy" (p. 428). Baily (1956) foresees that reading can help the child overcome insecurity that grows out of repeated failures, economic factors, physical factors, or relations with peers and members of the family. Cianciolo (1965) concludes that through bibliotherapy children have an opportunity to identify, comprehend, and relive in a controlled manner a problem that they are aware of. It is important to note that bibliotherapy is a process that not only has an effect on an existing individual problem but also raises consciousness and invites empathy and understanding of emotional issues that affect society.

For those who constantly debate who should conduct bibliotherapy and what training they should possess, Bohning (1981) and Sullivan (1987) provide some advice. Bohning suggests: "[Using] bibliotherapy effectively requires certain knowledge, materials, and methods on the part of the teacher [or librarian]" (p. 167). However, Sullivan argues: "Neither teachers nor [librarians] have to be trained therapists to lead a good class [or library] discussion about life's problems, all they need is to be sensitive when tackling such issues" (p. 874). Perhaps a combination of the two perspectives is best: Adults should acquaint themselves with the psychological, sociological, and political theories surrounding such issues as death, divorce, and other manifestations of loss. They should understand the developmental levels of childhood and should know the individual children well, and an array of excellent children's literature that handles these issues well. Only then can they be most effective in bringing together the child-reader and the books.

References and Bibliography

Adams, Marilyn J. *Failures to Comprehend and Levels of Processing in Reading.* Technical Report No. 37. Urbana, Ill.: Center for the Study of Reading, University of Illinois, 1977, and Cambridge, Mass.: Bolt, Beranek & Newman, 1977.

Applebee, Arthur N. *The Child's Concept of Story: Ages Two to Seventeen.* Chicago, Ill.: University of Chicago Press, 1978.

Appleberry, Mary H. *Bibliotherapy.* A paper presented at the Thirty-First Annual Conference of the International Reading Association, Philadelphia, Pa., May 1986. Reprinted by permission of Mary Hilton Appleberry, Ed.D. Professor, Elementary Education, Stephen F. Austin State University, Nacogdoches, Texas.

Axelrod, Herman, and Thomas R. Teti. "An Alternative to Bibliotherapy: Audiovisiotherapy." *Educational Technology* 16 (November 1976): 36–38.

Baily, Matilda. "A Candle of Understanding." *Education* 76 (May 1956): 515–521.

Beardsley, Donna A. "Using Books to Change Attitudes toward the Handicapped among Third Graders." *Journal of Experimental Education* 50 (Winter 1981): 52–55.

Bergenske, M. Dianne. "The Missing Link in Narrative Story Mapping." *The Reading Teacher* 41 (December 1987): 333–335. Reprinted with permission of the author and the International Reading Association.

Bernstein, Joanne E. *Books to Help Children Cope with Separation and Loss.* 2nd ed. New York: Bowker, 1983.

Bohning, Gerry. "Bibliotherapy: Fitting the Resources Together." *Elementary School Journal* 82 (November 1981): 166–170.

Boothroy, Bonnie, and Jean Donham. "Listening to Literature: An All-School

Program." *The Reading Teacher* 34 (April 1981): 772–774. Reprinted with permission.

Borden, Sylvia D. *Plays as Teaching Tools in the Elementary School.* West Nyack, N.Y.: Parker, 1970.

Brown, Eleanor Frances. *Bibliotherapy and Its Widening Applications.* Metuchen, N.J.: Scarecrow Press, 1975. Reprinted with permission.

Brown, Margaret Wise. *The Runaway Bunny.* New York: Harper, 1942.

Burke, Eileen M. *Early Childhood Literature for Love of Child and Book.* Boston: Allyn & Bacon, 1986.

Carbo, Marie. "Making Books Talk to Children." *The Reading Teacher* 35 (November 1981): 186–188.

———. "Teaching Reading with Talking Books." *The Reading Teacher* 32 (December 1978): 267–273. Reprinted with permission.

Carlton, Lessie, and Robert H. Moore. *Reading, Self-Directive Dramatization and Self-Concept.* Columbus, Ohio: Merrill, 1968.

Chadbourne, Sherry P. *Bibliotherapy: An Overview and the Librarian's Role,* 1976. ED 131 426.

Cianciolo, Patricia. "Children's Literature Can Affect Coping Behavior." *Personnel and Guidance Journal* 43 (May 1965): 897–903.

Clarke, Barbara K. "Bibliotherapy through Puppetry: Socializing the Young Child Can Be Fun." *Early Child Development and Care* 19 (1985): 338–344.

Cleland, Craig J. "Highlighting Issues in Children's Literature through Semantic Webbing." *The Reading Teacher* 34 (March 1981): 642–646.

Collins, Allan, and Edward Smith. *Teaching the Process of Reading Comprehension.* Technical Report No. 182. Urbana, Ill.: Center for the Study of Reading, University of Illinois, 1980.

Criscuolo, Nicholas P. "Book Reports: Twelve Creative Alternatives." *The Reading Teacher* 30 (May 1977): 893–895.

Davison, Maureen M. "Classroom Bibliotherapy: Why and How." *Reading World* 23 (December 1983): 103–107.

Dreher, Mariam Jean, and Harry Singer. "Story Grammar Instruction Unnecessary for Intermediate Grade Students." *The Reading Teacher* 34 (December 1980): 261–268.

Dreyer, Sharon S. (ed.). *The Bookfinder: A Guide to Children's Literature about the Needs and Problems of Youth Aged 2–15.* Circle Pines, Minn.: American Guidance Service, 1981.

Durkin, Dolores. "What Classroom Observations Reveal and Reading Comprehension Instruction." *Reading Research Quarterly* 14 (1978–1979): 481–533.

Eberle, Robert F. "Developing Imagination through SCAMPER." *Journal of Creative Behavior* 6 (Fall 1972): 192–203.

Evans, Ronald V. "Poetry Theory." Paper presented at the Fiftieth Anniversary of the Florida Council of Teachers of English State Conference, Daytona Beach, Florida, October 17–19, 1974.

Feinberg, Susan. "The Classroom's No Longer Prime Time." *Today's Education* 66 (September/October 1977): 78–79.

Fowler, Gerald L. "Developing Comprehension Skills in Primary Students through the Use of Story Frames." *The Reading Teacher* 36 (November 1982): 176–179.

Fox, Barbara J., and Helen S. Collier. "Skill Focused Bibliotherapy." Unpublished manuscript, North Carolina State University, Raleigh, N.C., 1983. Reprinted with permission.

Freedman, Glenn, and Elizabeth G. Reynolds. "Enriching Basal Reader Lessons with Semantic Webbing." *The Reading Teacher* 33 (March 1980): 677–684. Reprinted with permission.

Galda, Lee. "Playing about a Story: Its Impact on Comprehension." *The Reading Teacher* 36 (October 1982): 52–55.

Gates-MacGinite Reading Test. Boston, Mass.: Houghton Mifflin, 1978.

Gemake, Josephine. "Interactive Reading: How to Make Children Active Readers." *The Reading Teacher* 37 (February 1984): 462–466. Reprinted with permission of the author and the International Reading Association.

Gordon, Christine J., and Carl Braun. "Using Story Schema as an Aid to Reading and Writing." *The Reading Teacher* 37 (November 1983): 116–121. Reprinted with permission of the authors and the International Reading Association.

Griffin, Barbara K. *Special Needs Bibliography—Current Books for/about Children and Young Adults Regarding Social Concerns, Emotional Concerns and the Exceptional Child.* DeWitt, N.Y.: Griffin, 1984.

Harms, Jeanne McLain, and Lucille J. Lettow. "Poetry: Invitations to Participate." *Childhood Education* 63 (October 1986): 6–10.

Heitzmann, William Ray, and Kathleen Esnes Heitzmann. "Sports Literature and the Librarian: Opportunities to Mend, Mold and Motivate—Part I." *Catholic Library World* 48 (December 1976): 207–213. Reprinted with permission.

Hennings, Dorothy G. *Communication in Action.* Chicago, Ill.: Rand McNally, 1978.

Jalongo, Mary Renck. "Bibliotherapy: Literature to Promote Socioemotional Growth." *The Reading Teacher* 36 (April 1983): 796–803.

———. "Using Crisis-Oriented Books with Young Children." *Young Children* 38 (July 1983): 29–36.

Jett-Simpson, Mary. "Writing Stories Using Model Structures: The Circle Story." *Language Arts* 58 (March 1981): 293–300.

Johns, Jerry L., and Linda Lunt. "Motivating Reading: Professional Ideas." *The Reading Teacher* 28 (April 1975): 617–619. Reprinted with permission.

Johnson, Dale D., and P. David Pearson. *Teaching Reading Vocabulary.* 2nd ed. New York: Holt, Rinehart & Winston, 1984.

Johnson, Dale D., Susan D. Pittelman, and Joan E. Heimlich. "Semantic Mapping." *The Reading Teacher* 39 (April 1986): 778–783.

Johnson, Dale D., Susan Toms-Bronowski, and Susan D. Pittelman. *An Investigation of the Effectiveness of Semantic Mapping and Semantic Feature Analysis with Intermediate Grade Level Children (Program Report 83-3).* Madison, Wis.: Wisconsin Center for Education Research, University of Wisconsin, 1982.

Kinney, Margaret M. "The Bibliotherapy Program: Requirements and Training." *Library Trends* 10 (October 1962): 131–132.

Kintisch, Lenore S. "Journal Writing: Stages of Development." *The Reading Teacher* 40 (November 1986): 168–172.

Kircher, Clara J. *Behavior Patterns in Children's Books: A Bibliography.* Washington, D.C.: Catholic University Press of America, 1966.

Kukla, Kaila. "David Booth: Drama as a Way of Knowing." *Language Arts* 64 (January 1987): 73–78.

Larrick, Nancy. *A Parent's Guide to Children's Reading.* 5th ed. Philadelphia: Westminster Press, 1982.

Lundsteen, Sara W. *Children Learn to Communicate.* Englewood Cliffs, N.J.: Prentice-Hall, 1976.

———. "A Thinking Improvement Program through Literature." *Elementary English* 49 (April 1972): 502–512.

McGee, Lea, and Gail Tompkins. "The Video Tape Answer to Independent Activities." *The Reading Teacher* 34 (January 1981): 427–433.

———. "The Young Child as a Story Consumer." Paper presented at the Southeastern International Reading Association Conference, Orlando, Florida, February 26, 1982.

McGinley, William J., and Peter R. Denner. "Story Impressions: A Prereading/Writing Activity." *Journal of Reading* 31 (December 1987): 248–253.

McInnis, Kathleen M. "Bibliotherapy: Adjunct to Traditional Counseling with Children of Stepfamilies." *Child Welfare* 61 (March 1982): 153–160.

Madison, Ann B. "Read and Rock—A Special Kind of Reading Center." *The Reading Teacher* 30 (February 1977): 501–503.

Marshall, Nancy. "Using Story Grammar to Assess Reading Comprehension." *The Reading Teacher* 36 (March 1983): 616–620.

Martin, Charles E., Bonnie Cramond, and Tammy Safter. "Developing Creativity through the Reading Program." *The Reading Teacher* 35 (February 1982): 568–572. Reprinted with permission.

Miccinati, Jeannette L., and Stephen Phelps. "Classroom Drama from Children's Reading: From the Page to the Stage." *The Reading Teacher* 34 (December 1980): 269–272. Reprinted with permission.

Miller, G. Michael, and George E. Mason. "Dramatic Improvisation: Risk-Free Role Playing for Improving Reading Performance." *The Reading Teacher* 37 (November 1983): 128–131.

Moldofsky, Penny Baum. "Teaching Students to Determine the Central Story Problem: A Practical Application of Schema Theory." *The Reading Teacher* 36 (April 1983): 740–745. Reprinted with permission.

Monroe, Margaret E. "A Bibliotherapeutic Model for Library Science." In *Bibliotherapy Sourcebook.* Rhea Joyce Rubin, ed. Phoenix, Ariz.: Oryx Press, 1978.

Munson, Diane. *Adventuring with Books: A Booklist for Prekindergarten to Grade 8.* Urbana, Ill.: National Council of Teachers of English, 1985.

Nauman, Ann K. "School Librarians and Cultural Pluralism." *The Reading Teacher* 41 (November 1987): 201–205.

Newhouse, Robert C., and Suzanne Loker. "Does Bibliotherapy Reduce Fear among Second-Grade Children?" *Reading Psychology* 4 (January–March 1982): 25–27.

Nichols, James. "Using Paragraph Frames to Help Remedial High School Students with Written Assignments." *Journal of Reading* 24 (December 1980): 228–231.

Noyce, Ruth M. "Team Up and Teach with Trade Books." *The Reading Teacher* 32 (January 1979): 442–448.

Noyce, Ruth M., and James F. Christie. "Using Literature to Develop Children's Grasp of Syntax." *The Reading Teacher* 35 (December 1981): 298–304.

O'Bruba, William S., Donald A. Camplese, and Mary D. Sanford. "The Use of Teletherapy in the Mainstreaming Era." *Reading Horizons* 24 (Spring 1984): 158–160.

Olsen, Henry D. "Bibliotherapy to Help Children Solve Problems." *Elementary School Journal* 75 (April 1975): 423–429.

Olson, Mary. "A Dash of Story Grammar . . . Presto! A Book Report." *The Reading Teacher* 37 (February 1984): 458–461.

Painter, Helen W. *Poetry and Children.* Newark, Del.: International Reading Association, 1980.

Pearce, Phillipa. *What the Neighbors Did, and Other Stories.* New York: Crowell, 1973.

Pearson, P. David, and Dale D. Johnson. *Teaching Reading Comprehension.* New York: Holt, Rinehart & Winston, 1978.

Peck, Pauline C. "Poetry: A Turn On to Reading." In *Using Literature & Poetry Affectively*. John E. Shapiro, ed. Newark, Del.: International Reading Association, 1979.

Pellegrini, A. D., and Lee Galda. "The Effects of Thematic-Fantasy Play Training on the Development of Children's Story Comprehension." *American Educational Research Journal* 19 (Fall 1982): 443–452.

Pickert, Sarah M., and Martha L. Chase. "Story Retelling: An Informal Technique for Evaluating Children's Language." *The Reading Teacher* 31 (February 1978): 528–531.

Pittelman, Susan D., Kathy M. Levin, and Dale D. Johnson. *An Investigation of Two Instructional Settings in the Use of Semantic Mapping with Poor Readers (Program Report 85-4).* Madison, Wis.: Wisconsin Center for Education Research, University of Wisconsin, 1985.

Ross, Elinor, and Betty Roe. "Creative Drama Builds Proficiency in Reading." *The Reading Teacher* 30 (January 1977): 383–387.

Rubin, Andee. "Making Stories, Making Sense." *Language Arts* 57 (March 1980): 285–293.

Rudman, Masha K. *Children's Literature: An Issues Approach.* 2nd ed. New York: Longman, 1984. Reprinted with permission, from *Children's Literature: An Issues Approach,* 2nd ed., by Masha Kabakow Rudman. Copyright © 1984 by Longman Inc. All rights reserved.

Russell, David H., and Caroline Shrodes. "Contribution of Research in Bibliotherapy to the Language-Arts Program." *School Review* 58 (September 1950): 335–342.

Rutstein, Nat. "Kids and TV: Challenge to Teachers." *The Reading Teacher* 26 (November 1972): 134–137.

Sadow, Marilyn W. "The Use of Story Grammar in the Design of Questions." *The Reading Teacher* 35 (February 1982): 518–522.

Saint-Exupery, Antoine D. *The Little Prince.* New York: Harcourt, Brace & World, 1943.

Salup, Bernice J., and Alane Salup. *Bibliotherapy: An Historical Overview,* 1978. ED 200 896.

Sebesta, Sam L., James W. Calder, and Lynne N. Cleland. "A Story Grammar for the Classroom." *The Reading Teacher* 36 (November 1982): 180–184.

Shachter, Jaqueline. "Children's Authors on Videotape." *The Reading Teacher* 28 (May 1975): 773–778. Reprinted with permission.

Sherman, Louise. "Have a Story Lunch." *School Library Journal* 33 (October 1986): 120–121.

Sides, Nita K. "Story Time Is Not Enough." *The Reading Teacher* 36 (December 1982): 280–283.

Silverstein, Shel. *The Giving Tree.* New York: Harper, 1964.

Smith, Marilyn, and Thomas Bean. "Four Strategies That Develop Children's Story Comprehension and Writing." *The Reading Teacher* 37 (December 1983): 295–301.

Social, Education Research and Development, Inc. *Institutional Library Services: A Plan for the State of Illinois.* Chicago: American Library Association, 1970.

Spache, George D. *Good Reading for the Disadvantaged Reader.* Rev. ed. Champaign, Ill.: Garrard, 1975.

Stahl, Steven A., and Sandra J. Vancil. "Discussion Is What Makes Semantic Maps Work in Vocabulary Instruction." *The Reading Teacher* 40 (October 1986): 62–67.

Stein, Nancy L., and Christine Glenn. "An Analysis of Story Comprehension in Elementary School Children." In *New Directions Discourse Processing.* Roy Freedle, ed. Norwood, N.J.: Ablex, 1979, pp. 53–120.

Stein, Nancy L., and Tom Trabasso. *What's in a Story: An Approach to Comprehension and Instruction.* Technical Report No. 200. Urbana, Ill.: Center for the Study of Reading, University of Illinois, 1981.

Stephens, Jacquelyn W. *A Practical Guide in the Use and Implementation of Bibliotherapy.* Great Neck, N.Y.: Todd & Honeywell, 1981. Reprinted with permission.

Stewart, Oran J. "Audio-Visual Stories: Pre-Reading Activities for Bilingual Children." *Reading Horizons* 22 (Spring 1982): 218–222.

Sullivan, Joanna. "Read Aloud Session: Tackling Sensitive Issues through Literature." *The Reading Teacher* 40 (May 1987): 874–878.

Thorndyke, Perry W. "Cognitive Structures in Comprehension and Memory of Narrative Discourse." *Cognitive Psychology* 9 (January 1977): 77–110.

Tierney, Robert J., and P. David Pearson. *Learning to Learn from Text: A Framework for Improving Classroom Practice.* Reading Education Report No. 30. Urbana, Ill.: Center for the Study of Reading, University of Illinois, 1981.

Torrance, E. Paul. "Creative Problem Solving." Unpublished manuscript. University of Georgia, Athens, 1979.

Vawter, Jacquelyn M., and Marybelle Vancil. "Helping Children Discover Reading through Self-Dramatization." *The Reading Teacher* 34 (December 1980): 320–323.

Way, Brian. *Development through Drama.* Atlantic Highlands, N.J.: Humanities Press, 1967.

Weinstein, Stuart H. "Bibliotherapy for Children: Using Books and Other Media to Help Children Cope." Paper presented at the Annual Conference of Health Educational Media Association, Miami, Florida, April 1977.

———. "Choosing Media to Help Children Cope." *Audiovisual Instruction* 23 (February 1978): 26–29.

Whaley, Jill Fitzgerald. "Story Grammars and Reading Instruction." *The Reading Teacher* 34 (April 1981): 762–771. Reprinted with permission of the author and the International Reading Association.

Yawkey, Thomas D. "Effects of Social Relationships Curricula and Sex Differences on Reading and Imaginativeness in Young Children." *Alberta Journal of Educational Research* 26 (September 1980): 159–168.

Zaccaria, Joseph S., and Harold A. Moses. *Facilitating Human Development through Reading: The Use of Bibliotherapy in Teaching and Counseling*. Champaign, Ill.: Stipes, 1968.

4

Writing about Loss

Notable Authors Discuss Their Work

MASHA KABAKOW RUDMAN,
JOANNE E. BERNSTEIN,
AND MARIE LOUISE SORENSEN

A number of authors have made enormous contributions to children's literature dealing with loss. They are a varied group and approach their work from diverse perspectives. Some of them are teachers or librarians as well as writers; some have served or work now as editors of other authors' work. Their writing takes the form of fiction, nonfiction, and poetry. All are talented; all understand people's feelings; all are distinctly in tune with children and adolescents.

There are, of course, many more authors who write movingly and effectively about loss than are described here. A glance at the Author Index will demonstrate that there is a long list of people who focus on these deep feelings in their work for children. A few notable authors are interviewed here in order to provide readers with some insight into the writing of books where loss is an important theme, and how this writing is viewed by its creator.

A selection of these authors' in-print works can be found at the end of this chapter; other titles mentioned here are currently out of print.

Mel Glenn

Mel Glenn teaches in the same high school that he attended as an adolescent. He thinks that this is an important influence on his work "because part of me has never left this school. I once read somewhere that every writer is emotionally 14 years old. I try to listen to that voice, so that when I see a kid, third row, second seat, or a kid comes to me with a problem, part of that is me. I've seen it; I've felt it; and hopefully I can write about it."

Glenn's books, *Class Dismissed! High School Poems* and *Class Dismissed II: More High School Poems,* contain a number of poems about loss. When asked to comment, Glenn said, "Maybe I'm projecting, but I think that every kid feels loss at one time or another. It could be something minor: yesterday a girl came into my office; she was hysterical. I said, 'My God, what happened? Who died?' She had had a fight with her boyfriend. To her that was a loss, and a big one. In another case, a girl, one of the brightest we have this year, is suicidal. There are always losses. There is emotional loss, and there is pain. I don't think you can be a teenager without experiencing pain. I don't think you can be an adult without experiencing pain. But teenagers go through life majoring in theater. Everything is a crisis. Everything is monumental. Everything is 'NOW.' And whether it's a car they can't live without, or a teacher they can't get along with, or the loss of a best friend, or a breakup with a sweetheart, there are losses."

The poems in both of the *Class Dismissed* books are drawn from real life. For example, the poem "Stella Kolsky" (*Class Dismissed!,* p. 91) is based on actual fact. The poem dramatically and movingly reveals the impact that a suicide has on the rest of the family. It begins:

> "Last week my brother jumped from the roof of our apartment house
> And in the process killed a whole family."

It ends:

> "It's as if he had taken my hand when he jumped.
> Martin, what were you thinking on the way down?"

In response to the question "What do you hope for in your readers' response?" Glenn answered, "I want a kid to read the poem and know he's not alone . . . to say, 'Oh, that kid is me. It sounds like me, or I've felt that way.' I think many times kids are too tight to know how to articulate their feelings. If they see a poem where the characters are real to them, that they say something to the readers, then the poem can serve as an emotional bandage."

Glenn feels for the children he writes about. He says that it may be a way of reliving his own adolescence. In response to the suggestion that sometimes writing is a way of trying to undo our own losses, he responded, "Mark Twain said that all writing is autobiographical. No matter what you write, you write of yourself and through your own perceptions. It's a way of reliving."

One poem that has special appeal for Mel Glenn is "Elizabeth McKenzie" (*Class Dismissed II,* p. 32). Elizabeth is a young woman who is a secret writer of plays. She is afraid to show her writing to her teacher for fear of criticism. The teacher does not respond to her tentative attempts to talk to him. And so, in the end, she puts her writing away, hoping that one day she will "have the courage to get my act together."

One reason Glenn feels so strongly about this poem is that as a teacher, he tries to encourage his students "to show me if they have something in their drawer that they've stuffed away. It wasn't done for me, so let me do it for somebody else." A recurrent theme in Glenn's writing is the attention that he thinks youngsters want from the significant adults in their lives. As he says in the poem "Lisa Goodman" (*Class Dismissed!,* p. 15):

"I once read in a play,
'Attention must be paid.'
Not really."

Glenn states, with passion, "An English teacher has about 150 kids a day. That's a minute a kid. That's not proper; that's not right. And many of these kids cry, beg, not overtly, for some kind of attention. And often the quiet kid, and I was a quiet kid in high school, doesn't get it. Many people go through school untouched by human hands, and that's a shame." Mel Glenn's work touches young readers and helps them to see that they are not alone.

Elaine Landau

Elaine Landau's writing is nonfiction and is aimed primarily at young adults of junior high and high school age. Her topics include Alzheimer's disease, child abuse, eating disorders, the elderly, homosexuality, the homeless, teenage prostitution, and sexually transmitted diseases.

Landau does reams of research for each of her books. Her status as public librarian in a large urban system (her full-time job) affords her access to many resources. She looks at sociological, psychological, and medical sources. "I've always been a researcher, but I've never wanted to produce dry textbook materials. Usually I try to combine interviews with traditional research. If I interview a well-known authority on a subject I feel that it adds immeasurably to the books' value and interest."

In all of her books she goes out of her way to present information honestly and in an unbiased manner. "I think it's very important to present the whole spectrum of an issue. In writing nonfiction for young people, you have a special obligation to present the truth. I don't write books with a message. Everyone has experienced loss—it's a universal feeling. If you can bring the feeling home to your reader, then you've done your job as a writer."

Even with books where the specific situation is not a universal one, such as *On the Streets: The Lives of Adolescent Prostitutes,* Landau says, "I think that there's a part of everyone in everything that I write. We've all known pain. Young readers will recognize the feelings expressed in the book, but hopefully none of them (although I know that there are some) will come to experience that kind of life."

"The human fight, the human failure—all those kinds of feelings are universal and real. In *The Homeless,* even if young people have a home, they can identify with what it is like to perhaps lose a sense of structure and security that they are used to. Homelessness is a very real thing; it could happen to anyone. The people I interviewed for the book could have been anybody. Homeless people can no longer be stereotyped as eccentric recluses. They are simply human beings who want to tell what happened to them. It is very moving because what they've lost is a basic human right—the right to shelter. When you lose your shelter, terrible things happen to you. You lose your stature as a human being in our society. You become dejected; you're viewed as a skid row person. If you can't get to a restroom you begin to develop body odor, and you can't get to a restroom because you are immediately thrown out of a restaurant or bus station lavatory. It's a self-perpetuating thing that is replete with humiliation and a good deal of pain."

"Children who are homeless don't want to go to school because one of the first things that comes up is 'Where do you live,' or 'Can I come to your house?' It's terrible that there are people without shelter in the United States. It affects everyone, whether you're in that situation or not."

"My book, *Alzheimer's Disease,* clearly reflects my opinions and feelings about loss. It deals with what it is like to lose a loved one, as well as to lose a part of yourself. It's all about what it is to be alive with part of you missing, and keeping on missing more and more. At first you may forget only parts of things, and then, as your brain further deteriorates, you won't know your cousin; you won't know your child. And the fact that it's slow and inexorable makes it even more difficult."

"I didn't know anyone with Alzheimer's disease before I wrote the book, but I felt that it was an important thing to write about. Alzheimer's disease victims and their families have to deal with what's happened to their lives. Their reality is inescapable. One woman who I interviewed said, 'Everyone tells me to make the best of the life I have left. How can I do that?' The situation has a strong resemblance to a terminally ill person, but not entirely. That person will die, and you'll lose them, but that person will die whole. These people know they're deteriorating. They know that perhaps they'll eventually have to wear a diaper. They know that they're going to be saying bizarre things, that they may leave their house and be unable to find their way back."

Landau goes on to explain why she writes as she does. "I write about things that touch my life, things that I want to talk about with people. I write about things that I think should be written about, things that should be supported, that people should touch and very often don't. It's very important to me to write books that are meaningful and relevant. I want my books to be useful to the young people who read them. I hope that they won't just read a chapter for a school assignment and not want to read more."

"I want the people who read my books to see themselves in the profiles presented. I try to dispel stereotypes. If I can move my readers, if I can reach out and connect with a person, that makes the writing worthwhile."

Patricia MacLachlan

Patricia MacLachlan consistently provides readers with high-quality writing, memorable characters, keen observations, humor that never demeans, and plots that hold our attention and reflect our feelings in a way that extends our understanding of ourselves and others.

MacLachlan's writing deals with everyday losses as well as massive ones. "I love children's insights and their humor. I think that they understand pain. I feel childlike. I feel their vulnerability. Children live on the edge of loss and loneliness. Children live with it on an intimate basis. In a sense they live bittersweet lives of joy and sorrow. Children are lightning rods who reflect and absorb our feelings."

MacLachlan herself keeps wondering and questioning. "It's hard for me to let some things be. I need to know why. I want to find out how things can be changed. I question everything." This sense of investigation and of understanding that nothing is perfect pervades MacLachlan's writing. All of her books focus on what people are rather than what they are not. The elderly, such as the grandfather and grandmother in *Through Grandpa's Eyes,* and Old Pepper in *Unclaimed Treasures,* help young people to see the world in a different-from-the-ordinary way. It is not unusual for the elderly and young people to be friends and to engage in conversations that are philosophical, mutually respectful, and serious.

In *Seven Kisses in a Row,* the children's parents leave them in the care of a young aunt and uncle who are expecting their first child. The young couple learns a great deal about how to parent while they are baby-sitting for their niece and nephew. Emma, the young girl in the story, contributes most of the education, but she, too, finds herself adjusting to her parents' temporary absence, and to the new personalities in her home, so that, after five days, she has broadened her views.

Arthur, for the Very First Time introduces us to an assortment of people and situations that reflect not only many different perspectives but also a number of losses. In this book Arthur is also in the temporary care of an aunt and uncle, only this couple is elderly, and it is to their house that Arthur goes, rather than remaining at home. The books deals with foster care and desertion as well as the prospect of a new sibling for Arthur. Primarily it helps readers not only to understand how to handle loss but also to view the world and themselves in a different way.

Cassie Binegar contains another child protagonist who, with the aid of her grandmother, comes to terms with loss. Cassie is not perfect, sweet, or unselfish. She has a very difficult time adjusting to her grandfather's death, and to the family's move to a new location. She fears for her father's and brother's safety when they go out fishing. Throughout the course of the book she is helped to handle all of her fears and negative feelings. Readers learn with her how her behavior affects those she loves, and how what we think is not always what is.

Mama One, Mama Two deals with the feelings of fear and loss that a foster child has, and provides us with a model of a loving, understanding, and nurturing foster mother. *Sarah, Plain and Tall,* the 1986 Newbery Award winner, echoes this mother, but Sarah brings her own perspective of the world, and she broadens the vision of the children and their father, to whom she has come as a mail-order bride. Here again the author deals with themes of loss. Everyday life and relationships are juxtaposed with the sorrow that each of the characters feels. In *Sarah,* the language is spare and immediate, reflecting the outer landscape of the prairie setting for the story. Indeed, the inner-outer landscape becomes an important feature of the book. Its leanness invites readers to add, interpret, and reread for more and more depth. It's a book that can be read by any age reader, including adults. When MacLachlan's father read a piece of the book aloud to her mother (who suffers from Alzheimer's disease and lives in a nursing home), it touched her in a way that ordinary conversation could not, and she cried.

MacLachlan is not conscious of using any theory or rules to treat issues of loss. "Not, certainly at the beginning when I'm writing the story. As I'm going over it I have a little external Patty MacLachlan that sits over my shoulder and helps me be more honest, more realistic, and less self-indulgent. I try to make the characters speak their lines instead of the author. I think it's wonderful when you forget that the author is there and let the characters speak."

But she is conscious of trying to be honest and "to reflect what I know and to show that it's not simple to deal with loss. However, it is very important to me to show that children can cope and take power."

Katherine Paterson

Although many of Katherine Paterson's books deal with loss: death, desertion, foster care, war, sibling jealousy, and being an outsider, it would be a gross error to imagine that she writes them to be part of a trend, or simply to exemplify a theme of loss. "When I wrote about death it was because my family had come through a very traumatic experience; when I wrote about a foster child, it was because I had gone through the experience of being a foster mother myself."

"My more recent book, *Park's Quest,* is about a boy whose father died in Vietnam, who wants to know about his father and what happened there. One of the elements that I've put into this book is the overpowering image of the Vietnam War Memorial where the memorial is to those who died, not to the glory of war. Another element is the question of Parsifal: 'What ails thee?' Even though my readers will probably not be aware of it, the young protagonist really lives out the legend of Parsifal."

Paterson was born in China, the daughter of Southern Presbyterian missionary parents. After earning her master's degree in the English Bible, she served for four years as a missionary in Japan. It is no wonder that her books reflect not only her familiarity with these cultures but also a strong foundation in religious thought, and that her characters face universal dilemmas.

In all of her work Paterson celebrates the ordinary and humanizes the exotic. Her balanced perspective on life and her sense of humor are also important features of all of her books. "People fuss at me because I've made them laugh in *Bridge to Terabithia.* As though they would have cared one whit for Leslie, if they hadn't laughed earlier! Of course the tragedy and the sadness of death is because it happens in the midst of life. And we don't want it to happen."

Her engagement with the characters, an identification her readers share, comes across powerfully in all of her books. Many people write, asking her why she permitted Leslie (in *Bridge to Terabithia*) to die. In her 1978 Newbery Award acceptance speech, Paterson revealed that the book had been written in response to her own encounter with cancer, and to the death of her son David's closest friend. As she wrote the book and came closer to the inevitable moment when Leslie would die, because, after all, this was to be a book dealing with the death of a young person, Paterson found herself unable to continue the writing. She had to take time to mourn, not only the character's death but also the death of the young child who had been her son's friend. And as one of Paterson's friends pointed out, she had to come to terms with her own mortality. This was the challenge that led to the completion of the book.

Paterson's books feature characters who tackle problems that would confound many adults. They exhibit great strength, though all of them are human and possess flaws. There are many lessons to be learned within the context of the story, but Paterson says, "I do feel very strongly that, although I have learned a great deal from books, and I owe more than I could ever repay for who I am and what I believe to books, I think it's only when the author has not set out to teach me something, that has allowed the book to be what is true for himself or herself, so that it's my choice what I want from this book, that the learning has taken place. Then, you go back and read the same book, and you've learned something different. That's because the book is whole; the author is giving it to you whole. And so when I set out to write I guess my conscious thing is not that I'm going to teach a message but that I'm going to tell a true story, and then I will trust the reader to learn from it whatever he or she wants to or is able to."

By her own account, three principles drive Paterson's writing. She believes that children are entitled to stirring stories. These stories should be written in language that is vibrant and respectful of the reader. And the stories must deal honestly and truthfully with important issues.

Certainly, all of her work reflects these principles. The twelfth-century protagonists in her books set in Japan must cope with death, war, betrayal, violence, and rejection. In stories like *The Great Gilly Hopkins* and *Come Sing, Jimmy Jo,* the talented young protagonists must face the fact that their birth parents are not what they would wish, and that they must learn to know who the adults are who are trustworthy and loving. In *Bridge to Terabithia,* Jesse must decide to continue the kingdom of fantasy and promise that he and Leslie created. In *Jacob Have I Loved,* in which the force of jealousy is palpable, Louise triumphs in a way that acknowledges the need to compromise. And on through all of the others, Paterson brings us rich stories, peopled with strong characters, which we return to again and again, to find fresh sources of challenge, inspiration, and solace.

Norma Simon

Norma Simon is a prolific writer whose work is intended to involve young children in confronting, honoring, and coping with their own feelings. The career path that leads to this special interest and ability runs through a lifetime of professional work with young children.

Simon's story begins with an encounter with Dr. Abraham Maslow, one of her early teachers and mentors, when she was a student at Brooklyn College in the 1940s. "When I went to him and told him that what I'd like to do more than anything is to help emotionally disturbed children, his answer was, 'Well, if you're going to help children who have problems, you should first know about healthy children, and the best place you can learn about that is Bank Street College.' And that did it. It changed the rest of my life. My experience at Bank Street was the primary source of my understanding and respecting young children. My teachers and advisors were all giants in their fields. Each of them made a very deep impression on me as a young student and their influence continues to this day."

"I also find that the work of Viktor E. Frankl, the psychiatrist, was particularly important in my books that deal with death and loss. Frankl's books speak about the role of the survivor and about the transcendence that's necessary in order to give life meaning and make it possible to survive. His theme was that if you live a meaningful, responsible life you thereby have a right to live. He wrote his books about Holocaust survivors, but, in the final analysis, we're all survivors."

Simon's work, more than 40 books spanning many years, is primarily aimed at young children and is remarkable for its ability to take a whole picture into consideration. Even though she usually focuses on one issue (diverse families, accepting one's feelings, death, anger, single-parent families, adoption, weddings), she does not lose sight of other elements. In a poetic way she conveys information and empathy so that the stories never become tract. As always, the magic involved in this conversion of fact to "literature" defies explanation.

To help give some insights into how she works and develops these concepts into finished books, Simon adds some background information. "First and last, I think about my work as creating children's literature. Then, I've observed and lived the realization that all of life involves small and large losses, so you're always coping, one way or another. The subjects I write about, serious ones about children's emotional concerns or funny ones about their intimate experiences with animals, real or stuffed, are all very important to explore inside of myself and then to verify my expression with children. I visit many schools where I talk to children about work in progress, and then they write their ideas or tell them to me to help me expand my own thinking on these subjects. I visit our local school each week, to help with the children's creative writing, and for many years now the children are used to hearing my new ideas, telling me what they think and feel, drawing pictures on a book topic, and finally, seeing the finished book, which is often dedicated to them."

In response to the question of what makes her think that a book is worth writing, Simon replies, "It's usually something I hear or see from my time in the classroom that gives me a clue for a concept book. Adult books, newspapers, and magazines will contain ideas to inspire me to write a new book, as well as the excellent suggestions of my editors and my husband. The inspiration comes from many sources, but, when I turn it back to my own thoughts and feelings, it needs to feel right before I begin to write about it."

Simon collects everything that feeds into the emotional truth of the child's life. She is, above all, a listener and an observer. Then she translates what she has heard and seen into language with which young children can identify and appreciate and transforms the whole into a book that is true and enduring.

Cynthia Voigt

Cynthia Voigt's *Homecoming* was accepted as an unsolicited manuscript by Atheneum, and so began the saga of the Tillerman family. This family, the four children—Dicey, Sam, James, and Maybeth—and their grandmother, demonstrates survival. Each character has sustained massive loss: The children's father deserted them and their mother when they were very young, and then their mother abandoned them and subsequently died in a mental institution. Mrs. Tillerman, their grandmother, endured marriage with a cold and analytic man who was emotionally abusive of their children, all of whom either died or left home without any further contact. Each of the subsequent stories in the saga, *Dicey's Song, A Solitary Blue, The Runner, Come a Stranger,* and *Sons from Afar,* extends and deepens the story by focusing on a different character and perspective. Loss is an important ingredient of each story, but it is in the coping rather than the trauma that the stories reside.

The stories reflect all sorts of losses in addition to the devastating ones of abandonment and death. Jeff, one of Dicey's friends, and the protagonist in his own right of *A Solitary Blue,* must come to terms not only with his mother's desertion but also his father's personality, his relationship with his peers, and his understanding of the variety of human responses. In the end he recognizes his mother for what she is and accepts her limitations. He ceases to blame himself or to hope for what can not be. Mina, the center of attention in *Come a Stranger,* is another character we have met previously as a friend to Dicey. Her experiences as the only black person to be admitted to a dance camp, her unrequited love for Tamer, Bullet's running partner in *The Runner,* and her relationship with her family are meaty issues for her own story. It is certain that the audience is eager for more stories about this community readers have come to care about.

The Tillerman family and their friends are so rich in experience and character, and have so many narratives yet untold, that it is no wonder that they can fill many books. Voigt tells us, "I knew by the time I was through with *Homecoming* that I was going to be writing *Dicey's Song,* because even I knew that it would be too long to include it all in one book. I think of *Dicey's Song* as part three of *Homecoming.* I also knew at that point, roughly, Bullet's story *(The Runner).* That's a story I seem not to be able to let go of." This, of course, is the story of Sam, known as Bullet, the children's uncle who was killed in Vietnam. One of the characters in this book, Tamer, comes back again in *Come a Stranger.*

When asked how she copes with the deaths of her characters, particularly Bullet's death, Voigt replied, "I really wanted to save his life. And I thought of a way to weasel it. I came to the last chapter of *The Runner* and I thought, 'Wait a minute! I don't really have to.' I could write the last conversation so that it was possible to save him. And I could hear my own character saying inside my head, 'Come on, lady. . . .' "

"I think that the characters are as false or artificial or as true and as real as the things in any book I read. How do I cope with the loss of Hamlet? How do I cope with the loss of a friend this Fall? Somehow, I don't know, it all winds together, and is enough the same so that there is an interplay. It's not that you don't feel it, and it's not like playing with paper dolls. It isn't that way at all. I really did have a terrible time killing off Bullet because I really liked him. I really liked him. He would have grown to be quite something. And it was, of course, necessary that he die. So that I knew that I had to do it. I have a feeling that it affects my daily life more than I understand, which is to say that I'm quite capable of becoming depressed when I write that section. I'm thinking about it as if in fact I were having a real loss. It's real and unreal at the same time, and maybe because it's partly unreal that it's possible to do. But things that are real are in fact often easier to cope with than those things that are imaginatively approaching. The anxiety is different when it's factual."

Voigt has been a teacher for many years, and she uses her experience with children as a source for her writing. She and her colleagues understand that "the reason for talking about things like love and death and misery in a classroom is because the kids are going to have to face them, and if you've thought about something like that before you face it, then you may have something to bring to what may otherwise be a situation that's impossible to handle." She does not underestimate her audience. She treats them with respect. She pays attention to them, and partly because of her experience as a mother, partly because of her coming into contact with so many young people as a teacher, she knows them well.

Voigt's teaching style also guides her in her writing. "The only conscious principle that I can think of is to just query the matter and not act as if there are any answers. I think that writing is like thinking-around, thinking-it-out, trying to understand this problem. And it seems to me that there are never any answers, except that it's better when you ask the questions. Telling the truth is an operating principle throughout. At least attempting to tell the truth, even recognizing that it's impossible to tell." Because of her success in telling the truth and reaching readers through characters who engage in the struggle to endure, Cynthia Voigt's work makes an enormous contribution.

Jane Yolen

Jane Yolen is a storyteller, an editor, a mother, wife, and mentor for other writers. She has recently been selected to have her own imprint for Harcourt Brace Jovanovich and will be responsible for the publication of four to six children's books a year. The recipient of such honors as the 1988 Kerlan Award for a body of work in children's literature, Yolen is one of the most prolific of modern writers for young readers. Her books include fantasy, realistic novels, picture books, poetry, adventure stories, books with outrageous puns, songbooks, humor, and some nonfiction. A number of her works deal directly with loss. *The Gift of Sarah Barker* is about leaving home and about abuse, as well as the universal theme of growing up. *The Moon Ribbon and Other Tales* contains a number of tales that deal with loss in one form or another. The search for identity and leaving home recur, as does the necessity of dealing with death. *The Stone Silenus* confronts the issues of serious emotional disturbance as well as suicide. *Children of the Wolf,* a poignant story of feral children, provides a look at adoption as well as death and understanding one's feelings. The Pit Dragon trilogy contains global themes of independence and power, but it very movingly treats the death of a dragon as one of the more traumatic events in the story. *Cards of Grief* describes a society in which there are mandated rituals of mourning, and "grieving is the highest art." It is a death-centered fantasy. *The Girl Who Loved the Wind* deals with leaving home, with the implication that the child will never return. And this list is by no means all-inclusive.

Yolen says, "Sometimes it takes me days, weeks, and even months, when I'm writing about a loss, to actually set the loss down on paper. When I'm reaching the point in the book that involves the death of a character, often I have trouble dealing with it because I'm so involved with the people in the story. In the second book of the Pit Dragon series I put off writing the chapter in which Heart's Blood dies for weeks. I tried to find other ways, besides actually killing her—plot twists in which the emotional impact would be the same. Or a way in which the characters could resolve the story in as effective a way. I just couldn't find a different solution. It was very hard for me to accept the death of this character."

Yolen researches all of her books. Even the fantasy books require information and specificity that sends her to libraries, historical societies, archives, and experts. For *The Devil's Arithmetic,* her book about the Holocaust, she engaged in three kinds of research: secondary sources, that is, books about the Holocaust from a psychological and historical perspective; firsthand accounts in book form; interviews with survivors, and asking other people to interview survivors when she thought that the questions would have to be of too intimate a nature (such as, "What color was the ink on the number tattooed on your arm?"). The result is a book whose authenticity is without question, and whose impact is extraordinary. The child in the story who experiences the Holocaust firsthand through the device of time travel is so real to the reader that the experience becomes one that the reader is drawn into from the start.

Yolen writes the losses of her own life into her books. "*Cards of Grief* was written while my father was dying. *Bird of Time* and 'The Boy Who Sang for Death' were really about my mother's death. *The Boy Who Had Wings* was about a nonloss of mine: the fact that despite much pressure to do so, I did not give away (or deny) my talents as a writer. So *The Boy Who Had Wings* was a story that made a positive recognition of something that had not occurred. The first two or three times that I drafted *The Stone Silenus* it was the character of the mother who died. But after my own mother died, it was too painful for me to have the mother die in the book, so I changed it to the father. Of course this was before my own father's death."

The issue or theme never overpowers the story in any of Yolen's books. And the poetic language makes the emotion and interaction of the characters even more effective. Yolen tells the story about *The Girl Who Loved the Wind,* "a story I wrote for myself, out of my own history. I received a letter from a nurse who told me that she had read the story to a dying child, and the story had eased the little girl through her final pain. If I can continue to write with as much honesty and love as I can muster, I will truly have touched magic—and passed it on."

Charlotte Zolotow

A giant in the field of children's literature, Charlotte Zolotow is an accomplished and respected author, as well as a long-time editor for Harper & Row. She has the distinction (with two other authors, Jane Yolen and Tomie dePaola) of having her own imprint. This means that she is in charge of selecting books to be published under her exclusive aegis.

Zolotow's books reflect her respect and empathy for children. She says that she works from the double exposure of her own memory of having been a child, and of still being aware as an adult. "I think all adult emotions are the same as the child's except that we've found ways to protect ourselves. The intensity even the degree are very similar."

When asked what governs her writing about themes of loss, Zolotow commented, "There is no set of principles I use. It's something that I'll feel deeply, so there is an overflow of emotion that has no place else to go, and shapes into a story. Sometimes my writing comes from a memory of my childhood experience, compared to a child I see going through the same thing. Or sometimes it comes from an adult incident and reminds me of something that did happen to me as a child—when I felt the same way as the present adult incident makes me feel."

Zolotow's writing talks of everyday losses as well as massive ones. *When the Wind Stops,* a simple story of a child's going to bed, reflects some questions about the constant loss and renewal in the world: The sun goes away; where does it go? Where is the wind when it has stopped blowing? The book handles the philosophical issues of cyclical appearance and disappearance, and the need to be reassured that the child and the world will be there in the morning. *Timothy Too* reveals the issue of a younger sibling, and *My Grandson Lew* sensitively uncovers the mutual remembering and mourning by a young boy and his mother of his dead grandfather, his mother's father.

In all of her books, Zolotow conveys a clarity and truth that connect with the reader's feelings. She says that this comes as a result of "the distillation of the way I feel about my life. I do feel that there's both a sadness and beauty in all things. Even in joy there's sadness because you know it's not going to last at that intensity forever. The sadness has a bittersweet quality that reminds me of a garden. The garden is beautiful and transient so that in its moment of greatest beauty you know it will disappear, but come back again. The feeling of cycles recur in many of my books and poems. One of the mysterious paradoxes of life is that it includes death."

Early Sorrow, a book of short stories that Zolotow has recently compiled, contains stories that reflect the losses that adolescents endure in their everyday lives. Zolotow says, "Adolescence is one of the most intense periods in a human's life because you do have adult emotions but not the experience and knowledge of how to cope with them. I can remember so clearly that perfectly well-meaning and loving adults just couldn't cope with the intensity, with the quality of emotion that I felt when I was a young girl; they just didn't believe that I was grown up enough to feel that way. It is very hard to cope with someone else's intensity, particularly if you think that you're wiser than they. And this is what happens so often with adults: they don't give younger people credit for being as wise as they are. Adults may be more knowledgeable, but they are not always wiser."

One of the hallmarks of Zolotow's books is that she does, indeed, respect the wisdom of the young. In *Someone New* (a book some people call a book about "epiphany"), a young boy slowly and uneasily recognizes that he is not what he once was, and that, therefore, the world, too, has changed. The boy, in putting aside what he once enjoyed, and moving toward a new stage in his life, reflects the constant change and development of all of us, no matter how old we are. The boy has sustained a loss in leaving some of the pleasures of his childhood, but he is gaining too, and we, as readers, keenly feel with the boy.

Zolotow's books are not didactic, although they powerfully teach. They are not tract, although there is a spiritual quality to them. They are not complex, but they are deep. Her books are a mixture of the sensory and the philosophical, the commonplace and the ephemeral. They are poetic prose. They comfort and enlighten, speaking to the youngest and the oldest of readers.

These authors and more share among them a respect for themselves and their craft, and a responsibility for telling the truth to children. They deal with themes that can invite bathos and banality, didacticism, and moralizing. But the best of them avoid any hint of these. The best of them write from the heart and reach the hearts of readers.

Titles in Print by the Notable Authors

Glenn, Mel

Class Dismissed! High School Poems. Illus. by Michael Bernstein. Houghton Mifflin, 1982.
Class Dismissed II: More High School Poems. Illus. by Michael Bernstein. Clarion, 1986.
One Order to Go. Clarion, 1984.
Play-by-Play. Clarion, 1986.

Landau, Elaine

Alzheimer's Disease. Watts, 1987.
Child Abuse: An American Epidemic. Messner, 1985.
Different Drummer: Homosexuality in America. Messner, 1986.
Growing Old in America. Messner, 1985.
The Homeless. Messner, 1987.
On the Streets: The Lives of Adolescent Prostitutes. Messner, 1987.
Why Are They Starving Themselves? Understanding Anorexia Nervosa and Bulimia. Messner, 1983.
(and Hermelie Heimlich). *Sexually Transmitted Diseases.* Illus. by D. Armstrong and H. Haundsfield. Enslow, 1986.

MacLachlan, Patricia

Arthur, for the Very First Time. Illus. by Lloyd Bloom. Harper, 1980; Scholastic, 1982, pap.
Cassie Binegar. Harper, 1982; 1987, pap.
Mama One, Mama Two. Illus. by Ruth Bornstein. Harper, 1982.
Sarah, Plain and Tall. Harper, 1985; 1987, pap.
Seven Kisses in a Row. Illus. by Maria P. Marella. Harper, 1983.
Through Grandpa's Eyes. Illus. by Deborah Ray. Harper, 1980; 1983, pap.
Tomorrow's Wizard. Illus. by Kathy Jacobi. Harper, 1982.
Unclaimed Treasures. Harper, 1984; 1987, pap.

Paterson, Katherine

Angels and Other Strangers: Family Christmas Stories. Crowell, 1979; Avon, 1980, pap.
Bridge to Terabithia. Illus. by Donna Diamond. Crowell, 1977; Avon, 1979, pap.
Come Sing, Jimmy Jo. Lodestar, 1985; Avon, 1986, pap.
Gates of Excellence: On Reading and Writing Books for Children. Lodestar, 1981.
The Great Gilly Hopkins. Harper, 1978; Avon, 1979, pap.
Jacob Have I Loved. Harper, 1980; Avon, 1981, pap.
The Master Puppeteer. Illus. by Haru Wells. Harper, 1976; Avon, 1981, pap.
Of Nightingales That Weep. Illus. by Haru Wells. Harper, 1974, 1980; Avon, 1980, pap.
Park's Quest. Lodestar, 1988.
The Sign of the Chrysanthemum. Illus. by Peter Landa. Harper, 1973; Avon, 1980, pap.
Yours Brett. Lodestar, 1988.

Simon, Norma

All Kinds of Families. Illus. by Joe Lasker. Whitman, 1975.
Cats Do, Dogs Don't. Whitman, 1986.
Children Do, Grownups Don't. Illus. by Helen Cogancherry. Whitman, 1987.
Cuando Me Enojo. Illus. by Dora Leder. Whitman, 1976.
Elly the Elephant. Illus. by Stanley Bleifield. Whitman, 1982 (repr. of 1962 ed.).
Every Friday Night. Illus. by Harvey Weiss. United Synagogue, 1982.
Go Away, Warts! Illus. by Susan Lexa. Whitman, 1980.
Hanukah in My House. Illus. by Ayala Gordon. United Synagogue, 1960.
Hanukkah. Illus. by Symeon Shimin. Harper, 1966.
Happy Purim Night. Illus. by Ayala Gordon. United Synagogue, 1984.
How Do I Feel? Illus. by Joe Lasker. Whitman, 1970.
I Know What I Like. Illus. by Dora Leder. Whitman, 1971.
I Was So Mad! Illus. by Dora Leder. Whitman, 1974.
I Wish I Had My Father. Whitman, 1983.
I'm Busy, Too. Illus. by Dora Leder. Whitman, 1980.
My Family Seder. Illus. by Harvey Weiss. United Synagogue, 1961.
Nobody's Perfect, Not Even My Mother. Illus. by Dora Leder. Whitman, 1981.
Oh, That Cat! Illus. by Dora Leder. Whitman, 1986.
Our First Sukkah. Illus. by Ayala Gordon. United Synagogue, 1959.
Passover. Illus. by Symeon Shimin. Harper, 1965.
Purim Party. Illus. by Ayala Gordon. United Synagogue, 1959.
Rosh Hashanah. Illus by Ayala Gordon. United Synagogue, 1961.
The Saddest Time. Whitman, 1986.
Simhat Torah. Illus. by Ayala Gordon. United Synagogue, 1960.
Tu Bishvat. Illus. by Harvey Weiss. United Synagogue, 1961.
Wedding Days. Whitman, 1987.
What Do I Do. Illus. by Joe Lasker. Whitman, 1969.
What Do I Say. Illus. by Joe Lasker. Whitman, 1967.

Where Does My Cat Sleep? Illus. by Dora Leder. Whitman, 1982.
Yom Kippur. Illus. by Ayala Gordon. United Synagogue, 1959.

Voigt, Cynthia

Building Blocks. Atheneum, 1984.
The Callender Papers. Atheneum, 1983; Fawcett, 1985, pap.
Come a Stranger. Atheneum, 1986; Fawcett, 1987, pap.
Dicey's Song. Atheneum, 1982.
Homecoming. Atheneum, 1981; Fawcett, 1987, pap.
Izzy, Willy-Nilly. Atheneum, 1986; Fawcett, 1987, pap.
Jackaroo. Atheneum, 1985; Fawcett, 1986, pap.
The Runner. Atheneum, 1985; Fawcett, 1986, pap.
A Solitary Blue. Atheneum, 1983; Fawcett, 1985, pap.
Sons from Afar. Atheneum, 1987.
Stories about Rosie. Atheneum, 1986.
Tell Me If the Lovers Are Losers. Fawcett, 1987, pap.

Yolen, Jane

The Acorn Quest. Illus. by Susanna Natti. Harper, 1981.
All in the Woodland Early: An ABC Book. Illus. by Jane Breskin Zalben. Putnam, 1983, pap.
Children of the Wolf. Viking, 1984.
Commander Toad and the Big Black Hole. Illus. by Bruce Degen. Putnam, 1983, hb and pap.
Commander Toad and the Dis-Asteroid. Illus. by Bruce Degen. Putnam, 1985, hb and pap.
Commander Toad and the Intergalactic Spy. Illus. by Bruce Degen. Putnam, 1986, hb and pap.
Commander Toad and the Planet of the Grapes. Illus. by Bruce Degen. Putnam, 1982, hb and pap.
Commander Toad and the Space Pirates. Illus. by Bruce Degen. Putnam, 1987.
Commander Toad in Space. Illus. by Bruce Degen. Putnam, 1980.
Dragon Night and Other Lullabies. Illus. by Demi. Methuen, 1980.
Dragon's Blood. Delacorte, 1982; Dell, 1984, pap.
The Gift of Sarah Barker. Scholastic, 1983, pap.
The Girl Who Cried Flowers and Other Tales. Illus. by David Palladini, Harper, 1974; Schocken, 1981, pap.
The Girl Who Loved the Wind. Illus. by Ed Young. Harper, 1972; 1987, pap.
Heart's Blood. Delacorte, 1984; Dell, 1986, pap.
An Invitation to the Butterfly Ball: A Counting Rhyme. Illus. by Jane B. Zalben. Putnam, 1983, pap.
The Lullaby Songbook. Illus. by Charles Mikolaycak. Harcourt, 1986.
The Magic Three of Solatia. Illus. by Julia Noonan. Harper, 1974.
Mice on Ice. Illus. by Lawrence DiFiori. Dutton, 1980.

Neptune Rising: Songs and Tales of the Undersea Folk. Illus. by David Wiesner. Putnam, 1982.
No Bath Tonight. Illus. by Nancy W. Parker. Harper, 1978.
Piggins. Illus. by Jane Dyer. Harcourt, 1987.
The Rainbow Rider. Illus. by Michael Foreman. Harper, 1974.
Ring of Earth: A Child's Book of Seasons. Illus. by John Wallner. Harcourt, 1986.
The Robot and Rebecca the Missing Owser. Illus. by Lady McCrady. Knopf, 1981, hb and pap.
The Seeing Stick. Illus. by Remy Charlip and Demetra Marasalis. Harper, 1977.
A Sending of Dragons. Illus. by Tom McKeveny. Delacorte, 1987.
Shirlick Holmes and the Case of the Wandering Wardrobe. Illus. by Anthony Rao. Putnam, 1981.
Sleeping Ugly. Putnam, 1981, hb and pap.
The Stone Silenus. Putnam, 1984.
The Three Bears Rhyme Book. Illus. by Jane Dyer. Harcourt, 1987.
Touch Magic: Fantasy, Faerie and Folklore in the Literature of Childhood. Putnam, 1981.
The Transfigured Hart. Illus. by Donnal Diamond. Harper, 1975.
Uncle Lemon's Spring. Illus. by Glen Rounds. Dutton, 1981
(ed. by Jane Yolen, Martin H. Greenberg, and Charles G. Waugh). *Dragons and Dreams.* Harper, 1986.
(ed. by Jane Yolen, Martin H. Greenberg, and Charles G. Waugh). *Spaceships and Spells.* Harper, 1987.

Zolotow, Charlotte

The Beautiful Christmas Tree. Illus. by Ruth Robbins. Houghton Mifflin, 1983, hb and pap.
Big Brother. Illus. by Mary Chalmers. Harper, 1960; 1982, pap.
Big Sister and Little Sister. Illus. by Martha Alexander. Harper, 1966.
The Bunny Who Found Easter. Illus. by Betty F. Peterson. Houghton Mifflin, 1959, hb and pap.
But Not Billy. Illus. by Kay Chorao. Harper, 1983.
Do You Know What I'll Do? Illus. by Garth Williams. Harper, 1958.
Everything Glistens and Everything Sings. Illus. by Margot Tomes. Harcourt, 1987.
A Father Like That. Illus. by Ben Shecter. Harper, 1971.
Flocks of Birds. Illus. by Ruth L. Bornstein. Harper, 1981.
The Hating Book. Illus. by Ben Shecter. Harper, 1969.
Hold My Hand. Illus. by Thomas Di Grazia. Harper, 1987.
I Have a Horse of My Own. Illus. by Yoko Mitsuhashi. Crowell, 1980.
I Know a Lady. Illus. by James Stevenson. Greenwillow, 1984.
I Like to Be Little. Illus. by Erik Blegvad. Harper, 1987.
If It Weren't for You. Illus. by Ben Shecter. Harper, 1987.
If You Listen. Illus. by Marc Simont. Harper, 1987.
It's Not Fair. Illus. by William Pene Du Bois. Harper, 1976.
Janey. Illus. by Ronald Himler. Harper, 1973.
May I Visit? Illus. by Erik Blegvad. Harper, 1976.

Mister Rabbit and the Lovely Present. Illus. by Maurice Sendak. Harper, 1962; 1977, pap.
My Friend John. Illus. by Ben Shecter. Harper, 1968.
My Grandson Lew. Illus. by William Pene Du Bois. Harper, 1974; 1985, pap.
The New Friend. Illus. by Emily A. McCully. Harper, 1981.
One Step, Two. . . . Illus. by Cindy Wheeler. Lothrop, 1981.
Over and Over. Illus. by Garth Williams. Harper, 1987.
An Overpraised Season. Harper, 1987.
Park Book. Illus. by H. A. Rey. Harper, 1944; 1986, pap.
The Poodle Who Barked at the Wind. Illus. by June Otani. Harper, 1987.
The Quarreling Book. Illus. by Arnold Lobel. Harper, 1963; 1982, pap.
River Winding. Illus. by Kazue Mizumura. Harper, 1978.
A Rose, a Bridge and a Wild Black Horse. Illus. by Robin Spowart. Harper, 1987.
Say It! Illus. by James Stevenson. Greenwillow, 1980.
The Sky Was Blue. Illus. by Garth Williams. Harper, 1963.
Some Things Go Together. Illus. by Karen Gundersheimer. Harper, 1983; 1987, pap.
Someday. Illus. by Arnold Lobel. Harper, 1965.
Someone New. Illus. by Erik Blegvad. Harper, 1978.
The Song. Illus. by Nancy Tafuri. Greenwillow, 1982.
Storm Book. Illus. by Margaret B. Graham. Harper, 1952.
Summer Is. . . . Illus. by Ruth L. Bornstein. Harper, 1983.
The Summer Night. Illus. by Ben Shecter. Harper, 1987.
Three Funny Friends. Illus. by Mary Chalmers. Harper, 1961; 1982, pap.
Timothy Too. Houghton Mifflin, 1985.
The Unfriendly Book. Illus. by William Pene Du Bois. Harper, 1975.
Wake Up and Goodnight. Illus. by Leonard Weisgard. Harper, 1971.
When I Have a Little Girl. Illus. by Hillary Knight. Harper, 1965.
When I Have a Son. Illus. by Hillary Knight. Harper, 1987.
When the Wind Stops. Illus. by Howard Knotts. Harper, 1987.
The White Marble. Illus. by Deborah Ray. Harper, 1982.
William's Doll. Illus. by William Pene Du Bois. Harper, 1972.
(ed.). *Early Sorrow: Ten Stories of Youth.* Harper, 1986.
(and James Stevenson). *I Know a Lady.* Penguin, 1986, pap.

PART II

Reading about Separation and Loss: An Annotated Bibliography

5

Learning to Face Separation

Siblings

Children who gain a new sibling also lose. They lose a coveted place in the family—that of only child or youngest, that of only boy or only girl. Especially if they were only children or the youngest, they also lose the enjoyment of being the apple of everyone's eye. All youngsters, no matter what their position in the family, lose much of the parental attention they have relied on when a new sibling arrives on the scene. The anger, fears, guilt, and depression aroused are part of the mourning for what once was and now can never be. Unusual births, such as cesareans, may heighten these feelings and foster additional questions.

Even after the birth of the new baby, sibling interaction can continue to involve feelings of loss. Loss of parental attention, loss of self-esteem (especially from the perspective of the younger sibling), and the loss of control that accompanies sibling rivalry can be palpable. Books that offer solace and coping strategies are helpful.

1. Arnold, Eric H., and Loeb, Jeffrey, eds. *I'm Telling: Kids Talk about Brothers and Sisters.* Illus. by G. Brian Karas. Boston: Little, 1987. 160 pp. Nonfiction.

   Interest level: Ages 8–13 Reading level: Grade 4

The producers of a National Public Radio children's issues show have put together preteens' taped observations about family life from the radio program "Hole in the Sock" and presented it with all its natural humor, pathos, and idiosyncratic wisdom. The editors hardly interject at all; their words only appear in a brief introduction alerting children to read the book for guidance or for curiosity's sake. Chapters cover such issues as family position, negatives and positives, jealousies and competition, tattling, sharing rooms, and good times. The book also ventures into such special spheres as being an only child or becoming part of a stepfamily. It's all very exuberant and, with next-to-no changes by the editors, childlike, filled with normal kids who trick their sibs with fibs, bribe them, look up to them and down on them, and otherwise do very normal brother–sister things. The full range of life's experience is here, and on balance, being part of a family is very enjoyable, as this book is as well.

Genuine and down-to-earth, this reassuring book is likely to get passed around from child to child, and occasionally brought to a parent with a plaintive plea for change or a self-justifying "I told you so."

2. Brown, Marc. *Arthur's Baby.* Illus. by the author. Boston: Little, 1987. 32 pp. Fiction.

   Interest level: Ages 4–7 Reading level: Grade 2

Although Arthur would prefer the surprise to be a bicycle, the fact is that his parents are going to have a baby. Arthur has enough trouble coping with his younger sister, D.W., but his parents and D.W. are thrilled. Arthur's friends warn him about the problems of an infant, including the noise, the odor, and the infringement on Arthur's free time.

When the baby comes Arthur is still not delighted. He is reluctant to have anything to do with the baby until one day the baby is crying and no one can stop her. Then Arthur holds the baby so that she burps, and she is happy again.

The ending is predictable: Arthur is the instrument of the baby's satisfaction. The burp is an amusing surprise. The illustrations and the dialogue between Arthur and the other characters make this a sibling book that stands out above the rest.

3. Cole, Joanna. *The New Baby at Your House.* Photos by Hella Hammid. New York: Morrow, 1985, hb and pap. 48 pp. Nonfiction.

   Interest level: Ages 3–7 Reading level: Grade 1

Preparing for life with a new baby is sensitively handled here. In a full, detailed note to parents is the warning "a parent's job is not to 'fix things' so the negative feelings will go away and everyone will be happy all the time." Rather, it's to acknowledge the scope of feelings, make siblings feel included, and allow time for adjustment. The note gets down to helpful specifics, for example, "Experts urge parents to say good-bye to their children before they leave for the hospital, even if it means waking them up to do so." The note also recommends pressing for sibling visits in hospitals through intercession by the doctor or midwife.

The children's portion of the book has large black-and-white photos showing several families of varying races. There are few words on each page. The process is laid out chronologically, from siblings "talking" to the baby in the uterus, to visits in the hospital, to picking up Mommy there. It immediately becomes apparent that siblings are involved with the pregnancy at every point. The observations of siblings are a strong focus, such as the still-attached umbilical cord and infants' lack of tears initially. The emphasis is on fascination with development and becoming an active scientific participant in what is observed, for example, seeing baby's sucking capacity firsthand with a clean sibling finger. This aspect of being participants distinguishes Cole's book from others in the field, where children are merely encouraged to be helpers.

The emotional sphere is not left out, however, as children's jealousies and angers are expressed and parents make time for explanations, reassurances, and time with the sibling alone. The book shows good modeling for a family where "love can grow as big as it has to." An excellent job.

4. Dragonwagon, Crescent. *I Hate My Brother Harry*. Illus. by Dick Gackenbach. New York: Harper, 1983. 32 pp. Fiction.
   Interest level: Ages 3–8 Reading level: Grade 1

The little girl who narrates the story vividly describes her brother's teasing and practical jokes. She reiterates how much she hates him and provides evidence for the validity of her feelings. Harry truly is a big tease, but he can also be tender and thoughtful. The little girl realizes this and wishes he were like that all of the time. She does have hope, however, because he responds positively to her question about whether he wants to be friends.

This story is unusual because it is told from the perspective of the younger, rather than the older, sibling. Both elder and young siblings will empathize with the characters while they are chuckling over the diabolical ways Harry dreams up to torment his little sister.

5. Edelman, Elaine. *I Love My Baby Sister (Most of the Time)*. Illus. by Wendy Watson. New York: Lothrop, 1984; Puffin, pap. 32 pp. Fiction.
   Interest level: Ages 4–7 Reading level: Grade 2

In this amiable book the older sister fully understands the positive and negative features of having a baby sister in the house. For the most part, the older sister can tolerate the baby's yanking of hair, nose-grabbing, and lack of speech. She also knows how to attract her mother's attention when the baby is receiving too much of it. All in all the entire family, including the parents, is actively involved in the nurturing and the management of the family's activities.

Watson's illustrations contribute enormously to the appeal of the book. A sense of affable mess pervades each picture. Clothing, toys, food, and household utensils are strewn around the house; leaves and pebbles clutter the outdoors. The overall effect is that of a busy, informal life-style in which people matter much more than things, and in which neatness is not the primary goal.

6. Greenwald, Sheila. *Alvin Webster's Surefire Plan for Success (and How It Failed)*. Illus. by the author. Boston: Little, 1987. 95 pp. Fiction.

   Interest level: Ages 9–12 Reading level: Grade 4

Alvin's parents are going to have a new baby and Alvin is jealous and anxious about it. His parents are eager for him to love and want the baby. They show Alvin the ultrasound of his soon-to-be-baby brother, and they place the picture on the bulletin board next to Alvin's math test. Alvin's parents give him all sorts of books on how to be a big brother. They also go off to take a birthing and parenting course.

Alvin is in the gifted program at school, and he is very competitive, as are his parents, particularly his mother. She wants him to be the best in everything he does. When Alvin is assigned to tutor a child in math, he determines to be the best tutor of all. He learns a lot from Bone, the child he tutors, because Bone is happy with himself and doesn't even mind an occasional failure.

Everything Alvin does he turns into an occasion for intellectual analysis. Thus, he writes a book about how to be a tutor. Bone is upset when he sees the book because he feels that Alvin has dehumanized and exploited him. By the end of the story Alvin hasn't exactly reformed, but he is much more comfortable with the idea of possible failure, and his parents have become somewhat more open as well.

Greenwald pokes fun at the parents who are going about the process of parenting intellectually rather than intuitively. She also implies that gifted children are anxious and competitive. On the other hand, she portrays Bone as a character who is very talented and bright, but whose values are more cooperative and style more easy going. Bone's mother is as delighted with his ability to draw birds as are Alvin's parents about his grades. One wonders if, in the end, both sets of parents aren't more alike than different. Alvin is given a guinea pig to care for so that he may experience firsthand a process analogous to parenting. It works. He understands what it means to accept and love a creature no matter what it looks like or what its talents are. The story is humorous, and the reader is interested in what happens to the characters. There may even be some lessons to be learned here.

7. Hazen, Barbara Shook. *If It Weren't for Benjamin (I'd Always Get to Lick the Icing Spoon)*. Illus. by Laura Hartman. New York: Human Sciences, 1979, hb and pap. 32 pp. Fiction.

   Interest level: Ages 3–6 Reading level: Grade 3

Told from the perspective of the younger brother, this book explores the child's feelings about his relationship with his older brother, Benjamin. He is jealous of Benjamin's prowess and position in the family. He fears that he is not loved as much as his brother, but his parents and grandmother reassure him of their love. They all explain to him that it is not necessary for him to be and do the same as his brother; he is loved for who and what he is.

The child is also helped to respond appropriately to his negative feelings. He learns to channel his anger into constuctive actions, such as kicking a ball. He learns to deal with his frustration at being excluded from Benjamin's games by inviting over a friend of his own. And he learns to savor the rare times when he beats Benjamin in a game, rather than sulking over losing most of the time.

This book is helpful in showing children ways to defuse their negative feelings, while at the same time acknowledging their validity. It is also helpful to see that not only older siblings have problems, but younger siblings have problems, too. The book also shows that younger siblings are entitled to their own point of view.

8. Heide, Florence Parry. *Time Flies.* Illus. by Marylin Hafner. New York: Holiday, 1984; Bantam, pap. 97 pp. Fiction.
   Interest level: Ages 9–12 Reading level: Grade 4

Noah is not happy about having a younger sibling. His mother is somewhat scatterbrained and disorganized and his father is an efficiency expert, and between both his parents Noah's life is somewhat harried. He loves visiting the Quayles, their next-door neighbors, because Mrs. Quayle is an excellent cook, and there is always lots of food around. He doesn't even much mind the Quayles' baby.

When Noah's mother returns home with his new sister, Noah finds that he can help take care of her and that he enjoys it. Furthermore, he inadvertently supplies his father with a new logo, slogan, and ad campaign, for which Noah wins prize money. All is now well in Noah's life.

This amusing story will never serve as a model for anyone's behavior, but it is such good-natured fun that children will enjoy that interaction and zaniness of the characters. It is unfortunate that Noah's parents are both such inept characters. The story would not suffer if they were accorded some respect.

9. Hendrickson, Karen. *Getting Along Together: Baby and I Can Play.* Illus. by Marina Megale. Seattle: Parenting, 1985, pap. 23 pp. Nonfiction.
   Interest level: Ages 3–7 Reading level: Grade 3

The narrator of the book speaks directly to older siblings in a respectful and informative tone. The book celebrates the importance of older brothers and sisters, acknowledges both their positive and negative feelings, and recommends specific activities for the older children to do in response to their negative feelings. It also presents some excellent ideas for how to play with the babies when the older children are in the mood to do so.

The activities progress from such relatively passive ones as playing where the baby can see the older child to cuddling and stroking, picking things up that the baby drops, playing peek-a-boo with toys and people, and crawling and chasing. The author wisely recommends thinking ahead to when parents are too busy to attend to the older children. Hendrickson recommends that the older children create a special box of items to play with and do while their mother is nursing the baby. She discusses a number of negative feelings and how to handle them, and then ends with the assurance that the baby is lucky to have such a special and important older brother or sister.

Included at the back of the book is a set of notes to parents to guide them, not only in the use of this book but also to help them with the issue of sibling relationships in general.

10. Hest, Amy. *The Mommy Exchange*. Illus. by Anne D. Salvo-Ryan. New York: Four Winds, 1988. 32 pp. Fiction.

    Interest level: Ages 4–7 Reading level: Grade 3

Jessica thinks that Jason's house is infinitely preferable to hers, and Jason feels that way about Jessica's. Jessica has twin siblings, toddlers who seem to dominate her household. Jason's house is quiet and orderly. Both Jason and Jessica are angry and impatient with their mothers. They decide to arrange an exchange, one in which fathers will be permitted to visit, but not mothers. They view the exchange as a permanent one, although their parents, who go along with the idea, assure them that they will be welcomed back when they decide to come home.

Of course it turns out that neither child is happy away from home, and that they prefer their own mother's style of managing and nurturing. The child's perspective is clearly transmitted, but the resolution is not as convincing as it could be. The sibling relationship is never resolved, and, as a matter of fact, it turns out that Jason's potential problems are about to begin because his mother is pregnant with twins. The book is amusing and well illustrated, and could be the spark for children's discussions of their family's life-style and their methods for coping with younger siblings.

11. Hooker, Ruth. *Sara Loves Her Big Brother*. Illus. by Margot Apple. Niles, Ill.: Whitman, 1987. 32 pp. Fiction.

    Interest level: Ages 4–7 Reading level: Grades 1–2

This story gives ample evidence that there is more than one perspective on every event. Told from the younger sibling's point of view, this book's illustrations make clear how the older sibling is feeling. As far as Sara, the younger sibling, is concerned, she and her brother have an idyllic relationship. Never mind that he is wearing roller skates when she hugs him and so she unbalances him. Never mind that her constant physical proximity causes countless small mishaps. Never mind that she enjoys entering his room and making a mess of it, disregarding the "KEEP OUT" sign. Her remarkably tolerant brother accepts all her behavior, lovingly reads to her, and puts her to bed with the assurance that he loves her.

This is a description of a younger child's taking advantage of the good nature of her older brother. Where are the parents? Why don't they protect the brother's privacy and right to do things on his own? Why aren't they putting the little girl to sleep? Although the model of the adoring-though-bratty little sister is charming and amusing, some discussion and sympathy for the plight of the older child would be in order here.

12. Jenkin-Pearce, Susie. *Bad Boris and the New Kitten.* Illus. by the author. New York: Macmillan, 1987. 26 pp. Fiction.

    Interest level: Ages 4–8 Reading level: Grade 2

Poor Boris the elephant can't seem to do anything right after a kitten moves into the house. Maisie, their caretaker, delights so much in the kitten that Boris is terribly jealous. When the kitten gets trapped in a tree, and no one knows where she is, Boris does not miss her. When Maisie, in the course of a conversation, indicates that she loves both Boris and the kitten, Boris is astounded. This knowledge cures him instantly of his jealousy. He finds and rescues the kitten and all is well until Maisie brings home a goldfish from the fair, and it looks like the cycle will begin again.

The illustrations and writing are charming, but it is difficult to believe that jealousy can be cured in an instant. Nevertheless, Boris's feelings are those of any older sibling who feels displaced and unloved, and young readers will probably identify with him.

13. Kitzinger, Sheila. *Being Born.* Photos by Lennart Nilsson. New York: Grosset, 1986. 64 pp. Nonfiction.

    Interest level: Age 9+ Reading level: Grade 4

Children expecting a new sibling in their household will get both a feeling-evoking and technical education about the process going on in their mothers' uteruses. Against a black background, award-winning photographer Nilsson's astounding full color intrauterine photos are even more striking. Kitzinger, a childbirth educator, has prepared a sensitive narration to match the photos, taking the reader from conception through birth. Her analogies are memorable, comparing the beginning fetus to a beanlike projection, then to a seahorse, and so on, until the face and body become increasingly clarified and evident. By 9 to 10 weeks you could open and close your mouth; by 12 weeks you could frown and make funny faces. "Yet you still weighed only as much as a hen's egg in its shell."

Intercourse is described as follows:

> When your mother and father felt very loving, they kissed and cuddled each other. Your father's penis became hard so that it could slide into your mother's vagina, the soft opening between her legs which leads to the uterus. As your mother and father held each other in their arms, a liquid called semen spurted out from his penis into her vagina.

Childbirth itself is shown in the photographs, with the baby's head popping out from the vagina. Likewise, a baby is shown sucking.

The photographs are truly impressive and awe inspiring, but other reactions may also ensue. For example, how the photographs were achieved is not explained adequately, and some readers may therefore find them distasteful. Are some of the pictures of the well-developed fetuses (for example, at six months) taken from miscarriages?

14. Lakin, Patricia. *Don't Touch My Room.* Illus. by Patience Brewster. Boston: Little, 1985. 32 pp. Fiction.
    Interest level: Ages 4–8 Reading level: Grades 2–3

Aaron's room is being torn apart and redone because his parents are expecting a new baby. Aaron is not happy about the new baby or his room change. It seems as if he is no longer in control of his world. He tells people not to touch his things, but they do, anyway. He still has some misgivings after his new room is all ready, however, it has a special, small compartment that he loves. Into this compartment he puts his treasures.

After the baby, Benji, is born Aaron relies increasingly on the sanctuary of his secret compartment. Benji has displaced him, and Aaron feels most secure in his own special place. After a number of months, Benji grows old enough to get into mischief and to have people call him a bad boy. Now it is Aaron who comes to his brother's defense, and, ultimately, he rescues Benji from being punished by bringing him into the security of his, Aaron's, secret place.

Aaron progresses through the sequence of "Don't touch my room"; to "Don't touch my things"; to "Don't touch my baby." His parents don't seem to understand either of their children's feelings at any point in the book. They summarily override their children's wishes and contribute to the children's sense of displacement. They appear to be well meaning, but inept. Perhaps they can serve as examples of what not to do when expecting a new baby.

The story is told from a decidedly childlike perspective, and young children will probably identify with Aaron. The author does not make the mistake of having Aaron's negative feelings suddenly disappear. It takes quite a while before Aaron considers his baby brother a suitable companion. He takes on the protector's role in a believable way. The book is filled with humor. The illustrations show us the specifics of the children's many wonderful possessions as well as capturing the feelings of the youngsters.

15. Lakin, Patricia. *Oh, Brother.* Illus. by Patience Brewster. Boston: Little, 1987. 32 pp. Fiction.

    Interest level: Ages 4–8 Reading level: Grade 3

Aaron, who was introduced in *Don't Touch My Room,* is now eight years old, and he is still resentful of Benji, his younger brother, who is now three. Benji gets lots of attention and special favors, while Aaron is expected to be responsible for himself now. Even when Aaron tries to behave like a three-year-old, it doesn't work out well for him. His attentive parents respond to his unpleasant feelings by once again rearranging his room. This time they build him a treehouse bed and provide him with a space for his work. When Benji is frightened by Aaron's stories of monsters, Aaron invites his younger brother to join him in bed, and he reassures him that there are no monsters lurking.

Lakin is well aware that sibling rivalry does not end with the adjustment of the older sibling to the baby. It is an issue that must be confronted in an ongoing manner. This family tackles the situation with a change of environment. It works for them, and it may provide a solution for some readers as well.

16. Lasky, Kathryn. In the words of Maxwell B. Knight. *A Baby for Max.* Photos by Christopher G. Knight. New York: Aladdin, 1987. 48 pp. Nonfiction.

    Interest level: Ages 3–7 Reading level: Grade 2

This book is the story of Max Knight, a five-year-old child whose mother is going to have a baby. The story is told in Max's own words, with the text written by his mother and the photos taken by his father.

The book is an excellent presentation of the "new baby" issue. It can serve as a model for both the adjusting child and the parents expecting their second child. Max is involved with his new sibling's arrival from the start. He goes to the doctor with his mother, visits the hospital where she will have the baby, is given a lesson by the nurse on how to diaper the baby, visits other newborns in the hospital nursery, and helps his father make a changing table. All of these activities involve Max in the birth of the baby, provide him with a sense of his own importance, and show him how he can help the family.

Max's experience is related in realistic language easily understood by the young child. He talks to the baby through his mother's belly button. When he accompanies his mother to the doctor he hears the baby's heartbeat, which he describes as being like the "ocean water washing and somebody hammering and fish splashing."

Although the book focuses on his excitement, Max's apprehension and resentment about his new sibling are also shown. On the day the baby is born, Max is happy at first, but he becomes sad later in the day because his parents are not there and because of all the excitement the new baby's arrival has caused. After the baby has been home for a few days Max tells about his anger because people are not paying enough attention to him. When his mother shows him how to zip the baby into the carrying sack, Max wonders if, after they zip the baby into the sack, they could sell it.

Max looks forward to when the baby will be old enough to play with him. Although he sees and acknowledges his feelings of anger and jealousy, Max often reminds himself of the things he is able to do that the baby cannot.

The photographs add to the book's realistic nature. By reading this book, children are helped to understand that feelings of jealousy and misplacement are normal.

17. McCully, Emily Arnold. *New Baby.* Illus. by the author. New York: Harper, 1988. 32 pp. Fiction.

    Interest level: Ages 3–6 Reading level: Wordless

In this wordless picture book children can see themselves in the next-to-youngest member of the mouse family's reaction to the newborn baby mouse. Nothing the mouse child does distracts others' attention from the baby. Even behaving like a baby doesn't work. Finally, with the help of a loving older sibling, and with the discovery of some interest in the baby, the jealous sibling is permitted to help with the baby, and the household returns to normal.

The images of this busy family are cheerfully depicted, and the jealous older sibling is never in terrible trouble, even when she runs off to be by herself (to a spot where she can see but not be seen). The amiability of the family augurs well for the harmony of the family to be restored. Again, including the older siblings in the care and feeding of the newborn is a good way to dispell negative feelings. Young children will enjoy inventing their own dialogue to this story.

18. Manushkin, Fran. (Created by Lucy Bate.) *Little Rabbit's Baby Brother.* Illus. by Diane de Groat. New York: Crown, 1986. 29 pp. Fiction.

    Interest level: Ages 5–8 Reading level: Grade 3

Little Rabbit fears that she will be displaced by her expected baby brother. Her parents are very busy planning for the new baby's arrival, and they seem to be paying less and less attention to Little Rabbit. After the baby arrives, he is too noisy, he can't eat the food Little Rabbit wants to feed him, and their parents are so solicitous of the new baby that they seem always to be reprimanding Little Rabbit. Finally, Little Rabbit hops outside the house and threatens to hop around the world. She hops right outside their house until after the sun goes down. At last her parents each make it clearly and loudly known that they miss her and want her to come home. Little Rabbit then hops into the house and is welcomed by her parents as a Big Sister. She decides that she will designate her robe a Big Sister Robe to wear when she helps with the baby. Her father decorates the robe with medals, bells, and stars, for her being such a wonderful baby, maker of snow angels, and big sister. She helps quiet the baby, holds him, and dreams of the day when she can play with him outdoors.

Manushkin wisely does not have the character really run away from home to attract her parents' attention. Little Rabbit stays within the range of her parents' vision and hearing. She adopts a ritual that helps her to overcome many of her jealous feelings. She is a Big Sister only when she is wearing her special robe. At other times she is simply herself. Her role is also aided by the knowledge that she is competent in her parents' eyes, hence the symbolic medals. Children going through the throes of sibling rivalry may be able to take from this book some good ideas on how to overcome their negative feelings.

19. Naylor, Phyllis Reynolds. *The Baby, the Bed, and the Rose.* Illus. by Mary Szilagyi. New York: Clarion, 1987. 32 pp. Fiction.

    Interest level: Ages 3–6 Reading level: Grade 3

David and Tom try to comfort their baby sister, Molly, when she is crying. The boys help entertain her, change her, and feed her, but when she is returned to her crib the crying begins again. Finally, they realize that Molly is fascinated by the pink rose painted on the footboard of her crib.

In this simple story, the family models how a new baby is incorporated into the family by enlisting the aid of her siblings, her mother, and her grandfather. Research has demonstrated that when older siblings are encouraged to take responsibility for some of the nurturing of the new baby, they form a close relationship. It is clear that Molly's brothers are delighted by her progress toward standing up and creeping. They willingly interrupt their games to take care of the baby.

The father is absent from all of the pictures, including the one at bedtime when the rest of the family is standing around the crib. No mention is made of him. Nor is there a grandmother. Older children might want to discuss the possible reasons for their absence. Younger children will enjoy and benefit from the joyousness of the family's appreciation for one another.

20. Ormerod, Jan. *101 Things to Do with a Baby.* Illus. by the author. Harmondsworth, England: Puffin, 1984, pap. 27 pp. Nonfiction.
    Interest level: Ages 5–8 Reading level: Grade 2

This catalog of activities, all doable and practical, is a merry romp for siblings, from saying "good morning" to exercising, bathing, whispering, and tickling (including some things to watch out for, such as ankle biting and Granny's glasses), and finally to the good night kiss. The book exemplifies a helpful and loving relationship in a family whose members clearly care a lot for each other.

The illustrations make it clear that the older sibling is every bit as valued and attended to as the infant. The author obviously understands that the more an older sibling is involved constructively with the new baby, the easier it will be for the child to bond with the baby.

21. Pankow, Valerie. *No Bigger Than My Teddy Bear.* Illus by Rodney Pate. Nashville: Abingdon, 1987, pap. 28 pp. Fiction.
    Interest level: Ages 4–8 Reading level: Grade 3

Dustin is a little boy whose mother has just given birth to a premature baby. Through Dustin's eyes we learn how hospitals care for premature babies. This approach also lets readers understand how older siblings and the family feel about the new baby. It helps Dustin to compare the baby with his teddy bear and to treat the teddy bear as a surrogate baby sibling.

The information in this book is given in an accurate and straightforward manner. The comparison with the teddy bear is a good one, and it makes the facts more interesting and accessible.

22. Patent, Dorothy Hinshaw. *Babies!* Photos. New York: Holiday, 1988. 40 pp. Nonfiction.
    Interest level: Ages 4–9 Reading level: Grade 3

A noted author and zoologist, Patent tackles the human development of babies and achieves glorious results. She is abetted in her task by intriguing, appealing photos produced by some of the most well-known photographers of children—Suzanne Szasz, Bruce McMillan, and others. The babies are multiethnic.

Birth, the biggest change one goes through in life, is the start of the book, and the reader is instantly involved: "Have you ever seen a newborn baby?" Patent has simple ways of explaining the baby's beginning and growing traits: "Its tongue is designed for sucking. The baby can wrap it around a nipple and pull the milk out easily."

Without being stuffy, Patent taps what are obviously the interesting results of scholarly studies: "By the time it is six weeks old, it can tell the difference between the touch of its mother and father. It knows if its brother or a stranger has picked it up." Always the reader is invited to participate, as regarding babies' many forms of communication: "You can learn what it is trying to say if you watch and listen closely."

The development focuses mostly on the first year, but travels into the second as well. Particular attention is paid to the second half year of life, when babies get upset if the mother leaves the room. "No one else, even a brother or sister, can ease the pain. This stage can be difficult for everyone. Mother can't always be with the baby, and other family members may feel hurt that they can't provide comfort." Patent shows a great deal of understanding regarding the development of babies. And she gives advice, too, like this, about babies who don't seem to talk at the so-called right time: "Each family needs to be patient and accept the pace set by its own toddler." A delicious book for sharing and learning about the new sibling.

23. Polushkin, Maria. *Baby Brother Blues.* Illus. by Ellen Weiss. New York: Bradbury, 1987. 26 pp. Fiction.

    Interest level: Ages 4–7 Reading level: Grade 2

The little girl's baby brother is a mess and a nuisance as far as she's concerned. He can't talk or even stand up, he is sometimes smelly, he is often noisy, and he throws things on the floor and gets into everything. All the grown-ups adore him and think he is wonderful. At last, when the baby is crying and no one can comfort him, the little girl makes him stop crying. This endears him to her, and she acknowledges that he is likable after all.

The book is charmingly and amusingly illustrated in cheerful cartoon-like pictures, with some of the characters' reactions floating out of their mouths in comic-strip balloons. The contrast between the child's reactions to the baby and the adults' adoration is amusing and telling. The ultimate shift is predictable and not quite believable, but it is, by now, an accepted happy ending for a sibling rivalry book. Adults might want to discuss with children how to handle their negative feelings, and, perhaps, indicate that they understand that siblings feel differently toward new babies than adults do.

24. Rogers, Fred. *The New Baby.* Photos by Jim Judkis. New York: Putnam, 1985, hb and pap. 32 pp. Nonfiction.

    Interest level: Ages 3–8 Reading level: Grade 2

Rogers's approach to a new sibling, as expressed in the introduction to adults, is to assure the older sibling that he or she has a special place in the family that no one else can ever take; to find special time to be alone with the older child; to encourage talk about feelings; and to enable the older child to feel active and important in the care of the newborn.

In the text, Rogers engages the reader, for example, "Is it hard to imagine what your family will be like with a new baby there?" Using two families to illustrate, one black, one white, one with an older sister-to-be, one with an older brother-to-be, he brings the older children back to their baby pictures and points out how good the parents feel about being parents and proud of their child. "They like taking care of you *and* they like taking care of the new baby." The underside is noted, though: "But moms and dads sometimes spend so much time looking at their new babies and holding them and making faces at them . . . that they seem to have less time with you." Rogers goes on to comment about the presents babies get, older siblings' wish to be babies again, and new constrictions (for example, be careful, be quiet). "A person could get very grumpy." If that happens, Rogers recommends doing angry things that don't hurt anyone (Judkis's photo illustrates knocking down blocks). Selfhood is emphasized when a child sees his crib used by another but doesn't have to share his teddy. At the close, Rogers tells of the many things an older sibling can teach someone younger. "Soon you'll even be able to help the baby understand about pretending and sharing." In the end, this book is about feeling—feeling good and feeling bad—and both are all right.

25. Root, Phyllis. *Moon Tiger*. Illus. by Ed Young. New York: Holt, 1985. 32 pp. Fiction.
    Interest level: Ages 5–8 Reading level: Grade 3

The little girl is angry at her mother and younger brother. She feels that it is unjust that she should have to go to bed at the same time as her brother just because she refused to read him a story. She was busy playing with her tiger, and now she uses the tiger as her vehicle for an imaginary journey far away from her house. During the journey she resolves her anger and decides to tell her little brother the story of her journey.

The illustrations evoke the feelings of magic and power that the little girl needs to overcome her anger. The text helps readers to experience the little girl's feelings of anger, escape, and competence. Together the blend of words and pictures creates a mood, a story, and an experience that is very satisfying.

26. Ross, Dave. *Baby Hugs*. Illus. by the author. New York: Crowell, 1987. 32 pp. Nonfiction.
    Interest level: Ages 4–8 Reading level: Grade 2

One of a series of more general hug-humor books, this one starts off, "You can hug a lot of things . . . but everyone agrees the best hugs of all are when you hug a baby." Ross goes on to explain what hugs do for the baby's health and happiness; moreover, what they do for the hugger. He claims, probably rightly, that it is almost impossible to frown while hugging a baby. Hugs are then classified, such as in welcome for newborns and newly adopted babies. Then there are meet-the-new-baby hugs, in which everyone from siblings to office buddies likes to participate. Also, among feeding hugs are nursing hugs reserved "just for Mommy and baby." Sharp-edged black-and-white cartoons really show off the essence of the varied hugs, as in a bleary-eyed 3 A.M. feeding hug given by a dad. Additional hugs include wake-up, going-places, play, baby-sitter, comfort, and family hugs that are aptly named (sandwich, reach-around, and so on). As if these weren't enough, there are special hugs for twins, triplets, and quintuplets. Ross includes a most enjoyable small segment on ways babies ask for hugs, from flirting to lip quivering. One only wishes siblings were pictured more often in the book.

27. Samuels, Barbara. *Faye and Dolores*. Illus. by the author. New York: Bradbury, 1985; Aladdin, pap. 36 pp. Fiction.
    Interest level: Ages 4–8 Reading level: Grades 2–3

Faye and her younger sister, Dolores, sometimes argue, but most of the time they are very kind and loving to each other. The story tells of some of their arguments (for example, Dolores breaks Faye's crayon and Faye hurls several insults at Dolores). It also describes a number of incidents where they care about each other's feelings and play happily together. The book can serve as an affectionate and amusing model for sibling interaction.

28. Schaffer, Patricia. *How Babies and Families Are Made: There Is More Than One Way!* Illus. by Suzanne Corbett. Berkeley, Calif.: Tabor Sarah, 1988. 48 pp. Nonfiction.
    Interest level: Ages 5–9 Reading level: Grade 4

This book's intention is to help children from various backgrounds feel welcome and included. The author calls it an "updated facts of life." As such, the narrative discusses a wide range of circumstances and loses its focus. In these pages are descriptions of miscarriage, twins, in vitro fertilization, stepparents, adoption, prematurity, stepchildren, babies with disabilities, and artificial insemination. Some pages have the simplicity of a first-grade basal reader; others offer more science and technology than most children of the age group want or can grasp. In trying to create a large umbrella, the author may have created confusion instead.

29. Shreve, Susan. *Lily and the Runaway Baby*. Illus. by Sue Truesdell. New York: Random, 1987, hb and pap. 62 pp. Fiction.

    Interest level: Ages 7–10 Reading level: Grade 3

Lily believes that no one in her family loves her or cares about her. Her parents have acknowledged that the birth of their "sweet surprise" baby would be hardest on eight-year-old Lily, but they still seem to pay more attention to the baby and to the twins than to Lily. When Lily reasons that they might not miss her, but they will miss the baby, she decides to take the baby with her.

She and the baby board a train from Scarsdale to New York City. On the way, an elderly woman helps Lily with the baby, and, while Lily is in the bathroom washing up, the woman steals her baby sister. The police, her parents, and many people are involved in the search for the baby, but Lily is the one who finds her. Lily then solemnly promises never to run away again. It is important that Shreve points out how dangerous it is to run away, or to leave a baby in the care of a stranger.

Although Shreve based her story on an incident that happened to her when she was six years old, in print it does not ring true. Lily's emotions are certainly understandable, but her actions as presented in the story are not believable. Young readers might benefit from discussing Lily's alternatives.

30. Smith, Anne Warren. *Sister in the Shadow*. New York: Atheneum, 1986. 69 pp. Fiction.

    Interest level: Ages 11–15 Reading level: Grade 6

Beset by confusion and jealousy when her younger sister becomes more popular than she, Sharon tries to take a break from the family tension by getting a summer job as a mother's helper 60 miles away. Preschooler Tim is precocious and miserably spoiled, but more challenging is his cold mother, who wants to care for him but won't let him live a normal life. Why is she so tense and overprotective? In unfolding the tragedy of crib death that lies behind the mystery Sharon gains perspective about her own past year. Smith gives the characters both quick-paced action and sharp, cerebral dialogue and internal monologue. Tim, the world's original monster, is totally credible, and although Sharon is occasionally too wise and can solve the problems of the adults around her, she is usually believable, too. Sharon's funny introspection is exemplified by her questions to herself: "What would Mary Poppins have done?" An excellent book about the effects of family constellations.

31. Smith, Dian G. *My New Baby and Me*. Illus. by Marie Madeline Franc-Nohain. New York: Scribner, 1986. 44 pp. Nonfiction.

    Interest level: Ages 3–8 Reading level: Grade 1

This clever album is designed to include older siblings in the practice of recording special firsts, talents, events, and activities. Instead of focusing on the baby, there are spaces in this book for the older sibling to insert his or her accomplishments. The new sibling is always referred to as "My baby." Comparisons are invited that help the older sibling to put things into perspective. There are spaces for indicating the number of teeth, books, stuffed animals, cousins, rattles, freckles, and siblings both the baby and the older sibling have. This is an excellent strategy for helping children overcome their feelings of loss of attention and gain respect for their attributes.

32. Steptoe, John. *Mufaro's Beautiful Daughters: An African Tale.* Illus. by the author. New York: Lothrop, 1987. 32 pp. Fiction.

Interest level: Ages 7–11 Reading level: Grade 3

In this retelling of a Kaffir folktale, Steptoe presents readers with a gift of lavish paintings that convey a palpable sense of the beauty and majesty of the southern African people and setting. The text respectfully tells the story of two beautiful young women, Nyasha and Manyara, one gentle and thoughtful, the other competitive, selfish, and vain, who respond to the invitation issued by the king to appear before him so that he may choose a wife. Of course, Nyasha, the generous and loving one, is selected.

The story has value beyond its exquisite illustrations. It is refreshing that the selfish woman is beautiful. Children need to get the message that one cannot tell from physical appearances what the character of a person is like. It is also a valuable factor that the king knows Nyasha and what she is like. He has lived near her, in the guise of a snake, before issuing his proclamation. This is not love at first sight for him; it is love born of knowledge. One wonders why he had to invent the ploy of the competition, but it suits the story to have the nasty sister try to become queen and fail because of her own behavior and character.

The competition between the sisters is not really resolved. Undoubtedly Manyara will cause trouble in the castle unless she has learned her lesson. Perhaps children can discuss how they would help Manyara to become a better person. This is a deeply satisfying book because of its beauty, its respect for the people and culture of the story, and its careful wording.

33. Titherington, Jeanne. *A Place for Ben.* Illus. by the author. New York: Greenwillow, 1987. 24 pp. Fiction.

Interest level: Ages 4–7 Reading level: Grades 1–2

When Ben's baby brother is moved into his room, Ben decides that he needs a place of his own where no one will intrude on him. He fixes up such a place in the garage, but then he gets lonely and wants company. His baby brother is the only one who responds to his wish, and Ben is glad to see him. The simple story carries a familiar and perhaps simplistic message, but the illustrations of Ben and his family are wonderfully realistic and appealing, and the look of genuine joy on Ben's face as he greets his baby brother is unmistakably authentic.

34. Voigt, Cynthia. *Sons from Afar.* New York: Atheneum, 1987. 214 pp. Fiction.

    Interest level: Age 12+ Reading level: Grade 7

This story is another in the Tillerman family saga. This time we learn much more about Francis Verricker, the father who deserted Dicey, Maybeth, Sammy, James, and their mother. James and Sammy search for their father in an attempt to find out more about themselves. They never quite catch up with him, but they do find out all sorts of information, not only about him and their family but also about themselves and their relationship as brothers.

Readers can appreciate the protagonists' stamina and determination at the same time that they empathize with their feelings of self-doubt and conflict. Here are two siblings who manage, despite their antagonism and tensions, to carve out a working relationship with each other.

As always, Voigt presents us with characters and situations that are far from the ordinary, but which contain elements that every reader can relate to. We are not permitted the luxury of hating villains unalloyedly; there are no real villains. All of the characters are notable for their fallibility as well as their virtues, and what emerges is their humanity.

35. von Königslöw, Andrea Wayne. *That's My Baby?* Illus. by the author. Toronto: Annick, 1986. 24 pp. Fiction.

    Interest level: Ages 3–7 Reading level: Grades 1–2

Lexi, told by Mom and Dad that there will be a new baby, is very excited—what a great toy to show off, she tells her stuffed dinosaur, confusingly named Teddy. As the months go on, Teddy and Lexi count off the days and watch the changes in Mommy's belly (there seems to be no lap left for them to sit on). They visit the female doctor with Mommy, and soon it is time to be brought to a friend's house late one night. There is some humor as Lexi asks, "Am I going to be a brother if it's a boy?"

Teddy becomes the voice of reason as the action unfolds. When Lexi is jealous and wants to leave the baby at the hospital, Teddy tells her, "Mommy and Daddy love us more than ever. They're just busy." Lexi tries nursing but doesn't like it; in general, she's unhappy with this new baby who can't yet play. Again Teddy reminds her that her new sister will be bigger soon and encourages Lexi to hold the baby when she isn't so sure about that. And what Teddy said would take place, does. Soon they do play and bathe together. And then she won't trade her for anything.

The action is a bit hard to follow, but this is an affectionate story nonetheless.

36. Walker, Mildred Pitts. *My Mama Needs Me.* Illus. by Pat Cummings. New York: Lothrop, 1983. 32 pp. Fiction.

    Interest level: Ages 3–7 Reading level: Grade 3

Jason's mama comes home from the hospital with his new baby sister, and Jason is eager to help his mama. He refuses all invitations from friends and neighbors with the response "My mama needs me." But it seems to be only wishful thinking that his mother needs him. The reality of the situation is that Jason's mama and baby sister want to sleep most of the time. When the baby wakens briefly, Jason rubs her back and both baby and mother are appreciative. Afterward, Jason is permitted to help bathe the baby. For the most part, Jason feels unwanted and unloved until his mother assures him that he can go and play with his friends because he is needed all the time, but he can also enjoy himself. When his mother gives him a big hug and tells him she loves him, Jason realizes that this reassurance was what he was really looking for; he wanted his mother to need him, want him, and love him.

In addition to verbalizing the fears and behaviors of young children who feel displaced by their new siblings, the book has beautiful illustrations of a close and loving black family that add to its value.

37. Watson, Jane Werner; Switzer, Robert E.; and Hirschberg, J. Cotter. *Sometimes I'm Jealous.* Illus. by Irene Trivas. New York: Crown, 1986, pap. 32 pp. Fiction.

    Interest level: Ages 2–8 Reading level: Grade 2

Newly illustrated and revised in content, this book offers parents guidance in the preface and gives sound advice and thoughts for its young listeners who now have a baby to contend with. As doctors Switzer and Hirschberg intone, "Gradually Baby learns that even though he may have to wait for what he wants, he can count on Mommy and Daddy." The unisex child in the story to be shared is right up front, starting off with: "Do you know what I like? I like having my own way. . . . I like having Mommy and Daddy pay attention to me—nobody else, just me!" The child then takes the listener through some of the development that has already been accomplished, for example, slowly learning that some things make parents happy, others do not. Attention is paid to children's inner lives, as when the child comments that when Daddy and Mommy were angry, "they seemed further away." And now, after all this development, there's a new baby. And what do you know, it's not a "plaything" for the child.

38. Wilhelm, Hans. *Let's Be Friends Again.* Illus. by the author. New York: Crown, 1986. 32 pp. Fiction.

    Interest level: Ages 3–7 Reading level: Grades 1–2

When the little boy's sister releases his pet turtle into the pond, the little boy is furious. In general he has a good relationship with his sister, but this time he wants to kill her. He dreams of all sorts of dire punishments for her, notices that she is enjoying herself while he is seething, and decides to go and make up with her. When she suggests that they buy a new turtle, he declines, but decides to buy two hamsters, instead, one for each of them. The hamsters will live in the turtle's old aquarium.

The idea of the story is a good one, but there seems to be no explanation for why the brother is so willing to forgive his little sister. His replacement of his lost pet so quickly is another flaw in the book. If he were so devastated by his pet's loss, how is it that he is going to be satisfied so easily with a new pet? Children will benefit from discussion of these questions.

The illustrations are charming and convey the children's emotions very well, perhaps more so than the text.

39. Zolotow, Charlotte. *Timothy Too!* Boston: Houghton Mifflin, 1986. 32 pp. Fiction.

    Interest level: Ages 4–7 Reading level: Grade 2

Timothy adores his older brother, John, and he emulates his every word and act. John is impatient with Timothy and considers him a pest, but Timothy continues to worship his older brother. When Timothy finally begins to play with a little boy his own age and does not need to shadow his older brother all the time, John misses the attention and invites Timothy and his new friend to join him.

Although the message is a familiar one, the story is presented in an amiable and positive manner. It is, perhaps, a little too pat, but the idea is believable, and the book may help younger children in this situation decide to try to find friends of their own.

New School

When youngsters enter a new school, they must separate themselves from the familiar. The warmth of the family circle is lost when children go off to their first day of school. Whatever the age and no matter how many school experiences children have had, the fear always remains that there will be no friendly faces to welcome them in a new situation.

40. Brown, Tricia. *Hello, Amigos!* Photos by Fran Ortiz. New York: Henry Holt, 1986. 48 pp. Nonfiction.

    Interest level: Ages 5–9 Reading level: Grade 2

A day in the life of one San Francisco first grader is the focus here. Frankie Valdez takes a long bus ride from his Mexican-American neighborhood. At his school, he and his sister are happy in a bilingual environment. Brown gives a full flavor to the book by showing the dual cultural life Frankie has in his large family. Spanish words are intermixed with English, for example, piñata, mariache, and corona. A realistic, well-photographed essay.

41. Bulla, Clyde Robert. *The Chalk Box Kid.* Illus. by Thomas B. Allen. New York: Random, 1987, hb and pap. 59 pp. Fiction.

    Interest level: Ages 7–10 Reading level: Grade 3

In a story somewhat reminiscent of Eleanor Estes's *The Hundred Dresses* (Harcourt, 1974), Gregory, a nine-year-old boy whose family has had to move to a new neighborhood because his father has lost his job, draws with chalk the garden he would love to have if he had ground on which to plant it. Gregory's artistic ability is the only thing that saves him from despair. His self-centered young uncle monopolizes his room; his parents are too preoccupied with trying to make ends meet to pay much attention to him; and the children at school reject him.

A visit from a local nursery owner gives Gregory the idea for his garden. Although his classmates have not been welcoming, and he doesn't feel as if he belongs, one child in school, Ivy, who has won a prize for her artwork, recognizes Gregory's talent and succeeds in bringing it to other people's attention. In the end even Gregory's uncle appreciates his ability, and the children in school become friendly.

The book avoids sentimentality because of its unadorned style and characterization. Gregory is not a wimp; he is a sensitive, motivated, and coping boy. The reader knows that he will go far.

42. Carrick, Carol. *What a Wimp!* Illus. by Donald Carrick. New York: Clarion, 1983. 89 pp. Fiction.

    Interest level: Ages 9–12 Reading level: Grade 4

After their parents' divorce Barney and his brother have moved with their mother to the town where their grandmother spent her summers as a young girl. The first week that they are there Barney encounters a bully, who continually menaces him. His new school is also a disaster. His teacher is unfriendly and critical, and he finds it difficult to keep up with the unfamiliar work.

Barney's problems with the bully increase, but although he pleads for help from everyone, including his father, no one can help him. Even after his older brother has come to his aid, the bully keeps up his attacks. School gets a little better, Barney has a friend, and his teacher seems to be a little more understanding. One day, after some conferences between his mother and teacher, and after a particularly frightening incident with the bully, Barney decides not to be a wimp anymore. He refuses to run from the bully or cry. This behavior so confuses the bully that he lets Barney go, unharmed. From now on Barney will be in command of his own behavior.

The story tells clearly of the problems a single parent encounters, and of the issues that some children must contend with in a new neighborhood and school. The ending is satisfying, but not quite believable. The bully is a little too one-sided; it is difficult to read his motives. Nevertheless, the book succeeds in its presentation of a picture of a family in stress that manages to cope.

43. Delton, Judy. *Kitty from the Start.* Boston: Houghton Mifflin, 1987. 141 pp. Fiction.

Interest level: Ages 8–11 Reading level: Grades 3–4

The story is set during the Great Depression. Kitty's family must move to a new neighborhood because their landlord is selling their house. Kitty has loved her old school and is so terribly apprehensive about going to a new one that she has nightmares about it. When the time comes, despite a mix-up at the outset, she settles in well at the school. The nuns are similar to those in her former school, the children are friendly, and she is a good student.

Much of the story deals with the climate of the Catholic school in the 1930s. When a lay teacher comes to substitute for Sister Charlene, Kitty is astonished to discover that she is of normal health and intelligence, and that she is a good teacher. Some other encounters with Catholicism and its tenets (such as a trip to the movies where one of Kitty's friends mortally fears they are witnessing a "B" rated film) form the basis for some amusing and provocative incidents.

The book is engagingly written, and the protagonist is an attractive one. Although adjusting to the new school is the major theme, and Kitty gets a chance to make another newcomer feel at home at the end of the book, there is much more to the story. The look at Catholic life in the Midwest of the 1930s flavors the book enormously.

44. Frandsen, Karen G. *I Started School Today.* Illus. by the author. Chicago: Childrens, 1984. 32 pp. Fiction.

Interest level: Ages 4–7 Reading level: Grade 1

Jaunty, colorful cartoons and simple sentences that nonetheless convey the tension and import of a first day at school make this book a potential winner. From the moms waiting outside the school then leaving (shown on the kids' faces in looks of surprise, terror, and frowns) to individual reactions, the author tries to tell all through simplicity. ("Susie started crying. Jason couldn't find the bathroom.") The protagonist (unnamed) just wants to go home to see if a stranger is taking his toys.

Unfortunately, Frandsen carries the humor too far and the boy purposely puts a half-eaten cupcake on his teacher's chair, saying "I like surprises." She sits on it but smiles anyway. It is difficult to tell if this is a prank or he genuinely wanted to share it (as he says) and his efforts went awry. The book goes further afield and is actually frightening when the school bus passes his house, lets him off at the corner, and no one is there for him. A friend then tries to convince him to run away with him! He goes home instead (to see if his toys are still there), and plans tomorrow's surprise for teacher—a dead lizard, because he "likes" his teacher.

It is doubtful that the target age children will be as sophisticatedly hip (or malicious?) as this child; therefore, the humor falls flat and can actually frighten with its hostility. This book is not nearly as successful as it might have been.

45. Howe, James. *When You Go to Kindergarten.* Photos by Betsy Imershein. New York: Knopf, 1986, hb and pap. 48 pp. Nonfiction.
Interest level: Ages 3–6 Reading level: Grades 3–4

Husband and wife Howe and Imershein worked at New York area schools for this photoessay, including the famed Little Red Schoolhouse. It is unique in presenting a variety of schools, rather than just one. An introduction to parents suggests discussing differences between what is shown and what the child's situation will be. More important, they also discuss the difficulty for the parent in letting go of the child's hand as well as the child's difficulty in taking the big step.

The narrative talks to children directly: "This book will tell you about kindergarten—and what it's like to go there." Children are shown both walking to school and going by bus. Some schools have long halls, some have stairs; most have a principal's office, we're told. Parents reading aloud may have to explain what a principal is, as well as a custodian, but this book is meant for sharing aloud. The photographs capture tense children on the first day: "They're all starting out—just like you." Howe emphasizes the nitty-gritty. There is an introduction to the bathroom, water fountain, cubbies, taking attendance, fire drill, and so forth. Also such concepts as getting in line, sharing, learning the alphabet, and the classrooms shown have some advanced prereading curriculum that remains controversial and may be a source of unnecessary pressure on young children: "Your teacher will help you learn to print your letters and to hear the sounds that the letters make." More is made of this issue, showing that children are indeed thinking about this, perhaps feeling pressured: "Some children do not know how to read when they are in kindergarten. Other children do know how. This doesn't mean that they are better or smarter. It just means that they are ready to read sooner. Everybody reads whenever he or she is ready." The photos are large and clear, and in one of the classes, the teacher is a man.

Some of the ideas are especially inviting: "Your teacher will be your best grown-up friend in school." Mostly, the attempt to show everything, everywhere, at home, at school, and so on, works. One problem is that there is an attempt to show too much, such as a fire drill and a birthday party, and some children who can't prepare in one sitting (who can?) might be a bit overwhelmed. This is a book to share over and over so that its many pieces can be absorbed.

46. Janeczko, Paul B. *Bridges to Cross*. Illus. by Robert J. Blake. New York: Macmillan, 1986. 162 pp. Fiction.

    Interest level: Ages 10–14 Reading level: Grades 5–6

Set in the early 1960s, this novel of stumbling into selfhood is easy to identify with. Freshman James Marchuk must reconcile hypocrisy with everything he's been told about honesty and following rules. What should he make of his Catholic high school, where strident brothers slap the boys and visit pornography stores? At home, he wants to break away from being "Helen's boy," but his perfectionist mother won't listen, so he begins to lie. Through believable dialogue and a logical, fast-paced buildup of incidents, James comes to view the intrigues of the adult world in new, more complex ways. In a satisfying conclusion, James dares to cross the shaky symbolic town bridge of the title, gets hurt, and comes out able to stop spiting his mother. He confronts her, calls a halt to the web of deceit, and begins to pick and choose among rules to find his own ethical direction.

47. Kraus, Robert. *Spider's First Day at School*. Illus. by the author. New York: Scholastic, 1987, pap. 32 pp. Fiction.

    Interest level: Ages 4–7 Reading level: Grade 2

Spider experiences all the anxieties and negative feelings about the first day of school that most children suffer. His teacher and the children are, for the most part, friendly, with the exception of one group, the bedbugs. The school activities are relevant and fun for him. Spider is a friendly person who shares generously with his classmates. When the class has a football game Spider is the hero of the game, and at the end of it all the children are admiring of Spider, and are all friends.

School is depicted as a place where problems can be solved by positive social interaction. It is also filled with activities that make sense and that are appropriate to the children's needs and interests. It is unfortunate that Spider must become a hero in order to be totally accepted. In fact, he is happy before the game, but the game becomes the icing on the cake. Lots of good ideas are incorporated into the book about how to make school a successful experience.

48. Krementz, Jill. *Katharine Goes to Nursery School.* Photos by the author. New York: Random, 1986. 14 hardboard sides. Fiction.

Interest level: Ages 2–5 Reading level: Grades 1–2

In this photo-essay, Krementz follows a young girl to school. Katharine speaks directly to her audience, and though this is not a first experience the narration sensibly balances delighted independence with contact and reminders of Mommy and Daddy. Specifics are explained through chronology: the teacher's greeting, parent's good-bye, games and activities, snack, story, nap, reunion. Katharine speaks like a three-year-old that readers can identify with.

Most pages have two or three photographs, all well composed, asplash with hearty color, joyful, and caring. Katharine's love for school will be contagious, just as Krementz intended.

49. McCully, Emily Arnold. *School.* Illus. by the author. New York: Harper, 1987. 32 pp. Fiction.

Interest level: Ages 3–6 Reading level: Wordless

This wordless picture book treat tells the tale of a curious little mouse who watches his many siblings trek off to school on a fall day. He sneaks off to follow them, is welcomed in, and becomes part of the large class. (All the mice are brown and without clothes, but he can be identified by his size and a watch on his wrist.) Of course, his mother has missed him. She comes hurriedly in, sees he is safe, is happy, and they leave together to go back home. Children use books to get their first idea of what a new experience will be like, and this one, in its unique form, offers a peaceful view of a school in which everyone learns and gets along.

50. Magorian, Michelle. *Back Home.* New York: Harper, 1984. 375 pp. Fiction.

Interest level: Age 12+ Reading level: Grade 7

Magorian, author of *Good Night, Mr. Tom* (Harper, 1982), has again given us a thoughtful and dramatic story with strong characters and a plot that contains themes of loneliness, coming of age, knowing oneself, abuse, and the aftermath of war. The book also treats the issues of clashing values, adjusting to a new school, and striving for independence and understanding.

The protagonist is a feisty girl nicknamed Rusty by her foster family, with whom she stayed in America when she was evacuated from England during World War II. She left her parents when she was seven, and now, five years later, she has been forced to return. She has loved her foster family and her life in America, and has become thoroughly Americanized in outlook, speech, and manner, but the war in Europe is over and her mother wants her back.

Her new life in England is a difficult one for her. Her mother, Peggy, has changed over the five years from a passive, helpless creature into a woman who is an adroit auto mechanic and has friends of her own. Peggy lives in Devon with her four-year-old son, Charlie. She has been stationed here as part of her Women's Voluntary Service group, and it is to this place that Rusty has come, and where they remain for a while until the Japanese surrender.

They return to their permanent home, where Rusty's grandmother lives. Her grandmother is a snobbish, unbending woman who disapproves of everyone but her own son. When her father returns from the army, he is cold, punitive, and removed. One person who has been kind to Rusty, and whom Rusty has grown to love, dies and leaves her house in Devon to Rusty's mother.

Rusty is forced to go to an oppressive boarding school where no one likes her. She takes refuge in a bombed-out cabin in the woods where she retreats regularly. After a set of minidisasters, Rusty runs away from school and returns to Devon. Although she returns to the school, she is expelled. In the end her mother and father separate, and she and her mother and brother move into the small house in Devon. Rusty and her brother go to a day school that is Summerhillian in philosophy, where Rusty and her brother are welcomed and will flourish.

For some reason, Rusty is not angry at her father. She does hate her grandmother, but she is strangely sympathetic to her father. She wishes that her father would come with them; nevertheless, she is happy to be in Devon. She realizes that she loves her mother, and that she would probably not fit in any more in America. This conclusion is a little too pat, but the power of the rest of the book makes up for the small flaws in the logic of the narrative.

51. Robinson, Nancy K. *Veronica the Show-off.* Illus. by Sheila Greenwald. New York: Four Winds, 1982; Scholastic, pap. 128 pp. Fiction.
    Interest level: Ages 8–11 Reading level: Grade 4

Veronica desperately wants friends, but no one in her new school seems to be interested in becoming her friend. Veronica tries her best to attract children by inventing what she thinks are interesting stories about how rich she is and how many things she has. She can't understand why the children are not interested.

As the story progresses, we realize that Veronica's father never comes to see her, even when he is in town. He also doesn't invite her to come to visit him. Veronica's mother is also too preoccupied with her own interests to pay any attention to Veronica. So Veronica is really a deserted child, even though she lives with her mother. Her showing off is a way of getting attention, but it doesn't work.

Quite by accident, Veronica does become friends with an understanding classmate who defies stereotyping. She is petite and gentle, and she takes karate lessons. Her house becomes a haven for Veronica.

Veronica also practically lives in the public library. She loves to read, and she is furious when a book that she has been waiting for is renewed by another child. Veronica and the girl, Melody, engage in a sort of warfare for a while, but when they meet each other they discover more similarities than differences, and they become friends. They are both distraught and angry when they learn that their library has been closed due to lack of funds. Together they send a letter to the newspaper to demand the reopening of the library.

Because she now has friends, and she also has some real issues and interests to share with her friends, the other children in the class begin to view Veronica differently. There may be little hope of her receiving satisfaction at home, but in school and in her social life Veronica has made great gains.

The story may help children better understand those of their peers who always seem compelled to brag about their exploits and possessions. It may also provide a mirror for those children whose behavior is inappropriate if their aim is to establish friendships.

52. Rogers, Fred. *Going to Day Care.* Photos by Jim Judkis. New York: Putnam, 1985, hb and pap. 32 pp. Nonfiction.

    Interest level: Ages 2–6 Reading level: Grade 2

Acknowledging that increased numbers of children are attending day care, Rogers has written about the situation's differences from school (mixed age groups, for example). He also calls the adult staff day-care givers, as opposed to teachers. In his note to parents, Rogers emphasizes taking the time (and he acknowledges it may take a lot of effort) to find a good day-care situation about which both parent and child can be happy. Also important are talking about feelings, being reassured they *will* come home at day's end, and letting children know how loved and valued they are at home. With these steps, new attachments can begin to be forged.

In this book, two children (boy and girl; black and white) are pictured going to day-care centers or day-care homes. The settings look warm, colorful, cheerful. Rooms in the day-care center are shown—kitchen, bathroom, and so forth. The emphasis is on balance—some things children can do by themselves (for example, washing hands); other things children need help with (for example, shoe tying). Children are shown helping grown-ups and each other, eating, resting, playing inside and out, and being in a group and playing alone. They have the day-care giver to themselves, too: "It feels good to know that there are times when you can have someone you love all to yourself." The day ends happily with a father picking up a child and a proud day-care giver discussing his child's activities during the day. And then at home there's a lot to talk about, too. This book is recommended for its warmth, clarity, and respect for early childhood development.

53. Roth, Harold. *Babies Love Nursery School.* Photos by the author. New York: Grosset, 1986. 14 boards. Nonfiction.
    Interest level: Ages 2–6 Reading level: Grades 1–2

This small-sized book shows a multiethnic classroom with close-up shots of children painting, drawing, eating, and participating. The reader is drawn in with such sentences as: "Nursery school is a busy place. You can draw with crayons . . . or try sponge painting." It's an all-day affair, it seems, with children eating lunch, and it's a happy place. But the children shown are not babies but preschoolers, as the nursery population is. The title is cause for wonder, as babies might be in day care, which usually starts at around age 3, but not nursery school. Recommended. Children will enjoy the book's size—tiny like themselves, and the colorful presentation will keep them interested.

54. Schwartz, Amy. *Bea and Mr. Jones.* Illus. by the author. New York: Bradbury, 1982; Penguin, pap. 32 pp. Fiction.
    Interest level: Ages 4–9 Reading level: Grades 1–2

Bea Jones, one sophisticated child who's "had it with kindergarten," is ready for a change. Her father commiserates, "Do you think I like my job?" Naturally, they decide to switch places. Off Bea goes in her father's suit to the advertising world. And her dad? He does cartwheels and feels better immediately. The humor in the black-and-white illustrations comes from the reader who knows all. The teacher looks askance but allows Bea's father to stay because he has brought a note from Bea—"the child's father." He delights in school games and tasks because he uses his adult skills—what quicker way to become teacher's pet? And Bea brings children's activities to the office meetings and saves the day by bringing a simple children's rhyme to an advertising account. Do the two go back to their original roles at the end? No way. And so, in this unusual book, it's not a child who goes to a new school, but a bald, roundish fellow with a mustache. Recommended as a way for children to gain perspective and enhance their sense of fun.

55. Schweninger, Ann. *Off to School!* Illus. by the author. New York: Viking Kestrel, 1987. 32 pp. Fiction.

Interest level: Ages 4–7 Reading level: Grade 1

A happy mixture of washes, inks, and pencils, this full-color book uses few words (and they appear in cartoon balloons) to tell how Button Brown, a rabbit, goes off to school. The first chapter is called "Getting Ready" and tells what is in Button's pencil box. There are touches of humor, as the "child" takes Super Rabbit, a doll, along for the day. The parents walk him to Peter Cottontail School, where, in spite of owning a pencil box with a tiny globe inside, he is indeed a preschooler. Lo and behold, Button is not the only child to bring Super Rabbit to class. Another chapter is devoted to names, and the teacher has the children lie down on paper to trace their body shapes (a highly unlikely first day activity). The children also magically get right into routines of line up, clay play, blocks, and the playground, too. At story time, the teacher tells the story of—guess who—Peter Rabbit. All is smooth, and Button goes home to imitate what has taken place so he and his younger siblings can play school.

Although this book is fun, the activities are far too advanced for a first day at school and therefore misleading. Also, Button only expresses minor hesitation (will the teacher like him and vice versa). In addition, early childhood teachers currently have quite a problem battling children's insertion of superheroes into class curriculum; many teachers feel that superhero worship leads to unnecessary aggression. In this class, superhero fun is encouraged.

56. Smith, Jennifer. *Grover and the New Kid.* Illus. by Tom Cooke. New York: Random/Children's Television Workshop, 1987. 32 pp. Fiction.

Interest level: Ages 3–7 Reading level: Grade 1

In something of a reversal of the usual situation, Barry, the new child in school, is the one who doesn't want to share, and who is mean to the other children. Grover tries to befriend Barry, but the new boy doesn't seem to appreciate it, and even ruins Grover's painting. At last Barry sees that Grover is unhappy and apologizes, and begins to share. He confides in Grover that he was afraid to come to this new school, and tells him how much he appreciates his friendship.

The story's use of the popular Sesame Street muppets serves as a good stimulus for talking about the plight of the new child. In this story, it is not only the new boy but also Grover and the other children in the class whose feelings we are invited to understand. Admittedly, Grover is extraordinarily empathic for a young child, and Barry does come to his senses a bit suddenly. But the story is gentle and positive.

57. Stolz, Mary. *Ivy Larkin.* New York: Harcourt, 1986. 226 pp. Fiction.
Interest level: Age 11+ Reading level: Grades 5–6

The story deals with the changes that Ivy goes through as she confronts going to a snooty private school and her family's deteriorating situation during the time of the Great Depression. The characters in the book are well developed. They could easily have become stereotyped. The father is a jovial and poetic Irishman whose love for his family sometimes suffers because of his pride. The mother is a hard-working nurse who is willing to sacrifice anything so that her children will get good schooling. Frank, the independent older brother, hangs around with the local gang, but refuses to miss his family's weekly outings, is sensitive to his youngest sister's fears, and gives his lunch to a poor man on the street. Megan, Ivy's younger sister, is so beautiful and sensitive that no one can deny her anything, yet she is so fearful that one of her siblings must always be with her. Ivy, the main character, is 13 years old. She is not as attractive or as outgoing as her siblings. She is jealous of their talents but her love for all of them always keeps her balanced.

The story tells of how difficult it is for the family when the father is out of work for a number of months. It also details the problems that Ivy encounters in the private school to which all three siblings have won scholarships. Although Ivy sees the advantages in the school, she decides in the end, despite her father's prejudice against it, that she will go to a parochial school. She pledges, however, that she will always think for herself.

58. Surat, Michele Maria. *Angel Child, Dragon Child.* Illus. by Vo-Dinh Mai. Milwaukee: Carnival, 1983. 32 pp. Fiction.
Interest level: Ages 5–9 Reading level: Grade 2

Written poetically and with almost overwhelming feeling, this is the story of Ut, who has come with her sisters, brother, and father to the United States from Vietnam. There is no money yet for her mother to join them. School is a misery, where instructional methods are different and she is teased mercilessly by Raymond, a classmate who (naturally) turns out to be as insecure as she. "Pajamas," he calls out to her, mocking her clothes. The seasons proceed this way, with Ut finding solace in her mother's photo. She is less able to be the Angel Child or brave Dragon Child her mother had told her to be. Instead she is an Angry Dragon. When Raymond goes too far, the principal intervenes, cleverly creating a task whereby he must write down her story as she tells it to him. The principal, now the hero, and a weakness in the story, then rallies the student body to raise money for Ut's mother to come to the United States through a Vietnamese Fair. The writing is as gentle and poetic as Ut herself: "We slid through icy winter. . . . We splish-splashed through spring rain."

59. Wirths, Claudine G., and Bowman-Kruhm, Mary. *I Hate School: How to Hang In and When to Drop Out.* Illus. by Patti Stren. New York: Crowell, 1987, hb and pap. 128 pp. Nonfiction.

    Interest level: Age 12+ Reading level: Grades 5–6

This is a most unusual, needed book that can help kids make decisions that might lead to attending a new school. At last someone (in this case, two people with teaching, administering, and writing experience) has addressed the needs of alienated students. In a question-answer format the authors address issues as varied as building concentration ability, stepping out versus dropping out, alternate routes to degrees, and dealing with authority figures. Accompanying cartoons are sophisticated and meaningful (for example, a character saying "I wouldn't mind school if it was just a few weeks a year"). Successfully chatty, this book has great value: how to get over homework hurdles, study skill buildups, tips for reading faster and writing better, ways to remember material, report outlines, and test-taking strategies.

Wirths and Bowman-Kruhm also attend to deep personal problems that students may be having, realizing this influences attitudes toward school and ability to function there. In this section they switch from the question-answer format and wisely become more authoritative in their discussion. Example of a heading: "Serious Family Problems (physical abuse, sexual abuse, divorce, abandonment, criminal or racial threats to family safety, illness, money, and so on)." And underneath that heading are guidelines—whom to talk to, agencies to call, for example, "Call the main number for county offices and ask the operator who answers to connect you with a family service agency." This is a down-to-earth treatment that will appeal to many alienated students because it doesn't view the only possibility as staying in school.

New Neighborhood

Moving means the loss of friends and surroundings that have grown familiar. The move may necessitate separation from people, schools, habits, customs, and attitudes that have been taken for granted. In order to cope, children must eventually accept changes in the setting for the drama of their lives; the management of these changes implies adjustment to a new environment and the creation of fresh patterns of living.

60. Ashabranner, Brent. *Dark Harvest: Migrant Farmworkers in America.* Photos by Paul Conklin. New York: Dodd, 1985. 160 pp. Nonfiction.

Interest level: Ages 9–14 Reading level: Grade 6

This book provides portraits of farm workers and their families, along with an explanation of migrant workers' way of life. There are maps of individual travel patterns, along with an analysis of why these workers are needed. The emphasis is on sociology and economics, with amplification of how the crew leader system works. The often bleak picture is elucidated: an average life span of 49 years; infant and maternal death rate at two and one-half times the national average; health and workplace hazards; pesticide poisoning; status as the poorest paid workers in our country, including a child labor law that exempts agricultural work, enabling 14-year-olds to be legally employed and 12- and 13-year-olds to do so with parental consent. Of farm workers' children, 60 percent drop out of school before grade 9.

The sharp, cheerful photographs almost belie the above statistics, showing happy family groupings, but chapter subtitles such as "Being Poor" bring back the larger feeling of the book as a whole. Segments on migrant childhoods are especially poignant, and the book ends with chapters on the future—hopes and movements for change that, in spite (or perhaps because) of corporate conglomerates' increasing control over farming, is not yet on the horizon. Informative and moving. Bibliography, index.

61. Auch, Mary Jane. *The Witching of Ben Wagner.* Boston: Houghton Mifflin, 1987. 132 pp. Fiction.

Interest level: Age 11+ Reading level: Grade 5

Because their father has a better opportunity in another town, the family must move. None of the children is happy about the move, and the ride in the car to the new town is an agony for all of them, as they squabble and suffer from the heat. Ben's first day at school is equally disastrous. He cannot find his way to his first class, is embarrassed about telling anyone, and is reprimanded for cutting class. Ben's older and younger sisters seem to make a better adjustment than he does, but in reality, Ben's sister, Susan, is so anxious about making friends that she lies to her friends about where she lives and how much money she has. She also tells stories about Ben to get him into trouble.

Then Ben meets Regina near the lake and becomes friendly with her. He suspects that she may be a witch, because he has heard that witches haunt this area. She knows a lot about herbs and cures, and she speaks of trances and brews. Both her parents have deserted her, and she lives with her grandmother. Ben believes that it is Regina's magic that is helping him to do better at school and to feel less unhappy there. He also believes that it is Regina's spell that enables him to rescue his younger sister, Liz, from drowning.

In the end, Ben discovers that Regina is not a witch, that his accomplishments have been his own, and that his family can get along together once the truth about all of their behavior is uncovered.

The story is believable, even to the point where the reader is not sure whether Regina is a witch. The family is an ordinary family trying its best to get along. The mother has no individuality, but Ben's plight is worthy of investigation, and young readers will empathize with him.

62. Banks, Ann, and Evans, Nancy. *Goodbye, House: A Kids' Guide to Moving*. Illus. by Marisabina Russo. New York: Harmony, 1980, pap. 64 pp. Nonfiction.

Interest level: Ages 5–8 Reading level: Grades 2–3

A combination of advice book, journal, and scrapbook, this slim volume is a helpful stimulus to activities and discussions that can help children cope with the trauma of moving. Starting with preparations for the move, such as looking at a map to locate where they are moving and how far away it is, children are encouraged to make all sorts of lists, to give friends self-addressed postcards to ensure getting mail, to create an address book so that they can keep in touch with friends, and to decide on ways to be helpful to their parents. The focus is on the child's feelings, but the book wisely acknowledges that the move is a family event, and that children must learn to be part of the family enterprise.

Banks and Evans also recommend helpful activities to do after the move has taken place, such as drawing a map of the new neighborhood so that the children won't get lost; planning their first day of school; making more lists; and, perhaps, finding a secret hiding place in the new house. Part of the coping strategy is to collect a list of pleasant memories of the old house, and also think of the things children are glad to be rid of.

The parents' notes are as thoughtful as the primary content. Banks and Evans have themselves experienced many moves and have talked to many children in their research. They remind parents to be honest about the reasons for moving and give a reasoned analysis of the debate about timing for moving: Should it be in the summer or during the school year? They offer ways to include the child parents might not have thought of, for example, getting enough change-of-address postcards from the post office in order to give some to the child. The authors also offer ideas that can reassure the child, such as allowing the child to fantasize and suggesting a flashlight for the first night in a new room. And they're very practical in their reassurance, too, as when they suggest having the van filled with the children's things last so they can be emptied first—the kids' rooms can then be set up reassuringly quickly and thus give the children a place to stay out of the way; the children can do final arrangements of the rooms while the rest is unpacked. This book is a wonderful helpmate for a difficult time!

63. Bargar, Gary W. *Life Is Not Fair.* New York: Clarion, 1984. 174 pp. Fiction.

Interest level: Age 10+ Reading level: Grade 5

Although the story is told from the perspective of Louis, a white seventh grader, a key figure in the book is his black friend, DeWitt, a boy who has moved in next door. The year is 1959, and Louis knows that it is not "cool" for a white boy to have a black friend. And Louis desperately wants to be cool.

Louis's white friends seem to be bullies, cheats, and bigots. After DeWitt is almost killed when a group of hoodlums beats them both up, Louis comes to understand that it is much more important for him to live with himself than to be accepted by people he does not admire.

The difficulties of adjusting to a new neighborhood and school are presented in a somewhat simplistic fashion here. Louis's need to be accepted by the "in" crowd when he attends junior high is understandable, and may provide a basis for youngsters to consider their own feelings and behavior. The racial situation is less realistically handled, but certainly worthy of discussion.

64. Black, Sonia. *The Get Along Gang and the New Neighbor.* Illus. by David Gantz. New York: Scholastic, 1984. 32 pp. Fiction.

Interest level: Ages 3–6 Reading level: Grade 2

Rudyard Lion is a visiting student from a distant country. Although he enjoys playing with the Get Along gang, he is homesick for his own country. The animals in the gang plan a surprise birthday party for him, but while they are planning it they give him the impression that he isn't wanted. Tearfully, he writes a good-bye note and goes to the airport. The gang discovers his departure just in time, and they fetch him back to stay for "a long, long time."

The impression that the author gives is that it is Rudyard's fault that there was a misunderstanding, when, indeed, it was the insensitivity and preoccupation of the others that caused the misunderstanding. The illustrations are cartoonlike. The plot is somewhat simplistic, but young children may be able to discuss the behavior of the friends in the light of Rudyard's feelings.

65. Booher, Dianna Daniels. *Help! We're Moving.* New York: Messner, 1983. 144 pp. Nonfiction.

Interest level: Ages 12–16 Reading level: Grade 5

In this entry in the Teen Survival series, Booher tells of her own fright at moving during high school, in her case from a junior class of 25 on up to one of more than 500. Booher weaves stories to get her points across, particularly about resiliency, which she brightly calls "snapbacktivity." There is an emphasis on the positive, true, but there is also good advice on wrapping up loose ends. Insightful self-quizzes can help youngsters decide if they want to stay behind when the family moves if the school year is not over: "Have you ever been with the relative's or friend's family when they've been upset or angry?" Adjustment to the new locale is filled with practical ideas ("call the Y," for example), as is the chapter on coping with newcomer blues ("give your pets extra care"), on making friends, and on finding one's way around the school. The aim throughout is ego-building, finding lots of ways to feel good, and Booher presents a bouncy, lively list. Bibliography, index.

66. Carlson, Nancy. *Loudmouth George and the New Neighbors.* Illus. by the author. Minneapolis: Carolrhoda, 1983; Penguin, pap. 28 pp. Fiction.

Interest level: Ages 5–8 Reading level: Grade 2

When he finds out that his new neighbors are a family of pigs, George, a rabbit, decides he will have nothing to do with them. But he changes his mind after he sees all of his friends playing happily with the Pig children. When a family of cats moves into the neighborhood not long after, George grudgingly agrees to go and play with them despite his prejudices about cats.

The issues here include not only the difficulties of moving into a new neighborhood but the book also indicates the prejudices that people have about each other. George would perhaps never overcome his bigotry if he weren't abandoned by his friends in favor of the new neighbors. The message here is intended to be a positive one.

Children should take care to avoid thinking that just because a bigot decides to try out the company of people he formerly despised, that that constitutes a victory for equality. George is very much the "Archie Bunker" type: tolerated for reasons unknown, and loud in his defaming of other groups.

The book is charming enough that children will enjoy tackling a discussion of George and his bigotry.

67. Cone, Molly. *The Big Squeeze.* Boston: Houghton Mifflin, 1984. 114 pp. Fiction.
    Interest level: Ages 9–12 Reading level: Grade 4

Dudley is a high school sophomore, but he looks more like a seventh grader. What is more, he and his family are constantly on the move. His father fixes up old houses, sells them, and moves on. Dudley has never been a part of any of the schools he has gone to and he feels this loss keenly. He is very sociable, and he makes friends easily, however. This time he develops a crush on a girl named Donna, whom all the boys ogle because she has large breasts. Dudley is attracted to her because of the role she plays in the school production of "The Fantasticks." He takes part in the play and is sure that Donna is attracted to him, but in the end she selects another boy for her affection. Dudley is not dismayed; he realizes that he loved the character in the play, not the girl. And he also finds out that his family is moving again, this time to a brand new city.

Dudley is a competent young man. Despite his longing for some sort of permanence, he comes to understand that he is fortunate to be with parents who love each other and him. They are his security; they are his permanence. Cone provides for young readers a different perspective on the problem of moving because of this awareness of the importance of the internal family structure.

68. Davis, Jennie. *Julie's New Home: A Story about Being a Friend.* Illus. by Pat Karch. Chicago: Dandelion, 1983. 30 pp. Fiction.
    Interest level: Ages 6–9 Reading level: Grade 3

Julie is unhappy and lonely in her new home. She sees children in the neighborhood, but they are busy with each other. Her mom says it takes time to adjust to a new place. Julie, however, becomes upset and cries. Mom gives her this advice: "Be a friend," instead of just wanting a friend. So Julie adds a big welcome sign to the house, made with cardboard boxes, and invites a girl passing by to come see it. Soon several other neighborhood kids are dropping in. Julie is happy and has made new friends by being a friend.

The solution is certainly a reasonable one, but it is made all too facile here. Nevertheless, this sort of helpful advice can stand some children in good stead, and let them know that there are active things they can do to get used to and become accepted in a new place.

69. Finsand, Mary Jane. *The Town That Moved.* Illus. by Reg Sandland. Minneapolis: Carolrhoda, 1983. 48 pp. Nonfiction.
    Interest level: Ages 6–9 Reading level: Grade 1

Children who are overwhelmed by their family's moving might regain a sense of humor from this beginning reader account of a town that moved because iron ore was discovered beneath it. It is a rousing true story of seeking economic benefit and preserving an entire town at the same time. It began in the early 1900s in Hibbing, Minnesota, and lasted into the early 1950s, such was the magnitude of the task. After discussing alternate methods, the mine owners and townspeople separated all the buildings from their basements, then dug new basements for the buildings. With cranes they lifted buildings onto log rollers and then had horses pull the log rollers to the new locations. Clean attractive drawings fill each right-hand page in a compelling book.

70. Fisher, Leonard E. *Ellis Island: Gateway to the New World.* Photos and drawings by the author. New York: Holiday, 1986. 64 pp. Nonfiction.
    Interest level: Age 10+ Reading level: Grade 6

By all means join Fisher on his majestic journey, the "largest movement of human beings in history." Through his evocative writing, along with the immigrants, we too "fall silent with excitement and expectation." On the way there's the area's history from colonial times until today and stories and remarks by individuals who went through the process there: the first to arrive on the actual island (Annie Moore, Ireland, 1892), the fire that destroyed all records from 1855 through 1897, the painful eye exam, the heartbreak of being sent back. Perhaps most lingering, the "hollow din of . . . the talk, laughter, tears, sobs, and screams all melting together like a wavy sigh." Well-chosen National Park Service photographs of varied ethnic groups, in combination with Fisher's dark scratchboard drawings, effectively convey emotion, making this a wonderful book.

71. Fleming, Alice. *Welcome to Grossville.* New York: Scribner, 1985. 104 pp. Fiction.
    Interest level: Ages 9–12 Reading level: Grades 4–5

Not only are Michael and Jenny's lives changed by the sudden news that their parents are getting a divorce, their anguish is compounded when their mother tells them that they are moving from Glenville to a new town, selling much of their furniture, and dismissing their housekeeper and gardener. Their new house is much smaller than the one in which they have lived all of their lives (Michael is 11; Jenny is 8). The third bombshell explodes when their mother tells them that she will have to find a job.

Michael finds it difficult to make friends in the new neighborhood. Although both their former and present towns are suburbs of New York, Glenville is a high-income area, and Humboldt, the new town, is middle class. Michael calls it "Grossville." A group of boys in the new neighborhood think he is snooty because he has a fancy bike and wears trendy clothes. Jenny, on the other hand, makes a friend right away, which causes Michael to be envious and resentful. He spends most of his time snacking and watching television. With his father on Sundays, he is sullen and argumentative.

At last he starts to meet children his age who are friendly and with whom he enjoys himself. With his new friends' help he eventually becomes friends with the group of boys he first encountered as a hostile group. At the end of the story he has adjusted happily to life in Humboldt, and he is well on his way to coping with the divorce.

The book is helpful in many ways. Through the elements of a good story the reader is able to build a repertoire of strategies for coping with divorce and with the stresses of moving to a new neighborhood. Positive thinking, permitting others to get to know you, and letting go of petty resentment and preconceptions are all part of the process. And Fleming presents it with humor and balance.

72. Greenwald, Dorothy. *Coping with Moving*. New York: Rosen, 1987. 140 pp. Nonfiction.

    Interest level: Ages 11–15 Reading level: Grade 5

With snappy chapter titles like "Pity Party or Great Adventure," free-lance writer and real estate agent Greenwald sets out the mixed emotional luggage moving may represent. Reminding readers of other past good-byes (visits, summer camp, and so on), she sets the stage for making moving less devastating.

Greenwald puts the teenage love relationship and the prospect of leaving it up near the front of the book. At first, this seems to be disjointed disorganization, but perhaps she is really right on target about what truly matters to teens who must leave. She is also very concrete about additional losses other books of this type haven't covered, for example, leaving a favorite teacher. Other topics include possibilities of staying behind, making sure the school transition is smooth with all courses credited, using community resources such as the YMCA or YWCA, planning ahead, garage sales, getting ready for the big day, the actual day, and beyond, when one must adjust to a new school, home, and town. Making new friends is the subject of not one chapter, but two, with practical ideas for joining established groups. Index.

73. Grove, Vicki. *Good-Bye, My Wishing Star*. New York: Putnam, 1988. 128 pp. Fiction.

    Interest level: Ages 9–12 Reading level: Grade 4

Grove's intent in writing this book was to help make children aware of what is happening in the country today and to convey the resilience that people have, even in a time of hardship and loss. The story tells of Jens, a 12-year-old, whose letter, to whoever moves into her house, begins the book. In her letter Jens tells of the people of the community that she and her family are now leaving. She tells of the hardships that other people endure, and she describes her own difficulties with her friends and her family. Most of all, the thread of her family's serious economic problems runs through the story, leading to the family's decision to leave their beloved farm and move to the city.

Each of the characters comes alive through the author's perceptive eye. When Jens and her friends try to do something nice for Brenda, a child whose father has just died, they present her with a gift that they think she will enjoy, and instead of reacting with pleasure or thanks, Brenda asks them why they did this. The memory of this incident comes back when, on learning that Jens is leaving, her friends give her a surprise party. Jens is so distraught over the fact that she must move that she feels that a party is totally inappropriate. She asks her friends why they did this and then she leaves. But she recovers her good sense when she learns that her friends gave the party because they wanted to show her how much they will miss her. One lesson to be learned is that good intentions do not always make up for insensitivity. Another is that different people grieve in different ways.

With the help of her family and friends Jens is finally reconciled to the fact that she must go. She knows that she will keep this home in her heart forever, but she also knows that wherever she and her family are will be home to her.

The story is well told and refreshing in its directness. The characters are neither petty nor stereotypic. They are interesting people with recognizable traits and problems, but they transcend these problems by their determination not to let these difficulties defeat them.

74. Hickman, Martha Whitmore. *When Can Daddy Come Home?* Illus. by Francis Livingston. Nashville: Abingdon, 1983. 38 pp. Fiction.
Interest level: Ages 5–8 Reading level: Grades 2–3

Andy's father has been imprisoned for robbery and Andy must deal with the fallout. Some of his former friends abuse him, and some are not permitted to play with him any more because of his father's crime. His family moves away from their old neighborhood in order to be closer to the prison so that they may easily visit the father. At school Andy meets Joel, another newcomer, whose father is very ill, probably with cancer. Joel and Andy have much in common and enjoy each other's company.

Andy often goes to visit his father. They are allowed to picnic on the prison grounds. When Andy's father is granted parole, Andy shares the happy news with his family, Joel, and his understanding teacher.

Hickman conveys graphically the difference that acceptance of a child makes when he is going through the trauma of an absent parent, and in particular, a parent who is in prison. She helps children to see that it is the parent who made the mistake, not the child, and that the parent's crime should not cause the child to be unduly punished. The only flaw in this otherwise carefully thought-out book is that Andy's mother at first told her son that his father was on a trip. Andy then had to learn the truth from other sources, at which point the mother dealt well with the issue. It is too bad she didn't have the foresight to tell her son the truth from the start. Nevertheless, the book is a helpful one in dealing with this not-so-rare problem.

75. Kaufman, Curt, and Kaufman, Gita. *Hotel Boy*. Photos by Curt Kaufman. New York: Atheneum, 1987. 40 pp. Nonfiction.
    Interest level: Ages 4–8 Reading level: Grade 2

After an apartment fire, five-year-old Henri and his brother have to live in a hotel with their single-parent mother. This book tells of the crowded conditions and the loss of the usual amenities of home—the clothes, toys, and books are gone. Henri must also go to a new school (Gita Kaufman actually was Henri's kindergarten teacher). This much starting over often seems like too much starting over.

Henri tells the story of the city help his family received, of how hotel children make their own meager entertainment, and how the wide open streets often are more appealing than the single room that three must share. And yet, while the family endures as Mom searches for a job and they await a new apartment, other family traditions and milestones of growth remain—a trip to the zoo, buying pizza, learning to tie a shoe. When the big day comes and the family gets a new apartment, there's excitement all around. This book is a valuable look at an increasingly prevalent problem.

76. Komaiko, Leah. *Annie Bananie*. Illus. by Laura Cornell. New York: Harper, 1987. 32 pp. Fiction.
    Interest level: Ages 4–8 Reading level: Grade 1

    Annie Bananie,
    My best friend,
    Said we'd be friends to the end.
    Made me brush my teeth with mud,
    Sign my name in cockroach blood,
    Tie my brother to the trees,
    Made me tickle bumblebees.

No easy children, these girls. The rhyme only intensifies her friend's reaction to Annie's move. She wouldn't be Annie Bananie without her, for she'd given her the nickname and tried to make her over in a particular image. Why must she go away? How can she go away? At last the friend must say good-bye, but not without reminding Annie Bananie she'll never ever ever find another friend like herself. The full-color illustrations fit the mood, for this is a colorful, lively, almost wild friendship, the kind where you hide under the bed together rather than have to go home. Children's intense feelings about the friendship they must leave behind when they move are given credence and respect.

77. Lord, Bette Bao. *In the Year of the Boar and Jackie Robinson.* Illus. by Marc Simont. New York: Harper, 1984. 169 pp. Fiction.

    Interest level: Ages 9–12 Reading level: Grade 4

Shirley Temple Wong is the heroine of this story of moving to a new land and adjusting to new customs and circumstances. Shirley and her mother have just come to Brooklyn to be with Shirley's father. He has been in America for a long time preparing the way for the rest of the family to be together again. Shirley misses her extended family and home in China. She has trouble learning English, and she faces the problem of some antagonistic and pugnacious classmates. And to compound matters she is placed in class with children at least a full year or two older than she, because of the difference in the Chinese way of counting age (that is, she was considered a year old at birth and a year older each New Year's Day).

Shirley is bright, feisty, and imaginative. She is generous and enthusiastic, and cares deeply about people. The author introduces us to Chinese customs and to Shirley's feelings through her escapades and her interactions with people. The story is full of humor, information, excitement, and sentiment. The triumphant moment, when Shirley is introduced to her idol, Jackie Robinson, has an authentic ring to it, as does the rest of this endearing book.

The book demonstrates how children can cope with separation from homeland and family, and with the challenges of moving to a new neighborhood, entering a new school, and dealing with differences in heritage and custom.

78. Lovik, Craig. *Andy and the Tire.* Illus. by Mark Alan Weatherby. New York: Scholastic, 1987, pap. 32 pp. Fiction.

    Interest level: Ages 7–10 Reading level: Grade 3

When no one becomes his friend in the new school or neighborhood into which Andy, his sister, and his parents have moved, Andy is unhappy and resentful. He finds an old tire on his way home from school and spends almost all of his time learning to ride on it and do tricks with it. Although Andy does become quite accomplished at everything except stopping, no one seems to appreciate his performance. His mother makes him take the tire out of the bathtub, and his grandmother exiles his tire to the outdoors after Andy gets tread marks on her carpet. Things come to a head when Andy and his tire wreck the Founders' Day parade. The officials are very tolerant, however, and explain to him that next year he had better apply for a parade permit. When Andy's parents realize the reason for his exhibitions, they help Andy tie the tire to a tree and convert it into a swing. Now many children come to play in the swing, and Andy acquires some friends. But he also unties the tire from time to time and practices on it to be ready for next year's parade.

In a charming and amusing story, the message is communicated that there are many ways to attract friends, that parents can help, and that being a new person in school and in the neighborhood is hard. Andy is a competent and inventive boy whose sense of self is well established.

79. Malone, Nola Langner. *A Home.* Illus. by the author. New York: Bradbury, 1988. 32 pp. Fiction.

Interest level: Ages 4–8 Reading level: Grade 1

"One cold day in the middle of March, Molly moved to a new big house. Good-bye Rock. Good-bye Pond. And Good-bye Creaky Swing." And so Molly goes off to her new, bigger house, where nothing feels right. But a friend quickly materializes. Will all be jim-dandy, as it first appears? No, there is a pinching, poking, pushing fight. The making up (which simultaneously leads to everything in the new house feeling right) is probably the way children actually do it in real life—they just do it, with full heart and with the ability to say "I missed you." But, ironically, in the book, it somehow feels abrupt and of lesser authenticity.

80. Mango, Karin N. *Somewhere Green.* New York: Four Winds, 1987. 174 pp. Fiction.

Interest level: Age 11+ Reading level: Grades 6–7

Not only has Bryony's family moved to Brooklyn, a neighborhood she hates, but then her parents go to Brazil on a three-month expedition and leave Bryony and her older but dreamy sister and younger brother in the care of a housekeeper. When the housekeeper leaves after only a week, the three siblings decide to withhold the news of her departure from their parents, neighbors, and relatives. They encounter many serious problems, including a mugging and a beating, but they also meet interesting people and begin to appreciate the variety and spice of their Brooklyn surroundings. When their parents return they are very proud of their children.

Although the young people in the story are admirable and accomplish a lot, they aren't quite believable. Nevertheless, the story is an interesting one and can challenge young readers to imagine what they would do in a similar situation.

81. Nida, Patricia Cooney, and Heller, Wendy M. *The Teenager's Survival Guide to Moving*. New York: Atheneum, 1985, hb and pap. 148 pp. Nonfiction.

Interest level: Ages 12–16   Reading level: Grade 6

Nida runs a consulting firm specializing in helping families and organizations deal with the human side of moving. Heller is a journalist. Together, they make strong emotions the centerpiece here, being admirably cognizant of the losses involved in moving. Breaking the process into phases (for example, disconnect, change, reconnect), the authors try to make the inevitable less stressful. They also regard moving as a family affair, rightly so, and address the likely concerns of others in the group besides the teen reader, thus giving that reader insight into the five-year-old, a grade school child, and the child's parent. Influenced by rational-emotive therapy and its proponents, the authors advocate "thinking straight" to control emotions and make the situation turn out for the best. Readers are given mini-training in not jumping to conclusions.

Helpful sections relate to saying good-bye, preparing to say hello, and getting oriented to the new surroundings. In keeping with the rational-emotive point of view, readers are told to talk to themselves continuously to remind themselves that their new vulnerability is only a fleeting condition. Of particular value is the discussion of boarding and *not* moving along with the family. As this is often an option chosen by teens close to their high school graduation dates, it's a welcome addition. Other unique features of this book include a section on moving overseas, returning from overseas (which is often regarded as harder), and guidelines for forming a Welcomers Club at a high school.

This is an unusual book that is at once appropriately chatty and blessed with quite a bit of depth to its exploration. Clearly, the authors have been around.

82. O'Donnell, Elizabeth Lee. *Maggie Doesn't Want to Move*. Illus. by Amy Schwartz. New York: Four Winds, 1987. 32 pp. Fiction.

Interest level: Ages 5–8   Reading level: Grades 2–3

The charming illustrations complement the amusing and authentic text in this book, in which a young boy, Simon, tries desperately to persuade his mother not to move. He uses the ploy that his baby sister, Maggie, a cheerful toddler who never utters a sound in the story, is the one who does not want to move. His mother and all of the neighbors are sympathetic and understanding. Simon and Maggie's mother takes them to the new neighborhood and introduces them to their new neighborhood and to Simon's new school. The fact that he will have some friends, and that his new teacher is a man, plus his mother's wisdom at acquainting him with how the neighborhood looks, convince Simon that Maggie will be happy there, and that she doesn't want to stay in the old neighborhood without their mother.

The household is obviously a single-parent family. The mother is wise and understanding of her son's anxiety. Simon's feelings and the ploy he uses to express them are respected and handled well. This is a good model book that is entertaining and thoughtful as well as useful.

83. Park, Barbara. *The Kid in the Red Jacket.* New York: Knopf, 1987. 113 pp. Fiction.

Interest level: Ages 7–11 Reading level: Grades 3–4

Ten-year-old Howard Jeeter has to move from Arizona to Massachusetts despite his protests. The book covers his moving and his handling of the most humiliating (and scary) position of his whole life: being the new kid! He has to make new friends and also deal with his six-year-old new neighbor, Molly Thompson, who desperately wants his friendship.

Howard narrates the story. It is consistently humorous and believable. The book portrays the anxieties of moving, making friends, relating with siblings (Howard has an infant brother, Gaylord, with whom he has serious talks), and the problem of desertion (Molly has been deserted by both parents after a divorce and is now living with her grandmother). Molly's attachment to Howard is explained by her circumstances. The book ends with Howard's writing a positive letter to his best friend in Arizona.

Readers will enjoy the humor and wit of the story, while at the same time sympathizing with the plight of the characters.

84. Rabe, Berniece. *A Smooth Move.* Illus. by Linda Shute. Niles, Ill.: Whitman, 1987. 32 pp. Fiction.

Interest level: Ages 5–9 Reading level: Grades 2–3

Gus shares his journal with us detailing a month and a half of events from the time he hears that he has to move from their Portland, Oregon, home to after he and his family are settled in Washington, D.C. Gus and his family experience very little trauma; the worst things that happen are that the moving men mistakenly pack an unbaked clump of dough, some wet laundry, and some dirty dishes from the sink; and that the moving van gets stuck in Utah, delaying their move from a hotel to their house for more than a week.

The whole family is very good-tempered about the move; it must be a step up in the father's career. Gus is a gregarious, bright boy, and his family is clearly a loving and cheerful unit. Many details of the plane trip, the hotel, and the move itself are included. Gus leaves a large group of friends, but despite his early anxieties, he meets a new friend almost immediately. This book certainly provides a model for a smooth and pleasant move.

85. Rogers, Fred. *Moving.* Photos by Jim Judkis. New York: Putnam, 1987. 32 pp. Nonfiction.

Interest level: Ages 2–6 Reading level: Grade 2

Like the other titles in the Mister Rogers' First Experience Books series, this one boasts a sensitive introduction for parents, similarly understanding content within, and outstanding photographic work. Rogers recommends including children in some of the moving process in order to give them a sense of continuity. He also advocates talking about their feelings, so that they can join in some of the adventure of moving, not just be overwhelmed by the hectic pace.

The book begins, "It's a good feeling to know the neighborhood where you live and to know some of the people who live there . . . but families don't always live in the same house forever." And, pictured, looking at the for sale sign, is a toddler dragging a blanket. Explanations of what's brought along and what's left behind, the inconvenience of packing, the crankiness that everyone feels, and finding time to talk and hug are helpful. The young reader is brought into the discussion: "Are there a few things you'd rather *not* pack so that you can play with them on the trip to your new home?" Then the moving van comes and that process is shown. Again, children are encouraged to ask questions. And again, children are given signals for decision making. "You may be able to help decide where your bed and clothes and books and toys will go in your new room."

The sense of discovery is paramount here, made possible by acknowledging that leaving is hard and by bringing the child in the story into the process. The book ends with a discussion of identity. The old house is still there. Your old friends are still your friends. And wherever you are, "You're still the same person—the same person your old friends will be remembering."

86. Rosenberg, Maxine B. *Making a New Home in America.* Photos by George Ancona. New York: Lothrop, 1986. 48 pp. Nonfiction.

Interest level: Ages 6–10 Reading level: Grade 3

Through the words of four seven- and eight-year-old children, the author reveals mixed emotions about the changes involved in coming to the United States. The children have left Japan, Cuba, India, and Guyana; two are here temporarily, and two have come to stay. The reasons range from a parent's job transfer to the need for freedom of speech.

The children's reactions are explored with candor that is authentic and engaging, and are easy to identify with. Japanese Jiri's misbehavior in school is given as much attention as Guyanan Carmen's awe at the material splendor she finds here. Rosenberg has intertwined the four profiles to look at central themes of adjustment. We see the commonalities of the four experiences.

Ancona's top-notch sharp, slick photos draw us into natural home, neighborhood, and school scenes. The children's sparkling eyes look terrific on exceptionally fine paper, adding to the desire to view, re-view, and understand.

87. Sharmat, Marjorie Weinman. *Gila Monsters Meet You at the Airport.* Illus. by Byron Barton. New York: Macmillan, 1980; Puffin, pap. 32 pp. Fiction.

Interest level: Ages 6–9 Reading level: Grade 3

A young boy must move with his parents from New York to someplace "out West." He has many preconceived notions of life in the West, and these ideas add to his fears of moving. The boy arrives at the airport and briefly meets a youngster moving to New York. This boy's fears of life in New York bring about an understanding that life in the West will be neither as different nor as bad as our hero first imagined.

This is an enjoyable book written with humor. It has a lesson for all of us. Sometimes our imaginations create situations far worse than reality.

88. Shura, Mary Francis. *The Search for Grissi.* Illus. by Ted Lewin. New York: Dodd, 1985; Avon, pap. 128 pp. Fiction.

Interest level: Ages 9–12 Reading level: Grade 4

Peter, his sister, DeeDee, and their parents have just moved from Peoria to Brooklyn and Peter is very unhappy about it. To make matters worse, it is November, and all of the children already know each other and are settled into their routines. He has always been teased by his peers because he likes to draw, but now he is teased because of his former hometown and because he has to walk his younger sister home from school every day. She makes friends quickly and even finds a cat named Grissi to have for her own pet. Peter doesn't make one friend, and must endure a school he hates and the jibes of the boys in his class. His teacher proves to be very understanding of his situation and even explains to Peter the phenomenon of being the new boy in school. He assures him that all will be well as soon as the newness wears off, and he commends Peter's courage.

When Grissi runs off, the search leads the children to an area where there are many stray cats. During a series of events, DeeDee manages to find homes for all of the stray cats, an old man who has been a benefactor to the cats dies, and Peter not only finds a friend but he also receives much praise and respect for his talent.

Although the story deals with many issues, it works well as a story. The characters are interesting. The author leaves some loose ends untied, but perhaps there will be a sequel so that readers can follow the further adventures of Peter, DeeDee, and the gang.

89. Singer, Marilyn. *Archer Armadillo's Secret Room.* Illus. by Beth Lee Weiner. New York: Macmillan, 1985. 32 pp. Fiction.

Interest level: Ages 4–7 Reading level: Grade 3

Archer Armadillo loves the burrow in which he and his large family live. He loves its many rooms, and especially he loves his own secret room where he can go to curl up and get away from everyone and everything. His grandfather is especially understanding of Archer and his feelings, and Archer is happy. Then one day Archer's father announces that their water hole is drying up, and they must move. He goes off and finds a suitable new place, but Archer is very unhappy about moving. He runs back to their old house and determines to stay there alone. He has recognized that his plan is not a feasible one when he hears noises in the old burrow. It is his grandfather who has also decided to run away from the others and return to the old burrow. Archer persuades his grandfather that there will be no one to get food and take care of them if they stay at the old place, and so he and his grandfather go together to their new home where, the grandfather assures him, he is certain that Archer will again find a secret place for himself.

The pictures and text blend well to portray a very realistic and attractive story of the pains and pleasures of moving. The characters and the experience are easy to identify with. The solution of running away is presented not as one that stirs up the rest of the family, but rather as an episode in which Arthur figures out for himself that this is not a wise thing to do. The grandfather's ploy is, perhaps, gratuitous, but it does establish a link between the youngest and oldest family members, and it communicates well that moving is not only difficult for young children, but is a potentially traumatic event for older people as well.

90. Slote, Alfred. *Moving In.* New York: Lippincott, 1988. 167 pp. Fiction.

Interest level: Ages 8–11 Reading level: Grade 4

Robby and his sister, Peggy, hate the idea of moving yet again. Their father has been offered a partnership in a company; their mother died two years before, and this looks like a very good opportunity for him. His new partner is a woman, and Robby and Peggy are convinced that she wants their father to marry her. The two children behave rudely and concoct all sorts of plots to prevent this marriage from occurring. It turns out that although their father does, indeed, want to marry his new partner, she is in love with someone else.

Despite their anxieties, the children grow to enjoy their new town. They make friends, and they get used to the different environment. They even understand that their father needs female companionship, and they start to plot how they will find someone for him to marry.

Some helpful hints are given here about how to adjust to a new neighborhood. Robby knows that moving vans are attractions for neighborhood kids, and he looks forward to meeting some people on the day that they move in. When none show up, he goes to the nearby park, where he does meet a number of potential friends. He is outgoing, unselfconscious, and a good model for children who are anxious about moving.

91. Stiles, Martha Bennet. *Sarah the Dragon Lady*. New York: Macmillan, 1986; Avon, pap. 91 pp. Fiction.
    Interest level: Ages 8–11 Reading level: Grade 4

The move from New York to Kentucky is a big one for Sarah. Her parents' separation is a shock for her. Her mother, an artist, will draw horses while her father remains in New York. The story deals with making friends and with Sarah's strong desire to get back to New York.

Throughout the story there is very little communication between the parents concerning their separation. Sarah is basically left in the dark the entire year. She is a frightened and confused little girl. She does manage to make friends but the author locks her into a New York state of mind and she never fully enjoys any relationships for the relationships themselves. Everything feels temporary and results in a year of frustration for her. Even at the end of the book Sarah's mother continues to play games with her; instead of telling her outright "We're going back to your father," she simply says she is going to do a new book on a little girl in Paris, where Sarah's father is.

The book violates several important criteria for dealing with separation and divorce: It disregards the child's need to know, it mystifies the process of communication between the parents, and it supplies the "happy ending" of the parents' reunion without indicating a process to effect that reconciliation. When reading this book, children will benefit from some discussion about Sarah's parents' behavior, as well as from Sarah's attitude during her year away from New York. One wonders if Sarah will enjoy Paris if she does not get some help with her perspective. Also one wonders about the eventual success of the parents' marriage if they don't begin communicating with each other in a more open manner.

92. Storr, Catherine. *A Fast Move.* Illus. by Toni Goffe. Morristown, N.J.: Silver, 1987, hb and pap. 20 pp. Fiction.

Interest level: Ages 4–7 Reading level: Grade 2

Tom and Sally's family is moving to a new town. With their grandparents they travel by train to their new house while their parents go with the moving van. The grandparents are very absentminded, and part of the fun for the children is locating the items that their grandparents misplace. Young readers will also enjoy locating the objects that appear on the page at the very same time that the grandparents are searching for them.

The pain of moving is certainly not addressed in this playful book, but the fun of the children's trip with their grandparents, and the realistic, though amusing, drawings will help children recognize that a move need not be a solemn or traumatic event.

The book is one of the Let's Read Together series that invites parents and children to enjoy together the reading and discussion of a book.

93. Tsutsui, Yoriko. *Anna's Secret Friend.* Illus. by Akiko Hayashi. New York: Viking Kestrel, 1987. 32 pp. Fiction.

Interest level: Ages 3–6 Reading level: Grades 2–3

Anna and her family have moved to a new location, near the mountains. It is very beautiful, but Anna is lonely and bored. She receives mysterious, anonymous gifts of flowers, a letter saying that friends are nice to have, and a paper doll. When she sees the paper doll being inserted into the mail slot, Anna is finally quick enough to call out to the little girl who is the giver of these gifts. Then Anna and the little girl play actively and happily, and it is clear that they will become good friends.

Readers might want to discuss why the little girl didn't wait for Anna's response to her earlier gifts. If she was adventuresome enough to send a letter and to come regularly to Anna's house, why didn't she at least wait a few moments to benefit from Anna's reaction? Even though readers may not quite believe the behavior of the secret friend, they will enjoy the outcome. The appealing illustrations greatly enhance the text.

6

Separation Has Many Names

A great number of separations during childhood, many of them temporary, evoke feelings of loss in children: A child is left with a baby-sitter; loses a valuable object, a pet, or a friend; gets lost for a time; goes away for an overnight or an extended stay; or goes away to camp for the summer. Lacking a large body of experience in the world, such youngsters are unsure of eventual reunions. If not handled properly, terror can be the result.

Sometimes parental employment requires separation and becomes a loss situation for a child. If parents must travel or must work at a distance from home, children left behind feel the absence deeply for days, weeks, and sometimes months at a time. They lack the company of a necessary adult in their lives and sometimes do not know when or if that individual will return. The pattern of life of migrant workers or parents out of work also creates issues of loss for children in the family.

General Temporary Separations

94. Hickman, Martha Whitmore. *Lost and Found.* Illus. by Joe Boddy. Nashville: Abingdon, 1987. 28 pp. Fiction.

    Interest level: Ages 4–7 Reading level: Grades 1–2

Parallel statements defining losses and what it means to be found are presented on each set of facing pages. The children in the book bring up experiences such as losing a pet, toys, or objects and then finding them. It ends with the more profound loss of being in a new neighborhood and not knowing anyone, and then having someone come to the door and offer to be your friend. Although no specific strategies for coping with loss are given, the book is reassuring in its message that many losses are temporary or curable. It does not deal at all with the situations where the lost pets or objects are not found, or where the loss is more serious.

95. Mayper, Monica. *After Good-Night.* Illus. by Peter Sis. New York: Harper, 1987. 32 pp. Fiction.

Interest level: Ages 4–8 Reading level: Grade 2

This unusual book pays attention to the daily separation children must endure after they are sent to bed. Focusing on sensations, particularly what little Nan experiences, the author brings a rare insight into children's imaginations. "Nan is the eyes of the house: The dark is dark-dark in the corner where her chair has rocked her animals to sleep." There's a passing car, whose lights reflect on her ceiling, causing her to hold her breath until it passes. There's father's night walk, when he locks the door and jiggles the toilet handle. And as this and more goes on, Nan starts an imaginative ocean journey on a bed–boat, her way of greeting sleep.

Children reading this book may, in a discussion with a parent, bring to consciousness all they hear and see as they drift off. They are not alone. Others have similar journeys. They can even improve theirs.

The Baby-Sitter

96. Anderson, Peggy Perry. *Time for Bed, the Babysitter Said.* Illus. by the author. Boston: Houghton Mifflin, 1987. 32 pp. Fiction.

Interest level: Ages 3–6 Reading level: Grade 1

In attempting to get Joe to bed, his baby-sitter tries firmness, cajolery, fury, and wile. However, Joe manages to evade every strategy. Finally, after they have practically demolished the house, his baby-sitter asks him why he won't go to bed, and Joe informs him that it's because he didn't say "please." After the baby-sitter says "please" and Joe goes to bed, the reader will be amused to see Joe pop back into the room, reminding his baby-sitter that he didn't say "thank you."

Although this is not a model for a baby-sitter or child behavior, it is an amusing story. The text is simple enough for a first grader or younger child to read. The illustrations of the two frogs (for that is what the child and the baby-sitter are) leaping and playing are fun and filled with interesting details that carry the story along.

97. Barbato, Juli. *Mom's Night Out.* Illus. by Brian Schatell. New York: Macmillan, 1985. 32 pp. Fiction.

Interest level: Ages 5–8 Reading level: Grades 1–2

This book is about a big secret and power. Just who is important to children, their mother or their father? The jacket immediately gives a hint of giddy happiness, as we see two fiendish children laughing in the back seat of a car.

It's Mom's night out this particular summer evening. She's the one in charge of directing her husband regarding the children's care in her absence. "Take the kids out to dinner. It's too hot to cook." But the kids play a trick on Dad and guide him to the amusement park instead. He's a willing victim and goes along with being tricked. There, a good time is had by all, although Dad encourages them to play gambling games, which is not intrinsic to the plot, so one wonders why it is there. When they return, the children scamper into their pajamas so Mom won't know where they've been or that they've had a ball. In fact, when she announces her return, the father says, "And not a moment too soon," implying it's been a drain and a strain. Not a look at an honest family, this one. Children and parents can discuss what they would do differently. They can also rewrite the story from the mother's perspective.

98. Christelow, Eileen. *Jerome the Babysitter.* Illus. by the author. New York: Clarion, 1985, hb and pap. 32 pp. Fiction.

    Interest level: Ages 5–8 Reading level: Grades 2–3

Jerome, an alligator, asks his older sister, Winifred, to include him in her baby-sitting service because he needs some extra money. She sends him to the home of the infamous Gaterman kids without warning him of the problems he will encounter. Jerome is at first the victim of many practical jokes, but he catches on at last and performs some of his own, thus winning over the obstreperous children. He also manages to play a trick on his sister to repay her for sending him to the little monsters.

Although the book is not a model for how a baby-sitter should behave, it certainly is amusing. The fun is broad enough to discourage imitation on the part of the young reader.

99. Crary, Elizabeth. *Mommy Don't Go.* Illus. by Marina Megale. Seattle: Parenting, 1986, pap. 32 pp. Nonfiction.

    Interest level: Ages 4–8 Reading level: Grade 2

Part of the Children's Problem Solving Book series, this volume presents Matthew's problem: His mother's going on a trip, and he is staying with a baby-sitter. Matthew wants his mother to stay home. It's a solve-it-yourself book, with no right or wrong answers. The parent must read it with the child and go through the book based on the child's response. To the opening question, "What can Matthew do so he will feel better?" there are nine answers, among them, cry, tell the sitter he is sad, keep something special of Mom's, make a surprise for his mom, ask for loving, try to make Mom stay home, and pretend he doesn't care that she's going. When parent and child turn to the page appropriate to the child's response, they can read a ministory that demonstrates the action and its consequences. The bottom of the page asks, "What will he do now?" which leads to another ministory.

After some, the child is asked, "How do you like this ending?" And at the end, there's a blank page for writing and drawing your own ideas. Perhaps a bit complicated, but thinking is a complicated activity.

100. Havill, Juanita. *Leroy and the Clock.* Illus. by Janet Wentworth. Boston: Houghton Mifflin, 1988. 30 pp. Fiction.

Interest level: Ages 5–8 Reading level: Grade 3

Leroy goes for his first overnight stay away from home to his grandfather's house while his parents go on vacation. It is clear that grandfather has no idea about what a young boy needs. At one o'clock grandfather falls asleep in the chair, leaving Leroy without anything to do. Leroy does manage to amuse himself, but the old grandfather clock bongs and ticks loudly and frightens Leroy.

Grandfather is a clockmaker, and he doesn't want Leroy to play with the delicate clockworks. He gives Leroy a block of wood and nails, but Leroy soon becomes bored with aimlessly pounding nails into the wood.

At night, Leroy finds it difficult to sleep and wishes that the big clock would stop. Lo and behold, it does! In the morning grandfather reassures Leroy that wishing can't make a clock stop; lack of winding does it. He then realizes how Leroy has been feeling and offers to refrain from winding the clock. Leroy thinks, and then asks to wind the clock himself, which he does. Having conquered his fear, he is further delighted when grandfather informs him that they will go to the park together.

The book realistically points out that grandparents do not necessarily know how to be good baby-sitters for their grandchildren. In this pleasant and beautifully illustrated book, the grandfather and grandson eventually accommodate each other's needs, and all ends well.

101. Hooker, Ruth. *At Grandma and Grandpa's House.* Illus. by Ruth Rosner. Niles, Ill.: Whitman, 1986. 32 pp. Fiction.

Interest level: Ages 3–6 Reading level: Grade 2

Soft full-color watercolors portray the magical, cherished nature of things at two children's grandparents' house—a closet light that goes on when you open the door, a junk drawer for exploring, a long hall for running. Perhaps best of all, besides a staying-overnight room, there are toys and games, all on hand because their grandparents think of them, set aside space and time, and relish their role. Junk drawer and closet light or not, youngsters will nod in recognition.

102. MacLachlan, Patricia. *Seven Kisses in a Row.* Illus. by Maria Pia Marrella. New York: Harper, 1983. 57 pp. Fiction.

Interest level: Ages 7–10 Reading level: Grade 3

Emma, an outspoken and engaging seven-year-old, and her older brother, Zachary, who knows her idiosyncracies and understands her needs, spend five days with their aunt and uncle who are baby-sitting for them while their parents go off to an "eyeball convention." When her aunt and uncle first arrive, Emma is not happy. She has special routines and rituals, and she is sure that her aunt and uncle won't understand her. At first, they don't. The very first morning that her aunt and uncle are there they don't make Emma a divided grapefruit with a cherry, and they don't give her seven kisses in a row. So Emma "runs away" to a neighbor's house, where she always goes when she's running away. Zachary comes to pick her up, and he takes her back home where her aunt and uncle are ready to begin practicing being parents.

One of the reasons Emma's aunt and uncle turn out to be such good baby-sitters is that they respect their niece and nephew and are willing to learn from them. They also enjoy engaging in the activities the youngsters invent. When Emma decides to sleep in a tent in the yard (in order to avoid the "night rumbles"), first her brother, then her aunt, and finally her uncle all come out to join her, and they all sleep in the tent together.

Emma finds, to her surprise, that she's enjoyed her aunt and uncle so much that she doesn't want her parents to come home. Her aunt and uncle, who are expecting their first child, are so grateful to Emma and Zachary for teaching them about parenting that they give the children two bus tickets, so that they can come to visit as soon as the new baby is born.

This MacLachlan story contains all of the elements that make her such a popular writer. The humorously told story touches on serious themes of adjustment, separation, and preparation for parenthood. The happy combination of the inventive and lively children with the attentive and responsive adults makes a week they will all remember fondly . . . and so will the readers.

103. Martin, C. L. G. *The Dragon Nanny*. Illus. by Robert Rayevsky. New York: Macmillan, 1988. 32 pp. Fiction.
Interest level: Ages 5–8 Reading level: Grade 3

Nanny Nell Hannah has served as baby-sitter and nanny to the king's children for a long time, but he turns her out when he feels that she has become too old. Poor Nanny encounters a dragon and her babies and is sure that she will be killed, but she offers to baby-sit for the dragon babies and does an excellent job of raising them to be pleasant and gentle creatures. The dragon mother is angry when she discovers that her babies do not wish to breathe fire and do not engage in battle with the king's men. Nanny joins the dragon babies in prison, and they do breathe fire to rescue Nanny. All ends well as Nanny is rehired by the king and also continues to tend to her dragon charges.

The messages here are, for the most part, worthy and humane. It is admirable that Nanny has the energy to tend to her dragons. It is satisfying that she demonstrates to her former, ungrateful employer that he was wrong to fire her. It is unfortunate that she submits to constant harrassment from both her employers, but she stands up with spunk for herself and her dragons when the king accuses her of being a traitor. She also manages to bring two enemies together to live in peace. Rayevsky manages to make the dragon babies look almost cuddly.

104. Orgel, Doris. *My War with Mrs. Galloway.* Illus. by Carol Newsom. New York: Viking Kestrel, 1985. 80 pp. Fiction.

Interest level: Ages 8–11 Reading level: Grade 3

Rebecca has had a succession of baby-sitters since her parents' divorce. Her mother is a physician, and her father is an artist who now lives in Portland, Oregon, far away from Rebecca and her mother, who live in Brooklyn, New York. Most of Rebecca's sitters have been pleasant and relaxed, leaving Rebecca to her own devices. But Mrs. Galloway, Rebecca's new sitter, is more attentive and structured, and not as tolerant as Rebecca is accustomed to. Rebecca, therefore, declares war on Mrs. Galloway.

The story describes a series of misunderstandings and mishaps, most of which end up with Rebecca's being angry at Mrs. Galloway. But in the end Mrs. Galloway proves to have been a responsible and competent sitter, and Rebecca learns to adjust to her style.

The story is humorously told, and is sympathetic to Rebecca even when she is acting like a spoiled child. The story is fun, in and of itself, but children who are left regularly with baby-sitters will probably appreciate the book, as will parents who are trying to teach their children how to get along with their baby-sitters.

105. Rockwell, Anne, and Rockwell, Harlow. *My Baby-Sitter.* Illus. by the authors. New York: Macmillan, 1985. 22 pp. Fiction.

Interest level: Ages 3–8 Reading level: Grades 1–2

Martha is an ideal baby-sitter. This little book simply recounts the routine in which Martha engages when she is baby-sitting for the five-year-old narrator of the story. Martha makes a delicious dinner, dances with the little boy, makes sure that he brushes his teeth, watches television with him, reads to him, and puts him to bed. If he can't sleep, she talks to him and soothes him. He looks forward to her coming.

The book is designed to help children feel comfortable with the fact that their parents occasionally leave them in the care of someone else. Martha, a 15-year-old, is competent without being spectacular. The little boy doesn't expect much from her except for a certain amount of attention and security. This is a useful statement and model for children.

106. Viorst, Judith. *The Good-bye Book*. Illus. by Kay Chorao. New York: Atheneum, 1988. 32 pp. Fiction.
Interest level: Ages 3–7 Reading level: Grades 1–2

The young boy tries to cajole, threaten, bully, frighten, and nag his parents into staying home or taking him with them when they are about to go out for dinner. He imagines his baby-sitter as an unattractive person who will compel him to do terrible things, like eat vegetables. His parents stoically proceed with their preparations for going out, and when, at last, his attractive young male sitter arrives, he happily becomes engaged in activity with the sitter and cheerfully waves good-bye to his parents.

Both the text and Chorao's illustrations are amusing, true, and effective. It is unfortunate that the imagined sitter is a middle-aged heavy woman. Perhaps the "dreaded" fantasy sitter would have best been left to the child-reader's imagination, thus eliminating some negative stereotyping. But on the whole, this book is sure to be useful in homes where a child makes a fuss about parents' leaving for the evening.

Losing a Pet

107. Calders, Pere. *Brush*. Illus. by Carme Solé Vendrell. Trans. by Marguerite Feitlowitz. New York: Kane/Miller, 1986. 32 pp. Fiction.
Interest level: Ages 4–8 Reading level: Grades 2–3

An import from Spain, this tale tells of losing a family dog and what one might do to get over the suffering. There's plenty of flavor here, and the book starts out this way: "The day that Turco—a little pistol of a pup—ate Señor Sala's hat, Señora Sala decided that enough was enough and that it would take the patience of a saint to put up with this mischief any longer." Thus it was, after a family meeting, that the Salas' gardener's daughter was able to keep Turco at her house. Little Sala is so sad, and he tries to get companionship from a canary, a floor lamp, a flower, and other objects. Nothing will do. Finally, a brush in the attic seems to fit the bill. It feels like a dog, and he begins dragging it around on a string behind him.

This book changes from realism to fantasy in midstream, when the brush actually begins to act like a dog. "Soon Little Sala noticed that the brush was warm and was snuggling up against him for a hug. This, naturally, was very serious, because it's one thing to pretend to change a brush into a dog, but it's another thing if the change really happens." No one believes him, of course. But when Brush saves Señor Sala from a robber (or when Little Sala throws Brush at the robber, however one interprets it), the new "dog" earns a place of honor, even a doghouse with the inscription "WE'RE NOT SURE THAT IT'S ALIVE BUT IT DESERVES TO BE!"

Like *Where the Wild Things Are* (Harper, 1963), this book has droll illustrations and an energetic child. Both can be viewed in several different, philosophical ways, but like the Sendak volume it is sure to generate conversation regarding parents, imaginary friends, and life.

108. Delton, Judy. *I'll Never Love Anything Again.* Illus. by Rodney Pate. Niles, Ill.: Whitman, 1985. 32 pp. Fiction.
Interest level: Ages 6–10 Reading level: Grade 3

A young boy develops allergies and must give up his dog because of this. He is distraught, and imagines that no one will be able to love and understand his dog the way he does. The boy's mother is very understanding, and also unhappy about having to give their dog away. She arranges for a good home for the dog, on a farm where the boy will be able to visit in the summer.

The details of the relationship between the boy and the dog, the specifics of the dog's attributes, and the loving and intelligent help the boy's mother gives him combine with the boy's authentic responses to this unhappy situation to form a very helpful and well-crafted book.

109. Kuklin, Susan. *Mine for a Year.* Photos by the author. New York: Coward, 1984. 80 pp. Nonfiction.
Interest level: Ages 8–12 Reading level: Grade 4

Loss is preordained in this unusual book. Doug, a black labrador puppy, is meant to spend only a year with George and his family. Afterward, Doug will become trained to be a guide dog for a blind person. George is part of the preliminary training, getting Doug to be congenial and mannerly. This he accomplishes through pouring affection and good feeling onto the dog. The dog–boy duo is part of a project called Puppy Power, which places young pups with families through the auspices of the 4H.

The subjects of this particular book are doubly interesting. Besides taking on the training project, George is a foster son. Just barely a teenager, George has had three eye operations. He knows it is possible that one day he'll be a candidate for ownership of a guide dog. In a first-person narrative, Doug movingly tells of his training procedures, sharing his experience with others, visits to the vet, and more training procedures. Finally, there is the parting. Now that George is so good at training dogs, Yuri, a new puppy to train, arrives.

The Puppy Power project enables children to see that loss is not just a negative experience—rather, part of growing up. In loving the dog and then having to relinquish it, children have a counterbalanced experience. Usually it is not a good idea to replace a pet immediately when one is lost. In this case, as the loss was inevitable from the start and part of a service venture, it seems entirely appropriate.

110. Schubert, Dieter. *Where's My Monkey?* Illus. by the author. New York: Dial, 1987. 24 pp. Fiction.

Interest level: Ages 3–6 Reading level: Wordless

In this wordless book a young boy takes his pet toy monkey everywhere. It is clear that the boy loves the monkey very much. One rainy day, when the boy has been on a bicycle outing, the monkey falls from his arms without his noticing it. He and his mother search for the monkey, but they can't find him. They don't see that he has fallen into an opening near a large tree. A family of mice, then a hedgehog family, and finally a bird claim the monkey. After he has been dropped into a lake, a man who, fortuitously, is the proprietor of a doll hospital fishes him out, repairs him, and places him in his shop window, just as the unhappy young owner of the monkey comes by. Of course the reunion is a joyful one.

Not many toys are so miraculously found, and young readers will have to learn to cope with irretrievable losses. But this lovely fantasy is so much the fulfillment of children's dreams that it would be ungracious not to acknowledge its wonderful happy ending.

Losing a Friend

111. Eriksson, Eva. *Jealousy.* Illus. by the author. Minneapolis: Carolrhoda, 1985. 24 pp. Fiction.

Interest level: Ages 4–8 Reading level: Grade 2

When Rosalie recovers after having been in bed with the mumps for two weeks, she is dismayed to discover that her best friend, Victor, is enjoying playing with another little girl, Sophie. Rosalie is terribly jealous of the new-found friendship between Victor and Sophie, and she tries to get rid of Sophie. None of her schemes works. Through a misunderstanding the two girls find themselves together, each trying to emulate the other. They gain enough perspective to laugh at their own behavior, and when Victor reappears on the scene they are ready to share him and to be three best friends together.

Just as it is with sibling rivalry, where children must learn that their parents' love is expandable and all-inclusive, so too they must come to adapt to maintaining multiple friendships. This is a difficult concept, and this book, although somewhat simplistic, can be used as a starting point.

112. Gaeddert, LouAnn. *Your Former Friend, Matthew.* Illus. by Mary Beth Schwark. New York: Dutton, 1984. 75 pp. Fiction.

Interest level: Ages 9–12 Reading level: Grades 3–4

Since babyhood, and until the summer between fourth and fifth grades, Gail and Matthew have been best friends. That summer, each spends his or her vacation in a different part of the country. Gail thinks about Matthew all summer long and can hardly wait to see him again. When school begins in the fall, Matthew suddenly doesn't want to have anything to do with Gail. He has new friends and new interests. Gail is angry and hurt. She tries to entice Matthew to continue to be her friend, but he is not at all interested. He stays with a group of boys all the time now. Gail dislikes and is bored by most of the girls; she pines for Matthew's friendship. Finally, her mother advises her to make new friends, and she does, grudgingly. Not until Gail has the opportunity to help Matthew with a science project, after his new friends disappoint him, do Gail and Matthew become friendly, but not best friends, again.

Gaeddert realistically portrays some of the peer issues of 10-year-olds when they begin feeling pressure to associate only with children of their own gender. But the children's parents seem to condone this behavior. They do not see fit to help their children overcome this barrier in order to have friends of both sexes. It is clear at one point that even a very much younger boy is a preferable companion to Matthew than Gail, with whom he has been so close. And Gail's father and Matthew's father go along with the change. Even Gail's mother simply says that she was expecting this. Why did she not prepare Gail for it? Why was Gail permitted to focus all of her attention on one friend? Why didn't Matthew's parents help him to be more understanding of his new situation and of Gail?

The book can be a useful catalyst for discussion of peer pressure and friendship. Discussion about what makes people be friends and what is expected of friends could be a very helpful one.

113. Hansen, Joyce. *Yellow Bird and Me.* New York: Clarion, 1986. 155 pp. Fiction.

Interest level: Age 10+ Reading level: Grade 5

In this sequel to *The Gift-Giver* (Houghton, 1980), Doris, a sixth grader living in New York, pines for the companionship of her friend Amir, who left the Bronx and was sent to a group home in Syracuse when his foster family moved to California. Doris's fellow classmate Yellow Bird also misses Amir's supportive friendship and asks for her assistance with his homework. Through his letters Amir encourages Doris to help Yellow Bird battle his dyslexia. As Doris's friendship with Yellow Bird deepens, her mourning the loss of Amir lessens, and she learns to place his friendship in perspective as they continue to correspond through the mail.

Hansen used humor and insight into her characters' feelings in this lively story of friendship. The setting of the black community adds depth and reality, while reminding the reader of the universality of the characters' responses.

114. Ottens, Allen J. *Coping with Romantic Breakup*. New York: Rosen, 1987. 148 pp. Nonfiction.

Interest level: Ages 12–16 Reading level: Grades 5–6

This is a book, about the throes of adolescence, which will be most welcome. Ottens, a university psychologist, intends the book to speed the injured party's recovery from unilateral breakups. He speaks to both sexes and is quite practical, separating healthy emotions and desirable behavior from the negative emotions that can make you feel you're stuck in mud. Wisely, Ottens refers to two types of loss in the breakup: the loss of the individual and the loss of personal power implied when you are rejected. His understanding of loss extends to other areas of life, as he has readers understand parallels in losing a job, for example. Both are investments and both may have presented illusions of fair treatment.

Ottens seems to understand the language young adults sometimes resort to in expressing their hurts, from spying and threats, to promises, even to harassment and physical abuse of the other person or oneself. He presents a good analysis of relationships as they cool off, and makes suggestions on how youngsters can assess the present state of the romance.

For those who must cope with the end of a relationship, Ottens recommends avoiding hanging on by asking friends about him or her, looking for him or her to appear and just happening to be where that might happen, and so forth. Instead, Ottens recommends a clean break made possible by imagery exercises, for example, imagining an embarrassing consequence from the spying. Also recommended are drawing up a list of irritating habits and bad points to keep up your resolve, developing diversionary tactics for the hardest times of the day or week, and mental exercises that can soften the image of the person in one's mind, keeping both the good and bad aspects of the relationship in perspective. Ottens understands the feelings of loss and his hints will be useful indeed.

115. Perl, Lila. *Fat Glenda's Summer Romance*. New York: Clarion, 1986. 144 pp. Fiction.

Interest level: Ages 9–13 Reading level: Grades 4–5

Thirteen-year-old fat Glenda finds herself newly thin but waiting watchfully for the threatening ghost of her former self to return. The fast-paced action revolves around this and other changes—how to get along in an adult world away from home as a junior waitress at an inn, how to respond to a new boy's attention, how to get her mother to stop coddling, and most important, how to adjust when a dear friend is suddenly rejecting. Glenda's hopes for a glorious summer with her old friend Sara quickly crumble in lively, funny, and readily identifiable incidents, but other good things happen, such as being convinced by her new boyfriend to abandon the old fat self-image. It's a fast and thoroughly enjoyable read.

116. Voigt, Cynthia. *Izzy, Willy-Nilly.* New York: Atheneum, 1986; Fawcett, pap. 262 pp. Fiction.

Interest level: Age 12+ Reading level: Grade 7

The book contains powerful insights into the emotions experienced by a young person who has undergone an amputation. It discusses the difficulties and challenges of adjustment and the contribution that family and friends can make to this process. It also raises the issue of friendships lost and found.

Izzy, a junior in high school and a popular member of the "in" crowd, is devastated when she loses the lower half of her leg in an accident caused by the drunken driving of a date she didn't even like. Voigt, with great sensitivity and well-researched accuracy, explores the pain and success of Izzy's adjustment.

Izzy's sense of loss is compounded by the virtual abandonment by her three long-standing friends, also pretty, popular members of Izzy's crowd, who are unable to comfort her during her crisis. Symbolized by the uselessness and frivolity of her friends' gifts, which are brought to the hospital, Izzy realizes that these friendships were based on her looks rather than her essence.

A sincere friend enters her life in the person of Rosamund, an awkward and outspoken classmate whom Izzy had previously ignored. It takes time for Izzy to appreciate her, but it is with Rosamund's care and support that Izzy recovers. Izzy learns to face her feelings, and to appreciate and value her strengths and those of others with greater clarity and maturity.

117. Waber, Bernard. *Ira Says Goodbye.* Boston: Houghton Mifflin, 1988. 40 pp. Fiction.

Interest level: Ages 5–8 Reading level: Grade 3

Ira (of *Ira Sleeps Over* [Houghton Mifflin, 1972]) is losing his best friend, Reggie. Not only is Reggie moving away, but he seems to be happy and excited about the fact, and not aware that Ira is devastated by the impending loss. Not until the actual day of the move does Ira discover that Reggie, too, is overwhelmed by the knowledge that he and Ira are being separated. Only then can the two boys acknowledge that they will miss each other. They exchange precious gifts (two turtles and a favorite baseball card). That night, Reggie calls Ira and invites him to spend the weekend at Reggie's new house. Of course Ira accepts, and we know that the boys have not lost each other's friendship after all.

Using humorous dialogue, Waber has put his finger on a common fear and problem of childhood: the possible loss of a friend, not because of moving away, but really because of misunderstanding each other's feelings. If Ira and Reggie had not displayed their true emotions they would have harbored great resentment toward each other. The story is powerful and provides an outlet for children who need to learn to express their feelings of concern about friendship, or, for that matter, about any relationship.

118. Winthrop, Elizabeth. *The Castle in the Attic.* Illus. by Trina S. Hyman. New York: Holiday, 1985. 179 pp. Fiction.
Interest level: Ages 9–12 Reading level: Grade 4

William is crushed that Mrs. Phillips, his housekeeper and companion of 10 years, ever since he was born, is now leaving him to return to her original home in England. She thinks he is old enough to do without her, and she also thinks that her absence will make his parents spend more time with him. As a going away present she gives him a wonderful castle that has been in her family for generations. It is a lifelike replica of a real castle with a drawbridge and many rooms. One silver knight comes with the castle. William tells Mrs. Phillips that he would rather have her stay than have the castle, and that he will think of some way to keep her with him.

Before Mrs. Phillips leaves, William discovers that his touch has made the little knight come to life. He learns that the knight has an amulet that turns living things into a tiny size. He uses the amulet on Mrs. Phillips, and places her in the castle, thinking in this way to keep her with him forever. But Mrs. Phillips refuses to speak to him until he is her size.

William learns of the knight's story and because of his guilt over what he has done to Mrs. Phillips, he decides to permit himself to become small so that he can save the knight's kingdom and restore Mrs. Phillips to her proper size. He embarks on a long and dangerous journey, but, due to Mrs. Phillips' excellent influence, he succeeds in his quest. He vanquishes the wicked wizard, retrieves the amulet that restores people to their proper size, and returns home, magically arriving at exactly the same time that he left, with no one knowing he was gone.

His quest is, of course, one that will win him his independence over himself. Once he recognizes that he can be brave and strong, he knows that he must permit Mrs. Phillips to return to her home. This is a part of growing up for him, and he does it well.

Winthrop has handled a delicate subject well. No one is blamed for his or her feelings. The silver knight is not zapped back and forth from toy to human because of the whim of the child. He is a real person who has been enchanted, and who retains his dignity at all times. The story works very well.

Getting Lost

119. Blackwood, Gary L. *Wild Timothy*. New York: Atheneum, 1987. 153 pp. Fiction.
Interest level: Ages 9–12 Reading level: Grade 5

Timothy Martin is a "mama's boy." He is sickly and pampered. He has no friends and very few interests. His brother, Kevin, on the other hand, is competent at everything, physically fit, and a credit to his father. One August, Timothy's father insists on taking him camping in the woods. Timothy dreads the outing, but obeys his father. However, Timothy gets lost and spends three weeks by himself in the wilderness. He not only survives but he also learns to enjoy his own company and the sense that he is responsible for his own welfare. He sharpens his wits, his senses (he no longer needs his glasses), his physical condition, and his self-image. During this time he concentrates on himself and is never bored.

When he is finally found, rather than being relieved, he is apprehensive about going home and reluctant to leave his primitive campsite. He is silent about his experience and does not enjoy his new-found popularity at school. One gets the feeling that at the first opportunity he will return to the wilderness.

Blackwood admonishes readers not to use this book as a wilderness survival manual. As he points out, Timothy did a number of things correctly, but he also made many mistakes. It is a little difficult to believe that Timothy, given his background and past behavior, could have survived at all. He remained in one place for the three weeks rather than continuously searching for a way out of the woods. He ate plants that could have been poisonous. He is not happy to be rescued, and it is almost by accident that he reluctantly informs the hunters who find him that he is lost. No matter how excited he is about his ability to take care of himself, it is hard to imagine that he would not feel relief at being found.

Timothy's parents are not a likable couple. The mother is weak and hovering; the father is insensitive, macho, and a fraud. Neither of them seems to be interested in how Timothy feels. Despite these negative elements, the story is an absorbing one and is well written. It provides a different perspective on being lost, and causes the reader to wonder if, upon being found, Timothy is now really lost.

120. Crary, Elizabeth. *I'm Lost.* Illus. by Marina Megale. Seattle: Parenting, 1985. 32 pp. Nonfiction.

Interest level: Ages 4–8 Reading level: Grade 1

This title is an entry in the Children's Problem Solving Book series, in which the child gets to choose solutions to problems. The books in this series are best read along with a parent, and there is no right or wrong response. This story focuses on the alternatives facing Amy, who has become separated from her father at the zoo. Amy can think of seven ideas, all of which the child can follow in a sequence chosen by the reader. The ideas are: stay where she is, go hunt for her dad, cry, look for a police officer, find a woman with children, ask a clerk for help, or wait at the front gate. The child, in following the various options, gets to interact with the parent, responding to such activity questions as "How does Amy feel now?" or "What do you think Amy will do next?" As in the other books in the series, a final page is left blank for the child to fill in his or her own ideas.

121. Hines, Anna Grossnickle. *Don't Worry, I'll Find You.* Illus. by the author. New York: Dutton, 1986. 32 pp. Fiction.
Interest level: Ages 3–6 Reading level: Grades 2–3

Three females go shopping at the big, confusing mall: Sarah, her mother, and at Sarah's insistence, her doll Abigail. "Well, if you lose her, don't complain to me about it," Mama warns, adding that Sarah should stay put if *she* gets lost. All hands are held tightly as the reader eagerly anticipates one of the three getting lost; each pastel picture becomes a "what's missing" search. Suspense mounts as they choose clothing and have lunch. A pair of red sneakers is finally exciting enough to distract Sarah, and Abigail is left behind. Sarah runs back, and Abigail is indeed in the same spot. When she then can't find her mother where she'd left her, Sarah stays put, just as her mother had advised and just as Abigail had done. In a cute twist, it's the doll's presence that brings the two, mother and daughter, back together again. Spare, soft illustrations simultaneously show the dizziness of a mall and reassure readers that parents and child may be temporarily separated but will indeed reunite.

122. Paulsen, Gary. *Hatchet.* New York: Bradbury, 1987. 195 pp. Fiction.
Interest level: Age 11+ Reading level: Grades 5–6

Brian Robinson's plane crashed and he is the only survivor. He had been on his way to visit his father; his parents are divorced, and he is obsessed with the secret that he carries: he saw his mother embracing and kissing another man before his parents were divorced, and he knows that that is the reason for the divorce.

Brian matures through the course of the book. He is forced to rely on his own intelligence, strength, and instincts in order to survive. The language is specific and graphic, especially when it describes human bodily functions and reactions, and the sensations and odors of the wilderness. For example, when Brian catches and eats a bird and is faced with the dilemma of cleaning it, he pulls the skin off and likens it to peeling an orange. The bird's insides fall out, and a "steamy dung odor" arises from its entrails. There is much retching and vomiting and flatulation in the book, but the language is appropriate and respectful of the reader.

In addition to its being an adventure and survival story, the book also helps the reader to empathize with Brian, who is trying to come to grips with his parents' behavior before, during, and after the divorce. Contrary to what Brian had originally anticipated, he returns to his mother; and his father, after an initial show of interest and concern, returns to his self-centered ways. This is a good and realistic book on many levels and will be appreciated by many young readers.

123. Ravilous, Robin. *The Runaway Chick.* Illus. by the author. New York: Macmillan, 1987. 32 pp. Fiction.

Interest level: Ages 4–7 Reading level: Grades 2–3

This is the first book by this English writer-illustrator. The picture book has the spunk of its protagonist. "Spry's mother knew she was in for trouble the moment Spry hatched out. He started asking questions as he broke through his shell." He is urged to be easy, safe, and warm, like his sisters. Why are the girls content to seek safety while the boy is inquisitive, one wonders. Nevertheless, the mother hen has all five under her wing and tells them how dangerous the big world can be. Spry is unconvinced, and is soon into mischief from dawn until dusk, even convincing his sisters to mock their father behind his back, and getting them to hide with him whenever their mother calls.

One day these troublesome traits almost led Spry to a bad end. His new hiding place, a basket, got picked up and Spry was off "to who knew where." He was puzzled, frightened, and challenged in a new environment (a house) but used his old investigative resources. All was not smooth. Soon a cat was after him, but using his small size to his advantage Spry soon upset the cat's plan. A human being rescues Spry and brings him home, where he now has stories to tell. The stories do not compare to the warmth of his mother's feathery back, though, where he soon falls asleep.

The soft, hazy illustrations are counterpoint to the action. Not truly a runaway, Spry gives the story a sparkling originality that might help children in numerous new situations. However, it is surprising that publishers would in this day and age consent to have a boy be the active leader while girls follow, especially when the gender of the siblings is irrelevant to the story line.

124. Trivelpiece, Laurel. *Just a Little Bit Lost.* New York: Apple, 1988, hb and pap. 186 pp. Fiction.

Interest level: Age 11+ Reading level: Grade 6

The book is essentially a romance, and, as such, is predictable, but it is engagingly written and moves well. The plot revolves around two teenagers, Bennett and Phillip, who are lost in the high Sierras, manage to survive and protect each other, and, of course, fall in love. The two teens make many mistakes, but they generally figure out what they need to do and do it.

The story does not really help people learn to survive in the wilderness. In its focus on the relationship between the two young protagonists, it does not indicate how the adults in their lives feel about their disappearance. Nor does it tell what the adults do to find the two lost people. Even their return to civilization is too facile; there seems to be no aftermath of their experience. But the book serves well as a light excursion into a potentially terrifying situation.

125. Vincent, Gabrielle. *Where Are You, Ernest and Celestine?* Illus. by the author. New York: Greenwillow, 1986. 32 pp. Fiction.
Interest level: Ages 4–8 Reading level: Grades 2–3

In this adventure about Ernest and Celestine, Ernest seeks a museum position. Ernest, the older bear, will only take the job if Celestine, his young mouse charge, can come along each day. However, that isn't possible, he is told, so the two leave to look around the museum. Celestine fails to be intrigued by the paintings, even the Mona Lisa, who, Ernest adoringly says, smiles similarly to Celestine. When the tired mouse asks to go home, Ernest can't resist looking at a few more paintings. Quick as a flash, the two lose each other and are frantic, but a guard helps them get back together.

The job interview segment keeps the story from being as coherently pointed as it might have been and seems unnecessary as a device to show unconditional love. There's already enough abandonment, reunion, and declaration of love with which children can identify. With soft watercolors, Vincent has created angles that make Celestine seem small in contrast to the great halls, a common position for youngsters. And Celestine's feelings, when her caretaker momentarily sees to his own needs, are beautifully and simply expressed: "I thought you liked the pictures better than me," to which Ernest replies, "There is nothing I like better than you, Celestine!"

Working Parents—Unemployment

126. Berenstain, Stan, and Berenstain, Jan. *The Berenstain Bears and Mama's New Job*. Illus. by the authors. New York: Random, 1984, pap. 32 pp. Fiction.
Interest level: Ages 4–8 Reading level: Grade 3

Each member of the Bear family is very busy. They all have work that they do and hobbies that they engage in and enjoy. Mama Bear is the busiest of all, because she spends time not only doing her own work but also reacting to the others and helping them in their work and play, too. Mama Bear's hobby is quilting. When a number of people ask her to sell her quilts, she decides that she will, indeed, go into business. The family is apprehensive about it, but they help her fix up a shop for her quilts. Although dinner is late, and Papa Bear and the children are the ones who have to cook it, they are all delighted when Mama Bear's quilt shop is an instant success.

Although the message here seems a positive one of support for all of the members of the Bear family, the implication that Mama Bear is shirking her family duties must be guarded against. Her "extra" money is somehow trivialized in the text, although the family enjoys going to the Burger Bear as her treat. Adults reading this book to children would do well to discuss the genuine importance of each family member, and the responsibility of everyone to maintain the family's welfare.

127. Bograd, Larry. *Poor Gertie.* Illus. by Dirk Zimmer. New York: Delacorte, 1986. 103 pp. Fiction.
Interest level: Ages 8–11 Reading level: Grade 4

Gertie is the narrator of this story and her voice is clear and true. She is a spunky, funny girl, even though her father has deserted her and her mother. Her mother's job is one that not only doesn't pay enough but is also not a pleasant one. Things come to a head when the landlord threatens to evict them if they can't pay the back rent. Gertie and her grandpa hold a sale of Gertie's artwork and materials that he has repaired, and they earn the money needed to pay the rent. Gertie's mother gets a better paying job, and it looks as if the family will survive.

The seriousness of the story is lightened by the humor and quirkiness of the characters, but the message comes through that it is no fun to be poor. The ending is believable and satisfying, especially because Gertie's good fortune does not change her solid character traits.

128. Cleary, Beverly. *Ramona Forever.* Illus. by Alan Tiegreen. New York: Morrow, 1984; Dell, pap. 182 pp. Fiction.
Interest level: Ages 7–10 Reading level: Grades 3–4

Now in third grade, Ramona Quimby is experiencing a difficult year. Some of the problems that Ramona and her sister, Beezus, have are: they hate going to Mrs. Kemp, their baby-sitter, because they feel that she dislikes them; they discover that their mother is pregnant; their friends tease them because their father is still going to school, studying to be an art teacher, and does not yet have a "regular" job; money is scarce, and everyone is worried about it; their cat dies of old age; and their beloved Aunt Bea is going to marry a man they don't like. To compound their problems, their father receives an offer to teach in a one-room schoolhouse far away from their present home, and they don't want to move.

Everything turns out for the best, of course. Ramona's baby sister is born, and Ramona survives her initial worries about being displaced. She and Beezus grow to appreciate their new uncle. Their father accepts a full-time job at the supermarket rather than uprooting his family. And Beezus and Ramona are permitted to take care of themselves, rather than having to go to the baby-sitter they feel uncomfortable with.

It is strange that the girls do not mourn their cat, who, after all, was with the family for 10 years. They bury him and have a funeral, but then he is all but forgotten. The children do, however, freely express their anxieties and delights about all of the other happenings in this eventful year.

Cleary has produced a winner of a story about Ramona and her family. Children will certainly empathize with and enjoy the characters' escapades. They may grieve for Picky-Picky, the cat, more than Ramona and Beezus do, because the cat has been an integral part of many of the stories in this series. Nevertheless, the book deals well with most of the losses and displacements that normally occur in the life of a young child.

129. Delton, Judy. *My Mother Lost Her Job Today*. Illus. by Irene Trivas. Niles, Ill.: Whitman, 1980. 32 pp. Fiction.
Interest level: Ages 4–8   Reading level: Grades 1–2

When Barbara Anne's mother loses her job, the little girl is worried that everything is going to be different. She's afraid that all of the celebrations and happy rituals of her life with her mother will change. At first her mother is angry and upset that she has lost her job. However, when she sees how anxious Barbara Anne is, she comforts her daughter and reassures her that everything will turn out fine.

The relationship between the mother and child is clearly a close and supportive one. The author and illustrator combine to show the characters' emotions, and to help young readers identify with this single-parent family.

130. Hazen, Barbara Shook. *Why Can't You Stay Home with Me? A Book about Working Mothers*. Illus. by Deborah Borgo. New York: Golden, 1986. 28 pp. Fiction.
Interest level: Ages 4–8   Reading level: Grade 2

This entry in the Learn about Living series, like the others, includes a note to parents. The note urges parents to set aside time to talk uninterruptedly with their children, to give children the opportunity to share the day's activities, and to ask children for help with chores. The text itself opens with a typical family encounter: "Melissa's mother works, which means mornings are sometimes hectic. Everyone hurries. Everyone has to help. Everyone is busy." The accompanying picture shows the father doing dishes, but the text doesn't say *both* parents work. The implication is that the onus for creating all this busyness is on poor mother. "Melissa has to hunt for her homework herself, and make her bed, and braid her hair the best she can. Melissa's mother walks her to school, which is on her way to work. It's a special time when they can talk about all sorts of things."

Much of the rest of the narration explains Melissa's day and the times she is most likely to miss her mother—when someone else has to pick her up after school, when her mother's absence makes it hard to sit down to concentrate on homework, when there are school vacations but not mother vacations. But caretakers (grandma, a baby-sitter, another child's mother, an after-school-center teacher) provide fun and, occasionally, different, easier rules to follow.

Although the action probably does reflect the pattern in many households, in this one, the mother misses special events at school—field day, when Melissa hit her first home run, and a play in which Melissa had the lead role of Captain Cook (but her cousins came). As many mothers make special efforts to get there for their child's lead role, one wonders why this mother was away on both important events and not shown changing her work schedule for at least one time.

When Melissa says, "You like your dumb old job more than me," she is answered, "I love you a zillion times more than any job. . . . Always remember that. Now have a nice day with Mrs. Maxwell, and I'll call you later." The reader also sees the mother becoming available when there is an emergency. She takes a taxi to the playground when Melissa is hit on the head with a baseball.

The narrative tells what working can buy—more meals out, a new coat for Melissa, more vacations. Melissa reflects on the idea that she is also getting more grown-up by helping out, and better at waiting out her mother's grumpy periods at the end of the working day, realizing they are not personal. And when she goes to her mother's office and sees she keeps Melissa's picture on her desk, she realizes how dear she is. Somehow, though, in its particular dramatic portrayals, this book is sadder than it need be. A meal out and a coat don't seem to make up for not being seen as Captain Cook. As the books in this series were put together by an educational team and will be seen as models in thousands of families, one wishes they had had the mother attend at least one of the events.

131. Jarrow, Gail. *If Phyllis Were Here.* Boston: Houghton Mifflin, 1987. 132 pp. Fiction.
Interest level: Ages 9–12 Reading level: Grade 4

Libby's grandmother, Phyllis, has won the lottery and is now going to move to Florida with her boyfriend. Libby is bereft because her grandmother has been her primary caretaker, confidante, and source of emotional comfort. Although Libby's parents are both at home, they are preoccupied with their work, and they, too, rely on Phyllis to manage the house and to be there for Libby.

The mother is depicted as someone who is a competent lawyer but an inept homemaker. When Phyllis leaves, she hires a housekeeper who is more concerned with keeping the place neat than with Libby's feelings. Eventually, after several near disasters and some emotional trauma caused by a nasty girl at school, all is resolved, and it looks like Libby and her parents will manage well. The story is written with a light touch, but it provides young readers with some excellent insights into the dynamics of a working family as well as helping to blast some stereotypes about old people.

132. Kleeberg, Irene Cumming. *Latchkey Kid.* Illus. by Anne Canevari Green. New York: Watts, 1985. 102 pp. Nonfiction.

Interest level: Ages 9–13 Reading level: Grades 4–5

Kleeberg opens the book by combining statistics with her helpful point of view: "Imagine! Between two and six million kids coming home after school and managing things just fine." Topics include snacks, chores, homework, neighbors; also calls, brothers and sisters, occupying oneself (chapter heading: "What Is There to Do?"), friends; also illness, joining after-school clubs, summer; and housekeeping, safety and emergency, and when to call a parent. The advice is simply stated and clear, for example, how to receive a call for a parent without saying the parent isn't home. There are some original ideas, too—such as using office memo pads to take messages, beneficial because of their easy-to-fill-in boxes. Another area for original ideas is the author's activity section, for example, building an obstacle course that doesn't present a safety hazard as an afternoon activity. The safety measures are broad in coverage, showing good thinking regarding potential occurrences in a house. Besides the obvious—fire and the like—there is information about a toilet overflowing, no lights, thunderstorms, and water in the cellar. Helpful, respectful, and fun. Glossary.

133. Kyte, Kathy S. *In Charge: A Complete Handbook for Kids with Working Parents.* Illus. by Susan Detrich. New York: Knopf, 1983. 128 pp. Nonfiction.

Interest level: Ages 8–12 Reading level: Grades 4–5

Suggesting a family conference to get rules and procedures underway, Kyte recommends master lists and contact persons. Her guide is divided into such sections as child care, cooking, caring for your clothes, and coping with a crisis. She's big on charts that elucidate daily schedules and chores, certainly matters that can become more easily accomplished if put in writing.

The crises to which she attends are both little and big, little exemplified by a power outage, big by fire and crime. Her section on crime prevention is especially good, telling readers to do a homecoming check and helpfully reminding them that such sections deserve rereading from time to time. Her hefty section on cooking includes easy recipes that are very appealing (for example, apple toast).

This is a lively book. Kyte writes with chatty gusto and builds self-confidence in her readers. "You will astonish yourself with your In Charge, crisis-coping ability." In her illustrations, Susan Detrich provides reassuring laughs about what might otherwise seem overwhelming. In the section on plumbing, a boy is shown swimming in his basement trying to find the water valve, dressed in goggles and fins. Bibliography.

134. Leiner, Katherine. *Both My Parents Work.* Photos by Steve Sax. New York: Watts, 1986. 48 pp. Nonfiction.

Interest level: Ages 5–9 Reading level: Grade 3

Part of the My World series, this volume does what the series claims, opening up new experiences and horizons. The families portrayed demonstrate varied patterns—night, day, home, and office jobs. The people, of various races, hold jobs ranging from ones children are familiar with (police officer, farmer, manager of a fast-food restaurant) to vocations that will be very new to children (arbitrator, city planner).

The children who narrate the sections range in age from 5 through 12 and describe their parents' jobs and the schedule the family as a whole keeps. Varying child-care arrangements are discussed—relatives, day-care, baby-sitting, and so on. They also describe feelings, exemplified by David, who feels left out sometimes when his psychologist mother and musician father keep him out of the rooms where they are respectively practicing. The author and photographer maintain interest throughout, although they are profiling 10 children and their weekly family schedules. The book ends appropriately with a photo of a hand putting a key in the door.

135. Lewin, Hugh. *Jafta's Father.* Illus. by Lisa Kopper. Minneapolis: Carolrhoda, 1983. 24 pp. Fiction.

Interest level: Ages 4–8 Reading level: Grades 1–2

Jafta's father works in the city and must be away most of the time. Through the illustrations and the narrative it is clear that Jafta's father loves him very much, and that his mother trusts his father. Jafta remembers every detail of the activities he and his father engage in when his father is home.

These memories sustain him during the time that his father is away. Nevertheless, although he knows his father will return, there is always an edge of anxiety until Jafta sees his beloved father again.

This beautifully illustrated book tells, in simple but evocative language, of the feelings of a young child at his father's enforced absence. The flavor of the community and family come through in this story set in South Africa. Although the setting and some of the details are of a land far away, the interaction and emotions are universal.

136. Lowry, Lois. *Anastasia on Her Own.* Boston: Houghton Mifflin, 1985. 131 pp. Fiction.

Interest level: Ages 9–12 Reading level: Grade 4

Both of Anastasia's parents are good at their paid work. However, Anastasia's mother is not a good housekeeper. Nor does she enjoy organizing the household tasks. Anastasia and her father decide to take over the design of the household schedule. They construct what they think is a nonsexist schedule, but it is clear that the mother has the major burden for all the tasks. Not until she leaves to serve as a consultant does the family realize how complex the task of running a household really is. They encounter all sorts of unexpected emergencies, such as Sam, the baby brother, getting chicken pox, and an old girlfriend of the father's coming for dinner.

The story is amusingly told. It is too bad that the father is such a dolt when it comes to helping out or making intelligent decisions. He is pleasant, but he hardly displays the intellect that it must have taken for him to earn his Ph.D. He is the stereotypical male bumbler. The mother is expected to be all things to all people: housewife, mother, cook, and professional artist. Even at the end of the story, everyone breathes a sigh of relief when she figures out that she needs a microwave oven to solve all of her problems, and she takes charge again, resuming the responsibilities that the rest of the family, by rights, ought to share.

137. Mazer, Harry. *Cave under the City.* New York: Crowell, 1986. 152 pp. Fiction.

Interest level: Ages 9–12 Reading level: Grade 4

This book may be a painful one for young readers, even though it has a happy ending. It tells of Tolley and his five-year-old brother, Bubber, and their survival for a number of weeks on the streets of the Bronx during the Great Depression. The boys' father has gone to Baltimore to look for work. Their mother is in the hospital suffering from pneumonia and probably tuberculosis; she is a sweatshop worker and the air is always filled with bits of thread and dust. Their grandmother is also ill and hospitalized, and the boys don't want to be placed in a children's shelter.

For a while they live in their own apartment, buying groceries on account, and finding whatever bits of change they can. Then, when the grocery owner won't allow them any more credit, and the social worker keeps coming around to look for them, they take to the streets. They hide in a basement, try to earn money whatever way they can, and often are reduced to begging. Tolley steals two doughnuts and a bottle of milk when Bubber is sick, and this tortures his conscience.

After a number of weeks, when Tolley becomes too sick to function, the boys once again return to their own apartment. They are astounded and delighted when their father comes home and rescues them with the news that he will be staying home with them from now on.

The neighborhood in the Bronx is authentic. Mazer's detailed description of the setting and the burdens the boys bear makes the reading hard. But it is the kind of difficulty that comes from reality, not from elaborate prose or turgid description. The story brings home the pain and desperation that people felt during the time of the depression, and children were not exempt.

138. Mitchell, Joyce Slayton. *My Mommy Makes Money.* Illus. by True Kelly. Boston: Little, 1984. 32 pp. Nonfiction.

Interest level: Ages 4–8 Reading level: Grades 1–2

A number of occupations are elucidated from the first-person viewpoint of a child. Each annotation begins with something the person does, followed by a story, and culminating with formally naming the occupation. For example, one starts off: "My mommy plans trips" and then is followed by a story, ending with: "My mommy says it's fun to be a travel agent." The jobs include French horn player in a symphony, surgeon, ambulance driver, paperhanger, news photographer, car salesperson, and others. The child tells a typical story for the car salesperson: "She showed a big new car to a family with two children, a dog, two cats, and a grandmother. Everyone looked under the hood at the engine and checked the tires and tried the windows." Nonsexist language is present throughout, and funny cartoons accompany the words, for example, the appliance repairer is running to help a man whose washing machine has overflowed. "Fear not!" she announces. Although this book doesn't explore children's feelings about their mothers' jobs, it does help to clarify the act of going out to earn money.

139. Perl, Lila. *Tybee Trimble's Hard Times.* New York: Clarion, 1984. 145 pp. Fiction.

Interest level: Ages 9–12 Reading level: Grade 4

Tybee Trimble wants to go to the circus in order to be able to write about it for her class project. She is resentful when her parents tell her they can't afford the price of the tickets. She criticizes how they spend their money. It is hard for her to appreciate their situation: her father is an aspiring attorney who needs to take time off from his job in order to study for the bar exam. Her mother leaves her job at the library to become a painter of fancy designs on people's walls. Tybee is embarrassed that her parents are doing such nonconforming things. She worries about what people will think and say.

Tybee is a very determined young woman. She engages in a number of money-making schemes, and finally earns the price of her circus ticket, but she encounters near disaster when she tries to get to the circus on her own. She returns home and decides that she will save her circus money, and write her essay about her family and how they get along together.

The story is amusing in many ways. Tybee, for all of her prejudices, is an engaging character. She is very literal and for a long time thinks that she has to write something called an S.A. for school. She is embarrassed when she discovers that the word is essay. She also imagines her father jumping over some pole in order to win a prize when she hears that he wants to pass the bar.

She is indignant when she discovers that her parents have been concealing the fact that her mother is pregnant. The reader, too, wonders why they have done this. It is as if they do not include their daughter in the important information of the family. But the family is, by and large, an amiable one, and the reader has hopes that they will learn from their mistakes.

140. Quinlan, Patricia. *My Dad Takes Care of Me.* Illus. by Vlasta van Kampen. Toronto: Annick, 1987, hb and pap. 24 pp. Fiction.

Interest level: Ages 4–8 Reading level: Grades 1–2

"My stomach hurt when the kids in school asked, 'What does your dad do?' I didn't know what to say, so I said, 'He's a pilot.' " Actually, Luke's father is unemployed. Both of them have mixed feelings about this—it's good that Luke can come straight home instead of going to a baby-sitter, they can play games and cook together, and they talk more about feelings, but both wish he were employed.

The layoff from a factory job has meant a move from the country to the city, where the mother has gotten a new job with computers, at which she sometimes works nights. Luke likes both city and country living, but there are sometimes difficulties in this adjustment, like when he wants a bike and is told they can't afford it. And it's difficult to see his father grumpy and sad. Once, he cried when he didn't get the job he wanted. Luke tries to comfort him at times like this. The book has the ring of truth but doesn't develop gracefully. In spite of what are probably the world's most sensitive parents (who are made all the more attractive with the use of watercolors), Luke's shame doesn't clear up until he meets a classmate whose father is home, too. That father says his job is taking care of Jillian, and now Luke has something to say, too, and his stomach stops hurting when he is asked what his father does.

141. Ruby, Lois. *Pig-Out Inn.* Boston: Houghton Mifflin, 1987. 171 pp. Fiction.

Interest level: Age 10+ Reading level: Grade 5

Dovi's parents have moved around from place to place and job to job. Now they have landed in a place where they have opened up a restaurant, although none of them has any restaurant experience. They manage to surround themselves with colorful characters, and get involved in the custody battle of a nine-year-old boy's parents, one of whom has kidnapped him.

The story is full of interesting characters, all of whom are described in a light and humorous way. Even the potential tragedy of the child who is kidnapped is dealt with so that the reader knows that things will work out all right.

Serious issues, such as alternative life-styles and their effect on children, custody battles, and a young woman's coming of age, are incorporated into the plot, which relies heavily on the quirkiness of the main characters. Preadolescents will resonate to this book.

142. Snyder, Carol. *Leave Me Alone, Ma.* New York: Bantam, 1987. 148 pp. Fiction.

Interest level: Age 11+ Reading level: Grade 6

The main characters in this story are affluent people who live in New York City in a building with a doorman, and with no worries about money. Jaimie's parents are super-successes in their professions: Jaimie's mother is a financial wizard, and Jaimie's father produces television shows, Jaimie's widowed grandmother lives with them, and she is always available to Jaimie. But Jaimie is unhappy and resentful because she wants her parents to pay more attention to her. In truth, they are often out of town, and when they are at home they don't listen much to what Jaimie has to say. She becomes surly with her mother and nagging with her father.

Jaimie's friend, Amanda, who lives in the same building wishes that her parents would go out of town and pay less attention to her. Amanda is also jealous of the relationship that is developing between Jaimie and Amanda's brother, David.

Jaimie and Amanda meet a mysterious young girl named Marie and befriend her. They realize, one day, that Marie is one of the homeless children they have seen on a television special about the homeless of New York City. Jaimie writes a letter to the mayor about the homeless, and she recommends to her father that he do a television special following up the first one on which Marie and her family appeared.

One might think that encountering such a serious issue would help Jaimie and Amanda put their own gripes into perspective, but this never happens. Marie disappears from the story without anyone's knowing what happened to her. Amanda and Jaimie reconcile, and Jaimie and David become boyfriend and girlfriend. Jaimie's parents listen to a lecture from Jaimie and her grandmother and vow to reform. A happy, tidy ending to everyone's problems except, perhaps, for Marie and her homeless family.

The issue of parental lack of concern can be a serious one. Not all parents who work outside the home neglect their children, but it is a good idea to remind parents that they need to set aside time that is especially devoted to their children. These parents seem like children themselves, at first not seeing anyone's concerns but their own, and then becoming penitent and contrite. The young people seem self-centered and pampered, though likable and pleasant enough. The story is so laden with middle-class, white values that it bears discussion for this factor alone. It is well written and entertaining, and the author demonstrates considerable skill in depicting family conversations and characterizations. But it ignores many of the issues it raises in its own pages, and it misses out on demonstrating any growth in the characters.

143. Stanek, Muriel. *All Alone after School.* Illus. by Ruth Rosner. Niles, Ill.: Whitman, 1985. 32 pp. Fiction.

Interest level: Ages 5–8 Reading level: Grade 3

Josh's mother can't afford a baby-sitter for him, and she has to work, so she helps Josh prepare to be alone in the house after school. She discusses an important set of rules for his safety and security; she tapes a list of useful phone numbers on the wall; and she informs all the necessary people about the situation. She also demonstrates her empathy for Josh by giving him a special stone to hold, a talisman to help him feel brave.

On his first day alone he immediately calls his mother at work and they have a good, though short, talk. When his mother comes home they are both overjoyed to be together, and his mother tells Josh how proud she is of him.

Now, a year later, Josh is able to use his own good experience to help Becky, a new classmate, to overcome her anxieties at being a latchkey child. He is so secure now that he can give Becky his security stone.

The details of Josh's and his mother's preparations for his being alone, and the specifics of the activities Josh engages in when he is alone, help enormously. The book has an authenticity and respectful tone that makes it very effective.

Camp

144. Carlson, Nancy. *Arnie Goes to Camp.* Illus. by the author. New York: Viking Kestrel, 1988. 32 pp. Fiction.

Interest level: Ages 5–8 Reading level: Grades 2–3

Arnie is reluctant at first to go away to summer camp but his mother assures him that it is only for two weeks. When he arrives at camp he is somewhat homesick, but he quickly overcomes this feeling and enjoys all of the activities the camp has to offer. The camp is one that anyone who has ever been to camp will recognize. Nothing of significance, except for some bee stings, happens to Arnie. He not only survives the experience, he thrives on it. Perhaps this book can help youngsters who are anxious about their first summer camp experience to feel better.

145. Cole, Brock. *The Goats.* New York: Farrar, 1987. 184 pp. Fiction.

Interest level: Age 12+ Reading level: Grade 6

The details of the story are dramatic: An adolescent boy and girl are brought to a small island by their summer campmates, stripped naked, and left to fend for themselves. Apparently it has been a tradition at this particular camp to select the least popular campers, label them as "goats," and abandon them on the small island overnight. The two goats (they don't discover each other's names until almost the end of the book) decide not to wait for the other campers to come and claim them; they manage, by their wits and determination, to get off the island, steal some clothes, and survive for a week until the girl's mother comes to get them.

During their odyssey they gain greatly in strength and self-esteem. They help each other, and come to love and depend on each other. They are both, in a sense, abused children, although the abuse is emotional rather than physical. Laura's mother is a single parent whose work occupies so much of her time that she has little left to give her daughter. Howie's parents are archaeologists who have made it clear to their son that he was unplanned and unwanted, and that he is a nuisance and a burden to them, although they do not mean to be unkind. Their work is the overriding feature of their lives.

During the course of the book the reader is introduced to another summer camp where the campers are very helpful to Howie and Laura. These campers are poor, from the city, and wise in the ways of survival. For them the camp represents an opportunity, not a frivolous taking up of time.

The novel is just as much a coming-of-age story as it is one of survival.

Cole palpably demonstrates different kinds of abuse that youngsters are subjected to. The reader is never, for one moment, tempted to disbelieve, because the writing is powerful and graphic. The issue of the nudity is handled delicately, as is the relationship between the two adolescents. Other problems, such as those of Laura's and Howie's stealing clothing and money, and deceiving a motel owner into permitting them to stay in a room rented by someone else, are tackled in an ethical manner. The two youngsters steal, but they know they are doing something against their moral code, and they keep track of everything they are taking so that they can eventually reimburse the owners.

Cole masterfully demonstrates how the two main characters and Laura's mother develop and change for the better. He also introduces memorable minor characters in the person of the girls' head counselor and some of the campers in the "good" camp. The police, deputy sheriff, and camp director fare badly and are one-dimensional, but they are foils who are designed to lend drama to the situation. They do not damage the integrity of the story. The reader is left to speculate about what will happen at the end, but there are sufficient clues to reassure us that the ending has every possibility of working out for the best.

146. Gauch, Patricia Lee. *Night Talks*. New York: Putnam, 1983; Archway, pap. 156 pp. Fiction.

Interest level: Age 12+ Reading level: Grade 7

In this study a group of overprivileged teenagers attend camp with a group of poor teenagers and all of them learn about stereotyping and living together. The camp counselor is a well-respected, competent young woman who motivates the campers to rise above their differences, and to cooperate with and care for each other. One camper, Margaret, is particularly difficult. She is transformed by the end of the summer from a sullen, silent person to someone who trusts her friends and who is almost destroyed by that trust. The girls mistakenly try to interfere in her life at home by sending her mother a letter. They finally come to the conclusion that they should not interfere in matters that they do not understand.

The atmosphere of a summer camp is well portrayed here. The author communicates the intensity of the summer experience and the creation of a community set apart from the rest of the world.

147. Kroll, Steven. *Breaking Camp*. New York: Macmillan, 1985; Scholastic, pap. 169 pp. Fiction.

Interest level: Age 11+ Reading level: Grade 6

For the first time in his 15-year-old life, Ted is going away to summer camp. Ted is excited about it because it is a riding camp, and he loves horses. But

Camp Cherokee proves to be more of a trauma than a vacation. A bully named Jack, a vicious hazing ritual, and a near tragedy punctuate the experience. Although the bully is vanquished, and Ted makes friends with a few of the boys at camp, he decides he won't go back again.

The story shows how important it is for parents to investigate a place thoroughly before sending their children to it. It also, unfortunately, glorifies the act of keeping silent and not telling one's parents about the problems at camp. Ted could have been seriously hurt. Young readers would do well to discuss some alternate behaviors that he could have selected.

148. Marsoli, Lisa Ann. *Things to Know before Going to Camp.* Photos and illus. Morristown, N.J.: Silver, 1984. 48 pp. Nonfiction.

Interest level: Ages 7–11 Reading level: Grades 4–5

Part of the Look Before You Leap series, this one gives an overview divided into short sections: what camp is like in general, specific kinds of camps (specialty camps, camps for special needs, coed camps, day camp, resident camp), choosing a camp, and the camp layout; also, adjusting to camp, the kinds of activities, daily routines and chores, eating at camp, counselors, problems that may occur, expenses, and returning to camp. A special section deals with questions parents should ask before sending a child to a particular camp.

In choosing a camp, children are given a set of questions they can ask themselves, for example: Do I want a camp close to home? Do I want a camp that offers a lot of activities? Do I want to go to an all-boy or all-girl camp? Do I want to be close to a lake or an ocean? The mountains? Children are given a rundown on what to bring, and they are also helped on emotional matters. Marsoli seems to have thought of those little things that can cause anxiety, for example, sounds in the night. And the section for parents is helpful, too, with such questions as what percentage of staff/campers returns each year? What is the financial limitation of your liability insurance? What is the camp's philosophy? The photographs and illustrations don't match up to the verbal content in excitement. Index.

149. Martin, Ann M. *Bummer Summer.* New York: Holiday, 1983; Apple, pap. 152 pp. Fiction.

Interest level: Ages 9–12 Reading level: Grade 4

Kammy is upset about her new stepsiblings. They badger her constantly, and they ruin her things. She is also not very happy about her new stepmother, Kate. Although Kate tries to get along with Kammy, nothing she does seems to be right. Kammy's father is powerless to fix the situation, so he suggests that Kammy go to a summer camp. Kammy pleads with her father not to send her away, but they strike a bargain: Kammy will go for two weeks, and if, at the end of that time she wants to come home, she will be permitted to do so.

Kammy goes to camp and it is worse than she imagined. She is constantly in trouble. She has one friend, but she has one enemy, too. After some conversations with a sympathetic counselor and a remarkably understanding director, Kammy begins to enjoy camp. After two weeks, when her family comes to visit, she waits only until they tell her that they will take her home with them, and then she informs them that she wants to stay for the rest of the summer. She has reconciled with her stepmother and siblings and made up with her enemy.

One of the benefits of a camping experience is that children learn to adjust to difficult situations. That is the case for Kammy. The book is fun, and Kammy's coping strategies are useful.

150. Voigt, Cynthia. *Come a Stranger*. New York: Atheneum, 1986. 190 pp. Fiction.

Interest level: Age 11+ Reading level: Grade 6

Mina wins a scholarship to an otherwise all-white dance camp in Connecticut the summer she is ten years old. She loves the camp, and is praised for her dancing ability. When she returns home she is critical of her old friends and of almost everything about her close-knit Maryland community. Her father, a minister, and mother try to help her see herself more clearly, but she only lives for the next summer so that she can again go to the camp and be with her white friends.

Over the year, Mina grows and develops physically at a rapid pace. When she gets to camp she cannot help but see some slights and attitudes that she never noticed before. Although the other girls and the teachers are friendly to her, she has no roommate, and she detects subtle evidences of racism. To make matters worse, she is no longer a good dancer, and is sent home.

Over the next few years Mina develops a deep love for the summer minister in their community. His name is Tamer Shipp, and those of us who have read *The Runner* (Atheneum, 1985) remember him as Bullet Tillerman's friend. He is married, and has named one of his children for Bullet. Through her friendship with Dicey Tillerman, Mina brings Tamer together with the Tillerman family. Everyone is deeply moved by the encounter, and 14-year-old Mina is at last free to be her own woman and move toward relationships with men her own age.

This story, like every story by Voigt, is a complex one. In addition to welcoming this book as another set of information to link to the rich store of connections we have with the Tillerman family, the reader is given the opportunity to grapple with preconceptions, assumptions, philosophy about people and life, and the moral behavior of people toward each other. The characters are full-blooded mixtures of goodness and meanness, bigness and smallness. Mina changes as she grows older and wiser, but her essence remains the same, and most readers can identify with her humanity, while enjoying her individuality.

151. Weyn, Suzanne. *My Camp Diary*. Illus. by Ann Iosa. New York: Bradbury, 1986, hb and pap. 128 pp. Nonfiction.

Interest level: Ages 9–15 Reading level: Grade 3

This spiral-bound book is meant to be a fill-in companion to take along to camp. By using it, youngsters will have both a record of their experience to turn back to in later years (for example, names of bunkmates) and a way to sort out feelings. There are funny quotes from the books of well-known children's book authors (for example, Judy Blume and Ellen Conford) on the challenges of growing up and being independent. Also, there are charts for scoring every aspect of camp life, and then rescoring at the end to see how the scores compare. Weyn includes games for rest hour, tips for getting into and out of trouble, and self-analysis sections on such things as the homesick blues (for example, "The person I most want to see is . . ."; "Sometimes I start to feel homesick when . . ."; and "When I feel homesick, this is how I cheer myself up . . ."). A number of pages can be torn out and sent as instant letters, and a number of others become private pages for private notes to oneself. There's understanding of the minicrises that come about, such as getting an award but having your name misspelled on the certificate, or worse, not getting one at all. To these letdowns, the author provides solace in the form of imagined revenge: "If I gave the awards . . . ." With places for addresses, photographs, and important scraps as well, this chronology of the camp experience from arrival to departure will surely be worth its cost as a summer gift. A fine idea happily brought to fruition.

Traveling

152. Bernstein, Joanne E. *Taking Off: Travel Tips for a Carefree Trip*. Illus. by Kathie Abrams. New York: Lippincott, 1986, hb and pap. 190 pp. Nonfiction.

Interest level: Age 12+ Reading level: Grade 6

Ours is a time when youngsters desire and need to travel independently. It may be that they need to board plane, train, or bus to visit a parent who doesn't live with them. It may be that they are ready to leave home on a tour, traveling with other youngsters under supervision. Or that they may want to go off with friends by bike, car, or bus on a first jaunt without parents. This is a guide to those first travel experiences and adventures.

Topics are both psychological and practical. Along psychological lines, Bernstein develops questions readers can ask themselves regarding their likes and dislikes: How long should you be away? Should you have a schedule? Would you be better off traveling alone or with a companion? If with a companion, there are questions useful for choosing a compatible companion. There is also guidance on how to keep from feeling lonely while on the trip, how to stay in touch with relatives back home but still be independent, how to stay safe and healthy while traveling, and how to meet people. Practical information includes full information on all means of travel: train, bus, plane, and car. There is also discussion on how to get a ticket, how to get the best price, and luggage needs. Various places to stay are detailed, including advantages and disadvantages: hotels and motels, guest houses, colleges, YMCAs/YWCAs, and camping. There is a chapter on vacation ideas: theme parks, resorts, package plans, teen tours, hostel stays, and international education. The nitty-gritty is addressed in detail: getting passports, finding out about locales, and packing. An especially helpful section on caring for emergencies rounds out the material. Abrams's drawings add wry humor with just the right balance for teens serious about their new responsibilities. A full, annotated list of travel organizations is appended. Index.

153. Faulkner, Matt. *The Amazing Voyage of Jackie Grace.* Illus. by the author. New York: Scholastic, 1987. 42 pp. Fiction.

Interest level: Ages 5–8 Reading level: Grade 2

Jackie goes on a fantasy voyage in his bathtub, during which time he encounters the noisy crew of a sailing ship, a wicked storm at sea, and pirates. He leaves his tub on hearing his mother call him, and we hear a small "yoho" from the ship that has now been returned to the original toy size.

The illustrations are a wonderful blend of exaggeration and reality. The imaginary adventure lets children know that their fantasies are acceptable, and prepares them for the eventual real life adventure of leaving home.

154. Howard, Elizabeth Fitzgerald. *The Train to Lulu's.* Illus. by Robert Casilla. New York: Bradbury, 1988. 32 pp. Fiction.

Interest level: Ages 4–8 Reading level: Grade 1

Beppy and Babs take the train to Great-Aunt Lulu's, going from Boston to Baltimore, mirroring a trip the author took as a child each summer. They are on their own on this nine-hour trip, packed up for the entire summer. Their parents have given them detailed instructions: the conductor will take care of them, Travelers' Aid will see to it that only Lulu picks them up, and so on. The 1930s setting is painted beautifully in full color, each watercolor setting the mood as they change on the long trip—fear, excitement, and impatience. Beppy takes good care of her younger sister Babs and monitors the activities—eating, drawing, reading, resting, and eating again. When they arrive, not only is Great-Aunt Lulu there, but a large extended family as well, creating a warm circle. The parents and grandparents of the children reading or hearing this book will enjoy the feelings and adventures of these two black girls—in a time when milk could be bought on a train for 10 cents. And the book provides an excellent model for children traveling alone for the first time.

155. Huff, Barbara A. *Welcome Aboard! Traveling on an Ocean Liner.* Illus. and photos. New York: Clarion, 1987. 128 pp. Nonfiction.
Interest level: Ages 9–14 Reading level: Grades 5–6

Huff is a children's book club editor and an ocean crossing-enthusiast-fanatic. Here she presents a jubilant account of what such a crossing might be like, specifically based on her adventures on the *QE 2.* She draws the reader into a day-by-day diary right from the start: "You are among the hundreds of passengers who crowd the ship's railings. Some, like you, look down on the dock fifty feet below." In this brief passage one can see both the attention to a cruise's excitement and the accuracy of her research. (Youngsters feeling fretful about their trip away from home may be comforted to learn that the *QE 2* carries enough ice cream to create 24,000 cones.)

Along with the diary of her trip there are historical looks at cruising, stories of famous ships of the past and present, and innovations in today's cruising (theme trips, Mark Twain country, visiting Hawaii and Alaska, and so on). Throughout, Huff talks about games, activities, and opportunities for children; she tells interesting, real stories about children she has met on voyages, for example, the girl (shown in a photograph) who can knot a cherry stem within her mouth. With the exuberance that only a person in love with her subject can bring, Huff has created a delightful book that will get youngsters and their older relatives alike ready to pack their bags and leave the usual behind. List of resources, index.

156. Krementz, Jill. *Jamie Goes on an Airplane.* Photos by the author. New York: Random, 1986. 14 boards. Nonfiction.
Interest level: Ages 1–5 Reading level: Grade 2

Bright photographs make it fun to visit Grandma and Grandpa. This is not a first visit, as preschooler Jamie tells us, "We fly there on a big airplane." He seems to know the routine well—Mommy helps him pack his own suitcase the night before, the skycap puts tags on the suitcases so that they won't get lost, and the family of three gets seat numbers at the counter. Photographs show security and why ("to be sure we're not taking anything dangerous"), loudspeaker announcements, meeting the smiling pilot, fastening the seatbelt, takeoff safety procedures, meeting the stewards, snacks on board, a very adult looking meal, a little nap, and then a happy landing reunion with Grandma and Grandpa. "I love plane trips" says Jamie, in this happy introduction to temporary separation from the comforts of home.

157. Prestine, Joan Singleton. *My Parents Go on a Trip*. Illus. by Meredith Johnson. Los Angeles: Price/Stern/Sloan, 1987, pap. 24 pp. Fiction.
Interest level: Ages 4–8 Reading level: Grade 1

This story is part of My Special Feelings series. In the story, Terry tells about her parents' business trips, mostly in questions she asks her smiling mother and father at the dinner table. The questions are the best part of this book because they will enable readers to frame their own questions. Terry's questions concern practical things: where they're going, how long they'll be away, where and what they'll eat, and how they'll keep in touch with her. Conveniently, both parents are attending this business convention, as they do the same kind of unnamed work, so one is not accompanying the other. Terry smiles, too, in listening to the answers, until she actually goes to spend the five days with her grandparents. Then she misses them almost immediately in an abrupt switch. But Grandma and Grandpa talk about keeping busy to make the time go faster, and with fixing things, cooking, and playing with her dad's old toys, it quickly becomes time for hugs and kisses of reunion. The illustrations are old-fashioned brown and dull, but the questions may spark young readers to find out what they weren't previously fully conscious they needed to know and may encourage their parents to tell them more fully, so that the children can imagine what they're doing in that far-off place.

158. Roffey, Maureen. *I Spy on Vacation.* Illus. by the author. New York: Four Winds, 1988. 28 pp. Nonfiction.
Interest level: Ages 4–7 Reading level: Grade 1

With so much to see on vacation, the details readers must look for on these pages will make any earlier worries simply disappear. Each double spread shows a busy scene, and the few words start with the phrase: "I spy. . . ." The first page, for example, says: "I spy the sea." The family (two parents and three children) is shown arriving at a hotel, with other people looking out windows, boats on the ocean, palm trees, and so on. Subsequent pages let the child fill in the words, for example, "I spy a pair of sunglasses on the. . . ." They are pictured on the floor and the reader must spot them. And on it goes: "I spy the waiter bringing two . . . (ice cream sodas)." On and on goes the fun, ending with a plane ride bringing the family back to Grandma and Grandpa. This one will be enjoyed again and again, before a trip and afterward as well.

Sleeping Over—Visiting

159. Leonard, Marcia. *Little Kitten Sleeps Over.* Illus. by Karen Schmidt. New York: Bantam, 1987, pap. 24 pp. Fiction.

Interest level: Ages 3–6 Reading level: Grades 1–2

Hoping to lure an entirely new generation into the "choose your own adventure" genre, this book gives children a chance to participate actively with animal characters. In addition, there are really two stories in one! Some parents and teachers may question whether three-year-olds can handle this concept, but at least there are only two stories, not the several offered for older children. This particular entry is truly participatory in asking children to imagine themselves as the protagonist: "Pretend you are a little kitten and you're at your grandma and grandpa's house." Homesickness ensues on this sleepover and on page 4 the child must make a choice. "If you want to get up and find someone to keep you company, go on to page 5." Alternatively, "If you want to stay in your room and call for your grandma, turn to page 11." (Notice both these alternatives result in company.) In the first alternative, the kitten doesn't have grandma in mind, and would have been happy with brother or even the goldfish. A story from Grandma does the trick. In the second story, fear suddenly intrudes and the kitten sees danger where there is none. "There's something hiding in my closet!" Grandma explains the several frightening possibilities under the bed, out the window, and so on, but then partially ruins it by lacking understanding, "There's nothing to be afraid of." She comes through, however, offering a favorite old stuffed animal of the kitten's father. "Now it can be your special friend and keep you company all through the night."

160. Nilsson, Ulf. *If You Didn't Have Me.* Illus. by Eva Eriksson. Trans. by Lone Thygeses Blecher and George Blecher. New York: McElderry, 1987. 113 pp. Fiction.

Interest level: Ages 7–10 Reading level: Grades 3–4

A young Swedish boy and his little brother stay at their grandmother's farm while their parents are completing the building of their new house. In a series of chapters, each a complete little story in itself, the boy explores the world and learns about it and himself. He engages in rituals of controlling his fears as he tries to gain dominance over natural phenomena such as the singing of birds and the rising of the sun. He confronts the farm animals and tames his fear of them. He visits elderly people in an old age home and acquires some insight into his little brother's feelings. He finds a friend in the hired man and learns about books and history. And he tests his parents' need and love for him and finds them satisfyingly responsive.

The book is simply but profoundly written from the perspective of a young child, but with the insight of a wise adult.

161. Roberts, Sarah. *I Want to Go Home.* Illus. by Joe Mathieu. New York: Random/Children's Television Workshop, 1985. 32 pp. Fiction.

Interest level: Ages 3–6 Reading level: Grade 2

When Big Bird goes to visit his grandmother at the seashore for his first-ever trip away from home, he enjoys himself for a little while. But then, after his first day there, he grows terribly homesick. Granny wisely recognizes what is wrong with Big Bird and gives him picture postcards to send to his friends at home. She also listens to his stories about his friends, without feeling defensive or making Big Bird think that his feelings are not valid. Eventually he finds a friend, and his feelings of homesickness diminish.

Children will probably enjoy seeing their beloved Sesame Street characters experiencing the same sorts of feelings that real-life children do. The topic is lightly, somewhat simplistically, handled, but the book can be helpful in preparing a child for going away for an extended visit, or to camp.

162. Rockwell, Anne, and Rockwell, Harlow. *The Night We Slept Outside.* Illus. by Harlow Rockwell. New York: Macmillan, 1983. 48 pp. Fiction.

Interest level: Ages 6–9 Reading level: Grade 2

An entry in the Ready-to-Read series, this "chapter" book concerns two brothers and their new sleeping bags. After asking and being refused on a school night, they get permission to sleep outdoors on the weekend. Their sense of the special experience is captured in their plans not to bring pajamas—"You don't wear pajamas on an adventure." What begins as fun, of course, turns to higher adventure, when in the darkness, strange sounds become frightening. Ensuing escapades with a raccoon, cat, mouse, owl, and even a skunk bring out the two personalities: The younger sib is ready to call it a night and return home, the older one becomes protective. And in the morning, after a rainstorm does bring them inside, there's plenty of bravado from both of them. A good vehicle for discussions about sharing or hiding feelings.

163. Rockwell, Anne, and Rockwell, Harlow. *When I Go Visiting.* Illus. by the authors. New York: Macmillan, 1984. 24 pp. Fiction.

Interest level: Ages 3–6 Reading level: Grade 1

A little boy enjoys visiting his grandparents and tells readers what he packs. He's eager to see them because of the differences—he lives in a house, they live in an apartment. The Harlows capture the joy in differences, such as riding in the elevator. The grandparents are ideal—they make special room for him (he has to sleep on a cot in the living room); they shower him with attention such as taking him to the park; they show him photos of his mother as a child; they share interests with him, exemplified by grandfather's seashell collection and a visit to the library with grandmother. They sing. Both grandparents cook. Clear paintings show each aspect of the sleepover in appealing, calming fashion. The book has a feeling of real grandparents, perhaps a real relationship. And as it should be, the boy has a great deal of fun. "I almost don't want to leave when it is time for me to go. But if I stayed, my mother and father would miss me. So I do go home, until it is time to visit again."

Prisons

164. Gifaldi, David. *One Thing for Sure.* New York: Clarion, 1986. 172 pp. Fiction.

Interest level: Age 10+ Reading level: Grade 4

Dylan is a 12-year-old whose father is in prison. He faces the usual stigma attached to families of convicted people. His former "friends" torment him. Fortunately, he meets Amy, who is spending some time with her grandparents while her mother and stepfather are vacationing in Europe. Amy and Dylan become good friends, and together they overcome the nastiness of Dylan's tormentors.

Dylan is not only confronted with external abuse; he is also worried that perhaps he has inherited his father's bad traits—that he has "bad blood." He resents his father so much that he refuses to visit him in prison. His mother is understanding and clear about her feelings. She does not press Dylan to visit his father, but she does insist that he respond appropriately, and not with violence when he is teased about his father.

It is somewhat difficult to understand why Dylan was ever friends with the bullies. It seems as if they were never worthy of his attention. Amy is almost too good to be true, but her character is an engaging one. The author successfully portrays the pain of separation and the ensuing bitterness and misunderstanding surrounding the families of convicted prisoners.

165. Lichtman, Wendy. *Telling Secrets.* New York: Harper, 1986. 243 pp. Fiction.

Interest level: Age 13+ Reading level: Grade 7

Toby's father is in jail for embezzlement, and Toby's mother has sworn her to secrecy about it. Her mother even forbids Toby to tell Sharon, her college roommate and best friend. During the course of the four months that her father is in jail, Toby explores her feelings about herself, her family, and the world. She is desperate to talk about her father, and one night she tells the secret to a young man with whom she engages in sexual intercourse for the first time in her life.

Eventually Toby tells Sharon and feels the better for it. During the course of the story, some thefts get solved, a cousin confesses to having tried to kill himself, and other secrets get revealed. In the end, Toby and her family are much closer and more self-knowledgeable, and the future looks bright.

Too few books exist on the problem of separation from a parent who is in prison. This story helps readers to see the issues involved in keeping secrets of this sort.

166. Maury, Inez. *My Mother and I Are Growing Strong; Mi Mamá y Yo Nos Hacemos Fuertes.* Illus. by Sandy Speidel. Trans. by Anna Muñoz. Berkeley, Calif.: New Seed, 1979, pap. 28 pp. Fiction.

Interest level: Ages 5–10 Reading level: Grade 4

The left side is in English, the right side is in Spanish, and each page is given a title, for example, "My Mother Keeps Secrets." The narrator, Emilita, introduces herself and her mother. We meet them working in a garden and taking over a job the father had before he went to prison. (The secret is that the mother has taken over the father's jobs. The daughter approves when her mother keeps friends' confidences but not that she is keeping this important information from the father.)

Much of the book is commentary—"be fair to others," her mother says, how her mother and she are becoming self-sufficient and can now fix machinery, and so on. In this story, Emilita's father has been jailed for getting into a fight after being ethnically insulted. The man fell to the sidewalk and hit his head and Emilita's father must spend a year in prison. Emilita and her mother hope for parole. The mother visits the prison but does not take Emilita. "I wish she would take me, but she says a prison is too sad for children. I say why is it worse for children than for grown-ups?" A few pages later, under the heading "A Mother Can Change Her Mind," the mother does allow her daughter to visit. Sure enough, it is terrible. It even smells scary. Emilita is surprised at the change in her father—he is pale. Their visit is described emotionally and realistically in terms of today's society—the females cry, the male merely grows paler. Nonetheless, Emilita hopes to go again, but she will think of something funny to do on the next visit.

Alas, when there are family problems, too often children think they must make themselves responsible for making things right. That aspect of children's nature is shown well here. And, what do you know, on the next visit, Emilita's attempt to bring fun into the prison by carrying a bouquet of radishes brings about an emotional torrent from the father and he does cry. His tears mix with joy when he reveals that he will be freed in a week's time. This is a loving story about a loving family caught up in life's circumstance.

Understanding Feelings

167. Adler, C. S. *Always and Forever Friends.* New York: Clarion, 1988. 164 pp. Fiction.

Interest level: Ages 9–12 Reading level: Grade 4

Wendy, age 11, is bereft because her best friend has moved away. Wendy's mother has recently remarried, and, although Wendy likes her stepfather, she is having lots of difficulty with her new stepsister and stepbrothers. Both her mother and stepfather work, and Wendy is burdened with many responsibilities in addition to her personal problems. She is depicted as a cheerful, ingenious girl, but the other children in her class are either members of previously established cliques (Wendy is a relative newcomer to the school) or have personality problems of their own. One girl, Honor, seems to be a likely candidate for friendship, but she is mysteriously standoffish.

Wendy fixes on Ingrid, a new arrival at school, as the most likely person to be her best friend. The reader quickly sees that this is a mistake on Wendy's part, but Wendy doesn't discover this until the end of the book. Finally, after countless demonstrations of friendship, loyalty, and excellent advice on Honor's part, Wendy realizes that Honor is her friend. It is unfortunate that it takes her so long to come to this recognition.

Issues such as the trials and tribulations of stepparenting and being a stepsibling are also explored, as is Honor's dilemma of being a biracial child whose white mother has emotionally abandoned her. (Honor lives with her paternal grandmother. Her father is dead, and her mother's new husband doesn't want Honor because she is black.) Wendy's stepsister, Ellen, is disruptive and sullen throughout most of the book, but this situation is resolved as she and Wendy begin to get along. The story moves along briskly, and Wendy and Honor are likable and interesting characters.

Wendy's lack of perception occasionally becomes annoying, but, in general, the reader can empathize with her plight.

168. Adler, C. S. *Binding Ties.* Illus. by the author. New York: Delacorte, 1985. 183 pp. Fiction.
Interest level: Age 13+ Reading level: Grades 6–7

Anne is 16 years old, and in the throes of her first love. Her mother has been through a divorce, the accidental death of her young son, and now must cope with cancer. Because of her mother's mastectomy, Anne and she have moved in with Anne's grandmother and aunt. Anne's mother is a dependent, sweet, and wimpish woman who is still devastated that her husband divorced her. Anne's father is very happy in his new marriage, and Anne loves Dodie, her stepsister. Anne is astounded, at one point in the story, to learn that her parents' divorce resulted from her mother's affair with a neighbor. Anne is angry that she has been blaming her father for years, and that no one has told her about this before. She is also angry because her family disapproves so strongly of her boyfriend, Kyle.

It is difficult to believe that Anne has only one friend, her stepsister, Dodie, in addition to her boyfriend. Anne is bright, pretty, and generous. She seems to love Kyle, even though he treats her badly. They are lovers, and Anne is unabashed about her sexual relationship with him. She is willing to leave home and family to be with Kyle. Only when she discovers that he has been unfaithful to her does she return home and take up her old life again.

There is no assurance that Anne will change. Nor is there any guarantee that she has learned anything from the affair. But readers will probably be wiser than Anne. They will probably understand that Anne needs to be more concerned with herself as a person, and less concerned about potential rejection. Readers will be drawn into the story, which is well paced and excellently written. The characters are all interesting and well constructed. The issues are those that affect adolescents.

169. Berry, Joy. *Every Kid's Guide to Understanding Parents.* Illus. by Bartholomew. Chicago: Childrens, 1987. 48 pp. Nonfiction.
Interest level: Ages 9–12 Reading level: Grade 3

An entry in the Living Skills series, this book has a school lesson tone to it, starting off with a list of what the reader will learn:

There are different kinds of parents,
parents want what is best for their children,
parents are responsible for their children,
there are many ways parents take care of their children,

there are several ways parents supervise their children,
parents deserve to receive something from their children, and
parents are not perfect.

Under the many kinds of parents are adoptive, foster, and stepparents. After the introduction, it is made clearer that *most* parents want what is best for their children, not the implied unanimity of the earlier list. The book tries to cover a great deal with few words, often glossing over the complexities (for example, why children might be in foster care), which may have the consequence of creating anxiety. Perhaps the strongest part of the book, and really the most relevant to the title, is the categorization of disciplinary techniques parents use—explanation, logical consequences, isolation, and punishment. What Berry means by parents receiving something from their children is also worth thinking about, but some ideas on her list may be more than children can do, thereby increasing guilt: putting oneself in the parents' place, accepting parents as they are, praising and showing appreciation whenever possible, encouraging them when they are discouraged. These sound more like the responsibilities have been reversed. Other suggestions are more manageable for youngsters: help parents establish the rules, talk to them calmly and honestly when you disagree or are upset.

The cartoons are colorful, with wry captions ("Aren't lima beans taking 'healthy' too far?"); a wise-cracking dog also lurks in each picture, giving advice. Surprisingly, the name of the artist can't be found in the book and Berry is clearly stated as the *author.* The books in this series are available with audiovisual materials; perhaps as a teaching package the material works better, but as a book alone, without discussion, too much is covered with too few words. The result is a mite too preachy.

170. Bunting, Eve. *Ghost's Hour, Spook's Hour.* Illus. by Donald Carrick. New York: Clarion, 1987. 32 pp. Fiction.

Interest level: Ages 3–7 Reading level: Grade 3

When Jake is awakened in the middle of the night by some strange noises, he tries to turn on the light, but finds that the electricity doesn't work. He and his dog, Biff, cling to each other fearfully as they make their way to Jake's parents' room, only to find that his parents are gone. The noises of the wind, the branches of the trees scraping against the windows, the moaning of the dog, and the ordinary noises of the clock are frightening in the context of the time of night and the missing parents. When Jake's parents appear, they explain that they had been bothered by the noise of the branches so they decided to sleep on the sofa bed. And Jake explains that Biff was very frightened. They reassure Jake that everyone gets frightened sometimes, and they invite both Jake and Biff to spend the rest of the night with them on the sofa bed.

Bunting's prose, graphically describing the scary sounds, works well with the expressive illustrations to convey the sense of the child's fears. A plausible explanation of the parents' absence is important for the young reader. Some experts might frown on taking the child and the dog into bed, but it really is the humane thing to do in this case.

171. Bunting, Eve. *Sixth-Grade Sleepover.* New York: Harcourt, 1986; Scholastic, 1987, pap. 96 pp. Fiction.
Interest level: Ages 8–12 Reading level: Grade 4

Bunting combines a story about school readathons with a drama about overcoming fears. The Rabbit Reading Club's plan for an all-night session frightens Janey, who desperately wants to go, but can't seem to shake her trauma-induced terror of the dark night. Will this turn into the evening when everyone finds out she still uses a nightlight? The action mixes in preteen crushes and the embarrassment of puberty, giving a rounded feeling to the plot, and Janey's dread is finally resolved when another person in the class has an equally vexing problem. Newcomer Rosie also must move away from her fears, for she has thus far been able to hide her first-grade reading level. The events have a natural flow to them, so when the girls team up to be open about their problems it is perfectly believable. Both girls come out of their darkness and into the light in this subdued, elegant ode to the literacy theme.

172. Canty, John. *Shadows.* Illus. by the author. New York: Harper, 1987. 20 pp. Fiction.
Interest level: Ages 4–7 Reading level: Grade 1

"Benjamin hates the dark. Fierce creatures live there. Late at night he sees one move. Or at least he thinks he does." And so, in gray darkness, Benjamin tests the night, and in his mind, shapes form and grow. What was once a rabbit shadow becomes a monster. He tries to reason. "If I run, . . . it will always chase me. Always and forever. But this is my room, and I won't run from anything!" And with this assertion, Benjamin calms the room down; shadows whirl, swirl, and melt away, vanishing "into the farthest corners, back to where dark shadows belong." The boy conquers his fear of separation himself and makes his own safety from his bravery.

173. Conrad, Pam. *What I Did for Roman.* New York: Harper, 1987. 218 pp. Fiction.
Interest level: Age 12+ Reading level: Grade 6

Darcie's mother and father were never married. Now Darcie's mother has married and is on her honeymoon in Europe. She has sent 16-year-old Darcie to stay with her uncle and aunt, where she will work at a restaurant concession at the zoo for the summer. During the summer Darcie uncovers all kinds of information she never knew about her father. In the process of doing so she learns a lot about her family and herself.

The somewhat melodramatically told story involves an emotionally disturbed worker at the zoo who both befriends and endangers Darcie. It turns out that Darcie's uncle and aunt both betrayed her mother, and forced her father to go into the army, where he was killed.

At the end of the story there is the implication that Darcie will now be much happier, and that she will be ready to accept her mother and new stepfather. The story could have been one that many young readers could have related to, but because of the complexity of the characters and the plot, the book becomes somewhat of a potboiler and less a story that rings true.

174. Curtis, Robert H. *Mind and Mood: Understanding and Controlling Your Emotions.* New York: Scribner, 1986. Nonfiction.

Interest level: Age 12+ Reading level: Grade 6

Among this book's strengths is its historical approach to emotions, ranging from biblical and ancient Greek observations of human feeling to Darwinian explanations. To show the relationship between mind and body, internist Curtis uses unique cases such as "Tom's Stomach," in which doctors literally had a window into the coloration of one man's emotions. Curtis also deftly shows emotion's rich spectrum, for example, how trepidation, fear, dread, terror, panic, and horror differ from one another. Sections covering psychotherapy, behavior modification, endocrines, and the nervous system are commonly found in other volumes; the chapter on personality tests is fresh and will be of interest. A weakness, however, is the distant formal tone that doesn't make contact with the individual reader.

175. DeClements, Barthe. *I Never Asked You to Understand Me.* New York: Viking, 1986; Scholastic, 1987, pap. 144 pp. Fiction.

Interest level: Age 12+ Reading level: Grade 6

DeClements's novels for preteens have been immensely popular. This novel for an older group concentrates on students who have chosen or been forced to attend a casual alternative high school, a group DeClements understands from her work as a counselor in such a school. Didi is there because she becomes truant during her mother's terminal illness, terrified at being left with a distant father and a great-grandmother who sees illness as something we will on ourselves. The action revolves around Didi's struggle to see her own truth. How responsible are we for our destinies? Didi tries to find answers in the context of her new circle—teachers who stress self-actualization with kids who have seen the world through drug abuse, detention centers, and other tragedies. When she is able to help her desperate friend Stacy out of the dilemma of incest, Didi begins to find direction. Whether it's when Didi's father forgets a Christmas present or her friends party with drugs, DeClements creates memorable incidents with her large group of well-delineated characters.

176. Emerson, Kathy Lynn. *Julia's Mending.* New York: Orchard, 1987. 160 pp. Fiction.

Interest level: Age 10+ Reading level: Grades 4–5

When Julia's parents go to China to be missionaries, they send her to her cousins' house in upstate New York. Julia would have preferred to have stayed with her grandmother in New York City, but her parents want her to be with people who hold the same religious beliefs as they. Julia immediately hates her new surroundings and dislikes her cousins. They feel the same negative way about her. On her second day there she falls and breaks her leg. Julia begins keeping a journal with the intention of sending it to her parents so that they will see how she is suffering, and either send for her or permit her to go to her grandmother's.

Life in a rural community in the nineteenth century is not easy, and Julia misses the coddling and luxury of her New York grandmother's home. During and after her convalescence, Julia engages in some energetic self-reflection and decides to change her attitude and her behavior. She makes friends with her cousins, helps to solve a mystery, and looks forward to a much happier stay.

Emerson has written the story from materials and memories from her own family. The situation and characters have the ring of truth. The characters are all three-dimensional and interesting. Julia's predicament and separation from her family will probably strike chords in a number of readers who have had to endure a prolonged separation from their parents.

177. Emmens, Carol A. *The Abortion Controversy.* New York: Messner, 1987. 124 pp. Nonfiction.

Interest level: Age 12+ Reading level: Grades 6–7

Leaning a bit toward the pro-choice mode, free-lance writer Emmens nevertheless presents a highly balanced, truly informative treatise on this troubling topic. Topics include the biology of fetal development and a description of spontaneous and induced abortions, as well as a historical perspective on the subject of abortion, ranging from biblical times and the days of Aristotle (pro) and Hippocrates (anti) to the present. She looks at the subject sociologically, assessing who seeks abortions (the majority of women are in their twenties, followed by teenagers) and why some adolescents have the wrong ideas about conception. The methods of abortion, as well as relative safety, complications, after-effects, and emotional trauma are examined, as are religious viewpoints, which, surprisingly, are more complex than many would imagine—there are times in the Mormon and Catholic religions, for example, when abortion is condoned. The points of view of pro-choice and pro-life contingents are investigated fully. Finally, there is an in-depth exploration of court decisions, including up-to-date looks at the Reagan administration's response to the problem.

178. Gay, Kathlyn. *Changing Families: Meeting Today's Challenges.* Hillside, N.J.: Enslow, 1988. 128 pp. Nonfiction.

Interest level: Ages 10–14 Reading level: Grade 6

This is a sociological overview of today's family structures and dilemmas. Beginning with a look at the purposes of a family, the author moves on to examinations of today's varied patterns: the working family; split families; single-parent families; other structures, such as gay parents, extended families, foster care, and adoptees; older families; families at risk and families who hurt (e.g., families in which there is child abuse and other violence, homeless families); and the family of the future. The innovations of the 1980s are investigated, such as joint custody, but by including so much, the book becomes statistical rather than feelingful and is more likely to be used for reports than leisure reading. Resource list, bibliography, index.

179. Glenn, Mel. *Class Dismissed II: More High School Poems.* Photos by Michael J. Bernstein. New York: Clarion, 1986. 96 pp. Fiction.

Interest level: Age 12+ Reading level: Grade 4

Glenn has written 70 new poems about high school life, accomplishing the admirable task of sounding like each person who speaks. Glenn, a high school teacher himself, seems to record their words, feelings, and manner, and it comes out powerfully in these first-person vignettes. Bernstein's close-up photographic portraits of a multiethnic high school student body heighten the effect, whether the emotion is fear, despair, ebullience, pride, bravado, or one of many others.

Among the poetic–photographic portraits in this volume are Paul Hewitt, who wants books that can help him deal with real life ("I'm never going to fight the Civil War. And I certainly don't live in the Dust Bowl."); Candie Brewer, who has heard every line in the book at the rock club she frequents; and Veronica Castell, who has seen schools in seven states, courtesy of the Air Force. Many will identify with Robert Ashford, whose parents have usurped his power in picking out colleges for him, and Juan Pedro Carrera, who wants to return to his home country, where he doesn't "have to act so strong." A strong book all around.

180. Gordon, Sol. *When Living Hurts.* Photos. New York: Union of American Hebrew Congregations, 1985, pap. 140 pp. Nonfiction.
Interest level: Age 12+ Reading level: Grade 5

Sex and family life educator Gordon offers an inspirational guide on what to do when one feels depressed, lonely, suicidal, trying to help youngsters look seriously at what they deem the purpose of life. The concept that we are all our brothers' keepers is entwined in the pages, and as such, the author wisely recommends talking to someone immediately if a teen feels terrible, before reading the book. As such, he also gives step-by-step instructions to readers on how to help others who are having anxiety attacks or expressing suicidal thoughts.

After emergency measures are taken, the reader may be ready to learn why depression occurs and how it relates to either bad or good happenings. The art of giving caring messages while at the same time sharing the secret suicidal feelings with an adult figure who can help is stressed.

Short-term ways to help oneself or a friend get out of a depression (go to a park, write to someone who will be surprised to hear from you, and so on) are coupled with suggestions for long-term help (therapy, seeking help from the clergy, and so forth). Other topics covered include substance abuse, minimal self-esteem, sexual worries, anger, and boredom as they may have an impact on depression. The book offers exercises to think and write about, for example, when looking at the worst thing that ever happened to you, reflecting on what you learned, and if anything good came out of it.

Additional areas of exploration are disappointments in religion, not getting along with parents (and here, he offers advice to parents as well as children on how to keep communication avenues open), and special family situations (divorce, stepfamily, and so on). The segments are individually short but neither glib nor empty. Instead, Gordon is reassuring in his terse, forthright presentation and trustful manner in presenting philosophies to children. The ideas of Frankl, for example, are related to help teens find meaning in life. Gordon also doesn't fear to recommend additional reading and inject his own life—anecdotes, poems, sayings he values in trying to recover from life's batterings. Renewal, forgiveness, and being kind to oneself are folded into every page, and the message will uplift teens thoughtful enough to work with this book. Appendix of crisis intervention/suicide prevention centers and hotlines.

181. Havill, Juanita. *Jamaica's Find.* Illus. by Anne Sibley O'Brien. Boston: Houghton Mifflin, 1985; Sandpiper, pap. 32 pp. Fiction.
Interest level: Ages 4–8 Reading level: Grade 3

From start to finish, this is a story about feelings. Jamaica finds a stuffed dog on the playground. She loves it and wants to keep it, but her parents help her to empathize with the child who has lost the dog. She returns it to the office of the park administration. Later on she meets a little girl who is looking for her lost dog. Jamaica takes the little girl to the office where she is reunited with her toy. Jamaica has lost the dog, but has found a friend.

The illustrations are wonderfully realistic and warm. The plot is filled with interesting details (parents who express their opinion but let their child find her own way to a decision) and speaks to readers' hearts without moralizing. The children have personality, and make the situation an interesting and believable one. An added plus is that Jamaica is portrayed in the watercolors as a black child, but being black has nothing to do with the story line. A useful book to spark discussion about values and socializing.

182. Hermes, Patricia. *Who Will Take Care of Me?* New York: Harcourt, 1983. 99 pp. Fiction.
Interest level: Ages 9–12 Reading level: Grade 4

Mark and Pete's parents were killed in an automobile accident, and their grandmother, who took care of them after their parents' death, has now died, too. Aunt Agnes wants Mark to live with her, but she plans to send Pete to a special school for retarded children. Mark is as violently opposed to Pete's being sent away as his grandmother was. He runs away with Pete to their family cottage, but just after they arrive, Pete disappears.

After Pete is found, Mark, Aunt Agnes, and Dr. Ramirez, their family doctor, have a discussion about what they will do. Mark is included in the decision making, and he is invited to go to see a potential school for Pete. Relieved at being permitted to participate, and beginning to understand that his aunt is not against him, Mark finally recognizes that sending Pete to school is probably in everyone's best interest.

The important element in this story is the one of understanding that children need to be permitted to help in the decision making about their own lives. However, the resolution is somewhat confusing: Is Pete's school a residential institution, or is it a day facility from which he returns home every evening? If that is the case, why does Mark try to prevent his enrollment? If not, how is it that Pete comes home in the afternoon?

Despite the confusion, the story is a good one. It has suspense, a real sense of the dilemma children confront, and several models of nurturing adults.

183. Herzig, Alison Cragin. *Shadows on the Pond.* Boston: Little, 1985. 200 pp. Fiction.

Interest level: Age 12+ Reading level: Grade 7

Jill's parents' marriage is deteriorating and Jill and her mother arrive at their summer home in Vermont for the first time without her father and sister. Her sister has detached herself from the situation. Jill cannot do that, but she is able to resume her friendship with her neighbor, Megan, and to work together with Megan to defeat the cruel trapping of beavers in their secret pond. When an accident keeps Megan at home, Jill continues the work with the help and friendship of a new friend, Ryan, who is on vacation in this same area.

Ryan and Jill's friendship blooms while her mother and father's once loving marriage has cooled to the point of estrangement. Jill's mother is learning to live alone and finds difficulty managing the tasks that were once the province of her husband. The tension that exists between her parents is overwhelming and frightening for Jill, who must guess at much of what is going on, because her parents do not confide in her. She is hurt and confused and constantly longs for the way life used to be. Ryan, whose parents divorced many years previously, represents a person who has become reconciled to a similar situation and has come out of the pain. He is able to help Jill gain a different perspective on her agonizing situation.

The book deals with many issues but the overriding theme is reconstruction. The beavers will rebuild their dams, Ryan and Jill will continue their friendship in New York, and it also seems hopeful that, with effort, Jill's parents can resolve their own crisis. The book concludes with Jill's recognition that despair can be overcome through acceptance.

184. Mayle, Peter. *Sweet Dreams and Monsters: A Beginner's Guide to Dreams and Nightmares and Things That Go Bump under the Bed.* Illus. by Arthur Robins. New York: Harmony, 1986. 32 pp. Nonfiction.

Interest level: Ages 7–12 Reading level: Grades 4–5

With droll, sly humor, author and illustrator actually bring the reader to the brink of monstrous nightmares half-remembered. The cockroach nightmare with which the book starts tells you right away if this is the book for you. Not afraid to venture forth? If so, there are subject headings like "Free Movies Every Night," which explores dream physiology and our ability to remember nightly separations from those we love. Also included is information about what winds up in our dreams, our subconscious storehouse, and a beginning list of common dreams, for example, forgotten dreams, memory, the future, and nightmares. Mayle explains how real life actually influences dreams that seem to come true. Once you get past that eerie cockroach, this book is sort of fun and can help ease children's minds for that daily time we must be alone.

185. Paterson, Katherine. *Come Sing, Jimmy Jo.* New York: Dutton, 1985; Avon, pap. 178 pp. Fiction.
Interest level: Age 11+ Reading level: Grades 6–7

James's family has been a singing group for many years, but James only sings for the family. He has terrible stage fright. When James is 11 years old, an agent discovers his wonderful voice, and he is drawn into the singing profession despite his fears. He acknowledges that he has a gift when the fans go wild about him.

James feels closest to his grandmother and father. His mother is a flighty young woman who James later discovers is having an affair with his uncle, his father's brother, also a member of the singing group. Then, one day, a stranger tells James that he is really James's father. It turns out to be true, and James is dismayed to find that the two people he loves most in the world are not his blood relatives.

It takes some thought and some help, but James finally comes to realize that his grandparents and "adopted" father are his real relatives, and his biological father is no more than an accident of biology. He reconciles with his family, and even begins to understand his mother's needs, as he joins the family publicly in singing, "Will the Circle Be Unbroken?"

Katherine Paterson is masterful with language and characterization. She demonstrates again the ability to take a particular set of characters in their own special circumstances and transform them into universal representatives, while taking care that they retain their individuality and vitality. The issue of raising a child who is not your biological offspring is powerfully conveyed, as is the practice of understanding and forgiving people their weaknesses.

186. Prestine, Joan Singleton. *Love Me Anyway.* Illus. by Meredith Johnson. Los Angeles: Price/Stern/Sloan, 1987, pap. 24 pp. Nonfiction.
Interest level: Ages 4–8 Reading level: Grade 1

This entry in the My Special Feelings series concerns expressing emotions and finding appropriate words. Susan, the protagonist, tells of times she miscommunicates because she doesn't know how to use words. For example, "Sometimes I pull Billy's hair, when what I want to say is, 'Mommy, pay attention to me!' " Miscommunication follows miscommunication, though without a break or example of what might happen if Susan were able to use words. The book would have worked better by use of contrast, which is a shame, because the author had a fine idea. The only hint of resolution is in the last pages, when Susan says, "Sometimes I'm just awful, when what I want is to say, 'Hug me and love me anyway.' " That kind of resolution, thinking of what to say but not being able to say it, simply isn't good enough. Pass on this book, a worthy notion inadequately developed.

187. Rylant, Cynthia. *A Fine White Dust.* New York: Bradbury, 1986. 106 pp. Fiction.

Interest level: Age 10+ Reading level: Grades 5–6

Thirteen-year-old Peter Cassidy tells his own story in retrospect to help himself finish an episode in his life that has taught him many hard lessons, among them that he can count on his parents, but not to expect anything, and, "If somebody loves you, it's because he wants to. And it's never because it's what he's supposed to do."

Peter has always loved going to church, even though his parents do not accompany him there. When he meets an itinerant revivalist preacher he falls under his spell and plans to abandon his best friend and parents in order to accept the preacher's invitation to go away together. However, instead of meeting Peter at their appointed time and place, the preacher runs off with Darlene Cook, a young woman who works at the drugstore.

Crushed, Peter returns home; his parents and loyal best friend provide him with love and understanding, and his life returns to normal, except that he is now wiser about people and what can be expected of them. The story moves quickly and is accessible to readers aged 10 and up, even though the topic is one that might be more appropriate to older readers who are grappling with issues of whom to choose as heroes, how different to be from one's parents, and how to establish a value system. Unfortunately, Cynthia Rylant does not let us in on what motivates Peter, either to his religious fervor or to his willingness to abandon his friends and family for the preacher. His religious convictions remain unshaken, but he now attends church less regularly and certainly less passionately. "But it's a real quiet thing for me now. Sort of like a nice swim in the lake."

Rylant never clears up the mystery of why Peter's parents feel as negatively as they do about going to church. At one point, when Peter confronts them, his father says, "There's more to it than you can see, Pete . . . things you might not understand." Peter is alarmed, because he is afraid to learn his parents' secrets. Peter's mother intervenes just as his father is about to explain it to him, and so neither Peter nor the reader ever find out what the secret is.

Such deep issues as autonomy and independence, religious fervor, hero worship, and betrayal are explored in this book. Rylant has a gift for conveying the voices of the characters and for providing the reader with an authentic sense of place.

188. Thomas, Marlo, et al., eds. *Free to Be a Family . . . A Book about All Kinds of Belonging*. New York: Bantam, 1987. 176 pp. Fiction.
Interest level: Age 8+ Reading level: Grades 4–5

Here, after many years, is a welcome follow-up to *Free to Be You and Me* (McGraw, 1974). The latest anthology conceived by Marlo Thomas and edited by her, Christopher Cerf, and others contains works by well-known writers, illustrators, composers, and entertainers. Numbered among them are Shel Silverstein, Judith Viorst, John Steptoe, Susan Jeffers, Charlotte Zolotow, Carly Simon, the Dillons, Kris Kristofferson, Arnold Lobel, Jane Wagner, and Lucille Clifton. Some of the works are older and familiar (for example, *A Father Like That* by Zolotow; *I'll Fix Anthony* by Viorst; Silverstein's poem about a girl who actually *does* die when her parents won't get her a pony, and the foster care depicted in Steptoe's *Stevie*), some less familiar. Some of the stories have been given new illustrations, for example, Lobel's *I'll Fix Anthony*. All stress the beauty of family regardless of its size or constitution. In the introduction by Letty Cottin Pogrebin and in a story she includes called *My Grandmother,* the idea of feeling different and perhaps ashamed of one's family is exposed and worked through.

Variety works well for the anthology, and it's only occasionally heavy-handed on the message-giving. There's a comic strip about Superboy and a poem about being forced to perform for guests. There is a song that combines concepts about the extended family caused by divorce, remarriage, and adoption ("Friendly Neighborhood"), and a rewritten Cinderella who is more dedicated to writing book reports than prince-chasing or being chased. The families depicted here live in the United States, Central America, and elsewhere. They are of many colors, sizes, and arrangements. Some features are brief, others longer; occasionally they try to cram in too many ideas, such as a one-page piece that mixes stepdaughter-stepfather relationships with the child teaching the parent to read, but throughout the works the general theme is one of being able to say what's on your mind and acceptance of differences.

189. Voigt, Cynthia. *Dicey's Song*. New York: Atheneum, 1982. 196 pp. Fiction.
Interest level: Age 11+ Reading level: Grade 5

It is difficult to place this 1983 Newbery Award-winning book in a particular category of loss. It is the sequel to *Homecoming* (Atheneum, 1981), which describes the journey that Dicey and her younger sister and brothers made when their mother abandoned them in the parking lot of a supermarket. They are now with their grandmother in the tidewater area of Maryland, and they are secure in the knowledge that their grandmother loves them.

The book deals with the issues of abandonment, displacement, coming to terms with differences, adjusting to a new community and a new school, learning about themselves, and, finally, accepting their mother's death. Dicey, her siblings, and her grandmother are all strong and unique characters. But so is every other character in the book. They are not eccentric; they are real. Each has his or her own story to tell, as does every human being. Each deals with loss and challenge in different ways, but all are valid. This book should be read by everyone because there is something for everyone in it. It is told with beauty, empathy, warmth, and wisdom.

190. Wright, Betty Ren. *Christina's Ghost.* New York: Holiday, 1985; Scholastic, 1987, pap. 105 pp. Fiction.
Interest level: Ages 9–12 Reading level: Grades 3–4

Christina and Jenny are supposed to stay with their grandmother on her farm when their parents go off to Alaska for the summer. But when the girls get to their grandmother's farm, they find that she has been hospitalized, so Chris must go with her grumpy old uncle to an out-of-the-way cottage he has consented to take care of as a favor to a friend. Chris already feels abandoned by her parents and now she must face the rejecting behavior of a man who clearly prefers to be alone. When Chris and her uncle arrive at their destination they soon discover that there is a mystery about the cottage. As it turns out, two ghosts haunt the place, and a murder was committed there.

Wright cleverly presents the story of an alienated child who gains self-acceptance and self-confidence by befriending a mournful young ghost, solving a mystery, and learning to get along with her gloomy uncle. The story is full of suspense. The mystery is handled adroitly, so that the reader is very willing to suspend disbelief. The mixture of fantasy and reality works well here.

191. Zolotow, Charlotte, ed. *Early Sorrow: Ten Stories of Youth.* New York: Harper, 1986. 212 pp. Fiction.
Interest level: Age 12+ Reading level: Grades 6–7

Carson McCullers, E. L. Doctorow, Stephen Vincent Benet, and Katherine Mansfield are among the authors of the short stories in this book. Each of the stories deals with a loss of some sort: the death of a father, divorce, loss of a friend, or desertion. Each story respects the emotions and burgeoning maturity of adolescents. None of the stories has a conventional happy ending, and each provides the reader with much food for thought.

Growing Up

192. Blos, Joan W. *Brothers of the Heart.* New York: Scribner, 1985; Macmillan, pap. 162 pp. Fiction.

Interest level: Age 12+ Reading level: Grades 7–8

The story tells of a pioneering family in which Shem, the only son, runs away from home in anger over an argument with his father. Shem has a disability: One leg is shorter than the other, and he has found it difficult to find work. But when he runs away he finds work immediately, has many adventures, proves his manliness, and is able to return home to his family and the young woman who eventually becomes his wife.

The story tells of the strength necessary to endure the hard times and many losses the pioneers had to endure. It also conveys the indefatigable spirit of the unlikely hero. The author, who won the 1980 Newbery Medal for *A Gathering of Days* (Macmillan, 1979), brings authenticity and scholarly research to her story.

193. Bridgers, Sue Ellen. *Permanent Connections.* New York: Harper, 1987; Harper Keypoint, pap. 264 pp. Fiction.

Interest level: Age 12+ Reading level: Grade 7

Rob's parents are at their wits' end. He has a problem with alcohol and marijuana; he is running with the wrong crowd, and they can't get through to him. There seems to be no explanation for Rob's behavior; he doesn't seem to know, himself, why he feels the way he does. Rob and his father go south to his paternal grandfather's house. There they stay in the somewhat ramshackle house where Rob's father grew up. Rob's uncle has been in an accident, and it is decided, much against Rob's will, that he will stay to help take care of his uncle and his other elderly relatives.

Rob meets a girl who seems to harbor the same angry feelings inside her that he does. They have a rocky but steamy relationship and she helps him to mature. It takes a brush with the law involving Rob's smoking marijuana, and a nearly fatal injury to his grandfather, to make Rob feel that he is part of his family, and that he has a worthwhile direction to follow.

No one in this novel is so fully fleshed out that the reader gets to know his or her motivation or thoughts. We see the surface behavior, and there are hints as to the influencing factors in their lives, but, on the whole, the characters remain remote. Some adolescents might see in these turned-off youths something to which they can relate. The solutions are somewhat pat, and no one really takes responsibility for his or her behavior. But there is potential here, and the characters are quirky enough to arouse some interest.

194. Cole, Joanna. *Asking about Sex and Growing Up: A Question-and-Answer Book for Boys and Girls.* Illus. by Alan Tiegreen. New York: Morrow, 1988, hb and pap. 128 pp. Nonfiction.
Interest level: Ages 8–12 Reading level: Grade 4

In a matter-of-fact tone, Cole packs a punch in her openness with preteens. In sections on girls' and boys' development, masturbation, crushes, intercourse, birth and birth control, homosexuality, and self-protection from abuse and disease, she provides nitty-gritty information that parents would wish they could as smoothly offer. For example, many women enjoy having their breasts caressed, how a tampon is removed, how each sex masturbates, how a girl can view her sexual organs by using a mirror. There's an occasional fact parents might not know, too, for example, why one testicle hangs lower than the other. The section on child abuse is strong and helpful for this age group, as the author delineates more types of abuse than are commonly acknowledged, such as being kissed in an adult way and unable to stop it. The material on AIDS is up to date and, although the readers are young, Cole trusts them with precautionary strategies against AIDS (for example, using condoms and washing the sexual organs before and after intercourse). Cole's comforting manner reassures and, most important in a book of this kind, makes it absolutely, positively all right to want to know. Bibliographies for parents and children.

195. Frank, Elizabeth Bales. *Cooder Cutlas.* New York: Harper, 1987. 311 pp. Fiction.
Interest level: Age 13+ Reading level: Grades 7–8

Because Cooder is still grieving over the death of Maude, his girlfriend, he decides to pack up and move to Paradise Beach, New Jersey, with his friend, Eddie, who is joining a rock band. Cooder remains a loner at heart, although he establishes close friendships with the band members. Then he meets Macky, a young aspiring model who has run away from home, and subsequently from an abusive boyfriend. Macky joins the crowd of girls who travel with the band, and she and Cooder fall in love.

Even after Cooder and Macky become involved with each other, Cooder is still haunted by his relationship with Maude. He doesn't talk about her much, but he is constantly reminded of her and even carries photos of her in his Bible. His relationship with Macky seems doomed because she cannot possibly compete with a dead girlfriend who is portrayed as being as nearly perfect as any human can be. However, Macky's unconditional love helps Cooder to learn that although Maude can never be replaced he can continue to live and love without her. A measure of his self-development is demonstrated when he doesn't run away when he and Macky temporarily break up.

The sleazy life of the rock band is the backdrop for the story. None of the characters is admirable. Sex is cheap and everyone is promiscuous. Fame and fortune are the overriding goals, and most of the people are failures in their own eyes. Undoubtedly, there are many people like this in today's society. This story holds up a harsh mirror to those who would emulate them.

196. Klein, Leonore. *Old, Older, Oldest.* Illus. by Leonard Kessler. New York: Hastings, 1983. 48 pp. Nonfiction.

Interest level: Ages 6–10 Reading level: Grades 1–2

Old, Older, Oldest is a concept book about the relative nature of age. The author takes a humorous approach that gets right to the heart of that relative nature. For example, "Is 'old' when your bones feel achy and cold?" The next page shows that eight-year-old Michael must therefore be old because he has the flu and his bones feel achy and cold. Next, "Is 'young' when you kick up your heels and dance?" In that case, Grandma is young although she is 65 years old, and the jaunty illustration shows her kicking up her heels. The rest of this useful book examines different animals, explaining their typical life spans. Additional concepts are examined, the most interesting of which is "How old would you like to be?" Well done and likely to provide the perspective the author and illustrator tried to offer.

197. McGuire, Paula. *It Won't Happen to Me: Teenagers Talk about Pregnancy.* New York: Delacorte, 1983, hb and pap. 244 pp. Nonfiction.

Interest level: Age 13+ Reading level: Grade 5

Fifteen young women from varied backgrounds are interviewed by the author, who is a writer and editor of educational materials. All seem to want to talk so that others can benefit from their experiences. Some have decided to have abortions, some get married very young and keep the baby, some opt for adoption. The interviews are broad in scope, covering the varied roles and nonroles the fathers of these children have chosen to play in the unfolding drama. Other topics include pregnancy by rape, reasons the teens had sex, and discussion of venereal disease. The interviews are made into first-person narrations, with the editor's words hardly appearing at all. Occasionally others participate in the narration, such as a young woman's mother. As the narrations are based on real people talking, they have a poignant power that simple information dispensing is less likely to offer. Bibliography, resource list, index.

198. MacLachlan, Patricia. *Unclaimed Treasures*. New York: Harper, 1984, hb and pap. 118 pp. Fiction.

Interest level: Ages 10–12 Reading level: Grades 5–7

Although the book describes a summer that begins with a death and a funeral, and nearly ends with one, this treasure of a story is about life and helps readers contemplate and value life's ordinary and extraordinary events. As with all of MacLachlan's books, the characters are individuals who capture readers' attention with their particular actions, observations, and feelings and move the reader with the universality of their situations, and the thoughtful and appropriate way in which they handle their problems.

In this story, Willa, twin sister to Nicholas, searches continuously for her true love. They have just moved into their new home, and they soon meet Horace Morris, the boy next door, who lives with his tall, solemn artist-father, and several aunts whom he calls "Unclaimed Treasures" because they are elderly women who never married (that is, they were never claimed). One of the aunts has just died. Horace's mother has deserted him and her husband. She's "out in the world looking for something that needs her." Willa is not happy with her mother at the moment, because after 11 years her mother is pregnant, and Willa wishes that her mother were out in the world doing something extraordinary.

Other characters in the book include Old Pepper, who demonstrates that old age need not be synonymous with self-centeredness and crotchety behavior. Old Pepper teaches Willa to do more than "just look." He pays attention. He helps the children to think about and cope with the idea of death as he contemplates the fact of his eventual death.

Love and death and friendship and understanding are interwoven. Although the reconciliation of Horace's parents is a romantic rather than realistic outcome, it is appropriate for this book, whose tone is gentle and wise and extraordinary in its valuing of the ordinary.

199. Mills, Claudia. *The Secret Carousel*. New York: Four Winds, 1983. 138 pp. Fiction.

Interest level: Ages 8–12 Reading level: Grade 4

Lindy Webster lives with her grandparents, because her parents were killed in an automobile accident. Her sister, Joan, has gone to New York to live with an aunt, because Joan is a ballerina and needs the city for her career. Lindy must decide what she wants for her own life, and that is what the process of the story is about. She builds a knowledge of herself and her grandfather, as well as an appreciation of the small town in Iowa where they live.

The story is a good one for young people to read. Not only does it move well, but the characters are interesting and have depth. Lindy suffers from loneliness, boredom, self-doubt, and jealousy, but she is also generous, loving, talented, and introspective. The family support system is an honest one. The problems and issues include the grandfather's retirement, the grandmother's concern, and the dilemma of the older sister who has a passion for ballet. A very satisfying book.

200. Pople, Maureen. *The Other Side of the Family.* New York: Henry Holt, 1988. 165 pp. Fiction.

Interest level: Age 12+ Reading level: Grades 6–7

Katherine Tucker is sent by her parents from her home in England to be with her maternal grandparents in Sydney, Australia, until World War II ends. But when, soon after her arrival, Japanese submarines are sighted in Sydney harbor, it is decided that she now be sent to her paternal grandmother in the safety of the country inland. Katherine is shocked when she hears this news. She has never met her other grandmother, and she has the idea that her grandmother hates her and her family. Her mother has told her terrible stories about how awful this grandmother is, and no one has ever contradicted them.

All of the myths she's heard about her grandmother explode as Katherine gets to know more about her own background. Her grandmother was never wealthy; her grandfather was a charming ne'er-do-well who deserted his wife and son; her father was a selfish snob who was ashamed of his mother and who invented stories about his upbringing. Also, her grandmother is deaf, and can only lip read to understand what is said to her. All of this and more Katherine learns in the brief month that she is away from Sydney. But she uses what she has learned to become a kinder and more honest person. Her absence from home turns out to be a homecoming in its deepest sense.

The story unfolds dramatically, and is a believable one. All the characters are interesting and hold the reader's attention. The themes of war and desertion are blended, so that the reader understands more of the events and the times of World War II and its effect on the Australian people. A worthwhile book.

201. Rogers, Fred. *Going to the Potty.* Photos by Jim Judkis. New York: Putnam, 1986, hb and pap. 32 pp. Nonfiction.

Interest level: Ages 2–4 Reading level: Grade 2

In his introduction to this particular volume in his First Experiences series, Mr. Rogers of the "Mister Rogers" television program stresses that parents apply a balance of gentleness and persistence in their toilet-training approach. He uses those very qualities in his writing as well, explaining that children need help in many ways but as time goes on they need less help. First, several babies are shown being helped to dress and eat, and then he moves into the ideas behind training, explaining the seat and stressing children's readiness: "Children need to take their time about things like that." He's cognizant of aspects of the big toilet that can be frightening, such as the noise of the flush and the forbidding nature of the seat: "At first it may feel a little hard and cold." He involves his reader, too: "Do you have a chair or seat like that?"

Rogers uses adult words in the book (urine, bowel movement), but in his introduction for adults understandingly states, "You may be more comfortable substituting the words with which your own family is familiar." The full-color photographs of two families going through the training process are sharp and pleasant. They also show older children age four or five sitting on the toilet. One wonders how these models felt at being asked to be photographed this way, but knowing the care and sensitivity with which the Mr. Rogers's neighborhood projects are undertaken, one is reassured that it was likely done with the utmost intelligence, perhaps explained by Mr. Rogers himself. This is indeed the book they hoped to have, one which would promote the mastery and stronger sense of self that the toilet-training process, ideally realized, accomplishes.

202. Rosenblum, Richard. *My Sister's Wedding.* Illus. by the author. New York: Morrow, 1987. 32 pp. Fiction.

Interest level: Ages 6–9 Reading level: Grade 3

A nostalgic look back to the 1940s gives this book charm as it touches on a common theme—big sister's getting married. Will her younger brother get her room? And how can that younger brother make friends with his new brother-in-law and his intriguing army and navy cohorts? The first-person account, speaking from the vantage point of an 11-year-old harkens back to the author's actual experience, and each memory of planning and being at the wedding feels real, from the much-listened-to radio in the living room and the synagogue traditions to the servicemen's uniforms and conga line at the wedding. Oh, and brother never gets the room, because sister's husband goes overseas and sister stays home after all.

203. Snider, Dee, and Bashe, Philip. *Dee Snider's Teenage Survival Guide: How to Be a Legend in Your Own Lunchtime.* New York: Dolphin, 1987, hb and pap. 264 pp. Nonfiction.

Interest level: Age 12+ Reading level: Grade 6

Who would think that a teen guide acknowledging Alice Cooper and Ozzie Osbourne would be terrific? Written by a musician from the rock group Twisted Sister with the help of a heavy metal journalist, it is highly intelligent, full of nitty-gritty self-revelations, funny, and altogether a winner.

Snider and Bashe cover the usual—school, parents, career plans, drugs, sex, child abuse, family problems including death, suicide, divorce, and stepfamilies, but the honest, fascinating stories Snider tells about himself will make readers want to read every word. These range from his father's erratic, violent mood swings to a turnaround when a girl "uses" Snider in seducing him out of his virginity. Under his admittedly bizarre exterior, Snider is (and always has been) quite straight; he's against drug use, quitting school, early marriage, and other potential problems for youth. Parents can offer this book without fear—there are good values inside, and Snider's style is one teens will heed.

Snider's gift may be in his insight and memory of what it is like to be young. Using a three-generation perspective—his parents, himself, and his son—he gets right to the heart of the matter as few self-help writers do. He *does* remember being embarrassed to be seen with his parents in public, and he *does* touch the heart with the dramatic specific, such as different meals now being prepared in a joined stepfamily household. Only very occasionally is Snider's wit offensive, as when he interjects allusions to sexual intercourse in the midst of talking about grief caused by death. "Others, who are normally stoic and rarely display their emotions, grieved long and hard. And deep and penetrating and thrusting and plunging and—oops, sorry, wrong book." An unfortunate lapse in an otherwise thoroughly delightful book. Bibliography, appendix of community agencies for seeking help with problems.

204. Watanabe, Shigeo. *I Can Take a Walk!* Illus. by Yasuo Ohtomo. New York: Philomel, 1984, hb and pap. 32 pp. Fiction.

Interest level: Ages 2–6 Reading level: Grade 1

As a book in the I Can Do It All by Myself series, this volume features Bear, a character seen in other books. This time, he decides to take a walk by himself, and he's full of bravery and adventure. Wherever he goes, his imagination is at work, too, just as younger children's imaginations are. As he walks across a park bench, he says, "I can cross this high bridge." It is likewise with other happy adventures, such as shooing away birds that to him are flying dragons. But when he gets stuck on the edge of what to him seems like a cliff, he's very relieved when Daddy comes walking by, and he's most happy to join him for the walk home. This book beautifully captures the essence of the preschool child, who needs to step away but simultaneously needs to know that he or she can always come back and the parent will be there, just when a helping hand is needed.

205. Worth, Richard. *The American Family.* Photos by Robert Sefcik. New York: Watts, 1984. 128 pp. Nonfiction.

Interest level: Age 12+ Reading level: Grade 6

An overview of the American family—where it's been, where it is now, and its future. Covered are the history of families in this country, with particularly interesting colonial material. The twentieth century is covered in most depth, with the sexual revolution and women's movement being important aspects of family change. Worth involves the reader in various personality tests, for example, a test for marriage readiness. The family at various stages is a focus of much of the book—before marriage, early marriage, getting ready to be parents. Then young parenthood, being parents of adolescents, and being parents of grown children who then begin families of their own.

Photos show families of varied races. In keeping with today's times, there is a helpful chapter on divorce, enumerating common causes and investigating how it feels for children at various ages. "Among older children—between ages 6 and 12—guilt feelings are far less common. Yet these children commonly share with their younger brothers and sisters a deep sadness when a parent departs, as well as an intense loneliness." Interestingly, Worth also lets young readers in on what the divorce feels like for the parents. An entire chapter is delegated to the single-parent family, another to a death in the family.

In point of view this is a book for adults as well as teens. Bibliography (addresses adults as well as children).

Leaving Home

206. Alexander, Sue. *Dear Phoebe.* Illus. by Eileen Christelow. Boston: Little, 1984. 32 pp. Fiction.

Interest level: Age 9+ Reading level: Grade 3

It's time for Phoebe Dormouse to leave home and be out on her own. She and her mother outwardly pretend that everything is just fine. They hide their true feelings from each other, but both are actually very anxious and unhappy about this move. Once Phoebe is in her own place, they miss each other very much, but keep up the pretense that nothing is wrong. They write cheerful letters to each other until in one letter Phoebe's mother confesses that she misses her daughter. This admission helps Phoebe to feel better about being away from her mother and she can now look forward to visiting her in the spring. This book is in picture-book format and appears to be aimed at a young audience. But it really concerns the older teenager's issue of leaving home and living independently. Perhaps the author wants to prepare youngsters for their impending move far in the future, or perhaps she wants younger siblings to understand the fears and feelings of their older, more independent family members.

The text and illustrations are well crafted, but certainly too simplified to be of great use to a young person now in the main character's shoes. The story might also be used to show how important it is for people to communicate their true feelings to each other, and in that case, as a story about two characters, it would be appropriate for its young audience.

207. Angell, Judie. *One-Way to Ansonia.* New York: Bradbury, 1985; Berkley-Pacer, pap. 183 pp. Fiction.

Interest level: Age 11+ Reading level: Grade 6

This story conveys an authentic sense of the hardships and life-style of some of the poor immigrant Russian Jews on New York City's Lower East Side at the turn of the century. Far from romanticizing the poverty-stricken, crowded, dehumanizing environment where children were expected to work to help support the family and where people jammed themselves, their families, and their friends into small tenement apartments, this book introduces us to the reality of the situation. Angell also does not fall into the trap of idealizing the people. Although we meet kindness, honesty, and intelligence, we also note the weaknesses and selfishness of many of the characters.

The story's protagonist is Rose Olshansky, who, at eight years of age, was sent to earn money as a housekeeper, and was known as "The best housekeeper in Neschviz." At the beginning of the book, she and her three sisters and brothers have just arrived from their small village in Russia to join their father, Moshe, in America. He is something of a scoundrel, having married two women in Russia since his wife died three years earlier. Having divorced neither of them, he is now getting married again, on the very day that his children arrive. He keeps them a secret from his new wife, Mume, until after the wedding. Then, when he tells her about the children, she firmly informs him that there is room for only the youngest girl, Celia. The others will have to find other places to live. Moshe appeals to all of his landsmen at the wedding, extolling his children's virtues. He manages to find beds for all of them but his son, Meyer, who has to sleep in a stable with the peddler's horse.

The children know their father's faults, yet they obey him unquestioningly and they love him. To his credit, he responds appropriately when Rose comes to him and lets him know that the father of the family she is staying with has tried to molest her. He immediately arranges for her to be placed in another home. Although she now has to share a bed with her sister, she finds it more palatable, and manages to maintain her energy and thirst for knowledge. She attends night school, learning English and math, works during the day, and does piecework at night and on weekends. She gives her father most of her money, as do the other children. It is not until several years later, when he tries to arrange a marriage for Rose that she does not find appealing, that she disobeys him, and instead, at age 14, marries Hyman Rogoff, a young man whom she has been dating.

The story contains many details of the tragedies of the era. One of Rose's dearest friends is killed accidentally by a policeman because she happened to be observing a labor dispute. Women die from bearing too many children and not having the proper nourishment. But there is also the more positive side of their existence: the parties where they meet together as a community, the excitement of the new wave of unionism, the genuine opportunity for education and advancement, the maintaining of certain of the old and cherished rituals, and the fact that they are free from the terror of the pogroms.

At the end of the story, Rose leaves her husband, her father and siblings, and her friends. She takes her infant with her and buys a one-way ticket to Ansonia, Connecticut. She plans to find work and send for her husband when they can be assured of some financial security. Hyman never attempts to stop her; in fact, he recognizes that this spirit is what he loves in her. The reader must wait for a sequel to see what happens.

In this story the author provides us with the many facets of leaving home. The heroic act of coming from Russia to America without knowing what awaited them was a common experience for many immigrants. Once they arrived in New York it was difficult for them to go further, and it was not until the second and third generation that people began to feel that they had freedom of movement. But Rose, in this story, is determined to make a better life for herself. Some of the questions readers are sure to ask concern the people she leaves behind. How will they communicate with each other? What will happen to Rose and her child in a place where there are few, if any, Jews, let alone immigrants? What is the reader's judgment of Rose's action? This book is certain to spark much research, discussion, and interest.

208. Carey, Mary. *A Place for Allie.* New York: Dodd, 1985. 250 pp. Fiction.
Interest level: Age 11+ Reading level: Grade 6

It is the turn of the century, and the story begins in Nova Scotia. Allie and her sister, Gertrude, are happy and active girls who adore their father, love their mother, and feel secure in the midst of their extended family. But the year that Allie is 12 and Gertrude is 9 their father is killed in a boating accident and their lives change completely. Their mother cannot abide remaining with her husband's family in her husband's country. She moves with her daughters to her sister's apartment in Boston, and the two girls enter a new school there.

The school is a disaster. Children are cruel to the two sisters, and Gertrude is constantly harassed by a bully. Their only friend is Rosa, whose

Italian heritage makes her the butt of the other children's jibes. Schoolwork is dull and focuses on American history, with which the girls are unfamiliar.

Their Aunt Susan is a sympathetic listener, and she is their only comfort. Their mother is withdrawn and unhappy until she finds a position 50 miles away as a housekeeper and cook for a wealthy man. She plans to place the girls in a Catholic Academy, and this is fine with them, until Rosa's aunt requests that Allie be permitted to come and live with her. To the girls' and Susan's dismay, their mother consents, because she thinks that Allie will have a wonderful opportunity.

In order to escape separation, Allie and Gertrude run away to their grandmother's house in Nova Scotia. When their mother comes to claim them the family arranges that Allie and Gertrude will, after all, go to the Academy, and they will come home to Nova Scotia for the summers. The arrangement is a satisfactory one for everyone.

Many issues are uncovered in this book. The mother's reaction to her husband's death is to reject and resent all things that relate to her life with her husband. She is a bitter and ungiving person. She has not gotten past the denial and anger stage of mourning. The girls, on the other hand, grieve for their father, but they go on with their lives, as they know he would have wished. The themes of adjustment to a new school, coming to terms with loss, and running away are also handled in a thoughtful and helpful manner. The story moves quickly. The characters are all three-dimensional and the author weaves them skillfully into the plot.

209. Geras, Adele. *Voyage*. New York: Atheneum, 1983. 193 pp. Fiction.
Interest level: Age 10+ Reading level: Grade 5

Mina is a spirited young woman, just entering adolescence. She has many burdens to shoulder: She, her mother, and her young brother, Eli, are on a ship journeying from eastern Europe. They are traveling in steerage along with hundreds of other passengers, all of them too poor to pay for better passage, all of them pinning their hopes on what they will find in America.

We become familiar with a number of these passengers: Clara, a wise and brave old woman; Mr. Kaminsky, an old man who has seen his family and friends destroyed in a pogrom, and who no longer wants to live; Mrs. Katz and her son, Yankel, two nasty, selfish, small-minded characters; and several young men and women, all of whom we come to know and respond to. We learn about the past history of some of the characters; we become familiar with their hopes, fears, virtues, and flaws.

In all, it is a moving story of the displacement of people and their eventual accommodation to a new place and a new society. It is also the story of coping with such massive losses as death and the devastation of persecution. Geras is a gifted writer whose books are all well worth reading, and who has much to say through her stories and characters.

210. Goble, Paul. *Her Seven Brothers.* New York: Bradbury, 1988. 32 pp. Fiction.

Interest level: Ages 9–12 Reading level: Grade 4

Although Goble was born in Haslemere, England, he has made the art and culture of the Plains Indians his life's interest and work. He is an adopted member of the Yakima and Oglala Sioux tribes and he now resides in the Black Hills of South Dakota. His well-known books, among them *The Girl Who Loved Wild Horses* (Bradbury, 1978), *Star Boy* (Bradbury, 1983), and *Buffalo Woman* (Bradbury, 1984), all respectfully and authentically reveal to children the culture of these native-American nations.

In this story a young woman who is gifted at embroidering beautiful designs into clothing finds herself impelled to sew and embroider seven sets of men's clothing. She explains that there are seven brothers who live in a faraway land, and she must go to them and make them her brothers. Her mother accompanies her on part of her journey, but at a certain point the young woman sends her mother home and continues by herself. Her mother and father are saddened by the knowledge that they will not see their daughter again, but they know that it has been ordained that she go alone on this journey toward her own independence.

The young woman and her adopted brothers live contentedly together for a while, until the chief of the Buffalo Nation demands that the young woman be surrendered to him. When the brothers and the young woman refuse, and the Buffalo Nation comes stampeding after them to claim her, the brothers and sister escape to the sky where they can now be seen as the Big Bear constellation.

The symbolic leaving of the home that the young woman in the story undertakes is the same in any culture. It is always a wrench when a young person is ready to become independent, and there are always fears that contact will be lost. The way is paved with dangers that must be overcome. Sometimes a tragedy is transformed into a triumph, and sometimes the outcome is less dramatic. But it is important for children of any culture to acknowledge that there are universal anxieties and events that are part of the human condition.

The Sioux designs are faithfully and aesthetically rendered in this dramatically beautiful book.

211. Lasky, Kathryn. *Beyond the Divide.* New York: Macmillan, 1983. 254 pp. Fiction.

Interest level: Age 12+ Reading level: Grade 7

Meribah Simon chooses to join her father, Will, who has been excommunicated by the Amish community, in his westward journey. The story tells of the hardships and vicissitudes of the wagon train in its attempt to reach California. But the story tells far more: It is the story of Meribah's strength of character and personal courage, and her anger at injustice; it is a portrait of the values and attitudes of nineteenth-century America; and it is a tale of tragedy and survival.

Meribah, like her gentle father, finds the punitive, restrictive, and rigid atmosphere of their Amish community stifling. She and her father are disappointed to find the same sorts of attitudes prevalent among their fellow pioneers. When times grow difficult, Meribah sees "civilized" people who are quick to criticize low-class behavior performing acts of cruelty and cowardice. Until the Great Divide, there is a sharing of food and labor, and spirits are high. But once these mountains loom they are not only a physical barrier, but the symbolic separation of what is veneer from what is real among the travelers.

Rape, death, selfishness, theft, and wanton destruction as well as illness, abandonment, and broken promises are part of their everyday existence now. Finally, when Meribah's father becomes very ill, and he and Meribah lose one of their oxen and most of their wagon in a landslide, they are heartlessly abandoned by the consensus of the group.

Death and the loss of friendship and loved ones are important themes in this book. Death becomes more and more familiar to Meribah and then, alone, she experiences the death of her father. It is then that she understands the words spoken by another pioneer who died, "Dying is horrible, death is not." Eventually, in order to prevent her own rape, she kills a man.

The book describes how Native Americans are designated as savages by the emigrants. Will helps Meribah to understand their plight, and George Goodenough, an artist, vividly describes to her the inhumane treatment of the Native Americans by the white settlers. Meribah's personal experience provides her with her own basis for respecting this group of people. She is adopted into the Yahi tribe after they save her life.

Despite all her ordeals, the book ends hopefully for Meribah. She discovers who she is and what she wants. *Beyond the Divide* is a useful book for young readers. It raises issues of separation from cultural background, it critically examines the pioneer experience for those who might otherwise over-romanticize this period of American history, and it brings an understanding of the pain of dying and the possibility of coping with death.

212. Levitin, Sonia. *The Return.* New York: Atheneum, 1987. 213 pp. Fiction.

Interest level: Age 12+ Reading level: Grade 7

It is unusual to find the topic of Ethiopian Jews in a book for young readers. This story tells of a rescue mission called Operation Moses, in which thousands of Ethiopian Jews were airlifted secretly from the Sudan to Israel during a brief six-month period in 1984–1985. The Ethiopian Jews are persecuted in their own country and called Falashas, which means "stranger."

The story tells of three siblings who leave their home to find religious freedom in Israel: Desta, her brother, Joas, who is killed before they arrive at their destination, and their younger sister, Almaz. It is at Joas's insistence that Desta consents to leave her beloved homeland and her extended family. But after Joas is killed, Desta assumes leadership and protects her younger sister on their strenuous journey.

Levitin skillfully blends factual information with story so that the effect is one of a true-to-life adventure that instructs and inspires the reader. The characters seem drawn from life, and the fact that this is based on a true event makes the book all the more compelling.

213. Meyer, Carolyn. *Denny's Tapes*. New York: McElderry, 1987. 209 pp. Fiction.

Interest level: Age 13+ Reading level: Grade 8

The story revolves around 17-year-old Denny, who leaves his mother and stepfather's house because his stepfather has called him a black bastard. Denny and his stepsister, Stephanie, have become involved with each other. Denny's father is black, and Denny has been raised in a white world. Now he goes cross-country to find his father. On the way he stops off at both his grandparents' homes. He connects with his heritage, and when he arrives at his father's house, even though his father is away and will not return for a couple of months, he decides that he will go to school to be a musician like his father.

The book brings up not only the usual identity and coming-of-age problems of adolescence, but also the special problems of this biracial young man. The author has not succeeded in bringing the level of the book beyond the particular, and we really don't get to know any of the characters very well. But the story moves quite quickly, and the main character is an engaging young man. In addition, the topic will probably stimulate thought and discussion on the part of young readers.

214. Murrow, Liza Ketchum. *West Against the Wind*. New York: Holiday, 1987. 232 pp. Fiction.

Interest level: Age 10+ Reading level: Grade 6

Abby and her family are journeying westward in a wagon train, hoping to rejoin her father, who has gone on ahead to pan for gold. Now he sees great promise in the new land and has urged his family, including his brother, to come and settle in the West. The group takes on Matthew as a hired hand to help with the driving of the wagons and with the chores. Matthew, whose father was killed in a fight, is a mysterious but attractive young man. The wagon train encounters many hardships and tragedies along the way. Abby recounts the details of their journey in a series of letters to her sister, which she accumulates in a diary. Her strength of will and her determination to reach her father carry the rest of her family through the hard times.

The story is one of survival and determination rather than one of homelessness. Throughout the book the importance of family and loyalty are stressed. The spirit of the young woman is an inspiration.

215. Turnbull, Ann. *Maroo of the Winter Caves.* New York: Clarion, 1984. 136 pp. Fiction.

Interest level: Ages 9–12 Reading level: Grades 4–5

The unusual setting for this book is Europe at the end of the last Ice Age, more than 25,000 years ago. Maroo, a young girl of the Madeleine people, is called on to bring help to her family, who are trapped in the mountain snows. Her father has been killed while hunting for meat, and she and her brother are sent across the mountain passes as a last resort to save the starving family. The story then tells of how Maroo succeeds in her quest.

The culture of the cave people is communicated well in this book. Maroo is a heroine of any age, but the setting seems to be an authentic backdrop for her adventure. Her father's death is a terrible loss that she must overcome through her own strength and fortitude. Her success is believable because the author has built up an image of Maroo as a competent and courageous young woman, even before it was necessary for her to embark on this journey. Interesting details about the life of these early people enliven the story even further.

216. Yep, Laurence. *The Serpent's Children.* New York: Harper, 1984. 277 pp. Fiction.

Interest level: Age 12+ Reading level: Grade 7

Yep tells us that his original intent in writing this story was to discover his identity as a Chinese person. In the unraveling of the complex plot he presents to his audience an image of the complexity of the Chinese people, and a glimpse into their history, not only in their own land, but also here, in America.

The story revolves around one family, whose father has been absent for a long time, fighting to keep his country, China, safe from the British invaders. When he returns to his home in the Kwangtung province, he finds that his wife has died, and his two children, Cassia and Foxfire, are struggling to maintain themselves.

The hardships and fighting have injured the father, and Foxfire does not agree with his father's devotion to what Foxfire thinks is an outmoded cause. He decries the poverty of their land, and holds out no hope for it. His father disowns him, so he leaves home and travels to San Francisco.

It is clear that war and changing times have made life very different for the Chinese people. The father acknowledges that his children will face a new set of challenges in a new way. He forgives his son for differing with him, and lets Cassia know that he appreciates her contributions. Although Foxfire sends money from America, and Cassia remains with her father, the reader understands that all of them have a hard road ahead. Their salvation lies in the fact that they are a coherent family unit, and therein lies their strength.

Yep's writing provides access to a complicated and tradition-laden society. The aspects of the deprivation of war and poverty are universal, as are the characters' feelings and interactions. But the special qualities of the Chinese society that he describes are communicated clearly and with passion.

Old Age

217. Auch, Mary Jane. *Cry Uncle!* New York: Holiday, 1987. 212 pp. Fiction.

Interest level: Ages 9–12 Reading level: Grade 4

Davey is the narrator of this story. He and his family have recently moved from the city to a farm. Everyone except their mother hates it, and to make matters worse, Davey is menaced by a bullying set of twins. He and his brother don't get along, either. The last straw is when his mother's seemingly senile uncle must auction off his farm and is invited to come and live with Davey's family.

All the problems except the move to the country are worked out. Uncle Will finds a sympathetic and loving woman who wants to marry him; Davey figures out a way to stop the twins from menacing him; even his older brother, Brad, comes around and helps find Uncle Will when he is lost in the woods. But the mother is still an inept farmer and cook, and it looks as if neither the mother nor the father have very good decision-making skills.

In general, the story is well intentioned and good-humored. But the author seems to have little respect for several of her characters, most especially the mother. Although the mother is good-hearted and well meaning, she is incompetent in just about everything she tries. Much of the humor of the book is at her expense, although it is clear that everyone loves her. The father is a nonentity who permits his life to be run for him. The older brother is a nasty person who finally becomes more sympathetic when he grudgingly joins in the hunt for the old man. Davey, the protagonist, is a likable 11-year-old who seems wiser than the adults.

Despite its flaws, the resolution of the plot is satisfying, and Davey is a character with whom many children can identify. The treatment of the old man is somewhat confusing: His erratic behavior is attributed to the fact that his brother died and he lost his farm. Hope is expressed that with his marriage he will completely recover. He is a colorful, knowledgeable, and lovable character.

218. Berenstain, Stan, and Berenstain, Jan. *The Berenstain Bears and the Week at Grandma's.* Illus. by the authors. New York: Random, 1986, pap. 32 pp. Fiction.

Interest level: Ages 4–8 Reading level: Grade 3

Although the Bear cubs love their grandma and grandpa, they are anxious about the idea of spending a whole week with them while their mother and father go off on a second honeymoon. The cubs are pleasantly surprised when their grandparents prove to be able to entertain them wonderfully well. They go fishing and dancing; they build ships in bottles and feed birds; they play with yo-yos and jacks. The Bear cubs are very impressed with the abilities of their grandparents. When their parents return, the cubs are already eagerly discussing a possible third honeymoon, so that they can visit their grandparents again.

This little story certainly confirms the ability of aged people to be interesting and full of life. It is somewhat strange that the cubs had never visited their grandparents before this; the house was unfamiliar to them, and they acted as if they did not really know their grandparents. But all in all, the book is a useful one for allaying children's fears about being left by their parents for a short period of time, especially with grandparents. It can also serve as a discussion starter on the characteristics and capabilities of the elderly.

219. Clifford, Eth. *The Remembering Box.* Illus. by Donna Diamond. Boston: Houghton Mifflin, 1985. 70 pp. Fiction.

Interest level: Ages 7–10 Reading level: Grades 3–4

Grandma Goldina often cries tears of remembrance when she tells Joshua stories of the olden days sparked by the treasures in her remembering box. From the time he was five years old, Joshua has gone to visit his grandmother. He is now 10, and he promises he will visit her until he grows old. They have a special relationship that does not end when the grandmother dies. This tender story has much to offer young readers. It is a story of love, growing old, valuing one's heritage, and wisdom. Diamond's realistic drawings enhance the flavorful text.

220. Coutant, Helen. *The Gift.* Illus. by Vo-Dinh Mai. New York: Knopf, 1983. 48 pp. Fiction.

Interest level: Ages 7–10 Reading level: Grade 3

Anna, a shy young girl, moves into a new town and befriends Nana Marie, an old woman who has also recently moved here to live with her son and daughter-in-law. Anna and Nana Marie have lengthy conversations and see each other every day. When Anna finds her friend absent from the house one day she fears that Nana Marie has been taken to a nursing home and that she will never see her again. Instead, it turns out that Nana Marie has been in the hospital with some mysterious illness that has left her blind.

When Anna discovers the news of her friend's blindness she is devastated and spends the rest of the day trying to think of an appropriate gift to bring to her friend. She finally decides to bring her a complete and detailed description of her day as Nana Marie has taught her to see it. In essence, she is continuing to bring Nana Marie the priceless gift of friendship.

The story reminds us that friendship knows no age barriers, and that old and young people can contribute to each other's happiness just as importantly as people the same age can. It is unfortunate that Nana Marie's family did not think about informing Anna of her friend's hospitalization. The temporary separation could have been made easier for both friends had Anna been told earlier.

221. Fosburgh, Liza. *Mrs. Abercorn and the Bunce Boys.* Illus. by Julie Downing. New York: Four Winds, 1986. 115 pp. Fiction.

Interest level: Age 10+ Reading level: Grade 6

Otis and his older brother, Will, are close friends. They understand each other and are always in each other's company. Ever since their father died of cancer, and Bink, a beer-drinking construction worker, moved in with their mother and them, they have been unhappy and unsure of their mother's deep concern.

Bink has found a construction job in the Berkshires, so they all go there from their home in Ohio. The boys are at odds and lonely because their mother has taken a waitressing job. They are fortunate to meet Mrs. Abercorn, a lusty, hardy, fast-driving old woman who has made a good living as a mystery book writer, and who opens her home and heart to the two boys. She teaches them to fish, lends them books, and takes them places. They spend every day together and grow to love each other. Mrs.

Abercorn's son and grandson never come to see her; they are waiting to inherit her money. But she understands enough about human beings to help the boys see their mother and Bink in a more sympathetic light, and to help them deal with their father's death. At the end of the summer, when the boys must return home to Ohio, they leave their cherished puppy with Mrs. Abercorn.

The book is very well written. The characters are appealing and three-dimensional. Their situation is realistic. There is much to be learned from each of the incidents that the boys and Mrs. Abercorn encounter, and the author builds each of their characters so that as the book progresses we get to know and like each of them more and more. It is to be hoped that we hear more about the boys and Mrs. Abercorn.

222. Fox, Mem. *Wilfrid Gordon McDonald Partridge.* Illus. by Julie Vivas. New York: Kane/Miller, 1985. 32 pp. Fiction.

Interest level: Ages 5–9 Reading level: Grade 2

Wilfrid Gordon McDonald Partridge lives next door to an old people's home and knows everyone who lives there, having an individual relationship with each, but his favorite is Miss Nancy Alison Delacourt Cooper. He likes her best because she has four names, as does he. To Miss Nancy he tells all his secrets. She's a good choice—she can't tell, because she can't remember. But his parents feel sorry for her for losing her memory, so Wilfrid tries to find out just what a memory is. The old folks give him varied definitions, from something that makes you cry, to something that makes you laugh. Wilfrid then searches for memories to give Miss Nancy, because she's lost her own. Finding objects that would match each definition, he brings her a basket of things. And they do spark memories, mostly from long ago.

This beautifully illustrated, respectful, touching book doesn't offer miracles, only little pieces of help along lines that can actually take place. Highly recommended.

223. Hewett, Joan. *Rosalie.* Illus. by Donald Carrick. New York: Lothrop, 1987. 32 pp. Fiction.

Interest level: Ages 7–10 Reading level: Grade 2

Rosalie is an old dog, almost 100 years old by human standards. Although she is slow and infirm, she is still loved and appreciated by her human owners. Every member of the family values her and does whatever is possible to keep her happy. This is a lovely model for human behavior to humans as well as to animals. The fact that the dog is still alive at the end of the book is a plus. Too often, children see only that the elderly die, not that they are cherished while still alive.

224. Hickman, Martha Whitmore. *When James Allen Whitaker's Grandfather Came to Stay*. Illus. by Ron Hester. Nashville: Abingdon, 1985. 48 pp. Fiction.

Interest level: Ages 4–9 Reading level: Grade 3

After James Allen's grandmother dies, his grandfather comes from Massachusetts to North Carolina to stay with James Allen's family. He is a wonderful old man who keeps busy and is genuinely helpful. He detects when his daughter, James Allen's mother, is being patronizing or overly solicitous, and he puts things into context for everyone. Even though he tries to make the best of it, he misses his home dreadfully. And, perhaps even more, he misses his independence.

The grandfather lovingly builds a birdhouse that is a replica of his house in Massachusetts, and when it is completed he presents it to James Allen and his parents, and informs them that he is returning to his home. He has made arrangements to have renters stay there with him so he won't be alone, and he invites his family to spend summers with him. His decision is based on his own needs, and he is caring and firm about it. There is no acrimony, but there is the ability to face the situation with dispassion and clarity.

The grandfather is an excellent model of a senior citizen who is not senile or infirm, but is temporarily displaced because of the loss of his lifelong partner. It is clear that his decision is a good one, and that his life will continue to be a fulfilling and active one.

225. Khalsa, Dayal Kaur. *Tales of a Gambling Grandma.* Illus. by the author. New York: Potter, 1986. 32 pp. Fiction.

Interest level: Ages 7–10 Reading level: Grade 3

The author–illustrator has given young readers a colorful story about her grandmother and their special relationship. Her grandmother emigrated from Russia as a very young girl and settled in Brooklyn. She married a plumber and had two children. In order to supplement their income Grandma learned to play poker. She won by marking the cards and hiding aces up her sleeve. In later years, after the death of her husband, Grandma moved into her daughter's house in Queens. This coincided with the birth of her granddaughter, Dayal (the author). Because both of her parents worked outside the house, the girl and her grandmother were always together.

Grandma's activities included sitting and knitting; telling stories; giving advice; and taking her granddaughter to Coney Island, vaudeville shows, movies, Chinese restaurants, and the Sunshine Ladies Card Club, a gambling club for the local elderly women. She also taught her granddaughter how to play poker. One day when Dayal came home from school, her grandmother was ill. Then she died, leaving the young girl with her memories of a vibrant woman and a special relationship.

The beautiful color illustrations lend a kind of fairy-tale quality to the book. This is appropriate because the reader gets the sense that the grandmother was an accomplished weaver of tales, and that the book is somewhere between fiction and nonfiction and, therefore, a fitting tribute to this vibrant, warm, loving, strong-willed, and nonstereotypical woman.

226. Landau, Elaine. *Growing Old in America.* Photos. New York: Messner, 1985. 148 pp. Nonfiction.

Interest level: Ages 11–15 Reading level: Grades 5–6

The usual statistics are here, but some unusual ones, too, such as polls that show senior citizens have more self-esteem than is usually assumed. The challenges of retirement are elucidated and a typical day at an active senior center is given account. The pros and cons of living in an adult community are explored. The medical, financial, and legal sides of having an aging population in the United States are topics for individual chapters, citing present laws and customs, model programs, and varied possibilities for the future. There is interesting material on aging in other cultures, the Israeli kibbutzim, France, and Japan among them. Individual profiles of older people's opinions and strategies for handling the aging process are very illuminating. The approach or attitude is summed up in a chapter subtitled, "A Time to Grow." Some of the photographs are interesting, for example, a white-haired woman, suitably togged, taking a martial arts pose and carrying a book entitled *Karate Self-Taught.* Bibliography.

227. Leiner, Katherine. *Between Old Friends.* Photos by Michael H. Arthur. New York: Watts, 1987. 32 pp. Nonfiction.

Interest level: Ages 5–9 Reading level: Grade 2

In four separate stories, children tell of their friendships with older people. Among them is a girl who meets her neighbor when her family runs a garage sale. As it turns out, he buys and sells books, and they have a lot in common. He is a philosopher on growing older: "It's like when a book gets old, your pages yellow a little and your cover fades, but you still know what you know and want to share it with an old friend." The emphasis in this book is on activities together—a girl meets a fellow violin player on the bus, and a boy comes to terms with his grandmother's participating in what seems to him an unseemly activity, creating a city garden. By the end of their profile, the boy participates as well.

228. LeShan, Eda. *Grandparents: A Special Kind of Love.* Illus. by Tricia Taggart. New York: Macmillan, 1984. 128 pp. Nonfiction.

Interest level: Ages 8–13 Reading level: Grade 4

Encouraging understanding between grandchildren and grandparents, LeShan tells why grandparents are so pleased to be such—it's a second chance to try to be a good parent, the family is continuing, they don't have to worry as much and are less insecure than they were as parents, and they don't have to teach as much. "All they have to do is love you." Yet, LeShan notes, even such special love can be complicated, because no matter what the age, we are all different and we have different moods.

LeShan helps children understand that grandparents may be different from their grandchildren because of the times they grew up in, those times perhaps being less casual and more restricted in terms of personal honesty. Through this book, children can also come to see their grandparents as continuing their parental role, and they can learn about how the history of the extended family affects them as children. Traits that are good and bad in grandparents are discussed, for example, when a grandparent boasts about a grandchild, it can either be gratifying or mortifying, perhaps even both at the same time! The author encourages oral biography and history, investigating how the world was when the grandparents were children. She also encourages time alone for each grandchild with a grandparent and gives children the words to ask for these things.

Special situations are dealt with in the same understanding manner: living together in an extended family; when grandparents are strangers; when a grandparent is kept away from a grandchild; grandparents' rights; when there are more than four grandparents because of remarriage; when relationships are unhappy between grandparent, parent, and/or grandchild; when a grandparent changes because of illness; and when a grandparent dies, including ways to remember the good and bad in order to hold onto the whole person. This is a valuable book drawn from the author's experience as a new grandmother and her memories of being a beloved grandchild.

229. Lloyd, David. *Grandma and the Pirate.* Illus. by Gill Tomblin. New York: Crown, 1985. 26 pp. Fiction.

Interest level: Ages 5–8 Reading level: Grades 1–2

Robert spends an idyllic day at the beach with his grandmother. She participates actively in his games and is an enthusiastic partner in his fantasies. She is a model of a fully capable person who is in her late middle years. The illustrations reinforce the message of the book: This is no extraordinary person; this is a woman who is not beautiful or svelte, but a person who is shining with health and love for her grandson and for life.

230. Skorpen, Liesel Moak. *Grace.* New York: Harper, 1984. 87 pp. Fiction.

Interest level: Ages 9–12 Reading level: Grade 5

Sara is suffering from loneliness. Her friends have all progressed into a stage that Sara is not yet ready for. She feels isolated and alienated, not only from her peers, but also from her family. She meets Amy, whose mother has run off, and who is contemptuous of all things conventional. Under Amy's influence, Sara participates in rude behavior to Grace, an old, senile woman who lives alone next door to Sara's family.

Not until Sara is forced by her parents to apologize to Grace does Sara realize how lonely and afraid the old woman is. Sara befriends her throughout the summer. She visits the old woman regularly and promises to keep secret the fact that she is ill and almost helpless. In turn, Grace teaches Sara some old songs and serves as a friend to the lonely girl. Grace is terrified of dying in an institution; she wants to die in her own bed in her own house. At the end of the summer she has her wish, and she bequeaths to Sara her Bible, her hymns, her Grimms Fairy Tales, and the pearl her father gave her for her wedding day.

After Grace's death, Sara can make contact with her old friends again, and determines to tell her parents about her experience with Grace. Sara has come of age.

The story is written in a style that is spare but flavorful. The reader is invited to fill in some of the details, but the implications and tone are sufficient to carry the story. Both Grace and Sara are characters who will stay with the reader after the book is ended.

231. Smith, Robert Kimmel. *The War with Grandpa.* Illus. by Richard Lauter. New York: Delacorte, 1984; Dell, pap. 140 pp. Fiction.

Interest level: Ages 9–12 Reading level: Grades 3–4

Peter's grandfather is still grieving over the death of his wife. His daughter, Peter's mother, invites him to come and live with them, and he accepts. The problem is that he will be taking over Peter's room, and Peter will have to use the upstairs guest room. Peter is unhappy and furious over the arrangements, and he decides, on the advice of a couple of his friends, to engage in warfare with his grandfather until he regains his old room.

At first Peter's grandfather is sedentary and spiritless. Then, after Peter has played some tricks on him and let him know about the war, Peter's grandfather perks up and engages in as many dirty tricks as Peter does. He actually seems to gather strength from the battle of wits. Eventually, Peter capitulates because he realizes that he has gone too far, and he and his grandfather figure out a solution that is acceptable to everyone.

One of the messages that is conveyed by this essentially good-natured and amusing story is that it is important to communicate your feelings. Another is that the elderly are happier when they have something to occupy their energies; they wither away when they feel useless. Despite the potentially silly situation, the author never loses respect for his characters. They may be mischievous and self-centered, even stubborn, but they are not demeaning or dehumanized.

232. Worth, Richard. *You'll Be Old Someday, Too.* Photos. New York: Watts, 1986. 128 pp. Nonfiction.
    Interest level: Age 11+ Reading level: Grade 6

Worth has a dual purpose: first, to present a realistic picture of the condition of old people in American society; second, to start each of us thinking about the question "What kind of old age will I have?" To accomplish his goals, Worth examines Americans' history, attitudes, and points of view. He interviews numerous people, both the well-known and not-so-well-known. For Worth, old age presents an occasion "to pause and look back—to sum up and gain perspective on life."

Worth offers statistics of the elderly and their economic conditions, physical aspects of aging, and health care and death-related issues. His voice is present in the accounts, for example, "I visited . . . ." He points up model programs, such as peer support counseling, and coordinated efforts between the young and old such as pen pal programs and visitations. Other notions to consider include life-care facilities, phased retirement, and retirement villages (complete with an amazing aerial photograph of Sun City, Arizona). There is also in-depth attention to the family, looking at the elderly as relatives—parents and grandparents.

Perhaps the most compelling aspect of the book is the examination of what Worth calls the "ageless ones." These are men and women whose lives and talents seem untouched by time, people who are creative until their deaths. The detailed profiles of such people may serve to inspire. Subjects include Benjamin Franklin and Margaret Mead, and in the same chapter, Worth includes other less famous people who meet the same criteria, showing you don't have to be a genius to live well throughout life.

7

Coping with Tragic Loss

Death

The death of a significant person in a child's life means that the world will never again be the same. Every role played by that person in the child's life leaves a void. The changes in the youngster's feelings, called bereavement, come about because the child must now redefine existence and continue to grow without the support of that person. One aspect of facing the eventual death of important people in a child's life is the confrontation with the child's own mortality, which may take place even during these early years.

When a child dies, the separation encountered at life's end is the largest of all, for in leaving life, the child departs from everyone and everything that is cherished.

233. Adler, C. S. *Carly's Buck*. New York: Clarion, 1987. 166 pp. Fiction.
Interest level: Age 10+ Reading level: Grades 4–5

Carly's mother has died of cancer, and Carly blames herself and her father for not having been as good to her mother as she thinks they should have been. Carly asks to leave her father after her mother dies. She goes to stay with her aunt, her father's younger sister. Carly's home is in California; her aunt and uncle live in the Adirondack region of New York.

When Carly starts attending the school near her aunt's home, she finds, to her surprise, that she is having trouble making friends. She has always been a gregarious and popular girl, and she is puzzled and disturbed by her lack of success. She also refuses to have anything to do with her father, although she recognizes that she still loves him. She feels that his cold-hearted treatment of her mother is too great a sin for her to forgive. At last, with the help of her friends and her aunt and uncle, she decides to change her style of interacting with her peers, and she can begin again to build a relationship with her father.

One factor that helps Carly to change her ways is her preoccupation with a deer, which she hopes to save from a hunter's bullet. The father of her closest friend accidentally kills the buck, and Carly must cope with her own anger and grief over the loss of the buck. Her friend helps her to see her father and herself in a different light, and the pain that has engulfed Carly for so long starts to recede.

Deer lore was carefully researched by the author, and its authenticity is one of the book's excellent qualities. Carly's pain over her perceived failure to be good enough to her mother is palpably described. We feel with Carly her guilt, and her disappointment and anger at her father. We also become involved enough with her to hope fervently that she will be able somehow to resolve her feelings and come to terms with her pain and self-hatred. Adler accomplishes these aims masterfully and engagingly. The book is a welcome addition to the literature on mourning and coping with the death of a loved one.

234. Alexander, Sue. *Nadia the Willful.* Illus. by Lloyd Bloom. New York: Pantheon, 1983. 46 pp. Fiction.
Interest level: Ages 7–10 Reading level: Grades 3–4

Nadia, a feisty Bedouin girl who is called Nadia the Willful because of her stubbornness, is bereft when her father decrees that the name of his dead son, her brother, Hamed, must not be spoken. Nadia's father, the Sheik Tarik, is known as a kind and good man, but he cannot face the reality of his son's death, and he does not understand that silence prolongs grief.

At first Nadia unwittingly mentions Hamed's name, because she notices that her brothers are making errors when they play the games that Hamed taught them. Nadia reminds them of the right way. She then moves on to share with the women, as they sit at their looms, the stories that Hamed told her. Once she begins, Nadia cannot stop. She goes all over the camp, talking with everyone about Hamed and her loving memories of him.

One evening, after Tarik has exiled a shepherd who said Hamed's name, Nadia confronts her father. She confesses to him that she has been reminding everyone of Hamed's life, and in so doing has kept his image alive. The sheik is moved and persuaded by her good sense, and he renames her Nadia the Wise. The shepherd is returned to the group, and Hamed is permitted to live again in everyone's heart.

The story is beautifully told, and the pencil drawings by Bloom add dimensions of flavor and emotion.

235. Arnold, Caroline. *What We Do When Someone Dies.* Illus. by Helen K. Davie. New York: Watts, 1987. 32 pp. Nonfiction.
Interest level: Ages 6–10 Reading level: Grade 3

Feelings start the narration, but the author moves quickly into funeral purposes and practices. The current idea of explaining death in terms of machinery that no longer functions is the approach taken in the section "All Living Things Die," and a hefty chunk of information is delivered on each page. For this reason, a care giver may want to explore the book in segments with a child. For example, on two of the pages in the section named above, topics range from ways we die, to the machine analogy, to what ends when death occurs, to life sustenance machinery, to brain death, to organ transplants. Whew!

Another segment is "What Happens to the Body," in which autopsy is discussed, also enbalming, morticians, caskets, funeral homes, and burials. Here, cross-cultural references are made, for example, India and cremation. Life insurance policies are also discussed. This is confusing, because of the picture-book format. Few children will need to know this aspect of the death experience. The third section, "Death Announcements," includes discussion of obituaries, sympathy cards, and visitors. "The Funeral Ceremony" discusses religious services, eulogies, pall bearers, the hearse, and graves. Again, more detail is offered than the age group needs to handle: "Occasionally, a funeral service may be held in one city even though the body may be buried in another city. Then the casket is sent by airplane or train to the other city."

"After the Funeral" covers feelings of mourning, and "Remembering the Dead" deals with memorial services, anniversary commemorations, charity contributions, naming monuments, and visiting grave sites. "What Is a Will?" gives nomenclature such as "executor" and "intestate." "Belief about Death" is again cross-cultural, and the book closes with the universality of death and ways we share our sadness and keep our memories. In summation, the material is certainly accurate. And children do want to know. The question is whether children of picture-book age will want to know this much. Content doesn't seem appropriately wedded to form. With the large, soft watercolors and 32-page format, one will not expect a middle grade, almost preadolescent, investigation of ideas. Index.

236. Avi. *Wolf Rider: A Tale of Terror.* New York: Bradbury, 1986. 202 pp. Fiction.

Interest level: Age 11+ Reading level: Grade 6

Fifteen-year-old Andy receives a phone call from a stranger named Zeke, telling him that Zeke has just killed a girl named Nina Klemmer. Zeke goes on to give specific details about Nina and the murder. Andy and his father have just moved to a new neighborhood, and their phone is not yet listed. Andy's mother died a year ago and there have been a number of deaths in his family, so he is particularly sensitive to the idea of death. Andy reports the call to the police and to his father, all of whom say it was a sick joke. He calls Nina after finding her number in the college phone book and she, too, thinks that it is a prank. Andy does not give up. He contrives to meet Nina and is terrified to discover that she fits the description Zeke gave him over the phone.

Because of Andy's concern, the local police think that he needs counseling and he is required to see the school guidance counselor regularly. The adults think that Andy is having a hard time adjusting to his new neighborhood and the fact that his mother was killed in an automobile accident. Even worse, Andy's father does not believe him, and reacts to Andy's obsession by deciding to send him away to stay with his aunt.

Andy discovers that Zeke is really a professor in the math department and he forms a scheme to catch the potential killer. His scheme works, but Andy is in terrible danger as a result of it. Zeke and Andy have a confrontation, and Zeke is killed in a car crash while trying to kill Andy. Andy has torn a cuff link from Zeke's shirt. He puts it in his pocket. Later, after Andy has been put safely on his flight to his aunt's house, his father, who has found the cuff link and now knows that what his son has told him was true, tearfully deposits the cuff link into a trash barrel. The reader is left to speculate about how this incident will affect the lives and relationship of Andy and his father.

The story is mostly a vehicle for suspense. But within it is the issue of how death affects a survivor, and how important it is to listen carefully to people when they are stressed.

237. Bauer, Marion Dane. *On My Honor*. New York: Clarion, 1986; Dell, pap. 90 pp. Fiction.

Interest level: Age 10+ Reading level: Grades 4–5

A summer afternoon's escapade turns to tragedy when Tony, challenged by Joel to swim in the treacherous Vermillion River, drowns. After desperately and unsuccessfully trying to rescue Tony, Joel is overwhelmed with grief and guilt at the loss of his best friend. He fears telling the truth about the accident to his and Tony's parents. His father has expressly forbidden him to swim in the river. Joel concocts a story that hides his involvement, but he becomes obsessed with his guilt and, at last, confesses.

In this swiftly moving 1987 Newbery Honor book the author explores Joel's dilemma with extraordinary insight and sensitivity. Joel perceives the world as a punitive one. He feels powerless to exercise control over his own behavior when Tony persuades him to disobey their parents' injunctions, and they go on a treacherous bike path. He then feels so frightened at what happened that he conceals the truth. He is angry at Tony for goading him into his behavior, and he is angry at his father for being duped into permitting him and Tony to go on their bicycle trip.

Joel is astounded when his father, on learning the truth, apologizes for misjudging the situation. Although this response alleviates Joel's pain, the reader cannot help but wonder when and how Joel will learn to take responsibility for his own decisions and actions.

238. Bernstein, Joanne E. *Loss: And How to Cope with It.* New York: Clarion, 1977, hb and pap. 160 pp. Nonfiction.

Interest level: Age 10+ Reading level: Grade 7

Brought back into print by popular demand, this book regards life as a series of losses. The author seeks to help young people deal with one of life's most serious losses, the death of a loved one. In order to celebrate existence, loss must be faced, grappled with, and managed. Utilizing research data, personal anecdote, and the opinions of individuals ranging from Shakespeare to Dick Cavett, the following topics are covered: what happens when someone dies, children's concepts of death, feelings of bereavement, living with survivors, handling feelings, the deaths of particular individuals (parent, grandparent, friend, pet, and so on), unusually traumatic death (suicide, war, murder, and so forth), and the legacy of survivors. The author tries to achieve a warm and reassuring manner as she deals with practical issues. Bibliographies of nonfiction and fiction titles treating death are appended, as well as listings of film resources and service organizations. Index.

239. Boyd, Candy Dawson. *Breadsticks and Blessing Places.* New York: Macmillan, 1985. 210 pp. Fiction.

Interest level: Age 10+ Reading level: Grade 4

Toni has two best friends, Susan, who is flighty and fun, and Mattie, who is serious, loyal, and academically minded. Mattie is musically talented, and knows that she must work hard to earn a scholarship to college, because her widowed mother cannot afford to pay tuition. Toni and Mattie want to get accepted to King Academy, an excellent public preparatory school in Chicago. Mattie's parents impress on her the importance of black people's getting a good education.

When Susan is struck down and killed by a drunken driver, Toni is inconsolable. She goes through all of the stages of mourning: She denies that Susan is dead; then she pleads and bargains with God to make her be alive. She is angry at her classmates and her teacher for removing Susan's things from the classroom. She cannot eat or sleep. Mattie helps her to ease her grief by admonishing her to do the hard work of mourning for herself. When Toni conducts her own special funeral service for Susan she is finally ready to come to terms with her grief and set about the business of her own life. At the end of the story both Mattie and Toni are accepted into King Academy.

The book conveys an authenticity, not only of voice but also of character, setting, and situation. The grappling that the characters must do over the death of people dear to them is a model for readers.

240. Boyd, Candy Dawson. *Circle of Gold.* New York: Scholastic, 1984, pap. 124 pp. Fiction.

Interest level: Ages 9–12 Reading level: Grades 4–6

Mattie Benson, an 11-year-old black girl, lives with her mother and her twin brother, Matt. Her father died six months ago in a car accident. From that day on, everything changed in Mattie's life. Her mother is always tired and angry, having lost all interest in anything. Her mother has also had to work two jobs since her husband died. Mattie wants to help her mother and make the family happy again. She does the housework and she baby-sits for extra money. She also works hard in order to win the local newspaper's writing contest on the subject of what your mother means to you. She reasons that if she wins, she can earn enough money to buy a beautiful pin for her mother for Mother's Day. Warm memories about her father help her through every hard time. Her best friend is also a great support. Finally, she wins the contest and buys the pin. Mattie's courage touches her mother deeply and they become a happy family again.

The family's sorrow over their loved one's death and how they try to build a new life as a family are presented sympathetically in this book. The author tells the reader that death can bring gigantic sorrow to a family, but that the other family members can share love among themselves and try to soothe each other. It is unfortunate that so much responsibility is placed on Mattie's shoulders. Why isn't her brother as involved as she in helping out? What sort of relationship do they have with each other? It is not a good idea for a book to continue the myth that only females can be nurturing. Otherwise, the book succeeds in presenting the image of a caring family reacting to a massive loss with strength and dignity.

241. Burningham, John. *Granpa.* Illus. by the author. New York: Crown, 1984. 32 pp. Fiction.

Interest level: Ages 3–8 Reading level: Grade 2

Most of the book explores the loving and active relationship between a little girl and her grandfather. They garden together, play at make-believe, argue, go to the park and the beach, and go fishing and sledding. The grandfather reads to the little girl, tells her stories, and respects her questions and concerns. Then the grandfather gets confined to the house, and, ultimately, we see his empty chair, and a sad and pensive little girl taking her baby sibling for a walk, and we assume that she will pass on to her sibling the love and companionship she enjoyed with her grandfather.

The text is sparse but evocative. The whimsical crayon-and-ink pictures have a spontaneous, expressive line quality and a childlike style full of action and texture. *Granpa* is a loving book to share with young children.

242. Buscaglia, Leo. *The Fall of Freddie the Leaf: A Story of Life for All Ages*. Photos. New York: Slack, 1982. 32 pp. Fiction.

Interest level: Ages 5–10 Reading level: Grade 3

In an anthropomorphic tale, "personhood" acclaimant Buscaglia enters the children's book arena. The leaves on a particular park tree are given names. Freddie, the protagonist, becomes the last leaf left on the tree as fall approaches, but until then he listens to Daniel, the wise leaf, who explains life.

According to Daniel, when you die, you change your home. When Freddie expresses fear of dying, Daniel glibly explains: "We all fear what we don't know. . . . It's natural. . . . Yet, you were not afraid when Spring became Summer. You were not afraid when Summer became Fall. They were natural changes. Why should you be afraid of the season of death?" When Freddie asks about the purpose of life—"Why were we here at all if we only have to fall and die?"—this is the response: "It's been about the sun and the moon. It's been about happy times together. It's been about the shade and the old people and the children. It's been about colors in Fall. It's been about seasons. Isn't that enough?"

When Daniel dies and falls to earth, he alludes to the mystery of afterlife by saying, "Goodbye for now." And when Freddie himself must die, he becomes proud to be a part of life as in the descent he sees the strong, firm tree's grasp. The mystical atmosphere may be inspirational to some readers, perhaps the adults buying the book, but it is disconcerting that Buscaglia refers to death as sleep and readers should be alert to this puzzling misconception. "In this new position (dying on the snow) he was more comfortable than he had ever been. He closed his eyes and fell asleep." To children unfamiliar with the nuances of metaphor, this allusion can be very disturbing, and poor sleep patterns can be a possible result.

Surprisingly, although he is so staunch an advocate for "personhood," Buscaglia doesn't give the photographers credit until the end, almost as an afterthought.

243. Clardy, Andrea Fleck. *Dusty Was My Friend: Coming to Terms with Loss*. Illus. by Eleanor Alexander. New York: Human Sciences, 1984. 32 pp. Fiction.

Interest level: Ages 5–10 Reading level: Grades 2–3

Benjamin, the eight-year-old narrator, describes in detail his feelings when he learns of the death of his friend, Dusty. He goes through the stages of mourning and discusses his reaction during each stage. He talks to his parents and they respond helpfully and informatively. He never stops missing and loving Dusty, but he goes on with his life and remembers the good times he and Dusty shared.

Although this is clearly a didactic book aimed at helping children cope with the loss of a young person, it is well-crafted and gentle in its approach. Young readers will feel with Benjamin, while at the same time taking to heart his message of permission to grieve and to mourn.

244. Clifton, Lucille. *Everett Anderson's Goodbye.* Illus. by Ann Grifalconi. New York: Henry Holt, 1983. 32 pp. Fiction.

Interest level: Ages 5–8 Reading level: Grades 2–3

Written, like all the Everett Anderson books, in poetic form, the story takes us through the five stages of grief: denial, anger, bargaining, depression, and acceptance. Everett Anderson's mother is with him throughout the process, but she cannot help him actively until he emerges from his depression. She is always there to accept his feelings and to guide him to his next step, but he must come to the understanding himself that just because his father died does not mean that love dies.

Grifalconi's illustrations are enormously expressive of both the mother's and the child's feelings. This is a loving and helpful book.

245. Coerr, Eleanor. *The Josefina Story Quilt.* Illus. by Bruce Degen. New York: Harper, 1986. 64 pp. Fiction.

Interest level: Ages 5–9 Reading level: Grade 2

An evocative addition to the I Can Read series, *The Josefina Story Quilt* gives focus to the wagon train experience. It is 1850 and Faith's family is heading to California. Faith's father doesn't want to take Josefina, her beloved elderly hen. He can't break his daughter's heart, but he warns that if Josefina gives trouble, "Out she goes!" This becomes a repetitive phrase, as Josefina causes near disasters. The trip is compelling every inch of the way, with events sewn together with Faith's diary quilt patches and Coerr's sensuous language—"the wheels began their creaky song." The starvation and hardships of the wagon train are given appropriate attention, with people dying and being buried alongside the trail—"Nobody laughed or sang or smiled anymore." And, as might be expected, Josefina, not thrown out—becomes a heroine.

There are a couple of confusing jumps: It's not clear how Josefina dies after she squawks the robbers away, and a cabin abruptly materializes for the family in California, more like a waiting motel than an immense building task. These are outweighed by suspense and appreciation for family life. Children in any generation will well recognize the persuasion process by which "Ma gave Pa a special look." From that look, Josefina gained passage on the wagon train.

246. Cohen, Daniel, and Cohen, Susan. *Heroes of the Challenger.* New York: Archway, 1986. 115 pp. Nonfiction.

Interest level: Age 10+ Reading level: Grades 5–6

This book is highly accessible, from beginning to end. Starting off by reminding us how we felt on January 28, 1986, the Cohens then lead into profiles of the seven lost astronauts that emphasize their teen years and hobbies. (Did you know Christa McAuliffe liked Ms. Pac-Man?) In-depth use of research sources enables the authors to provide a sense of the continuing drama surrounding the investigations as well as a history of near misses and actual tragedies in the American and Soviet space programs. Closing with a probing analysis of the need for space exploration and the shuttle in particular, the Cohens offer a balanced picture of the scientific and emotional reasons behind manning spacecraft at the close of the twentieth century.

247. Cohn, Janice. *I Had a Friend Named Peter: Talking to Children about the Death of a Friend.* Illus. by Gail Owens. New York: Morrow, 1987. 32 pp. Fiction.

Interest level: Ages 4–8 Reading level: Grade 3

The first section of this sensitive book is for parents, answering questions about children's development of separation/loss concepts, how to explain death in general and particularly of a young child, and pitfalls to avoid (for example, comparisons with sleep, or a concept of heaven wherein the dead look over a potentially naughty child). Social worker/consultant Cohn stresses the importance of honest simplicity and describes children's emotional reactions—from the giddiness of anxiety to boisterousness and sadness.

In the children's section, Betsy, a child of about six, is told by her parents that her best friend, Peter, has been hit by a car. Her parents are attentive and models of what to say and do. "Peter was hurt so badly that the doctors couldn't make him better, and he died." Betsy wants to go to the funeral, so they describe the service and burial. Betsy shows the varied reactions likely—a stomachache, a bad dream, guilt about their fights, a short sadness span, and then back to grief. Her parents share their sadness, too, explaining they, too, can't sleep. A lovely feature of this book is the tapping of a child's natural capacity and desire to comfort. It's not syrupy but real when Betsy offers to help Peter's parents, likewise, when the children in school the next day remember Peter with discussion and drawings. The sad pastels heighten the emotion in this finely tuned, valuable book.

248. Conrad, Pam. *Prairie Songs.* Illus. by Darryl S. Zudeck. New York: Harper, 1985. 176 pp. Fiction.

Interest level: Age 11+ Reading level: Grade 5

The story is narrated by Louisa, the older child of a family living in a sod house on the Nebraska prairie. It is an important day when a doctor and his wife move from New York City into their community. Emmeline, the doctor's young wife, is apprehensive about living on the prairie and always talks of her home back East. The author includes enough foreshadowing so that the reader knows that something dreadful will happen to her and her unborn child. Sure enough, the baby dies at birth. Louisa's younger brother, Lester, is afraid that he or his mother will die, too, and needs reassurance, but it is clear that to survive in this land one needs to be able to live with death.

The beauty of the land contrasts with its cruelty. Emmeline dies; she cannot tolerate the losses. There is always the danger of death from the elements, from Indians, from natural causes, and the settlers must be strong to endure it. The author writes sparingly but forcefully of the land, the situations, and the strength of the surviving characters.

249. Davis, Jenny. *Good-bye and Keep Cold.* New York: Orchard, 1987. 210 pp. Fiction.

Interest level: Age 12+ Reading level: Grade 7

The story is told in retrospect from the voice of Edda, now a young adult. When Edda was eight years old her father was killed in a strip mining accident. Her parents had a close and warm relationship, and Edda's father had been especially loving to her. The father's death was a devasting blow to the entire family, and Edda details clearly how each person responded.

Henry John Fitzpatrick enters the family constellation immediately after the death of the father. It is he who inadvertently caused the father's death, and at first he helps the family as a way of expiating his guilt. After a few months, however, he falls in love with Edda's mother. Edda does not recognize their relationship until a family friend reveals it to her, in a troubling conversation in which Annie, the friend, says, "People will talk, that's what I'm worried about." When Edda confronts her mother in confusion and anger, her mother wisely reassures her, "Whatever happens, you won't be losing me." She explains that Edda's father goes on loving her, even though he is dead, "And we go on loving him. No matter what."

The relationship between Henry John and Edda's mother continues and ripens, and Edda resents it greatly. In a dramatic turnaround, Henry John leaves, because Edda's mother refuses to marry him, saying she is still married to her dead husband. And there is more drama. Edda finds out that her father and Annie, her mother's best friend, had had an affair.

Edda's mother breaks off with Annie, and, after an interlude of near insanity, devises her own ceremony and ritually divorces her dead husband.

Even more plot complications ensue: The family moves to the city; and Henry John and his new wife have a baby with a clubfoot who is rejected by her mother and adopted by Edda's mother. In the end, Henry John and Edda's mother marry; Edda goes off to college and is ready to take her place in the adult world. Edda has the reader's attention throughout the book, although the book is somewhat marred by the intrusion of unnecessary and underdeveloped problems. At times the book has the flavor of a soap opera.

Davis, who lives in Lexington, Kentucky, where some of the story takes place, is a teacher of English and sex education. This, her first novel, reflects her familiarity with the setting as well as her understanding of the feelings of preadolescents about death, love and sex, and growing up.

250. Deaver, Julie Reece. *Say Goodnight, Gracie.* New York: Harper, 1988. 214 pp. Fiction.

Interest level: Age 12+ Reading level: Grades 5–6

Morgan and Jimmy have been friends since birth. Their parents are close friends, too, and the two families are always together. Jimmy and Morgan love each other, communicate directly to each other, and depend on each other for support. They are both interested in the theater, and both experience setbacks that make them rely even more on each other's nurturing.

When Jimmy is killed in an automobile accident by a drunken driver, readers experience the sense of a genuine loss. This is no literary device; it is real. Morgan refuses to acknowledge her feelings. She is numbed by the extent of her loss. She cannot go to Jimmy's funeral or speak to his parents. She feels withdrawn from the world and thinks that she cannot go on without Jimmy.

Morgan's parents are very understanding. They permit her to stay home from school, to try to engage in theatrical activities, and they take turns sitting up with her when she cannot sleep. They finally take her to her aunt, who is a psychiatrist, and who has prescribed tranquilizers and sleeping pills, but who now refuses to permit her to take any medication. She helps Morgan to confront her denial, anger, guilt, and fear. Morgan finally decides that she will choose life and try to cope with Jimmy's death in a more constructive manner.

Deaver conveys the sense of loss very well. Because Jimmy is so alive, and such a vibrant character, we commiserate with his family and friends when he is killed. We also respond to each of the characters in their grief. Deaver is adroit at describing the everyday events that affect a grieving person, such as the encounter with people who have not yet heard of the death, or the having to deal with disposing of the deceased's possessions. This novel is a well-crafted, moving story.

251. Dolan, Edward F. *Matters of Life and Death.* New York: Watts, 1982. 128 pp. Nonfiction.

Interest level: Ages 12–16 Reading level: Grade 6

Today's controversies as they reflect on our concepts of life and death are explored here: abortion, contraception, euthanasia, in vitro fertilization, artificial insemination, and cloning. For each, free-lance writer Dolan instructs on the core of the procedure, then investigates the heart of the controversy, as it has existed over long periods of time and as it exists in the 1980s in the United States. The many controversies are presented fairly and in depth, as exemplified by examining abortion in history, as seen by churches, through the eyes of the law, and as a political arena. Newspaper stories on these issues are part of Dolan's story, such as the story of Karen Ann Quinlan. Bibliography, index.

252. Fenton, Edward. *The Morning of the Gods.* New York: Delacorte, 1987. 184 pp. Fiction.

Interest level: Age 12+ Reading level: Grades 6–7

Carla Lewis has come to Greece to spend some time with her great aunt and uncle, who raised her mother. Carla's mother has recently died, and Carla needs this time to come to terms with her mother's death and her own grief. She is visiting the people who knew her mother best, and she wants to see and touch all the places her mother told her about as she was growing up. Carla becomes very much involved in the Greece of the 1970s, as well as the place that her mother knew and loved. And she discovers things about her mother that she had never known, such as the fact that she wrote poetry.

The political situation cannot be avoided because Greece is now ruled by a dictatorial junta. Carla helps to prevent the military from capturing a poet who is a national hero. She risks her own safety by doing so, but she is deeply gratified to have been successful. She returns to America, but only for a while. The next Autumn finds her back in Greece, where she has made spiritual contact not only with her mother, but with herself. Fenton has done a masterful job of blending the setting with the emotional tone of the work. Carla's conversion is the reader's as well.

253. Fleischman, Paul. *Rear-View Mirrors.* New York: Zolotow (Harper), 1986. 128 pp. Fiction.

Interest level: Age 12+ Reading level: Grade 7

A cryptic telegraphic invitation begins Olivia's journey to meet the almost reclusive father she's never known. It seems he wants an heir and Olivia is given the doubtful privilege of auditioning. Their visit starts with a volley of hyperarticulate one-upmanship-type barbs, he digging at Olivia's mother, Olivia digging at him. Bright high school kids—equally standoffish, cynical, and needy in turn—will appreciate the characters' glib tongues; they will also enjoy the inspired description ("legs stiff as beef jerky") and unexpected slapstick humor.

Olivia is a junior in high school when she hears from her father for the first time. Her mother and father were divorced when Olivia was eight months old, and she and her mother have lived in the San Francisco area of California, while her father has remained in New England. After all these years he has written to invite her to come to spend the summer with him. She goes, and during the summer Olivia's father acquaints her with who he is, what he likes, and, especially, what he doesn't like. She also discovers that he feels that he will die soon, partly because his heart is weakening, and partly because of an inner contest he wages with death that he knows he will lose. Indeed, he does die, shortly after the summer that he and Olivia share, while he is fixing the roof during an electrical storm.

Part of the story is told in flashback, and part of it is in the present as Olivia returns to her legacy, the house and land that her father left her. She undertakes a ritual bicycle ride that her father used to do, with special rules and conditions. She encounters a number of obstacles, but she succeeds in completing the ride and upholding all of its conditions. She now feels that she can lay her father to rest, and that she can go on from here, the stronger because she knows both her parents, is like both of them, but has an individuality of her own.

The idea of a ceremony or ritual to complete the process of mourning is a valid one, especially when a person decides for herself what that ritual will be. The marathon bicycle ride is the symbol of Olivia's father's life and spirit. It is something that she can claim as her own as well, and it works well in this story. The first-person narrative is also effective. The book is unblemished by the intrusion of an artificial romance, and none of the characters is glorified.

254. Gerstein, Mordicai. *The Mountains of Tibet.* Illus. by the author. New York: Harper, 1987. 32 pp. Fiction.

Interest level: Age 7+ Reading level: Grade 3

The book begins with the birth of a little boy, high in the mountains of Tibet, who grows to enjoy flying kites. He lives out his life in one place, but always longs to visit different lands and come to know different sorts of people. When he dies, he is given the choice of rebirth, and he takes it. He is given one choice after another and consistently chooses that which feels most like home to him. His last choice is whether to be a boy or a girl, and he chooses to be a girl because he seems to remember that he was once a boy. The book ends with the birth of a little girl in the same high mountains of Tibet, and she also enjoys flying kites.

Aside from the notion of reincarnation, the book deals with the philosophical issue of choices and how we make them. Children will certainly enjoy speculating about what their choices might be if they were given the option of rebirth again on any spot in the galaxy, in any universe, on any planet, in any country, as any creature of either gender.

The illustrations in this beautiful picture book are framed almost as snapshots in the real world and take the form of mandalas when the story takes place in the world beyond. The details of the options the main character is offered are interesting and attractive. Truly an unusual book.

255. Gould, Deborah Lee. *Grandpa's Slide Show.* Illus. by Cheryl Harness. New York: Lothrop, 1987. 32 pp. Fiction.

Interest level: Age 6+ Reading level: Grades 2–3

This story will arouse memories and stir emotions in the many people, children and adults, who fondly remember a family member, particularly a father or grandfather, who entertained them with slides of vacations and family gatherings. In this case the grandfather, who has been the primary photographer and master of ceremonies for the slide shows, has died. After the funeral and after all of the well-wishers have left, the immediate family gathers around for a slide show of the miscellaneous vacations the family has taken. The slides and memories are cathartic for everyone, especially the little boy who goes to sleep and dreams of his smiling grandfather.

The brothers' reactions are depicted well. For example, Douglas is confused by the fact that his grandfather is dead and, in his confusion, he acts silly. Later, he tries to grab his grandfather's image from the screen. The details demonstrate what children are likely to notice during a family gathering and throughout a family crisis. The author and illustrator demonstrate that rituals and happy memories help in the process of mourning a loved one. This tender and true book will be a treasure in many homes.

256. Greenberg, Judith E., and Carey, Helen H. *Sunny: The Death of a Pet.* Photos by Barbara Kirk. New York: Watts, 1986. 32 pp. Nonfiction.

Interest level: Ages 5–9 Reading level: Grades 2–3

Sunny, Ken's dog, likes to nap in a sunbeam, hence her name. One day she doesn't get excited at the sight of the leash, and she's barely wagging her tail. She hardly eats. An appointment at the veterinarian is scheduled, and she is given medicine for old age heart ailments.

Sunny dies while Ken is in school, and the photographs appropriately show him thinking of her while he has to be away. Ken's mother tells him with feeling, "I have some sad news for you. Sunny died this afternoon." Ken's emotions are shown well—he doesn't feel like playing. His friend Bill comes over to keep him company anyway, an appropriate action for these children who seem to be about age nine. The two friends talk about times with Sunny, and she is later buried in the yard. Other emotions and actions given attention here include dreams about the dead and imagining seeing the loved one. Another good idea is shown when Ken puts Sunny's leash and toy bone in a box and looks at them when he misses her.

In this story, boy gets dog in the end, but it's handled with understanding. Bill's aunt's dog has had puppies and Ken is offered one. "I want Sunny, not a dumb new dog." But then looking at Bill's new pet makes him think a puppy would like Sunny's bone, too. This wise mother tells her son, "Getting a new dog doesn't mean you have to stop loving Sunny." And the new puppy is allowed her own personality, being named Lacey "because she chased his shoelaces."

257. Greene, Constance C. *Beat the Turtle Drum.* Illus. by Donna Diamond. New York: Viking, 1976; Dell, pap. 120 pp. Fiction.

Interest level: Ages 9–12 Reading level: Grade 3

"Nothing will ever be all right again," says 13-year-old Kate, after her 11-year-old sister, Joss, is killed instantly in a fall from a tree. Joss was a unique, gay, ethereal child, especially devoted to horses—the family favorite, thinks Kate. In celebration of her birthday, Joss accumulates enough money to rent an old horse for a week. Ironically, it is in looking after the nag that she falls and loses her life.

The story is exquisitely crafted. Unlike most stories of loss, the character dies almost at the end; instead of treating the family's adjustment in detail, the author spends most of the pages creating a picture of the loving, warm family. In fact, in the end, readers are left at the height of acute grief—mother is looking toward pills for solace, father toward alcohol, and Kate is miserably isolated in her home. Yet the hint that grief will fade—found in the comfort of condolence, in overtures made by adults outside the family, and in Kate's expression of feeling in poetry—is enough.

Without equal are the passages in which bereavement is described. So few words are used, but those chosen are almost unbearably precise and sensitive, never hitting a false note. About the immediate shock: "I don't know how we got home, my mother and I. One minute we were in the emergency room at the hospital, the next we were standing in our living room." On the somatic symptoms of grief, as experienced by Kate: "My bones feel hollow with loneliness." And as experienced by Joss's friend: "Tootie was huddled on our back steps." On denial: "I imagine I can hear her breathing in the next bed. . . . It's all in my mind. I know that, but I can't stop myself from turning on the light to make sure." Finally, the handling of unspeakable pain, when Tootie asks Kate if Joss knows how much she is missed: "I have to turn away and pretend I'm tying my shoe or something. I don't want him to see how much he upsets me." Also: "I weep inside my head." Each and every character in this outstanding novel is memorable.

258. Grollman, Sharon. *Shira: A Legacy of Courage.* Illus. by Edward Epstein. New York: Doubleday, 1988. 96 pp. Nonfiction.
Interest level: Ages 8–13 Reading level: Grade 4

Shira Putter died of a rare form of diabetes while still in elementary school. For three and one half years she suffered, spending months on end in hospitals all over the United States and Canada, undergoing many operations and for most of that time, moving about with a foot pole and insulin pump attached to her, a last resort because she couldn't seem to benefit from more standard approaches. She was surrounded by love throughout her ordeal and she tried to make the best of her ever-worsening situation. In the hospital, she would put on plays, go trick-or-treating, and attempt to do schoolwork. She also wrote poetry and kept an intermittent journal, and those sometimes funny, sometimes confused, sometimes sad writings became the basis for this book. Grollman, a psychologist and author, took Shira's writings and after interviews with her family reconstructing the illness and the child's point of view, created a fuller diary of what Shira might have said and thought.

The result is a most moving piece, in which we see the many ups and downs of a girl and her family in agony: A teacher doesn't understand she must snack when she needs to and scolds her. Shira changes schools. Shira experiences the attempts of her classmates at the new school to include her, but as her condition worsens her classmates eventually withdraw. Shira gets close to hospital personnel and children as well, keeping her sense of humor enough to play a trick on a newcomer to the hospital. Shira is treated insensitively at a roller rink—"Why don't you stay home, where you belong?" someone shouts. In response, her friends skate around her in a circle of love, a thrilling moment. Shira comes home for the Passover Seder and she and her family are unafraid to cry together at the predicament of her illness. Shira's emotions are many. She faces fear, not just the fear of pain and death, but the fear of losing her parents' love because she is a burden, and the fear of being forgotten after death because her short life was so sad.

With the help of a psychiatrist, Shira learns visualization techniques and tries to master pain. The doctor also helps her talk about death. In time, as she weakens, she is eager for death because life seems so hard. In discussions with her mother, she helps her parents get ready to let her go, something children often do, according to the introduction by Rabbi Harold Kushner. Unlike many unfortunate children, Shira had not needed to keep her feelings bottled up so as not to upset her parents. Instead, there was much openness. This story of love, hope, and courage will help readers realize the truth of the "Song of Songs" phrase "Love is stronger than death." The book closes with an epilogue by Shira's mother. Glossary, bibliography, index.

259. Guernsey, JoAnn Bren. *Five Summers.* New York: Clarion, 1983. 180 pp. Fiction.

Interest level: Age 11+ Reading level: Grade 5

The story centers on Mandy from the time she is 13 until she is 18. During this period, her grandmother comes to live with Mandy and her family, causes untold problems, moves to a nursing home, returns to them again and, after a while, dies; her aunt and uncle are killed in an automobile accident, and her young cousin comes to stay and selects Mandy as his surrogate mother, then goes away to live with another aunt; her mother is diagnosed as having cancer and undergoes a mastectomy, then another, and then more surgery. And Mandy meets Peter, and they fall in love with each other. All of these events happen during the summers across the five-year span.

A portrait of the family emerges as the story unfolds. The father and mother love each other dearly and understand Mandy very well. Mandy goes through a period where she wants to take her mother's place, but her father wisely puts her behavior into perspective and helps her to know she is loved. The grandmother is cantankerous but strong and responds well in crises. Mandy is self-centered and not always pleasant or respectful to her elders. As she matures she increasingly understands how to acknowledge her feelings without behaving in a nasty fashion.

At the end of the story we don't know if the mother will live; we suspect not, but she and Mandy have confessed their fears to each other and have agreed to go on with their lives in as sensitive and honest a way as they can.

260. Guest, Elisa Haden. *Over the Moon.* New York: Morrow, 1986; Bantam, pap. 201 pp. Fiction.

Interest level: Age 12+ Reading level: Grade 5

Kate's parents were killed in a car crash. Kate, her brother, Jay, and their older sister, Mattie, went to live with her father's older sister, Georgia. Mattie and Georgia did not get along, and Mattie ran off one day with a ne'er-do-well boyfriend. Now, four years later, she has gotten in touch with Kate, and Kate goes, without Georgia's permission, to visit her sister in Canada. On the way Kate is robbed of her wallet. A pleasant and helpful young man assists her, and they fall in love. When Kate gets to Mattie's house she finds her sister with a child, but deserted by her lover. Kate manages to persuade Mattie to come home with her, and we get the feeling that all will be well.

The story is a romance that has as its main focus the idea that a loving family is strong enough to overcome all sorts of obstacles, including death. Kate is an interesting and sensitive protagonist. Her ingenuousness might be dangerous in real life, but it works well for her in the book. Her newly acquired boyfriend is ideal for her, and his family is also ideal. Her aunt is Mother Earth, and her sister and brother fall neatly into line. There is little reality here, but as an escape into romance it is well done.

261. Hastings, Selina, adapter. *The Man Who Wanted to Live Forever.* Illus. by Reg Cartwright. New York: Henry Holt, 1988. 28 pp. Fiction.

Interest level: Ages 7–10 Reading level: Grades 3–4

Bodkin enjoys life so much that he wants to live forever. He turns to several aged people for help, and all advise him how he can live as long as they, but he is not satisfied until he comes to the man who will live as long as a mountain shall stand. This is long enough for Bodkin, who stays with the old man for several hundred years. Then Bodkin, who miraculously has not aged, longs to return to see his old village. He does so despite the old man's warning, and when he returns he is devastated to see that a city now stands where his village once was. He tries to go back to the mountain, but he meets someone along the way who persuades him to dismount from his horse, counter to the old man of the mountain's instructions, and he finds himself captured at last by Death.

There are many messages here, and they are somewhat confusing. Is the ending a just one? Bodkin dismounted to help a poor old man and was rewarded for his generosity by death. But was the existence he led really living? He gave up a joyous and full life to stay alive with an old man in the mountains. Yet the text says that he was content for several hundred years.

The illustrations, paintings that look almost like paper sculptures, enhance the book. One puzzling factor, though, is that Bodkin has not aged in appearance even though he is several hundred years old. Nothing is said in the text about eternal youth. Another puzzle is that Bodkin does not put up a struggle with Death and permits himself to be led away. This is confusing behavior for a man so determined to live forever.

As with most allegories and folktales, this story will spark much discussion and speculation. Depending on the child's developmental level of knowing about death, the responses will vary enormously. The book is an interesting one.

262. Hazen, Barbara Shook. *Why Did Grandpa Die? A Book about Death.* Illus. by Pat Schories. New York: Golden, 1985. 24 pp. Fiction.

Interest level: Ages 5–8 Reading level: Grades 2–3

Molly has much in common with her grandfather. They both have dimples and enjoy pink lemonade; and they spend time in the park together. One day when she finds a dead butterfly, she asks her grandfather why it is not moving. He explains that it will never move or fly again because it is dead. They bury it.

The next day Grandpa was going to take Molly sailing, but he has chest pains. He is taken to the hospital, where he dies. Molly denies this fact. She cannot believe her beloved grandfather is dead. Her father holds her and explains that her grandpa was old and could not be fixed up despite the best care. Molly wriggles away and goes into her room, where she feels awful and frightened, but she does not feel like crying. Her father reminds Molly that Grandpa was his father whom he loved very much. He adds that he knows that the love between Molly and her grandfather was very strong. In these statements, he binds them all together with the enduring, common bond of love. When Molly asks why her grandfather died, and her father explains that everything that lives must die eventually and that death is the end to everyone's life.

Over the next time period, Molly's mother brings her some pink lemonade, but Molly rejects it because she misses her grandfather too much. Her mother acknowledges Molly's grief and joins in it. She affirms that they can never see him again except in pictures and memories.

Molly and her family and many friends, relatives, and colleagues of her grandfather assemble. They go to the graveyard and Molly picks daisies for his grave. She still thinks he will return sometime.

As time passes, Molly's feelings of missing Grandpa grow less painful, but there are still reminders—the pink lemonade, the leaves falling. . . . When school starts, she tells her classmates about her grandpa's death. That night, at last, she cries. By the next summer when the flowers she and Grandpa planted are blooming she is not as sad. As Molly grows up, she keeps her loving memories of her grandfather and shares them with other members of her family.

This is an excellent book about death and grieving. It could serve as a model for all people. The information to parents in the blurb at the front is accurate and helpful. Euphemisms for death and dying are not used. Molly's parents are available to her and supportive of her feelings. The process of grieving, including the postponed crying, is quite accurate. The illustrations support the narrative. The expressions in the pictures complement and expand our appreciation for the feelings and content in the narrative. The notion developed in the last part of the book, of storytelling as a means of holding onto and passing on a family's traditions and connections, is an important one.

263. Hermes, Patricia. *You Shouldn't Have to Say Goodbye.* New York: Harcourt, 1982; Scholastic, pap. 117 pp. Fiction.

Interest level: Age 10+ Reading level: Grade 4

Although dealing with the death of a 13-year-old girl's mother from cancer, the author also deals with the affirmation of life. Love and courage are the themes here. While Sarah goes through the stages of mourning for the life she once had, her mother prepares her for the inevitable. Even after death occurs, Sarah's mother helps her by means of a diary, which she (the mother) has kept throughout her illness. This is good fiction, told through Sarah's eyes and feelings. The plot moves quickly; there are very few flashbacks, which can be confusing to less able readers; the print is large; and there is enough white space so that the book is not intimidating.

264. Hickman, Martha Whitmore. *Last Week My Brother Anthony Died.* Illus. by Randie Julien. Nashville: Abingdon, 1984. 28 pp. Fiction.

Interest level: Ages 6–10 Reading level: Grade 2

Julie's baby brother died four weeks after birth. She is despondent. And though her mother talks to her, it is finally the family minister and the passage of time that help her put her grief aside.

Told through the perspective of a very young child, the text recognizes all of a child's feelings, including the confusion, anger, and grief at losing a sibling. The minister's recounting of his own loss helps the little girl feel as though he is a companion she can share her feelings with. They eat ice cream together, and this symbolizes the permission the child now has to go on with her life and enjoy its pleasures, while at the same time acknowledging her loss.

265. Horwitz, Joshua. *Only Birds and Angels Fly.* New York: Harper, 1985. 186 pp. Fiction.

Interest level: Age 12+ Reading level: Grade 7

Danny is in the middle of his freshman year at college when he receives a phone call from his father informing him that his friend Chris has had a serious accident and is near death. Danny quickly suspects that Chris was under the influence of drugs. He immediately leaves for home, even though he and Chris haven't seen each other for several years.

The rest of the book is a retrospective of Danny and Chris's friendship, and how it went wrong. They were both heavily involved with drugs, but Danny stopped and Chris didn't. As a matter of fact, after the funeral, Danny goes into Chris's room at the request of another friend of theirs to find Chris's drugs and paraphernalia, and to get rid of them before Chris's parents find them. This part does not ring true because surely the parents have had the opportunity to look at Chris's room while he was in the hospital.

Nevertheless, the story is chilling enough to use as yet another warning to young people of the disastrous harm that drug abuse can cause.

266. Howker, Janni. *Isaac Campion.* New York: Greenwillow, 1986. 80 pp. Fiction.

Interest level: Age 12+ Reading level: Grades 7–8

Isaac Campion was 12 years old when his older brother, Daniel, died. Daniel's death was due to an accident, a result of a dare that a neighbor's son had leveled at him. The two families were always feuding, and now the hatred was worse than ever. Young Isaac witnessed his brother's death, and it affected him for the remainder of his long life.

Isaac's father is a hard man, and at times Isaac hates him. But in the end, when Isaac knows that he must leave home for good, he feels compassion for his father and for the life that his father leads.

The dialect and style of narrative are somewhat difficult to manage, but the power of the setting and the force of the narrator's words sweep the reader along. The hatred and bitterness are palpable. The death is a horrifying one, and the young boy's response is well charted.

267. Jukes, Mavis. *Blackberries in the Dark.* Illus. by Thomas B. Allen. New York: Knopf, 1985. 48 pp. Fiction.

Interest level: Ages 8–11 Reading level: Grades 4–6

Austin is a nine-year-old boy who has visited his grandparents every summer for a number of years. This summer, however, is different. Grandpa will not be there; Grandpa died. With constant reminders of what summers used to be like, fishing gear hanging on the barn wall, tractor sitting in the barn, Austin painfully remembers his grandfather. With his grandmother's help, Austin is able once again to take part in family traditions.

Jukes does an excellent job dealing with a child's reaction to death. She provides the reader with a touching scene in the barn that had not been cleared of Grandpa's things, where Austin and Grandma hug each other thinking back to the promise Grandpa made to teach Austin to fly-fish this summer. The stage of acceptance is portrayed by Austin and his grandmother using Grandpa's fishing gear and eating blackberries in the dark for supper—a family tradition.

Besides revealing the pain and joy of a relationship, Jukes also does a wonderful job of nonstereotypical writing. Grandma is not a feeble, broken down woman dependent on her family to take care of her. Rather, she is old but spunky and capable of taking care of herself. She is willing to take on a grandson for the summer, fish with waders in the stream, and run the tractor to cut the tall grass.

268. Kaldohl, Marit. *Goodbye Rune.* Illus. by Wenche Owen. New York: Kane/Miller, 1987. 32 pp. Fiction.

Interest level: Ages 7–10 Reading level: Grade 3

Sara and Rune are best friends, playing, planning, and imagining a future romance together. One day, not paying their best attention to Sara's mother's instructions, they venture too near the lake and Rune is drowned. Sara is blessed with understanding parents who try to help. She's filled with questions that might be expected: "Can she see Rune again?" "No, he can't talk to any one, see or hear." But Sara discovers that she can remember Rune and see him smiling, just the way he always did. But when she remembers that she can never play with Rune again, her sadness returns.

Sara attends Rune's funeral, along with nearly all the townspeople. Later, when winter has come and gone, she visits his grave, where, her mother explains, Rune's body is slowly turning into earth. Despite the factual information, this experience brings Sara a great longing to have Rune again as her friend. The author is a poet, and her collaboration with painter Owen is felicitous; the ethereal paintings demonstrate empathy with a little girl's needs. A flaw, however, is that Sara does not question her possible role in the death, although she was there and did not insist that Rune stay away from the water. This detracts somewhat from an otherwise masterful job.

269. Keller, Holly. *Goodbye, Max.* Illus. by the author. New York: Greenwillow, 1987. 28 pp. Fiction.

Interest level: Ages 5–9 Reading level: Grade 2

Ben has to deal with the death of his pet dog, Max. Max was old, and the vet did everything he could, but Max died while Ben was in school. In the process of mourning, Ben and his friend Zach begin to remember some of the funny things that Max did while he was alive. Then Ben and Zach cry over the loss. Ben can now accept Max's death, and he is ready to love his new puppy and give it a name.

Children may feel that Ben recovers too rapidly from the loss of his beloved pet. Although it is helpful that the author conveys a sense of relief through the memory of pleasant times, it is not usually a good idea to suggest that a replacement can be found, especially so soon after the death of the beloved pet.

270. Klein, Norma. *Angel Face.* New York: Viking Kestrel, 1984; Fawcett, pap. 208 pp. Fiction.

Interest level: Age 12+ Reading level: Grade 7

Jason is the narrator of this story. His mother and father are bitterly divorced, and of four children Jason is the only one left at home with his mother. His brother and sisters are away at school. When he falls in love with a girl, his mother is jealous of their relationship. She depends too much on Jason, and she complains constantly about his father as well as his siblings. Jason bears the brunt of it all.

When Jason decides to go away for the summer, his mother is bereft. There is a tearful parting scene at the airport, and then Jason's mother is killed in a car crash while she is returning from the airport. Jason's sister thinks that their mother has committed suicide, but Jason isn't sure. He does know that he feels guilty and confused. Their father insists that three of the four children come to live with him and his new wife in California (Jason's sister remains at Harvard Law School), and at the end of the story it looks as if they will forgive their father and adjust to the changes in their lives.

The book contains explicit sex and some obscenities, but the focus is on people's relationships and their reactions to loss.

271. Koertge, Ron. *Where the Kissing Never Stops.* Boston: Atlantic, 1986. 217 pp. Fiction.

Interest level: Age 14+ Reading level: Grade 7

Walker's father has been killed in an automobile accident; Rachel's mother died suddenly of a heart attack. The two of them have much in common, including problems with their living parents. Walker's mother has taken a job as a stripper, not only to earn money, but also because she enjoys dancing. Rachel's father is a real estate operator, and Rachel is ashamed of how he duns people into selling their property. Although Walker's mother is practical and loving and understanding, Rachel's father is dependent and self-centered.

Walker did not really know his father as well as he would have liked, and this fact complicates his feelings about his father's death. A bizarre occurrence at the funeral (Walker and his mother were pushed into the father's grave) seems to be the symbol for the mother's rebirth and transformation from a mousy, passive wife into a strong and determined woman.

The problems in the book are mainly those of a teenager who is trying to deal with his hormonal explosions, his independence, his future, the loss of his father, and his shame about his mother's job. He is also trying to establish his self-identity. Walker and Rachel develop an ideal relationship, sexually as well as emotionally. The language is often explicit and vernacular. The writing is reminiscent of a romance; all of the characters are upper-middle class, and their problems seem to be resolved with little real effort. But the character of the mother is an interesting and earthy one, and Walker does learn tolerance for himself, his mother, and even his dead father.

272. Lasky, Kathryn. *Home Free.* New York: Four Winds, 1985. 252 pp. Fiction.

Interest level: Age 11+ Reading level: Grades 5–6

Fifteen-year-old Sam and his mother return to Salem, Massachusetts, after his father's death in a car accident. He becomes involved with Gus Earley and the reintroduction of eagles into Quabbin. It is through this project that Sam meets Lucy, an autistic girl with whom he works to help overcome her handicap.

The book revolves around the theme of Sam's adjustment, not only to his life in New England but also to his problems with life and death. It penetrates the mind and actions of the adolescent Sam and his discovery of the purpose and meaning of life through his relationships with his mother—who is struggling to recover from the loss of her husband; with Lucy—who has already died once from the cruelties she experienced in an earlier existence; with Quabbin Valley; with Gus—whose life is purposeful although he is dying; and with the eagles themselves. The reestablishment of the eagles becomes important and meaningful to each character as a symbol of faith in the future.

The book sensitively discusses the issue of death in the violent and untimely demise of Sam's father, and Gus's slow, painful bargaining with death as he dies of cancer. Although both deaths seem to be final, the very existence of Lucy, and Gus's sitting on the hill after his demise, suggest to the reader that nothing is really final. Sam's father is very much alive in his continued influence on Sam's intellect and interests, and Gus's work will be continued by Sam and others in Quabbin.

Sam is portrayed as a compassionate and sensitive boy. He is able to see beyond Lucy's disability, recognizing that her spirit cannot be limited by the psychologists' tests and labels. He is courageous, can face solitude, enjoys hard work, and is able to plan and organize his own time. Although his father has obviously influenced his thinking, his mother's strengths are never belittled, even though he does not share her enthusiasm for restoring their New England home and finds it hard to relate to her family.

Sam cares for and communicates with his mother; each understands the other's grief but cannot penetrate or assuage it—each has to work it out alone. The eagle project and Lucy are the catalysts for Sam's self-realization and the reconciliation of life and death.

This wonderfully written story can convey to the reader a sense of the purpose and integration of life—past with present, nature with man, life with death—and is highly recommended.

273. Lester, Julius. *This Strange New Feeling.* New York: Dial, 1982; Scholastic, pap. 166 pp. Fiction.

Interest level: Age 11+ Reading level: Grades 6–7

These three stories are love stories with a difference. They all deal with the issue of the displacement of black people as slaves, and their winning of their ultimate freedom. The middle story, "Where the Sun Lives," tells of a woman who did not actually gain physical freedom from slavery, although her free black husband had freed her in his will. After he died, she was used to pay his debts, and when she sued, she lost her case. Nevertheless, she never again became enslaved in spirit. She knew that any white man who bought her would be sorry. In the other two stories, "This Strange New Feeling" and "A Christmas Love Story," the main characters do gain their physical as well as spiritual freedom.

All three stories are important because of how the characters cope with loss, and how they use their wits and sense of personal power to gain their freedom. Many stereotypes are blasted, such as the one of the generous and good slave owner, and the passive and contented slave. A number of points are made about the duplicity of the so-called liberal northern white who seems to be in sympathy with the slave, but who, in reality, is more concerned about his own economic gain than about people. The book is poetically and dramatically written. Its authenticity is unquestionable. The author used historical records to construct the stories; the language rings true; and the characters breathe and live. The models they present are notable.

274. Little, Jean. *Mama's Going to Buy You a Mockingbird.* New York: Viking Kestrel, 1984; Puffin, pap. 213 pp. Fiction.

Interest level: Age 11+ Reading level: Grade 6

For the first half of the book the story tells about Jeremy, his younger sister, Sarah, their mother, and their dying father. The father, a teacher, has cancer, and the children are not informed about this until they overhear someone else talking about it. In general, the children are excluded from much that goes on. They are not permitted to visit their father in the hospital, except for occasional Sundays, and then not for very long. Isolated and uninformed, they are, therefore, confused and angry about the whole situation. Once the father is hospitalized he seems to be already dead, because there is no interaction and no real communication going on. Before his hospitalization, however, the reader comes to know him as a kind and thoughtful man. He gives his family some gifts that later become symbols for his presence.

After the father's death, the children, especially Jeremy, are required to take more and more responsibility for their welfare. They are required to move to an apartment, and their mother goes to school to equip herself with some skills for earning money. Jeremy becomes friendly with a girl, Tess, whom his father had especially wanted him to befriend. Tess's mother has deserted her and she is an outcast in school because she looks, dresses, and behaves differently from the other children.

During the course of the story the author deals with small losses of material objects and a pet. All of the lost items are found. When Jeremy finds it in his heart to give his mother a ceramic owl his father had given him, the message is conveyed that Jeremy has finally been able to accept the loss of his father and to share his memories and grief with his mother.

The support of other people is an important element in this book that deals with many losses, massive and slight. Tess cannot cope with her mother's desertion until she is befriended by Jeremy and his mother. Jeremy needs Tess's support. Tess's grandfather offers himself as a substitute grandfather to Jeremy and Sarah. They accept his offer, but Jeremy knows that although they are all a family now, it will never be the same as when their father was alive. He does not view a new "grandfather" as a replacement.

Little writes well. Interspersed in the story are references to other children's books, such as Kipling's *Kim* (Penguin, 1987), Paterson's *The Great Gilly Hopkins* (Harper, 1978). The idea of using books therapeutically is accepted as beneficial here. The withholding of information from the children seems to be accepted as common practice, but the reader can certainly see the harm in it. And, even though the mother offers the children the option of staying away from the funeral, they are wise enough to decline. The funeral, however, is not a personally tailored one; it seems to be a time of distress rather than healing. Children can be invited to discuss these problems, and to come up with their own solutions. In general, and because the story is such a good one, the book is a good one.

275. MacLachlan, Patricia. *Cassie Binegar*. New York: Harper, 1982, pap. 120 pp. Fiction.

Interest level: Ages 8–11 Reading level: Grade 4

Cassie mourns for her grandfather and dreams about him all the time. She bitterly regrets her behavior the last time she saw him, because she yelled at him and didn't apologize when he asked her to. She thinks that had she apologized he might not have died. She keeps this as a bitter secret to herself for a long time.

To compound Cassie's problems, her family has moved to a place near the sea, where her father and brothers can fish and her mother can tend a group of cottages in order to make a living. Cassie's family are all unconventional in some way, and Cassie longs for a more traditional sort of family, one more like that of her new friend, Margaret Mary. Margaret Mary's parents ask polite, dull questions; their house is very neat; and they use matching dishes at every meal. Margaret Mary wears matching clothes with matching ribbons and socks.

Cassie is a poet. She can express in writing some of the fears and feelings that she does not dare to express out loud. When her grandmother comes for an extended visit, Cassie is able, at last, to talk about her bad feelings, and her grandmother helps her to overcome them.

MacLachlan is a master of character creation. Each character is unique, yet each carries a universality that communicates itself to the reader. The author respects her characters and their situation. She accords them permission to express themselves in deep and thoughtful ways. The reader benefits from the product of the characters' thoughts, and from the questions that they ask. Often the questions are not answered, but they are, nevertheless, important to explore.

276. Marsoli, Lisa Ann. *Things to Know about Death and Dying.* Photos and illustrations. Morristown, N.J.: Silver, 1985. 48 pp. Nonfiction.

Interest level: Ages 7–12 Reading level: Grades 4–5

Short chapters on many subjects inform the reader about death's basics. Some of the topics are the usual found in nonfiction today—what death is physically, funerals, suicide, death of a pet, the death of a relative, the death of a child. Others are more unusual—dying in hospitals or at home or a hospice, death as portrayed on television, ceremonies at military funerals or for police or fire personnel who die in duty, obituaries, and afterlife.

Marsoli manages to give a great deal of information but also attends to emotions, with a fine tone at that. She tells readers death is not a punishment, but a natural eventual end for every animal and living thing. She reminds them that death can never be caused by people's thoughts. She alerts children to the idea that not everyone will know how to comfort them if they have had a death in the family and that anger the children may feel when they see this deficit in those around them is perfectly acceptable. She also reminds children that dying people have emotional needs, and if someone in their home should be dying she suggests they help that person with emotional needs by sitting and talking, reading to them, and so on. Marsoli is unafraid to talk about difficult subjects. Bibliography, index.

277. Martin, Ann M. *With You and Without You.* New York: Holiday, 1986; Scholastic, pap. 179 pp. Fiction.

Interest level: Age 11+ Reading level: Grade 5

Liza's father has been told that he will die in the next six months to a year. His heart is failing and nothing can be done to save him. The entire family responds by vowing to make his last days memorable and pleasurable. Their energy becomes focused on their last Christmas celebration together. When he dies, each of the family members responds differently to the loss. Liza, the protagonist, seems to be the most affected. She cannot visit her father's grave; she is angry at him for dying; she feels guilty about accepting invitations from friends, because she doesn't think it's appropriate to enjoy herself. Further, she thinks that the other members of her family have forgotten their father, and that they are not grieving. Once Liza realizes that her siblings and her mother are also mourning their loss, but in their own ways, she permits herself to accept the fact that she must, indeed, go on with her own life.

Martin realistically portrays a loving and normal family coping with an incalculable loss. The father and mother form a partnership to do all they can to prepare the children for his death. They do not pretend that there are no problems, but they try to create an idyllic time for everyone to remember. They try to ensure that there will be no guilty regrets later on.

But it is also made clear that no matter how carefully people prepare, the reality of this massive loss is larger than the expectation. The financial burdens and the pressure of time and obligations are difficult for everyone. Martin does her audience a service by providing characters at different developmental levels: Hope, the four-year-old, finds it difficult to believe that her father won't return; Brent, the eldest, must work hard in order to be able to afford to go to college; Carrie, the next oldest, baby-sits to earn money and plunges herself into activity so that she won't have time to think; the mother tries to pretend that she is stoic and strong enough for all of them.

Through constant communication and mutual affection the family works out their problems. They make some hard decisions, such as moving from the home that has been in their family for generations, but they are together, and they are functioning. The story is well written, realistic, and inspiring.

278. Mayled, Jon. *Death Customs: Religious Topics.* Photos. Morristown, N.J.: Silver, 1987. 32 pp. Nonfiction.

Interest level: Ages 7–12 Reading level: Grade 6

This book is one in a series imported from England called Religious Topics. Other titles include birth customs, initiation rites, and pilgrimage. Within this book's pages, which include large color photos, the author tries to describe the ways of seven different religions: Buddhism, Taoism (Chinese), Christianity, Hinduism, Islam, Judaism, and Sikhism. As a result, the coverage has to be superficial and can most benefit readers if an adult interprets the information. As this book is most likely to be used for short reports, and as most adults do not know that much about religions other than their own, it is unlikely the young reader will get the help he or she might need. For example, citing the beliefs of Jews, Christians, and Muslims, the introduction states, "When you die, God will decide if you have been a good or a bad person and whether you will go to heaven or should be punished." What is that punishment? No room to say, and the introduction ends.

Mayled doesn't have room to attend to emotions but tries to give the basics, for example, describing how some groups show their sadness by crying, although other groups may rarely cry because of a belief that dying and being reborn and a succession of such sequences brings one closer to God. The brevity does remain a problem, though, both in understanding ways so different from one's own and in terms of presenting cultures accurately. For example, the book states: "The last words a Jew says before death are called the 'Shema': 'Hear O Israel, the Lord our God is one God.' " The readers of this book may take that literally, as a form of last rites, but it is not accurate to interpret that literally. Who can say what people of any religion say last in their lives? Glossary, reading list, video list, index.

279. Mazer, Harry. *When the Phone Rang*. New York: Scholastic, 1985, hb and pap. 181 pp. Fiction.

Interest level: Age 11+ Reading level: Grade 6

Billy and his younger sister, Lori, are at home awaiting the arrival of their parents from the Caribbean when a phone call informs them that their parents' plane has crashed and that there are no survivors. The two teenagers go through the reactions of denial, anger, guilt, fear, and grief as they mourn their parents. They, together with their older brother, Kevin, who comes home from college and takes a job as a paramedic, decide to stay as a family, without any other adults to take care of them.

The three encounter many problems. They must sell a number of their valued possessions in order to get along financially. Kevin loses his job. Lori develops a friendship with a girl who is a bad influence on her, and she begins shoplifting. The boys bicker and finally get into a violent fistfight. They realize how serious matters are when they find Lori sitting on the edge of the roof.

Together the three siblings recognize that they are reacting to their parents' death, and that they must make some changes in order to remain a healthy family. When various family members offer to take them away to live, the three reiterate their commitment to each other. They all determine to do what is necessary to continue to live together.

Although the situation is a plausible one, it is unlikely that the siblings would not have collected a large sum of money from the airline and from insurance. Aside from this discrepancy, it is a little hard to believe that their concerned relatives would not be more actively intervening in the three siblings' lives. But the characters' emotional responses ring true, and their behavior can form the basis of much discussion among young readers.

280. Mellonie, Bryan. *Lifetimes: A Beautiful Way to Explain Death to Children.* Illus. by Robert Ingpen. New York: Bantam, 1983, pap. 40 pp. Nonfiction.

Interest level: Age 5+ Reading level: Grades 2–3

The exquisite paintings are the centerpiece of this Australian import, immediately stirring inspiration and appreciation for life and lifetimes, no matter how long. Each illustration is captioned in tiny print (for example, Young Apple Growing), framing it as a work of art. And the words? They are simple, poetic, and inviting: "There is a beginning and an ending for everything that is alive. In between is living. All around us, everywhere, beginnings and endings are going on all the time."

The paintings show animals and plants going through the process, explaining that although most of the time living things recover, illness or accident can hurt living things so much that "they die because they can no longer stay alive. This can happen when they are young, or old, or anywhere in between." But, reassuringly, the author adds: "Each one has its own special lifetime." For trees, therefore, it's one hundred years or more. For flowers and vegetables, it's seasonal existence. Butterflies live as butterflies only a few weeks. In each of these and other instances, the repetitive line appears: "That is their lifetime."

Toward the end, the author asks, "And people?" A painting showing four generations of women is accompanied by the answer: "Well, like everything else that is alive, people have lifetimes, too. They live for about sixty or seventy years, sometimes even longer, doing all the things that people do like growing up and being grown up." Then the reminder is repeated that sometimes illness or hurt interferes to cause earlier death. "It may be sad, but that is how it is for people. It is the way they live and it is their lifetime. So, no matter how long they are, or how short, lifetimes are really all the same." Quietly philosophical, this is a book that, in its beauty, contributes to acceptance.

281. Mills, Claudia. *All the Living.* New York: Macmillan, 1983; Skylark, pap. 114 pp. Fiction.

Interest level: Ages 8–12 Reading level: Grade 4

A family inherits a camp on Mooselookmeguntic Lake, Oquossoc, Maine. The parents go there intending to prepare it for sale, but the son and daughter fall in love with the area and hope to keep the camp and return each summer.

Although they appear to be a normal family, the father's attitudes and cruel insensitivity interfere with family relationships. Jamie, the son, is made to feel like a loser because he is not the superathlete that his macho father desires, but a quiet introspective boy who loves to read and do science projects and gets straight As on his report cards. Karla, a very independent and determined girl who is experiencing difficulty dealing with the concept of death, decides to become a vegetarian when she can no longer consider the thought of eating dead animals. Her father responds in an exasperated and derogatory manner rather than trying to understand his daughter's concerns. The mother diverts herself by writing articles that she hopes will be published. She attempts to pacify the family rather than deal with its conflicts

Karla's trauma with death is the result of an experience in school. For a science project, she had been studying the life cycle of a butterfly, caring for it as it metamorphosed through its stages. While the whole class watched her butterfly emerge and dry its wings, one classmate intentionally stomped on it. Karla was so horrified by this experience that she was not able to deal with it openly. Consequently, she began to dwell on the tragedy of each dead animal she saw on the highway. She was also anxious about the idea of living at her dead uncle's camp. She worried about which of the beds he might have died in.

Conflict arises between the usually loving and supportive brother and sister when Jamie tries to please his father by learning to fish. Karla cannot tolerate the idea. It erupts when the family picks more blueberries rather than leaving them for the birds. When the children are caught out in the lake during a sudden storm, Karla slips, hits her head, and falls overboard. Jamie jumps in and saves his sister and they are rescued by their father in a motorboat. When Karla wakes in the hospital realizing she had almost died, she starts to consider the joy of life rather than her concerns with death. From her Bible she reads Ecclesiastes and decides to join "All the Living."

Although the parents decide to keep the cabin and the conflicts between the brother and sister appear to be resolved at the end of the story, there is no clear indication that the father understands that he has been emotionally abusive. It does appear that he may have altered his priorities and is going to try to behave differently.

282. Oneal, Zibby. *A Formal Feeling.* New York: Viking, 1982; Fawcett Juniper, pap. 162 pp. Fiction.

Interest level: Age 12+ Reading level: Grades 6–7

The title is taken from an Emily Dickinson poem that describes the feelings that come after great pain, until finally the person who is suffering can let go. The story revolves around 16-year-old Anne, who has so idealized her dead mother that she cannot tolerate the idea of her father's remarriage. Her mother died only a year before, and she resents the idea that her father has been able to remarry in so short a time. She is now at home for her first vacation from school since her father's remarriage, and she is cold and unresponsive to her father and her stepmother.

The real problem is that Anne has not yet come to terms with her mother's death. In the year that has passed since her mother's death, she has cried only once, and she is determined not to do that again. She and her brother, Spencer, differ over what life was like when their mother was alive. Anne remembers only the good; Spencer remembers more dissent and errors.

At last, Anne remembers how difficult life with her mother really was. She remembers the time that her mother left them, and how she felt that she was to blame. She remembers her mother's insistence on self-control and lack of display of emotion. In the end she can let go of her hurt and anger and begin to live her own life again.

Oneal's prose is crisp and clean. She paints images for the reader of the characters, the setting, and the emotions of all of the characters. We get to know and understand even the minor players in this drama, and they all contribute to the impact of the story. Anne develops important insights during the brief period that she is at home, and the reader knows that they will serve her in good stead.

283. Osborn, Lois. *My Dad Is Really Something.* Illus. by Rodney Pate. Niles, Ill.: Whitman, 1983. 32 pp. Fiction.

Interest level: Ages 5–8 Reading level: Grades 2–3

Ron, a new boy in school, keeps bragging about his father to Harry. Harry loves his father dearly, but he is a little disappointed when his father won't even try to live up to the ideal description of Ron's father. Finally, at the school's open house, Harry and his family discover that Ron's father is dead. Harry is devastated by what he considers to be his friend's deception, but with the help of his father and mother, Harry begins to empathize with Ron's predicament. He arranges for Ron to accompany him and his father on some outings after that, and Ron now has a new father figure to brag about in school.

Osborn's intention of helping children learn to empathize with children for whom the death of a parent is still a difficult problem to cope with is a noble one. This book is somewhat oversimplified, but the solution of providing a surrogate parent is a practical one. We never encounter Ron's mother, so we don't know how helpful she is to her son, but the fact that Ron's father died a number of years ago suggests that she should have sought help for her son long ago. Nevertheless, this book is a gentle and constructive one for young childen to read.

284. Paterson, Katherine. *Park's Quest.* New York: Lodestar, 1988. 148 pp. Fiction.

Interest level: Age 11+ Reading level: Grades 6–7

The book's title prepares us for the actual and symbolic quest that Park, the 11-year-old protagonist, undertakes. Park's father was killed 10 years ago in the Vietnam War. His mother refuses to talk to Park about his father, or, indeed, even about his father's family. Park yearns to hear about his father. He longs to know about his own background. Park has always felt multiple loss, because not only is his father dead, but when his mother refuses him any information, it's as if he never existed. Paterson ably demonstrates what an error it is to try to keep the truth from children. In the end, the mother recognizes her mistake. This recognition helps the mother as well as Park.

Ever since he was little, Park has actively fantasized that he is a knight who lives in the time of quests and daring and chivalrous acts. He plays out these fantasies in scenarios with courtly language and knightly deeds. He reads voraciously, mostly books of high fantasy.

Park has found a picture of his father in a book of poetry. He resolves to unlock the mystery of his father's (and his) identity, first by reading his father's books, and second, by finding his father's name on the Vietnam Veterans Memorial in Washington, D.C. A librarian has told Park that people can be known by the books that they read, and he has seen evidence that this belief holds true. His father's books include all of Conrad's work, and when Park has read his way through his father's books, he goes to the memorial and does, indeed, find his father's name. This gives him the courage to confront his mother, who finally consents to contact his paternal relatives and arranges for Park to visit them.

During this two-week visit Park discovers that he has an uncle and a grandfather. He also finds out, eventually, that his mother divorced his father after she learned that he had had an affair with a Vietnamese woman, and that they had had a child. After this divorce, Park's father returned to Vietnam for a second tour of duty, during which time he was killed. The child now lives with Park's Uncle Frank, who has married the child's mother.

Park comes to recognize that he has been feeling guilty all these years for his father's death. But Park also discovers that his grandfather and his mother have also felt guilty about the same thing. Only when Park can ask the question of Parsifal, the archetype of grail-seeking knights, "What ails thee?" can he set himself and his grandfather free. There is also the hope that he can do the same for his mother. He has accomplished every knight's quest: He has reached the holy grail.

Religion plays an important role in Paterson's life. And her books reflect this religious and philosophical base in their ability to ask the deepest of questions and to tackle the most profound of human emotions. They deal with issues of morality, life and death, guilt, and the way people choose to live their lives. Her characters are often called on to be more than themselves, to rise to greater levels than what can reasonably be expected of them. And they do. Park's quest is an individual one, but it echoes the search that everyone must conduct, for one's own sense of self, and the expiation of one's own culpability for the errors of the past.

285. Payne, Bernal C., Jr. *The Late, Great Dick Hart.* Boston: Houghton Mifflin, 1986. 133 pp. Fiction.

Interest level: Age 10+ Reading level: Grade 5

Dick Hart, Tom's idolized best friend, has died of a brain tumor at age 12. Six months later, Tom is still bereft over his friend's death. One night Tom is taking a lonely walk to the town square when he meets Dick, looking as though he were alive. Dick explains that the world in which he now resides is filled with former residents of their town, all of whom have died, and all of whom have selected the age at which they wish to remain, no matter how long the passage of time. Thus, while Tom is now 13 years old, Dick is still 12.

Dick and Tom enter Dick's world through a special opening in a tree. After they have spent some time together, Tom becomes aware of the gap between him and Dick, and the changed perception he is developing about his relationship with Dick. When Dick gives Tom the opportunity to accept an early and sudden death, and to come to stay in Dick's world forever, Tom realizes that he must decline. He wants the opportunity to find out what his life will be in his own world. He knows that Dick's company is not sufficient for him any longer. He reenters the world of the living and says good-bye to his friend for what he knows will be many years, but he is comforted by the knowledge that they will meet again. Dick reluctantly returns to his world beyond the living, and the special exit that he used is closed forever by the One in charge.

The book invites a consideration of such philosophical issues as what happens to people when they die, and if there is an afterlife, what does it look like? Readers will undoubtedly ask such questions as "How did Dick get away with his escape and his bringing Tom into the afterlife? Where was God?" and "If all the people who died from this town were supposed to be in this small location, why wasn't it enormously overpopulated?

Tom's supernatural encounter with his friend helps Tom to value and appreciate life. Perhaps young readers will also take this opportunity to look at their own lives. The author also invites a look at changes that occur without our even recognizing that they are happening. Tom tries to deny that he is taller and stronger than Dick. He wants to keep within himself the image of the friend who outshone, outran, and outsmarted him. This may lead readers to ponder the issue of friendship.

Payne deals well with the issue of coping with the death of a dear friend. Tom's mother is very understanding and helps Tom to name his emotions and to accept his angry and negative feelings. Although the book contains a number of logical inconsistencies, it is well worth reading because it is well written, contains an interesting premise, and will stimulate much thought on the part of readers.

286. Pomerantz, Barbara. *Bubby, Me, and Memories.* Photos by Leon Lurie. New York: Union of American Hebrew Congregations, 1983. 32 pp. Fiction.

Interest level: Ages 5–9 Reading level: Grades 1–2

In the foreword, early childhood educator Pomerantz says: "When children ask questions, they need answers. When children feel grief, they need comfort. When children see us mourn, they need our open permission to comfort us. When children are curious about death, they need to be shown the purpose of life." With these aims in mind, her protagonist, a young girl of eight or nine, tells the story of her *Bubby,* the Jewish word for grandmother. Large photos illustrate the girl's memories: walking in the park, being hugged and read to, receiving presents, baking challah together, and sharing jokes. Then, "A few days ago my Bubby died." The girl relates what her parents have told her, among which are the concepts "It's okay to cry" and "Everything that is alive dies some day. That means old people and very, very sick people, and plants, and animals." Some may question limiting death to the old and sick and wonder if a qualifier such as "usually" would have been more courageous, but the rest is on target. The child then tells of her feelings and how her parents responded (for example, denial relating death to sleep, to which her father responds, "Bubby will not wake up again"). The child also shares Jewish mourning customs of the Shiva condolence period, the Kaddish prayer for the dead, and the book concludes with an honest appraisal of what grief is like and how we work through it: "Sometimes she feels lonely, but she remembers the things they did together and begins to feel better."

287. Prestine, Joan Singleton. *Someone Special Died.* Illus. by Meredith Johnson. Los Angeles: Price/Stern/Sloan, 1987, pap. 24 pp. Fiction.

Interest level: Ages 4–8 Reading level: Grade 1

One of several books in the My Special Feelings series, this entry takes the concept of universality a bit too far. The first-person protagonist opens the book this way: "My name is Rick. Someone special I knew died." Then we learn how he feels as he talks and walks with his mother and dog. We know the special person is male, because reference is made to "he," and from pictures Rick draws we see "he" may be an adult, possibly a father, but "he" may also be used for simplicity of expression. The author seems to have wanted the deceased to stand for anyone the reader fills in. What happens as a result, however, is that the question "Who in the world was this someone special?" becomes dominant, and it's hard to concentrate on how the child misses him, how everyday things will not be the same, how Rick wanted him to get well, and what the death process is. It's a shame, too, because the process is described well: "His body stopped working." Rick's way of coping, by remembering through the creation of a scrapbook, is a good idea, too. Why couldn't they just spell it out, though, thereby allowing readers to concentrate on the otherwise fine content?

288. Richter, Elizabeth. *Losing Someone You Love: When a Brother or Sister Dies.* Photos by the author. New York: Putnam, 1986. 80 pp. Nonfiction.

Interest level: Age 10+ Reading level: Grade 5

The grief of 15 adolescents is expressed in their own words. The passages vary in length, and the teens differ in their stages of bereavement and ability to verbalize agony, but the halting quality of their narration enhances the book's piercing reality. Their siblings have died from crib death, vehicular and drowning accidents, cancer, blood disorders, murder, and suicide. The person lost was usually a teen (in one case, a twin), but sometimes a younger child, toddler, or infant. Some of the deaths were recent, others many years ago. Regardless of the circumstances, Richter allows survivors to speak whatever is on their minds now. The composite, edited result is an unobtrusive, natural overview of likely emotions—fear for one's health, guilt at survival, abandonment, pervasive sadness or depression, the need to try to recover.

Except for recommending the sibling and teen groups of The Compassionate Friends (see Appendix under Death, Bereavement), Richter wisely doesn't give step-by-step procedures for that recovery. What she offers instead are the details other survivors and their friends want over and over again as reassurance that they're not alone—a father's scream on hearing the news, watching a crypt be sealed, having trouble falling asleep. As she did in *The Teenage Hospital Experience* (Coward, 1982), Richter provides one compelling doorway out of the loneliness.

289. Rodowsky, Colby. *Fitchett's Folly.* New York: Farrar, 1987. 166 pp. Fiction.

Interest level: Ages 9–12 Reading level: Grade 4

Sarey's father died while he was trying to save the lives of Faith Wilkinson's family. He did not succeed in doing so, and Sarey's stepmother has taken Faith to live with the family. Sarey's younger brother, Henry, and Sarey's friends accept Faith and even seem to favor her over Sarey. But Sarey cannot forgive Faith for being the cause of her father's death.

Sarey has a history of not accepting adversity. When her mother died as a result of giving birth to Henry, Sarey's aunt, her mother's sister, came to take care of them. Eventually Sarey's father and aunt marry. In Sarey's eyes it is a marriage of convenience rather than love. She calls her stepmother Aunt-Mama, and so does Henry, even though he has never known another mother. Sarey never changes her attitude toward her stepmother; her birth mother is always her "real" mother in her mind.

There are some problems in this otherwise excellent and absorbing book. Sarey behaves somewhat inconsistently. If she is so unforgiving of Faith for having been the cause of her father's death, why does it not occur to her that Henry was, in the same way, the cause of her mother's death. She seems to harbor no resentment against him. She is a bright child, but many of her actions belie this quality. She also has a best friend to whom she confides much, but she never lets her friend know of her newly acquired terror of the sea, or her feelings about Faith and her father. Nevertheless, the story brings up issues that children who have lost a parent must face. And the behavior and attitudes toward stepparents and stepsiblings will invite much discussion on the part of young readers.

290. Rofes, Eric E., ed., and the Unit at Fayerweather Street School. *The Kids' Book about Death and Dying: By and for Kids.* Boston: Little, 1985. 128 pp. Nonfiction.

Interest level: Age 10+ Reading level: Grade 5

"The Unit" is a voluntary discussion group/class in the private Fayerweather Street School, Cambridge, Massachusetts. Rofes, a teacher, along with his pupils created a course of study that resulted in this book. The youngsters, ages 11 through 14, shared ideas, saw related movies, read related books, and interviewed kids, parents, and other adults. They visited and talked to professionals in hospitals, suicide prevention centers, hospices, funeral homes, and cemeteries. To start off, they talked about the responses they had to the first deaths they were aware of; those responses form the introductory material. They also did exercises, the results of which are here to be learned from. For example, what would death look like if it were a person or an animal?

The chapters cover causes of death; what death is; legal death; euthanasia; autopsies; funeral customs; burial; cremation; death of a pet, parent, sibling; suicide and other violent deaths; death caused by illness; and life after death. The tone is chatty, and children are quoted frequently. What the authors have provided is a summation of real feelings, not the experts' feelings disguised in children's voices. As such the authors offer good ideas. For example, when a child has lost a parent, the teacher should consult with the child before discussing it with the class. The book is also filled with dramatic specifics that are very memorable, for example, a girl whose father had always had sherry and a slice of bologna after dinner. When that tradition was gone, it was hard for her to sit at the table at the close of the meal. The ideas throughout give an insight into childhood—from the discussion of mounting Roy Rogers's horse Trigger to children with cancer learning not to ask their parents certain questions if those questions brought tears to the parents' eyes. Very worthwhile. Bibliography.

291. Schwandt, Stephen. *Holding Steady*. New York: Henry Holt, 1988. 161 pp. Fiction.

Interest level: Age 12+ Reading level: Grade 7

Brendon Turner is the only person in his family who has not yet come to terms with his father's death. His younger brother seems to have accepted it almost immediately, and his mother, although she misses her husband, feels numb, and sometimes cries when she thinks of him, has resumed most of her usual activities. But Brendon has cut off most of his old friends and refuses to go on vacations. Now he has reluctantly consented to spend a month with his mother and brother at a remote island resort where they have gone before as a family, and where his mother and father first met.

On the island he meets Courtney, a girl to whom he is very attracted, and he meets a number of his father and mother's old friends. Over the course of the summer he realizes that he is jealous of his younger brother because he thinks that his father favored him. He almost kills himself proving that he is brave and worthy, and he realizes that he has been a fool. His brother sets him straight about his father's true feelings—he loved and admired Brendon—and Brendon ends the summer having come back to a sense of himself and having forgiven himself for his father's death.

Other issues in the book include Courtney's father's alcoholism and

Courtney's desire to have a good relationship with her father, who is divorced from her mother because of his problem with alcohol. A bully, coming of age, and ecology are also part of the plot, but the major theme is that of coming to terms with the death of a loved one.

292. Simon, Norma. *The Saddest Time.* Niles, Ill.: Whitman, 1986. 40 pp. Fiction.

Interest level: Ages 4–8 Reading level: Grade 3

In poetic prose and faultless understanding of children's development, Simon recounts three situations in which people die and are mourned. In each case, there are knowledgeable and sensitive adults to help the children cope with their loss. The deaths of a young child, an old woman, and an adult but not-quite-middle-aged man are dealt with honestly but delicately.

When Teddy, an eight-year-old, is killed in an accident, the children recall with sadness the times they weren't nice to him, or quarreled with him. Their teacher explains that no one is perfect and that the children's feelings are natural. He helps them to express their feelings on paper in letters to Teddy's parents. When Emily's grandmother dies, Emily cries with her grandfather, but also remembers the good times with him as well. Similarly, with Michael's Uncle Joe, who dies after a long illness, Michael is frightened at the thought that perhaps his parents will die young, too. His family helps him to feel more secure and to think of ways to help his aunt, and in that way to handle his own grief.

The stories are the stuff of which literature is made. They are gentle and true. The language is strong and flowing; the characters are appealing.

293. Smith, Doris Buchanan. *The First Hard Times.* New York: Viking, 1983; Dell, pap. 137 pp. Fiction.

Interest level: Age 10+ Reading level: Grade 5

The story centers around 12-year-old Ancil's adjustment to her mother's remarriage and to the fact that her father is not coming home from Vietnam. He has been missing in action for over 10 years, yet Ancil clings to the hope that he is alive, and that he will return. No one in her family talks to her about her obsession, nor do they seem to really understand it, with the possible exception of her grandmother.

Harvey, her stepfather, tries to woo Ancil and her sisters with elaborate gifts. He seems like a very kind person, and Ancil's mother and he love each other very much. It takes a long time, but finally Ancil is ready to relinquish some of her grief and become part of the family again.

It is difficult for the reader to understand the source of Ancil's preoccupation with her father. She was only two years old when he disappeared, and she has no real memory of him. The missing-in-action status is barely discussed, although the grandmother does allude to dealing with the government. Although the story is an interesting one, and the issue of MIAs is timely, the author never really addresses the issues. Ancil's recovery is as inexplicable as her long period of mourning.

294. Stevens, Margaret. *When Grandpa Died.* Photos by Kenneth Ualand. Chicago: Childrens, rev. ed. 1985, hb and pap. 32 pp. Nonfiction.
Interest level: Ages 5–9 Reading level: Grades 1–2

The first-person narrator and her grandfather spent lots of time together because he lived with her family. Once they found a dead bird in the garden, and this became a reason to discuss why things die—illness, accident, age, and other reasons. The two ceremoniously buried the bird in the yard and continued to discuss death, the grandfather saying, "Death is natural." The narrator informs the audience: "Natural means that things turn out the way they are supposed to." Some children (and adults, too) might question this concept when it comes to premature death of children or young adults; others may find it comforting. Also discussed are the changes in the living, and even after death, as the bird's body changes would help the flowers to grow.

The next phase of the book concerns the grandfather's illness and death in the hospital. The girl is allowed and encouraged to express her emotions—to be angry, to want to keep contact by staying near her grandfather's things, to cry, and to say good-bye at his funeral. In the final pages, time has passed and the girl knows her grandfather will not return to be with her; a strange afterthought is the presence of a little sister, seen for the first time: "My sister is too little to understand about Grandpa. Someday when she's older, I'm going to tell her all about him." Does this mean a secret's been kept from the child (who looks about age four or five), or she's been told but can't grasp it fully? The ambiguity doesn't serve the book well. Aside from this, the book's format consists of a large, full-page photograph on one side, and narration of a paragraph or two on the other works well for its purposes of informing of the permanence of death.

295. Talbert, Marc. *Dead Birds Singing.* Boston: Little, 1985; Dell, pap. 224 pp. Fiction.
Interest level: Age 12+ Reading level: Grade 7

Matt Smythe had just won a swim meet and was reliving the sweetness of victory in his mind as he was riding home with his mother and sister. Without warning, a car driven by a drunk driver swerves into their lane, killing his mother and fatally injuring his sister. As Matt's father had been killed in the Vietnam War, and Matt has no other relatives, his best friend's family takes him in.

No matter how hard his new family tries to make Matt feel at home he cannot overcome his feelings of anger, guilt, grief, and loneliness. Matt cannot even comfort himself with happy memories; they have all been erased by the awful memory of the accident. Only when Matt can finally say "good-bye" to his mother and sister can he begin to live again in the present and think about the future.

The book is an accurate portrayal of the trauma of sudden and violent death. It contains language that is somewhat sexually explicit, and there is profanity, but it is in the context of the story, and mature readers will be able to handle it.

296. Tallmountain, Mary. *Green March Moons.* Illus. by Joseph E. Senungetuk. Berkeley, Calif.: New Seed, 1987. 28 pp. Fiction.

Interest level: Ages 11–15 Reading level: Grade 5

This is a story of native-Alaskan life. During the winter camps, a young Koyukon girl suffers yet finds the indomitable spirit to carry on. In this year, 11-year-old Tash loses her mother to spreading disease. Already mature, she helps prepare her mother's body for the burial rituals and takes full part in the ceremony. Later, the terrible winter takes its full toll when Tash is sexually abused by an uncle given to drunkenness. In spite of it all, she finds value in herself and makes plans for the future. Readers not familiar with native-Alaskan ways may need introduction to the life circumstance, as this book leaps into the culture. Readers may find the death rituals of interest, particularly the custom of placing the body in a sack and hoisting it on a rope above ground on a tree branch.

297. Tarlton, Gillian Leigh. *The Two Worlds of Coral Harper.* New York: Harcourt, 1983. 150 pp. Fiction.

Interest level: Age 10+ Reading level: Grade 6

As the story begins, the reader finds Coral, a 14-year-old gifted pianist, traveling from her fishing-village home to live with her aunt in the city of Auckland, New Zealand, and to study at the School of Music. Through a series of flashbacks we learn about Coral's life with her creative, artistic mother and her fisherman father; about the accidental drowning death of her mother five years earlier; and about the stages of mourning that Coral and her father have progressed through toward an understanding of each other. In addition to the mourning process we observe Coral's maturation from a little girl who believed that her father was omnipotent, to a young woman who understands her own goal, her father's grief and fallibility, and her mother's gifts.

Coral's initial reaction to her mother's death was strong denial. On finding her mother's body washed ashore, she tried to keep her warm and to treat her as though she would wake up. She felt that her father had deserted her when he was not there to rescue her mother. By blaming him and refusing to acknowledge his grief, she isolated herself from him, and he alienated himself from her in his own despair. Only when threatened by the intervention of outsiders were both father and daughter able to move beyond their deep depression to an acceptance of the mother's death.

Coral and her father are strong characters who have both been caught in their unreasonable expectations. When they recognize that they are each human, and that the woman they mourn was also human, they are able to transcend their grief and embrace life again. The book moves well and conveys the lesson that the acceptance of loss takes time and willingness to forgive oneself.

298. Van Oosting, James. *Maxie's Ghost.* New York: Farrar, 1987. 118 pp. Fiction.

Interest level: Ages 9–12 Reading level: Grade 4

Maxie and Mercy's parents have been killed in a plane crash. The children's grandmother is recovering from a broken leg, and from the shock of learning about the death of her son and daughter-in-law. The grandmother and Maxie are very close; they write to each other every day, and they love each other's company. The children's aunt keeps them for a while, but finally has to place them in an orphanage because she has a demanding full-time job. Grandma has promised to come and get them as soon as she is well.

Meanwhile, Maxie has developed a keen interest in ghosts. His friend, Judy, has seen her father's ghost, and Mrs. Becker, a teacher he admires, has seen her brother's ghost. Now, on a day when his class is enjoying an outing at the orphanage, Maxie sees a shadowy figure he is sure is a ghost.

Maxie, Judy, and Mrs. Becker are badly hurt when lightning strikes a tree. Maxie is in a coma, during which his grandmother appears to him as a ghost, and together they fly off. Grandma has just died. In this mystical experience Maxie is given the choice of whether to die now or later. Because of his little sister, Mercy, he decides to come back to life. But he will always remember his grandma and this experience. And he is ready to face the difficulties of his life, because he now knows there is something beyond life.

It is interesting that it is his grandmother, not his mother or father, to whom Maxie feels the closest. She is certainly a remarkable character, lively even in death. The author deals with the orphanage in an amorphous way; we are not quite sure what is going on there, but it does not seem to be an abusive place.

The characters in the story merit a sequel. Children will wonder what happened next. Perhaps they can be invited to speculate in writing. The issues of out-of-body experience and ghosts are handled respectfully and persuasively by the author. The book will appeal to many young readers.

299. Varley, Susan. *Badger's Parting Gifts.* Illus. by the author. New York: Lothrop, 1984. 24 pp. Fiction.
Interest level: Ages 7–10 Reading level: Grade 3

In poetic prose and illustrations reminiscent of Ernest Shepard, the story tells of Badger, who was much loved by all of the woodland creatures. He tried to prepare his friends for his death, but when he finally died they grieved. During the springtime, Badger's friends gather and remember the kind and good things that Badger did. From cutting out paper figures to skating, from knotting a tie to baking, Badger had given his friends many gifts that they could now recall with love and gratitude. And whenever his name was mentioned it brought happiness. That is a legacy many people would covet.

The book is helpful in conveying a process of preparing for death and in affirming the value of a life well lived.

300. Wilhelm, Hans. *I'll Always Love You.* Illus. by the author. New York: Crown, 1985. 32 pp. Fiction.
Interest level: Ages 4–7 Reading level: Grade 2

Elfie and her young master grow up together, but, as a dog's life is much shorter than a human's, Elfie grows old and dies when her master is still quite young. His grief over her death is ameliorated by the knowledge that every night he has engaged in a ritual of telling his dog that he'd always love her. And now, even in death he knows that his love will continue. He refuses an offer of a new puppy, even though he knows that Elfie wouldn't mind. He is not yet ready for a new pet, but when he does decide to have a new pet he knows that he will tell the new pet, every night, "I'll always love you."

The story meets many of the criteria that are recommended for helping children to cope with loss. The child knows that Elfie will not return; he is permitted to mourn, together with his family; he does not accept a new pet as a replacement for the one that died; and he takes comfort in the relationship that he had with his dog while the dog was still alive.

The illustrations admirably convey the sense of love and caring that the boy and his dog share.

301. Wood, Phyllis Anderson. *Then I'll Be Home Free.* New York: Dodd, 1986. 256 pp. Fiction.
Interest level: Ages 11–15 Reading level: Grade 6

In spite of the tragedy of her parents' death when she was an infant, Rosemary has been generally fortunate. She has been raised by loving, imaginative grandparents, and we'd all like to meet someone like her lifelong neighbor Kevin, who's perceptive, sweet, and smart—the model of a nonmacho future man. In junior year, she begins to see her schoolmate differently. It is Kevin who stays close when Rosemary's grandmother dies suddenly. He is the only outsider at the funeral. Now, when Rosemary finds herself "parentified" in caring for her suicidal grandfather, she must ask herself if she dares respond to the overtures of Kevin's extended hand. Might loving mean losing? The contrast of the everyday world with the despondent world of mourning is portrayed well, as is the trendy hug-a-pet program that brings comfort to her grandfather. But does a Kevin really exist? If so, where can we get a clone?

302. Yolen, Jane. *A Sending of Dragons.* Illus. by Tom McKeveny. New York: Delacorte, 1987. 240 pp. Fiction.

Interest level: Age 12+ Reading level: Grade 5

Jakkin and Akki have been through many adventures separately and together in *Dragon's Blood* (Delacorte, 1982) and *Heart's Blood* (Delacorte, 1984), the first two books in the Pit Dragon trilogy. In this third book of the series they make use of their ability to send mind messages to each other and to the dragons, and they prepare to become useful citizens of their world. In the process they decide to save the lives of dragons who have been condemned to a bloody death in an underground human subculture. Jakkin has found it difficult to recover from the death of his dragon, Heart's Blood, and almost all of his actions are in response to his intense and lingering grief over her death. By the book's end, however, he has turned his grieving—with Akki's help—into a positive thing.

Although the books are high fantasy, the emotions and challenges in them reflect the coming of age and coping with loss that we encounter in life. The author poetically and dramatically portrays the characters as real people, making mistakes, atoning for them, and learning from experience.

Suicide

A suicide is one of the most traumatic deaths faced by a family. A significant person in a child's life may be motivated by great unhappiness to lose everyone and everything by rejecting life itself. Often it is not death the family member seeks, but help with a problem. However, if the suicide attempt is successful, it is too late to help, and both the one who cries for help and the survivors lose. Too often the member of the family who attempts self-destruction—and often succeeds—is a child, performing the ultimate act of separation.

303. Bennett, Paul. *Follow the River.* New York: Orchard, 1987. 190 pp. Fiction.

Interest level: Age 13+ Reading level: Grades 7–8

"Lighthorse" Harry Lee falls in love with Nancy Sutton. It is a difficult match: Lighthorse, his five brothers, and his father are laborers; Nancy's father is a banker. Nancy's mother is an alcoholic, and a discontented, snobbish adultress. Lighthorse's family is close-knit "salt-of-the-earth." A romance develops between Lighthorse and Nancy, especially after Lighthorse rescues Nancy from the school bully. Tragedy strikes when Nancy's mother kills one of Lighthorse's brothers and then commits suicide. Eventually Nancy and Lighthorse get back together, planning to go to the same college.

Bennett is a poet, and the story is written in the elusive language that poetry sometimes has. References are made that are not easy to follow; events happen in a few brief words, and then much language is spent reflecting on the events. Not enough information is given about the source or the evolution of the characters' problems; they are just there. Certainly no hint is provided of how to help the troubled characters, and none is forthcoming. Elmo, the good brother, dies; another brother, Ed, remains an alcoholic with not much chance of changing; Mrs. Sutton dies. This is not a book to use for any sort of information gathering. But the story is a challenging one and might be attractive to young teenagers who are grappling with some of the problems of growing up in families whose values are at odds with theirs.

304. Bunting, Eve. *Face at the Edge of the World.* New York: Clarion, 1985. 158 pp. Fiction.

Interest level: Age 12+ Reading level: Grade 7

Seventeen-year-old Jed Lennox must contend with problems that would overwhelm a mature adult: his best friend, Charlie, has just committed suicide; Jed's mother died when she gave birth to him, and his father blames him for her death. As a consequence, Jed's father is rarely at home, leaving Jed to fend for himself. Nevertheless, Jed is a bright, sensitive young man. He is an outstanding photographer and has won several prizes for his photographs.

Charlie's suicide is not the only one in the story. Another boy at the same high school kills himself, and a retarded young man attempts suicide. Such issues as drug abuse, media hype, bigotry, guilt, and fear of punishment emerge as contributing factors. Guilt, anger, and despair lead the list of reactions to the suicides. A variety of young people are presented to the reader, supporting the understanding that each person is an individual. Peer pressure is strong, but individual relationships are stronger.

The story takes the form of a mystery to be solved, with Jed the protagonist and detective. Through a series of events and a building up of clues, Jed uses his powers of observation and his love for his friend to uncover the answer to why Charlie killed himself. The ending is positive but realistic. A masterful book.

305. Gardner, Sandra, with Rosenberg, Gary. *Teenage Suicide.* New York: Messner, 1985, hb and pap. 128 pp. Nonfiction.

Interest level: Age 12+ Reading level: Grade 6

A free-lance writer and a psychiatrist collaborate to tell the stories of six who tried to commit suicide and the signals they gave off. The narrative is concrete and thus affecting: "Every night for a month, Debbie cut skin off her wrists with a razor blade. The only way she knew she was alive, she says, was when she saw the blood."

Gardner and Rosenberg wisely relate a lot of suicide feelings to previous losses such as death and divorce, loss of childhood, and loss of self-esteem. Rich with psychological concepts (for example, "the expendable child," trying to kill off unwanted portions of the self), these ideas are useful in trying to find reasons for suicide and attempts. Pressures for success are also attended to here, as well as social and cultural factors (for example, fear of pregnancy as a factor in suicide).

Some adolescents participate in other self-destructive risk taking and the authors have examined such taking of fatal risks. Perhaps some readers will identify themselves in the stories of anorexia, sexual acting out, and so forth. There is also a chapter on the romance of suicide in the media, including suicide clusters. This insightful book concludes with a section on prevention, highlighted by the travails of Kim Fields, an actress on the television program "Facts of Life." Her own feelings made her become active in suicide prevention work. Prevention programs are described, along with warnings not to keep secrets of suicide intentions if one knows someone is feeling that way. Resources for help, bibliography for adult readers and suggestions for further readings, index.

306. Hall, Lynn. *If Winter Comes.* New York: Scribner, 1986. 128 pp. Fiction.

Interest level: Age 12+ Reading level: Grade 7

The United States is threatened with nuclear annihilation within 36 hours. In the time left to them, Meredith McCoy and her boyfriend, Barry, draw close to those who are important to them and in the process discover what is meaningful in their own lives.

The dominant theme of Hall's sensitively written book is living with the thought of imminent death. Given the opportunity of knowing what their "end" will be, Meredith and Barry, who are high school sweethearts, look beyond their own relationship to discover what is of value and of purpose in their lives.

Barry is a young man materially indulged but denied love and understanding by a stereotypically domineering, "successful" father and a mother who long ago escaped into the world of tranquilizers. Barry views death as a promise of relief from a world without affection. He has courted death's power since he attempted suicide "to get what he wanted" while still a young child. Faced with the reality of death, however, his romantic notion of it becomes apparent; the thought of suffering after a nuclear explosion is intolerable. He panics, denies the possibility of suffering, and then plans to kill himself before the bomb explodes, although it becomes apparent to the reader that, as when he was a child, he will not go through with it. Barry has a faith in eternity, and he turns again and again to a comforting book that promises life after death.

Meredith, on the other hand, with the background of strong, loving, though separated parents, sees the world as beautiful and wants it to continue. The book presents a good contrast between the adolescents' perspectives on the world. It offers its readers the opportunity to think about what really matters to them in this life.

307. Harlan, Elizabeth. *Watershed.* New York: Viking Kestrel, 1986. 224 pp. Fiction.

Interest level: Age 12+ Reading level: Grade 6

Why is one sibling resilient, while the other breaks like the branch of a young apple tree, unable "to carry the burden of the fruit it bears"? Treacherous pitfalls in familial devotion are given startling plotlines as vulnerable Noel, unable to get Jeb to join him, angrily sets forth to relieve summer heat by unleashing a trickle of water from the town blockhouse. There is a flood and not even a lawyer father can avert Noel's detention. When released, he has lost all hope and commits suicide. Does Jeb's ability to go on in the face of unspeakable tragedy come from sports, loving his girlfriend, somehow seeing the same flawed parents differently? While played out in sweeping gestures, Harlan's response to the question is open-ended but richly textured; like Jeb, readers will find varied answers in their own strengths.

308. Kolehmainen, Janet, and Handwerk, Sandra. *Teen Suicide: A Book for Friends, Family, and Classmates.* Minneapolis: Lerner, 1986, hb and pap. 72 pp. Nonfiction.

Interest level: Ages 10–16 Reading level: Grade 4

Kolehmainen and Handwerk, counselors and developers of community programs on suicide prevention, offer an analysis of what is known about suicide, including the statistics, myths, and warning signs. Narrative profiles of attempters, friends of attempters, and those who succeed demonstrate through dramatic specific what can happen. For example, with Steve, a boy with suicidal thoughts, the value of a friend and counselor listening comes through. Other chapters demonstrate involving an adult, anger, regrets, risks, the aftermath of a suicide attempt, and grief shared by a community. A final chapter discusses ways we can help ourselves and others, professional help, and community resources. Of books in this genre, this one is simply structured, not laden with sociological analysis. The stories are readable and make the points smoothly. Those who are not deep readers will find its straightforward information and advice valuable.

309. Kunz, Roxane Brown, and Swenson, Judy Harris. *Feeling Down: The Way Back Up*. Illus. by Mary McKee. Minneapolis: Dillon, 1986. 48 pp. Fiction.

Interest level: Ages 8–13 Reading level: Grades 3–4

Important words are given bold print in this educational book—words like feelings and suicide. Sam and Kirk's teenage sister, Stephanie, has tried to commit suicide, and no one in the family understands why. Together, they go to a therapist (another word in bold letters) to try to find out what went wrong and clear it up. It turns out that Stephanie feels the burden of pressures—to get As in school, baby-sit, do chores, practice piano, and act and look like a young lady. However, with a change in schools and no new friends, she's flunking.

Soon, Kirk, who relates the story, becomes angry at Stephanie's selfish deed, which now takes up all the family time. He's embarrassed as the neighbors talk, too, and slugs a kid in school. The therapist later calls this inappropriate behavior, as opposed to talking, which is appropriate behavior (both in bold). She teaches them to communicate better—to neither ignore nor shout, how to listen, and how to record their feelings. In their talks they also realize that Stephanie had given body language signals to her feelings for quite a while. In time, Stephanie is ready to leave the hospital, and the family is better able to communicate. Although didactic, the book will be of help to siblings, the primary group addressed.

Appended are a glossary, danger signals, an adult resource guide, which includes questions for discussion, and stress reduction activities (for example, reading books, using art, music, and physical exercise). There are also games for communication, resources in the community, and a bibliography.

310. Langone, John. *Dead End: A Book about Suicide.* Boston: Little, 1986. 176 pp. Nonfiction.

Interest level: Age 12+ Reading level: Grade 7

In Langone's tradition (*Goodbye to Bedlam,* Little, 1974, and so on), *Dead End* is both scholarly and thoughtfully expressive (for example, suicide is "murder's blood brother"). Chapters on history, psychology, social attitudes, and suicide notes are given added punch by citing such unusual sources as high school newspapers and interspersing comments of teen attempters and survivors. Its considerable superiority over other recent volumes about the second leading cause of teen death lies in several areas: lengthy, informed discussion of the role of biochemistry and genetic links in depression and impulsive behavior; inclusion of a wide range of research results (for example, stress is greatest at the start of a school term, not at exam time); differentiations between attempters and committers; and highly detailed checklists, warning signals, and guidelines for prevention. Perhaps most important is the investigation of controversies such as the right to die and the possibly contagious influences of music and media, even daring to ask if and how we can openly balance talk about the topic without yielding larger numbers of suicides through our focus.

311. Leder, Jane Merskey. *Dead Serious: A Book for Teenagers about Teenage Suicide.* New York: Atheneum, 1987. 160 pp. Nonfiction.

Interest level: Age 12+ Reading level: Grade 6

Journalist Leder provides good warning signs, cites experiences of the founders of Loving Outreach to Survivors of Suicide, and correctly views separations (some smaller than we'd imagine) as major causes of suicide. There's also a moving interview with someone who has attempted suicide. These are all positive aspects of this book. On the negative side, however, the presentation is not as coherently organized as it might be. The author will suddenly shift from an in-depth presentation of one case to comment briefly on another. There is also strange, disjointed, almost extraneous material here and there (for example, countering depression through resetting the body clock). Even more important, readers might be more frightened than they need to be when they read about suicides after what appears to be minor provocation. And can't doctors seem to help? Are we to be helpless after our initial losses? These are unintentional images presented by Leder, but there is not enough to counter those impressions for readers to become comfortable. It's also unusual that although Leder lost a brother to suicide and alludes to this briefly, she is unable to discuss it and leaves the reader wondering if one ever really can recover from the grief of a suicide in the family.

312. Martin, Ann M. *Slam Book.* New York: Holiday, 1987. 154 pp. Fiction.

Interest level: Age 12+ Reading level: Grade 7

Anna is terrified at the thought of starting high school. She learns from her cousin about a "key to popularity." It is a slam book. Anna starts one as soon as she enters school, and soon she and her friends are getting lots of attention. But the slam book backfires: People start writing ugly things in it that hurt other students. One item, a cruel joke, is the catalyst that causes one young woman to commit suicide and another to attempt it.

Fortunately for Anna, her parents are understanding and intelligent enough to explain to her that although what she did was wrong, the girls who harmed themselves were emotionally disturbed and would not have reacted so extremely if they had not already had many problems. They recommend that Anna go for therapy. Some readers may want to discuss this and speculate on what might have happened if Anna had not brought the slam book to school.

The story carries a bitter lesson about the cruelty of young people to each other, and the necessity for people to empathize with each other.

313. Peck, Richard. *Remembering the Good Times.* New York: Delacorte, 1985; Dell, pap. 181 pp. Fiction.

Interest level: Age 12+ Reading level: Grade 7

Buck, Katey, and Trav are inseparable friends. Buck lives with his divorced father, and Katey lives with her great-grandmother and her divorced mother. Trav's parents are together, but he resents them, and their relationship is a tense one. The story focuses on the friendship that the three build over the course of a few years, with Trav the newcomer at the beginning of eighth grade.

Trav is a disturbed young man, and his problems reach a head when he is caught shoplifting. He is sent away by his parents, and when he returns he is greatly upset by a number of changes that have occurred in the town, among them the killing of Scotty, a family friend who owned a gasoline station. Trav gives his friends two possessions that he values highly, and then he kills himself, leaving his friends, his parents, and the town angry, guilty, and confused.

The issue of suicide is dealt with well, as are the other themes in this swiftly moving and poignant book. Humor and warmth temper the chilling effect of the suicide. Katey and Buck are bereft but determined to make themselves heard after the tragedy. They will endure.

314. Smith, Judie. *Coping with Suicide: A Resource Book for Teenagers and Young Adults.* New York: Rosen, 1986. 128 pp. Nonfiction.

Interest level: Age 12+ Reading level: Grades 5–6

Smith, an expert on suicide and crisis intervention, begins her book with the story of a teenager who committed suicide, told by her mother. Then she looks at the issues—suicide over history, statistics, the legal issue, rational suicide, and dispelling the myths (all suicidal people want to die, for example). Theories of why a person would want to die are explored (for example, crisis theory). Other reasons for attempting suicide are also looked at: sociological factors, suffering a loss, depression, rebellion, low self-esteem, and loss of communication. Warning signs are carefully laid out.

The second half of the book is what makes this particular volume so unusual—a manual on crisis intervention communication skills. Smith explains about feelings and their importance, letting readers in on the possible strength or mildness of each potential feeling. Exercises help the reader separate thoughts from feelings. Once that concept is grasped, the reader is ready to learn what a teenager can and cannot do—how to promote understanding in speaking with people who are in crisis, and how to get additional help. Exercises help build up skill. A final chapter deals with surviving the loss of a friend or relative who has committed suicide. Each chapter has a summary, discussion questions, and references. Resource list, bibliography, index.

315. Thiesman, Jean. *The Last April Dancers.* Boston: Houghton Mifflin, 1987. 206 pp. Fiction.

Interest level: Age 12+ Reading level: Grade 7

Cat St. John's sixteenth birthday is marked by ecstacy and agony. She receives beautiful and exciting gifts, spends most of the day with Cameron, the young man she loves, and earns her driver's license. But this is the day that she lets her father know how angry she is at home; and this is the day that her father commits suicide. Cat's father is a shadowy character throughout the book. Together with Cat, the reader discovers more and more about him and about Cat's mother and grandmother. Cat also discovers more about herself as this engrossing, well-crafted novel unfolds.

One of the major discoveries in the book is that things are not necessarily as they seem. A number of mysteries are presented in the book; many characters are introduced along with their conflicts; no issue is completely resolved. The reader is not left dissatisfied, however. The ambiguity of the resolutions acts in the book's favor, because the reader is respected enough to work out the possible endings. For example, we know that the relationship between Cat and her mother is strained and volatile. We are furious with Cat's mother for pushing her out of her house after her father's death. The mother is afraid that Cat will become sexually involved with Cameron in reaction to her father's death. Cat's mother is also very self-involved, and she can't handle her own grief and guilt. But there is enough evidence of both Cat's and her mother's conscious willingness to change, to indicate that they may be able to resolve their difficulties. On the other hand, we suspect that Cat's grandmother will never accept the reality of her son's act.

All of the characters are believable and interesting. Even the minor characters command our attention. Cat, herself, is a strong, intelligent, and attractive individual. And Cameron is a worthy companion for her.

The issue of serious mental illness is dealt with in the context of the story. No new information is transmitted, but the author clearly conveys the dangers of ignoring symptoms and creating a fantasy in which there is the pretense that nothing is really wrong. Cat's feelings of guilt over her feeling certain that she has killed her father are presented in an authentic manner. We feel with Cat, even when we know she is mistaken. Adolescent readers will take much from this book. It deals with many of the concerns in their lives.

316. White, Ellen Emerson. *Life without Friends*. New York: Scholastic, 1987. 250 pp. Fiction.

Interest level: Age 12+ Reading level: Grade 7

After Beverly's parents were divorced, her mother became drunk more and more frequently, and finally was killed in an automobile accident, which most people believe was intentional. Beverly came to live with her father, a professor at Harvard, and her stepmother and young stepbrother. Beverly is a very disturbed young woman, but no one seems to take strong action about helping her until she becomes involved with a young man who is a drug dealer and, eventually, a murderer. Beverly is finally instrumental in having the young man arrested. After that her father insists that she go into therapy, and he is very strict about keeping a close rein on all of her activities.

Beverly is very talented academically. She gets high grades in all of her school subjects. But she is socially retarded. She is uncomfortable with everyone, including her family. One day she meets Derek, a young park attendant, and they become friends. On his insistence she introduces him to her family and is surprised when her father accepts him. The combination of Derek's support and love, her stepmother's steady and positive responsiveness, her father's easing up and beginning to talk to her, and the therapist's ear helps her to free herself from much of the guilt, the suicidal feelings, and the anguish she has felt at not being able to prevent all the deaths from occurring.

The reader's interest is maintained throughout the book. The characters are well drawn and three-dimensional. The situation, extreme as it is, is believable, as is Beverly's recovery. Adolescents may find in Beverly's situation a warning or, perhaps, a path to follow for extricating themselves from situations that hold potential danger.

317. Yolen, Jane. *The Stone Silenus.* New York: Philomel, 1984. 127 pp. Fiction.

Interest level: Age 11+ Reading level: Grade 6

Melissa adored her father. Now, a year after his death (probably a suicide), she still remains in the denial stage. She meets a young man whom she calls Gabriel, who believes himself to be possessed by her father's spirit, and for a while Melissa believes it too. The story takes us through Melissa's near suicide and her memories and veneration of her father, to her eventual realization that Gabriel is psychotic, and that her father is truly dead.

For Melissa the most difficult task is to relinquish her romanticized vision of her father and to see him as the man he was. Until she can acknowledge his imperfections she cannot accept his death. It takes some dramatic and dangerous encounters with Gabriel to finally bring Melissa to her senses.

Yolen uses her considerable poetic skill to convey to the reader the dual pictures of Melissa's real father and the idealized version that her father wanted the world to have of him. Melissa's mother colluded with him in his attempt to fool, not only the world, but also his own children. The message here is an important one, and it comes through to the reader by means of Melissa's awakening to the truth, and her ability to bear it.

Divorce, Marital Separation, and the Single-Parent Family

Divorce and marital separation imply loss for the child, not only because of the destruction of the parents' marriage but also because of the added element of rejection. This was no accident—the separation was deliberate, conscious. Divorce and marital separation are additionally difficult for children because society offers no rites with which to commence bereavement. There is no service, no condolence call, no formal machinery for mourning the end of a marriage. Many psychologists evaluate the impact of divorce on a family as more traumatic than a death.

For many youngsters, there has always been only one parent. Either a mother or a father has never been on the scene, perhaps because no marriage has taken place. In such cases, there is loss because the unique support given by either a mother or a father is missing. The young person usually wonders what the missing parent was like and what contribution might have been made by him or her.

318. Baum, Louis. *One More Time.* Illus. by Paddy Bouma. New York: Morrow, 1986. 24 pp. Fiction.

Interest level: Ages 4–8 Reading level: Grade 2

Simon and his father spend an idyllic Sunday together, and the reader is surprised when Simon's father says good-bye to him after depositing him at his door. Only then is it clear that Simon's parents are divorced, and that Simon spends only one day a week with his dad.

There is a bittersweet element about the joy that Simon and his father experience during their day together. At the end, Simon is reluctant to let his father go, but he is more willing to do so knowing that he will see his father again soon. This issue is a difficult one with young children. Even when their parents have demonstrated that they are trustworthy, the fact of the separation causes anxiety. This book may help serve as a catalyst for discussion and the airing of feelings.

319. Boegehold, Betty. *Daddy Doesn't Live Here Anymore: A Book about Divorce.* Illus. by Deborah Borgo. Racine, Wis.: Western, 1985. 28 pp. Fiction.

Interest level: Ages 4–8 Reading level: Grade 2

As in the other Golden Learn about Living books, this has a note to parents in the preface, advising on how to reassure their children during a difficult adjustment period. The story itself concerns Casey, who returns from school wondering if her mom and dad will be fighting. She thinks, "No. They'll pretend everything is okay. As if I didn't know better!" But Casey returns to find Dad's car gone and Mom crying again. Trying to forget that her father has left by playing the scene out with her dolls in a dollhouse helps for the moment. At dinner, though, Casey's mother informs her that her father isn't going to live with them anymore and her parents are going to divorce.

Casey's mother tries to reassure her that her father loves her a lot, but the two adults don't love each other anymore and can't get along. "I don't want to have no daddy," Casey cries. Again, her mother tries to comfort: "Daddy will always be your daddy. He'll just live in a different place. You'll see him lots of times, but most of the time, you'll live with me." It's too much to hear at once, and Casey runs to her room and her own doll children. There she tries to bargain and get Daddy to come back by being sick. Mom does call Dad, and he explains that they just can't live together anymore. The next ploy is to run away, but not so far that mother can't come and woo her back. This time the mother reassures her that her father's leaving wasn't anything Casey did. Casey's next doll play involves putting the father doll in a separate place and exclaiming: "And you better have the kids come over to visit a lot—I'm telling you." And it's Casey's turn to reassure her dolls. The usual emotional reactions are explored, however briefly, and the resolution is realistically not complete at book's end; the device of using dolls is helpful.

320. Brown, Laurene Krasny, and Brown, Marc. *Dinosaurs Divorce: A Guide for Changing Families.* Boston: Atlantic, 1986, hb and pap. Nonfiction.

Interest level: Ages 5–10 Reading level: Grade 3

Starting off with a glossary cum invitation, the authors say, "The starred (*) words are in the book. See if you can find them." And then readers are off into a comic strip style assessment of divorce, culled from the authors' experiences as "a parent, stepparent, and for Laurie [the author], as a child herself." Marc Brown's children gave numerous ideas, too.

It's hard to put the many complex ideas about divorce, remarriage, and stepsiblings into a picture-book format, but these authors succeed in touching children's hearts and feelings. They do this in several ways. First, their point of view is stated squarely in the first sentence: "Divorce takes place between mothers and fathers. You are not to blame if your parents get divorced." Second, humorous dinosaur children and parents portray the action, bringing an amazing repertoire of emotion with them, from ashamed to angry, from relieved to confused. Through the fine wedding of words with illustrations a great deal is brought out that children can infer. For example, the words say, "If you feel angry, tell your parents why and look for ways to show anger that don't hurt others or yourself." Accompanying pictures show a child dinosaur in animated hostile dramatic play with dolls and an airplane. The illustrations also convey jokes that can be enjoyed on rereading, for example, the logo on a truck: "Tyrannosaurus Truckers/Since the Jurassic Period." Third, the authors touch on such complicated issues as scapegoating and self-destructive behavior.

The book assumes helpful parents who, although getting divorced, can sit calmly and answer questions. It also offers good advice and words to say that children can adopt and adapt. For example, "You don't have to listen when parents say bad things about each other. Say you love them both and hearing this upsets you. You may have to tell them more than once." On occasion, the authors gloss over difficult issues or expect too much of children's capability for maturity. For example, "Living with one parent almost always means there will be less money. Be prepared to give up some things" (an illustration shows a child longingly looking in a toy store window). Another example is: "Some parents feel too guilty or unhappy to visit you. Sometimes you can keep in touch by calling or writing." A third example is: "Try to be open to these changes."

Perhaps adults sharing this book with children can bring their own ideas to it, reassuring children they don't have to be that mature and giving. Other than these occasional shortcomings this is a book of deep understanding that is highly admirable: "It may feel strange at first to show your love for one parent in front of the other. Try to remember it's okay to love both and to show that you do."

321. Clark, Margaret Goff. *The Latchkey Mystery.* New York: Dodd, 1985. 128 pp. Fiction.

Interest level: Ages 9–12 Reading level: Grade 4

Minda has moved with her young brother, Joey, and their mother from Buffalo to Florida because after her father's death the only place they could afford to live was a house Minda's mother had inherited. Minda makes friends at her new school, and together they try to tackle the problem of a recent rash of burglaries in their neighborhood. They decide to form a neighborhood watch. In the process of trying to catch the criminal, they acquire some important information, such as the idea of taping the police telephone number to their phones, which helps them as latchkey children.

Minda's mother gets a full-time job, and things are looking up for the family. She will arrange for Joey to be in a day-care facility so that Minda will no longer be solely responsible for baby-sitting. Minda and her friends form a list of suspects for the burglaries. They also design a plan for catching the thief. And it works! The children are careful to keep the local police informed at all times of what they are doing. Their behavior is always such that young readers can glean some good ideas for how to protect themselves while at the same time having a good time. The mystery is handled well, and readers can also enjoy being detectives. The book also serves as a model for a single parent who needs work outside the home.

322. Cleary, Beverly. *Dear Mr. Henshaw.* Illus. by Paul Zelinsky. New York: Morrow, 1983; Dell, pap. 134 pp. Fiction.

Interest level: Ages 8–11 Reading level: Grades 3–4

Leigh Botts has been writing to an author named Henshaw since second grade. He is now in sixth grade, adjusting to a new school in a new town because his parents have been divorced. He is angry at Mr. Henshaw because in his last letter, Mr. Henshaw asked Leigh to answer some questions about himself. Although Leigh claims to want to be a writer, he resents having to do added work; his letters to Mr. Henshaw have usually been prompted by a school assignment.

During the course of his correspondence with Mr. Henshaw, Leigh writes about what bothers him and what he wishes, which mostly has to do with his father, although he hardly sees or hears from him. His father is a truck driver on the road a lot, but most of the problem is that his father is not a very attentive or loving person to Leigh or his mother. Another of Leigh's problems is that someone is stealing his lunches at school. He's also lonely, especially because his father has custody of their dog, Bandit.

Leigh's continuing correspondence with Mr. Henshaw reveals that the author is too busy to read much of what Leigh writes. He suggests that Leigh keep a journal, perhaps in the form of letters to someone. So Leigh writes letters to Mr. Henshaw in his journal rather than mailing them. He does manage to send some fan mail in response to the author's new book. And Mr. Henshaw answers with postcards from wherever he happens to be.

Meanwhile things are going badly for Leigh and his father. When Leigh calls his father one night, he hears a boy's voice asking when they will go out for pizza. To add to Leigh's misery, Bandit has been lost.

In the process of becoming a writer and adjusting to his new school as well as his new situation as a stepbrother, Leigh learns a lot about himself. He manages to solve his new-school problems; Bandit is found; and his mother comes to terms with the fact that her ex-husband will probably never change.

The book is written in Cleary's inimitable style. It is truthful but light; important issues are not sidestepped; and the characters are respected. Divorce is presented as a wrenching experience for everyone involved, but it is also clear that the problems can be surmounted. Leigh learns, develops, and succeeds in his efforts to become better adjusted to his situation.

323. Clifford, Eth. *The Man Who Sang in the Dark.* Illus. by Mary B. Owen. Boston: Houghton Mifflin, 1987. 112 pp. Fiction.

Interest level: Ages 8–11 Reading level: Grade 3

Leah and her little brother, Daniel, have forged a close and loving relationship. Although their mother is attentive and concerned, especially since their father died, they have depended on each other for emotional support, for entertainment, and for dealing with the rest of the world. Their mother is a hard-working, honest, creative, and imaginative woman who is not as demonstrative as they would sometimes wish, but who, nevertheless, shows her love for them in many ways.

The story is set in the time of the Great Depression. The father's death has not only left an emotional void, but has also caused an economic crisis. The family moves from their comfortable home to a small apartment with secondhand furniture that the mother spruces up with paint and decals. The children are well behaved and thoughtful.

Eventually, the family adjusts to their new surroundings, and even to a blind neighbor, who at first inadvertently frightens Leah. The ending is somewhat predictable and romantic, but it is a satisfying one for young readers. The family is idyllically good, but their relationship and methods of coping provide a fine model. The wrenching problem in the story hinges on the issue of whether four-year-old Daniel will be better off living in poor economic circumstances with Leah and his mother, or with a wealthy couple who love him and want to adopt him. Of course, this problem is resolved satisfactorily and they all live together happily ever after. The book is well written, and the reader is drawn into the setting as well as the activities of the characters.

324. Colman, Hila. *Just the Two of Us.* New York: Scholastic, 1984, pap. 168 pp. Fiction.

Interest level: Age 12+ Reading level: Grade 6

Samantha, nicknamed "Indian" by her father, likes to move. She is now 14; her mother died when she was a year old. She and her father have moved 6 times in the past 10 years, and she enjoys it. She loves having her father all to herself; she does not want any attachments or roots. She feels as if she has never had a mother, especially because her father won't talk about her mother's death. She knows that her father and mother married young, were very much in love, and that her mother's death from pneumonia has some mystery surrounding it. She later discovers that her father feels guilty about not having been able to save his wife's life.

When her father decides to buy a house and a restaurant in a small New England town, Samantha is worried that their idyllic relationship will change. She knows that he is settling down in order to make a better life for her, but she is fearful of the changes that will occur.

Samantha makes friends with a woman named Liz, who eventually falls in love with Samantha's father. Samantha is horribly jealous and nearly destroys her father's relationship with Liz, but when her father has an accident and Liz comes to the family's rescue, Samantha becomes more acquiescent about the idea of having Liz as her stepmother. It also helps that Samantha has Josh as a boyfriend to provide a relationship different from the father-daughter one.

Samantha has an advanced case of the electra complex. She is so enamored of her father that she cannot develop any relationships with either boys or girls her own age. It is incredible that Josh would continue to put up with Samantha's bad humor and worse behavior. Liz is too perfect, as is Samantha's father. The story's ending is totally predictable. There's little here that is real, but as a romance it's a good read.

325. Conrad, Pam. *Holding Me Here.* New York: Harper, 1986; Bantam, pap. 184 pp. Fiction.

Interest level: Age 12+ Reading level: Grade 6

Conrad sensitively addresses the issues of the difficulties children encounter when their parents divorce. Robin, whose parents have divorced, decides to help Mary, a secretive boarder, get back together with her children after she discovers that Mary has left her husband and two children. Robin does this partly because she feels guilty that she has failed to reconcile her own parents.

The author conveys the message that secrecy on the part of adults during the difficult time of separation and divorce can be the cause of misunderstanding and anxiety for the children involved. Robin's mother's quest for privacy means that she doesn't tell Robin that she has been dating for a number of months. Robin is left to speculate about what is going on, and she feels a resentment toward her mother's new friend that could have been avoided. Robin's scholarly father, though seeming to her to be most open with his feelings, has never discussed with her why he "walked away" from the family, leaving Robin to surmise that it must have been an easy thing for him to do, and that one of the reasons he left was Robin's untidiness.

Robin is uncertain of her father's love for her and thrives on his compliments and approval. She is never sure how she can fit into his academic life. It is her father, however, who is able to ask the right questions to help Robin understand the traumatic failure of her attempt to reconcile Mary with her family. Mary's husband turns out to be an abusive alcoholic who beats Mary. Although Mary has left her children as well, she has a plan to retrieve them, which Robin unwittingly ruins. The reader never learns what happened to Mary and her children. This part of the story is the least believable. Why didn't Mary report her husband? Why didn't the social worker remove the children from the husband's presence?

Eventually Robin's parents recognize that she has been "too good" in coping with the divorce. She has hidden her true feelings in order to be acceptable to them. There is no dramatic change in Robin's life after this, but she does feel closer to her father and more accepting of her mother's right to date other men. Most important, she is respectful of her own needs and feelings and is learning how to communicate them.

326. Delton, Judy. *Angel's Mother's Boyfriend.* Illus. by Margot Apple. Boston: Houghton Mifflin, 1986, hb and pap. 176 pp. Fiction.

Interest level: Ages 7–10 Reading level: Grade 3

Angel is off on her mental trampoline again, jumping to the wrong conclusions. She misconstrues the sudden changes in her mother as crimes, and quick-witted Angel is ready for the rescue. But her mother isn't in trouble, she's just met a man. Or is this an even worse crime? After all, when Rudy comes to visit he seems to stay forever; he practically moves in. Then he brings all his belongings to their town. And he gets a job as a TV clown. What could be more embarrassing?

Angel's acceptance of this marvelous man is paced well, and the page-turning sprightly humor of characters they can touch will help readers overlook the path's being too straight and smooth.

327. Dragonwagon, Crescent. *Always, Always*. Illus. by Arieh Zeldich. New York: Macmillan, 1984. 32 pp. Fiction.

Interest level: Ages 6–10 Reading level: Grades 2–3

The young girl lives with her mother in New York for most of the year, but every summer she visits with her father, who is a carpenter in Colorado. Her parents' life-styles and values are very different from each other, but they are wise enough not to catch their daughter in the middle. They do, however, do things that they ask her not to tell the other parent about, such as permitting her to chop wood and giving her a manicure.

When the girl asks her parents why they ever were married, they each tell her that their marriage was a mistake, but that she wasn't and that they love her dearly. Despite her parents' differences the girl seems very well adjusted. She has a fine relationship with each parent; accommodates to each life-style with ease; and has friends and possessions in each place, and it looks as if she will continue to live a balanced and secure life.

Dragonwagon is good at helping children to understand and respect differences in life-style as well as opinions and values. She is nonjudgmental and conveys the notion that life is joyous and to be savored.

328. Galloway, Priscilla. *Jennifer Has Two Daddies*. Illus. by Ana Auml. Toronto: Women's Educational Press, 1985, pap. 32 pp. Fiction.

Interest level: Ages 3–8 Reading level: Grade 2

Jennifer is very fortunate. She has two of almost everything, and her mother and father and stepfather love her very much. Her parents have joint custody, so Jennifer commutes weekly from one place to the other. She's generally content until her father has to go away for three weeks. He tries to prepare her for his absence, but she becomes terribly anxious and tries to call him in the middle of the night. Even though she has dialed a number in Bombay, India, her mother and stepfather are very understanding, and they help her to dial her father's number. He helps her to deal with his absence in a loving and practical way. Jennifer is enveloped in love and concern and the reader knows that she will be fine.

329. Girard, Linda Walvoord. *At Daddy's on Saturdays*. Illus. by Judith Friedman. Niles, Ill.: Whitman, 1987. 32 pp. Fiction.

Interest level: Ages 3–8 Reading level: Grades 2–3

Katie's daddy and mommy separate, and they will be divorced. They are both very solicitous of Katie and discuss all of her worries with her in an open and loving way. She goes to visit her father in his new apartment, and he assures her that he will always love her, always be her father, and always tell her the truth. Katie's mother is also in tune with Katie's feelings. She lets Katie know that it is not Katie's fault that her father doesn't live with them any more. Both parents seem respectful of each other as well as Katie's feelings. The narrator of the book acknowledges that Katie may never be free of a hurt feeling about the divorce, but at least she knows that she is loved and wanted by both her parents.

The author is clearly aware of the criteria for helping children deal with divorce. She is in touch with children's anxieties and reactions, and she does not fall into any of the traps of "happy" endings or false hopes. This book may help serve as a model for some parents who wonder how to handle the topic of divorce with their young children.

330. Hurwitz, Johanna. *DeDe Takes Charge.* Illus. by Diane de Groat. New York: Morrow, 1984; Apple, pap. 121 pp. Fiction.

Interest level: Ages 8–11 Reading level: Grades 3–4

DeDe's parents are divorced. Her father demands perfection in everything; her mother is less than perfect, but DeDe loves them both. The book is written in a light and humorous style and moves quickly. DeDe is a likable girl, who thinks about the feelings of others even when she is concerned about herself. She does her best to please both her parents, and she even tries to make a match for her mother.

A number of DeDe's plans backfire, but in general life goes well for her, even with the hated divorce. DeDe's mother gradually starts to look better and feel better about herself; she has been the less fortunate person in the divorce. DeDe's father will probably relocate across the country, to California, but DeDe will get to visit him on holidays.

The story affirms the message that even though parents no longer love each other, they still love their child. Although the father comes across as a less sympathetic character, he clearly cares about his daughter. He is not irresponsible or abusive, although he certainly is demanding and unrealistic. DeDe is an attractive protagonist. Readers would enjoy hearing more about her.

331. Ives, Sally Blakeslee; Fassler, David; and Lash, Michele. *The Divorce Workbook: A Guide for Kids and Families.* Illus. with children's drawings. Burlington, Vt.: Waterfront, 1985, pap. 147 pp. Nonfiction.

Interest level: Ages 4–8 Reading level: Grades 1–2

Designed to give children ownership of their own responses and coping strategies, this workbook provides excellent activities for children to engage in. It takes them from thinking about why people get together to what happens when people have decided to separate. It uses children's words and drawings to encourage young readers to respond with their own words and drawings.

The *Workbook* contains some good ideas that children advise other children to try, such as punching a pillow or batting some balls when they are angry, and talking to someone when they are confused or upset. There is information about lawyers, judges, and psychologists and their roles in the separation process. This is a useful book for youngsters, and for their parents as well. It is similar in format to another book by the same authors, *Changing Families: A Guide for Kids and Grown-Ups* (Waterfront, 1988), which explores more deeply the aftermath of divorce and the changing constellation of the family as a result of marital separation. It does not deal with families whose different life-styles have nothing to do with divorce, but it is a useful workbook to complement the first one.

332. Joosse, Barbara M. *Jam Day.* Illus. by Emily Arnold McCully. New York: Harper, 1987. 32 pp. Fiction.

Interest level: Ages 4–8 Reading level: Grades 2–3

Ben is envious of families that are noisy and large. He lives with his mother, and he often thinks his life is too quiet. But Ben's perception changes when he and his mother go to visit his grandparents and the rest of his extended family for a family outing and a special jam-making day. Ben now realizes that he is, indeed, part of a large and noisy family, and this knowledge will sustain him even after the visit is over and he returns home to live with just his mother again.

The story is a good one for helping children see that their family circle extends well beyond the limits of their own home.

333. Krementz, Jill. *How It Feels When Parents Divorce.* Photos by the author. New York: Knopf, 1984. 128 pp. Nonfiction.

Interest level: Age 8+ Reading level: Grade 4

This book contains 19 profiles of children's views and experiences. The children range in age from 7 through 16, and their parents encouraged photojournalist Krementz to speak to and photograph the children. Krementz thanks the children: "It took courage for them to talk openly about their fears, their sorrows, their confusions, knowing full well that what they were revealing about themselves would not only be read by strangers but by the very people whose actions had caused much of their pain."

And talk to this author (a child of divorce) of their pain they certainly do. She has captured the real thing and in the rawness of the children's experience she touches home. There is the child who gets caught in the middle of money problems; the divorced mother who embarrasses her former husband and child by wanting to kiss her ex-husband "good night" at a class play; the exploited child who is kidnapped and, so that the parent doesn't have to produce records that would expose location, is left back in school; and that very exploited child who still misses the parent who kidnapped him (he's back with the other parent, now). Children's feelings are very strong—wanting half siblings, not wanting them; wanting stepparents or not wanting them. One child asks for broadening of the Catholic Church's views: "Being divorced is bad enough, but feeling God is mad too only adds to the feeling of guilt and makes the situation worse."

The families are of varied races. The family constellations are varied—some remarried, some live-ins, some boy and girlfriends. Custodial arrangements vary, too, with nearly every conceivable plan included (parents switch, children switch, brief spans, long spans). Here's one reasonable holiday solution: "During the summer we alternate every six weeks, and we always spend Christmas with my father and Easter with my mother. On our birthdays it's whoever we're with and then the other parent calls."

The profiles are lengthy, with few pictures, usually an individual portrait of the child and a portrait or action shot with at least one parent. The leisurely length allows for the expression of deep feeling, for example, one boy's idea of what a custody battle would be like—fighting over a restaurant check, but secretly neither party wants it. Such haunting images are frequent in Krementz's book, making it compelling, instructive reading for both children and adults.

334. Kroll, Steven. *Annie's Four Grannies.* Illus. by Eileen Christelow. New York: Holiday, 1986. 32 pp. Fiction.
Interest level: Ages 4–8 Reading level: Grade 2

A humorous look at what divorce, remarriage, and the stepfamily has wrought for one child, who now becomes mediator in a sea of grandparents.

> Annie has four grannies,
> Annie loves them all.
> One is six feet seven,
> One is four feet tall.
> One is large and heavy,
> One is thin and strong.
> It's too bad for Annie
> They don't get along.

Funny cartoon "photographs" show her with each grandmother. Annie tries to have them get along on her birthday, when they all arrive in a rhyming sweep. She eventually gets them to unite over a fine cup of tea. Some readers will find the episode hilarious; others may not find it funny that it falls on a child to create harmony. Where are the many parents here, after all? Nevertheless, this may be a comfortable way to bring children around to discussing their own bewilderments and social burdens.

335. Leroe, Ellen W. *Personal Business*. New York: Bantam, 1987, pap. 135 pp. Fiction.

Interest level: Age 11+ Reading level: Grade 4

Danny Coleman's parents are divorced. He has done his best to reunite them, but they stay divorced. His dreams are really shattered when his father decides to marry a woman he has met at his health club. Danny then turns his attention to trying to find another husband for his mother. He places an advertisement in the "Personals" section of a magazine, and then he and his friend Melanie sort out the responses and arrange for a rendezvous. He does select one response, sets up a meeting with the man, and tries to introduce him to his mother. His plan backfires when his mother discovers what he has done and is embarrassed and infuriated. But eventually his mother consents to go out with the man, and the book ends with the hope that Danny's dream will come true.

Although the plot is somewhat contrived and farfetched, Danny is a bright, amiable, and energetic young man. His mother is not a passive, pathetic creature, and the story is not without humor. The greatest flaw in the book lies in the youngsters' reliance on physical appearances, their interfering in Danny's mother's life as if she were helpless to handle her own social life, and in their lack of feeling for the men who don't measure up to their expectations. They do express some sympathy for one man's loneliness, but after that, they have no compunctions at all about judging the men unfit because of their appearance.

The idea that without a husband a woman is nothing is a subtle message here, and despite the humor and good intentions of the book, this negative feeling pervades.

336. McGuire, Paula. *Putting It Together: Teenagers Talk about Family Breakups*. New York: Delacorte, 1987. 184 pp. Nonfiction.

Interest level: Age 12+ Reading level: Grade 7

McGuire interviews 20 adolescents and social service professionals who specialize in family problems, and the end result "tells it like it is" in feelingful vignettes. Raw emotion with little held back of the pain felt after death, separation, or divorce is the rule. The kids' fantasies touch the heart (brothers Peter and Quentin wanted to follow Mom to a 100-acre farm; "it was going to be really good"). Reality was disappointing (Mom was never reliable, so it probably never would come to pass). Some of the teens involved come from middle-class homes and are college-bound youngsters; others are those more on the periphery who have run away, live in shelters, or are flirting with a lengthy future in the prison system.

The sadness of such a broad panorama becomes the book's power, reflecting on not just one group of teens, and making it different from most books of this sort. It shows us aspects of this generation and the one to follow.

337. Miner, Jane Claypool. *Split Decision: Facing Divorce.* Illus. by Vista III Design. Belmont, Calif.: Crestwood, 1982. 63 pp. Fiction.

Interest level: Age 10+ Reading level: Grade 5

Part of the Crisis series under the aegis of Fearon Education, this story deals with the custody decision a young girl is asked to make when her parents decide to divorce. At first Ann spends all of her energy trying to reunite her parents. When that doesn't work she figures out a way to solve her problem: She demands joint custody. Although her parents agree on little else, they decide to accept her decision.

Although the purpose of the book is didactic, the author does portray accurately the conflicting feelings of the child placed in this position. The parents are also realistically described. At first they are so angry at each other that they don't even want to speak to each other. They place Ann in the middle and complain to her about each other as well as sending each other messages through her. As time elapses they are able to be civil to each other, and to express their feelings of love for Ann. The book can probably serve as a catalyst for young people who are going through this situation and as a source of empathy for those who are onlookers.

338. Nelson, Theresa. *The Twenty-Five Cent Miracle.* New York: Bradbury, 1986. 214 pp. Fiction.

Interest level: Ages 9–12 Reading level: Grades 4–5

The book introduces us to a memorable character in Elvira, whose mother is dead, and whose father, Hank, is more often than not out of work. He is neglectful of 11-year-old Elvira, not because he doesn't love her, but because he is so caught up in his own grief and inadequacy that he fails to see how much Elvira needs and loves him.

Elvira and Hank have moved from place to place and are now in a trailer camp. Elvira tries to make the place a home by planting a rose bush in the sandy soil outside their trailer. She goes to the library in a quest for information about how best to nurture her roses and finds, in a sympathetic librarian, her ideal friend. Miss Ivy is a divorced mother of two boys slightly younger than Elvira, and she provides Elvira with love and company as well as a model for behavior. In exchange for Elvira's help in her garden, Miss Ivy gives Elvira the proper soil and fertilizer for her roses.

When Hank decides that Elvira will be better off with his sister, whom Elvira does not like, Elvira hatches a plan to get Hank and Miss Ivy together. It is to the author's credit that although Hank and Ivy and the children become friends and go fishing together, the great romance that Elvira hoped for does not materialize. Elvira runs away, taking her beloved rose bush with her, rather than submit to life with her Aunt Darla. When she is found, Hank recognizes his need for his daughter and gets a job that will enable him to keep Elvira with him. The friendship with Miss Ivy and her family remains secure. And Elvira's faith in her own actions and in the goodness of people is affirmed.

The author writes poignantly of the serious problems that this feisty and engaging child must overcome. At age 11, Elvira has responsibilities for caring for herself and her father that many adults would not be able to handle. She emerges as a human being with quietly heroic qualities, as does Miss Ivy. Although the story is very moving, it never crosses the line to sentimentality. It is unfortunate that Elvira has to run away in order to bring across her point to her father. She certainly endangers her life in doing so. But her desperation is palpable, and the running away is not presented as the ideal solution. This book is a winner.

339. Nickman, Steven L. *When Mom and Dad Divorce.* Illus. by Diane de Groat. New York: Messner, 1986, hb and pap. 80 pp. Nonfiction.
Interest level: Ages 8–14 Reading level: Grade 5

Pediatric psychiatrist Nickman uses seven stories of typical situations to lead on to generalized insight: The subjects include analysis of what leads to divorce, how it feels at first, joint custody, stepfamilies, and actions that can help. Nickman's central thrust might be: "Kids have a right to be kids." And with this in mind, he offers concrete suggestions for getting through a tough time. Letting kids in on the reality that things will likely get worse before they get better, Nickman describes what happens in separation for kids who haven't yet gone through it. His ability to capture that reality is down-to-earth, for example, "Your eyes may fill with tears when you least expect it." He also gives a full account of one child's therapy and what she derived from it. Among Nickman's many practical suggestions for coping with a situation that seems out of control are remembering other tough things you've navigated and *yelling* if you're stuck in the middle.

Although similar in tone to Eda LeShan's *What's Going to Happen to Me? When Parents Separate or Divorce* (Four Winds, 1978), this book has something new to say in its author's emphasis on looking at and insisting on each party's rights and his willingness to share adult insights about the pathways of marriage with youngsters.

340. Okimoto, Jean Davies. *Jason's Women.* Boston: Atlantic, 1986. 210 pp. Fiction.

Interest level: Age 11 Reading level: Grades 5–6

The main character is a shy 16-year-old boy with divorced parents who are both very involved in their own lives. The story concerns his close relationships with an 80-year-old woman who is dying of cancer and a young Cambodian girl, Thao, who has escaped her country, leaving her family.

This book was a lovely surprise. The jacket leads one to believe it will be about a shy, lonely boy learning to face social challenges. That it is, yet it is also about a remarkable old woman whom Jason learns to respect and love, and the Cambodian girl she has sponsored. In helping Thao and learning her brave story, Jason learns more about himself. Interracial and intercultural relationships are sensibly and sensitively developed. Jason lives with his father, and their relationship is clearly and realistically portrayed. The mother seems more two-dimensional. There is humor; the characters are interesting; the plot is fun.

341. Paris, Lena. *Mom Is Single.* Photos by Mark Christianson. Chicago: Childrens, 1980, hb and pap. 32 pp. Nonfiction.

Interest level: Ages 6–10 Reading level: Grade 2

When a youngster is assigned to make name tags for his parents' visit to school, he feels left out because he only can write one tag. It seems (to him) everyone else gets to put two names down. The boy has a dad, but he will have to work that night, and he is not "part of our family" since the divorce.

The divorce has meant that Mom has obtained some additional schooling and gone to work. It has meant stricter budgets and staying at a baby-sitter's after school with his sister. It has meant household chores as well. When they visit their father they do some of the same things they do with their mother—share meals, do chores, shop, visit the zoo.

The boy says the hardest part is saying good-bye after a visit with his father. Another hard part is when his father can't join him for some of the same events they used to share—a camp-out, for example. A grandfather has filled in, and sometimes an uncle, but it's not the same. The book closes with the boy knowing that his parents won't get back together but that each cares for the children. "It doesn't mean that things are better than before or worse. They're just different." Somehow, however, because the arguing or chaos that may have existed in the household before the breakup are not described, things do sound worse. Realistic, but, yes, worse.

Emotions are mostly indirectly handled, through events, but they come through, nevertheless, and are handled by a network of people active in the boy's welfare. The mother reassures her son, as when the child fears he is being taught household tasks in case *she* leaves.

342. Pomerantz, Barbara. *Who Will Lead Kiddush?* Illus. by Donna Ruff. New York: Union of American Hebrew Congregations, 1985, pap. 32 pp. Fiction.

Interest level: Ages 4–8 Reading level: Grade 2

Divorce occurs in all groups, and this book's purpose is to reflect on how parental separation might affect a religious Jewish household. The author tries to find predictable, reliable aspects for a child to hold onto, and in the Sabbath there is such stability. The tradition can help strengthen a child, she says, while other traditions are less stable. As such, holiday traditions can also be a source of continuity.

The first-person story begins with a single-parent family already past the marital separation. "Tonight, it is my turn to lead Kiddush with Mommy." The female protagonist then remembers how it was when Daddy lived with them. Then Daddy moved away. This is a portrayal of a father who plans to be active in the life of his daughter (phone calls every night, visits together several times a week), in fact, in the life of his wife, too, as he will still be partially responsible for building the sukkah, an outdoor structure for the Feast of Tabernacles. And the child spends every other Sabbath with her father; on their first together, he gives her a present—her own kiddush cup to make the wine benediction. The kiddush becomes a way to think of one another, even if they are apart. A loving, thoughtful portrait that can help many families bridge distances.

343. Savitz, Harriet May. *Swimmer.* New York: Apple, 1986. 89 pp. Fiction.

Interest level: Ages 8–11 Reading level: Grade 4

Just after Skipper's tenth birthday his father moves out of their house. Now he and his mother have to move into a small bungalow they own in order to turn their large house into a summer boarding house. They have to manage it by themselves, because Skipper's older brother, Paul, is in the navy.

Everything goes wrong that summer, and Skipper and his mother find it difficult to cope with the situation. Then, to make matters worse, Skipper's father decides to move away to New York City. Both his parents want Skipper with them, and Skipper feels torn.

The only saving factor of the summer is Swimmer, a dog that Skipper has found, fed, and cared for. Skipper's mother does not permit pets at the boarding house, so Swimmer has to stay in an abandoned house nearby.

Skipper faithfully tends the dog, but one day he finds out that the house is being torn down. He rushes to rescue Swimmer, but the dog is gone.

After Swimmer is found, when Skipper's mother realizes how dependent he is on the dog, she permits him to keep the dog. Skipper also takes it on himself to call his father and ask him to send the payments he has been withholding in the hope that Skipper's mother will send Skipper to him. Skipper has made the decision to stay with his mother, his dog, and his home.

The story brings out how difficult it is for children when parents battle with each other for custody, and when one parent deserts the other. No one is really a villain here, though the father is portrayed as inconsiderate. The situation is a realistic one. The author does not fall into the trap of having the dog rescue the boy's life in order to be permitted to stay. The mother is sensitive enough to see how much the dog means to her son. This is a good story with a helpful treatment of a difficult issue.

344. Severance, Jane. *Lots of Mommies.* Illus. by Jan Jones. Chapel Hill, N.C.: Lollipop Power, 1984, pap. 34 pp. Fiction.

Interest level: Ages 4–9 Reading level: Grade 3

Emily is the only child in her household. She and her mother live in a big house with three other women. Each of the women likes to do special things with Emily, and the activities are explained, along with each woman's vocation (carpenter, school bus driver, healer, student-electrician). It's a multiracial household: Emily and her mother of Asian background, two white women, and one black woman. The plot centers around a first day of school. At school, when the discussion turns to mommies, no one believes Emily has so many until they all come running, after hearing Emily has taken a fall in school. As a story about alternative life-styles, in spite of an occasional strained line (for example, a girl in school wishes *she* could hammer when she sees Emily's carpenter "mother"), this book works well at conveying the happiness that one girl finds in a warm household.

345. Shreve, Susan. *How I Saved the World on Purpose.* Illus. by Suzanne Richardson. New York: Henry Holt, 1985; Random, pap. 65 pp. Fiction.

Interest level: Ages 9–12 Reading level: Grade 4

Miranda's mother is a peace activist; her father is a somewhat pedantic lawyer. Miranda has wanted to save the world ever since she was a little girl. She's now in fourth grade, and she decides to form a club for latchkey children. When 24 latchkey children show up at Miranda's house, her family recognizes that she has, indeed, identified a problem. They all pitch in to help her. They decide to invite elderly people who are otherwise unoccupied to help oversee the children. Miranda's father enlists the aid of the newspaper to help find a place for them. The local priest offers the use of two of the Sunday School classes five days a week, and they begin a thriving enterprise, all free of charge.

Trouble comes when a classmate of Miranda's, because he is jealous of her success and fame, bribes one of the children to come away with him from the Latchkey Club. Miranda finds the child, but in the meantime a number of people have become very upset. Miranda's father points out to Miranda that perhaps her motivation has been less than altruistic. Miranda takes his message to heart and invites the jealous classmate to join her. She doesn't relinquish her dream of saving the world, but she is somewhat less imperious about it now.

Susan Shreve has drawn a generous, delightful character in Miranda. It is unfortunate that more nine-year-olds are not like Miranda.

346. Simon, Norma. *I Wish I Had My Father*. Illus. by Arieh Zeldich. Niles, Ill.: Whitman, 1983. 32 pp. Fiction.

Interest level: Ages 5–8 Reading level: Grades 1–2

The little boy dreads Father's Day. Every year he is forced to make something for Father's Day, and he feels terrible because he never sees or hears from his father. He doesn't really know anything about him except that his father left his mother and him a long time ago.

His teachers always say that he can make something for any man he knows, but that doesn't alleviate his longing. He knows one child whose father is dead, and he knows another whose parents are divorced. It helps him to have other children in his situation. It also helps that he has several adult males who are surrogate fathers to him, but he wishes that he could have his own father with him, even if it were for only one day a year.

The story helps adults and children to understand the difficulties of coping with nontraditional family situations. How sad that so many teachers and adults assume that all children live in traditional surroundings. This book clearly presents the dilemma of those children who, in increasing numbers, do not live in two-parent families. Perhaps the book will help adults to become more sensitive to all the children they serve.

347. Slepian, Jan. *Getting On with It*. New York: Four Winds, 1985. 171 pp. Fiction.

Interest level: Age 11+ Reading level: Grade 6

The story tells of 13-year-old Berry Brice and the summer she spends at her grandmother's cottage while her parents arrange to get a divorce. Berry is furious at her parents and feels that she has been exiled to her grandmother's house. She is a romantic dreamer who creates scenarios in her mind for herself and everyone she meets. She leaps to conclusions and lets her first impressions color her responses to people. As the story unfolds, her impressions change and she realizes that there is more complexity to people and their interactions than she had ever imagined.

In the process of telling the story the author blasts a number of stereotypes. The older woman next door is not a mouse; she is emotionally and sexually involved with Sonny, the younger man who was adopted into her family by her older sister. The recluse in the woods is not a crazy man or a thief, but a person who feels that he causes trouble for people, and who is afraid to harm anyone else. He is Sonny's father, and, although Sonny wants to take care of him, he goes off by himself at the end of the book. Berry becomes friends with an 11-year-old boy, much against her initial intent. And Berry's parents do not reconcile, even though Berry does not understand the cause of the divorce. She is especially taken aback by her parents' decision, because she has never heard them fighting. All these stereotypes are dispensed with, not only for Berry but also for the reader.

Berry's grandmother is another interesting character. She is a Holocaust survivor who never discusses her story. In a moment of weakness she discloses that her family sent her to safety, but all of them were killed. She cannot understand why she survived. She doesn't like to talk about her emotions or her experiences, and she never permits Berry to talk about hers, either. She doesn't change at the end of the story, but Berry does. Here again, the author lets us know that everything doesn't always come out as we wish it to, and that life is often unpredictable because people are unique.

348. Smith, Doris Buchanan. *Return to Bitter Creek.* New York: Viking Kestrel, 1986. 174 pp. Fiction.

Interest level: Ages 9–12 Reading level: Grades 4–5

Lacey has lived in Colorado with Campbell, her mother, ever since she can remember. Now, after 10 years, they are returning to Bitter Creek, North Carolina, where Campbell was born, because David, Campbell's partner and lover, has accepted a position as a resident blacksmith at the Mountain Craft School. David is a wonderful father to Lacey, and a supportive and loving partner to Campbell. Campbell's mother does not approve of Campbell's life-style. She is an overbearing and stubborn woman who keeps trying to persuade Lacey that Campbell has done something wrong.

Despite her discomfort with her grandmother, Lacey likes having an extended family. She, her mother, and David settle into their new home well. Lacey likes the school she attends, and she enjoys being in class with her cousin Tam. But she and Tam quarrel, because Tam is loyal to her grandmother and sides with her against Campbell.

One day David is killed in an automobile accident. Campbell and Lacey are bereft. The reader is also shocked by the suddenness and unexpectedness of the loss. David was such a lovable character that the reader mourns along with Lacey and Campbell. It is only after David's death that Lacey's grandmother finally understands the depth of the relationship her daughter and granddaughter had with this wonderful man. Her including a special patch in a quilt she makes is her symbolic means of expressing, at last, her acceptance of her daughter.

The book is extraordinary in its use of detail to help convey emotion. Names play a large part in the uncovering of people's feelings and in expressing their personalities. Names become symbolic of people's interactions with each other. Campbell has changed her name from Ann; David's name is pronounced "Dah-vid" with the accent on the second syllable. Lacey learns the names of all the wildflowers to please David, and she names a newborn foal "Trillium" to perpetuate David's memory. The grandmother uses names to drive a wedge between her daughter and herself, as does Campbell. The notion of being called what one wants to emerges as an important theme in the book.

Campbell's unconventional life-style juxtaposed with the traditions of the family provide an intense backdrop for the characters' interactions. Smith has written another strong and effective book that handles deep emotions gracefully and with truth.

349. Stinson, Kathy. *Mom and Dad Don't Live Together Anymore.* Illus. by Nancy Lou Reynolds. Toronto: Annick, 1984. 23 pp. Fiction.
Interest level: Ages 3–7 Reading level: Grade 1

The book opens with the picture of a sad child thinking about the fact that her mom and dad do not live together anymore. It deals with this little girl's feelings—her wish for them to get back together, her desire to see both parents every day, her anxiety about her dad's relationship with another woman, and her worry about where she and her brother will celebrate Christmas. It deals with separate residences, vacation spots, and days on which the parents see them. She even asks, "Mom, when I grow up, will I get married and then get apart?" In the final pages, both parents tell her that she makes them happy, and she realizes that she likes to be with both of them and that they love her, "just not together."

This simple, well-written, and realistically illustrated book presents a reassuring approach to children of divorce. Young children reading this book will feel more comfortable about separated parents and realize that they are still loved by both, even though they don't live together anymore. One flaw is that the author has paid little attention to the brother. Boys have feelings too!

350. Vigna, Judith. *Grandma Without Me.* Illus. by the author. Niles, Ill.: Whitman, 1984. 32 pp. Fiction.

Interest level: Ages 4–8 Reading level: Grade 2

A young boy feels cut off from his paternal grandmother after his parents' divorce. He particularly hates celebrating Thanksgiving without her. To help make each other feel better, the boy and his grandmother initiate a correspondence. The boy keeps a scrapbook of letters and memorabilia that his grandmother sends him. He also hits on an excellent idea to help lessen his grandmother's sadness at his absence from the Thanksgiving dinner. He has his mother trace his shape on a large piece of paper. He sends the shape to his grandmother's house so that he will be represented there in a tangible form.

His mother is very angry at his father. His father has remarried and will be at the grandmother's dinner with his new spouse. The boy lives with his mother, who is clearly very bitter about the divorce. But after seeing the boy's anguish, she promises him that he will be permitted to attend his grandmother's Thanksgiving celebration next year.

The author honestly and clearly portrays a family in the throes of bitter and unhappy feelings after a divorce. The child and the grandmother are the victims of the situation. No one wants them to be unhappy, but that, nevertheless, is the result. The boy and his grandmother do their best to cope with a bad situation, and the reader is left with hope because of the genuine bonds between them that they are working hard to maintain.

351. Vigna, Judith. *Mommy and Me by Ourselves Again.* Illus. by the author. Niles, Ill.: Whitman, 1987. 32 pp. Fiction.

Interest level: Ages 4–8 Reading level: Grade 2

Here is a sad tale of today's times. Amy has lost not once, but twice. Her parents have divorced and her father doesn't come to see her, and now her mother's romance with Gary has ended. But Gary was kind; he gave Amy a charm on her last birthday and promised her one every year for the rest of her life. Or was he kind? Amy misses Gary, and so does her mother. Mom tries to help on this crucial day, knowing Gary will not come. She takes Amy on an outing, and she exclaims, "Lots of times it's fun, Mommy and me by ourselves." But the pain lingers, as there is no father figure. She berates herself and vows never to love again. She worries, too. Will Mommy leave? The book ends with six relatives arriving, each bearing a charm, and each better able to keep a promise.

The illustrations are in soft pastels, the sentences are brief, but Amy's mother tells the painful truth: "It's hard to find someone who's special enough to be a good husband for me and a good father for you, but I hope I will someday." Many families live through this situation—impulsive behavior that unintentionally causes hurt and confusion. The book offers a sensitive, realistic treatment of this situation.

352. Willey, Margaret. *Finding David Dolores*. New York: Harper, 1986. 150 pp. Fiction.

Interest level: Age 12+ Reading level: Grades 6–7

Suddenly, Arly can no longer tolerate her mother. She has no use for any of her former friends, does not care about school, and starts dressing in a slovenly manner. The author would have us believe that this is simply a function of her emerging adolescence. Arly meets a new girl, Regina, who seems to have the same attitude about life that Arly now does. The two of them commiserate with each other about their terrible mothers, although, in truth, each girl thinks that the other one's mother is fine.

Arly also has an obsession about a boy, David Dolores, whom she has never met. Regina, on her part, develops an even stronger obsession about David's mother, a professional photographer. (It turns out that Regina's father has deserted the family, and even when he was home he treated Regina badly. Now Regina is taking out her unhappiness on her mother.)

The story doesn't really work. The reader is hard pressed to empathize or sympathize with the two young teenagers. There is no reasonable explanation for their behavior; they are neither logical nor likable. The author provides no genuine rationale for their actions or feelings. It is the parents in this book who are the aggrieved and positive characters. The two girls seem hysterical and self-centered. The story ends well for everyone, but there is not much in the book to substantiate the change.

353. Wright, Betty Ren. *A Ghost in the Window*. New York: Holiday, 1987. 152 pp. Fiction.

Interest level: Ages 9–12 Reading level: Grade 4

Meg is frequently angry at her mother, especially since her mother and father were divorced. Meg is very much like her father, and her mother notes the resemblance with irritation. Now it is summer, and 14-year-old Meg is furious because her mother is sending her to be with her father, when Meg wants to stay home and accept the starring role in a play and thinks she is old enough to take care of herself. But her mother perseveres, and Meg must travel to the small town near Lake Superior, to stay in a boardinghouse with her father. It turns out that her father is in love with Kathy, the woman who owns the house, and Meg is ferociously jealous and upset. She had hoped that one day her parents would get back together again. Now her hopes are dashed and her summer is ruined.

An attribute that Meg has is one that she shares with her grandmother: the ability to dream what will happen in the future. She has several such dreams while she is visiting her father, and because of them she helps to solve a mystery that has been plaguing Kathy and her son, Caleb. Caleb and Meg become friends, and together they discover where Caleb's father hid a valuable ring before he died. He and his partner had stolen a great deal of money, and Caleb's father's share was converted to this ring. Through Meg's dream, she and Caleb find the ring and Caleb and his mother return the ring to the police. With the laying to rest of his father's ghost, Caleb is freed from a terrible burden. Meg, in turn, freed from her burden of anger and resentment, gives her father and Kathy her blessing.

The author is a master at inserting a mystery into a story of real human dilemma. Meg's feelings are understandable, and her ability to see into the future seems believable in the context of the story. Young readers will empathize with her situation.

Kidnapping

Many kidnapped children are taken by one of their parents because of custody battles. These children are often torn in their loyalties to either parent. They lose, not only their parent, but also their familiar surroundings, their extended family, and their friends. They are often anxious because of the constant fear of being found out. They sometimes are kept on the move in order for their parent to avoid detection. Children who are the victims of kidnapping by a stranger are justifiably in terror for their lives. Even when they are returned home, kidnap victims need much support in order to recuperate from their trauma.

354. Duffy, James. *Missing*. New York: Scribner, 1988. 144 pp. Fiction.
Interest level: Ages 9–12 Reading level: Grade 5

Ten-year-old Kate has a history of wandering away from home. She lives with her mother and 12-year-old sister, Sandy. Their parents are divorced, and her father is an alcoholic. The story revolves around Kate's abduction by an emotionally disturbed man who has been watching Kate for a long time because she reminds him of his own daughter who disappeared several years ago. His wife has left him, and he has fixed on Kate as the means of his salvation. He tricks Kate into getting into his car and holds her prisoner at his house. With the help of a woman who is a retired police officer, Sandy is finally the instrument of Kate's rescue.

The story is suspenseful. We get to know each of the characters very well, and, as in any good detective story, we are invited as readers to predict what will happen next and to imagine what we would do if we were any of the protagonists. The reader is also given some good advice about staying away from strangers, no matter what they tell you. Kate behaves in an intelligent way once she has been captured. She catches on to her sister's plan quickly and cooperates in her own rescue.

Although the book does not inform us quite enough about the background of the characters, enough clues are given for us to construct much of their history for ourselves. Why Kate and Sandy don't have friends is something of a puzzle; they are likable and bright. That they are from a single-parent family and that their mother works are not reasons enough, particularly because Sandy plays several sports. Kate's previous runaway escapades are not sufficient explanation either. Children might be asked what they would do to help someone like Kate, if they had the opportunity. They can certainly discuss rules of self-preservation when accosted by strangers.

355. Hyde, Margaret O., and Hyde, Lawrence E. *Missing Children.* Photos. New York: Watts, 1985. 112 pp. Nonfiction.

Interest level: Ages 11–16 Reading level: Grades 5–6

Who are the missing? They are runaways, victims of parental abduction, victims of stranger abduction, and lost children. This book explores the attempts to find such children, and such problems in this task as a lack of cooperation among agencies involved. The Hydes evaluate changing attitudes toward these problems from colonial times until the present. Case studies punctuate the narration and point up the use of such community social tools as hotlines and shelters. Causes of runaways and family abductions are looked at in depth, with ample attention to the psychological impact on a child. Likewise, profiles of various strangers who might abduct a child are helpful (pedophiles, childless psychotics, profiteers involved in pornography and sex rings, serial murderers). From this book readers can learn of common lures used by child abductors (asking for help, saying a parent is hurt, and so on) and ways to thwart would-be assailants.

Such controversial issues as fingerprinting programs are discussed, as are the efforts of such individuals as the families of Etan Patz and Adam Walsh, the latter being influential in having the Missing Children Act enacted into law. This very helpful, informative book ends with programs and legislation designed to get at the heart of the problem, including a section on how teens can help in their schools. An appendix of resources includes hot lines, action agencies, and organizations that assist. Bibliography.

356. Marsano, William. *The Street Smart Book: How Kids Can Have Fun and Stay Safe!* Illus. by Richard White. New York: Messner, 1985, pap. 80 pp. Nonfiction.

Interest level: Ages 8–12 Reading level: Grades 4–5

A serious book about a most serious subject—kidnapping. The author respectfully addresses children who are on their own for the first time in playgrounds, malls, school yards, and elsewhere. Marsano explains that there are several types of kidnappers (noncustodial relatives, people who actually like children and neurotically act out their need for a child, strangers who want a ransom and endanger life, and child molesters). He then alerts children to tips for staying safe (keeping eyes open, being especially careful on stairways, not emblazoning one's name on clothing, and so on). A section tells a child how to get away if he or she feels in imminent danger (who to tell, how to tell, the value of noise, and so forth). The book concludes with several stories of children who found themselves in danger and what they did. Appended are resources including the FBI and various missing children's bureaus.

357. Martin, Ann M. *Missing since Monday.* New York: Holiday, 1986. 165 pp. Fiction.

Interest level: Age 11+ Reading level: Grade 6

Courtenay, the four-year-old half-sister of Maggie and Mike, has disappeared. She was in her older siblings' care because their parents were away on vacation. The rest of the book describes the search for the little girl. Along the way we meet other characters and learn of Maggie and Mike's mother, who was not granted visitation rights after her divorce from their father.

It turns out that Maggie and Mike's mother was the person who kidnapped Courtenay. She is a disturbed woman who did not harm the child, but who needs extensive psychiatric treatment. There were hints that she might have been the one who took Courtenay, so it was not an enormous shock when this turned out to be the case.

Included in the narrative is a set of instructions of what to do if a child is missing, and also what to do to prepare children for being accosted by strangers. The book is a good blend of story and information.

358. Morris, Judy K. *The Crazies and Sam.* New York: Viking, 1983; Puffin, pap. 136 pp. Fiction.

Interest level: Age 10+ Reading level: Grade 5

Sam, who has been living with his father since his parents' divorce, feels both neglected and overorganized through lists, schedules, and routines by his protective but busy father. He has little contact with his mother, but he loves and admires his adventurous and high-spirited Aunt Kristen. He has a friend, a Burmese boy who is an expert artist and reckless cyclist. Sam often has the urge to follow the "crazies" (the tramps, homeless, and mentally ill people). Sam considers himself somewhat crazy, too, and he is fascinated by what he perceives to be their freedom.

Disappointed at being left alone one Saturday, Sam hitches a ride with a "crazy" lady who takes him to her small apartment. He enjoys her erratic and eccentric behavior, until it dawns on him that she intends to keep him. He uses his wits to free himself. Through this traumatic experience he comes to understand the true strength and value of his father's love and the real meaning of freedom.

Sam is a casualty of divorce. His mother is too busy with her job to maintain contact with him. Although Sam's father is sensitive to the problems of being a single parent—he makes a genuine effort to create a healthy and efficiently organized environment for his son by joining a food co-op and planning nutritious meals, in addition to maintaining his job outside the home—Sam resents his father's "mental notepad" and misses the element of mothering that his father cannot supply. The end of the story is no panacea, but Sam's father does promise to try to be home more on weekends, and Sam realizes that he cannot force his mother to be something she isn't.

Judy K. Morris brings to the readers' attention some problems of single parenthood that are as much societal as personal, and she presents the issues well.

359. Rardin, Susan Lowry. *Captives in a Foreign Land.* Boston: Houghton Mifflin, 1984. 218 pp. Fiction.
Interest level: Age 12+ Reading level: Grades 6–7

An important conference on nuclear arms control is being held in Rome, Italy. While the adults are meeting, the families of the delegates tour the city. An Islamic group takes some of the American children hostage to try to force a ban on nuclear arms. They take the children to a desert hideout in the Middle East, and the children are kept there until they are rescued.

The author vividly reflects the children's fears and responses while they are being held captive. She also describes, somewhat less clearly, the people who took the children hostage. The children are treated in a more humane manner than they expect, and it is through the children's efforts that one of their group manages to be brought out of captivity and tells where the rest of the children are being held.

The book succeeds best when it describes the children's reactions. It is well paced and transmits suspense to the reader. It is not as successful in conveying its message of antinuclear idealism. The children's message to the world and the Islamic group's supposed idealism deteriorate to slogans and rhetoric, noble though the intent is.

360. Sommers, Beverly. *Starting Over.* New York: Crosswinds, 1987, pap. 157 pp. Fiction.
Interest level: Age 10+ Reading level: Grade 5

For nine years Richie and his younger brother, Paco, now called Paul, have been living with their father in El Salvador. Richie thinks that it was because he begged his father to let Richie live with him that their father kidnapped them. He had visited every weekend, but that wasn't sufficient for Richie, who was upset when their mother was granted custody in the divorce settlement. The father had been an automobile salesperson and very well-to-do before he decided to simplify his life and move to a poor and rural country. He became a chicken farmer in El Salvador and taught his sons that too much material wealth was a burden and was selfish.

Now they have been stolen back from their father's house (he was away in town), and they have been returned to their mother in California. They discover that their mother has spent a small fortune over the years trying to find and recover them. They also find that they must learn to eat, dress, and behave differently from the way they have become used to with their father. They are illiterate and ignorant of math, geography, and world events. Their mother arranges for a tutor for them and the tutor is dismayed at their lack of knowledge but encouraged by their intelligence.

Both boys find the changes easier to bear when they make friends. Paul confesses that he likes his life in California much better than with their father because they do not have to work all the time, and their material wealth pleases him. Richie's friend Arlie is the best friend he ever had, but he misses his father and he wants to go back to him. He and Arlie plan how they will run away to El Salvador together. They actually begin their journey, but Arlie hurts her foot and they have to return. This turns out to be fortunate because the boys' father shows up and declares that he will once again become a car salesperson and live nearby. Richie decides to live with his father; Paul stays with his mother, and although the two parents are so different from each other, and the father has withheld the boys from their mother for nine years, it appears that the two will get back together again.

If the ending were not so artificial and romantic, the book would have much more substance. It is difficult to believe that this father could have been so uncaring about the boys' future in El Salvador, and then perform an about-face when they were returned to the United States. The response of the mother, although understandably an angry one, is far milder than what one might expect of a woman who has been put through such torture. The mother is not portrayed as a very sympathetic character. She knows that one son enjoys the material things she can give him, and the other son does not like her, but neither she nor the reader is given much more information about how that came about. As a matter of fact, we don't really get to know the motivation or the makeup of any of the characters.

The issue of a parent kidnapping his or her children is a serious and frequent one. It should be handled with much more insight and concern.

Desertion

In desertion situations, loss is keenly felt. A member of the family has chosen to leave, withdrawing physical and emotional support from the rest of the family. Those who are left behind express bereavement, rejection, and a lack of confidence, coupled with the nagging questions: Will the missing member of the family return? What did they do wrong? Can anything be done to bring him or her back?

361. Adler, C. S. *Roadside Valentine.* New York: Macmillan, 1983. 185 pp. Fiction.

Interest level: Age 12+ Reading level: Grades 5–6

Jamie's mother deserted him and his father. After a few years she dies in an automobile accident. Bereft of her loving and exuberant warmth, Jamie tries to please his strict and hard-working father, but nothing seems to work. His father is a silent, undemonstrative man who has found it difficult to express his emotions. After a stage of drug taking and alcohol abuse, Jamie settles into a more self-constructive life, but he still cannot seem to please his father. After Jamie builds a gigantic snow valentine expressing his love for a young woman who has another boyfriend, Jamie and his father get into a terrible argument and Jamie moves out. Not until Jamie gets a job, rents an apartment, and sends out college applications does he and his father reconcile and begin to understand each other better. With his new-found independence and self-esteem Jamie wins the girl he loves, gets accepted to college, and establishes a solid relationship with his father.

The author demonstrates that moving out of one's parents' home is not necessarily the worst or most destructive thing to do. It is only when Jamie is truly independent that he can forge an interdependent relationship with his father. All the characters in this story are believable and authentic. Readers can identify with the situation as well as the people.

362. Blue, Rose. *Goodbye, Forever Tree.* New York: Signet, 1987, pap. 155 pp. Fiction.

Interest level: Age 13+ Reading level: Grade 6

Heather seems to be the only person in the trailer park who is stable and has a vision of the future. Few of the families have both parents living there, and there is much sexual promiscuity among the inhabitants. Heather is part of a large crowd of teenagers who are aimless, bitter, and self-destructive. She is an attractive young woman who is talented in art. Her teachers support and encourage her to achieve her ambition of becoming an art therapist. She wins a scholarship and makes plans for a secure future, the symbol of which is a tree that she dreams about and that an elderly friend of hers paints, the "forever tree."

The book has the patterns of a romance novel, because it focuses heavily on the characters' romantic entanglements and on their physical appearance. But the theme of desertion and its effects on the families of the deserted ones is consistent, and it provides readers with a perspective that goes beyond the thinness of the plot. We come to know several characters, although there are a number of characters who seem to be present more as parts of the scenery than parts of the plot. Heather somehow manages to rise above her background, her mother's neglect, and her father's and brother's desertion. She manages to resist the sexual pressures her boyfriend puts on her, and she is also able to become involved with two potentially appropriate partners for her future.

The author conveys Heather's dilemma well. The issue of transience and its attendant complications are clearly described. Although some of the characters are cardboard figures, those whom we get to know have attractive as well as self-destructive qualities. This could be a useful book to help teenagers who are in this situation find some support. It could also be a help to young people who have never had to deal with the issue of abandonment and uncertainty to become more empathic with those who are in this circumstance.

363. Brooks, Bruce. *Midnight Hour Encores.* New York: Harper, 1986. 263 pp. Fiction.

Interest level: Age 13+ Reading level: Grades 6–7

Sib's mother deserted her when she was 20 hours old. Her father, Taxi, has brought her up, but Sib feels that although her father has been a good father, she has brought herself up. She has never asked him about her mother, or wanted to see her until now, at age 16. Now she not only wants to know all there is to know about her infancy and her mother, but she tells Taxi that she now wants to see her mother.

So Sib and her father begin an odyssey, visiting the places of her father's youth and meeting people who were important to him during the 1960s. Her father tells her of how he nurtured her when she was an infant. She learns things about the care and feeding of babies that she had never thought about before. She learns about her father, and she also learns about her mother as seen through her father's memory.

Before they get to San Francisco, where her mother lives, Sib informs her father that she really wanted to go on this journey in order to audition for a new music school in San Francisco. Sib had originally intended to go to Julliard. She is a champion cellist, of international reputation. Her father is crushed that she wants to leave him, but he understands her wishes and is gracious about her decision.

Both Sib and her father are surprised when they discover that her mother, Connie, is no longer a drug-taking, impoverished hippie. She is a very wealthy businesswoman. She accepts Sib into her home, buys her expensive clothes, and assumes that Sib will stay with her when she is accepted into the music school. Sib is accepted into the school, but at the last moment she decides to return with her father. The reader is left to wonder what she will do with her considerable musical talent and with the rest of her life.

Interesting issues are raised in this compellingly written book. We expect to hate the mother; and in truth, we never love or admire her, but rather we understand her. More important, her daughter understands her. Some of the relationships are dealt with too cursorily. And many specific questions about some of the characters and their eventual outcomes remain. However, the ending is satisfying, and the reader ends up more informed about important matters than in books where the endings are neatly tied up packages.

364. Cleaver, Vera. *Sweetly Sings the Donkey.* New York: Lippincott, 1985. 150 pp. Fiction.

Interest level: Age 10+ Reading level: Grade 5

Fourteen-year-old Lily is the anchor of the Snow family. Her father, Judson, is a junk collector and a dreamer. He has never managed to support his family adequately. Martha, their mother, is pretty, delicate, and dependent. Lily is the most practical member of the family, and it is she who carries most of the responsibility for caring for her two brothers. After they move to Florida because Judson has inherited some property there, they discover that Judson is ill, the land does not have any dwelling on it, and the impoverished family will have to scrape for a living.

Martha finally leaves them; she runs off with a man who has befriended the family. Lily and her friends build a house for the family, and by the end of the book we know that, thanks to Lily, the family will survive, and even, perhaps, prosper.

It is ironic but true to life that Martha was deserted by both her parents when she was a child. She tells Lily that she has stayed with Judson because she didn't want to do to her children what was done to her. Yet she does it. In the end she cannot withstand the same sort of self-centeredness that her own parents exhibited.

This book contains the same ingredients that the other books by Cleaver and her late husband have always contained: a strong and individualistic female protagonist, an accurate sense of setting, and a cast of memorable characters woven into a gripping story.

365. Furlong, Monica. *Wise Child.* New York: Knopf, 1987. 228 pp. Fiction.

Interest level: Age 12+ Reading level: Grade 7

The story is an interesting combination of fantasy and reality. Wise Child's mother is a witch who deserted her when she was very young. Her father has left on a voyage, and it is unlikely that he will return soon. Wise Child is placed with a mysterious woman, an outcast named Juniper, who instructs her in languages and expects her to work hard.

When Maeve, Wise Child's birth mother, discovers that she is with Juniper, she comes to try to woo her away. Wise Child does go to her mother, but runs back to Juniper when she discovers that Maeve is a wicked witch. She realizes that your true mother is not so much the mother who bore you, but rather the person who nurtures and loves you.

There is magic and mystery in this story set in Scotland in early Christian times. The values of loyalty, hard work, as well as education come through, and the fantasy is engaging.

366. Grant, Cynthia D. *Kumquat May, I'll Always Love You.* New York: Macmillan, 1986; Bantam, pap. 182 pp. Fiction.

Interest level: Age 10+ Reading level: Grades 4–5

Livvy's father died, and now her mother has deserted her. She receives an occasional postcard from her mother that says her mother loves her and will return, but it has been more than two years now, and still her mother has not come home. Livvy is now 17. She has not told anyone except her two best friends that her mother is gone. She does not want to be sent to other relatives; she wants to wait in her own house for her mother's return. She lies to family and other adults, and she devises elaborate schemes for making people think that her mother is living with her. When her boyfriend (a third person she has told that her mother is gone) pushes her too far, she sends him away and he tells the authorities that her mother is gone and that she is living alone. They come to investigate, and her mother returns home at that moment.

Livvy's mother is portrayed as a disturbed and limited woman who is, nevertheless, a survivor. Her daughter is much stronger than she. The end of the story is ambiguous: The mother has once again left the house on an errand, and it is not certain that she will return. But the reader knows enough about Livvy to feel confident that Livvy will manage.

The story is a strange one. The author is persuasive enough to have the reader suspend disbelief up to a point, but the intrusion of the boyfriend, Raymond, weakens the story, as does the less-than-full depiction of Livvy's best friend, Rosella. Livvy herself is an interesting and strong character and her predicament involves the reader in her problems.

367. Hahn, Mary Downing. *Following the Mystery Man.* New York: Clarion, 1988. 180 pp. Fiction.

Interest level: Age 10+ Reading level: Grade 5

Madigan lives with her grandmother. Her mother died when she was four years old; Madigan's father deserted them just after she was born. When a handsome and mysterious stranger named Clint comes to town and rents a room from her grandmother, Madigan fantasizes that he may be her father. It turns out that Clint is not her father. Madigan's friend Angie has a sister, Alice, who has had a baby, Chad, out of wedlock, and Clint is Chad's father. He is also a thief. Madigan is devastated when she discovers the truth. She is abducted by Clint and Alice because she has caught them in the act of making a getaway. After she escapes and returns home, Angie learns more about her real father and begins to better understand herself.

It is unfortunate that the author reinforces a stereotype about unwed mothers in this story. Angie's parents forbid her to have anything to do with her sister and nephew. Angie's brother is vicious in his reaction to his older sister. Why Alice would want to live in the same town as her parents is a mystery. Clint is also a mystery. He seems to be a pleasant and intelligent young man. He is sensitive to Madigan's feelings, and he genuinely seems to like her. He also seems to be sincere in his desire to take care of his son and Alice. He says he is a thief because he has a talent for it, but this does not have the ring of truth.

The story is a fast-moving one that keeps the reader's attention, but the characters and plot are a little too thin.

368. Hahn, Mary Downing. *Tallahassee Higgins*. New York: Clarion, 1987; Camelot, pap. 180 pp. Fiction.

Interest level: Age 10+ Reading level: Grades 4–5

Tallahassee's mother, Liz, has sent her daughter to live with Liz's older brother and his wife in Maryland, while she goes off with the latest in her string of boyfriends to seek an acting career in Hollywood. Twelve-year-old Tallahassee (Tally) fears that her mother will forget her, as she seems to have forgotten her past boyfriends, the family cat, and her family of origin. At the same time, she loves her mother deeply and is fiercely loyal and protective of her. Indeed, her mother does not communicate regularly with her, and the Hollywood plans fall apart.

Most of the story involves Tallahassee's learning to cope with her mother, her nasty aunt, and, especially, her feelings about herself and her situation. One of the interesting features of this book is its exploration of different life-styles and the choices people make. We come to know a number of characters, each of whom manages everyday living in a different way. Tally's best friend and her family, Tally's aunt and uncle, Tally's mother, her grandmother, and the other children at school all provide distinct options.

Tallahassee discovers for the first time who her father is when she sees some pictures in an album belonging to a former friend of her mother's. She meets her grandmother, who until now never knew of her existence. She learns some facts about her mother as well as her father. And, ultimately, she comes to terms with her own situation.

The mother here is reminiscent of the mothers in Cynthia Voigt's *A Solitary Blue* (Atheneum, 1983) and Katherine Paterson's *The Great Gilly Hopkins* (Crowell, 1978). All three women are physically attractive, terribly self-centered, and totally unreliable. All three have children who love them and want to be with them. And all three ultimately disappoint and desert their children. Like Jeff and Gilly, Tallahassee is intelligent, introspective, and hopeful that her mother will somehow become a person who can be counted on. Like the other two, Tally must learn to adjust to a family life without her mother.

369. Hamilton, Virginia. *A Little Love.* New York: Philomel, 1984. 207 pp. Fiction.

Interest level: Age 12+ Reading level: Grade 7

Sheema lives with her grandparents. Her father left her immediately after the death of her mother. She attends a vocational high school and has a talent for cooking. She is a generous-hearted, obese young woman who, until she became involved with a young man named Forrest, was promiscuous and self-deprecating. Forrest loves and admires her. He sees in her qualities that she doesn't even know exist. Her grandparents, too, love her dearly and she is fiercely loyal to them.

Sheema decides that she must see her father and come to terms with her grief over his not remaining with her when her mother died. She has long ago accepted her mother's death, but her father is alive; he sends money for her support, but she never hears from him. She and Forrest drive off together, with her grandparents' blessing but without Forrest's father's knowledge, to seek her father. They find him, and Sheema at last lays to rest the expectations she had of him. He is a sad man who mourns his losses and has not really recovered from them, even though he has a new family and is successful in business.

With new knowledge and self-respect, Sheema returns to her grandparents, and she and Forrest pledge to marry each other. All the characters are well drawn and rich, as might be expected in a Hamilton novel. Forrest, in particular, is a remarkably insightful, gentle, and loving person. The book deals with the complexity of people's responses to loss and recognizes that desertion is but one of these responses.

370. Highwater, Jamake. *I Wear the Morning Star.* New York: Harper, 1986. 148 pp. Fiction.

Interest level: Age 12+ Reading level: Grade 6

Sitko is a frightened, isolated, and unhappy boy, whose parents have deserted him, and whose older brother, Reno, is ashamed of being a Native American. The two boys have been placed in a home called Star of Good Hope, but it is an abusive and terrifying place for Sitko, who is a sensitive artist, and who has a love for his Cherokee heritage that was instilled in him by his beloved grandmother. Reno, on the other hand, hates being a Cherokee, denies that he is, and tries to bully his younger brother into rejecting his heritage.

In poetic prose, the author conveys the complexity of desertion and the agony of self-hatred. The story is filled with people who hate, not only Native Americans but also Jews, and, if truth be told, themselves. No noble beings emerge. Even the grandmother, who is a brave and wise person, is so filled with hatred for the white man who gives her and her family shelter that she poisons any possibility of a truce among them. Sitko is the last hope. The story is a tragedy in one sense, because the boys' father kills their mother, and their lives are seldom more than painful exile. But there is triumph here, too, because the grandmother transfers her store of knowledge and tradition to the young artist, Sitko, and the reader knows that he will carry it on.

371. Mahy, Margaret. *The Catalogue of the Universe.* New York: McElderry, 1986; Point, pap. 185 pp. Fiction.
Interest level: Age 13+ Reading level: Grade 9

Angela May has heard many stories about her father, whom she has never known. Her mother has tried to help Angela feel loved, and she has succeeded. But when Angela finally meets her father, she discovers that her mother did not tell her the truth, and she is furious. Over the course of this novel Angela falls in love, battles with her mother, and finally reconciles with her. Both she and her mother are strong and independent women. By the end of the book Angela has come of age; she can function as her own person, and even, perhaps, come to terms with her father and grandmother. The story's interest is heightened by its New Zealand setting.

372. Rinaldi, Ann. *But in the Fall I'm Leaving.* New York: Holiday, 1985. 250 pp. Fiction.
Interest level: Age 12+ Reading level: Grade 6

This book has a very complicated plot with many twists and surprises. The story tells of Brieanna McQuade and her older brother, Kevin, who were deserted by their mother when Brie was two years old. Her older sister, Celia, lives with their mother; Brie and Kevin, who is now a priest, remained with their father.

Unknown to Brie, her maternal grandmother, Miss Emily, lives in town. Brie is an angry and rebellious young girl, and at one point she vandalizes her grandmother's house. Not until her grandmother dies does she find out it was her grandmother. In the interim she has come to know and love the old woman, whose death is a terrible shock to her, as is the newfound knowledge about her relationship to Miss Emily.

Everyone colludes to keep the secret from Brie. No really good reason is given for this deception, and the author never satisfactorily explains it. It also strains the reader's credulity to believe that Miss Emily is a reformed person who at one time nearly destroyed the whole town by closing the mill, then had the audacity to return to it when she grew old. She is also supposed to have driven a wedge between Brie's father and mother. She and her daughter stop speaking to each other when the daughter leaves.

There are a suicide, several side issues of moral and societal responsibility, and Brie's emotional volatility. Many issues are raised, and in one way or another resolved, but a number of issues are left unsatisfactorily dangling, not the least of which is the personality of the mother. She is drawn as a totally selfish, malicious, vindictive woman. We never meet Celia, and she seems unnecessary to the book. This is a case where there is basically a good idea, but the author doesn't develop it in a satisfactory fashion.

373. Rodowsky, Colby. *Julie's Daughter.* New York: Farrar, 1985. 231 pp. Fiction.

Interest level: Age 12+ Reading level: Grades 7–8

Using the strategy of telling the story with the voices of the three main characters, the author has successfully conveyed the necessity to view a situation from different perspectives. The three characters are Julie, Slug, and Harper. Julie ran away from her mother's home when she was 17, leaving her newborn baby, Slug. Now that her mother has died, Julie returns to take Slug to live with her. The two of them find a common ground in their caring for Harper, their neighbor, who is dying of cancer. The chapters alternate among the three characters, and each has her own story to tell. It is to the author's credit that although the stories blend, each one remains individual, like the themes in a fugue.

Harper is an artist and keeps creating art until the cancer kills her. The book tells not only of the losses caused by desertion of a child but also of the loss of ability and the contemplation of the loss of one's own life. None of the characters is a stereotype; the reader learns that none of them can be judged, although they have been guilty of harmful acts. Perhaps the most powerful feature of this book is its invitation to consider the subtlety and pain of these acts rather than to leap to pat conclusions.

The plot is an interesting one, but the holes are a little too many and too deep for the reader to stay absorbed and willing to suspend disbelief.

374. Voigt, Cynthia. *A Solitary Blue.* New York: Atheneum, 1983; Juniper, pap. 240 pp. Fiction.

Interest level: Age 12+ Reading level: Grades 6–7

Deserted by his mother, Melody, at the age of seven, Jeff Greene lives with Horace, his distant, scholarly, and considerably older father. Four years later, while he is recuperating from a debilitating illness, his mother reenters his life and invites him to spend the summer with her. Oblivious to her faults, Jeff is infatuated with her beauty and charm. When he returns to his father, he is lonely and aches for his mother and her family, even though he knows that she is dishonest and superficial. A friend of the family, Brother Thomas, helps Jeff and his father to reach out to and appreciate each other. Together, they renovate a property overlooking the marshes of Chesapeake Bay. There Jeff meets Dicey Tillerman and they develop a strong bond. Decisively choosing to remain with his father when Melody sues for custody and the divorce is finalized, Jeff is able to develop a strength and eventual detachment that enables him to see Melody's immaturity and selfishness clearly, and to value the honesty of genuine relationships.

Jeff is the victim of self-centered emotional manipulation by Melody. Neglected from a very early age, at seven, Jeff is expected to feel guilty about wanting his mother to stay with him. His father is preoccupied with the academic world of the university, and Jeff is constantly apologizing for his existence, careful to disguise his feelings lest his father desert him too.

Although Horace never speaks ill of Melody, she sabotages Jeff's relationship with his father by undermining and devaluing him as a person and as a father. Once Horace recognizes the depth of Jeff's suffering and loneliness, he becomes more open with his son and takes responsibility for helping him to heal. He reassures Jeff of his always being wanted and loved and apologizes for his neglect. Once his father and he have been emotionally reunited, Jeff is able to become independent and strong. The lesson is an important one. The story is a moving one.

375. Zindel, Paul. *The Amazing and Death-Defying Diary of Eugene Dingman.* New York: Harper, 1987. 186 pp. Fiction.

Interest level: Age 12+ Reading level: Grade 7

Eugene Dingman is a sensitive, intellectual, and passionate 15-year-old who lives with his mother and older sister. His emotional outpourings are too much for his mother, who sends him away to a summer resort to work as a waiter. Eugene's father never comes to see him, although Eugene writes poignant letters pleading for his father's advice, understanding, and presence.

Eugene's peers are no more empathic than his parents. He is an oddball. His summer is filled with put-downs and betrayals, including two that are the most painful: The girl he has a crush on lies to him and goes out with many other males; and his father "sweeps" through the resort without even speaking to him. The ultimate blow is revealed to him in a letter from his mother: She will not be there when he returns home; she has married someone Eugene does not like, and she indicates that she feels that Eugene must change if he is to be a happy person.

Eugene is an open, aching wound, but his brilliance and his willingness to confide all to his diary make this a book that attracts the reader to him. Zindel's perception of young people communicates well. He conveys the results of Eugene's parents' physical and emotional desertion of the boy in a style that engages the audience. His use of the diary form is an excellent strategy for involvement. Eugene's problems, painful though they are, become wryly amusing because of the context and format of the story. Adolescents will probably identify with Eugene and his situation.

Serious Illness

Serious illness requiring hospitalization or isolation constitutes a loss experience because of traumatic separation from family members at a time of crisis. Children who are hospitalized feel understandably anxious about medical procedures, wondering what they have done to merit the "punishment" of treatment. If hospitalization of themselves or others is prolonged, children go through the phases of mourning that follow death: protest, despair, and finally detachment. Hospitalization and treatment for mental illness, anorexia, or substance abuse may also prompt the same feelings.

376. Adler, C. S. *The Shell Lady's Daughter.* New York: Coward, 1983, pap. 140 pp. Fiction.

Interest level: Age 11+ Reading level: Grade 5

Fourteen-year-old Kelly has been her mother's best friend for a long time. Her father is a pilot and is away more often than he is home. Kelly has noticed certain danger signs of her mother's mental illness, but her father prefers to make light of them. Kelly's mother's lethargy; her mentioning that it feels as if her skin is crawling; her pricking her hand with a needle so that the needlework becomes bloodied; her telling sad stories about a doomed shell lady all come to a head one day, and she is hospitalized. Kelly is sent off to stay with her grandparents in Florida despite her protests and her concern that no one will visit her mother in the hospital. According to her father it is the doctor's orders that she not see her mother. Kelly feels very guilty, certain that she has been the cause of her mother's illness.

Kelly's grandparents are wealthy. Her grandfather had been a college president, but is now senile. Despite her ferocious loyalty to her husband, her grandmother is, to the rest of the world, a detached, rigid, snobbish, somewhat cold woman who does not want to discuss anything that has to do with feelings. She disapproves of Kelly's mother because her background is not as upper class as Kelly's father's. She angrily tells Kelly that her mother didn't think enough of her to refrain from attempting suicide. Kelly is shocked, and even more guilt ridden, but she is angry, too.

Fortunately, Kelly makes friends with the next-door neighbor, Evan, a wealthy man confined to a wheelchair because of polio. He reassures Kelly that her mother's illness is no one's fault. He also helps Kelly to see that physical disabilities need not affect a person's relationships. He tells Kelly that love and support made him strong enough to be independent and happy. Largely because of what Evan has told her, but also because she has matured, Kelly makes the decision to return home to help her mother get well. Kelly will have a life of her own and will be there not only for her mother but also for her own sense of self-esteem.

Adler has written a novel that is strong enough to stand on its own as a good story. She has also incorporated some sound psychological information about mental illness, people with disabilities, abusive families, and the normal process of growing up. This book is a winner.

377. Adler, C. S. *With Westie and the Tin Man.* New York: Macmillan, 1985. 194 pp. Fiction.

Interest level: Age 12+ Reading level: Grades 6–7

Greg's mother is an alcoholic and Greg has been jailed for a year for repeated offenses, notably shoplifting. On his release from jail, he finds that his mother, who hasn't had a drink in a year, and a friend whom she met at AA, Manny Horowitz, have set up a business. Greg doesn't feel welcome or comfortable, except with Manny's dog, Westie. As the days go by, Greg learns that Manny has much to offer him, that his mother has changed for the better, and that telling the truth is an important task he must learn to do.

Adler is a prolific and popular writer. She manages, in the space of this one story, to convey a lot of information about alcoholics and their families. She also presents a believable picture of a 15-year-old boy who is angry at the world and at himself, yet manages to overcome his problems. This book is well worth reading.

378. Avraham, Regina. *Substance Abuse Prevention and Treatment: Encyclopedia of Psychoactive Drugs.* Photos and illus. New York: Chelsea, 1988. 128 pp. Nonfiction.

Interest level: Ages 12–16 Reading level: Grade 6

This is one entry in an encyclopedia of more than 60 volumes devoted to drug study. Approaches to prevention and control are the crux of this volume, with treatment alternatives and controversies demystified. Detoxification, maintenance, and residential programs are the three most often tried approaches. The historical analysis of how drugs slowly became part of the mainstream is interesting. In a country where opium was once an ingredient in over-the-counter cough and aspirin products, it's not surprising we have had a long history of problems. The history of treatment is also of interest, the establishment of AA being a pivotal event. A chapter on how addiction affects the family is insightful, and specific treatment centers and their approaches are explained. What comes through, however, is the vast failure over time. The tone is as one would expect, statistical and dry—encyclopedialike. Occasional stories of teenagers and their families are not as lively as those in other volumes, so this book is likely to become reference material instead of psychological self-help fodder. Bibliography, resources, glossary, index.

379. Berger, Melvin. *Germs Make Me Sick!* Illus. by Marylin Hafner. New York: Crowell, 1985; Trophy, pap. 32 pp. Nonfiction.
Interest level: Ages 4–8 Reading level: Grades 1–2

An entry in the Let's-Read-and-Find-Out Science series, this book explains such basic illnesses as sore throats. Just how do we get sick? From germs, those "tiny, tiny living beings." There are two specific kinds: bacteria and viruses. Colorful illustrations demonstrate how bacteria and viruses look under the microscope, where they are found, and how they behave. "Many germs are not harmful. Also, your body keeps germs out most of the time." The accompanying illustration shows a knight on horseback combating germs. The means of protection are enumerated: skin without cuts, the nose, and the mouth. And if germs get in, the white cells and antibodies often come to the rescue. One of the most interesting explanations is of what happens to make us feel sick: "The bacteria give off waste products. Some of these wastes are poisons. The poisons can damage or kill the cells that make up your body. When enough cells are harmed, you feel sick." Specific kinds of bacteria are explored—the kind that stay in one place, to cause cavities, for example. Viruses forcing their way into body cells and then popping more viruses out are explained. Home care and doctor's visits are part of the book, too, ending with a general list for health care so children can help to keep well.

380. Brooks, Bruce. *The Moves Make the Man.* New York: Harper, 1984, hb and pap. 280 pp. Fiction.
Interest level: Age 12+ Reading level: Grade 7

Jerome Foxworthy is the single black student in an otherwise all white high school. He is very bright, very happy with his family, and an excellent athlete as well. He befriends a boy named Bix Peters, who is also an excellent athlete, but who is by no means as well adjusted as Jerome. Bix cannot compromise; he cannot tolerate uncertainty or deception. When Bix's mother is hospitalized because of her emotional problems, Bix and his stepfather handle the entire situation badly. A visit to his mother (after he and his stepfather engage in a vicious competition to determine whether Bix will be permitted to visit her) is disastrous. Bix runs away, and Jerome is left to speculate about what happened to his friend.

The differences between the way Jerome and his brothers deal with the temporary loss of their mother when she is hospitalized after being in an accident and how Bix and his stepfather handle Bix's mother's hospitalization provide an instructive contrast. Bix and his stepfather have an antagonistic, closed relationship. They do not seem to care about each other. And they blame each other for the mother's emotional problems.

The story is told in Jerome's voice. Bix is his first best friend. The friendship is the primary factor in his narrative, but issues of differences between black and white people, the relationship between parents and children, and the emotional upheaval of adolescence are also themes in this well-written, engrossing novel.

381. Carter, Alden R. *Sheila's Dying.* New York: Putnam, 1987. 207 pp. Fiction.

Interest level: Age 13+ Reading level: Grade 7

Jerry's girlfriend, Sheila, has had a difficult life for all of her 16 years. Her parents were killed in a plane crash when she was an infant, and her grandparents raised her. Now Sheila is dying of cancer. Her grandmother is not a strong or stable woman, and at the onset of Sheila's illness is frequently drunk. Jerry was just about to break up with her, but when she suddenly needs to be hospitalized, and her illness begins to escalate, Jerry and Bonnie, Sheila's friend, take most of the responsibility for her care. At one point, when the burden becomes overwhelming for the two friends, they enlist the aid of a social worker, and she arranges for more housekeeping and cooking help for Sheila and her grandmother.

Alden Carter graphically describes Sheila's symptoms, treatment, and agony. He brings out the information that had Sheila visited a doctor when her symptoms first surfaced, there might have been hope for her. But it is clear from the first, at the time of her emergency operation, that there is little if any chance for her survival. The story is told in Jerry's voice, and through his perspective. The dialogue is sprinkled with profanities, but it is consistent with the language of teenagers. Carter's transitions are sudden, and at times the reader is left a little confused about what happened between the end of one chapter and the beginning of another, but, in general, his style is readable and clear. The topic is one that a number of teenagers face, and the author certainly conveys the particular perspective of the adolescent characters.

Sheila's reaction to her illness is frequently one of rage. She is not gracious to her visitors or her doctor. She is furious at the world for having done her in. At the end of her life she becomes more resigned to her dying, but the change is not a believable one, except for the fact that she is growing weaker. Nevertheless, it is useful for young readers to see that not all dying people are martyrs, or sweet-tempered, or grateful to their friends for helping them and loving them.

The ending is predictable: Jerry and Bonnie get together. Sheila never seems more than a poor, unfortunate, somewhat limited victim, whose illness and death are the impetus for Jerry's maturing into a responsible adult.

382. Carter, Sharon, and Monnig, Judy. *Coping with a Hospital Stay*. New York: Rosen, 1987. 110 pp. Nonfiction.

Interest level: Ages 10–16 Reading level: Grade 5

This is a truly valuable book written in an easy, straightforward style by a free-lance writer and a nurse. Its chatty tone and slim size seem just right for the concentration ability those facing up to hospitalization can muster. The authors cover a variety of topics, ranging from the expected (for example, what to bring to the hospital and pertinent questions to ask the doctor) to the pleasantly surprising, perhaps even more useful (for example, getting along with a roommate, depressing visitors and how to turn them off, and how to handle dumb questions about such things as cancer). Even in its few pages, there is considerable depth of exploration about attitudes, such as people who seem to tell the hospitalized it's their fault. And throughout, the authors admirably give young readers assertive lines to say back: "Hey, I don't like that! That doesn't make me feel very good!"

Along with instructions on assertion are guidelines for being a good patient as well, ensconced in a chapter titled "Don't Be a Patient the Nurses Want to Kick." This alerts readers to the scope of a nurse's job and ways to develop patience. Other chapters include checking into the hospital; long-term stays; ideas to avoid boredom; ways to keep up with schoolwork; admissions from an emergency room; hospitalization for cosmetic surgery, cancer, and psychiatric care; accidents; and having an uncertain medical future. There's also a diary of a typical hospital stay, this one caused by a car accident.

The chapter organization is not the best and chapters contain more than what their heading describes (there's a full discussion of guilt and other feelings in the chapter on the emergency room). Readers should therefore be advised that skipping around is fine. From page one on, this book is a fine mix of information and acknowledgment of the many feelings attendant to a sudden hospitalization.

383. Check, William A. *AIDS: Encyclopedia of Health.* New York: Chelsea, 1988. 128 pp. Nonfiction.

Interest level: Ages 12–16 Reading level: Grade 6

This look at AIDS is written by the former editor of the *Journal of the American Medical Association* who previously won the American Medical Writers Association Book Award for *The Truth about AIDS.* The volume boasts a lengthy, insightful introduction by Surgeon General C. Everett Koop.

Check offers the necessary biological understanding, but his entry in the growing adolescent AIDS bookshelf is primarily an epidemiological, sociological perspective. One-third of the book is devoted to tracing the early cases as they turned up in New York, San Francisco, Africa, and other places around the world, discussing the patients and pioneering doctors involved, and examining the roles of various medical centers in putting the pieces of the puzzle together. The stories are told in a fascinating manner, even though they are tragic—fights between the United States and France over honor, nations reluctant to share statistics for fear they'll be labeled country of origin, and the power of denial making it difficult to provide information for prevention. Chapters are devoted to the search for drugs and a vaccine, blood testing and its attendant controversies, and the heartbreaking dilemmas AIDS has wrought—how to give medical care to such large numbers; how to help drug addicts in the face of a federal government that talks about a war on drugs yet won't pay for treatment; and how to care for dying infants whose parents are dying as well. The author emphasizes behavior change (safe sex only with partners who are known well and in a caring relationship) as the only hope to avert worldwide disaster, believing that this can come about through information, counseling, and the brave societal response we are already seeing, as exemplified by the gay community and people of influence in film and other media.

Check is a graceful writer and his sympathies won't elude the adolescent reader, who is likely to read this book from cover to cover. One hopes readers will take up his idea of the only preventive treatment available today, "behavioral vaccination." List of resources, glossary, index.

384. Cohen, Susan, and Cohen, Daniel. *A Six-Pack and a Fake I.D.: Teens Look at the Drinking Question.* New York: Evans, 1986. 180 pp. Nonfiction.

Interest level: Age 12+ Reading level: Grade 6

Teenagers will make their own decisions, the Cohens know, so their attempt is to give a balanced picture with "reliable and believable information." Their task is difficult because while it's generally agreed that alcoholism is a serious national problem and drunk driving deaths are rampant, alcohol is also an integral and accepted part of our culture. Their wisdom is in acknowledging this paradox. Then, without moralizing, the authors examine the role alcohol plays in our culture and educate teens about the effects of drinking. They use science in describing the chemical changes that occur in the body, and they tap social science as well, including a short history of the laws that have been created (and sometimes uncreated) around alcohol consumption.

A strength of this book is the Cohens' tips for dealing with the kinds of situations teens are likely to find themselves in—the party that threatens to go overboard, peer pressure, and so forth. They give practical hints for successfully preventing situations from escalating and for confronting pressure. A section deals with communicating with parents, another with knowing when help is necessary and where to get it. This matter-of-fact approach will appeal to both teenagers and their parents. A recommended handbook.

385. Cohen, Susan, and Cohen, Daniel. *What You Can Believe about Drugs: An Honest and Unhysterical Guide for Teens.* New York: Evans, 1988. 180 pp. Nonfiction.

Interest level: Age 12+ Reading level: Grade 6

Starting off by asking readers to imagine a world in which tobacco is banned, the Cohens offer a balanced look at drugs: From coffee and tea through steroids, heroin, narcotics, speed, cigarettes, and marijuana, they answer teens' likely questions. Can cocaine kill? Looking at the example of Len Bias, yes, occasionally, but it's rare. They thereby confront the hysteria seen in the media. One might say their outlook is: There is no such thing as a devil drug, although there are excellent reasons not to use them. This is an erudite book, offering the history of marijuana, hallucinogens, and narcotic use and the various fashions through the decades, including why and how they became illegal. Through its pages the Cohens weave allusions from literature and the arts (for example, *Long Day's Journey into Night*).

Also included is an overview of ways these substances are ingested, which, although informative, might seem to give new ideas: "Some affluent teenagers play around with heroin by injecting it under the skin or sniffing [snorting] it. Either method is less likely to lead to addiction than injecting heroin directly into a vein. Others try to avoid addiction by injecting themselves intravenously only occasionally, say before a party." One hopes teens will also read the red alert signals the Cohens add to these antics: "But playing with narcotics is like playing with fire. It's like speeding along in your car with your foot pressed down on the accelerator, surviving, and telling yourself, 'Hey I'll never crash.' People who drive wildly often end up dead and people who use heroin often end up addicted." Other topics include drug testing and, most important, ways to find highs without drugs. Alcohol is not included because it was the subject of their earlier *A Six-Pack and a Fake I.D.* (see entry above). Sources of help are appended. Bibliography, film list.

386. Colman, Warren. *Understanding and Preventing AIDS.* Chicago: Childrens, 1988. Photos and illus. 128 pp. Nonfiction.

Interest level: Age 12+ Reading level: Grade 5

An audiovisual specialist who has become an expert on AIDS tries to tell where we are in the battle against this epidemic. In giving history and origin—the African connection, the first appearance in the gay population here, and rumors—Colman concludes: "Perhaps no one will ever know for certain how AIDS got started." And it probably doesn't matter, he adds. The presentation is scientific, statistically thorough, and up-to-date. In the stories of individuals (such as Ryan White) and question-answer chapters there is invaluable information teens may not have thought of—you can't tell by looking; the virus inactive in a partner can become active in you; sharing razor blades might be unwise. It's a caring, daring treatment that bends toward the conservative but is aware of adolescent behavior. Thus in one and the same book is discouragement of sexual involvement ("Most experts believe that teens really aren't emotionally ready for a deep, committed relationship—the kind of relationship many feel should accompany sex") and instructions on how to put on and take off a condom. The color photographs are medical, sometimes grisly—closeups of Karposi's sarcoma, a sad picture of a hospital boarder baby, and a microscopic view of AIDS. A unique feature is the accounts of plagues from other eras. Here is a mature, technically informative yet feelingful account, fully cognizant that knowledge is rapidly changing. A first-class, highly recommended book on the subject. List of organizations and hotlines, bibliography.

387. Cooney, Caroline B. *Don't Blame the Music.* New York: Pacer, 1986; Berkley, pap. 172 pp. Fiction.

Interest level: Age 12+ Reading level: Grade 6

The blackmail power of a person out of control is an unusual theme. High school senior Susan's older sister, Ashley, had dropped out of sight several years earlier, and now she's back, age 25 but ragefully infantile. Failing to achieve the only thing that matters—fame—Ashley vengefully lashes out. Is punk rock to blame for her bizarre, violent history? While coping with the everyday snide hostilities of her preppy school environment, Susan must also endure the ravages of a tragic mental illness. How long will her parents deny Ashley's illness as she destroys their very safety? One might wish for deeper exploration of character motivation, but that's because each and every character—Susan, her parents, boyfriends, school rival, and of course, Ashley—are memorable and their intriguing actions are consistently on the mark.

388. Crawford, Charles P. *Split Time.* New York: Harper, 1987. 183 pp. Fiction.

Interest level: Age 12+ Reading level: Grade 7

Evan and his father retreat like wounded animals to a new apartment after Evan's mother leaves them to be with her lover. Evan is furious with her, especially after she invites him to have dinner with her, and he discovers that she has also invited her lover. He is rude and insulting to both, and he comes home in a rage, only to find his father with a young woman who works as a clerk in Woolworth's having dinner at the apartment.

Living in the same building is a pair of old women and Lamia, a lovely young woman, seven years older than Evan, who is 15 years old. Evan is enormously attracted to her, and she consoles Evan and eases his fury. Evan doesn't know it, but Lamia is seriously disturbed. Her mother committed suicide when Lamia was just emerging into adolescence, and Lamia cannot recover from this act. Evan and Lamia become sexually involved, and Evan feels uncomfortable about it, but he still takes advantage of Lamia's willingness to go to bed with him. When Evan wants to be less involved, Lamia threatens to commit suicide. When Evan leaves her a note breaking off their relationship she hangs herself. Evan gets there just in time to save her life. She is taken to an institution and Evan never sees her again.

Meanwhile, Evan's mother has been abandoned by her lover, but even after her lover goes back to his wife, Evan's mother remains separated from Evan and his father. Evan is no longer furious with his mother and father; he is learning that people have their own needs and must fulfill them.

The first-person narrative helps the reader to empathize with Evan. Although his treatment of Lamia is shabby, he is, after all, only 15 years old. His pain and anger at his parents are understandable, and the author resists falling into the trap of a "happy" ending where the parents reconcile.

389. Delton, Judy, and Tucker, Dorothy. *My Grandma's in a Nursing Home.* Illus. by Charles Robinson. Niles, Ill.: Whitman, 1986. 32 pp. Fiction.

Interest level: Ages 6–10 Reading level: Grades 2–3

Jason finds it very difficult to adjust to his grandmother's Alzheimer's disease. He misses her and he wants her to come home where they can garden together the way they used to. She is in a nursing home, and when Jason and his family go to visit, there are people who discuss their fantasies, people without teeth, and his grandmother who does not remember his name. Jason's mother keeps shushing him when he tries to correct people's misimpressions. Eventually Jason learns to be quiet when it is appropriate, talkative in response to the old people's needs, and accepting of his grandmother's condition.

Although the presentation is somewhat oversimplified, the message is a useful one: People with Alzheimer's disease, and people who are old, lonely, and need institutional care, have their own human needs and can enjoy the company of their loved ones. The illustrations are realistic and informative.

390. Erglanger, Ellen. *Eating Disorders: A Question and Answer Book about Anorexia Nervosa and Bulimia Nervosa.* Minneapolis: Lerner, 1988. 64 pp. Nonfiction.

Interest level: Ages 12–16 Reading level: Grade 5

The author, a school counselor and administrator, effectively latches onto the reader's attention by introducing her book with a list of famous women who have struggled with eating disorders. Next comes an individual story, through which basic concepts of the disorders are explored. Questions and answers come to the fore afterward, encompassing signs and symptoms, causes (emotional, physical) and cautions, and help and hope. A range of therapies is explained, from nutrition counseling and behavior modification to individual and group therapy and support groups. Besides offering information on helping oneself, there is advice on how to aggressively encourage someone else to get help. The effectiveness of helping others is seen in some of the first-person stories in the book as well. The illustrations are black-and-white drawings of women from earlier, often Victorian, periods—an interesting choice for modern problems that had antecedents before they were given names. The information is up-to-date and thoughtful, hard to achieve in a book that is so short. Its brevity will attract many readers who might be intimidated by more detail. List of relevant organizations, bibliography, index.

391. Ferris, Jean. *Invincible Summer.* New York: Farrar, 1987. 167 pp. Fiction.

Interest level: Age 12+ Reading level: Grade 7

Robin is diagnosed as having leukemia. When she is in the hospital for tests she meets Rick, a charming young man who also has leukemia. Rick helps

Robin through the hardest time of her condition: from first discovery through chemotherapy. When Rick's condition suddenly worsens, and it is discovered that his cancer has spread so that it is irreversible, it is Robin's turn to try to help him and herself.

The story is explicit in its description of both the physiological and the psychological effects of this serious illness. The story is more than a clinical description. The reader gets involved with Robin and her family. Although Rick dies, Robin has learned to value herself and life, and the story ends on a note of hope.

392. Fine, Judylaine. *Afraid to Ask: A Book about Cancer.* New York: Lothrop, 1986, hb and pap. 177 pp. Nonfiction.

Interest level: Age 12+ Reading level: Grade 8

A highly valuable resource on a difficult subject; Fine offers solid information through a writing style that enables her to make complex concepts understandable and memorable. Originally a Canadian imprint, the book has material that is up-to-date and future-oriented, including trends in prevention, palliative care, and treatment techniques (pion radiation, monoclonal antibodies, and so on).

Information about more than 20 specific types of cancer is offered in question-answer format. For each, there is a description of the body part and its function, what the particular cancer involves, who is at high risk, symptoms, diagnosis, and treatment. Fine's admirable gift for simile helps harness the scientific puzzlements of how cancer cells function. Her useful comparison objects are diverse, ranging from Indian corn and photocopy machines to "multicoloured marble cake before it has been baked," the last image describing cancer cells under a microscope.

Though potentially frightening and depressing, the material is not, because the author joins the reader as a student herself, always learning. As such, although the author's voice is heard throughout, she never intrudes. Instead, she asks the same logical questions her readers would ask, tries to solve the same problems, and airs the same confusions. Whether relating the anger of bereaved teens or explaining the scientific basis for body pain, she is the teenager's ally.

Some will read this excellent reference volume in its entirety; others will check out only the sections that concern them because of their own illness or those of relatives. A book that makes things so clear and treats readers so respectfully should certainly be on hand. Bibliography.

393. Fleischman, Paul. *Path of the Pale Horse.* New York: Harper, 1983. 144 pp. Fiction.

Interest level: Age 11+ Reading level: Grade 6

It is the year 1793, and a plague of yellow fever has erupted in Philadelphia. Dr. Peale and Lep, his 14-year-old apprentice, go there to gather supplies and to rescue Lep's sister, Clara, who is in the city to help the family's benefactor, Mr. Botkin. The inhabitants of Philadelphia and its environs are in a panic because of the plague. Lep becomes separated from Dr. Peale and finds that Mr. Botkin has moved from his house, taking Clara with him. It turns out that Mr. Botkin is an impostor who sells magical rings guaranteed to cure the plague. Lep is contemptuous of people who are quacks and who hold out false promises. But his medical treatment turns out to be no more curative than the quacks' remedies. Lep and Clara return home with Dr. Peale sadder and wiser than when they went to Philadelphia. The brother and sister will strive to remain honest and kind, but their illusions are gone.

As the author points out in his note at the end of the book, people did not know the cause of yellow fever until 1902, when Walter Reed discovered that it was not contagious and that it was caused by mosquitoes. Until that time the disease was a scourge. It killed 4,000 people in Philadelphia during the time this story takes place. The same helplessness and panic that accompany any unexplained killing illness were present at that time and are ably described in this story. Ultimately the story depicts the coming of age of Lep, the idealistic and courageous young protagonist who must come to terms with the lack of knowledge that his chosen profession of medicine must cope with.

394. Fox, Paula. *The Moonlight Man.* New York: Bradbury, 1986; Dell, pap. 179 pp. Fiction.
Interest level: Age 12+ Reading level: Grade 6

Catherine calls her father the moonlight man, in contrast to her mother, whom she considers the daylight woman. Each of her parents has remarried, and Catherine spends most of the year at a Canadian boarding school. Her father is a charming man, a writer. He is also an alcoholic, and irresponsible. He lies and cheats and cannot be counted on to keep his word, even to his daughter. The month that she spends with him is like a ride on a roller coaster. She loves his company; she hates his vices. Fox's writing is as vivid and empathic in this book as in her other fine books. The dialogue, the characterization, and the situations compel the reader's attention. This is no clinical case study of an alcoholic, but it is as authentic as any text, and it has the advantage of being clothed in the truth of story. A worthwhile book.

395. Frandsen, Karen G. *I'd Rather Get a Spanking Than Go to the Doctor.* Illus. by the author. Chicago: Childrens, 1987. 32 pp. Fiction.
Interest level: Ages 3–8 Reading level: Grade 1

With a snappy title like this, the choice of cartoons to illustrate one little girl's feelings is not surprising and right on target. She's too busy to get her shots, and besides, she doesn't need them. (As she says this, her back is to her mother and the reading audience—she wants nothing to do with this business, but all the while she's adding humor and helping kids who see her laugh at themselves.) Other tactics include feigning illness, getting busy with chores, crying, wanting ice cream to feel better, even asking for the titled spanking instead. Finally, they get in the car to go, and she is still crying. The doctor says "Hi" and that she's getting big. Too big for shots, perhaps, she muses. Then the doctor (unseen on the pages, by the way) distracts her by asking her to count the balloons on the wall. It's over in a flash and then, probably, they are off for the ice cream that the little girl had asked for instead of the shot way back before the car trip. Different and effective.

396. Frank, Julia. *Alzheimer's Disease: The Silent Epidemic.* Illus. with photos and diagrams. Minneapolis: Lerner, 1985. 80 pp. Nonfiction.
Interest level: Age 11+ Reading level: Grade 6

Julia Frank, a professor of psychiatry, makes her children's book debut with this volume. According to *School Library Journal,* her debut was also the debut of the first book for children about Alzheimer's disease.

Sarah, a hypothetical older woman who is victimized by Alzheimer's disease, is the focus of the book. Medical procedures, progression of the disease, and the state of current knowledge are explained through her case. We become interested in all this, starting with Sarah's growing confusion, and moving into more advanced stages of the disease. Frank makes the material memorable by tagging it to Sarah's hypothetical experiences. For example, she relates that at the beginning Sarah could find her way to the store because it was familiar, but she had trouble navigating the zoo with her grandchildren. Brain physiology, heredity, diagnosis, and controversies of causality become easier for readers to navigate because intermittent anecdotes about Sarah make the path easier.

The book will be particularly valuable for youngsters trying to understand their relatives who have changed, for ample attention is given to fluctuations in temperament, loss of bodily functions, and such psychological problems as paranoia. From the book they will also glean understanding of the kinds of help Alzheimer's victims and their families need and the kinds of community resources that are developing to provide that help. The book closes with a moving poem-essay by Dr. Marguerite Rush Lerner, a victim in the early stages of Alzheimer's. (Dr. Lerner may be known to some as an author in the Lerner Publications backlist.) Dr. Lerner feels she has lost everything—her career as a physician, her ability to write, aspects of her family. "I've lost a kingdom," she says. Glossary.

397. Gaes, Jason. *My Book for Kids with Cansur: A Child's Autobiography of Hope.* Illus. by Tim Gaes and Adam Gaes. Aberdeen, S.D.: Melius and Peterson, 1987. 32 pp. Nonfiction.

Interest level: Age 6+ Reading level: Grade 3

At age six, Jason comes down with Burkitt's lymphoma. As time goes on he copes by recording his thoughts for other similarly afflicted children. His aim is to say kids don't always die. He relates how his cancer was discovered, describes operations, radiation, and chemotherapy. He gives advice on what to do in the hospital. He sounds candid and like a real little boy, albeit one blessed with fine, understanding parents. Jason tells one good effect of baldness—no shampoo in the eyes. Yet he doesn't play down the bad parts of cancer, such as endless blood tests. He's wise—kids who laugh at baldness are not very good friends anyway. Along the way he folds in ideas for parents, such as get your mom to rock you when you're afraid. He even leaves his phone number for readers to call. The childish illustrations by his twin and older brothers and squiggly beginning writing are effective. Allowing Jason's early school spelling is overly cute; words like "toomer" (tumor) are distracting. Children deserve editors, too. Three years later Jason is considered cured, but his dedication to another child touches home regarding the purgatory that living with cancer implies: "We're both waiting to see if our cancer comes back." Readers will root for him to indeed attain his aspiration to be a cancer doctor. On the whole, this book is well done and deserves wide attention by families who need it.

398. Graber, Richard. *Doc.* New York: Harper, 1986. 150 pp. Fiction.

Interest level: Age 12+ Reading level: Grade 7

Brad adores his grandfather. He finds it impossible to acknowledge that his beloved grandfather, who is suffering from Alzheimer's disease, is any less competent than he always was. When his Aunt Susan tells him of how terrible a husband and father his grandfather was, Brad does not want to hear it. He makes all kinds of excuses for his grandfather.

When there is a terrible car crash, and Brad and his grandfather are at the scene of the accident, Brad is gratified to see that his grandfather martials all of his energies and is able to handle much of the first aid that is necessary. But the effort is too much for the old man, and he dies. The family is more relieved than grieved that his death comes when and as it does.

The story is interesting in its raising the issue of how we idealize the people we love and find it difficult to believe that they are fallible. It is also painful to see our loved ones deteriorating and sometimes we like to pretend it is not happening. The book is honest and revealing and invites thought.

399. Gravelle, Karen, and John, Bertram A. *Teenagers Face-to-Face with Cancer.* New York: Messner, 1987. 128 pp. Nonfiction.

Interest level: Ages 11–16 Reading level: Grade 6

The authors, a science editor and hospital psychologist, tell the stories of a group of teenagers who have had cancer. The point of view is one of adolescence normally being a time of tumultuous change resulting (one hopes) in some control over the changes, a reasonable self-image, and plans for the future. Cancer throws a monkey wrench into all of this, for the teenage patient and for his or her family and friends.

Chapters cover the initial shock, varied treatments, surgery including amputation, and types of cancer. Feelings are attended to throughout and the chapter on dealing with doctors should be read by the doctors themselves as well. Possibilities of recurrence are looked at statistically and from an emotional point of view. The chapters on relationships are especially rich with nuance (for example, taking on the hero image and then having it backfire with friends by seeming to be on another plane). Specific relationships are looked at individually—with parents, friends, siblings, school officials, and so forth. With an air of hope, the book offers a hefty section on planning for the future: career, marriage, and family.

All are looked at realistically, for example, the medical aspects of having children while on chemotherapy or afterward. Finally, coming to terms with possible death is explored, again realistically, and the words of the teens are picked up most eloquently here, echoing many frames of mind, from denial to fighting spirits to philosophies. Glossary, bibliography, index.

400. Guthrie, Donna. *Grandpa Doesn't Know It's Me: A Family Adjusts to Alzheimer's Disease.* Illus. by Katy Keck Arnsteen. New York: Human Sciences, 1986. 32 pp. Nonfiction.

Interest level: Ages 4–8 Reading level: Grade 2

This book was produced in cooperation with the Alzheimer's Disease and Related Disorders Association. The note to parents that precedes the text states that the book is designed to answer young children's questions: "What is wrong? Is this an illness that happens to lots of grownups? Did I do anything to cause it? Will *you* get it? Will I get it? Why did it happen to us? What do I tell my friends?"

In the text, young Elizabeth remembers happy times with her grandfather. But when Elizabeth was in first grade, Grandpa started forgetting things and liked to sit and watch instead of do. The narrative describes specific kinds of losses—remembering the long ago as if it was yesterday, the mounting forgetfulness that eventually becomes dangerous (for example, leaving a pot boiling), leaving independent living to live with relatives, and hostility in the face of growing deficits. The book ends with the grandfather still alive, living with his children. He doesn't know Elizabeth, but with the guidance of her parents, she remembers and still loves him.

All the questions above are answered gracefully, and additional information is nicely interspersed, such as existence of day-care respite centers. Illustrations in peach, black, and white gently complement this sad but necessary story.

401. Halvorson, Marilyn. *Cowboys Don't Cry.* New York: Delacorte, 1985; Dell, pap. 160 pp. Fiction.

Interest level: Age 11+ Reading level: Grade 6

Shane's mother was killed in an automobile accident when he was 10 years old. The terrible thing about the accident is that Shane's father was driving and he had had too much to drink. After his wife's death, Shane's father does not stop drinking. As a matter of fact, his problem worsens. When Shane is 14, his maternal grandfather dies and leaves him a ranch. Shane hopes against hope that they will now be able to settle down and be a family again.

Although Shane's father embarrasses him on his first day of school, and Shane gets into a fight with a bully, the other students are welcoming and pleasant, and he is encouraged about the prospects of making a success of it. He does make a success of school, but his father cannot hold to his intent to remain sober. It takes an almost fatal accident to make his father realize that he seriously needs to take hold of himself.

At the end of the story it looks as if Shane and his father will try harder to express their feelings to each other. The main point is that they love each other, and they are able to say so.

Marilyn Halvorson vividly demonstrates how painful it is to feel responsible for the death of a loved one. She also details well the healing process and the importance of loving friends in that process.

402. Harris, Jonathan. *Drugged Athletes: The Crisis in American Sports.* New York: Four Winds, 1987. 104 pp. Nonfiction.

Interest level: Ages 11–16 Reading level: Grade 5

A highly intelligent book, this examination of a current problem broadly brings together the concerns of the professional athlete with the aspiring high school team member. Drugs seem to be everywhere—drugs to relax muscles, drugs to improve performance, drugs to mask pain, and drugs for sheer pleasure. Using statistical evidence of abuse of cocaine, steroids, and other drugs, social science writer Harris relates these to the stories of people who died from drugs (for example, Mercury Morris), athletes who came back (for example, Tony Elliott), and those who came close to abuse but escaped (for example, Kareem Abdul-Jabbar). The stresses of sports contribute to the problem—starting young, being pampered, getting injured, being pawns in the larger money-making goals of college and professional sports, and so forth.

Harris points to national shames—racism that exploits black athletes but fails to prepare them academically, coaches who stress winning over everything, shaving points, and so on. Chapters deal effectively with drug tests (and the controversies surrounding them) and treatment programs. How interesting it is to see the intense effort that goes into treating a valuable commodity on the playing field—daily therapy sessions, group sessions several times a week, and so on. Harris hopes the future will come from policymakers aiming at prevention. Glossary, bibliography, index.

403. Hautzig, Deborah. *A Visit to the Sesame Street Hospital.* Illus. by Joe Mathieu. New York: Random/Children's Television Workshop, 1985, hb and pap. 32 pp. Fiction.

Interest level: Ages 2–7 Reading level: Grade 3

An introductory note in this "pictureback" volume talks about parents and children sharing calmly together. The story content concerns Grover, a Jim Henson muppet, who has had one sore throat too many this year. His doctor (not a muppet, but a human) recommends a tonsillectomy and arranges for a tour of the hospital for the Sesame Street gang. A nurse explains about the funny smell of disinfectant and allows them to visit the pediatric ward and get close to the children, which might not take place in an actual prehospital tour. There Grover tries out the call button and looks at a menu. The group visits the playroom, where a child explains about the hospital bracelets. The group also sees X-ray machinery and the operating room and tries on special surgical clothing. The visit closes with a visit to the gift shop, where it's hinted someone might bring Grover a present. The doctors shown are male, female, black, and white. There's also an emphasis on reasons for things, such as the reason for sterile clothing. Each hospital visitor on this tour thinks a different thing is best about the hospital, but Grover knows "the best thing about the hospital is getting well!"

404. Hawley, Richard A. *Think about Drugs and Society: Responding to an Epidemic.* Illus. New York: Walker, 1988. 168 pp. Nonfiction.

Interest level: Ages 11–15 Reading level: Grade 6

This is an overview of the history of drug use and its present-day use and abuse. Written by a writer who is an expert on drug matters, the book opens by classifying various substances and telling the history of each from ancient times until the present. As befits the book, a great deal of attention is paid to the growing drug subculture that mushroomed in the 1960s and

1970s as part of antiestablishment sentiment. The most important drug controversies are also discussed: What is the best drinking age? Should there be mandatory drug testing? Is drug use a victimless crime? What would be the consequences of decriminalization? The author's tone is downhearted, perhaps appropriately: "Government policymakers, customs officials, and police officers are periodically paid to look the other way from major drug dealings." Does that mean it is a matter of policy? In spite of his grim, conservative outlook, the first entry in the appendix materials (which take up one-third of the book) is a plea and plan for youngsters to become "American Civic Animals" who try to change society. The rest of the appendix is organizations, drug laws, bibliography. Each chapter has textbooklike bold print for new concepts, a summary, and review questions.

By failing to insert stories of individual teens, Hawley has failed to give the book life. In spite of adequately giving both sides of the many controversies, this entry in Walker's new Think About current affairs series is probably too dull to be used for anything more than school reports. And how truly current might it be if AIDS, mostly spread by intravenous drug users at this point, is not in the index?

405. Hill, Eric. *Spot Visits the Hospital.* Illus. by the author. New York: Putnam, 1987. 28 pp. Fiction.

Interest level: Ages 3–6 Reading level: Grades 1–2

Spot, the popular talking dog of Hill's previous books, makes an ill-fated trip to the hospital—ill-fated for the reader, that is, for this book's attempts at humor would have been better spent on a different topic. Spot and his friends go to the hospital to visit their friend Steve, a monkey with a broken leg. The mayhem they create there doesn't serve well to introduce the hospital. Those seeking a book where children will be informed and comforted about a hospital should look elsewhere. If you want to see animals get carried away with a bed crank or hide under the X-ray machine the reader might warm to this book. One wonders if children of the younger target age group for this book can understand some of Hill's jokes.

406. Howard, Ellen. *Edith Herself.* Illus. by Ronald Himler. New York: Atheneum, 1987. 132 pp. Fiction.

Interest level: Ages 9–12 Reading level: Grade 4

After Edith's mother and then her father die, her siblings send her to live with an older married sister. Edith is devastated at being sent away, even though her siblings live in the same general geographic area. She has a very difficult time adjusting, especially because John, her sister Lena's husband, is a very serious and stern person. John and his mother, who lives with them, are devoutly religious. Lena and her father-in-law are less strict in their religious observance. The story is set in the late nineteenth century and is flavored with customs of the period.

Although the adjustment is very difficult for young Edith, she finally manages to make friends with Lena's surly little boy, Vernon, and to tolerate the frequently nasty old grandmother. Edith is subject to epileptic seizures, but eventually even this disability does not deter her from going to school with Vernon, making friends, and even surmounting the negative effects of her seizures at school. Surprisingly, it is John who insists, over Lena's tearful resistance, that Edith attend school. He points out that Edith is bright and capable and that she needs to feel competent and independent.

This book is successful in a number of ways. It provides the reader with a number of complex characters who defy stereotyping. It presents a story in a historical context that is relevant to today's children. It reminds us that no person is all good or all bad, and that sometimes people can smother others in the name of love. It also gives some accurate information about epilepsy. It treats the issue of mourning with compassion and wisdom. There is much for the young reader to discuss in this interesting and fast-moving book.

407. Hughes, Monica. *Hunter in the Dark.* New York: Atheneum, 1983; Avon, pap. 131 pp. Fiction.

Interest level: Age 12+ Reading level: Grade 7

Mike's parents have protected and pampered him for all of his 16 years. They continue to try to protect him when it is discovered that he has leukemia. They keep the news from him, but Mike wants to know what is wrong. He finds out for himself what his illness is, by researching his symptoms and treatment in the library. He handles the situation well, telling his parents that he knows, and getting support and comfort from his closest friend, Doug.

Mike's treatments and his response to them are graphically described, but this is no clinical study. Mike's feelings of panic and desperation communicate to the reader. Mike doesn't want to die. He rages against his body, the illness, the treatments, and the world. He goes in and out of remission, and he determines to accomplish a goal of his, or die in the attempt. He wants to hunt and shoot a white-tailed buck.

Doug and Mike had planned this hunting expedition for a long time, but now Mike wants to go alone, as a rite of passage, as a talisman against death. His solitary hunt serves as the setting and backdrop for the story, which is told in a series of flashbacks. Mike does find a deer, and he has the opportunity to shoot it, but he decides not to. He returns home, having made his peace with death, and with the understanding that no matter what happens he will have the courage to face it.

The story is beautifully written. The strategy of the flashback works well to relieve the dual tensions of the inexorable course of the illness and the sustained suspense of the hunt. Mike is a likable, fallible character, as are his parents. Doug is unrealistically perfect, but he is a good model of the best friend everyone wishes he or she had. The story transcends cliché and invites the reader's compassion.

408. Hyde, Margaret O., and Forsyth, Elizabeth. *AIDS: What Does It Mean to You?* New York: Walker, 1986. 128 pp. Nonfiction.

Interest level: Age 12+ Reading level: Grade 6

A "catastrophic collapse of the immune system"—the authors' definition bespeaks compassion. Theirs is a difficult task—to reassure in midst of battle while governmental response remains hopelessly inadequate. The picture may be too rosy in early comment, "It seems likely that most people have nothing to fear from AIDS." News stories about inaccurate statistics and rapid spread among heterosexuals give pause, supported by even the authors' own estimate: "Each day . . . as many as two thousand people . . . who belong to the high risk groups, may be acquiring the virus." Aiming at balance between sensible precaution and concern for sufferers, information on spread, medical progress, and research studies are given human dimension through profiles of sufferers, comparisons with plagues in other times, and controversies (for example, testing by insurers and employers). Up-to-date, scientific yet journalistically accessible—a very worthwhile overview. Glossary, organization list, index.

409. Hyde, Margaret O., and Forsyth, Elizabeth. *Know about AIDS.* Illus. by Debora Weber. Walker, 1987. 80 pp. Nonfiction.

Interest level: Ages 8–12 Reading level: Grade 4

The authors of a book on the same subject for teens, *AIDS: What Does It Mean to You?* (see above entry), this prolific reporter-psychiatrist team now brings the message to a younger group. Their aim is to answer children's questions and help teachers in that task. Most of the time they succeed, as the book explains the possible origins of AIDS, virus mechanisms and how this particular virus seems to work, the primary risk groups, who might need a test, and the search for a cure. On occasion, however, they falter, as in their statement (which might be misconstrued): "People do not get better when they have AIDS." This doesn't allow for small improvements or small recoveries, only a steady decline. Also not reassuring is the story of the child afflicted with AIDS who lets herself cry only during therapy sessions. Why can't she cry at other times? She certainly has something to cry about. On the whole, though, the individual stories strengthen the work and help children to have beginning empathy (for example, foster care of an AIDS child, and a child whose bisexual father is afflicted). The book has another strength: crediting the gay community for its role in creating awareness. Interestingly, adults who read this book may come on new information, such as the notion that the disease has different character in varying geographic locations, or that pregnancy can bring about full-blown AIDS in an AIDS Related Complex infected woman.

410. Hyde, Margaret O., and Hyde, Lawrence E. *Cancer in the Young: A Sense of Hope*. Philadelphia: Westminster, 1985. 96 pp. Nonfiction.
Interest level: Age 11+ Reading level: Grade 6

This accounting of the current state of cancer treatment for young people offers balanced facts and an up-to-date picture of the outlook victims currently face. Topics include a description of cancer cells and how they multiply and spread; specific cancers are given full elaboration, including leukemia, bone cancer, brain tumors, lymphoma, neuroblastoma, retinoblastoma, and others. A large section of the book is devoted to diagnosis and treatment plans, and the possibilities, for each (spinal tap, for instance), and the reader is given a helpful description of how such a procedure might be conducted. As many seeking this book will already be diagnosed or have relatives/friends in that situation, this comprehensive quality is very helpful. Throughout, the words and feelings of young cancer patients give the book a humanity and help the reader make a connection. The increasing attention given to support of cancer patients and their families is also elucidated, in discussion of special hospitals, support groups, camps, and so on. An extensive glossary and lists of cancer centers, organizations, camps, and hotlines are appended. A fine reference tool.

411. Kesden, Bradley. Produced by Oralee Wachter. *Sex, Drugs and AIDS*. Photos. New York: Bantam, 1987, pap. 76 pp. Nonfiction.
Interest level: Age 14+ Reading level: Grade 6

This is a book based on a film produced by the New York City Board of Education. It was scarcely shown to its students because, in the opinion of some of its critics, it did not stress abstinence enough. As a film adaptation, it has a magazine format and approaches AIDS from several viewpoints. There are first-person stories and worries, friendly advice from Rae Dawn Chong who starred in the film, and common questions and responses. Throughout, the message "AIDS is hard to get" is repeated. That does not mean precaution is not necessary, and the book discusses drug abuse and straight and gay sex. Homophobia is also discussed, and the short magazine format makes the material easily digestible, somehow retaining the active voice that film allows, for example, "Remember, just one fix with an infected needle can give you the AIDS virus." Some of the profits from this sensible book have been set aside for AIDS research.

412. Klein, Norma. *Going Backwards.* New York: Scholastic, 1986, hb and pap. 182 pp. Fiction.

Interest level: Age 12+ Reading level: Grade 6

Charles's grandmother has Alzheimer's disease. She lives with Charles and his family in their big, expensive apartment, but she wanders around aimlessly, frightens her younger grandson, and seems frantically unhappy most of the time. When the decision is made to place her in a nursing home, Charles's father, a pathologist, administers an overdose of sleeping pills, and she dies in her sleep. After that his father's health deteriorates and he dies soon after.

The grandmother's behavior is graphically described, as is the father's anguish. He loves his mother and is grateful to her for raising him. (It seems that he and his mother disdained his father, and that the two of them, mother and son, were very close.) He hates seeing her in her confused and undignified state, and he hates even more the idea of how she will suffer in a nursing home.

The boy, Charles, narrates the story. He seems singularly insensitive and self-centered. He reports what people say and do but he does not understand their motivation or feelings. He is the vehicle through whom the story is told, and the other characters all like him, but he does nothing to help anyone.

Unfortunately, Klein has her main character make generalized negative comments about Jewish people. ("He can't understand the average Jewish family where everyone is at each other's throats about the utmost trivia.") Charles's grandfather is disdained and criticized because he observes certain Jewish rituals. The grandmother makes nasty remarks about the housekeeper's race. All of these distract from rather than flavor the book.

Alzheimer's disease is alluded to as the normal condition to be expected when a person grows old. This sort of inaccuracy also detracts from the effectiveness of the book. The grandmother is painted as a tragic figure, and the reader cannot help but sympathize with her. She is a victim of a dread illness, and her humanity has been damaged. The author writes poignantly of her plight, as well as that of her son, who is caught between loyalties to his current family and gratitude and love for his mother. Despite its flaws the story certainly sustains our interest.

413. Kolodny, Nancy J. *When Food's a Foe: How to Confront and Conquer Eating Disorders.* Boston: Little, 1987. 224 pp. Nonfiction.

Interest level: Ages 12–16 Reading level: Grade 6

Kolodny, a social worker, takes on the eating disorders of bulimia and anorexia nervosa (obesity is not a subject here). Written for boys as well as girls, Kolodny compares having an eating disorder to entering a maze alone. A special feature is the many self-quizzes and charts to fill out. Through these, readers examine their self-esteem and self-image and can begin to ascertain if habits are turning into obsessions. In other words, warning signs. She recommends defusing the disorder—usually with professional help—one step at a time, by isolating negative triggers. Kolodny compares a therapist who deals with eating disorders to a coach working with an athlete, probably a very apt analogy.

Lively and strong on practical advice (don't get a job in a food-related business if you may be susceptible), the book does not delve quite as deeply into causes. She speaks of power issues as important but does not stress perfectionism, which for many people with eating disorders plays a major role. She also talks about the social costs of being anorexic or bulimic, for example, becoming an outcast or self-imposed exile. This consequence is well worth pondering, especially for those who aren't yet fully caught up in the syndromes. Unique features include advice for helping those who are anorexic/bulimic, word-for-word suggestions on how to tell your family you need help, charts of caloric/fat content of fast foods, and insightful cartoons from the comic strip "Cathy." It will be helpful to those who in the author's words are finding the "dining table a battleground."

414. Kosof, Anna. *Why Me? Coping with Family Illness.* New York: Watts, 1986. 96 pp. Nonfiction.

Interest level: Age 11+ Reading level: Grades 5–6

A serious illness is a family affair says the author, a writer with an anthropology background. Through firsthand stories of adults and children, Kosof explores the world of cancer and heart patients, accident victims, and those born with birth defects such as spina bifida. The emphasis is on coping mechanisms, which are spelled out—overcompensation, intellectualization, anger, and so forth. In each case, we are brought into the family of the ill adult or child, with opinions expressed by all involved. The changes in daily routines are discussed (extra chores, perhaps) and the more emotional, internal changes are as well. The lesson chronically ill people have learned—how to be encouraged and live one day at a time—comes up time and again in the book, in varied forms as the cases differ. Each person in the book has changed as a result of the illness, and the doctors have changed as well. Highly readable and not at all depressing, this book wisely recommends honesty, keeping everyone informed, and considering emotional as well as physical needs. Index.

415. Kuklin, Susan. *When I See My Doctor.* Photos by the author. New York: Bradbury, 1988. 32 pp. Nonfiction.

Interest level: Ages 4–7 Reading level: Grade 2

Full, happy color accentuates the first-person account of a four-year-old named Thomas, a child of Asian background who, with longish hair, doesn't clearly look like a boy. He also has a Caucasian mother. One wonders why this very accomplished author-photographer added extraneous issues such as adoption to the content of the book. On one hand, by having interracial families merely an incidental, it does reinforce the idea that families come in all flavors, see, no big deal. On the other hand, it might take interest away from the action. Let the reader decide!

And on to the real action: Thomas does the talking about procedures involved in his checkup, but somehow he sounds like his mother, using sentences such as: "A fresh sheet is put down for the next patient." Few preschoolers would speak in this manner. Nevertheless, the book is extremely pleasing visually, and new instruments (lancet and hemoglobinometer) are given pictorial insets with pronunciation guides alongside. Dr. Mitchell is a most considerate doctor, warming the stethoscope up and taking other steps to make Thomas comfortable. Most important, Kuklin has Thomas explain the purpose of doctors' strange behavior—why they feel for bumps, and so on. If one gets beyond a little boy talking alternately in four-year-old sentences and mouthing the words of an older speaker, this is a book of great value.

416. Kurland, Morton L. *Coping with AIDS: Facts and Fears*. New York: Rosen, 1988, hb and pap. 220 pp. Nonfiction.
Interest level: Ages 12–16 Reading level: Grade 6

Historical battles against viruses are the beginning background the physician-author brings to readers' knowledge of how viruses have killed over the ages and how AIDS seems to work. Specific anonymous cases demonstrate how the virus is spreading. The emphasis, however, is not on the past, but on what can be done now—by individuals and by society as a whole. Condom use is encouraged strongly, with full knowledge that some youngsters will be sexually active. Unique in books about AIDS, this one gives numerous ideas for starting that very delicate conversation about birth control. There is material here for those infected, as well, or those who know people with AIDS-related illnesses. Kurland's medical experience is put to good use, as he relates advice he has given patients and talks of support groups. He is quite specific, recommending within the narrative books read in those support groups, for example. If one doesn't want to read the entire book, there is a lengthy chapter with common questions and answers. Glossary, bibliography, full list of crisis centers by geographic location, index.

417. Landau, Elaine. *Why Are They Starving Themselves? Understanding Anorexia Nervosa and Bulimia.* New York: Messner, 1983, hb and pap. 128 pp. Nonfiction.

Interest level: Ages 11–16 Reading level: Grade 5

"Mirror, mirror, on the wall, who's the thinnest one of all?" Each anorectic hopes it is she, according to Landau. The book is strong on describing the obsessions that bring this about and keep it going. The perfectionistic strains of people with these problems are given special attention, showing why they are so hard to treat, going through a hospital revolving door in their persistent attempts to starve and vomit. Individual stories complement general outlines and patterns, creating a narrative that remains interesting and brings the reader to understanding. The theories regarding reasons are well explained: "Some therapists believe that the anorectic's unconscious desire not to grow up but to remain a little girl is a factor in her illness."

The concluding chapters describe help that is available and approach it broadly, including self-esteem development, assertiveness training, self-help relaxation techniques, and organizational outreach. One treatment program described is designed by Ellen Schor, a recovered food disorder patient who now treats patients at a clinic in New York. Bibliography, index.

418. Lee, Essie E. *Breaking the Connection: Getting Off Drugs.* Photos. New York: Messner, 1988, hb and pap. 172 pp. Nonfiction.

Interest level: Ages 12–16 Reading level: Grade 6

This book examines how young people from all social classes—lower, middle, upper—have easily become involved with drugs and what some of them have done to get out of their predicaments. Lee, a professor of health education, relates stories of dependency on various drugs but emphasizes cocaine and crack because of their prevalence in today's society and their immense danger. It is surprising how simply crack is made, by combining cocaine with household baking soda. It is almost like a fast food—compact, popular, and profitable. Lee provides superb analysis of societal pressures that cause people to try the drugs and subsequently need treatment. Among them are the appetite suppressant qualities cocaine is reported to have, the high salaries some rather young adults command without concomitant maturity, and so on. She visits Phoenix House and other treatment centers and tells in depth about their procedures for accepting or declining to treat a particular patient. The detail-filled, fascinating stories of numerous young people who have overcome their drug problems are realistic and gritty and can serve as inspiration, for these people have used the many self-help programs and approaches she lists. Lee's list of agencies offering help is broader than that found in most books and will be very useful. Resource list, drug charts, index. Highly recommended.

419. Lee, Essie E., and Wortman, Richard. *Down Is Not Out: Teenagers and Depression.* New York: Messner, 1986. 112 pp. Nonfiction.
Interest level: Ages 11–16 Reading level: Grade 5

Lee, a professor of community health, and Wortman, a doctor, talk about adolescence as a constant state of becoming. Teenagers can become someone they like, someone they don't, or, often, both. The stresses as they become more aware are the focus of this book. First, depression is defined and contrasted with normal moodiness. Depression and its symptoms are categorized—reactive, chronic, major, manic. In each case, the lives of teens are used as examples, and the impact of the depression on broader areas of functioning is examined.

An exploration of events and characteristics that lead to depression, including losses, low self-esteem, and genetic disposition is up-to-date and research-oriented. The section on factors that affect teens regarding sexual development is especially helpful as related to early and late developers. The alienation in today's crowded teen society is also evaluated in terms of suicide risk. A shortcoming is the brevity of the book, which doesn't allow as full a presentation as one might have wished. A clear list of symptoms of depression is followed by an all-too-brief description of treatment, including discussions of individual and family psychotherapy, psychopharmacological treatment, and ECT (electroshock therapy). Bibliography.

420. Lee, Sally. *Donor Banks: Saving Lives with Organ and Tissue Transplants.* Photos. New York: Watts, 1986. 96 pp. Nonfiction.
Interest level: Ages 10–14 Reading level: Grades 5–6

Broader than blood donor banks in scope, this up-to-date book covers bone, corneas, skin, hearts, and other organs as well. In order to place the computerized networks that track, record, and bring substitute materials to needy patients in perspective, Lee first explains a bit about cell theory to show why substitutes can work when needed. With this in mind, the modern day magic becomes more understandable, for example, why cadaver bone can be inserted, then disappear after serving as a framework for new bone to grow into. For each type of donation, the process is detailed—with blood, from donor's decision through tests, identification, receiving, and transmission to a recipient. Specifics related to donation-type are discussed, such as questions about AIDS as related to blood donation. This is an entry in the First Book series; technical words are printed in boldface.

Lee works in the astounding opportunities in today's medical field most dramatically: On a small level, readers learn the temporal bone can help people with hearing or balance problems; looking at the larger picture, a harvest of organs can take place—one person's organs have benefited four people. The delicate care taken in preserving organs is discussed, as are controversies (sale of organs, animal experimentation, and levels of consent, for example). Photographs are dull in color but interesting in content (for example, rows of bones in differing sizes).

Lee ends with a plea for awareness in the face of the current donor bankruptcy (which resulted in Baby Faye receiving the heart of a baboon). Lee's dramatic details make the book work, so young readers will remember to plan for donation when they grow older and will talk to their parents, too. When Mary, going blind before her transplant, must bring her children to neighbors for care, they will grasp her need and the miracle that donor banks perform. List of organizations, glossary, index.

421. Lerner, Ethan A. *Understanding AIDS.* Illus. Minneapolis: Lerner, 1987. 64 pp. Nonfiction.

Interest level: Ages 8–12 Reading level: Grade 5

The author, a doctor with a Ph.D. specializing in immunology, makes a head-on attack onto AIDS and all the tension and fear it has brought to the world. Starting with a tittering classroom discussion about swollen lymph glands and strep throat, soon the sick child's classmates are asking if he has AIDS. And what is AIDS? "It's something that queers get," yells a classmate. And so we get the idea this is going to be a book that doesn't skirt around issues as they may be felt by countless people—denial by putting AIDS into just one category of people not at all like us. Soon enough, though, Lerner teaches readers not to be so confident that they are not at risk. By framing similar stories and supplementing them with question-and-answer paragraphs, the author provides full discussions of homosexuality and its connection to AIDS, transmission by blood transfusion, becoming infected through sharing drug needles, how children become infected, and so on. The chapters address most of today's newspaper issues as well, such as a description of condom use and questions about children with AIDS being allowed to attend school. (The answer here is that they can as long as they are mature enough.)

In one riveting chapter a young man named Stefan tells of his own life cut short. Not yet finished with college, he has AIDS, even though as a gay person he tried to be careful. Stefan tells of his earlier wish to believe it couldn't happen to him, of his shock, and of his current treatment. Through the device of Stefan (whether he is a real person or not we do not know, but the author has actually worked with AIDS victims), we learn of other people's reactions—most people stayed on the swim team when Stefan told them of his illness, but a couple thought the pool was permanently infected. He tells also of his growing weakness and eventual need to stop swimming, even of his AIDS dementia. Throughout, new concept words are highlighted. For the age group, this is a sensible discussion that is unafraid. As the months and years go on, however, it may become dated in its highlighting of special groups and de-emphasis on the general population.

422. LeShan, Eda. *When a Parent Is Very Sick.* Boston: Atlantic, 1986. 112 pp. Nonfiction.

Interest level: Age 8+ Reading level: Grade 4

With a warmhearted arrow right to children's hearts, LeShan gives them license to feel and encouragement to talk when faced with the confusion of parental illness. Knowing that angry, worried questions of "Who will take care of me?" predominate, LeShan clears the air about common happenings in families inexorably altered by accidents, cancer, heart disease, multiple sclerosis, and other sudden, chronic, or degenerative illnesses. Events include being scapegoated, having less money, school failure, and feeling shunted aside. Unafraid to look at both sides of the issue—recovery *and* death—LeShan also relates likely consequences for children who are only children or from single-parent homes. Her belief that feelings have impact on the immune system (perhaps influenced by the work of her psychologist husband, Lawrence LeShan, who works with cancer patients) is interesting, albeit controversial. Parents should model the conversational style of most of the adults in the book—they are ingenious, understanding, and helpful people.

423. Le Tord, Bijou. *My Grandma Leonie.* Illus. by the author. New York: Bradbury, 1987. 32 pp. Fiction.

Interest level: Ages 4–8 Reading level: Grade 1

In watercolors so delicate they are almost hard to grasp, Le Tord presents a story somehow reminiscent of M. B. Goffstein's work. "I remember when my Grandma Leonie came to live with us. She brought a small brown radio." And together the two laughed and listened to comedy shows and cried when Lassie didn't come home. The love between the two was expressed in little things, such as the child observing the grandmother's own observation of seasonal changes. Then one day Grandma Leonie got sick and left for the hospital. "When she didn't come back at all, I stared silently at the sky." Then the child, gender and name not given, tried to fill the emptiness by listening to the radio without Grandma Leonie and thinking how much Grandma Leonie showed her love.

This is an appealing but confusing book, with a grandmother who doesn't "come back at all." Did the author intend to make an all-purpose book, good for children whose loved ones are in the hospital or long-term nursing care, as well as those whose loved ones have died? Or is it only about death, and the author is afraid to use the word? The jacket says it's a "reassuring story about the loss of a loving grandparent," but a hospitalization is loss, too. Potential readers will have to decide if there really is a euphemism here, and if so, if they feel euphemisms are indeed reassuring.

424. Le Vert, Suzanne. *AIDS: In Search of a Killer.* New York: Messner, 1987. 140 pp. Nonfiction.

Interest level: Age 12+ Reading level: Grades 6–7

Le Vert offers a combination of reporting on epidemiological research and compassionate visits with affected individuals. Opening with questions and answers about AIDS, she covers the basics as known in 1987—who gets AIDS, how, and the biological basis of its spread. She follows with a scientific analysis of immunology, a history of the disease, and case studies. The book is especially strong on the heroic efforts of the gay community to fight for their survival, and on discussions of civil rights regarding insurance, housing, jobs, and testing. The author occasionally fails to meet issues head-on, as when she says, "Homosexual men contract AIDS more often (in this country) than heterosexuals because they frequently perform a certain sexual act common, but not exclusive, to the homosexual lifestyle."

In the late 1980s, parents are forced to discuss sex in much more graphic detail with their adolescents than they'd ever imagined they would, trying to give both warning and understanding. Those parents unable to muster the nerve to discuss sexual issues may rely on books to give the full story and say real phrases like "anal intercourse." It's a shame the author and/or publisher skirted the issue here.

Le Vert refers to AIDS as a clever disease. She makes an analogy between the search for its cure and a mystery, what with its killers, victims, false leads, modus operandi, and doctor detectives. Her analogies give the book its interest, heartbeat, and challenge. Index.

425. Levine, Saul, and Wilcox, Kathleen. *Dear Doctor.* New York: Lothrop, 1987, hb and pap. 256 pp. Nonfiction.

Interest level: Age 12+ Reading level: Grade 7

A compendium of advice by two Toronto physicians, one a psychiatrist with a newspaper column for youth, the other a specialist in adolescent medicine. Taking turns and giving lengthy responses, Levine and Wilcox air rather complex problems concerning physiology, growth and development, sex and sexuality, schooling, relationships, family life and problems, drug abuse, and psychological difficulties. Each chapter begins with an antiquated, now amusing quote from a guidebook used in the late 1800s. The doctors are strongest on the physical questions; on psychiatric issues, they are highly sympathetic, but occasionally don't look deeply enough at causes, skip steps, or don't provide enough highly specific advice, perhaps even the words to say. In one case, a boy who has humiliated his younger, handicapped brother and regrets it is told by the authors to apologize and that his brother needs help. Where is the help for the older boy in terms of understanding why he may have laughed at the handicap? In another example, a girl who has been "flogged" during much of her growing up complains she's too shy to get medical help with the scars on her legs. The answer assumes she may be able to approach her parents, which may not be so.

On balance, though, *Dear Doctor* is a solid piece of work that will be consulted often. Its encyclopedic nature allows for exploring many concerns not found in other books, from meeting potential stepparents to morning-after pills. The nitty-gritty answers found here are needed.

426. Levinson, Riki. *DinnieAbbieSister-r-r!* Illus. by Helen Cogancherry. New York: Bradbury, 1987. 96 pp. Fiction.
Interest level: Ages 6–8 Reading level: Grades 2–3

The title characters are siblings whose nicknames are always slurred together as one name in this atmospheric story of a Jewish family in Brooklyn during the 1930s. In those times boys seemed to have everything, according to the five-year-old girl, Jennie. They took the elevated train to go to yeshiva, they ran and hopped down the streets, seemingly "full of beans," while Jennie and her mother stayed behind talking.

The action takes place over a year's time, during which Abbie falls sick with an unnamed illness that keeps him from walking. The caring shown by all the family as Abbie is nursed back to health is movingly shown in vignettes, for example, Abbie is unable to put his heart into going to school without his brother. Likewise, the tone of real conversations—whose toes can reach highest on the wall, who can be funny with bananas across one's teeth—brings home even more strongly the bonds of family affection. And, in spite of the times that said, "Girls do this, boys do that," Jennie, too, becomes more than just little "Sister-r-r"—she's soon full of beans, too.

427. McFarland, Rhoda. *Coping with Substance Abuse.* New York: Rosen, 1987. 160 pp. Nonfiction.
Interest level: Age 12+ Reading level: Grade 6

McFarland, a certified alcoholism and drug abuse counselor, here looks at the effect of chemical (all drugs, including alcohol and prescription drugs) abuse on the body, the person, the family, and society. Part of the book discusses teenagers who abuse chemicals, the other part discusses living with a parent who is the abuser. The media, says McFarland, makes it seem that drug use is acceptable; hence from that attitude a myriad of social and emotional problems ensue.

McFarland is especially strong in discussing the implications for the family when a parent is addicted. Her exploration of the types of roles children may take—hero, scapegoat, mascot, lost child—is especially insightful. One unusual feature of this book, found almost nowhere else, is a chapter on coping with a sibling who is the abuser. Likewise, there is one on friends. In each case, just as McFarland did with the parents and the teen himself who is the abuser, she examines the addiction and its problems in stages—early to late stages. And, as she did with the parents, for siblings and friends, she explores co-dependent issues—how not to aid in the addiction, how to help get intervention, how to detach oneself from the need to save the person (which is impossible for another person to do anyway), and by doing so, becoming part of the solution, not part of the problem. There are also helpful quizzes to assess one's own attitude and behavior patterns toward chemicals and one's roles in others' patterns. Index.

428. Mazer, Norma Fox. *After the Rain.* New York: Morrow, 1987; Avon, pap. 290 pp. Fiction.

Interest level: Age 11+ Reading level: Grade 6

Rachel's grandfather, Izzy, is dying. He has a cancer caused by exposure to asbestos. Rachel goes to his house almost every day and walks with him. Until recently she has not really known her grandfather, but now that she spends so much time with him they get to know each other very well. Even though her grandfather is often irritable, and sometimes nasty, they develop a close connection. The author builds the relationship slowly, so that its intensity engulfs the reader.

The details of the inexorable disease are described with almost clinical precision, but they are as much a part of the story as any of the characters. As the disease progresses, Izzy gets weaker and weaker. His last days are spent in the hospital with Rachel at his side. She is with him when he dies. Her memory of him and the time they shared together enriches Rachel. She mourns, but she celebrates his life as well.

429. Miklowitz, Gloria D. *Good-Bye Tomorrow.* New York: Delacorte, 1987. 150 pp. Fiction.

Interest level: Age 12+ Reading level: Grade 7

Told through the voices of three of the characters, Alex, Shannon, and Christy, the story treats a topic of high interest in today's society: AIDS.

Alex is a clean-cut teenager who is neither gay nor a drug user. He has, however, had two blood transfusions because of an automobile accident. It turns out that Alex has AIDS Related Complex (ARC), and that he will have to be careful to avoid infections, but he does not have AIDS. His doctor tries to explain the difference to him and his family. Then Alex must explain the difference to his friends, teachers, and principal.

Miklowitz includes many details about AIDS and ARC within the context of the story. She also describes the reactions of Alex's friends and family. For a while it looks as if Alex will be ostracized, but in the end his closest friends stand by him, and the reader can hope for the best.

430. Naylor, Phyllis Reynolds. *The Dark of the Tunnel.* New York: Atheneum, 1985. 207 pp. Fiction.

Interest level: Age 12+ Reading level: Grade 7

Two themes are developed in parallel in this moving story. The major issue is that of Craig's mother, who is dying of pancreatic cancer. This is the more effective of the themes as it relentlessly details the mother's physical deterioration and its effect not only on her but also on Craig, his brother, and their uncle.

The other theme is an important one rarely found in books for young readers—the preparation for a nuclear attack. Craig's uncle is the county's civil defense chief and he is responsible for preparing a safe place to evacuate the people of the county in the event of a nuclear attack. He is very much involved in the planning of a drill that the entire county will participate in.

Other people agitate more toward influencing the government that it is futile to plan for survival of a nuclear blast, and that it is more important to work for peace. This cause is led by a man who has been devastated by war; his brother died in Vietnam, and he has been institutionalized because of his emotional response to his brother's death. He kills himself in a blast that destroys the tunnel that was to have been the shelter used in the drill.

It is clear that this is the author's message: It is better to work for peace than prepare for war. Although it has global implications, this message is less powerful here than the one of coping with the dying and eventual death of a parent.

431. Naylor, Phyllis Reynolds. *The Keeper.* New York: Atheneum, 1986. 212 pp. Fiction.

Interest level: Ages 11–15 Reading level: Grade 6

Honesty is the best policy, even when it hurts, perhaps especially when it hurts. Nick's father has changed jobs frequently; they are living in Chicago for only a couple of years when he slumps rapidly into paranoiac mental illness. At first Nick and his mother are baffled by his mysterious dropping out of work. As they realize what the problem is, they first try to ignore it, then cover for him, but tensions caused by his suspicions, sleeplessness, and suicide attempt soon overtake everyday life.

Nick's collapse in his junior high school gym class results in the vital contact that the family needs—the school and hospital staff finally get his father to consent to being hospitalized. Based on the author's experiences with her first husband, the book succeeds in moving the reader, especially when Nick realizes that he can call the school nurse in his emergency. Nick's final openness is not without consequence—he loses his first girlfriend, but without that realism the story would be inauthentic.

432. Osborne, Mary Pope. *Last One Home.* New York: Dial, 1986; Apple, pap. 180 pp. Fiction.

Interest level: Age 11+ Reading level: Grade 6

Bailey's mother left her family three years ago to be institutionalized because of her alcoholism and now lives in Florida. Bailey's brother is joining the army, and her father will soon marry Janet, a woman who has twin boys. Bailey is very upset. She doesn't want her brother to leave or her father to get married. Although Bailey is 12 years old, she begins behaving like a small child, complete with temper tantrums.

Bailey often stays at home with her brother while her father sleeps at Janet's house. Bailey is invited to sleep there too, but she doesn't want to. She feels deserted. Her emotions become so difficult to manage that she drinks a lot of wine, gets drunk, and becomes violently ill. Later she tries to run away, but her soon-to-be stepmother and her father find her and take her home. The reader is left with the assurance that Janet will take care of Bailey and that Bailey will flourish from her nurturing.

The book brings out how children of alcoholic parents can be damaged. It also uncovers the issue of the insensitive father who loves his children, but is more concerned with his own activities than with their welfare. He means well, but he seems incapable of responding in a way that his daughter wants and needs. The story is believable and consistent with what is known about families where a parent is an alcoholic.

433. Osborne, Mary Pope. *Love Always, Blue.* New York: Dial, 1983; Point, pap. 183 pp. Fiction.

Interest level: Age 12+ Reading level: Grades 6–7

Blue adores her father and is devastated that he now lives in New York, while she remains with her mother in North Carolina. Blue is an intelligent, lonely, and anxious young woman who can't let go of her fixation about her father. Even on her fifteenth birthday, when he has clearly forgotten about it, she calls him and is happy just to talk to him, and he claims to miss and love her.

Blue persuades her mother to let her visit her father in New York during school vacation. When she arrives in New York, Blue sees that her father is in bad shape, physically, economically, and emotionally. He cries a lot, is clearly very depressed, and cannot sleep or eat. Blue can't do anything to help him. She meets the son of one of her father's friends, and they immediately "click." Blue's father is jealous, becomes even more depressed, and leaves the house. Blue gets hysterical, runs out of the house without her keys, calls her mother, and is upset when her mother sends her uncle to New York to bring her home. When Blue's father returns he seems to finally see that he needs help and he promises Blue that he will seek it. She returns home wiser about her father's situation and clearer about herself and her relationship with her parents.

Blue's mother tries to help Blue understand her father and feel good about herself, but until Blue has seen for herself how ill her father is, her mother can't break through the barriers that Blue has erected. Now, perhaps, Blue won't blame her mother so much for her parents' divorce. She has been praying for her parents to get back together again, and the author has left the door open for a reconciliation, which may not be realistic. But the situation is one that young readers may find compelling, and which may invite them to think about how they would advise Blue and her parents.

434. Paulsen, Gary. *Tracker*. New York: Bradbury, 1984; Puffin, pap. 90 pp. Fiction.

Interest level: Age 10+ Reading level: Grade 5

John's grandfather is dying. The doctors have said that his cancer is so advanced that there is nothing more that they can do. John weeps and then spends lots of time denying that his grandfather will die. He has been raised by his grandparents; they are his closest friends, and he cannot bear the thought of losing his grandfather.

John and his grandfather have gone deer hunting together each season. Now John must go alone. He strikes a bargain with himself: If he can outstalk a deer, not kill her, but touch her, then his grandfather will not die. He does stalk a doe, one that has come to his grandparents' farm just before hunting season began. And he does outstalk her. He does not kill her, but touches her, and returns home to tell his grandparents of the experience. His grandfather is impressed and proud at John's feat, but John realizes that the bargain was a false one; his grandfather will die.

The spiritual conflict with and acceptance of death drives the story. It is poetically and sometimes mystically told. The inevitability of death and the mourning that precedes the actual death are palpably conveyed here.

435. Porterfield, Kay Marie. *Coping with an Alcoholic Parent.* New York: Rosen, 1985. 148 pp. Nonfiction.

Interest level: Age 12+ Reading level: Grade 6

Starting with a checklist to see if a parent might actually be alcoholic, Porterfield moves on to the multiple complications in the family because of the drinking, the alcoholic's many tricks, and the scope of children's feelings. In a section on myths, she reiterates the book's focus: "Alcoholism is a family disease."

Chapters include coverage of what alcohol does to the body, why various people may be alcoholic, family genetics, and how the problem affects various family members. A particularly interesting section concerns the often destructive unwritten rules families may live under, for example, "Don't trust yourself, don't let your feelings get hurt, and don't discuss the problem with the family or outsiders."

Also included is up-to-date information on coping styles and strategies that are common to alcoholic homes, for example, perfectionism, peacemaking, withdrawing, distracting, and rebeling. The pitfalls of these coping mechanisms are explained simply through profiles of youngsters. The book has full discussion of better ways to thrive, including specific lists of tactics to let go of the above deficient strategies. In addition, Porterfield lets readers in on overall strategies for better functioning: guided imagery, controlled relaxation, and exercise. The book culminates in hearty sections on getting help for oneself through Alateen and other organizations and ways to form a new, less responsibility-taking relationship with the alcoholic parent. There is also a good section on the new household with a recovering alcoholic and a helpful, tell-it-like-it-is chapter on the alcoholic's child as a potential future alcoholic. Appendix of organizations, bibliography. Thoughtfully done.

436. Richter, Elizabeth. *The Teenage Hospital Experience: You Can Handle It.* Photos by the author. New York: Coward, 1982. 128 pp. Nonfiction.

Interest level: Ages 11–16 Reading level: Grade 5

Nineteen teenagers tell of their experiences, hopes, fears, and disappointments. Some have been in and out of hospitals repeatedly, others are facing new problems such as cancer. Also interviewed are professionals in the hospital—a surgeon, a nurse, a psychiatrist, and a specialist in adolescent medicine. Elizabeth Richter has used the expertise of staff from numerous hospitals on the East Coast.

The professionals speak about the mechanics and what you can expect—getting admitted, how to deal with doctors and nurses, not being embarrassed to ask questions, and so forth. Richter also includes a position statement on the care of adolescents in health-care settings and provides a question checklist that teenagers may want to use, for example, "What's wrong with me? Is there a name for it? How did I get sick? What will be done about it? Will the treatment hurt? Will I look any different?" This last question is extremely important, as teens are just forming their self-image regarding looks, and hospitalization threatens that.

The patients are identified by name, hospital, and age, and their diagnosis and treatment are discussed matter-of-factly. Included are a ninth grader with gonorrhea and another teen who has been pregnant. Other maladies include broken bones, surgery, spinal damage, paralysis of a leg after a camping accident (and the adjustment that entails for the rest of one's life), and internal injuries. Each vignette feels real (for example, a girl with scoliosis relates that when her boyfriend found out about her condition, he dropped her). The teens' frustrations with their illnesses and with the system come out in first-person narratives that are sensitively recorded: "It took more than five doctors to figure out what's wrong with me." (He has blood clots.) The dramatic specifics of hospital life and being in a place you don't want to be make this a very worthwhile book to have on hand. The close-shot photographs handsomely show off a group of teenagers who were willing to tell their stories. Glossary, index.

437. Rockwell, Anne. *The Emergency Room.* Illus. by Harlow Rockwell. New York: Macmillan, 1985. 24 pp. Nonfiction.

Interest level: Ages 3–7 Reading level: Grade 1

Cheerful yellow endpapers tell us that it's not so bad at this hospital emergency room, and the Rockwells use their usual reassuring watercolor tones. The first page shows a boy coming to the emergency room with his parents, but we don't yet know what's wrong. He just tells us, "The emergency room is at the hospital. People go there when they are hurt or very sick." Then it's on to how they got there, the operating hours, and the equipment. After a few pages we get the boy's story when we see him in a wheelchair—a sprained ankle, it seems. The boy shows us more equipment, some named, some not, as in, "This machine shows how a heart is beating." On our journey we see patients and personnel of varied races and sexes. And soon the boy is off to X-ray. He lies still, even smiles. Then we see him, still smiling, with what looks like a cast or thick bandages and crutches.

Somehow, this book is not as full as it could be, because fear is never mentioned. And it's not quite believable that the boy would have all that time in midstream to learn about all the different machines, unless he were waiting forever, which, unlike real people in real emergency rooms, he is not. An incomplete introduction.

438. Rogers, Fred. *Going to the Doctor.* Photos by Jim Judkis. New York: Putnam, 1986, hb and pap. Nonfiction.

Interest level: Ages 2–6 Reading level: Grade 2

Part of the Mister Rogers' Neighborhood First Experience series, this book centers on young patients visiting two doctors—a black male and a white female. Starting with the premise that there are many ways parents help children take care of themselves, the narrative moves into the health sphere by discussing doctors. Doctors were once children themselves, Rogers tells his young audience. "They grew up and wanted to help take care of people." Covering where doctors work—offices, clinics, emergency rooms, the clear, sharp, easy-to-read photos then bring us into the waiting room (realistically crowded) and office, showing such instruments as the stethoscope.

Rogers brings to the action his usual understanding of children's notions, for example, regarding the stethoscope, the doctor can "look and listen, but can't see or hear what you're thinking or feeling." A lovely feature is Rogers's attention to the often unexplained. In doing so, he gives parents words. An example is the explanation of why we get undressed at the doctor's. "Doctors need to make sure children's bodies are healthy all over." Now, how often does that go unspoken! Rogers encourages children to ask questions of their doctors and parents and to use the real and play tools to explore their functions and have dramatic play.

439. Roth, Harold. *Babies Love a Checkup.* Photos by the author. New York: Grosset, 1986, pap. Nonfiction.

Interest level: Ages 1–4 Reading level: Grade 1

This full-color photography boardbook starts with a mother and father bringing their baby to the doctor's office. "It's time for baby's checkup." Baby is an unnamed girl, who meets with a friendly doctor carrying a stuffed doll. Baby sits on the scale, smiles as the doctor listens with his stethoscope, and allows her to check her throat with a tongue depressor. Baby looks apprehensive but doesn't cry when she gets "a shot to stay healthy," and soon the checkup is over and both doctor and patient blow a kiss.

The doctor is pleasant enough and so is the child, but perhaps the exaggeration in the title (part of a Babies Love series) and the noncrying shot will disturb some parents. Babies usually tolerate their visits to the doctor—it's not usual to love it, and most books on this subject today allow the patient to have more pain than a merely pensive expression.

440. Ryerson, Eric. *When Your Parent Drinks Too Much: A Book for Teenagers.* New York: Facts on File, 1985; Warner, pap. 144 pp. Nonfiction.

Interest level: Age 12+ Reading level: Grade 6

Eric Ryerson is the pseudonym of an author who has written many other books for teenagers. Here, he writes a personal story as the son of an alcoholic. His mother's alcoholism (from which she is now recovering) casts a black shadow over his house, he feels. Ryerson has taken an investigative approach, however, not limiting himself to his own family experience. Topics include why alcoholism is a disease, the limits of responsibility that a teen can take for that disease (in other words, you can't cure your parent's drinking problem), how family members may unintentionally aid the alcoholic in getting liquor, and how to stop that behavior. Also covered are how to find ways to detach yourself from someone else's problem; how to get over your own feelings of isolation, shame, and guilt; and how to deal with a crisis. In addition, Ryerson discusses several approaches to getting help for the alcoholic and the family.

There is much information here—why alcoholics drink, how to tell if someone is truly an alcoholic, how family members hole up and change their lives around the disease, understanding the sober parent's point of view, the role of intervention, the parent who becomes sober, and so on. But there is also a deep feeling side, understanding the many roles children of alcoholics can take: "If you are the super-responsible one, you may be angry at how the others aren't helping or aren't trying nearly as hard as you are to keep things from falling apart completely." Then Ryerson informs about why others may be behaving differently. Throughout, there's a balance of the author's own story and what he knows of other families, for example, before he learned detachment how he screamed, cried, and pleaded with his mother to stop. He tells of himself and then becomes more general. It's a technique that works well and will help many readers. List of resources, index.

441. Schein, Jonah. *Forget Me Not.* Illus. by the author. Toronto: Annick, 1988, hb and pap. 24 pp. Fiction.

Interest level: Ages 4–9 Reading level: Grade 2

Schein, who is 12 years old, has based the story on his family's experience as his grandmother lapsed into Alzheimer's disease. A photograph of his grandmother is on the dedication page, along with her name.

The story, written from the point of view of a young child, concerns a visit from the child's critically ill grandmother. Neither the child's brother Matthew nor the child like the grandmother. They manage to avoid her at the start of the visit, but they soon notice her confusion. As the parents have the grandmother diagnosed, the children come to understand that she isn't mean or crazy but sick. Soon after being diagnosed the grandmother is placed in a home. A postscript tells us that the grandmother has died. The child writes, "She may not have always been the Grandma most children hope for, but I know now in her own way she cared about me and my family." A photograph of Jonah Schein and his family follows the narrative.

The strengths of this book are many. The habits of those in the first stages of Alzheimer's disease are accurately portrayed (for example, suspiciousness of theft) and Schein is certainly on target about his feelings. On the negative side, though, for a 24-page picture book there are a bit too many words, and perhaps a professional should have done the pictures; the artwork is uneven.

442. Sebestyen, Ouida. *On Fire.* Boston: Atlantic, 1985; Bantam, pap. 207 pp. Fiction.

Interest level: Age 12+ Reading level: Grades 6–7

It is 1910. Twelve-year-old Sammy adores his 16-year-old brother, Tater. The two boys have a desperate time trying to get along with their alcoholic father. Tater had killed a man (the saintly black father from *Words by Heart* [Atlantic, 1979]), mistakenly thinking he was defending his father, but "Pap" is continuously abusive to the boy and often says that he wishes Tater were dead. The boys' mother and their four younger siblings are passive and victimized.

Tater and Sammy run away to a town where mining is the major industry, and where there is a terrible and bloody conflict between the union and the owners. The plot becomes very complex and intricate, and more characters are introduced, among them a young woman who rescues her dead sister's baby and who becomes a maternal guardian to the two boys. Tater sets a destructive fire and almost kills another man, but Sammy prevents him from doing so. At the end of the book the father has committed suicide; it looks like the mother has finally begun to make some decisions for herself; Tater seems to have reformed; and there is the hope that the family and the young woman will form an alliance and survive.

The ugliness of Tater's bigotry festers like a sore in this book. In the end he professes to have learned from the old black man, who, he confesses, was a better man than most. The family is pictured as the dregs of humanity, with no member having much of an identity except for Tater and Sammy. These are not lovable characters. But the seaminess of their existence and the desperation of their poverty may make some young readers think about the times in which this story takes place, as well as the time in which we now live.

443. Seixas, Judith S. *Drugs: What They Are, What They Do.* Illus. by Tom Huffman. New York: Greenwillow, 1987. 48 pp. Nonfiction.

Interest level: Ages 7–10 Reading level: Grades 3–4

Seixas has written about complex subjects in the easy-to-read format before, notably alcohol and tobacco. Here she covers psychoactive drugs, explaining that they are usually illegal but have been known for thousands of years as painkillers. The book's concrete style will help children understand the nature of drug use. For example, in discussing buildup of tolerance, she uses the example of jumping into cold water and then your body gets used to it.

Topics include how these drugs (stimulants, sedatives, hallucinogens, and narcotics) enter the body and work; their side effects, and difficulties with addiction. Dangers are clearly spelled out—stimulants can cause heart attacks; sedatives can confuse you into an overdose that may stop breathing. She also covers why kids try drugs and introduces such terminology as "gateway drugs" (tobacco, alcohol, and marijuana). Probably most convincing to this age group as reasons not to begin are Seixas's reliance once again on the concrete—"You won't be good at computer games." "You won't be able to catch or kick a ball." Continuing in the same concrete game, she lists ways to say "no"—actual excuses and words to say. Well done.

444. Stren, Patti. *I Was a 15-Year-Old Blimp.* New York: Harper, 1985. 185 pp. Fiction.

Interest level: Age 10+ Reading level: Grades 5–6

Told in the first person by Gabby Finkelstein, this is the story of a young woman who so thoroughly dislikes herself that she becomes obsessed with her weight, goes on fad diets, and becomes bulimic, making herself vomit every morsel of food that she eats. The story is most effective when the author is describing Gabby's weight problem. It becomes somewhat less so when the focus is on Gabby's wish to be admired by the "in" crowd. The young people in the supposedly popular group are shallow and cruel. Gabby has two friends who love her dearly and who are much worthier of her admiration than the group she craves acceptance from.

Gabby's parents are intelligent and concerned, but Gabby's mother is somewhat less capable of expressing her feelings than Gabby's father. The parents are well characterized here; the author escapes the trap of making the parents into cruel and uncaring stick figures. They help Gabby by reacting immediately when they discover that she is bulimic. They send her to a camp that focuses on healthful diet and exercise. And when she returns, thinner and healthier, they follow up with securing her some professional therapy.

The camp experience helps Gabby to put her problem into perspective. She is among girls who have the same issues to contend with that she does. Her counselor empathizes with her because she suffered from the same problem.

The book is engagingly written and moves quickly. The sections describing Gabby's condition in graphic terms are very effective. Unfortunately, weight and physical appearance, despite the characters' disclaimers about what really counts about a person, seem to be the major factors that make a person attractive and worthwhile. The book is, nevertheless, a great discussion starter and source of information.

445. Swenson, Judy Harris, and Kunz, Roxanne Brown. *Cancer: The Whispered Word.* Illus. by Jeanette Swofford. Minneapolis: Dillon, 1986. 40 pp. Nonfiction.

Interest level: Age 6–9 Reading level: Grade 3

Part of the Understanding Pressure series, this volume is very worthwhile. A child tells the story of his mother's cancer and her treatment. The upheaval the family goes through is not underplayed and it is well portrayed (for example, the child's embarrassment over the mother's loss of hair, and so on). Questions of contagion and inheritability are answered. Up-to-date resources for getting through the trauma, such as support groups, are used.

Advice is given on protection from cancer (for example, sun protection), and the warning signs are explained. New concept words are highlighted, and the book has a glossary, an adult resource guide, and two unique inclusions: activity suggestions, such as writing down feelings and methodically sharing responsibilities, and a short recipe section for easy cooking that children can do to help out. Very helpful.

446. Tapp, Kathy Kennedy. *Smoke from the Chimney.* New York: McElderry, 1986. 169 pp. Fiction.

Interest level: Ages 9–12 Reading level: Grade 4

Erin and her friend Heather want to go away to camp together, but Erin's family can't afford the fee, so Erin decides to earn the money herself. She and Heather write and present a series of puppet shows based on the Tarzan books that they love. They earn a good amount of money, but Erin's father, an alcoholic, has finally hit a new low, and he and Erin's mother have separated. Erin's mother now needs money for necessities, and Erin gives up her dream of going to camp.

The author clearly describes the issues that beset the family of an alcoholic. The family pulls together in the end, and there is even some hope that the father can overcome his condition. But it is not falsely optimistic hope: The mother knows that he has made this effort before, and he has failed. She is not again going to live her life based on what she wishes her husband would do. Erin does not go away to camp, but instead goes camping with her mother and two sisters, and it looks as if the family will function well.

447. Tiger, Steven. *Diabetes: Understanding Disease.* Illus. by Michael Reingold. New York: Messner, 1987. 64 pp. Nonfiction.

Interest level: Ages 8–12 Reading level: Grades 4–5

Tiger, a physician's-assistant, and an author in the Understanding Diseases series explains that diabetes is not a single disease and then gives a picture of who is likely to get diabetes. He also explains diagnosis and what can be done. Readers get a good idea of the role of metabolism and diet in various types of diabetes, each handled separately. The book is up-to-date, referring to laser procedures to fix burst eye blood vessels and other modern techniques. Prevention is also discussed in terms of diet. The illustrations are found in the center, in vibrant, attractive colors. On occasion they are confusing, as a picture of a pregnant woman, captioned thus: "Pregnancy causes a temporary diabetes—it disappears when the pregnancy is over." A check of the chapters indicates only one to two percent of pregnant women develop diabetes. Glossary, index.

448. Trull, Patti. *On with My Life.* New York: Putnam, 1983, pap. 144 pp. Nonfiction.

Interest level: Age 12+ Reading level: Grade 6

This extremely moving story tells of an adolescent's struggle with a sarcoma that cost her a leg. Trull was diagnosed around her fifteenth birthday but has gone on to beat a highly malignant disorder, becoming a hospital worker with young cancer patients herself. Down to earth and honest, the various chapters deal with the family's shock, her own very intense feelings, and her uphill battle with schools that didn't want to let her study toward her goal in occupational therapy. Trull tells of trying to be happy, although there is unhappiness in her life. She lets readers in on her world travels and romances as well as ways she found to get around with one leg. Each child whom she has helped as a therapist becomes vibrant, and through her work with them the reader comes to deep understanding of the trauma of cancer and the courageous sense of adventure meeting that trauma can bring.

Trull is unafraid of bringing complexity to her readers:

> As a therapist, my ability to deny things in order to cope was not as strong as it had been as a patient. . . . I never really believed a child was dying. When I worked with a patient I rationalized that the child had a chronic life-threatening illness—he or she might get better forever, temporarily, or never—but right then that child was alive. . . . However, I didn't "play games" with the kids, and I always answered their questions regarding death honestly and to the best of my ability. But I never took away their hope. Hope was a vital, necessary part of their lives and I never saw anyone die without it.

449. Vigna, Judith. *I Wish Daddy Didn't Drink So Much.* Illus. by the author. Niles, Ill.: Whitman, 1988. 40 pp. Fiction.

Interest level: Ages 3–7 Reading level: Grade 3

Lisa's daddy is an alcoholic. She is often afraid of her father, especially when he shouts at her, and when he storms around the house looking for something to drink. After her father has ruined their Christmas celebration, her mother explains to her that although Lisa sees that her father is drunk, he is really sick, and that her "true, kind Daddy" loves her and is a good person.

Lisa and her mother take their Christmas dinner to the house of Mrs. Fields, a friend, who helps Lisa to acquire some strategies for feeling happier. Mrs. Fields explains that she understands very well what is happening because she, too, used to drink too much. She also invites Lisa to come to visit her whenever she likes. Lisa knows that she can feel safe at Mrs. Fields's house.

The author tells this story from the point of view of a three- or four-year-old child. She uses simple illustrations and examples to help young readers understand that they are not alone in suffering from the problem of an alcoholic parent. The two suggestions she gives—that Lisa do something that she really enjoys, and that she visit a good and kind friend whenever possible—are helpful coping strategies for children.

450. Willey, Margaret. *The Bigger Book of Lydia.* New York: Harper, 1983. 215 pp. Fiction.

Interest level: Age 12+ Reading level: Grade 7

Lydia Bitte and her family are very small. They are not midgets, but it is clear that their size is a factor that influences other people's reactions to them. The father is killed in an accident, and Lydia wonders if he would have been spared if he were larger. In reaction to his death she constructs a book that she names *The Bigger Book,* into which she places all sorts of measurement statistics. It is almost as if she uses the book as a talisman to protect herself from harm.

For one year during high school Lydia becomes the girlfriend of a very tall, loud musician, with whom she has nothing in common. At the end of the year she breaks off with him and is glad to do so, despite the fact that she has no friends. At this point Michelle, a young woman who suffers from anorexia nervosa, comes to live with the Bitte family. The doctors have recommended that she not go to her parents' home; there is the implication that her parents are somehow the cause of her condition.

Lydia is astounded. For years she has been wanting to grow larger, and here is a young woman whose aim seems to be to become as small as possible. Michelle is haggard and sickly. The two girls become friends and try to overcome their weaknesses in order to please each other. Michelle starts to eat more and unburdens herself to Lydia. She tells of her feelings about her mother and father and indicates that it is her father's fault that she is as ill as she is. Her father is a surgeon who is overbearing and insensitive. Michelle feels that he has suppressed her mother, who has turned to alcohol for escape. This part of the story doesn't quite ring true. It is as if the mother has no personality or will of her own. Since we never get to meet Michelle's mother, there is no way of judging whether Michelle's perception is accurate.

Just before Christmas Michelle's father orders her to come home. Michelle relapses, but she does go, and there is some hope that she will be able to cope better this time. Lydia goes back to the high school she hates in order to please Michelle, and supposedly because she has now found new strength. Again, it is not convincing.

The characters are interesting but not substantial enough, except for Lydia. The information about anorexia nervosa is vague and misleading. Michelle remains a shadowy character whose self-destructiveness is never resolved, and whose condition is dramatic but mysterious, rather than clearly conveyed and pertinent to the story.

451. Wolfe, Bob, and Wolfe, Diane. *Emergency Room.* Photos by Bob Wolfe. Minneapolis: Carolrhoda, 1983. 40 pp. Nonfiction.

Interest level: Ages 6–10 Reading level: Grade 4

Captioned black-and-white photographs show the busyness of the emergency room (E.R.). In this visit, the staff is delineated and a potential registrant is shown the E.R. process with the explanation: "Long waits are common here since more serious cases are taken care of first and may require a lot of time, so don't think that you have been forgotten." Sample cases include Scott, an elementary schoolchild who fell from a tree, injuring his wrist; Joel, a teen who broke his finger in karate class; toddler Mike, who needs stitches over his eye after a cut suffered in a fall; grade school student Denise, who has a high fever; a girl a little older, Gretchen, who has burned herself on a barbecue grill. Each is shown according to his needs—an X-ray for Scott and Joel, a throat culture and other examination for Denise, bandages for Gretchen, a restraining board for screaming Mike so he can be sewn up. (His stitching process is shown in steps, too.) There is an adult, as well—a man who arrives with chest pain and is tested for signs of heart attack.

The text also explains much of the machinery available for use in the E.R.—an airway, oxygen, and trauma and burn equipment. The work of paramedics is also part of this information-rich, realistic look at the whirlwind activity of the E.R.

Abuse

Physical, sexual, and emotional abuse are coming more and more to the forefront of our attention. Whether this is true because of greater incidence, or because of better reporting strategies, it is still a problem of concern. Abused children experience a terrible loss of self-esteem and of confidence in adults. The loss may be compounded if the abusing adult is a parent, and that parent is removed from the house, or if the child is sent to a foster home as a result of the abuse being discovered. Children need to know that they are not at fault, and that they have a right to be heard. They also need to know that they are not alone.

452. Anderson, Deborah, and Finne, Martha. *Margaret's Story: Sexual Abuse and Going to Court.* Illus. by Jeanette Swofford. Minneapolis: Dillon, 1986. 48 pp. Nonfiction.

Interest level: Ages 5–9 Reading level: Grade 2

Few books exist on helping children cope with the process of testifying in court, a frightening ordeal for most. Using the fictional device of Margaret, who narrates, the authors (administrators of a child abuse service center) tell about a typical child's encounter. Margaret says:

> I had to go to court because of Thomas. He's a man who lived across the street. . . . One day . . . Thomas put his hand in my shorts. He touched me on a private place on my body, my vagina. He wanted me to touch his penis, but I wouldn't. I felt very mixed up. I didn't feel right about it. [Reprinted with the permission of the publisher.]

Margaret tells her mother, who explains there is something wrong with Thomas. She is very angry with Thomas, but not with her daughter. And she's glad her daughter told her. Both loving parents support their child and enable Thomas to come before the law, assuring Margaret that she is in no danger. A social worker helps get Margaret ready to testify by showing her the court and explaining procedures. An understanding lawyer has Margaret draw about her experience and shows her the details of the courtroom, having her sit in the chair to answer practice questions. Thomas lies about the abuse and is sent to jail, and he is given treatment. "That meant that people would help him learn that he shouldn't hurt children." Margaret expresses fears that continue through the trying trial period and beyond. "Mom and Dad said when I feel that way, I should ask for a big hug and a little talk."

The story is followed by information for the young reader about sexual abuse, explaining: "No one has a right to touch you on your private parts without a good reason." Good reasons include going to the doctor or being touched by parents or guardians if you are sick, hurt, or have gotten dirty. Other rights are explained in the context of the story, for example, Margaret saying "no." A list of places to get help is appended, plus a glossary and a note to adults regarding believing the child, being calm and reassuring, and reporting the abuse. The courtroom preparation Margaret receives is caring, competent, and thorough, a good model for professionals and families involved in abuse trials.

453. Anderson, Deborah, and Finne, Martha. *Robin's Story: Physical Abuse and Seeing the Doctor.* Illus. by Jeanette Swofford. Minneapolis: Dillon, 1986. 48 pp. Nonfiction.

Interest level: Ages 5–9 Reading level: Grades 2–3

The fictional child used to relate information about child abuse is Robin, whose early grade teacher notices she has a cut on her forehead. Robin's mother has thrown a cookie tin at her, causing the injury. She does that sort of thing when she gets angry, then she gets remorseful, but it happens again. And she instructs her child not to tell. "If anyone asks what happened tomorrow at school, tell them you ran into a door." But with gentleness the teacher elicits the real story. From there, the sequence of referral becomes: from teacher to social worker to doctor to child protective services worker. All the workers in this case are female. They are also all understanding, knowing how hard it is to tell the story over and over. Robin expresses her fears. Will she be sent to a foster home? The ending is not a foster home, of course, but help for both child and mother, so that the abuse doesn't continue. As is the case with the other books in this Child Abuse Books series, extensive end matter includes a discussion of physical abuse: differences between discipline and abuse, places to get help, and a list of whom to tell. Glossary, note to adults.

454. Bass, Ellen. *I Like You to Make Jokes with Me, but I Don't Want You to Touch Me.* Illus. by Marti Betz. Chapel Hill, N.C.: Lollipop Power, 1985, pap. 28 pp. Fiction.

Interest level: Ages 3–8 Reading level: Grades 2–3

The supermarket clerk, Jack, comes too close to protagonist Sara; his tickling and teasing become frightening. Jack claims, "Who me? I'm just a silly old man." But Sara's mother tells her, next time "you can tell Jack that you like him to make jokes with you, but you don't want him to touch you." When the child is too shy, her mother practices with her in a humorous fashion until she feels confident. Then, when the time comes, Sara carries it off, Jack understands, and the situation is solved. The story is developed believably and can teach children gently about one of the most irritating annoyances of childhood: Encountering the adult who, while not really dangerous, is not adequately cognizant of boundaries between people and, particularly, between adults and children. A good job on an unexplored subject that deserves mention.

455. Benedict, Helen. *Safe, Strong, and Streetwise: The Teenager's Guide to Preventing Sexual Assault.* Illus. Boston: Atlantic, 1986, hb and pap. 192 pp. Nonfiction.
Interest level: Age 12+ Reading level: Grade 6

This manual is blunt and to the point. It can save lives because it gives clear advice and doesn't shy away from difficult issues. Crisis counselor Benedict writes for girls *and* boys with an acceptance of possible teenage sex before marriage; she's also knowledgeable about youngsters' concerns as vulnerable beginners in adult life. The difficult subjects she deals with range from incest to doctors, teachers, and other professionals who betray their power of authority, yet she remains positive and empowering—"You can change that." Direct guidelines are offered for safety, from not working in a store alone, to safe places to park with a date. Also shown are physical self-defense techniques (for example, the Power Yell) and guilt-evoking date mind games (you know you want it) and how to turn them off. More broadly useful than just against sexual attack, the instructions for home, school, street, and job safety can also avert mugging, robbery, and other frightening crimes. Appendixes for both teens and parents add to this book's exceptional value. Truly outstanding.

456. Boegehold, Betty. *You Can Say "NO": A Book about Protecting Yourself.* Illus. by Carolyn Bracken. Racine, Wis.: Golden, 1985. 28 pp. Nonfiction.
Interest level: Ages 4–9 Reading level: Grades 2–3

In this book, part of the Golden Learn about Living series, the first-person narration of varied youngsters covers numerous anxiety-producing situations. For example, "I'm shopping with Mom—and Mom disappears! I can't find her anywhere. Either she's lost—or I'm lost!" Then the boy must choose among alternatives, including going with strangers, to which he says, "No. Absolutely not!" Other situations include: being approached by a stranger in the park and told his mother wants him home and he'll take him there; and countering abduction by running, yelling, hitting or kicking, and/or fooling the abductor.

A segment involves discriminating among people one knows. A girl will say "Hi" to the mailman and superintendent but not to the man who sweeps the sidewalk. "I don't like him. I don't like the way he talks to me. Or looks at me." The story goes on to this man's attempt to "comfort" her by patting her in between her legs, her running away, and discussing her fear with mother. Mother says, "Nobody is allowed to touch me that way—nobody. This is my own special body and nobody can fool with it." The second child talks of playing "funny games" with an uncle and, through a friend, getting the nerve to tell her mother.

This book has many situations covered in brief pages. Parents will want to share the book numerous times so youngsters can grasp the message, perhaps sharing only one segment at a time. The note to parents, always included in this series, tells parents what to teach their children for self-protection, including letting you know if someone wants to give a present or keep a secret between himself/herself and the child. Also included are signs of sexual abuse and what to do if a child is indeed assaulted.

457. Caines, Jeannette. *Chilly Stomach.* Illus. by Pat Cummings. New York: Harper, 1986. 32 pp. Fiction.

Interest level: Ages 5–9 Reading level: Grade 2

"When Uncle Jim tickles me, I don't like it." He also kisses Sandy (who appears to be about age 9 or 10) on the lips, and she gets a "chilly stomach." To make the point, this book about child abuse uses the contrast of affection that feels better. When Sandy's mom and dad "kiss me I feel nice and happy and cuddly." Sandy's initial strategy is to avoid her uncle. She asks to sleep at a friend's when Uncle Jim stays over. Her friend then advises her to tell her parents. Sandy fears her parents won't like her anymore, yet comes to terms with plans to talk. "But I want them to know." This story works in its simplicity and use of metaphor.

458. Chetin, Helen. *My Father Raped Me: Frances Ann Speaks Out.* Illus. by Karen Olsen. Berkeley, Calif.: New Seed, 1977, pap. 24 pp. Nonfiction.

Interest level: Ages 9–13 Reading level: Grade 4

This book concerns a grandmother and granddaughter sitting together and sharing their ideas into a tape recorder. The format doesn't work well for this type of material because although its 24 pages only have two illustrations, the book has the feel of a picture book (print size, dimensions of the book, and so on) rather than a pamphlet for the age group it is meant to serve. One must understand there is a mismatch in outward appearance and inner content, before one can judge the actual content. Thus, there is an obstacle to overcome before even beginning.

To make matters more confusing still, both have the same essential name. The grandmother, Frances, and her granddaughter, Frances Ann, live in an apartment together. The talk is chatty and casual between this 14-

year-old and her elder, and it takes them a good number of pages to get into the material related to the title. Many readers may not stick around through the family litany. The mixed emotions of a child of an alcoholic are played out in the dialogue between them. Frances Ann has even been accused of provoking her father, but she tells of his aggression toward her from early on. "I don't remember when he started doin' things to me. When I was real little. He'd catch me runnin' by and stick his fingers inside my panties. I was wearin' jeans he'd feel around a lot. He acted like he was just teasin' me, the way he roughhoused with the boys, but I knew it was different."

Frances Ann eventually feels dirty and that there must be something wrong with her. As the father's demands escalate (for her to undress and dance before him, for instance), he also threatens her with whippings. In time, after forcing her to masturbate him, he rapes her one drunken night. When she screams, he hits her. Sadly, the teacher doesn't realize the extent of the trouble and, noticing her looking scratched and bedraggled, says she must have been a bad girl to get such a spanking. But he does send her to the nurse, at which point everything starts to come out into the open. And now the family has been broken up; hence the living arrangement with the grandmother. Both are determined that Frances Ann will never be a victim again.

The dialogue is touching, but it takes too long to get into the emotional material, and the homey quality might have needed more rigorous editing. The value of telling one's story is affirmed, however, and people who have suffered similarly will be comforted by these women's wish to share.

459. Chlad, Dorothy. *Strangers*. Illus. by Lydia Halverson. Chicago: Childrens, 1982, hb and pap. 32 pp. Nonfiction.

Interest level: Ages 3–7 Reading level: Grades 1–2

Simply, a girl named Susie tells readers about strangers. "A stranger is someone you don't know. Be careful when you go to school . . . your friend's house . . . the playground . . . or the park." On subsequent pages a stranger beckons her into a car. She warns, "Never get in!" Beyond saying "no," she tells readers to try to remember what the stranger and the car looked like, the license plate, and so on. And tell your parents, brother (sexist?), or teacher. Instructions are also given for a stranger offering gifts. Say "no," and if the stranger touches you, "Scream as loud as you can. Kick as hard as you can. And run away as fast as you can." The book closes with the guidance that it's safer to stay with your friends and family than be off on your own. The illustrations show multiethnic children and adults. Strangers are both men and women.

460. Cleaver, Vera, and Cleaver, Bill. *Hazel Rye.* New York: Lippincott, 1983. 178 pp. Fiction.

Interest level: Age 10+ Reading level: Grades 5–6

When we first meet Hazel she is content to remain ignorant, unlettered, and unambitious. Her mother has abandoned her. She is her father's darling and his sole companion. She is dirty, quick-tempered, and self-indulgent. By the time we reluctantly leave her, she has begun her quest for knowledge and a wider circle of friends and interests. What is more, she now knows the extent to which her father has been involved in keeping her isolated and restricted. We wonder how Hazel will manage to overcome his destructive intervention in her life, but we are given some clues when we hear her planning how she will become more and more independent and self-sustaining.

The book's characters are all well drawn and memorable. Felder, a young boy who assists in Hazel's awakening, is a gentle, extraordinarily intelligent, talented person, reminiscent of Dicken in *The Secret Garden* (Lippincott, 1987), except that Felder is a voracious reader. He is particularly gifted in making things grow and in understanding human beings. We must believe that he and Hazel will meet again and that she will have the courage and strength to overcome her father's abusive and insidious hold on her.

461. Cooney, Judith. *Coping with Sexual Abuse.* New York: Rosen, 1987. 128 pp. Nonfiction.

Interest level: Ages 11–16 Reading level: Grade 5

Judith Cooney, a counselor and professor of psychology, draws the reader in immediately:

> As you read this book, some things may confuse you or frighten you. It is possible that one of the situations that are described will remind you of something that happened to you in the past or is happening to you now. It is essential that you talk over your questions, concerns, or reactions with someone who will take the time to listen.

The tone is straightforward; the examples used to define sexual abuse are to the point and, therefore, startling. Cooney makes a worthwhile differentiation between an anonymous molester and a sexual abuser, adding times when they may converge as one. Following this, a chapter explodes myths, for example, the sexual abuser is usually a stranger to the victim; or that sexual abuse is a twentieth-century phenomenon.

A subsequent chapter explores girls as victims of a father or father figure, breaking the abuse into periods such as encounter, engagement (second approaches and, thereafter, usually petting), marriage (actual intercourse), divorce (termination by whatever means—telling, leaving home, and so on). Not all abuse reaches the marriage stage, of course. A case study is presented. Boys as victims are given similar treatment. Then a chapter about the family context and particular family problems as they may influence patterns offers insight into the larger picture. This is followed by a chapter discussing the effects of abuse—physical and emotional—and one about treatment services available for individuals and families. As many readers will have great fears about reporting abuse, Cooney wisely devotes a full chapter to that, too. In this chapter, she uses a question-answer approach, which was not used in the rest of the book. Each chapter ends with a summary and discussion topics. Resource list, index.

462. Delton, Judy. *Near Occasion of Sin.* New York: Harcourt, 1984. 152 pp. Fiction.

Interest level: Age 14+ Reading level: Grade 7

This story describes the results of unconsciously abusive behavior as well as deliberate abuse. From the time she is a little girl, Tess is frightened and confused by the world. Her parents are devout Catholics, and she tries very hard to be obedient and respectful, and to avoid sinning, but neither her parents nor her teachers understand that their warnings and commands are threatening and terrifying to the sensitive child. She overreacts to her mother's leaving her in kindergarten; she is confused when a neighbor sexually abuses her and she thinks that it is her fault; she marries a man she does not know and permits him to abuse her emotionally. She listens to a nun's advice that she try to become more passive and obedient to her husband.

It is only at the end, when Tess finally recognizes that her husband is seriously disturbed, and she leaves him, that we sense that Tess considers herself a person in her own right. We are not given much evidence, however, that Tess will ever be able to go beyond her fears of sinning. We wonder if the abusive behavior will continue, as she has her newborn daughter baptized into the Catholic religion whose punitive strictures Tess has never been able to escape.

463. Froelich, Margaret Walden. *Reasons to Stay.* Boston: Houghton Mifflin, 1986. 181 pp. Fiction.

Interest level: Age 12+ Reading level: Grades 6–7

In a tangled story, three children live together with a weak mother and an abusive father. In actuality, the man is father to two of the children and the woman is mother to two of them. Babe, the eldest, has been taking care of the family as best she can, and when her mother dies, she tries to keep the two younger children from being further abused. Only after her mother dies, when Babe hears the neighbors shouting at her "father," does she discover that he is, in reality, not her father, and that her mother was not her "sister" Florence's mother. This confusing turn of events is as incomprehensible to the reader as it is to Babe.

Somehow, after a strange journey by mule and wagon, the children are deposited with a remarkably kind and generous family. This family, the Shaws, takes them in; the wicked stepfather is killed in a flood; Babe finds her family of origin; and all three children become a permanent and happy part of the Shaw family.

Despite the confusion and the needlessly tangled prose in some parts of the book, and despite the idyllic ending, there is strong writing here. Some of the sections are so painful as to cause the reader to have to pause in the reading. Babe is a heroic figure, and her character makes the book worth reading.

464. Gallagher, Sister Vera, with Dodds, William F. *Speaking Out, Fighting Back.* Seattle: Madrona, 1985, pap. 224 pp. Nonfiction.

Interest level: Age 12+ Reading level: Grade 6

Here, readers meet women who have triumphed over childhood sexual abuse to go on to marry, work productively, and help others. Sister Vera Gallagher has worked with the Good Shepherd Sisters for more than 30 years in helping oppressed women without regard to their religious affiliations. Sister Vera Gallagher put together some of the women's stories, looking at how the order helped the women come to terms with their fears, rage, and guilt. The portraits, told mostly in the first person, serve to show how a history of abuse can lead to a myriad of difficulties later in life—drug addiction, prostitution, violence, and/or perhaps a tendency to keep the abuse going in the next generation. Professional, caring help enabled these victims of abuse to find once again feelings of self-worth. Young people who are now victims themselves may find hope in reading about the drama of others who have made it through and who now join the professionals who helped them in saying, "Speak out, fight back." Bibliography, index.

465. Girard, Linda Walvoord. *My Body Is Private.* Illus. by Rodney Pate. Niles, Ill.: Whitman, 1984. 32 pp. Nonfiction.

Interest level: Ages 5–9 Reading level: Grade 3

Narrated by Julie, a young girl, the book explains in simple but respectful language that children are entitled to privacy in many situations, and especially to autonomy over their own body. Words like "vagina" and "penis" are used without embarrassment, and without the necessity to substitute nicknames or euphemisms. It is made clear that any kind of touching, if it is not acceptable to the child, is not acceptable. Julie's father does not permit her brother Rob to keep on tickling her when it is no longer a pleasant sensation for Julie. Julie's mother asks the doctor to inform Julie before he needs to examine her "in places that her bathing suit covers." Julie's parents give her permission to refuse to sit on her uncle's lap when he visits, because Julie doesn't like it when her uncle rubs her arms.

Julie and her mother have a conversation about what Julie could do if anyone wanted to touch her in a way that Julie did not want to permit. Julie's mother asserts that she will always want to hear about anyone who menaces Julie, no matter who it is, even if it is someone in the family. She explains that it is not good to keep things like this a secret.

The book distinguishes between good and bad touching, and it in no way prevents a child from enjoying the good kind of touching. It also models the importance of preparing children to be able to cope with any incidents before they happen, rather than reacting to them afterward. The book is sensible and careful. It is an excellent guide.

466. Girard, Linda Walvoord. *Who Is a Stranger and What Should I Do?* Illus. by Helen Cogancherry. Niles, Ill.: Whitman, 1985. 28 pp. Nonfiction.

Interest level: Ages 4–9 Reading level: Grade 4

The book is almost a manual for young children on how to deal with strangers. It points out that it is perfectly all right to talk to strangers if you are in the company of an adult. But when you are alone there are certain rules to follow. It explains the reasons for the rules, and phrases the rules in clear and simple language, so that children will not be frightened but will understand exactly what is being said.

The book provides a definition of strangers and tells where strangers may be encountered, including those who telephone or come to the house. There are rules such as "Never get into a car with a stranger," that must be followed. The book also provides a set of exercises for children to try that invite them to simulate what they would do in certain situations. All in all the book, although not imaginative or entertaining, is a useful guide.

467. Hall, Lynn. *The Boy in the Off-White Hat.* New York: Scribner, 1984. 87 pp. Fiction.

Interest level: Age 10+ Reading level: Grade 5

The story is narrated by Skeeter, a 13-year-old who is staying with 9-year-old Shane and his mother, Maxine, on their ranch in Arizona as a mother's helper for the summer. During the course of the summer a man named Burge becomes a regular visitor to the ranch. He courts Maxine and is a surrogate father to Shane, but for some reason, Skeeter doesn't like him.

Skeeter's instincts are accurate. Burge abuses Shane sexually and terrorizes him into continued submission. Even though Skeeter and Maxine notice that something is wrong with Shane, and that he seems afraid of Burge, they can't make Shane tell them what is wrong.

Then, one day, Shane claims that he is no longer Shane; he is John. It is in the guise of John that Shane is able to tell Skeeter what Burge has done. Burge is arrested. It turns out that he has a record of molesting young boys. Maxine is guilt ridden. Shane is taken for some psychiatric treatment and he and Maxine enter a program of therapy. The story effectively communicates the importance of helping children express their fears and learn to stand up for their rights.

The fact that the story is narrated by Skeeter gives it a detachment that rescues it from melodrama. The information given by the social worker at the end of the book is accurate and helpful. But the book itself reads more like a fictionalized case history than a story, perhaps because we never really get to know any of the characters well enough to think of them outside the context of the sexual abuse. Nevertheless, it is well written and interesting and can be useful reading for young people and their caretakers.

468. Hall, Lynn. *Flyaway*. New York: Scribner, 1987. 120 pp. Fiction.
Interest level: Age 12+ Reading level: Grade 7

Ariel and her sister, Robin, hate their father. He has never physically abused them, but he has been a tyrannical watchdog over them. He has forced them to obey him even in such mundane matters as insisting that they drink soured milk and watching them retch as they force it down. He has subjugated and menaced their mother as well. He is a cold, despicable man, and the two young women (Robin is 14, Ariel is 17) plot endlessly about how they will make their escape.

At one point Robin, by far the more abused child, runs away and prostitutes herself to earn some money. Of course her father finds her, insists that she spend a night in jail, and then takes her home. At the end of the book, Ariel manages to get away, promising herself that she will help Robin to do the same when it is time.

The father's ugliness is unrelieved. It is difficult to see why and how the mother stays with him. None of the characters is really three-dimensional enough to sustain the reader, but the plot carries us along. We want to see the girls escape. It is a measure of satisfaction that one succeeds, and we have some reason to hope for the other.

469. Howard, Ellen. *Gillyflower*. New York: Atheneum, 1986. 106 pp. Fiction.
Interest level: Age 12+ Reading level: Grade 6

Gilly regularly retreats to a fantasy world she has invented in order to shut out "the secret." Her father has regularly been abusing her sexually, and she does not know what to do about it. Her mother, a nurse, works the night shift, and her father has been out of work for a long time. Her father asks her to come to keep him company, and then he engages in sexual acts with her. Gilly thinks that it is her fault that her father is doing this. He warns her to keep it a secret.

The strain of keeping the secret affects Gilly's relationships with her friends. She becomes a loner. She fears that her father will abuse her younger sister, Honey, and she cannot tolerate that thought. When some new people move in next door, she is attracted to them because they plant a garden with beautiful flowers. They seem to be an ideal family. It is because of their friendship, and particularly because she thinks that her father has already molested Honey, that she gets the strength to tell her mother. Her mother moves out with her and Honey, and her father receives help. Gilly goes to a counselor, who helps her to see that it was not her fault.

The story is well told. It is suspenseful and moving, not a dry case study. The focus is on Gilly; her mother and father are somewhat shadowy figures. But she is a vivid and understandable character, and readers cannot help but empathize with her.

470. Irwin, Hadley. *Abby, My Love.* New York: McElderry, 1985; Signet, pap. 157 pp. Fiction.

Interest level: Age 12+ Reading level: Grades 6–7

Abby is beautiful, intelligent, and popular. It is difficult to believe that her father has regularly abused her sexually. She finally tells Chip, who loves her, and Chip tries to help her, but in the end Abby must help herself. She tries to tell her mother, but her mother can't or won't believe her. It is only with outside intervention that Abby manages to get her mother and sister to go to therapy with her. Her father, a successful dentist, leaves the family, and everyone is the better for it.

The book is helpful in informing the reader that incest is not simply a lower-class problem. On the surface Abby's father seems to be a doting father and pleasant person and Abby shows no outward signs of her ordeal. No indication is given of what drives the father, and the reader does not get to know the mother at all. Even Abby is a somewhat shadowy figure. The only character who emerges clearly is Chip, the narrator. The story would undoubtedly have been more sensational had Abby narrated it, but this secondhand account, veiled in mystery, distances the reader and lessens the impact of the truth. Nevertheless, the story is an important one to tell, and readers will undoubtedly benefit from it.

471. Kehoe, Patricia. *Something Happened and I'm Scared to Tell: A Book for Young Children Victims of Abuse.* Illus. by Carol Deach. Seattle: Parenting, 1987, hb and pap. 32 pp. Fiction.

Interest level: Ages 3–6 Reading level: Grades 1–2

A clinical psychologist offers a book for preschoolers about sexual abuse. A child sits beneath a tree lamenting, "Something happened to me. I don't know just what it was . . . and I don't know what to do." On the next page, a friendly lion offers, "Can I help?" The lion informs the child that promises under threat not to tell are not good to keep, and that people will still want to know the child afterward. After all, "You are still the one and only, very best you." The lion convinces the child to "tell and tell until SOMEBODY listens."

The child begins by telling the lion. The ensuing material implies that it is the father who is abusing the child ("I don't get spanked anymore"), and the lion explains bodily parts. The lion also names "what happened" to this child: "It's called sexual abuse and it can happen with anybody." The construction is occasionally awkward, for example, jumping from naming the penis, vagina, and anus, quickly on to hurt and hurtful feelings. Also, physical abuse is thrown in; discussion of the kinds of touches is handled in a way children of the readership age probably wouldn't understand: "There are all kinds of ways to show love. Some ways are just right for children, like hugs and cuddles. And some are just right for two grown-ups who love each other, like sex." Would most three to seven year olds know the word or concept "sex"? At the end, the child prepares to tell someone else besides the lion, who is very proud of the child. An afternote gives guidelines for reporting child abuse.

472. Kurland, Morton L. *Coping with Family Violence.* New York: Rosen, 1987. 141 pp. Nonfiction.

Interest level: Age 12+ Reading level: Grades 5–6

The psychiatrist author of this book tells of individuals who wisely sought counseling for problems of violence in the family. Episodes include examples of children caught in the crossfire of divorce; children victimized by confused, frightened parents who married or bore children too early; and families where drug abuse is the source of out-of-control behavior. Also discussed are murderous impulses and actions; sexual violence perpetrated within the family and on children who are not within the family by teachers, coaches, friends, and so forth. In an unusual section not found in books about abuse, Kurland pays attention to those occasions in which sibling rivalry exceeds normal bounds and becomes dangerous to those involved.

Woven into the case stories are pieces of information about psychology and how the human mind works (for example, when discussing sibling rivalry, Kurland notes that Freud was "Golden Siggy" to his mother). Each story also includes names of relevant organizations (Al-Anon, for example) that could be of help to readers, and the book culminates with steps to identify violence that is threatening, including recognition of the behavior, validation, and confronting those involved. An overview of the kinds of people who can be of service is included.

The book is broader than many often seen, reminding readers of experts they might otherwise overlook, such as religious experts. The stories are interesting and the lesson repeated throughout is valuable—violent behavior usually cannot be changed by family members alone. Professional help is a must.

473. Landau, Elaine. *Child Abuse: An American Epidemic.* New York: Messner, 1984. 128 pp. Nonfiction.

Interest level: Ages 11+ Reading level: Grades 5–6

Concentrating on child abuse in the family setting, Landau gives admirable in-depth attention to varied causes that might turn otherwise loving parents into abusive ones, citing among them past deprivations of the parents, familial isolation, and unwritten societal sanctions. Psychological abuse can be as devastating as physical abuse, says Landau, and as the book is geared toward teens she pays special attention to the particular concerns of abused teens, a broad variety of topics ranging from overly heated arguments to sexual abuse. Most important, she gives readers ideas as to why their parents might be acting as they do. As finding a way to get help often presents a double bind (Am I disloyal? Will I be further abandoned?), Landau offers helpful information about ways to seek help without running away or becoming a suicide statistic. Readers may find practical routes here, such as group living arrangements. A hefty portion of this level-headed book is also devoted to discussion of organizations that can be of service, such as the Clearinghouse on Child Abuse and Neglect. Bibliography.

474. Landau, Elaine. *On the Streets: The Lives of Adolescent Prostitutes.* New York: Messner, 1987. 112 pp. Nonfiction.

Interest level: Age 12+ Reading level: Grade 7

Landau writes frequently about social issues, and with the gaze of a reporter she has taken on the several worlds of teen prostitution. She offers an understanding perspective, combining in-depth sociological and psychological information with moving first-person profiles. She tells it honestly but somehow doesn't overwhelm her reader with the tragedy that abounds. There's the ugliness of a man who visits 13-year-old Lynn and insists on calling her by his own daughter's name. And the sadness of Chad, who had been repeatedly abused by his grandfather and gradually sold into prostitution by his own family. And there's the frightening story of a 15-year-old abducted into slavery until her escape six months later. How about 16-year-old Samantha who is back home, but already has needed a hysterectomy. About 50 percent of teen prostitutes live at home, it seems.

Landau's informative chapters on male prostitution, child pornography, and pimps are highly revealing, and the actual nonglamour of escort services is exposed. The long American history of prostitution, particularly on the frontier, where suicide before age 18 was frequent, is instructive, particularly because it reveals that the technique of getting girls drug-addicted is an old one. The chapter on pimps' techniques for getting teens into dependency and keeping them there is so highly detailed that readers may then be more savvy when they are approached. It may just save some lives. Health problems are discussed, including venereal disease, but surprisingly, AIDS, already hot in the media by publication time, is not given attention.

Landau offers an intelligent look at reasons kids become prostitutes. These are multitudinous, ranging from being thrown out (perhaps for promiscuity, homosexuality, so-called incorrigibility, and so on) to escaping a home of physical/sexual abuse, from abduction to economic destitution. Landau writes without an air of hysteria, yet her words serve indelibly as a warning to those who might be individually tempted or those who might be abducted into prostitution rings.

475. LeShan, Eda. *When Grownups Drive You Crazy*. New York: Macmillan, 1988. 144 pp. Nonfiction.

Interest level: Ages 8–12 Reading level: Grades 4–5

Noted parent educator LeShan here takes on the foibles of the parents themselves, bringing her knowledge to children so they can with open eyes learn to love themselves, try to be good people, and try to understand themselves and others albeit in their limitations. The chapters concern many kinds of interactions between children and adults, going beyond parents to teachers and others. Some are serious types of "craziness," such as abuse, others are persistent aggravations. Her information and advice center on adults who make children angry, frightened, or embarrassed. The range of the book is broad—from parents who keep secrets, or lie, to those who are out of control when drunk or otherwise abusive of those in their charge.

As in earlier books, LeShan shows great respect for children's capacity to understand. She therefore dares to share stories of her own parenting mistakes and her own sexual abuse by a trusted family doctor. Her many anecdotes about families will help readers differentiate between idiosyncracies and serious problems. Whichever kind children face, LeShan provides alternative ideas for action and samples of actual words children can say to show how they feel.

Surprisingly, LeShan makes little reference to outside help, but most of her focus is on becoming a good reader of behavior one's self instead. In her attendance to subtle matters that are nonetheless important (overprotection, immaturity, unpredictable mood changes, interference with privacy), LeShan speaks about points that haven't been addressed much in children's books. As youngsters are the ones most likely to bear the brunt of small problems as well as large, she performs a needed service.

476. MacLean, John. *Mac.* Boston: Houghton Mifflin, 1987. 175 pp. Fiction.

Interest level: Age 13+ Reading level: Grade 7

Mac is experiencing typical adolescent conflicts: He is bothered by his younger brothers; he is struck dumb when he encounters a girl to whom he is attracted; and he has friends with whom he engages in a bantering sort of rivalry. But something happens that changes Mac's life: He is sexually abused by a physician during a routine physical examination. The experience is so traumatic that Mac becomes unable to maintain any sort of relationship with anyone. He breaks up with the girl he adores, starts having fights in school, and, in general, behaves very differently from his usual self.

At last, his concerned principal connects Mac with an excellent counselor, who approaches Mac in an effective and appropriate manner and finally gets him to tell her what happened. She then helps him to realize that the assault was not his fault, and that he can, indeed, engage in normal relationships with the people he loves. She also takes him to a group meeting where other victims of sexual abuse talk to each other about their experience and their feelings. At the end of the book both the reader and Mac have learned a lot about how to cope with sexual abuse.

The factual information in no way detracts from the plot in this excellent book. Young readers would not only benefit from the information here; they will also be totally absorbed in the story. Some potentially objectionable language is used, however, it is in the context of the characters' interaction. This is not a book for children under 12, but teenagers will certainly be drawn to and get much benefit from it.

477. Nathanson, Laura. *The Trouble with Wednesdays.* New York: Pacer, 1986; Bantam, pap. 176 pp. Fiction.

Interest level: Age 11+ Reading level: Grades 5–6

Although Becky wants to have braces so that the kids at school will stop calling her "fang-face" and so that she can have her teeth straightened in time for entry in junior high, she hates going to her dentist. Her father and mother are having a hard time, economically, so they send her to her father's cousin, who fixes their teeth for what the insurance will pay.

Dr. Rolfman sexually molests Becky each time she is in his office. Becky tries to tell her parents about it, but her mother is too immersed in her own emotional doldrums to care about her child, and her father is too distracted by his economic problems to pay attention. Becky begins to feel as if she is a zero, worthless and unloved. An astute teacher rescues Becky after Becky has vomited on Dr. Rolfman and escaped from his office.

Afterward, Becky's teacher speaks to Becky's parents and reports Dr. Rolfman. It takes a while, but Becky's father finally redeems himself by demonstrating that he cares about what Becky thinks of him. Her mother is a lost cause, but Becky emerges strong and confident.

The story accurately indicates what the course of action should be if someone abuses a child. The teacher is a positive model of a helping adult. Becky's parents are weak and self-centered. They are inadequate to the task of parenting, but they are believable characters. The book can be useful in warning some children about the possibilities of abuse, and in helping those who have been or are being abused.

478. Parrot, Andrea. *Coping with Date Rape and Acquaintance Rape.* New York: Rosen, 1988. 140 pp. Nonfiction.

Interest level: Age 13+ Reading level: Grade 6

An unusual, valuable book that will meet a very special need. Writing for males as well as females, Andrea Parrot, a professor of sexuality and expert on date rape, recognizes that both men and women can be raped. Starting off by debunking myths (a rapist is always a stranger; rape victims are always attractive), she explains that most date rapes occur because a man has planned to have sex. When he is thwarted or his fantasies fall apart, the rape may be an attempt to get what he thinks he deserves. Drinking can compound the problem. Acquaintance rape can take place between other kinds of "pairs"—teacher/student, doctor/patient, employer/employee, friend of the family, and so forth.

Through examples culled from interviews, types of rapists are examined—such as the power rapist, the anger rapist, the sadistic rapist. The reasons behind rape are explored in terms of female socialization, influence of the media, male confusion about "no" possibly meaning "yes," and males who personify their penises, thereby abdicating responsibility for its actions. Many men do not even know they have committed a rape, having attached sexual meaning to gestures that may have merely meant friendly interest, or believed exaggerated reports of a girl's sexual availability.

As many people reading the book will have been victims of rape, Parrot goes into depth about the feelings that may ensue—distrust, fear of a bad reputation, anguish over being blamed although the victim. Other chapters include responsibility, ways and means for getting help, and advice about being careful about such matters as safety, alcohol consumption, and messages that may be confusing. Parrot's supplying of actual words people can use to get out of uncomfortable situations will be very helpful, as will the chapter devoted to people who have, knowingly or not, raped someone who has said "no." Appendix of resources, glossary, bibliography, index.

479. Patterson, Sherri. *No-No the Little Seal: A Story for Very Young Children That Tells about Sexual Abuse.* Illus. by Marion Needham Krupp. New York: Random, 1986, pap. 32 pp. Fiction.

Interest level: Ages 5–8 Reading level: Grades 2–3

No-No, the main character, was created as part of a Touch Safety program for elementary school children. The book is designed to help children understand what sexual abuse is and how to protect themselves. It also builds a strong support for self-worth and self-rights. The idea of using a little seal, instead of a child, having problems of sexual abuse is to help children not be unduly threatened.

The story tells about No-No being left with his uncle for two days while his parents go fishing. A close relationship develops between the small seal (child) and his uncle (grown-up). The child's confusion over his trusted uncle's abusive behavior is written in words that children can relate to and understand. A giant whale is the one No-No can turn to, showing children that if they are confused or afraid to discuss it with their parents, they can and should find a friend. The whale and the parents, when told, are supportive and caring for No-No. They make sure the little seal knows that it is his uncle who has a problem, not No-No.

Throughout the story, the focus is on No-No, his needs, his feelings, and finally his triumph in dealing with a very difficult problem.

This book supports children in knowing their rights, in taking control, and in seeking support to help resolve problems that are overwhelming. The ending may not be ideal in that the family does not always support the abused child but in fact denies the occurrence when they themselves cannot handle the problem.

480. Scott, Carol J. *Kentucky Daughter.* New York: Clarion, 1985, pap. 186 pp. Fiction.

Interest level: Age 12+ Reading level: Grade 5

Mary Fred Pratley leaves her rural Kentucky home to live with her aunt and uncle in Virginia. She wants to get a good education so that she can return to Kentucky as a teacher. Her father has been killed in a mine cave-in, and her mother, an excellent weaver and craftswoman, is struggling to support the four children in the family.

Mary Fred often acts as if she is too good for her family. She is ashamed of the coat her mother made her for her birthday; she always corrects her sisters' speech; and she is disdainful of an old man who is consistently helpful to the family. When she gets to Virginia she encounters a number of problems. Several of the girls are cruelly derisive of her because of her name and her Kentucky background. Her English teacher keeps grading her papers with Cs, and when she goes to speak to him about her work he molests her sexually.

Fortunately, Mary Fred has the good sense to speak to the principal about the teacher, and it later turns out that the teacher has also molested two other girls. The principal persuades the teacher to resign and she also informs the girls' families about the incidents. Mary Fred's aunt and uncle assure her that she can come to them for help whenever she needs it; Mary Fred receives word from home that things are looking up, and that her mother is beginning to receive recognition for her work. In the process of listening to how her family feels about her and her behavior Mary Fred begins to grow up and put things into perspective. She recognizes that her behavior has, indeed, been snooty, and she starts to value her heritage.

Carol Scott authentically presents us with the issues and dilemmas that can confront a young teenager in her search for a better future. The story clearly brings out the value of a supportive family. Scott also helps readers to find strategies for coping with such difficult problems as abuse from adults and peers, and the feeling of being different from and ashamed of one's background.

481. Stanek, Muriel. *Don't Hurt Me, Mama.* Illus. by Helen Cogancherry. Niles, Ill.: Whitman, 1983. 32 pp. Fiction.

Interest level: Ages 6–10 Reading level: Grades 2–3

After her father deserts her and her mother, life changes drastically for the young girl. She and her mother move to a city where no one knows them, and they are isolated. The mother can't get a job, and she begins to drink too much and to hit her daughter. One day she beats her daughter with a belt and admonishes her not to tell anyone. When the child gets to school, her teacher notices that something is wrong and sends her to the nurse, who discovers what is wrong, informs a social agency, and gets help for the family.

With today's focus on helping the abusive parent and keeping the child at home with the parent, this book helps readers understand that abusers are often victims too. As a matter of fact, it is the mother whose feelings we can empathize with. The little girl seems to manage unusually well, and she does not share her emotions with anyone. It would have been helpful for the author to let us in on how she feels. Although the ending in this book is somewhat unrealistic in its swiftness and total resolution of the problem, it serves to bring up the issue of abuse in a hopeful context.

482. Taylor, William. *Paradise Lane.* New York: Scholastic, 1987. 165 pp. Fiction.

Interest level: Age 11+ Reading level: Grade 6

The story is set in a poor section of New Zealand. Rosie Perkins is a loner, partly because her mother is depressed and an alcoholic, and her father is an overly possessive and abusive man. Rosie rescues a baby possum and raises it lovingly. She finds a friend in Michael, her next-door neighbor. When her mother's condition requires hospitalization, and her father's abusiveness reaches extremes, Michael's mother takes her to live with them and sets the father on the road to being helped.

None of the characters is as fully drawn as a reader might wish. The situation is clear, but the characters are shadowy. The abuse is vaguely alluded to until the end, when the father loses control and batters Rosie. The mother's condition contributes to the family's problems, but the family seems always to have been withdrawn from the small society in which they lived, and there is little explanation for their behavior.

The killing of the possum at the end of the story is a gratuitous violence. Perhaps the author meant it as a symbol that wild creatures cannot be penned in, but it is only when the possum is set free that it is caught and killed in a trap. Rosie's father lets the pet go, but Michael's trap kills it. Michael grieves in a strange way over his role in the accident; he says that he wishes he had never become involved with Rosie, but it is clear that he and she will be very much involved with each other for always. The book is unevenly written, but the plot is involving and the setting provides further interest.

483. Terkel, Susan Neiburg, and Rench, Janice E. *Feeling Safe, Feeling Strong: How to Avoid Sexual Abuse and What to Do If It Happens to You.* Minneapolis: Lerner, 1984. 72 pp. Nonfiction.

Interest level: Ages 10–16 Reading level: Grades 5–6

Using a pattern of story then discussion, this book discusses six situations of various abuse intensities: being forced to be kissed by a relative; being asked to model for a lascivious neighbor taking pornographic photographs, followed by coersive blackmail; exhibitionism; incest; obscene phone calls; and rape. Each story is portrayed in terms of an individual child, for example, Sarah, who meets up with an exhibitionist. In the stories, sometimes the child solves the problem alone, sometimes he or she needs a supportive adult to step in or give advice. In the effort toward believability, the stories tend to meander with too much detail. Sometimes, it's distracting (as in the story in which the name amuses—Ashley Montague Morgenstern); sometimes the point cannot be predicted until well into the story (five pages go by before it is evident that "You Can't Judge a Book by Its Cover" ends in exhibitionism).

Following each story, the discussion contains danger signals. An example is: "If you tell anyone . . . , no one will believe you." The discussion also contains psychological information and advice about what to do if confronted with the situation. The information and advice are very honest and down-to-earth, for example, in regard to exhibitionism, "Very few people go through life without encountering [exhibitionism]." In terms of practicality, to avoid abduction, the authors remind children not to wear clothing announcing their names. The authors, a child-development expert and a writer and director of a rape crisis center, convey important material about self-assertion, stating: "Before you can stand up for your personal rights, you must first recognize how you feel."

484. Voigt, Cynthia. *The Runner.* New York: Atheneum, 1985. 192 pp. Fiction.

Interest level: Age 12+ Reading level: Grades 6–7

Set in Maryland in the late 1960s, the story describes Bullet Tillerman, a strong 17-year-old long-distance runner. He trains regularly, is the best on the school team, and has been the state champion for two years. But he is a loner. His relationship with his father is an ugly and combative one. His father is an overbearing, abusive authoritarian who has repressed and subdued his wife into silence and has driven Bullet's older brother and sister from their home. For Bullet, running is his outlet, and he values it above everything else in the world.

The product of a southern white segregated and bigoted society, Bullet refuses to coach a promising black athlete, Tamer Shipp, and as a consequence is thrown off the team. Then Bullet discovers that his employer and only close friend, Patrice, is of black heritage. No longer so certain that his view of the world is the right one, he now realizes that his feelings for Patrice transcend any boundaries of color, so he agrees to work with Tamer. He neither offers nor expects friendship, but in the process of running and working together the two young men come to understand and respect each other, and together they win the state championship for their team.

Bullet leaves home on his eighteenth birthday, enlists in the army, and is sent to Vietnam where he is killed in action. His anger at his father never abates. He may know that his mother adored him, but if he does it is not because she reveals it openly to him. She travels miles to watch his last race, but she leaves without congratulating him. When she hears of his death she erupts into passionate anger at herself and the world.

The Runner gives us information about what happened before the events in *Homecoming* (Atheneum, 1981) and *Dicey's Song* (Atheneum, 1982), as well as *A Solitary Blue* (Atheneum, 1983) and, particularly, *Come a Stranger* (Atheneum, 1986). As with the other Tillerman family stories, it presents the reader with powerful insights into the relationships within families and the forces, internal and external, that shape the thinking and behavior of young people.

485. Whitley, Mary Ann. *A Sheltering Tree.* New York: Walker, 1985. 90 pp. Fiction.

Interest level: Age 10+ Reading level: Grades 5–6

The setting is a small Indiana quarry town in hard times. Lacey Foster lives with her mother and stepfather, Lonzie. Lonzie has no redeeming features: He is an alcoholic who drinks away most of the money he earns. He is mean-spirited even when he is sober. After he and Lacey's mother were married, he insisted that she send away her older daughter, Vernal, saying, "I won't support two kids that ain't even mine."

An unsatisfactory element of the plot is that the reader is given no clue about the whereabouts or circumstances of the girls' father. Nor is the reader informed about why the mother puts up with her situation. She ostensibly married Lonzie "to make things easier on herself, trying to raise two kids alone." But when it was clear that Lonzie wanted no part of raising any children, why didn't she leave him?

Vernal is sent off to a series of foster homes, and Adelle, the mother, makes no attempt to keep in touch with her. She avoids talking about her. Lacey longs to contact her missing sister. She is finally able to do this when she meets Christopher, a foster child with whom she quickly establishes a close relationship. Christopher is remarkable in his maturity and inventiveness. He discovers where Vernal is, makes all of the contacts, and persuades Lacey to enter an art competition in order to earn the money to go and see Vernal.

Another unsatisfying element of the plot is at the end of the story, when Lonzie, who has been nothing but abusive and churlish to Lacey, is shot, and Lacey comes to his aid. Adelle hopes desperately for his recovery and is relieved when she is informed that he will recover. Nothing is resolved, except that Lacey decides not to leave home, and the reader is led to believe that she will reestablish communication with her long-lost sister.

The information about foster care is shaky, at best. Christopher is a knowledgeable young man, but his description of the foster care process goes no further than to let the reader know that it has not worked well.

There is some confusion about the possibility of Vernal's being adopted, even though she is a foster child. Readers may be led to believe that all foster children may be available for adoption.

Lacey's "best" friend, Callie, seems shallow, unsympathetic, and self-centered. Why is Lacey so attached to her? On the other hand the friendship of the two main characters is portrayed in a convincing manner.

486. Woolverton, Linda. *Running before the Wind.* Boston: Houghton Mifflin, 1987. 152 pp. Fiction.

Interest level: Age 10+ Reading level: Grade 5

The story is an insightful and, at times, moving exploration into the feelings of a young girl in early adolescence who experiences conflicting emotions on the death of her abusive father. Kelly Mackenzie, who is 13, has a father who, on his good days, can be charming and fun to be with, but more often than not he displays a disagreeable and violent temper, which is mostly directed at Kelly. The explanation for the father's behavior includes the fact that he was abused by his family's housekeeper; that he is very unhappy in his work because he keeps getting passed by for promotion; and that he was once a very gifted runner but was stricken with polio and never came to terms with his disability.

Kelly loves running and has been invited by the junior high school track coach to join the team. Her father violently forbids her to do so. The idea that Kelly can be successful when he cannot seems to be too much for him to tolerate. Kelly is unable to find support from her mother or sister, both of whom are subdued by Mr. Mackenzie's outbursts as they desperately attempt to keep peace in the household at any cost. It seems to Kelly that they consider her to be at fault for her father's outbursts. She cannot discuss the situation with any of her friends; they are all involved with their own problems. Her only outlet is her running, which she does secretly.

When Kelly's father dies in a boating accident after a particularly violent incident during which Mr. Mackenzie beats both Kelly and her dog, Kelly is torn between her relief that the abuse has ended and her grief at losing the father she often loved and enjoyed. Her mother and sister are immersed in grief over their loss. Kelly is further confused and dismayed when she recognizes how alike she and her father were in many ways, and she sees in herself the potential for violence. Fortunately, Kelly confides in her gym teacher, an athlete and excellent coach, who both trains and counsels Kelly so that she can come to terms with her anger and guilt, understand and forgive her mother and sister, and bring closure to her rage at her father.

In addition to having written an engrossing story, the author has contributed enormously to helping young readers acknowledge the complexity of such a painful issue as abuse.

War and Displacement

Wartime presents many possible loss situations. In some settings, the father is gone from the family for an extended period. His eventual return is in question; if he does return, his mental and physical condition is uncertain.

When war takes place in a child's own country, the child continually faces circumstances in which physical comforts are diminished or are possibly nonexistent. The potential loss of home and family—even loss of the child's own life—is a frightening reality. At war's end, many of those who have been forced out of their homes cannot return and are destined to become displaced persons. Added to the tragic loss of members of the family and friends in such cases is separation from the familiar surroundings of home.

487. Abells, Chana Byers. *The Children We Remember.* Photos from the Archives of Yad Vashem. New York: Greenwillow, 1986. 48 pp. Nonfiction.

Interest level: Age 7+ Reading level: Grade 1

This is a large book with large pictures, a large subject, few words, and short sentences. This combination works together to form perhaps the most moving Holocaust book of all, and the one that is accessible to the largest age group. Each short phrase gets a photograph of its own, making the tragedy real:

> Before the Nazis . . . Some children lived in towns like this
> went to schools like this,
> prayed in synagogues like this,
> played with their friends
> or sat alone.
> Then the Nazis came.

The pages that follow tell the chronology of what befell Europe's Jewish children, from restrictions in clothing and schooling to the ultimate destruction. The photographs for "Sometimes they put children to death" show a mother shielding her toddler while both are shot by a soldier or policeman with a rifle.

The message is brought home with even more depth by showing a series of photographs of individual children killed by the Nazis, with the introducing caption: "These children were killed by the Nazis." After the series, readers are told (with accompanying photographs for each phrase) that children survived through various methods, such as going to Israel and other countries, going to non-Jewish homes, hiding in forests, or acting as non-Jews.

The heartbreaking series of pages ends with a break in pattern—five lines on one page to serve as warning for future generations:

The children who survived are grown now.
Some have children of their own.
They live in towns like yours,
go to schools like yours,
play with their friends, or sit alone. . . .
[And on the next page] Just like the children we remember.

488. Adler, David A. *The Number on My Grandfather's Arm.* Photos by Rose Eichenbaum. New York: Union of American Hebrew Congregations, 1987. 32 pp. Nonfiction.

Interest level: Ages 5–9 Reading level: Grade 2

A young girl tells the story, and photographs show her sitting with her grandfather, who, at last, reveals a history that continues to trouble the family. He tells her of his experiences in the Holocaust, Hitler's incendiary propaganda about Jews, Hitler's extermination plans, the concentration camps, his trying stay in Auschwitz, and the loss of his siblings and friends.

Adler is in touch with family emotions that go down the generations when confronted with something as overwhelming as the Holocaust, and we see the grandfather admonishing his daughter, "It's time you told her. . . ." The child comes to understand and also helps her grandfather with his problem regarding the number on his arm. The man wears long-sleeved shirts even in hot weather, but the girl tries to get him to change, explaining, "You shouldn't be ashamed to let people see your number. You didn't do anything wrong. It's the Nazis who should be ashamed."

The photographer is the child of survivors and the young girl posing is her own daughter. The grandfather (not actually related) is also a survivor and has been active in testifying at the Nuremberg trials and the trial of Adolf Eichmann. Here is a skillful attempt to tell the truth about an unbelievable horror—to bring the essential facts to the very young without terrifying them about tomorrow. It is a successful attempt that bridges emotion with history quite well.

489. Ashabranner, Brent. *Always to Remember: The Story of the Vietnam Veterans Memorial.* Photos by Jennifer Ashabranner. New York: Dodd, 1988. 101 pp. Nonfiction.

Interest level: Age 10+ Reading level: Grades 5–6

A father-daughter team is at work here, telling of the Vietnam Veterans Memorial's evolution in a most touching manner. The father, Brent Ashabranner, lets his voice and questions be heard—should he and other visitors read the notes others have left? Yes, he concludes, in his view the grief was meant quite deliberately to be shared. Putting himself into the narration is an appropriate personal touch that harmonizes well with the other living forces that enabled this wall, designed by a female undergraduate architecture student and paid for exclusively by private donations, to become the most-visited memorial in Washington. It's a very dramatic story, supported by moving photographs provided by daughter Jennifer Ashabranner.

Besides the history of the war itself, there is Jan Scruggs, the veteran who conceived the idea and held a news conference to announce fund-raising 10 years to the day of when he was wounded. And the time the whole project almost fell apart because H. Perot Ross and other big donors didn't like the chosen design. But most touching are the mementos and notes that are left: "I should have been with you guys. I'll see you guys in heaven 'cause we spent our time in hell." No wonder visitors come night and day to this "meeting of earth, sky, and remembered names."

490. Ashabranner, Brent, and Ashabranner, Melissa. *Into a Strange Land: Unaccompanied Refugee Youth in America.* Photos. New York: Dodd, 1987. 96 pp. Nonfiction.

Interest level: Age 10+ Reading level: Grades 5–6

This is a full account of the plight and triumph of recent young refugees who have come here to escape intolerable physical and emotional torture. Citing the history of the United States as a haven, the authors tell of numerous youngsters, mostly Vietnamese, who have escaped their homeland suddenly on boats, and Cambodians, who have arrived from camps. Talking with the teenagers and preteenagers themselves, their foster parents, and agency officials who light their way, the authors discuss the teens' and preteens' past, how foster families are chosen and why they get involved, adjustment for both children and adults to new cultural ways, the depression children may suffer after what seems to be a successful beginning, and sources for strength to get past it. The goal, whether with foster parents or in a group home, is to have a stable environment and gain life skills. Mutual happiness and love are welcome extras, not always forthcoming. Individual stories are moving—the fear of a new arrival who stays in bed three days, the loneliness of an Amerasian who seeks his father in this vast country, and a boy's poignant request to regain lost childhood years when birth records are found, "Do I have to be fifteen?" In this case, the family and agency allow him to live as twelve, in keeping with his needs and behavior.

A dramatic, balanced look at the successes and failures of these life-saving efforts, the end result is an inspirational testament to the human spirit.

491. Auerbacher, Inge. *I Am a Star: Child of the Holocaust.* Illus. by Israel Bernbaum, with additional photos. New York: Prentice-Hall, 1987, hb and pap. 96 pp. Nonfiction.

Interest level: Age 12+ Reading level: Grade 6

This is a moving combination of general and personal history during the Holocaust. As a child Auerbacher was 1 of only 13 people to survive Terezin concentration camp from her original transport of twelve hundred. Amazingly, 3 of the 13 were from her family.

This book differs from other Holocaust memoirs by intertwining rich, varied sources—Auerbacher's own strong, lyrical rhyming poetry, extant photographs of her town and family, and Bernbaum's appropriately crude, stark drawings. Auerbacher conveys the historical reasons behind anti-Semitism with clarity and sparks her narrative with expressive phrases (life or death is decided by "a flick of a finger"). It would have been instructive for Auerbacher to assess why her whole immediate family prevailed; this, however, is a minor flaw in an otherwise highly meaningful ode to the phrase "never again."

492. Avi. *The Fighting Ground.* Illus. by Ellen Thompson. New York: Lippincott, 1984; Trophy, pap. 157 pp. Fiction.

Interest level: Age 11+ Reading level: Grades 5–6

Jonathan is 13 years old, and he desperately wants to fight in the war. His father has already been wounded in battle, and he is afraid to permit Jonathan to leave home. One morning, when Jonathan hears the bell tolling a message, he goes to the tavern in the center of the New Jersey town and joins up with a group of men, led by a corporal, who are going to engage in a battle to try to prevent Hessian soldiers from penetrating into New Jersey. The battle is not at all what Jonathan expected; it is bloody and inglorious. He runs and is captured by three Hessian soldiers.

Ironically, after a while with his captors, Jonathan begins to wonder whose side he is on. The Hessians neither speak nor understand English, but they do not harm Jonathan. When the group reaches a small farmhouse, Jonathan milks a cow, and the four of them drink the milk and eat some bread that was in the kitchen. Jonathan finds a little boy in the barn. He then finds the boy's parents, who have been killed.

Jonathan escapes with the little boy after the soldiers have fallen asleep. He finds the corporal and the other men from his town. It turns out that it was the American corporal who killed the boy's parents, in the belief that they were spies. They were French and spoke no English, and, therefore, could not rebut the corporal's accusations. The corporal forces Jonathan to lead the Americans back to the farmhouse and the sleeping Hessians. Jonathan is sent ahead to make certain that the soldiers are asleep. He awakens them and tries to warn them, but they do not understand him, and they are all killed.

Jonathan returns home, after having heard the corporal and the others exclaim over their "victory." He now understands his father's feelings about fighting in the war. Jonathan has been gone only 24 hours, but this day has changed his life.

The story is written in segments of time rather than in chapters. Some of the segments last only five minutes; the longest is four hours. This structure dramatically demonstrates how important time is, and how conditions of life can change in a battle from one moment to the next. The book is a telling indictment of war, although it never discusses the merits of either side, or indicates what the causes or issues of the war are. It is important for children to understand that the American Revolution, although it is often painted as a glorious conflict, was as dirty and, at times, as meaningless as any other war.

493. Bauer, Marion Dane. *Rain of Fire.* New York: Clarion, 1983. 153 pp. Fiction.

Interest level: Age 11+ Reading level: Grade 6

Steve and his older brother, Matthew, were very close, until Matthew went to fight in World War II. Then, when Matthew returns he is morose and almost surly. He doesn't want to talk about his experiences in the war, and he seems to lack the energy even to go out to look for a job. Steve boasts about Matthew's exploits in the war, knowing that these are inventions that he has concocted so that his friends won't think badly of Matthew, and so that Celestino, a bully, will be impressed.

At one point, in an attempt to stop the war between Steve and his peers, Matthew passionately cries out against war and talks about its horrors. He confesses to being ashamed of what he had to do in the war. Steve foolishly constructs a series of lies about Matthew to make up for his inability to face the fact that Matthew killed people. Steve's "friends," under Celestino's leadership, construct a letter to J. Edgar Hoover, reporting Matthew's allegedly anti-American statements and actions.

After a series of terrible incidents, including the killing of the family cat, Steve finally learns that it is not possible to hurt someone else without hurting yourself. The book is a serious indictment of war. It is also a look at the effects of lying and concealing important information. Further, it reveals the damage that can occur when children are left confused and uncomprehending of adults' feelings.

494. Beatty, Patricia. *Charley Skedaddle.* New York: Morrow, 1987. 186 pp. Fiction.

Interest level: Age 11+ Reading level: Grade 5

Charley enlists in the Union army partly to avenge his brother's death at the Battle of Gettysburg, partly to escape his Bowery existence, and partly to see battle. He becomes a drummer boy, but longs to be a regular soldier, even though he can't help but notice how much drinking and gambling goes on in the camp. When he finally does see battle, he shoots a man and is so traumatized by this that he runs away from the army.

He is captured by the Confederates, but is released because of his young age. He wanders into the home of an old woman, with whom he stays, and whose life he saves when she is in an accident. He proves his courage and his character, and then he moves on to California, vowing to return to settle in the Blue Ridge Mountains when he is ready.

The story revolves around the strength of the two protagonists, the old woman and the young boy. It is persuasive and authentic. The author provides notes at the end that demonstrate the research that substantiates the events, actions, and incidental information in the story. The book's perspective on the war is important for young readers to understand.

495. Bergman, Tamar. *The Boy from Over There.* Trans. by Hillel Halkin. Boston: Houghton Mifflin, 1988. 182 pp. Fiction.

Interest level: Age 10+ Reading level: Grades 5–6

The setting is an Israeli kibbutz in 1948, just after the end of World War II and at the inception of the Arab-Israeli war, following the proclamation of Israel's independence and the partition of Palestine. We are introduced to a group of children who have lived on this kibbutz since birth. Avram, a newcomer from "over there," a survivor of the Holocaust, arrives with his Uncle Misha. Avram has been emotionally damaged by having to be in hiding for most of his young years, from seeing his father killed, and from not knowing what has happened to his mother since she was taken away to a hospital after the liberation of his town in Poland. He clings to Misha for a long time, and then forms a friendship with Rina, another child from the kibbutz. Rina's father has been killed in action in World War II. The two children share the feeling that their missing parents will one day return. The events of the story lead to their final understanding that their missing parents are, indeed, dead and that they must learn to bear that loss.

The writing is very moving and specific in its communication of the spirit and energy of the people of the kibbutz. We are introduced to a number of characters who have suffered losses of enormous impact, but who have managed, with the support of their comrades, to overcome their anguish. The author, by portraying characters who are far from angelic, helps the reader to understand that ordinary people, not saints and martyrs, endured these devasting events and emerged to lead constructive lives.

The agony of constant warfare and lack of security are presented here in a style that is intimate and straightforward. The author and translator convey their passion without seeming to lose a balanced perspective. This is an excellent addition to the literature about the aftermath of the Holocaust. It is also a valuable book to help people better understand the as-yet unended conflict in the bloody area of the Middle East.

496. Bernbaum, Israel. *My Brother's Keeper: The Holocaust Through the Eyes of an Artist.* Illus. by the author. New York: Putnam, 1985. 64 pp. Nonfiction.

Interest level: Age 9+ Reading level: Grade 5

This is truly an unusual book. A survivor has created symbolically laden paintings of Holocaust scenes, which he has shared with children in classrooms and, now, in book form. (Bernbaum dedicates his book to the 1.5 million children who didn't survive the Holocaust.) His aim in sharing is twofold: to prevent such a tragedy from recurring by knowing the past, and to learn the lesson of being one's brother's keeper.

The narrative is addressed directly to the reader, informing that two out of three Jews in Europe were killed. As Bernbaum transfers his feelings to canvas, red is the predominant color in the busy paintings, as the world, raging with flames, becomes soaked in blood. For Bernbaum, the Holocaust is "a fire engulfing any living being in its path." Much of the material in the narrative and artwork concerns the Warsaw Ghetto. He explains that where 80,000 previously lived, once the Jews were forced to live in a ghetto, 500,000 were jammed into the same living space. The sources for the paintings include newspaper photographs, some famous, such as the tragic shot of a young, shorts-clad boy on the street with the yellow Star of David on his coat, his hands up in the air before the police.

There are six paintings. They are titled: The Warsaw Ghetto Streets 1943; On Both Sides of the Warsaw Ghetto Wall; The Jewish Mother in the Ghetto; The Jewish Children in Ghettos and Death Camps; The Warsaw Ghetto Uprising—Heroism and Resistance; and My Brother's Keeper. The book's impact comes from Bernbaum's discussion of each painting. He first discusses each as a whole and then breaks it up into segments, showing the symbolism and inspiration for each piece. Newspaper and archival photographs (some of German origin) also demonstrate the times. The strongest works concern the Warsaw Uprising, in which young Jews fought for five weeks, successfully keeping the mighty German armies from destroying them, although they had few arms with which to keep the Nazis at bay.

The symbolism in each painting is broad-ranging. Some figures are symbols of continuity, for example, praying people, lighting candles. Other symbolic figures delve into details of history, for example, the silence of the Polish church and indifference of world powers to what was happening.

The paintings as a whole, in their agony, ask, "Civilization, where are you?"

Bernbaum has a flowing narrative style, in which he answers readers' questions. A sample: "You may ask: Is this possible? Aren't these images the pure imagination of an artist?" He answers the readers' questions: "I wish they were. Unfortunately, my images are only a slight shadow of the reality."

497. Buchan, Stuart. *All Our Yesterdays.* New York: Crosswinds, 1987, pap. 154 pp. Fiction.

Interest level: Age 12+ Reading level: Grade 7

Julie is now 15 years old. When she was five, she and her mother fled to England from the burning city of Singapore, where her family held estates. Her father remained and, along with many other Europeans, was imprisoned by the Japanese. Now Julie has returned, summoned by her father for a visit. Her mother died of heart failure, and Julie has not seen her father in 10 years.

Although a number of the characters in this book speak of the torture and deprivation of the war period, the reader is given little information. It is unclear what the war was, who the combatants were, and what the issues were. It looks as if, with the exception of some former landowners who were not very good managers, the status quo has returned. Julie's aunt has retained her faithful Chinese servants; Julie's father is wealthy, though sullen and seemingly scarred by his imprisonment. He has not until now sent for Julie, and we never satisfactorily find out why. He mourns the death of his wife, but we don't know much else about him.

We also meet a young man, Douglas, a year older than Julie, who remained in Malaya and was also imprisoned. He, too, seems scarred by the experience, but he is spoken of with a mixture of admiration and mystery. We never discover the mystery, but he and Julie fall in love. His father has decided to send Douglas to school in England, but he has not shared this decision with his son. Julie inadvertently reveals the secret, whereupon Douglas disappears. He reappears, and he and Julie go "home" to England together.

Although the book alludes to the devastation of war, it does not manage to convey it to the reader. The author's perspective seems to focus on the romance between the two attractive young people, with an exotic setting. No issues of depth are raised here; it is assumed that the rich white people deserve the land and the bulk of the wealth of the country. No character is three-dimensional. Not a book to be used for anything more than light reading.

498. Chaikin, Miriam. *Aviva's Piano.* Illus. by Yossi Abolafia. New York: Clarion, 1986. 43 pp. Fiction.

Interest level: Ages 7–10 Reading level: Grade 3

Aviva's piano has finally arrived from Argentina, where Aviva and her family have lived until their recent move to a kibbutz in Israel, near the Lebanese border. Aviva has waited months for her piano to arrive, and now that it is here she is dismayed to learn that it won't fit through any of the doors or windows of her house. In the midst of this dilemma, the members of the kibbutz must go to an air raid shelter because their kibbutz is under attack. After the attack, when the damage is assessed, it is discovered that a cow was killed and that one rocket has broken the upstairs wall of Aviva's house. Now the piano can be hoisted into the house, and Aviva rejoices that "something good came from something bad."

The story flavorfully conveys the life-style and activities of a kibbutz. It also authentically portrays the situation of having to live with the constant threat of possible annihilation. It is sad to read that these children are surprised to hear about a kibbutz near Tiberias that does not have a bomb shelter; such shelters are a fact of life for these children.

The story focuses on the arrival of the piano and, in so doing, makes the issue of war and its devastation a sidelight. This can be an excellent entré for adults to discuss the implications of the kibbutz children's different interactions and comments. It is a gentle but telling commentary on today's crises.

499. Chaikin, Miriam. *A Nightmare in History: The Holocaust, 1933–1945.* Illus. with photos and prints. New York: Clarion, 1987. 128 pp. Nonfiction.

Interest level: Age 10+ Reading level: Grade 6

Using simple, elegant writing that denotes deep understanding, this noted writer on Jewish themes tackles the hardest subject of all, the horror of one life disappearing and of being sucked into an unimaginably terrifying barbaric decline in its place. Her contribution is to bring a historical perspective, presenting a unique study of Hitler, who "stood out in no way as a boy." She also examines (from the time of Noah onward) how group differences began and the multiple directions in which anti-Semitism rose. Her chapter divisions are such that they powerfully drive home the little-realized concept that this was not a hatred merely gone wild. No, the Nazis planned the extermination of the Jews in elaborately charted stages. Whether it's discussion of school expulsion and ghettoization in stage one, or concentration camp lineups left and right in later stages, Chaikin keeps the book strong and vibrant with examples from real families.

Some of the individuals profiled perish, some survive. Although we know the protagonists die, the stories are rousing nonetheless, as in the account of the Warsaw Ghetto Uprising coinciding with the Passover seder: "Pulling triggers, throwing grenades, dodging bullets, they shouted to each other over the gunfire the events of the Exodus, telling how Moses freed the Jewish slaves in Egypt and led them out to freedom." A fine book. Extensive bibliography.

500. Clapp, Patricia. *The Tamarack Tree.* New York: Lothrop, 1986. 214 pp. Fiction.
Interest level: Age 12+ Reading level: Grades 6–7

Rosemary Monica Stafford Leigh, age 17, begins her narration of the story in Vicksburg, Mississippi, while that city is under siege during the Civil War. She and her older brother are British. They emigrated after both their parents died. From the beginning, Rosemary is appalled by the idea of slavery. Her brother tries to assure her that most slave owners are kind people and that she should try to understand Southerners' point of view.

Although Rosemary maintains her stance against slavery, she does make many friends in Mississippi, and she helps nurse the wounded during the war. Interwoven with the story are mentions and comments about the battles and the politics of the war. The ugliness of the war comes through clearly as Rosemary and her friends cope with the siege and afterward help with the wounded.

Rosemary is an excellent guide through the intricacies of the issues and the subtleties of human interaction. Included in the characters are southern whites, free blacks, and Northerners. All are treated respectfully by the author. This book is an excellent example of historical fiction; it teaches us, and at the same time we are involved in the story.

501. Collier, James Lincoln, and Collier, Christopher. *War Comes to Willy Freeman.* New York: Delacorte, 1983; Dell, pap. 178 pp. Fiction.
Interest level: Ages 9–12 Reading level: Grades 4–5

Willy, a young black girl freed by law because of her father's willingness to fight in the Revolutionary War, is forced to grow up quickly when she witnesses her father's death at the hands of British soldiers. On her return home from the battle, she discovers that her mother has been kidnapped by some other British soldiers and taken as a prisoner to New York City. Willy dresses as a boy and goes to search for her mother. Her search leads her to Fraunces Tavern in New York, where she is aided by Fraunces and a young worker, Horace.

Eventually Willy must cope with the death of her mother and with an attempt to return her to slavery. Her bravery and survival strategies are commendable. Her father and mother are slightly ambiguous characters: Her father is somewhat abusive of her mother and shows poor judgment; her mother seems stronger than she really is.

The authors—historians—have provided a close look at the ugliness of any war. They have also raised some disturbing issues about blacks and their involvement in the war. The soldiers who kidnap Willy's mother are black. They trust the British government more than the Americans to treat them as people after the war. The language the authors use ("darkies" and "nigger") is offensive to a modern audience. The authors explain their usage as the need for authenticity. Nevertheless, the language detracts from the message of the book and contributes to the demeaning of blacks. The authors probably could have avoided this offense, and the book would be the stronger for it.

502. DeFord, Deborah H., and Stout, Harry S. *An Enemy among Them.* Boston: Houghton Mifflin, 1987. 203 pp. Fiction.

Interest level: Age 10+ Reading level: Grade 5

It is always useful when a book contributes yet another perspective to a historical event. In this story about the Revolutionary War, readers get the opportunity to learn about the German-speaking community in Pennsylvania and their feelings regarding the Hessian mercenaries who were hired by the British to fight against the American colonists. We are also introduced to some Hessian soldiers who are not the beasts and cold-hearted individuals that they were reported to be in the newspapers of the time and in U.S. history books.

The story tells of one family living near Reading, Pennsylvania, whose sons fight for the Americans, and the Hessian prisoner they take in, who has fought for the British. Many points of view about the war are aired by the characters in their discussions and arguments with each other. One man, a former friend of the family, is a British spy. Christian, the Hessian prisoner, is responsible for the death of John, one of the brothers, but before John dies he and the Hessian become close friends and Christian winds up in the American army.

Readers cannot help but infer from the events of the story that there is often very little difference between enemies, that it is people's common humanity that emerges, even in times of warfare and bloodshed.

503. Dr. Seuss. *The Butter Battle Book.* Illus. by the author. New York: Random, 1984. 42 pp. Fiction.

Interest level: Ages 5–8 Reading level: Grade 2

The Yooks and the Zooks, two countries divided by a wall, are similar in all things except that the Yooks butter their bread on the top side and the

Zooks butter their bread on the bottom. Because of this crucial difference a fight begins and escalates to a war. The war intensifies until, at the end of the story, a Yook and a Zook stand on either side of the wall, each with a powerful bomb in his hand. The author leaves the outcome in doubt, and we never know if either side ever drops the bomb, or if they come to their senses in time to avoid total annihilation.

This allegory of our own times is meant to represent the futility and inanity of global confrontation. As with many allegories, the points are so oversimplified as to lose much of their impact. Although the story builds dramatically, the issue over the buttering of bread is nothing like issues of slavery, freedom, economic deprivation, and greed. The combatants are clearly more alike than different, and that could have been a powerful message had it been highlighted or articulated. Nevertheless, the message comes across that here are two nations that are brought to the brink of self-destruction over an issue that is not important, and that they arrived at their current situation through an ever-escalating development of weapons.

504. Finkelstein, Norman H. *Remember Not to Forget: A Memory of the Holocaust.* Illus. by Lois Hokanson and Lars Hokanson. New York: Watts, 1985. 32 pp. Nonfiction.
Interest level: Ages 9–13 Reading level: Grade 6

The strength of Finkelstein's convictions comes through in his every word. Finkelstein, a Hebraic scholar, writes with poetry of his feeling that the world must never forget: "The shocked world could only wonder how such a terrible event could have happened. It was an unimaginable tragedy, horrible and unbelievable; it was a savage firestorm of raging intensity—a Holocaust."

The book offers a historical overview, starting from 70 A.D. when the Jewish capital was destroyed, spewing the Jews into the diaspora. From this more scattered living pattern arose anti-Semitism, Finkelstein asserts, and from this came the most horrifying episode in long-standing anti-Semitic feeling, the Holocaust of the Third Reich. The history concludes with the establishment of the State of Israel, and, within its borders, the Yad Vashem Memorial and the Yom Hashoa yearly memorial day.

Woodcuts of simple clarity support the narrative well, bringing understanding to younger children. The tone is instructional but not pedantic, giving warning but not hysteria. For example,

> Anti-Semitism means a hatred of Jewish people, their religion, and their culture.
>
> Its causes are fear and lack of understanding.
>
> Its symptoms are name calling, unfair treatment, and violence.
>
> Even when the disease of anti-Semitism seems cured, the symptoms could break out again at any time.

505. Freedman, Russell. *Lincoln: A Photobiography.* Photos. New York: Clarion, 1987. 160 pp. Nonfiction.

Interest level: Age 10+ Reading level: Grade 6

This wonderful biography of Abraham Lincoln is so engrossing it almost reads like a novel. Freedman visited all the sites and archives associated with the sixteenth president and from his broad research has brought forth a lively account of his life. Complex issues are brought to bear, such as those he had to deal with during the Civil War. The young reader is also trusted with matters of the heart that are equally complex and are usually discussed only in books for adults, for example, how a born storyteller and wit can also be so melancholy. At every turn, Freedman makes us feel the way those who were connected with Lincoln might have felt, too—those who met him in stores, those who encouraged him to try politics, those who sadly waved to the funeral train. Lincoln's entire family history comes to life—the moving from territory to territory in search of homesteading, the death of his mother, the coming of a kind stepmother, his many jobs before becoming a statesman and lawyer, his courtship, his marriage, his children. This is a book to read again and again. The masterful telling is followed by a sampling from Lincoln's voluminous writings, a list of historical Lincoln sites, bibliography, index.

506. Fritz, Jean. *China's Long March: 6,000 Miles of Danger.* Illus. by Yang Zhr Cheng. New York: Putnam, 1988. 124 pp. Nonfiction.

Interest level: Age 10+ Reading level: Grade 5

Few authors can make history come alive the way Fritz does. Her series of books on American Revolutionary heroes is both entertaining and informative. Her autobiographical works on her youth in China illuminate the setting and time and help children understand the sense of leaving one's home, exotic as it may be, and coming into a new culture. In *China's Long March* she has provided young readers access to a period of history and an event of enormous magnitude that is rarely studied in the public schools. Because of her understanding of the people and of the process of history, Fritz is able to communicate the complexity of the issues without losing sight of the human element. The fact that she interviewed many survivors of the Long March adds to the authenticity of the work. She adds perspective to her admiration of Mao when she describes the Cultural Revolution, and that most people admit that it was a mistake. Most of all she conveys her respect for the people, the issues, and the facts.

507. Garrigue, Sheila. *The Eternal Spring of Mr. Ito.* New York: Bradbury, 1985. 163 pp. Fiction.

Interest level: Age 11+ Reading level: Grades 6–7

The story takes place in Vancouver, Canada, where Sara Warren, an English girl, comes to stay with her aunt and uncle during World War II. The book chronicles her experiences during the war, but more importantly it explores her relationship with Mr. Ito, a Japanese gardener who has worked for her aunt and uncle for many years, and who saved her uncle's life during World War I.

Mr. Ito's collection of bonsai trees represents his Japanese heritage, and his 200-year-old tree, which has been in his family for generations, becomes a symbol of Sara's hopes for the future and Mr. Ito's eternal life. After the bombing of Pearl Harbor, Mr. Ito is banished from the Warrens' house. Sara's uncle destroys all of his bonsai trees except for the ancient tree, which Mr. Ito manages to take with him, and one tree that Sara manages to rescue that Mr. Ito helped her to start.

Mr. Ito's family has been sent to an internment camp, but he refuses to go, and he hides in a cave to wait for death rather than sacrifice his pride. Sara finds him and he explains to her many of his Buddhist beliefs, including his conviction that his karma will pass on to a new life. When Sara returns again to bring him food, she finds that he has died. She takes his ancient bonsai tree and manages to deliver it to his family in the camp so that it can be passed on to the next generation.

The issues here of the bitter plight of the Japanese Canadians as a result of the bombing of Pearl Harbor is dealt with directly. It is difficult to believe that Sara's uncle would be so narrow as to blame Mr. Ito for what the Japanese government is doing. It is especially difficult since Mr. Ito had saved his life. In the end Mr. Warren begins to question the treatment of the Japanese Canadians in the internment camps, but this, too, is difficult to believe, given his previous irrational response. On the other hand, it is easy to see why Mr. Ito's daughter, Helen, is cynical about their ever reclaiming their confiscated property and their shattered lives. The devastation of war extends far beyond the battlefield, and this story palpably demonstrates that fact.

508. Gehrts, Barbara. *Don't Say a Word.* Trans. by Elizabeth D. Crawford. New York: McElderry, 1986. 169 pp. Fiction.

Interest level: Age 12+ Reading level: Grade 7

The story is set in Berlin during World War II. The protagonists are a family that is not Jewish but hates Hitler and the Nazis. The father is active in his opposition to Hitler's regime. The story tells of the dreadful events of the era as seen through the eyes of Anna, the teenaged daughter. Among the terrible things that happen is that Anna's friend Ruth and her family commit suicide rather than face the certain torture and death that they feel will come to them because they are Jews. Anna is, of course, devastated by this event, which is a precursor to her boyfriend's death on the Russian front, and, worst of all, her father's arrest by the Gestapo and his eventual execution.

Because the story reflects the author's personal experiences, it is unmistakably authentic. Some information contained here is shocking: The family is required to pay the costs of the father's imprisonment and execution! The author includes a copy of the bill in the text.

Although details of daily interaction and particular events are described, nowhere is there an inkling of the massive nature of the Holocaust. Readers will have to consult other books to find information about Hitler's plan and the course of the war. But just as Anne Frank's story tells more about the horror of the time than an entire chronicle of the war, so this book, with its focus on this one German family, brings us into proximity with the nightmare and bestiality of Hitler's Germany.

509. Gilmore, Kate. *Remembrance of the Sun.* Boston: Houghton Mifflin, 1986. 246 pp. Fiction.

Interest level: Age 14+ Reading level: Grade 8

Although this is fiction it is based on the author's experience in Iran during the late 1970s. The plot is simple—an American girl, Jill, and an Iranian boy, Shaheen, both talented musicians, fall in love. He is committed to revolution against the Shah; she deplores violence, especially when it endangers someone she loves. Their relationship evolves slowly and authentically so that it is believable to the reader. The characters are well developed and multidimensional. Jill's parents, caught in the conflict, are also presented realistically. In the end, Jill and her parents must leave Iran, and Shaheen has learned some hard lessons about the revolution.

The book could serve as motivation for young readers to research the complex issue of Iran and its current situation. It might be used to bring life and relevance into the study of the current conflict.

510. Gordon, Sheila. *Waiting for the Rain: A Novel of South Africa.* New York: Orchard, 1987. 214 pp. Fiction.

Interest level: Age 12+ Reading level: Grade 7

Frikkie is the white nephew of the owners of the farm. Tengo is a black employee who is the same age as Frikkie. The setting is South Africa. The story clearly outlines the inequality that poisons the country. Frikkie attends school free of charge. Tengo would love to go to school, but first, it is costly for blacks to attend, and second, there is no school nearby.

Despite the differences in their societal positions, Frikkie and Tengo are friends. As time passes the two boys are prepared to take their adult positions in life, but the hostile conditions in South Africa intervene, and one day the two young men meet as adversaries in battle. Frikkie is pressed into mandatory military service, and Tengo is an "agitator." In the end, although they both have their own point of view, based on their heritage, the two men remain friends but acknowledge that their country is in terrible trouble.

Nothing is resolved in the story, as nothing is resolved in the dreadful violence of apartheid in South Africa. Much of the book is wordy, especially the end, where the two young men talk at each other, and the story becomes tract. But this is an important issue for young readers to know about, thus it is a worthwhile book to help them understand some of the complexities of the South African battleground.

511. Haugaard, Erik Christian. *A Boy's Will.* Illus. by Troy Howell. Boston: Houghton Mifflin, 1983. 41 pp. Fiction.

Interest level: Ages 7–10 Reading level: Grades 3–4

The story takes place on the island of Valentia off the coast of Ireland during the American Revolutionary War years. Patrick, a young Irish boy, decides to go against his punitive and unloving grandfather and warn John Paul Jones of an ambush by the British navy. He steals out of his house late one night, takes a small boat, and races against time and the sea to reach the American ships before they are spotted by the British.

The story really revolves around the young boy's longing for his dead mother and father and his unhappiness with his grandfather. The boy, a Catholic, always empathizes with the underdog, whereas his grandfather, a smuggler, hates Catholics and is opposed to the American rebels' cause. It is clear that Patrick is aiding the rebels, not so much out of conviction as from desperation with his way of life. In the end he accepts John Paul Jones's invitation to stay with the rebels, but it is with mixed feelings that he leaves his own land and the site of his mother's grave.

Erik Christian Haugaard also provides young readers with other aspects of the American Revolutionary War and with some little-known information about the strategies and issues involved in the war.

512. Horgan, Dorothy. *The Edge of War.* New York: Oxford University Press, 1987. 112 pp. Fiction.

Interest level: Age 11+ Reading level: Grade 6

Because Anna and her younger sister and brother are dark-haired they are taunted and harassed by the other children in their German village. They are called "Gypsies" and "Jews," and they are pelted with stones and ostracized. (The author explains that the family is descended from Spaniards.) Their family is further suspect because the parents are not Nazi party members. Although the father is an officer in the German army, he, too, is treated badly because of his refusal to join the other officers in their admiration of Hitler.

The story tells of what ordinary German people endured during the war. It presents an interesting perspective, because most of the books about this era describe the Holocaust and its horrors. This family experiences loss: Their mother is killed in a bombing attack on the hotel where she was staying for just a few days. They also almost starve to death and witness many hard events.

Some of the sections of the book are confusing because they are left undeveloped. The family's escape from the eastern front where the mother was a teacher is managed with suspiciously little official notice. This is especially strange because they take up residence in their old house, and no one detects the discrepancy. At another point Anna discovers where her father is, but despite the fact that she manages to get to the hospital where he is kept and that she takes great risks to do so, she does not attempt to see him; she is content simply to know that he is alive.

Most of the family survives the war. Anna and her siblings are rescued by the Americans, and there is a strange lack of affect in the rescue. As a matter of fact, this is one of the disturbing qualities evident in the entire book: There seems to be little emotion evidenced, other than relief at the end of the war. Yes, the children wet their beds when their mother dies, but other than this physiological reaction, their feelings are unrecorded. Perhaps the author wants to convey a stoicism, but it seems hardly appropriate.

Another disturbing factor in the book is the objective way with which the elimination of the Jews is dealt. Anna and her family have been taking food to the starving Jewish family confined to living in squalor. But they make no attempt to do anything else, or even to communicate with their former neighbors. When, at the end of the book, the Jewish family's son, Joseph, who had emigrated to America, arrives at the family's former home, Anna remembers seeing a violin case half-buried in the ground outside the house. She leads the young man to the spot, and it is still there, with the violin inside in pristine condition. Because of this wonder, Joseph secures false papers for Anna's friend to protect him from having to return to Poland.

The events are believable but without passion or impact. It is difficult to summon much response to a family whose major accomplishment was survival. At the end of the war they start discussing some of the hard questions without coming to any conclusions. But perhaps that in itself is important. They promise to keep on asking the questions, but there is no guarantee, and very little indication that the ordinary German people have learned anything or will guard against monstrous things from happening again.

513. Kuchler-Silberman, Lena. *My Hundred Children.* Adapted by David C. Gross. New York: Laurel-Leaf, 1987, pap. 240 pp. Nonfiction.

Interest level: Age 12+ Reading level: Grade 7

Trying to find reason to go on living after her family died in the Holocaust, Kuchler-Silberman directed a postwar orphanage for 100 of the few Jewish children who remained alive in Poland. There she tried to give physical and emotional wholeness to these children who had lived in closets or forests and who often had seen their parents killed. It will not surprise many readers to learn that she and her charges encountered continuing aggressive anti-Semitism, in which the authorities would not care for them yet wouldn't let them leave the country. Finally leaving Poland for safer Czechoslovakia forms the crux of the first-person narrative, but as much drama is found in moving vignettes, such as the intoxicated hilarity the children and staff share the night they all dress alike in pink flannel pajamas, their first such warmth after the war. Kuchler-Silberman is truly a hero; her accomplishments were deservedly honored in a made-for-television movie starring Lee Remick.

514. Lawrence, Louise. *Children of the Dust.* New York: Harper, 1985. 183 pp. Fiction.

Interest level: Age 12+ Reading level: Grade 7

The starkness, deprivation, and terror of the aftermath of a nuclear blast are chillingly conveyed in this engrossing story. The book is divided into three parts, each of them symbolizing a separate phase of existence in a world devastated by the nuclear holocaust. Each section of the book has as its main character a representative of the situation, each one a member of the same family.

The first section, "Sarah," chronicles the immediate survivors' attempts to stay alive. Only Catherine, a young girl, manages to survive. Sarah, her older sister, sees that Catherine will live, and she takes her to the home of another survivor, Johnson, before killing herself and their younger brother. Catherine stays with Johnson, and together they find more people who escaped the immediate effects of the bomb, and with whom they build a utopian community.

In the next section, "Ophelia," it turns out that Catherine's father has survived in a shelter built to house hundreds of people. They have lived there for years, under a dictatorship, and are now commandeering food from the people who survived on the outside. Ophelia represents a dying form of society. She and her father meet Catherine and do what they can to influence their fellow shelter-mates to change their way of governing.

The last section, "Simon," represents the last of the homo sapiens part of the family and, indeed, of humankind. Simon is Catherine's grand-nephew, although they have never met until now. All of the people on the outside of the shelter are mutants. They are apelike in appearance and have fine white hair covering their bodies. The hair serves to protect them from the sun's killing rays. They are telepathic and can move objects by means of psychokinetic energy. They have designed a community where all people share with each other and are gentle and productive. The children of the community are repulsed by Simon. Their parents explain that he is more to be pitied than feared. He knows himself to be a freak among a new breed, homo superior.

The premise of the story is a dramatic one. It does not hold out the romantic hope that human beings can survive a nuclear war. It builds on the destruction of the human race by envisioning the evolution of a new group, one that will have learned from the mistakes of the past and build a functioning, self-constructive new world. There are lessons to be learned here, and they are all the more powerful because the story is so well crafted.

515. Meltzer, Milton. *Ain't Gonna Study War No More: The Story of America's Peace Seekers.* New York: Harper, 1985. 288 pp. Nonfiction.

Interest level: Age 12+ Reading level: Grades 6–7

As always, Meltzer's writing is eloquent and forceful, the result of exquisite research with primary documents. Here he looks at patriotism and its many expressions, highlighting the response to war known as conscientious objector. The book begins with one young man's letter about resistance: "Draft registration is preparation for war. To sign a registration card is to sign a promise—a promise to the United States government that it may take your body at any time, for any war it may see fit." In covering numerous periods in history, Meltzer compiles a book about courage—the courage to personally resist and to organize larger resistance in what he calls "a quarrelsome world." Among the eras discussed to show humankind's long propensity for war are biblical times and the Middle Ages, but most of the book deals with the United States: the Quakers, the Revolution, the Mexican War, choosing between two evils in the Civil War, the World Wars, Vietnam, the antinuclear movement, and so on.

Throughout, there is a balance between the accomplishments that momentum of large numbers can bring with the power of individuals. Examples of people who resisted war include: Fanny Fern Andrews who formed an American School Peace League to spread international understanding to children in the early 1900s and Senator Hatfield's calling the domino theory false in the Vietnam struggle and becoming influential in the war's eventual end. And as in all of Meltzer's work, there is fine interweaving of social forces at play in each period, bringing necessary complexity to what could have been merely propaganda. Bibliography.

516. Miklowitz, Gloria D. *After the Bomb.* New York: Scholastic, 1985, pap. 156 pp. Fiction.

Interest level: Age 12+ Reading level: Grade 6

In an isolated, nonwar-related incident, an atomic bomb has been dropped on Los Angeles, and Philip, his brother, Matt, his mother, and Matt's girlfriend, Cara, are caught in the blast together. Philip has always felt inferior to his brother, but in this crisis Philip responds more dependably than Matt. His mother is badly burned, and Philip manages to get her to a hospital and onto a helicopter to be flown to a burn unit. He also takes charge of an emergency procedure to bring water to the hospital. The story ends with the three teenagers going off, under Philip's leadership, to search for the boys' father, who had been at work when the bomb went off.

Miklowitz read a number of books and interviewed experts to try to piece out what would happen in the event a single one-megaton bomb fell on a large city. Supposedly the winds around Los Angeles could keep radiation from descending in drastic proportions onto the ground, but it seems hard to believe that people could emerge from shelters and basements and be safe outdoors. Although Miklowitz includes many details of the ravages of the bomb, the major elements of this story involve the human interactions between the brothers and among the survivors.

517. Miklowitz, Gloria D. *After the Bomb: Week One.* New York: Scholastic, 1987, pap. 137 pp. Fiction.

Interest level: Age 12+ Reading level: Grade 6

In a sequel to *After the Bomb* (see entry above), the author continues the story of Philip and his family, who were in Los Angeles when a nuclear bomb fell on the city. In this story Philip manages to locate his father, who had been in Pasadena when the bomb struck.

This book conveys the impossibility of dealing with the necessity of evacuating a large city in the event of a nuclear attack. It does not deal at all with the danger of fallout, because supposedly that will not become a problem until a few days after the bomb explodes. The story convincingly portrays how some people rise to the occasion heroically, and some people take advantage of the confusion and fear to loot and commit acts of violence. As in *After the Bomb,* a major element in the story is the relationship between the brothers, Matt and Philip.

518. Moore, Melinda, and Olsen, Laurie, with the Citizens Policy Center Nuclear Action for Youth Project. *Our Future at Stake: A Teenager's Guide to Stopping the Nuclear Arms Race.* Photos. Philadelphia: New Society, 1985, hb and pap. 72 pp. Nonfiction.

Interest level: Age 12+ Reading level: Grade 6

This book is divided into sections, the first defining "the problem," and the second asking "What can I do?" In the first, the potential problems of nuclear armament are seen through the eyes of teenagers age 13 through 16. Among their topics are the big debate over arms, the cost of the arms race, how wars start, what the bomb is. The second section involves educating and organizing others, how to amass voting power, how the government decides on its spending, and influencing the media. This is an attractive book, with sidebars including cartoons and insightful quotes from the famous and nonfamous regarding nuclear issues. Although the tone promotes peace and disarmament, there is no evidence of a sledgehammer approach. Instead there are voluminous charts and appendix materials. Included are a glossary, chronologies of U.S.-U.S.S.R. relations and key dates in arms control and disarmament, list of government agencies, resources, bibliography.

519. Naidoo, Beverly. *Journey to Jo'burq: A South African Story.* Illus. by Eric Velasquez. New York: Lippincott, 1985. 77 pp. Fiction.

Interest level: Age 10+ Reading level: Grades 4–5

Naledi, who is 13, and her 9-year-old brother, Tiro, journey alone to Johannesburg to fetch their mother to save the life of their baby sister. They encounter the terrible manifestations of racism that apartheid results in. They learn of the deaths of blacks, including children, who fight the system. They are exposed to the spirit of many of their people who are determined, one day, to change the system. In the end, their journey completed, their baby sister on the road to health, they vow to fortify themselves for the long struggle ahead.

In simple and dignified language, the author tells a story that is bound to have an impact on young readers. Too few books are available that inform this audience about the situation in South Africa. This story makes an excellent contribution.

520. Neimark, Anne E. *One Man's Valor: Leo Baeck and the Holocaust.* New York: Lodestar, 1986. 128 pp. Nonfiction.

Interest level: Ages 10–16 Reading level: Grades 5–6

This true tale is part of the Jewish Biography series. Leo Baeck is aptly the epitome of what it means to be noble. As Chief Rabbi of Berlin, Baeck chose to stay in Germany during the Nazi era, using his influence as a renowned scholar to help others escape. We see his dilemmas and are moved by them: Should he share the truth about Auschwitz? (He doesn't, favoring hope over despair.) Should he save family possessions when the Nazis will inevitably destroy them? (He doesn't, dumping silver menorahs and other treasured pieces into the sea so the Nazis can't seize them or the spirit they represent.)

Neimark uses Jewish symbols effectively to relate response to the Nazi menace. Baeck risks typhus in order to keep it from others; he spends more than two years in a concentration camp as the cost of pursuing his philosophy of patience and imagination in the face of adversity. But in the end, that philosophy, coupled with inordinate hard work, wins out. Baeck saves thousands of people from death.

There are few nonfiction biographies for this age group on the Holocaust and few books offer so much food for thought.

521. Orlev, Uri. *The Island on Bird Street.* Trans. by Hillel Halkin. Boston: Houghton Mifflin, 1984. 162 pp. Fiction.

Interest level: Age 10+ Reading level: Grade 6

This story of survival is set in the Warsaw ghetto during the Nazi Holocaust. Eleven-year-old Alex is in hiding in the ruins of a bombed-out house. He is alone. His mother has disappeared, but he hopes that his father, who has been taken away by the Germans, will return. During the five months that he lives in the house he feels like a person on a desert island, using his wits and his energy to survive.

The author and translator have done their jobs well. The story reads like an adventure and is all the more compelling because it is based on the author's own experiences. The details of Alex's everyday activities, the dangers he is exposed to, his final reunion with his father, and their escape into the forest to fight with the partisans make for exciting as well as inspiring reading.

522. Perez, N. A. *The Slopes of War: A Novel of Gettysburg.* Boston: Houghton Mifflin, 1984. 202 pp. Fiction.

Interest level: Age 11+ Reading level: Grade 7

This Canadian author has managed to convey an authentic sense of how people felt during the American Civil War. He portrays soldiers and officers on both the Confederate and Union sides, and he also lets the reader in on the events and reactions of the people who lived in Gettysburg at the time of that significant and bloody battle.

We are introduced to a family whose members are divided by the war, but who understand and love each other nevertheless. Perhaps the most important accomplishment of this book is to take war out of the realm of dates and names and place it in the perspective of human interaction. Southerners are seen here to be as much the victims of the war as northerners. The issues are not glossed over, but the human condition overrides the battle lines.

523. Pirtle, Sarah. *An Outbreak of Peace.* Philadelphia: New Society, 1987. 386 pp. Fiction.

Interest level: Age 11+ Reading level: Grade 6

The book chronicles the efforts of a group of students of all ages who take the initiative to create an art display about peace. It is an excellent example of a participatory process. The students form and organize their group without adult intervention. They learn to listen to each other and respect their strengths and differences. And they learn to continue despite setbacks and opposition. One of the book's most significant messages is that we cannot hope to achieve peace when there is hatred and war in one's own heart.

The book is a long one and may be difficult for young readers. At times the characters may seem too good to be true. The book's message is more compelling than its story and may be of value to children who are already trying to do something to win world peace. Those who have not yet been awakened to this issue may find the book more tract than literature.

524. Pringle, Laurence. *Nuclear War: From Hiroshima to Nuclear Winter.* Photos. Hillside, N.J.: Enslow, 1985. 128 pp. Nonfiction.

Interest level: Ages 10–15 Reading level: Grade 6

Tracing the history of nuclear warfare from the bombings of Hiroshima and Nagasaki to today's arms race and nuclear tensions, science writer Pringle takes readers from the beginnings during World War II to the prospects of nuclear winter if there ever were a full-scale nuclear battle. The research is thorough, yet this is more than a cold, scientific look. Pringle examines the lot of survivors in Japan, who have suffered cancer, malformed offspring, premature aging, even social discrimination. Using that background, he takes readers on a journey to a hypothetical city and shows how it would suffer in a limited nuclear war with today's stronger bombing capacity. As for large-scale war, Pringle feels the results are uncontrollable and untestable, but we "continue to uncover more and more unpleasant possibilities." In the end, after looking at the information scientifically, not politically, his point of view is this:

> Human curiosity is strong but nuclear war is not a fit subject for experimentation. There's very little we can learn until it is too late, until the weapons have been used. What we have learned, together with our unproved assumptions, strongly suggests that the nation that starts nuclear war will be making a murder-suicide pact with its opponent and threatening every living thing on earth.

Glossary, bibliography, index.

525. Ramati, Alexander. *And the Violins Stopped Playing: A Story of the Gypsy Holocaust.* New York: Watts, 1986. 237 pp. Fiction.
Interest level: Age 11+ Reading level: Grades 6–7

Told through the voice of Roman Mirga, a Gypsy who survived the Holocaust, this phase of the Nazi terror communicates itself very well. The story details the Gypsies' response, or lack of it, to their impending danger. They see the Nazi extermination of the Jews, but they doubt their informants' warnings that the Gypsies are next. And they are surprisingly callous about the Jews.

Young Roman and his father are among the leaders of the Gypsies who do recognize the Nazi threat. By the force of their persuasion they temporarily save the lives of their tribe, but they are eventually interned in concentration camps where they witness the slaughter of others of their heritage. Roman and his father incur the anger of some of their tribesmen, but in the end they are proven tragically correct. Roman and a few others escape from the camp, but most of the members of his family are killed. In total 500,000 Gypsies were killed in the Holocaust and received no recompense. This book helps to tell their story and makes an important contribution to Holocaust literature.

526. Rogasky, Barbara. *Smoke and Ashes: The Story of the Holocaust.* Illus. with photos and maps. New York: Holiday, 1988. Nonfiction.
Interest level: Age 12+ Reading level: Grade 7

This book examines Hitler's rise to power in the context of long-standing anti-Semitism. Whereas some books move readers by fleshing out stories of individuals, Rogasky eventually gets considerable power from an unexpected source—statistics and lists. A unique feature is comparison with the numbers and shapes of other holocausts—those suffered by American Indians, Armenians, and so forth, but the common denominator (such as relegating one group to lower human status) is disappointingly left unexplored.

Other areas of focus include the late, inadequate response of the United States and United Kingdom, and anti-Semitism rising again in the 1980s. Most powerful is attention given to rebellion and resistance by Jews, and so an individual like the butcher who leaped from a body-filled pit to tear out the throat of an SS commander with his teeth rises to stun the imagination from a list. Large numbers from lists also reverberate in memory, such as the acts of rescue by non-Jews, from an industrialist who saved 1,500 lives to the strong governmental leaders of Bulgaria, Finland, and Denmark whose steadfast refusal to cooperate also meant thousands saved. Perhaps the saddest statistic is that many were too weak to live even when liberated. "In the areas freed by the Americans, French, and British, 60,000 Jews were found alive. Within one week, 20,000 had died." Oddly, even with its many lists, *Smoke and Ashes* is perhaps one of the saddest Holocaust books because its numbers tell just how hard it was to escape, how few survived.

527. Rostkowski, Margaret I. *After the Dancing Days.* New York: Harper, 1986. 217 pp. Fiction.

Interest level: Age 11+ Reading level: Grade 6

Set in a small Kansas town in 1919, this book explores a young girl's emergence into maturity in the aftermath of World War I. The story revolves around 13-year-old Annie and her relationship with Andrew, a seriously burned, bitter young hospitalized veteran. In the process of making friends with Andrew, Annie confronts and constructs her own value system. She recognizes that she can no longer unquestioningly obey her mother, and she relentlessly seeks answers to some family mysteries even when she knows that the revelations will be painful to her and her family. In the process of unlocking these secrets she and her family become increasingly aware of how lacking in glory war really is.

The father and grandfather are wonderful models of quietly heroic and principled people. They are offset by the mother and grandmother, both of whom are self-centered and less admirable, but who are, nevertheless, sympathetically drawn. And although the grandmother remains a person who has decided to avoid active involvement in life, the mother does change at the end of the book, acknowledging the good example set by Annie and her father and grandfather.

The book is perceptively written and readers will find much substance to sustain their interest. They may even be motivated to discuss and do further research on the events and consequences of this and other wars.

528. Sender, Ruth Minsky. *The Cage.* New York: Macmillan, 1986; Bantam, pap. 245 pp. Nonfiction.

Interest level: Age 11+ Reading level: Grade 6

At age 16, Riva becomes the legal guardian of her three younger brothers. Her two older sisters and a brother have been sent to Russia for protection; her mother has been taken away by the Nazis, supposedly to a labor camp, but probably to a death camp. Riva and her brothers live in Poland. Their Christian neighbors, once their close friends, have turned against them and have aided the Nazis in pillaging their home. One brother dies, and Riva and her two remaining brothers are moved to the ghetto in Warsaw. There they stay until the ghetto is totally evacuated, and they are sent to Auschwitz, where they are permanently separated from each other.

Because of her ability to write poetry that elevates the spirits of the prisoners, Riva wins affection and attention, not only of her fellow prisoners, but also of one of the wardens of the camp. She manages to survive, as do the three siblings who were sent to Russia. She now lives in America, where she has married another survivor. She has a loving and understanding child, and her life is a full one, but she still has nightmares and fears that there will be another holocaust.

The book is not only Sender's personal account of her experiences in the Holocaust, but it is also the story of 6,000,000 Jews. She describes horrors and atrocities that were everyday events for several years and does not glorify anyone's courage; she lets the events convey their own effect. Sender demonstrates how futile it seemed for anyone to try to escape. She does not, however, discuss any of the process of her Polish friends' changeover to the Nazi cause. Perhaps this is because it is their story rather than hers that she would then have to tell. She provides evidence of the attitudes of the Polish people who were given the Jews' houses and possessions and thus benefited from the Jews' annihilation and describes the feeling of going to her old home, seeing her old furniture in the rooms, and being told that the current Polish occupants threw away all books and photos. Her story is dramatically and painfully told.

529. Siegal, Aranka. *Grace in the Wilderness: After the Liberation, 1945–1948*. New York: Farrar, 1985; Signet, pap. 199 pp. Fiction.

Interest level: Age 13+ Reading level: Grade 7

Piri and her sister, Iboya, have survived the torture of the concentration camps, but because they are Jews, now they have no home. They are sent to Sweden where they attend school and try to resume a normal life. They have witnessed unbelievable horrors, but they are grateful to be together and alive. They come to feel so secure in Sweden that the sisters consent to be separated: Iboya goes to work for the summer at a farm, and Piri stays behind with her new-found friends. This marks the first of several separations that the sisters weather very well. They live with Swedish families before they finally emigrate to America. The reader knows that they will survive; they have demonstrated their ability to weather almost any hardship, and they will continue to show this strength.

The author has clearly lived through all that she tells of in her story. The details are sometimes painful. She also talks of the difficult decisions that the survivors must make: Israel or America? Or should they marry Christians and remain in Sweden? How can they reconcile their current freedom with the pain of their past? The end of the war did not mark the end of their problems, but at least now they do have choices, and these are of the spirit and style of life rather than the threat of death. In some ways the story is even more powerful than its precursor, *Upon the Head of a Goat* (Farrar, 1981). There are included here tales of atrocities, but what dominates is the victory of the human spirit.

530. Siegel, Barbara, and Siegel, Scott. *Firebrats #1: The Burning Land.* New York: Archway, 1987, pap. 152 pp. Fiction.

Interest level: Age 11+ Reading level: Grade 6

More an adventure story than a scientifically accurate detailing of what a nuclear holocaust might bring, this book, nevertheless, conveys the psychological sense of what any survivors might feel. Sixteen-year-olds Matt and Danielle are accidentally thrown together at the time of a massive nuclear attack on the United States. They survive for more than a month in the basement of a theater, and when they emerge they find that most of the population has been killed, and that the rest are dying of radiation sickness. They manage, by means of their wits and courage, to escape from a menacing group of criminals and they decide to try to trek across the country in hopes of finding an area that has not been irretrievably damaged by the bombs and, perhaps, connecting with Matt's parents, who had been in California when the attack leveled the East.

Matt and Danielle are believable characters. Their inventiveness overcomes their terror, and their situation sparks their common sense. The story moves rapidly and convincingly, and young readers may be encouraged to discuss what they would do in the event of such a disaster.

531. Stein, R. Conrad. *World at War: Prisoners of War.* Illus. with photos. Chicago: Childrens, 1987, pap. 48 pp. Nonfiction.

Interest level: Age 12+ Reading level: Grade 6

The photographs of actual prison camps and prisoners of war (POWs) are the most dramatic and, at times, upsetting parts of this book. The text describes the conditions that POWs in Japanese and German camps suffered under in World War II and their everyday activities and their feelings at being imprisoned.

The book focuses on Allied POWs, but there is a section toward the end on Axis POWs imprisoned in the United States. It declares that these prisoners were fortunate and, in fact, better off than their countrymen who were not in prison. The book makes no mention at all of the Japanese Americans who were kept in camps as a protection against their possible subversion. Although the book is particularly biased, it is, nevertheless, a useful addition to the books for young readers on war, because it is so rare that this topic is even mentioned.

532. Stevens, Bryna. *Deborah Sampson Goes to War.* Illus. by Florence Hill. Minneapolis: Carolrhoda, 1984. 48 pp. Nonfiction.

Interest level: Ages 6–9 Reading level: Grade 2

This entry in the On My Own beginning reader series is an exciting biography of a woman during the Revolutionary War. New words that may be hard (regiment, probe, and so on) are introduced at the beginning, so children will be able to follow when they see them in the book.

A unique opening sets the stage for what was going on at the time of Deborah Sampson's birth and early childhood (for example, George Washington worked at pleasing his wife). Eventually Deborah's story is told. When her father is lost at sea, her mother can't support six children, so some are sent to live elsewhere. Living with the Thomas family, Deborah works hard but also goes to school, quite an accomplishment for a girl of the time. When the revolution starts, Deborah is only 14.

By the time Deborah is 21, the war is still going on. Strong and tall, she ties back her hair, dons a man's suit, and walks 35 miles to join the army. No one guesses "Robert Shurtleff" is a woman. The book recounts the tasks of her regiment. When a bullet hits her head, Deborah is of course afraid she will be found out at the hospital. She leaves before full recovery only to become ill under the terrible conditions soldiers had to endure. This time she is found out but a kind doctor takes Deborah home to his family without revealing her secret. Only at the close of the war is her secret revealed.

Besides offering a rousing view of this woman and the war, the book also points up times when people feel compelled to make hard separations for a larger cause. An afterword tells about Sampson's later life, which included marriage, children, and becoming the first woman lecturer in the United States speaking about her war experiences.

533. Strieber, Whitley. *Wolf of Shadows*. New York: Knopf, 1985. 105 pp. Fiction.

Interest level: Age 11+ Reading level: Grade 6

This is the story of the hunt for survival following a nuclear blast in the United States. The unusual perspective of this book is that the group seeking survival is a pack of wolves led by Wolf of Shadows, an intelligent, sensitive and courageous animal. The story is told from his point of view as he and his pack journey south, fleeing from the cold of a nuclear winter.

When a human mother and her daughter join the wolf pack, they are at first suspicious and uncomprehending of each other. But the wolves accept the humans, and the humans become genuine members of the pack, dependent on the wolves for survival. They encounter other humans and must do battle with them because of their intention of destroying the wolves.

In the end they have some slim hope of finding a warmer valley where it will be possible for them to live. The author is careful not to guarantee anything, but there is, at least, hope. The frigid atmosphere of the horror of a nuclear aftermath is well portrayed here, as is the perspective of a wolf leader toward his pack and toward the humans and their peculiar customs.

534. Swindells, Robert. *Brother in the Land.* New York: Holiday, 1985. 151 pp. Fiction.

Interest level: Age 11+ Reading level: Grade 6

The story is set in England, far in the future. The narrator is Danny, a young boy who has survived a nuclear bombardment. His story is one of devastation, human cannibalism and savagery, cruelty, and hopelessness. Danny meets Kim, and the two of them try to maintain a loving relationship despite the insanity of the world around them. The only hope that remains at the end is that if there is a future for the world, people will take to heart the lesson that there can be no survival after a nuclear holocaust.

Although the story is a dramatic one, it is not told especially well. The details are mostly of the battles and ugliness of human beings desperate to find food and willing to do anything to get it. None of the people emerges as an individual, not even the young protagonists. They are simply factors in the whole aftermath of the bombings. But the book succeeds in conveying the fact that there is no life after nuclear war.

535. Vigna, Judith. *Nobody Wants a Nuclear War.* Illus. by the author. Niles, Ill.: Whitman, 1986. 32 pp. Fiction.

Interest level: Ages 5–9 Reading level: Grade 2

The two young children in the story make a hideaway for themselves in case there is a nuclear war. Their mother finds them and explains that she understands their fears. She says that she felt the same way when she was a little girl. She tells them a little of the history of nuclear war, and she assures them that she and their father will try to be with them, no matter what.

She also tells them of the actions that different people engage in to help ensure that there will never be a nuclear war. The children decide to construct a banner, and take a picture of it to send to the president of the United States. The banner reads, "Grownups for a safer world to grow up in." The child narrator vows to work hard to prevent a nuclear war so that the world will be a safer place for her children to grow up in.

The message is clear and direct. The book may provide information, comfort, a base for questions and discussions, and inspiration for action.

536. Vinke, Hermann. *The Short Life of Sophie Scholl.* Illus. with photos and drawings from the Scholl family. Trans. by Hedwig Pachter. New York: Harper, 1984. 216 pp. Nonfiction.

Interest level: Age 12+ Reading level: Grade 8

Too few books for young readers tell of the underground movement called the White Rose, which young Germans engaged in during the time of the

Nazi regime. Although the movement failed, it remains a symbol of courage and sanity in a time when these qualities were in too short supply. Hermann Vinke interviewed the two surviving members of Sophie Scholl's family as well as friends who survived the war, and he uses their voices in addition to Sophie's diaries and letters to help tell the story.

Sophie's father was tried and imprisoned for "malicious slander of the Fuhrer." The entire family was opposed to the actions of the Third Reich. Sophie's brother, Hans, founded the White Rose, and Sophie joined him and his friends. They printed and distributed leaflets telling the German people what Hitler was doing. They caused quite a stir, as no one had been bold enough to speak out publicly against Hitler's actions.

The organization lasted for one year—1942. It was discovered and crushed by the Gestapo with the help of a janitor who reported that he had seen the leaflets scattered about the University of Munich. Sophie and her brother claimed total responsibility, hoping to save the lives of their friends in the resistance group. Sophie and her brother and six other members of the group were executed; more than 40 others were imprisoned. Sophie was 21 years old when she was killed. She was convinced, even at the end, that her cause had been a worthy one, and that her efforts had not been in vain.

The story is a dramatic one, told well. The use of Sophie's photographs and drawings adds to the reader's feelings of empathy with this courageous young woman. The letters and excerpts from diaries, as well as the authentic voices of the survivors, make this book a powerful one.

537. Wallin, Luke. *In the Shadow of the Wind.* New York: Bradbury, 1984. 203 pp. Fiction.

Interest level: Age 11+ Reading level: Grade 6

Caleb McElroy is a white adolescent who, despite his fear, befriends the Creek Indians in his community in Alabama in 1835. The story is a bloody and somber one of raids on Creek settlements and of deceit and betrayal. Caleb rescues Pine Basket and her mother from captivity. He and Pine Basket are married and when the Civil War comes he joins the Union army. Some of the facts about the Indian slave holdings and the arguments about the settlement of the Oklahoma Territory may be new to young readers. This is a book that makes history come alive and is worthwhile reading.

538. Watkins, Yoko Kawashima. *So Far from the Bamboo Grove.* New York: Lothrop, 1986; Puffin, pap. 183 pp. Fiction.

Interest level: Age 12+ Reading level: Grade 7

Although this is a fictionalized autobiography, it has the ring of truth. It is the story of Yoko, her sister, and her mother, and their flight from North

Korea to Japan. Their family is Japanese, and they are warned by a corporal in the army that the Russians will soon attack the Korean village where they are living, so they decide to flee to their extended family in Japan. The father and brother are away from the village, but the corporal tells the family how to leave messages for them. It is a dangerous journey that they undertake, and they narrowly escape being captured by the North Korean Communists who are looking expressly for them. Their home is ravaged, but they escape with their lives.

When they get to Japan, the mother immediately places them in school and journeys to their hometown. There she discovers that her parents and her in-laws have been killed. As a result of this catastrophic news she becomes very ill. She returns to her daughters and dies immediately after. The two young women manage, by salvaging from the trash and by sewing and selling various items, to survive. They receive a windfall when Yoko wins an essay contest. Their classmates ridicule them because they are in rags, but they both earn the highest grades and are undaunted in their efforts. The remarkable story concludes with the return of Yoko's brother. The epilogue tells us that the girls' father returned from a Siberian prison camp six years later.

This story describes a little-known series of circumstances stemming from the war. Its clear, unemotional prose is effective and moving. The author is testimony to the fact that even the "enemy" is human and deserves to be respected as such.

539. Yolen, Jane. *The Devil's Arithmetic.* New York: Viking, 1988. 160 pp. Fiction.

Interest level: Age 10+ Reading level: Grades 5–6

No story of the Holocaust is without horror and amazement at the cruelty of people to other people. But some are mostly recountings of the atrocities, and others attempt to overlook the pain and death and focus on the survivors. This story, by master storyteller Jane Yolen, transports the reader to the time and place, sounds and sights, and odors of the death camps and makes clear that the words of the Passover Haggadah are accurate: "This is what happened to *me* when I was a slave in Egypt." It is more than a vicarious experience; it is real.

In the story, Hannah, a modern Jewish child, is annoyed at having to go to her grandparents' house in the Bronx for a seder. She is embarrassed by the emotional outbursts of her grandfather who angrily displays his arm, tattooed with his concentration camp identification number. She feels a special kinship with her Aunt Eva, for whose dear friend she was named, but she feels no real connection with the rest of the family, or, for that matter, with the Jewish people.

During the part of the seder where she is asked to symbolically open the door for the prophet Elijah, she steps back in time into the shtetl of her grandparents, and into the fire of the Holocaust. She experiences the concentration camp as Chaya, her aunt's friend, all the while knowing that she is from a different time and place. After having been tortured and witnessing the hell of the camps, she is the only one of a group of four girls permitted to avoid the ovens. She swiftly substitutes herself for her friend Rivka (later, Eva) and goes to her death in her place. At that point she reenters the present and returns to the seder table, knowledgeable and forever a part of her people.

The story is a profound and moving one. The authenticity of the Yiddish phrases and customs helps to involve the reader. As always, Yolen has used not only her personal experience but also her impeccable research skills to weave a tale that is potent and unforgettable.

540. Ziefert, Harriet. *A New Coat for Anna.* Illus. by Anita Lobel. New York: Knopf, 1986. 32 pp. Fiction.

Interest level: Ages 7–10 Reading level: Grade 3

Set in the aftermath of World War II, and based on a true story, this book tells of the inventiveness and determination of Anna's mother in seeing to it that her daughter has a warm, new coat for the winter. Anna's mother designs a scheme to have a coat made for Anna, even though there is no money in the house. They have to wait almost a full year for the finished product, and they must part with some treasured belongings, but with patience, with some effort on their part, and by bartering several of their possessions, they enlist the cooperation of farmers and craftspeople, and Anna gets her coat.

Anita Lobel's illustrations dramatically convey the human and physical devastation of the war: Former soldiers, their injuries still evident, begging for coins; shuttered shops; empty provision baskets; and houses reduced to rubble introduce the reader to the setting of the story. The pictures and text combine to provide an inspiring story of human survival. Too often war is thought of in terms of battles and victories. Here is an accurate and accessible accounting of how people rebuild afterward.

8

"Who Will Take Care of Me?"

Facing Foster Care

Foster care for a child, even for a short period, implies the loss of one or both parents. The reasons for foster care, either by relatives or strangers, can be many: A parent has died, a parent is physically ill and must be hospitalized, a parent suffers from mental illness and is incapable of child care. For the child who is placed in a new home, life may be one of desperate uncertainty. The foster parents may be carefully selected and genuinely concerned for human welfare or they may be more interested in earning government funds.

"How long will I be wanted?" the foster child asks. "How will I be treated?" "Will I be abandoned once again?" The child usually does not know when or if the natural parent will ever return. At times natural parents know they can never care for or even visit the child but refuse to allow adoption by interested foster parents or others. This creates a legal and emotional bind for children who cannot allow themselves to love freely, not ever knowing the security of continuity.

541. Anderson, Deborah, and Finne, Martha. *Jason's Story: Going to a Foster Home.* Illus. by Jeanette Swofford. Minneapolis: Dillon, 1986. 48 pp. Nonfiction.

Interest level: Ages 5–9 Reading level: Grades 2–3

Part of the Dillon Child Abuse series, this book concerns seven-year-old Jason, who now lives with his mother, but had previously lived in foster homes. "A foster home is a home where adults take care of other people's children." His is a story of neglect, where his 16-year-old mother didn't change his diapers, hold or kiss him too much, or have an understanding of what babies need. But fictional Jason, representing more than just one child, was born into an extended family of troubles—grandparents who drank and fought, for starters. Jason hardly had a chance. Soon the doctor called Child Protection Services. Before long, the courts decided to put Jason in a foster home because he was in danger where he was. The book explains what happens in foster homes, who volunteers, how upset the foster family may feel when the biological mother wants her child back, and how confusing it feels to return to the biological mother's home. It does not explain, however, how the biological mother feels during the separation or how she solves her problems.

But the problems are not finished. Jason's shenanigans bring on heavy corporal punishment (for example, being locked in a closet and hit with a belt), and soon the day-care center is the one calling Child Protection. And so Jason, now guilt-ridden, is off to a second foster family, not as loving as the first. In time, Jason's mother gets serious help for her drinking and enters a program to help her be a better mother. The talky, heavy book ends with Jason back with his mother. "He and his mother went from having lots of bad troubles to just having little troubles, once in a while. Jason is glad about that."

After the narrative, the authors provide basic information about foster care—who's in it, how long, likely reasons, children's rights, and likelihood of return. An appended glossary of terms is curious in its inclusions—"court" and "Child Protection Services" are understandable, but why "diaper?" A final inclusion is a note to adults about the importance of foster care, urging them to be interested in volunteering. This book would seem best used in foster agencies themselves for social workers to help the children involved understand. It would have limited use in a general literature program because of the serious multiple problems the family has, even though many families are burdened with such heavy troubles. Glossary.

542. Bunting, Eve. *If I Asked You, Would You Stay?* New York: Lippincott, 1984; Harper, pap. 151 pp. Fiction.

Interest level: Age 12+ Reading level: Grade 7

Crow has been rejected by his mother and has been in a series of foster homes. He has run away from the last one, not because they were unloving to him, but because he was afraid of yet another rejection, so he left before that would happen. He finds a secret place to stay, behind a carousel. Into his hiding place he brings Valentine, whose life he has saved. Valentine, too, has been rejected. She has also been abused by her mother's new husband, and by the man to whom she ran in order to escape from her stepfather.

Crow and Valentine fall in love with each other and, in the process, learn to become more self-preserving. They leave, each of them for a different safe place, but this time they are going *to* a better life, not running away from anything. It is a measure of Crow's evolution that he is able to return to the foster home where he was loved and to trust that he will continue to be loved.

Foster care is, in general, a difficult situation for both the foster child and the foster parent. It is difficult to feel secure when the placement is, by definition, a temporary one. Both the characters in this story have been betrayed by their mothers and by their subsequent caretakers. It is important for them each to develop a feeling of self-worth before they can accept and give love again. The book helps readers to understand this fact.

543. Eige, Lillian. *Cady*. Illus. by Janet Wentworth. New York: Harper, 1987. 183 pp. Fiction.

Interest level: Ages 9–12 Reading level: Grades 4–5

After his grandmother dies, Cady runs away from his aunt who is abusive and neglectful of him. People think he has drowned. He stays for a while with a cousin, but one day she mysteriously tells him he must leave. She sends him to yet another person, Thea McVey, who enigmatically tells him that she is a friend who is interested in him, and will say no more. Ever since his birth he has been shifted from one relative to another (his mother died in childbirth; his father disappeared), never really feeling wanted. Now, at Thea's, he is taken care of; he makes friends with two other children who have also been sent away from their home, and he meets a stranger who, it later turns out, is his father.

Cady has lived with secrets and with secrecy for most of his life. It seems as if no one trusts him enough to tell him the truth. Even his Aunt Thea (who is really his father's older sister) withholds information from him until he can figure it out for himself. She makes a fuss about his taking a strange new surname and doesn't tell him why until the very end of the book. Through it all, Cady is very compliant. He has the foster child syndrome of not feeling at home or safe with anyone. Even at the end of the book, when all is seemingly tied up neatly, one wonders what will happen to this boy.

544. Hahn, Mary Downing. *Daphne's Book*. New York: Clarion, 1983; Bantam, pap. 178 pp. Fiction.

Interest level: Age 10+ Reading level: Grade 5

Daphne and her younger sister, Hope, live with their grandmother. Their parents are dead, and their grandmother is growing increasingly psychotic. Daphne is afraid to let anyone know about her grandmother because she doesn't want to be sent to an orphanage. But when Daphne's friend, Jessica, who is the narrator of this book, realizes that Daphne and her sister are in danger of being seriously hurt, she tells her mother about the situation. Daphne's worst fears are realized. She and her sister are placed in an institution. Her grandmother is hospitalized, and she dies soon after. Daphne feels terribly guilty. In the end, Daphne and her sister will go to live with a couple who sound as if they will care for the girls well. They are cousins, found by the social worker. Jessica is relieved that there will be a happy ending, and she reassures Daphne that they will always be friends.

The book describes a desperate situation, but perhaps readers will realize that sometimes children who seem to be different from the rest, who are shy or withdrawn, need some special understanding. The story is well told. The incidental issues of single-family parenting (Jessica's parents are divorced and she lives with her mother, who is at work most of the day) and adjusting to new situations are well handled.

545. Hall, Lynn. *Mrs. Portree's Pony*. New York: Scribner, 1986. 89 pp. Fiction.

Interest level: Ages 9–12 Reading level: Grade 4

It is seven years since Addie's mother, Gloria, prevailed on her old friend, Alice, to take in her daughter because her new husband doesn't want Addie living with them. Alice expects her third child soon and there will be no room for Addie anymore. Now Addie is 13, and she desperately wants to be loved. On her birthday Addie wanders into a field belonging to Mrs. Portree and falls in love with Ribbon, an elderly pony belonging to Mrs. Portree's daughter, who ran away to be with her father a long time ago and has never returned. The young abandoned girl and the old abandoned woman become close friends and find in each other the love they have been craving. It is no surprise that Mrs. Portree arranges with Gloria to become Addie's new foster mother.

The story is written with a spare, almost affectless prose that suits it well. Addie is a strong young woman who tries very hard to keep control of her loveless life. She is not abused, but she is certainly neglected. In the end she sincerely tells her mother that she understands that Gloria has done her best. The ending is a satisfying one.

546. McCutcheon, Elsie. *Storm Bird*. New York: Farrar, 1987. 176 pp. Fiction.

Interest level: Age 13+ Reading level: Grades 7–8

When Jenny's father must go to sea in order to make ends meet, he leaves her with Aunt Clara, his adopted sister. Jenny's mother has been dead for 10 years (she died when Jenny was two), and Jenny and her father have had a close and loving relationship. They both adored Jenny's mother, and now

Jenny feels that she has lost both her parents. Jenny is especially morose because it seems that Aunt Clara resented and disliked her mother.

As Jenny's stay is prolonged, she learns more and more about the history of this turn-of-the-century community. There are sad stories that help her to understand the people with whom she now lives. Old secrets are cleared up, and guilt is expiated. After it is thought that her father has died, he miraculously reappears and the reader is assured that all will be well. Jenny has matured into a person who will not be so quick to judge others. The story is a very complex one, and it reads something like a mystery because of all of the mistaken impressions the characters have had about people and events. The unraveling of the secrets forms most of the plot, but threaded throughout is the pain of separation and the responsibility of dealing with loss.

547. Nixon, Joan Lowery. *Caught in the Act (Second Volume of the Orphan Train Quartet)*. New York: Bantam, 1988. 150 pp. Fiction.

Interest level: Age 11+ Reading level: Grades 5–6

Mike Kelly has been adopted by the Friedrichs, a family of German immigrants. Mr. Friedrich is hard and punitive and beats Mike. Gunter, the Friedrichs' son, resents Mike and does all sorts of dreadful things to get Mike into trouble. After a series of mishaps and misunderstandings Mike succeeds in getting himself extricated from the Friedrichs' farm and going to live at Fort Leavenworth, Kansas, with a family he admires greatly.

This second novel in the Orphan Train Quartet continues the story begun in *A Family Apart* (see entry below). Mike is the boy who stole in order to feed the family, and, by coincidence, there is a tragedy in the Friedrich family involving a son who also stole to feed them. The flavor of the era is conveyed well, as is the setting of the Midwest in the mid-nineteenth century. The story is well told, and the dilemma of the foster family is as dramatically presented as is Mike's situation. The issue of poverty and the heartbreak of deciding to send children away to what is hoped will be a better life for them are poignantly portrayed in this series.

548. Nixon, Joan Lowery. *A Family Apart.* New York: Bantam, 1987. 162 pp. Fiction.

Interest level: Age 11+ Reading level: Grades 5–6

The six Kelly children, ranging in age from 6 to 13, are sent West, in 1860, on a train filled with orphans to be adopted by families, some of whom want cheap labor, and some of whom genuinely want children to love. Although the children are aware of the impoverished state their widowed mother is in, they feel that she has abandoned them. They feel even worse when they discover that they are to be separated from each other.

This book is the first in a series of four books that chronicles the adventures of the Kelly children. The story begins with modern-day Jeff and Jennifer who are visiting their grandmother's house and are bored. Their grandmother entertains them by telling them the story of her great-grandmother, Mary Frances Kelly, the oldest of the six Kelly children.

As the six children are assembled before embarking on the train that will take them to the West, and to new homes, Mary Frances overhears the adults talking about the fact that families want to adopt no more than two children at a time, and that boys are much more desirable as adoptees than girls. Mary Frances decides to masquerade as a boy so that she and her youngest brother can be together. The Children's Aid Society is managing the adoptions as humanely as they can. Eventually all six children are adopted, and Mary Frances's ruse works: She and Petey are adopted together by an attractive couple from New England who have come West partly to farm and partly to fight slavery. They are a part of the Underground Railroad.

All through the book Mary Frances fixes on the word "sacrifice." Her mother uses it, and many other adults use the word. She finally comes to understand the meaning of the term and to forgive her mother for sending the children away. At the end of the book she has proven her stamina, has forgiven her mother, and has regained her true identity. The reader has hopes for her and for young Petey. The book ends with the promise of another story about one of the other Kelly children.

549. Wosmek, Frances. *A Brown Bird Singing*. Illus. by Ted Lewin. New York: Lothrop, 1986. 120 pp. Fiction.

Interest level: Ages 9–12 Reading level: Grade 4

Anego is the only Native American in her entire school. Since she was small, she has lived with Mama and Papa and their daughter, Sheila, who are Anglos. She has lived with the knowledge that her father, Hamigeesek, a Chippewa Indian, may come and take her with him at any time, but she has never heard from him since he left her with Papa, his very close friend.

Some of the children in Anego's class make nasty remarks to her because of her Indian heritage, but Sheila, although not always kind to her, treats her like a real sister. Anego feels secure with Mama and Papa, and she wants to stay with them. She does not like being Native American, and she is shy and withdrawn because of her feelings of low self-worth.

When her father finally does arrive, he tells her that she may stay with her foster family if she wishes, but he leaves her with a memory of her birth mother's love and of his own proud heritage. The reader does not know what will happen in the long run, but the reader is sure that Anego will feel better about herself from now on.

The story is respectful of the Native-American heritage, but it focuses on the interaction between Anego and her foster family. Mama and Papa are unusually generous, intelligent, and understanding human beings. They consistently try to give Anego a feeling of pride in her father. They are the ideal foster parents, treating Anego like their own child but letting her know that the decision about whether to remain with them is hers.

The book is timely in its consideration of today's controversy over the advisability of Anglos adopting Native-American children. Much discussion and, perhaps, research can grow from a reading of this book.

Accepting Stepparents and Stepsiblings

If a child has already lost a parent because of death, divorce, or other permanent separation, the remarriage of the remaining parent does not in itself solve the child's bereavement problems. Instead, the feelings engendered by the child's loss may become intensified. Anger and fear may resurface. The child who has lost once now jealously senses that its sole source of support may be lost to another competing individual.

The child may reject the new parent, fearing abandonment once again. Before accepting the newcomer, the child must be convinced that the new parent has virtues that will make the child, as well as the other parent, happy. These feelings are compounded if stepsiblings are part of the package. The child may reject the stepparent and stepsiblings, fearing abandonment once again. The child may feel disloyal to the past. Before accepting the newcomers, the child must be convinced that the restructured family has virtues that might make him or her happy. Only then can the child allow the newcomers into the small circle previously shared with one parent only. The journey toward acceptance is rarely a smooth one, and to pretend instant love is misleading and cruel.

550. Ames, Mildred. *Cassandra-Jamie.* New York: Scribner, 1985. 135 pp. Fiction.

Interest level: Ages 9–12 Reading level: Grades 4–5

Even though Jamie's mother has been dead for three years, Jamie is not ready for her father to marry again, not, that is, unless he marries someone just like the mother Jamie remembers. Her new teacher is such a person, at least in Jamie's mind. But all of her efforts to get her father and teacher together fail. What is more, her father is involved with a woman named Sylvia, who Jamie is convinced is totally wrong for him, and to whom Jamie has been very rude.

Somehow, discovering that her adored teacher has a daughter brings Jamie to her senses. Jamie begins to see the similarity between Sylvia and her mother. The book ends with Jamie's grudgingly asking their housekeeper to invite Sylvia for dinner, and the reader knows that all will end well.

The issue of a child's blocking a new romance for a parent is a real one, as is the idealized image a child can develop of his or her dead parent. Jamie is an engaging, if sometimes cruel and obnoxious girl. Her feelings and her escapades are amusingly but feelingly recounted. The book helps bring to light some of the problems attendant on the end of the active grieving process.

551. Boyd, Lizi. *The Not-So-Wicked Stepmother.* Illus. by the author. New York: Viking Kestrel, 1987. 32 pp. Fiction.

Interest level: Ages 4–8 Reading level: Grade 2

Hessie knows there are two kinds of wishes—those that are possible, such as a new bike, and those that are not, such as after her parents' divorce, hoping they will reunite. That's particularly impossible now that Daddy has moved far away and remarried, to Molly, a woman whom Hessie has never met and only seen in photographs.

In going to spend the summer with Daddy and Molly, Hessie imagines Molly to be the wicked fairy-tale stepmother. "Stepdaughters have to stay inside and sweep and scrub and clean." Deciding Molly will be horrible to her, she makes plans to be horrible to her first. When they meet, Hessie makes horrible faces and refuses to eat, but no one seems to notice this behavior as she keeps doing it. This must be a trick, Hessie notes, everyone is so nice. So she snoops around to find stepmother clothes.

In time, Hessie forgets to make the horrible faces and becomes more interested in berry picking and learning to swim. The summer ends with a special story told by Molly as the three of them crowd into Hessie's bed: The story concerns Daddy-man Duck, Hess-a-bless Duck, and Molly-moo Duck—also a little girl who lives on the lake and feeds them—but when the summer is over the little girl returns to her mommy and the ducks go south. But then every summer, "the ducks came back, and so did the little girl."

Boyd has a good rhythm in her story, as exemplified by the story within a story. And she has a good sense of children's feelings, allowing them honest emotion, such as wishing to live alone with Daddy, and that Molly would drown to make that possible. But there is one inauthentic aspect to the book: The father lives a day's drive away. He thinks enough of his child to come and get her for the summer, and both he and his new wife are the models of sensitivity during the summer stay, yet he hasn't thought enough about her to introduce his wife-to-be before the marriage or the extended stay. It's a frightening thought indeed to go off for months with people who can give the courtesy of meeting and getting to know a person but don't. It's hard to believe these characters would have done that. On the other hand, it's in keeping with the book's theme of non-communication: Hessie doesn't communicate her thoughts and feelings about the "wicked stepmother" or about missing her mother, and the father hasn't communicated with his daughter adequately before marriage. How we send our strengths and weaknesses down through the generations!

552. Corbin, William. *A Dog Worth Stealing.* New York: Orchard, 1987. 163 pp. Fiction.

Interest level: Age 11+ Reading level: Grade 6

Jud is 16 years old. His mother has deserted the family to "find herself" in California. His father has remarried a woman, Carla, only 10 years older than Jud and 6 years older than Jud's older sister. Jud goes alone, without informing anyone, on a camping trip through the wilderness, because his father has reneged on his promise to accompany him. On the trip, Jud gets lost and comes across a marijuana field owned by a dangerous man who plans to train a dog to be an attack dog. Partly because Jud's own dog has recently died, Jud is sickened by the fact that a basically fine dog will be ruined. He "rescues" the dog and takes him home.

Carla tries very hard to establish a good relationship with Jud. Perhaps she would have succeeded earlier if Jud hadn't been so angry at his father. Carla is very sympathetic to his wish to keep the dog even though she is terrified of dogs. She helps persuade his father to permit him to keep the dog. After a number of adventures Jud, his father, Carla, and the dog become a solid and cooperative family.

The author tells a good story. Within its context the lessons of mutual respect and responsibility for the family's success come across very well.

553. Craven, Linda. *Stepfamilies: New Patterns of Harmony.* New York: Messner, 1982, hb and pap. 192 pp. Nonfiction.

Interest level: Ages 11–16 Reading level: Grade 6

Linda Craven is an editor of *Stepfamilies Bulletin* and speaks widely on the subject. She reveals her own crises in living in a stepfamily, moments they thought they wouldn't make it through, and this brings the book immediacy. Youngsters tell first-person stories and this, too, brings immediacy. Topics include myths about the stepfamily proposition (happily ever after, ugly stepmother, and so on); dealing with change by being good to oneself (creating a private space); roles and possibilities for stepchildren and stepparents; making roles clear; and confusions, hurts, and complexities in stepfamilies. A section on stepsiblings offers good practical advice on how to stay balanced when a stepparent's kids come by and there is a threat of displacement.

Her background as a stepparent gives Craven special insight into the particular problems of stepsiblings who are almost the same age. With openness, Craven discusses advantages and disadvantages of the stepfamily and doesn't shy away from the thorniest of issues: discipline and sexuality in a stepfamily. She seems to understand the pain youngsters can go through in watching a parent be lovey-dovey, for example. Craven never said living in a stepfamily was easy, but with her honesty about such issues as child abuse, incest, jealousy, and individuality, it may become less hard. Appendix of resources, index.

554. Delton, Judy. *Angel's Mother's Wedding.* Illus. by Margot Apple. Boston: Houghton Mifflin, 1987. 166 pp. Fiction.

Interest level: Ages 7–10 Reading level: Grade 3

Angel's mother is going to marry Rudy, a clown, and Angel and her little brother, Rags, are very happy about it. Rudy is an ideal stepfather. The family models excellent communication skills: They love each other and care about each other's feelings; they tell each other their worries, and they respect each other's concerns.

No character is depicted as a saint, although Rudy comes pretty close. When Angel has violated her mother's trust, by leaving Rags to fend for himself when she was supposed to be baby-sitting, and, into the bargain, has become lost, her mother is very angry. To top it off, Rags has painted the car in splotchy bright colors. Rudy comments that people are more important to him than splotchy cars, and a disaster is averted.

Angel's mother asks the children if they mind having their name changed; Rudy wants to adopt them. Angel is ambivalent at first, but in the end she agrees and is happy about her new status.

The book is written in a light tone, somewhat reminiscent of Beverly Cleary. This volume is the latest in a series of "Angel" books and should prove a welcome addition to those children who have become involved with Angel and her antics.

555. Drescher, Joan. *My Mother's Getting Married.* Illus. by the author. New York: Dial, 1986. 32 pp. Fiction.

Interest level: Ages 4–8 Reading level: Grade 3

Katy approaches life with a feisty nature, so while everyone else is delighted that her mother is marrying, Katy thinks "it stinks." Everything will change—dinner won't be flexible anymore and boring routine will enter her life. And what will happen to Saturday nights that were so happy and warm? Will her mother still call her Katydid? Maybe she'll be gone too often to remember that special nickname. And how can she possibly let Ben see her in her kitty pajamas? Katy's plots for revenge get put aside when she's given special attention at the wedding scene.

Although some readers may be comforted by the mother's calling her Katydid at book's end, others will get greater solace from Katy's earlier nasty words to her mother right before the honeymoon: "I hope you have a rotten time." This phrase may give realistic reassurance that anger is normal. Especially at the beginning, the stepchild-stepparent truce is impermanent at best and that's highlighted with spunk and irreverence here.

556. Durrett, Deanne. *My New Sister the Bully.* Nashville: Abingdon, 1985. 125 pp. Fiction.

Interest level: Ages 9–12 Reading level: Grade 4

Tom is very unhappy because his mother has remarried, and his name and hers aren't the same anymore; because they are moving; and because he has a new stepsister, Lydia, who is a bully. On the other hand, his stepfather seems like a decent, friendly sort, as does his stepbrother, Jeff. Tom does a lot of praying to God to help him be good at sports so that his relationship with his stepfather and stepbrother will be a good one. It turns out that Lydia can't tolerate the thought of Tom's being accepted into her family. Her deceit, tricks, and spiteful behavior seem to be working, and poor Tom feels helpless. Again he prays.

Tom makes friends with an old man named Grampa Jonah, whom Lydia dislikes, and Jeff likes. Tom finds a dog and brings it home. Everyone but Lydia likes the dog. Lydia finally engineers things so that when everyone is away, she gives the dog away and tells the family that the dog's rightful owners came to get it. Lydia makes Tom's life more and more miserable, and finally, after breaking his glasses, he gets lost. He wanders into a church to pray and meets Grampa Jonah, who whispers to him that Jesus wasn't Joseph's son, and that this knowledge should put Tom's predicament into perspective. When Tom arrives home he finds that Lydia has been punished for her behavior to him. Tom assures Lydia that he understands how she feels and that he will not report any of her nasty pranks. She and Tom acknowledge their fears of not being loved, and they agree to be friendly toward each other.

Abingdon Press, the publisher of this book, specializes in stories with a religious basis. But it is unfortunate that in this book the reader is talked at. Rather than providing the situation and letting the reader draw conclusions, everything is spelled out. Lydia is a monster at first with no redeeming characteristics. Tom is always a martyr and a goody-goody. Jeff is a tool. And the parents are well-meaning wimps for the most part. What could have been a good story turns into tract because of the frequent intrusion of comments about prayer, Christianity, church, and religious practices that really have nothing to do with the story or the characters. Too bad.

557. Getzoff, Ann, and McClenahan, Carolyn. *Step Kids: A Survival Guide for Teenagers in Stepfamilies . . . and for Stepparents Doubtful of Their Own Survival.* New York: Walker, 1984, pap. 182 pp. Nonfiction.

Interest level: Age 11+ Reading level: Grade 6

Meant primarily as a book for children of divorce, whose parent(s) have remarried, this book is a compendium of brief but very valuable, practical advice. Because of its breadth, depth may suffer a bit, but the breadth is nevertheless to be applauded for giving food for thought. For example, "When You Don't Like Your Stepbrother or Stepsister" is given but a page worth of attention, but its attendant section, "How to Cope," in only three-fourths of a page manages to fit in four different ideas. Breezy? Maybe, but the subject is complex and if but one good idea is gleaned, the book would be worth it.

Topics covered include sending messages, how to talk about feelings, why parents divorce, accepting your own feelings (including not loving or loving your stepparent), and getting along with stepsiblings. Also covered is how stepparents feel—with careful attention to pet peeves suffered by both sexes (for example, borrowing clothing without asking, complaining about food, and irresponsibility). Hints are given on how to get along with specific kinds of stepmothers (Mrs. Smother, Mrs. Clean) and stepfathers (the Dictator, Mr. Hot Pants), adding a touch of humor to what could be a grim situation. As can be seen from the epithet, problems of sexuality are openly addressed, and readers are given examples of words to say to counter overtures. Special situations are also given attention, such as not seeing one parent, being forbidden to see one parent, mental illness, sexual assault, parents in a homosexual relationship (an especially sensitively handled, informative section). Worthwhile and to the point. Appendixes include information on how to hold a family council meeting, nine ways for stepparents and stepkids to become friends, when to seek professional help, bibliography, material on the Stepfamily Association of America.

558. Hahn, Mary Downing. *Wait Till Helen Comes: A Ghost Story.* New York: Clarion, 1986; Avon, pap. 184 pp. Fiction.

Interest level: Ages 9–12 Reading level: Grade 4

When Heather was three years old she saw her mother die in a fire. Now she is seven, but she is still a troubled and troublesome child. Her new stepsiblings, Molly and Michael, find it very difficult to get along with her, but for their mother's sake, they try. Nevertheless, her jealousy, lying, and whining are a source of dissension among them.

Now they are going to move from Baltimore to the country, to a large old house that used to be a church. Behind the house is a graveyard, with a mysterious grave and a tombstone that bears Heather's initials. The ghost of the child buried there haunts Heather and Molly and almost kills Heather. But the mystery of the ghost-child's death is solved; the ghost's parents' bodies are discovered; Molly saves Heather's life; and Heather confesses to having set the fire in which her mother died. She's terrified that her father will no longer love her, but Molly, newly understanding the agony with which Heather has lived for the past four years, reassures and comforts her. In the end, the family is a close-knit unit, and the ghosts are laid to rest.

The ghost is real, as are many ghosts of people's fears and guilty thoughts. In this case the palpability of the phantom helps to resolve the terrible pressures that all of the family members have endured. The story is well told and the resolution is a believable one.

559. Henkes, Kevin. *Two Under Par.* Illus. by the author. New York: Greenwillow, 1987. 116 pp. Fiction.

Interest level: Ages 8–11 Reading level: Grades 3–4

Wedge's mother, Sally, has just remarried, and her new husband, King, who wears a crown instead of a hat, has opened a miniature golf course, complete with castle, just outside their home. Ten-year-old Wedge is embarrassed by his stepfather and confused over many events in his life, including why his father deserted him and his mother even before Wedge was born. He also does not like his five-year-old stepbrother, and he wonders why his mother married King.

Sally decides that it would be a good idea for her to go on a trip with Andrew, King's son, and for Wedge and King to be together so that they will get to know each other better. Everyone but Wedge is delighted at the idea. Sally returns home early when Wedge gets hysterical on hearing that his mother is pregnant with King's baby. King naively thought that Wedge would be pleased to hear this news.

Because King is such a loving and generous man, he eventually wins Wedge over, and Wedge's dream of one day having a real father comes true. The author paints portraits of real people grappling with real problems, and he does it well. Wedge's winning over is believable and satisfying.

560. Jukes, Mavis. *Like Jake and Me.* Illus. by Lloyd Bloom. New York: Knopf, 1984, hb and pap. 30 pp. Fiction.

Interest level: Ages 7–10 Reading level: Grade 3

Alex is a young boy, approximately seven years old, living out West with his mother and stepfather, Jake. Jake is a cowboy—complete with Stetson hat, silver longhorn steer belt buckle, tattoo of an eagle on his chest, and boots with yellow roses and "Jake" stitched on the sides. Virginia, Alex's mother, is pregnant with twins. Alex's father is an important although unseen character; Alex still cares for his father and sees him regularly, and his father has enrolled him in a ballet class when he stays with him. Alex feels he does not have much in common with his stepfather, who seems fearless and "macho."

Alex begins a discussion with Jake about wolf spiders (his father is an entomologist), without specifically mentioning the wolf spiders. Jake mistakenly thinks the conversation is about Virginia, Alex's mother. Their talk goes on for quite a while, making sense until Alex informs Jake about the spider that is in Jake's coat. Jake goes berserk; he is terrified of spiders. At this point Alex is able to help Jake. Through this humorous exchange a real bond forms between the boy and his stepfather. The last scene shows them "dancing" on the porch. Virginia says she feels the twins dancing inside her, too. "Like Jake and me," says Alex.

The differences between the father and stepfather make Alex's dilemma interesting. Different life-styles are presented as equally to be valued. The "bonding" between stepfather and son is accomplished humorously yet convincingly.

561. Kaplan, Leslie S. *Coping with Stepfamilies.* New York: Rosen, 1986. 176 pp. Nonfiction.

Interest level: Age 11+ Reading level: Grade 6

After defining what a stepfamily is, the author describes specific subcategories—those formed after the death of one parent differ in specific ways from those coming together following divorce. Attention is also paid to the differences that are likely to come about in children of varying ages, as well as the specific dynamics of how each gender might respond to a stepmother or a stepfather. The reader is encouraged to understand why parents might date or remarry, and what the remarriage is likely to represent to the children. There is full discussion of the dilemmas of lost dreams of reunion, social confusion, privacy, sexuality, getting along, being loyal or disloyal, and so on. Most helpful are the suggestions for making individual rules to fit individual families, not living by stereotypical expectations. Although the insights are good, the writing is somewhat disjointed, sometimes almost presented backward. An instance is reflected in the discussion of the specific problem of restricted mourning before launching into a general discussion of the stepfamily formed after a death. Bibliography.

562. Lowry, Lois. *Switcharound.* Boston: Houghton Mifflin, 1985; Dell, pap. 118 pp. Fiction.

Interest level: Ages 9–12 Reading level: Grade 4

Eleven-year-old Caroline and her 13-year-old brother, J.P., have seen their father only twice in the past nine years. He has not seemed interested in them, and they have reciprocated his negative feelings. Because their parents' divorce settlement stipulates that their father can have the children for the summer, they have no choice but to go to him now that he has summoned them for the entire summer. He is living in Des Moines, has remarried, and has six-month-old twins in addition to a six-year-old boy they call "Poochie."

It becomes clear at once to Caroline and J.P. that their father has invited them for the summer so that they can take care of the children. They agree to put aside their usual bickering and feuding in the face of their common enemy, and they begin to plot their revenge.

After a while, as they learn more about the family, Caroline and J.P. begin to change their opinions about their father and stepmother. Their father also changes his behavior and his misconceptions about them, once he gets to know them better. Through a series of misadventures and escapades, everything and everyone get straightened out, and the siblings enjoy their summer with their father and his family. Even their schemes of revenge turn out not to be as disastrous as they had feared.

The story is an amusing plea for people to listen to and sympathize with each other, no matter how difficult the task seems at first glance. It also makes readers think twice about assigning blame when they may not know all of the details.

563. McDonnell, Christine. *Count Me In.* New York: Viking Kestrel, 1986. 173 pp. Fiction.

Interest level: Age 12+ Reading level: Grade 6

Katie has mixed feelings about her mother's expecting a baby. She likes her stepfather, but she feels displaced and uncomfortable. A visit with her father doesn't help: He is not able to invite her to live with him.

During the course of the story Katie develops a new understanding about the feelings and responsibilities entailed in having a child. She also becomes very fond of one of her father's women friends and is genuinely pleased when they inform her of their intent to marry. Katie's relationships with her friends and her involvement with a young man help to assuage her feelings of being left out. Although the ending is predictable, it is satisfying.

564. Mark, Jan. *Trouble Half-way.* Illus. by David Parkins. New York: Atheneum, 1985. 129 pp. Fiction.

Interest level: Ages 10–12 Reading level: Grade 5

Amy is uncomfortable with her stepfather of six months. She doesn't know what to call him; he isn't like her father, who died fairly recently at a very young age; and his truck-driving job keeps him away much of the time. When she is forced to accompany him on one of his trips because her mother and baby sister had to go to help her grandparents, she learns a lot about him and herself, and she comes to admire, enjoy, and respect him. She even grows to think of him as her dad.

The story is set in England, and some of the words need defining in the glossary that is included. But the situation and the feelings of the characters are not bound by the setting. This is a respectful and unusual book in its exploration of the growth of the relationship between the girl and her stepfather.

565. Pevsner, Stella. *Sister of the Quints.* New York: Clarion, 1987. 177 pp. Fiction.

Interest level: Age 10+ Reading level: Grade 5

Natalie has chosen to live with her father and his new wife after her parents' divorce. Natalie's mother has moved to Colorado and is a teacher. She is crushed when Natalie refuses to go with her. But Natalie likes living in her familiar house with her father and Jean, her new stepmother. She is pleased when Jean gives birth to quintuplets. But after a while she begins to think that her father and Jean care nothing about her and are using her to help them with the quints. She revises her opinions when one of the quints is "borrowed" for a while by a disturbed young woman. She realizes then how much her mother must miss her, and, in fact, how much she misses her mother.

Natalie's father is very upset that Natalie is now choosing to return to live with her mother, but Natalie is firm in her decision. She knows how important her mother is to her, and she will continue to visit her father and his new family, but her place is with her mother.

Natalie's quandary is one with which a number of young readers will identify. Her decisions are each reached according to a reasonable process, and the author is convincing in the unfolding of the story.

566. Seuling, Barbara. *What Kind of Family Is This? A Book about Stepfamilies.* Illus. by Ellen Dolce. Racine, Wis.: Golden, 1985. 28 pp. Nonfiction.

Interest level: Ages 4–8 Reading level: Grade 3

This contribution to the Golden Learn about Living series asks readers to imagine themselves part of a new family—"with a new stepfather or stepmother, with a new stepbrother, or a new stepsister, or even a new stepbrother *and* a new stepsister, and maybe even a new pet or two—pets that didn't get along with your pet." Whew! But, then again, for Jeff, the fictional character who demonstrates the principles here, as well as for innumerable others, life is no less complicated.

The topics covered include appellations (Jeff resents it when his stepfather calls him "son"), new rooms, crowded conditions, and different household rules. Finally, Jeff erupts: "What kind of family is this? . . . I can't even go to the bathroom when I want to!" An argument with his stepbrother, Scott, results in a string across their shared bedroom, delineating territory. This and other familiar childhood tribulations are calmed a bit by his mother, who explains the only way she and Henry could live together with each other and with their children is if they all learned to be a family together.

In the end, an idea for playing brings Jeff and Scott to better terms. It was as his mother said, taking time, but he was getting used to it. A realistic resolution, not all sweetness and light, and utilizing common children's situations and dialogue.

567. Vigna, Judith. *Daddy's New Baby.* Illus. by the author. Niles, Ill.: Whitman, 1982. 32 pp. Fiction.

Interest level: Ages 3–6 Reading level: Grades 1–2

Many of the results of Daddy's having a new baby are negative ones for the young narrator of this story. She no longer has her own room at her daddy's house; her outings with her father are sometimes canceled because, for one reason or another, they have to stay home and watch the baby; and the baby seems to be ever-present, so that the little girl never gets to be alone with her daddy anymore. Further, her mother is anxious about the added expenses that the baby may cause, and she is fearful that her ex-husband won't have enough money for her and his first child. The little girl does, however, like to help take care of her baby sister, and she enjoys entertaining her. She also feels a kinship with this new child because they share the same daddy.

The issues brought up in this simple book are accurate and real. The story would be a good catalyst for discussion with children in the same situation.

568. Wallace, Bill. *Red Dog.* New York: Holiday, 1987. 185 pp. Fiction.

Interest level: Age 10+ Reading level: Grade 5

Although this is basically an adventure story of a boy and his dog, the issues of moving away from a community that is secure and the difficulty of accepting stepparents are important elements. Twelve-year-old Adam is resentful of Sam, his stepfather. He argues with his mother whenever she alludes to Sam as Adam's father. Adam steadfastly refuses to accept the fact that his father died two years ago, and he hates the fact that now he, his sister, mother, and stepfather have moved to the wilderness of the Wyoming Territory.

After Sam challenges Adam by calling him a boy and telling him that he must prove his courage and ability to behave like a man, Adam gets the opportunity to do so in a dramatic fashion. He overcomes the attempts of some vicious men to take over their land. The men have found gold in their stream, and now, while Sam is away laying claim to the land, they are ready to kill the entire family. Adam takes it on himself to escape and warn Sam. He endures pain and near death, but he manages, with the help of a mountain lion, to overcome two of the men and to return to help rescue his family. Everyone behaves heroically—his mother, sister, stepfather, and the dog.

To the book's credit, the story is always believable. Even the miraculous intervention of the mountain lion is explained. Adam now considers Sam his father, and the family will be strong and successful. The emotional issues are as important to the book's success as is the adventure. The greed and cruelty of the gold-crazed villains are palpably described, as are the courage and humanity of the family.

Understanding Adoption

Adoption is unique as a loss situation because it is often totally beyond the control of the persons experiencing it. Usually long before conscious awareness of family structure develops, adopted children permanently leave their original environment for another. Today psychologists are increasingly aware that the impact of adoption is strong. Many children seriously question their adoptive identity, unsure of their roles in the traditions and destiny of the families that have chosen them. Urged on by a sense of loss, they search to know more about the biological and environmental heritage that has been taken from them; for some, the longing develops into an active search in adulthood.

569. Bawden, Nina. *The Finding*. New York: Lothrop, 1985. 153 pp. Fiction.

Interest level: Ages 9–12 Reading level: Grade 5

Alex was found when he was a newborn in the arms of a statue of the Sphinx in the park. Alex is happy with his adopted family. They love him, and they have helped him to feel secure with them. Then the woman next door dies and leaves Alex and a missing daughter all of her fortune. The notoriety and fuss cause a problem at home, and Alex runs away, thinking that he is the cause of the trouble. He finds a woman who takes him home with her, and then things get complicated because he is kept in her house without being permitted to leave. At last he is taken to the scene of his original finding, whereupon he crawls into the arms of the Sphinx statue where he was first found, and it is there that his family locates him again.

The story is told in a masterful and suspenseful way. It escapes cliché because the author is always in control of the dialogue and characterization. The ending is satisfying and believable, and the issues of adoption, including the jealousy of the adopted child's siblings, are handled well.

570. Blume, Judy. *Just as Long as We're Together.* New York: Orchard, 1987. 296 pp. Fiction.

Interest level: Age 11+ Reading level: Grade 5

Friendship and its ups and downs, growing up, parents separating, fears of nuclear war, and adoption are but a few of the many themes running through this Blume novel that features three preadolescent girls and their families. Two of the girls, Rachel and Stephanie, have been best friends for years. When Alison, a Korean girl, joins them, there are a few minor problems, but the three girls become close-knit very quickly. Alison's mother is a famous movie star, but she is just Alison's mother at home.

Stephanie finds it very difficult to cope with her parents' separation. At the end of the book it looks as though her parents may get back together again. Alison is fearful that her parents won't want her anymore, because, after all, she is adopted, and now her mother is expecting a baby. Stephanie's younger brother awakens screaming in the night because of his fear of nuclear war. When he becomes active in lobbying for peace he feels much better.

As with all Blume books, there are large societal issues that the characters are confronted with, but the funny and effective parts of the book have to do with the everyday traumas of growing up. This one has too many main characters to sustain continuous attention, but young girls, in particular, will probably find that their concerns are being addressed here.

571. Bowe-Gutman, Sonia. *Teen Pregnancy.* Minneapolis: Lerner, 1987. 72 pp. Nonfiction.

Interest level: Age 12+ Reading level: Grade 6

This book is meant for three groups: pregnant teens looking for information and advice, sexually active teens who wonder or worry about pregnancy, and teens who feel they are not yet ready for sex but need reassurance. While giving statistics about sexual activity (about 40 percent of adolescents are sexually active), Bowe-Gutman urges that youngsters develop their own value system in order to be able to make important decisions. She sorts out the common reasons for having sex, listing those she considers poor (among them to be held, to defend against loneliness, or to be "in"). Once someone decides to be sexually active, a second decision must be made—whether or not to allow pregnancy.

The remainder of the book tells how to avoid pregnancy, including exploding common myths and illustrating what the various mechanisms look like, for example, a condom on an erect penis. Other chapters explain what a baby needs in terms of attention, health, and financial care, demonstrated through several case histories of teen relationships. The chapter "If You Think You're Pregnant" is actually disappointingly brief, giving signs of pregnancy, instructions on how to find a doctor, and the next steps, including brief mention of abortion but fuller attention to ways to keep the baby or give it up for adoption. The tone of the book as a whole is respectful and informative, telling readers of their legal rights, for example. List of organizations that can help, bibliography.

572. Cassedy, Sylvia. *Behind the Attic Wall.* New York: Crowell, 1983; Avon, pap. 315 pp. Fiction.

Interest level: Age 10+ Reading level: Grade 4

Maggie, an orphan who has been shuffled around from place to place, goes to live with two great-aunts in a large old house. She is careless in her dress, skinny and small for her 12 years, and she has a nervous habit of chewing her hair. Although her aunts and her peers show her no affection and fail to recognize her worth or needs, Maggie finds two dolls who come to life and become the objects of her love. After she becomes involved with the dolls she pays more attention to how she looks, and she stops chewing her hair. She even makes friends with a classmate, a first for Maggie. When her aunts discover the dolls, thus destroying the magic, Maggie reverts to her old behavior. Miraculously, when labeled as a failure and put up for adoption by the aunts, Maggie is adopted by a loving family, and we know that all will be well.

The author employs a technique of part realism and part fantasy. She makes it clear that the dolls are not part of Maggie's imagination. They are contrasted with a group of imaginary friends whom Maggie has invented. Maggie is portrayed realistically as a psychologically abused child. She has a low opinion of herself, takes things that do not belong to her, is angry most of the time, and expects to be treated badly. She is aggressive and unruly. It is unfortunate that only a magical intervention can save her. The book would be more impressive if the solution were more realistic.

573. Cohen, Shari. *Coping with Being Adopted.* New York: Rosen, 1988. 136 pp. Nonfiction.

Interest level: Ages 11–15 Reading level: Grade 5

Cohen discusses the common feelings about being adopted ("Why did she give me away?" for example), but goes a step further in offering ways to cope with offhanded remarks that may unintentionally hurt, with the longing to know the biological parents, with the extra frustrations adopted children might have.

Young people are interviewed and through them the reader learns the fantasies adopted children may have. ("*They* would let me go on the trip.") To counter fears and anger, she recommends removing the expression "because I'm adopted" from the inner and exterior vocabulary and searching for other explanations in events instead. Practical suggestions for handling anger and talking out feelings are offered. She also recommends using nonjudgmental responses to upsetting remarks, setting the situation straight, not ignoring what has been said.

There are brief sections on transracial and handicapped adoptees, reflecting some of the prejudices that they may encounter and how to handle them. In handling actions by family members who favor the birth children in a family (say, grandparents who give better gifts to them), Cohen is less strong, advising children to view the problem as that of the relative and ignore it. One would think the adoptive parent could play a role here. The sense of humor Cohen recommends may not be enough.

Cohen recommends finding out who you are before searching for biological parents and gives exercises to start the process going. The conflicts teens have with their parents are examined in light of adoption, and means of communicating better without running away are listed. As for the search that may ultimately be undertaken, studies show that if the subject is treated positively and honestly, the adoptee can be more at peace. Cohen gives examples of both positive and negative characteristics. Finally, there are informative chapters on parents' views (particularly on letting go) and how the mechanics of the adoption system works in this country. Although sometimes too brief on the depth and complexity of issues (such as accidental revelation of adoption and secret keeping), this book is somewhat unique in the literature, and thereby its many strengths will offer help to those who need it. Bibliography, index.

574. Fisher, Iris L. *Katie-Bo: An Adoption Story*. Illus. by Miriam Schaer. New York: Adama, 1987. 56 pp. Fiction.

Interest level: Ages 5–9 Reading level: Grades 2–3

What a happy book this is, with its colorful collages and pretty clothespin-decorated frames for the words. Seen from the viewpoint of her brother-to-be, the chronology of the story involves explaining that a baby is growing "in *a* mommy's tummy but not *our* mommy's tummy," and is being given up for adoption because the birth mother "loves her baby so much." (This part is not filled out adequately and is therefore unclear—why would someone give away someone loved so much?) Then the fat little social worker comes and asks the two children already in the family how they feel about adopting a sister. "We tell her GREAT."

The family then sets out learning everything they can about Korea, which is where the baby is being born. In time, the baby arrives, now two months old. There are touches of real family emotion here—one of the older children draws on the wall in combination of generosity and hostility, both mother and father cry when the baby arrives, and so on. The interchange with a judge closes the book, with Katie-Bo's older brother calling her (a combination of American and Korean names) his "forever sister."

575. Freudberg, Judy, and Geiss, Tony. *Susan and Gordon Adopt a Baby.* Illus. by Joe Mathieu. New York: Random/Children's Television Workshop, 1986. 20 pp. Fiction.

Interest level: Ages 3–7 Reading level: Grade 2

This story tells how Susan and Gordon become the parents of Miles by adopting him. The book emphasizes that now they will be Miles's parents forever, and that when someone new enters the family the love just grows and grows—so there is plenty of love to go around.

576. Girard, Linda Walvoord. *Adoption Is for Always.* Illus. by Judith Freeman. Niles, Ill.: Whitman, 1986. 32 pp. Fiction.

Interest level: Ages 4–8 Reading level: Grade 2

When Celia finally hears the words her parents have been telling her since she was a little girl, that she is adopted, she reacts with anger. She goes through various stages: grief, anger, pain, loneliness, fear, curiosity about her birth parents, resentment, longing, self-doubt, and, finally, acceptance. Her parents and the adults around her give her support, firm but loving responses, and understanding. They also reassure her that they will always be her parents, and that she belongs with them.

One of the things the parents do is get a book from the library on adoption. Celia rejects the book at first, but she soon uses it to comfort and inform herself. Her parents also do not make the mistake of coddling her; they understand her anger, but they do not permit her to break the rules that they have consistently set forth. She must still pick up her things and behave constructively. They remind her of how they felt when they first adopted her. They assure her that it was through no fault of her own that her birth parents gave her up for adoption. And an adult friend indicates that her birth mother must have loved her very much to let her go to a family that would love and care for her better than her birth mother could.

Some critics might argue that this is a somewhat didactic and simplistic book, but coupled with books presenting other perspectives, this book can probably be very useful not only for children who are adopted but also for children who want to understand how adoption works.

577. Greenberg, Judith E., and Carey, Helen H. *Adopted.* Photos by Barbara Kirk. New York: Watts, 1987. 32 pp. Nonfiction.

Interest level: Ages 5–9 Reading level: Grade 2

Sarah and Ryan are adopted siblings, both adopted beyond the newborn stage, Ryan just one week earlier as a toddler. A friend asks Sarah if adopted babies can be taken back if they cry too much. "Nobody can send Ryan back. . . . We adopted him and he's part of our family now." Sarah's mother overhears this conversation and works to help her daughter, explaining, "Sometimes a healthy baby can't grow in a mother's uterus. . . ." She continues that both children were born in the hospital, but she didn't see them until the adoption agency brought them together. Later, when Sarah asks who her real mother is, she tells Sarah, "I am. . . . I didn't help you to be born, but I am your mother because I take care of you and love you." She also tells of the goodness of her birth mother, who perhaps was alone or too young to care for her but let her be adopted so she "could have all the things she needed to grow up happy and healthy."

In a side note it is mentioned that Sarah has two friends who are adopted also, one of whom is Vietnamese and came here at age six. The picture of Sarah's extended family is warm and her grandfather advises, "Being adopted doesn't make you different or special. You are special because you are Sarah." He then tells what makes her special, and too much of it seems to hinge on kindness and sharing, but the photographs in this section are especially strong, allowing the extra sweetness to glide by.

578. Lindsay, Jeanne Warren. *Open Adoption: A Caring Option.* Buena Park, Calif.: Morning Glory, 1987, hb and pap. 256 pp. Nonfiction.

Interest level: Age 14+ Reading level: Grade 7

Equally useful to pregnant teenagers and their parents, this book explores current outlooks in adoption. The author is a teacher in a Teen Mother program, for pregnant teens who don't wish to remain in the regular classroom during their pregnancy. Through use of vignettes of various cases, the author presents changing drama in families, the law, and society. The chapters look at closed adoption, open adoption, the respective rights of birth parents and adoptive parents, and the role of the church—also, how an agency can move from closed to open adoption. Specific agencies are profiled to give readers an idea of the counseling and services they might expect, and results that can come from the new honesty. A special chapter looks at teen pregnancy. In its attentive look at such complex issues as confidentiality, reactions of birth grandparents, and grief, the author provides details of a new avenue teenagers might not have considered. A rich examination throughout. Annotated bibliography.

579. Lindsay, Jeanne Warren. *Pregnant Too Soon: Adoption Is an Option.* Rev. ed. Illus. by Pam Morford. Buena Park, Calif.: Morning Glory, 1988, pap. 224 pp. Nonfiction.

Interest level: Age 13+ Reading level: Grade 6

The author works professionally in a school system helping pregnant teens make decisions. Her primary aim is not to promote adoption over abortion but to discuss it as an alternative to premature and potentially disastrous marriage. Using the stories of people she has worked with—teenage mothers, the fathers, their parents, adoptive parents, and so forth—she informs readers sensitively about aspects of the teenage pregnancy and its outcome that they should consider. Topics include finding out if one is ready to be a parent, how agencies for adoption work, legal matters (birth certificates, who pays counseling fees, foster care, and so on). Also included are independent adoption and what each person's role is (lawyer, birth parents, and adoptive parents), adoption by relatives, fathers' rights (what they are and how to protect them), and the potential search when the child grows up. Special situations are also handled in this book, for example, releasing a toddler for adoption, open adoption where everyone knows who's who from the start and both birth parents and adoptive parents play important roles in the development of the child.

A chapter is devoted to feelings of grief and how to deal with them. The chapter on grief includes discussion of seeing the baby before adoption, hurting doesn't mean it is necessarily the wrong decision, rights as a birth parent, and fathers grieve, too. By reading the many stories of others, by the time readers come to the questionnaire at the end of the book from which they hope to find out more about their ability to parent right now, they know more about themselves and can answer these many questions and strive for a decision. More than 40 questions range from life-style decisions, to what one expects from a child, to communication between the pregnant couple. An appendix speaks to parents of the pregnant couple, informing them of where and how to help them find good counselors, matters to think about if their children choose to be parents now, and how to help themselves as birth grandparents. This is a well-thought out, very helpful book. Bibliography, index.

580. McDonald, Joyce. *Mail-Order Kid.* New York: Putnam, 1988. 125 pp. Fiction.

Interest level: Ages 9–12 Reading level: Grade 4

Flip Doty has received a live fox that he ordered through the mail without telling his parents he was doing it. Flip's parents have adopted Todd, a six-year-old Korean child, and somehow, for Flip, the fox and Todd are similar. Through taking care of the fox and getting fond of it, he understands more about what Todd is feeling.

Todd stays with Flip's family, but it is clear that the fox must go. With Todd's help, Flip relinquishes his pet to the wild, where he knows the fox will be much happier. By this time he loves his brother and appreciates what Todd has endured as a child who must make an adjustment to a place so different from his native land.

The parents are depicted as knowledgeable and sensitive people. The author does a fine job of balancing the benefits of adoption with the pain of adjustment.

581. Mayhar, Ardath. *Carrots and Miggle.* New York: Atheneum, 1986. 159 pp. Fiction.

Interest level: Age 10+ Reading level: Grades 5–6

Charlotte, familiarly known as Carrots, does not feel welcoming to her orphaned cousin who has come to her family's Texas dairy farm from England, where she was used to city life. As far as Carrots is concerned, Emiglia, dubbed Miggle, is just one more burden to Carrots's widowed mother, who already has Carrots, her younger sister, and her older brother and his wife to take care of.

It is a difficult adjustment for Miggle. She is used to the refinement of the academy and considers her relatives to be peasants. But she is a spunky young woman, and she is grateful to her family for taking her in. She complains regularly about the work, the heat, and their manners, but she becomes part of the family. She and Carrots have adventures with nasty girls at school and emerge victorious. At the end of the story she has the opportunity to move in with yet another relative who is very well-to-do, and who lives in a fine house in California. But Miggle likes the fact that she is needed and asks to stay. Everyone is pleased by this because they have all grown to love Miggle and to want her to remain with them.

Nothing of much import happens in this story, and Carrots and her family are too good to be true. This book is one of those old-fashioned, sweet stories where the heroes are all virtuous, and problems are overcome through gentleness and truth. As an example of this genre, the book does well.

582. Mills, Claudia. *Boardwalk with Hotel.* New York: Macmillan, 1985; Bantam, pap. 131 pp. Fiction.

Interest level: Ages 9–12 Reading level: Grade 4

After a baby-sitter inadvertently discloses to 11-year-old Jessica that her parents thought they couldn't have children, which was why they adopted her, Jessica thinks that perhaps she is second-best to her siblings, who are her parents' children by birth. From that moment on Jessica questions and mistrusts everything her parents do or say. She is convinced that they love her sister and brother more than they love her. She becomes sullen, argumentative, and nasty.

As the story progresses Jessica comes to learn more and more about herself. When she is a sore loser at Monopoly, she seeks solace from her best friend, who tells her affectionately that she is, indeed, regularly a sore loser. When she finally tells her father what has been bothering her, he is not effusive in his reassurance, but he is clear about his love for her.

Finally, when Jessica realizes that she loves her brother, even though she resents and dislikes him at times, she comes to terms with her feelings of rejection and understands how her parents feel. The author honestly and humorously presents a family's way of dealing with children, both natural and adopted, and makes it clear that it is not the fact of adoption, but the actions and character of the child that determine the parents' reactions.

583. Nickman, Steven L. *The Adoption Experience: Stories and Commentaries.* New York: Messner, 1985. 192 pp. Nonfiction.

Interest level: Age 11+ Reading level: Grade 6

Told from the point of view of a child psychiatrist who has subspecialized in the concerns of adoptive children (and who has also had adoptive family experiences), these stories and attendant commentaries are up-to-date in their attention to social change. Included are stories about searching for birth parents, foster care, adopting older and other special-needs children, transracial adoption, adoption of a child from another country, adoptions that never "took" (in which a child eventually had to leave), and a story about birth parents who are about to give up their baby. The commentaries offer insight and compassion to the reader, for example, about the importance and variations that can take place in bonding, both between birth parents and adoptive parents and their children. By reading the stories and commentaries children and their relatives and friends may for the first time dare to talk openly about the difficulties in the relationship. From this book they will also learn there are agencies and professionals who can help with problems that are coming up years after the adoptive agency may have left the picture. Perhaps because the author has tried to cram multiple concerns into seven stories, they are occasionally hard to follow, but to seek out the meat of this book, readers, who are likely to hunger for the information, will probably work harder.

584. Rosenberg, Maxine. *Being Adopted.* Photos by George Ancona. New York: Lothrop, 1984. 48 pp. Nonfiction.

Interest level: Ages 7–10 Reading level: Grade 3

Three children are introduced who have been adopted into three different American families: Rebecca, a 7-year-old Cheyenne girl; Andrei, a 10-

year-old boy from India; and 8-year-old Karin, a Korean child adopted by the author into a family where there are already three biological sons. Through sensitive text and wonderful black-and-white photographs the book brings out many issues pertaining to adoption that are not unique to these youngsters.

The fear of a new environment and family structure, the period of initial adjustment, the inevitable questions about birth mothers and the reason children were given up, and feelings of rejection and low self-worth are all functions of any adoption. The book also discusses the additional problems that pertain to multicultural adoptions: the issue of looking different from their adoptive parents and siblings; daydreams about life in their culture of origin; and the desire to look and be like the dominant culture. Rosenberg tempers the difficulties encountered by these children with the constant reassurance that it is the love and cooperation among family members that binds them rather than physical appearance or place of birth.

The author's perspective is clear, particularly because she is one of the adoptive parents. But she does not minimize the challenges that face both the families and the children in these augmented families.

585. Sobol, Harriet Langsam. *We Don't Look Like Our Mom and Dad.* Photos by Patricia Agre. New York: Coward, 1984. 32 pp. Nonfiction.
Interest level: Ages 5–9 Reading level: Grade 2

Eric (age 10) and Joshua Levin (age 11) are brothers by adoption; they have different biological mothers and both are Korean by birth. They were adopted as babies. Their Caucasian parents keep their Korean heritage alive by cooking Korean food, by reading books about Korea and Korean culture, and by saving the clothing in which they arrived. Both boys still have Korean middle names. Like children everywhere, they enjoy hearing their baby stories, in this case, about their arrival at the airport to join the Levins.

The Levins sought out Korean children because of the recognized need of children in Korea for parents. They were aided by an agency. Eric and Joshua do feel slightly different from the other children in their community, but they spend little time thinking about their origins. They're too busy with school and playing with friends. When in anger Eric says, "You're not my brother," their mother answers, "In this family, you're brothers."

Like many adopted children, Eric wonders why his mother gave him up for adoption. He is bothered that he didn't grow inside his American mother. For some of the boy's questions there are no known answers. His adoptive mother can only speculate that his biological mother cared about him and realized that she could not properly care for him. She assures him that his mother must have felt sad for a long time after she gave him up for adoption. Also discussed are the negative and inquisitive looks this family gets when they are shopping. This book honestly addresses both the joys and the problems that arise.

This seems to be a model book, addressing honestly both the joys and problems that arise. The Levins are not a typical family. No one in the family is biologically related to any of the others. Nevertheless they are a family because they choose to be one.

586. Yolen, Jane. *Children of the Wolf.* New York: Viking Kestrel, 1984. 136 pp. Fiction.
Interest level: Age 10+ Reading level: Grade 5

Yolen wrote this book after she had done considerable research, about feral, or wild, children and India. The story is based on an account by a missionary and rector, of an orphanage in India in 1920, of the discovery of two children who were found living with a wolf and her two cubs.

The setting of this story is also India, and the details of the finding of the two wild children coincide with the historical incident. But this book really focuses on the people who adopt the wild children rather than on the feral children themselves. The emotions of the children in the orphanage as well as the religious zeal of the director and his wife are important to the story. The responsibility for caring for the new children without jeopardizing the security of the others presents a dilemma. Mohandas, the orphan who most takes on the care of the new children, feels a kinship with the wild ones, but he also feels torn because he wants the friendship and approval of his friend Rama, who despises the Wolf girls.

The story is a complex and, ultimately, tragic one. Both girls die without ever really having rejoined the human society. Neither of them is ever happy in the orphanage, and the question is raised that perhaps it was a mistake to bring them out of the wild. However, they probably would have died earlier had they been left with the wolves; they were scrawny and full of worms and disease. Ironically, Mohandas is sent to England to be educated, and there he is treated as if he were a feral child by the other boys at school. Nevertheless, he perseveres, and he becomes a writer, indicating, perhaps, that there really is hope for the wild orphans of the world.

The Homeless Ones

Homeless children know loss because they are separated from the family life they sense is part of most children's lives. Without economic or emotional support, they struggle to maintain even physical well-being. Deprivation of the most basic needs implies greater losses, for without the satisfaction of these needs it is impossible for children to concentrate on the search for love or self-actualization.

Those who run away choose to lose, temporarily or permanently, the support of the family. Others are cast from their homes, throwaway children. Still others are children trying to survive abandonment on their own instead of appealing to the authorities. Some are street children. They all attempt to find the answer to the question "Who will take care of me?" by responding, "I will."

587. Aaron, Chester. *Lackawanna.* New York: Lippincott, 1986. 210 pp. Fiction.

Interest level: Age 12+ Reading level: Grade 7

It is difficult for many young readers in today's affluent society to comprehend what life was like for children their age during the time of the Great Depression. In this disturbing novel, six children of varying ages meet in a Hooverville constructed of shacks. All their parents have either died or deserted them in hopes that orphans would be more eligible for welfare than children with able-bodied parents. The children band together and declare themselves a family. They name themselves Lackawanna, for the freight trains they hop in search of food and money.

The six children find shelter in an abandoned building where Carl's father used to do bookbinding. They are warm and dry and somewhat comfortable there until the day that Herbie, the youngest of the group, gets kidnapped. Deirdre, Herbie's sister, is frantic. Willie, the leader of the group, gathers information from a railroad worker, and the five children go off in search of Herbie. He has been kidnapped by a hobo whose own son died. When the group finds Herbie, he is reluctant to leave the hobo, who has been like a father to him for several weeks. One of the children freezes to death; another is hospitalized because a policeman attacked him. In the end the remaining five survive because they help each other.

The details of the life of a hobo during the depression are shockingly specific. During this era many people starved to death, and many more were homeless. The story succeeds as a story, but it is also a history text from which young readers can learn.

588. Bell, William. *Crabbe's Journey.* Boston: Little, 1986. 169 pp. Fiction.

Interest level: Age 13+ Reading level: Grade 7

Intelligent, rich, and an alcoholic, Franklin Crabbe has everything except confidence in himself. He runs away into the wilderness to find himself through physical testing and challenge. Each mistake he makes during his journey is his own, and he must learn from it or not survive. With each success the reader sees his confidence grow and his acceptance of himself as a person increase.

Unfortunately, the other characters in the book remain fuzzy, in particular Franklin's parents. The author seems to have little regard for them or for their suffering when their son disappears. Their feelings are touched on lightly, but not understood or accorded any importance. Although as a metaphor, the trip serves its purpose well, in reality it is difficult to believe that an inexperienced person could survive alone without anyone knowing where he is. It is a dangerous example to set and readers should be warned against attempting to emulate the journey. Further, Franklin's decision to run away is not given the serious attention it should have. This was a foolhardy and potentially self-destructive act, and attention should be called to that fact.

589. Bentley, Judith. *Refugees: Search for a Haven.* Photos. New York: Messner, 1986. 160 pp. Nonfiction.
Interest level: Ages 12–16 Reading level: Grade 6

Today's refugees forced from their homelands are the subjects here, be it from Indochina, Latin America, Africa, or Afghanistan. Accounts of the decisions made to avoid political, religious, ethnic, or economic oppression are seen through exploring the plights of individuals and their families. Among them is a student, jailed for participation in a demonstration in Ethiopia; another is a family that left Cambodia, fearful for their lives. Bentley has done good research regarding statistics, public policy, the conditions forcing the emigration, and the dilemmas met afterward. Particularly interesting is the contrast of governmental efforts and some of the private endeavors of the sanctuary movement to reach out, which are sometimes more successful. Bibliography, index.

590. Carter, Anne. *Ruff Leaves Home.* Illus. by John Butler. New York: Crown, 1986. 28 pp. Fiction.
Interest level: Ages 7–10 Reading level: Grade 3

Even though mother fox feels that Ruff is not yet ready to leave home, he does. He explores his environment, stays in a park for the winter, and at the end of winter finds a mate. The cycle begins again in the spring when one of Ruff's cubs decides to go off on his own and explore. The illustrations, paintings that look like giant close-up photographs, elevate the simple story to a work of art. The young fox is appealing in his independence and curiosity. The message of the cycle of nature is communicated well.

591. Dumas, Jacqueline. *And I'm Never Coming Back.* Illus. by Iris Paabo. Toronto: Annick, 1986, hb and pap. 24 pp. Fiction.

Interest level: Ages 4–8 Reading level: Grade 2

Louise meets her mother as she returns from work. Louise has had a rotten day and has packed a bag, ready to run away from this household where her father and sister find her a pest. "Are you sure you want to go? We would all miss you so terribly," her mother says. In an original turn, the mother suggests they run away together. (She explains she hasn't had such a good day either. And she definitely doesn't feel like making supper.) The suggestion is to hop in the car and drive off, just the two of them.

After saying good-bye to her father and her sister, Jennifer, off they go to the country. They stay at a motel, where Louise can stay up late. When she finally does get to sleep, Louise says, "This is so much fun. We should have brought Jennifer." Delightful in the mother's understanding of her child, this is a winning book indeed. Wouldn't it be wonderful if every child could have a memory such as this spontaneous loving event?

592. Eige, Lillian. *The Kidnapping of Mister Huey.* New York: Harper, 1983. 153 pp. Fiction.

Interest level: Ages 9–12 Reading level: Grades 4–5

Willy is 14 years old. He has become friendly with an old man, Mister Huey, who lives in one of the houses on Willy's paper route. Mister Huey's grandson wants to place his grandfather in an old age home. Willy's parents have been fighting a lot, so when they decide to take a trip together so that they can come to terms with each other, Willy is pleased. They make arrangements for him to go to camp, but he has other plans in mind. He wants to run away with old Mister Huey in order to protect Mister Huey from having to go to a run-down, unappetizing old age home.

The two runaways find an abandoned town where they camp out for two weeks. They meet a young girl whose mother is emotionally exhausted after the death of her young son. The three characters understand each other and help make the two weeks they spend together a time they will all treasure.

When the inevitable occurs, and they are discovered, Willy prevails on his parents to help Mister Huey keep his house. All works out for the best as each of the characters emerges stronger and more hopeful. The running away has helped Willy to mature, and it has given Mister Huey confidence in his ability to maintain his independence.

It is usually not a good idea to offer running away as a solution to a family problem, but in this case the running away turns into a positive action and is justified.

593. Evernden, Margery. *The Dream Keeper.* Illus. by Eric S. Nones. New York: Lothrop, 1985. 173 pp. Fiction.

Interest level: Age 11+ Reading level: Grade 6

Although Becka is the main character in this complicated story of a musical family that lives in a large house belonging to an elderly great-grandmother, it is the old "bobe," Hannah, who is by far the most interesting of the characters. The story within the story, that of the old bobe's leaving her shtetl to come to America, is the powerful one in this book. It would have sufficed as the only plot, because the modern-day complications of the parents' marital problems and Becka's aspirations are intrusions that are never fully fleshed out.

Until the old woman's story is told, using the ruse of some old tapes that are found in the attic, the interaction of Becka's parents, as well as Becka's anxieties, are overshadowed by the bobe's strange and dramatic decision to be removed to a nursing home. It is not until the end of the book that Becka discovers that Hannah hoped, by leaving, to help Becka's parents to reconcile. This does not ring true, and if it were so, it would certainly be a vain hope.

Even though the rest of the family is shadowy, and their circumstances do not compel attention, Hannah's story is an interesting one. She is an attractive character as a young woman. She is energetic, talented, and intelligent. She is also independent and strong. Her determination to come to America and her ability to make a life for herself are admirable. The book is worth some notice for Hannah's tale of leaving home and surviving in a strange and new environment.

594. Garfield, Leon. *Fair's Fair.* Illus. by S. D. Schindler. Garden City, N.Y.: Doubleday, 1983. 32 pp. Fiction.

Interest level: Ages 7–10 Reading level: Grades 3–4

With lavish and flavorful illustrations to match, this story, which has a Victorian flavor, tells of two orphans, who, because of their bravery and generosity, find a home with a rich benefactor. Each of the children befriends a large dog and follows it to its home. They live in the seemingly empty house for a while, cleaning it and accepting gratefully the food that is left there each day. They finally meet their generous host, and he adopts them. The story is a fantasy, but it is a satisfying one where the blend of the illustrations and writing causes the reader to suspend disbelief.

595. Gondosch, Linda. *Who Needs a Bratty Brother?* Illus. by Helen Cogancherry. New York: Lodestar, 1985; Minstrel, pap. 118 pp. Fiction.

Interest level: Ages 8–11 Reading level: Grade 4

Kelly's rivalry with her nine-year-old brother, Ben, has gone beyond bickering. It is now out and out war. Eleven-year-old Kelly doesn't object to her little sister, Samantha, but she's sorry her mother ever gave birth to Ben. Ben puts worms in her water glass, competes with her for the prize in the cereal box, reads her library books and uses a mouse's tail as a bookmark, explodes balloons filled with icy water in her face, and, in general, is the bane of her existence.

Kelly plots to get rid of Ben. First, she earns some money to help contribute to the cost of sending him away to camp. Ben is such a disruptive influence that he is sent home after one day. Then Kelly arranges to have him sent to their grandparents' house. Again he is brought back after one day, but this time it is because he has chicken pox. The dreadful boy runs around Kelly's room touching everything in hopes of giving Kelly the chicken pox, too. Sure enough, Kelly contracts chicken pox and, to her chagrin, is prevented from attending the beginning days of school.

When Ben disappears, Kelly is as upset as everyone else in her family. It turns out that Ben feels unloved and has run away. The reaction to his deed is very satisfying to Ben: Everyone tells him how much they missed him and how worried they were about him. Even Kelly is glad to see that he is all right.

It is unfortunate that the pat solution of running away to make people know how much they love you is given here as a good idea. It is a dangerous act and should be viewed as such. Children need to know how much of a risk they take when they run away from home. Parents can communicate their love and concern without a child's having to resort to such an act.

In truth, Ben is a monstrous child. He has no regard for other people, and his pranks are ugly. His parents seem powerless to help him develop self-discipline, and when he runs away in response to well-earned punishment, they are sorry. Their behavior does not augur well for the future.

596. Guernsey, JoAnn Bren. *Journey to Almost There.* New York: Clarion, 1985. 166 pp. Fiction.

Interest level: Age 10+ Reading level: Grade 5

Alison runs away with her grandfather, Oliver, to rescue him from being placed in a nursing home. Her mother, his daughter-in-law, thinks that he needs to be in a home because of his Parkinson's disease. Although Alison is only 15, she drives them across country to be with her father, whom she hasn't seen since he deserted the family when Alison was a baby. He has been writing to her from Rockport, Massachusetts, for a year, so she has hopes that he will take her and grandfather in. In any case, she has an overwhelming curiosity about her father, and she wants to see him.

The trip is a difficult one because of Oliver's illness and his reaction to different medications. He hallucinates and behaves erratically because of it. He is hospitalized briefly, and then they continue their journey, with far fewer traumas. When they reach Rockport, they discover that Alison's father, Oliver's son, has again fled. He could not face them. Sadly, but with determination and new knowledge, Alison and her grandfather prepare to make the trip back home to Minnesota, where Alison's mother is eagerly awaiting them.

Running away should not be the solution to a massive family problem. It is always better if the family members can work out the issues without resorting to dangerous behavior. In this case the trip was tiring and nearly disastrous, but Alison and her grandfather came to know themselves and each other a lot more than they had previously. Alison also learned new information about her mother and about her own background. She learned that her father was a weakling and a failure, but she forgave him and prepared to live her own life more constructively.

597. Landau, Elaine. *The Homeless.* New York: Messner, 1987. 112 pp. Nonfiction.

Interest level: Ages 11–16 Reading level: Grades 5–6

The brutality of being homeless comes through on the first page in the story of "Mama," a homeless woman who is found dead in New York's Grand Central Station on Christmas morning. The varying reasons for being homeless are explored (mental illness, destitution, housing shortages, eviction, fires, alcoholism, eccentric preference, and so on). Landau shows sympathy for their plight. ("It is nearly impossible for someone in extremely dire circumstances to remain neat and clean.")

As in her other books, Landau combines research into public policy and statistics with individual first-person stories to make her story come alive. An example is Marybeth, who had four children in five years of marriage, then became widowed, was ill, then evicted. In telling the stories, Landau weaves in material about public shelters, treatment facilities, and so forth. Landau seems to have come to know homeless individuals and tells of their habits, again sympathetically: "Life on the street forces homeless people to become aware of the hours at which public rest rooms open and close. Whenever possible, they try to regulate their food and liquid intake in order to avoid middle-of-the-night emergencies."

A special chapter is devoted to homeless youth and their attempts to survive, albeit through illegal trading of body and substance, after running away or being thrown out. Like the rest of the book, it is moving and disturbing. To read that a nine-year-old prefers the abuse of a sex ring to the home environment tells of astounding levels of violence in this society. Unfortunately, according to Landau, the crisis is likely to continue, bright lights appearing from private and local sources, not the federal government. Bibliography, index.

598. Levoy, Myron. *The Magic Hat of Mortimer Wintergreen.* New York: Harper, 1988. 211 pp. Fiction.

Interest level: Ages 8–12 Reading level: Grades 4–5

This comic fantasy has serious overtones: Joshua and his younger sister, Amy, have been orphaned and forced to live with their evil and abusive Aunt Vootch. Amy, who is an artist, has stopped drawing human beings. She does not trust anyone over the age of 15.

Then, one day, the children meet the magical and eccentric Mortimer Wintergreen. He owns a magic hat that has a mind of its own and is very unpredictable. The children run away with Mortimer Wintergreen and have many adventures, all of them amusing and imaginative. With the aid of the magic hat they finally locate their grandparents with whom they feel loved and secure.

This is really a book about running *to* rather than away. Aunt Vootch is a cartoon villain. For those people who might be tempted to compare this book with some of Roald Dahl's fantasies, the differences are palpable. Although the characters have the flavor of a Dahl romp, the heroes are not vicious or cruel to others. No one gets mutilated or seriously hurt. The magician is eccentric, but he is more the captive of his magic than the master of it. He is good-hearted and willing to confess his shortcomings. His values are clear and constructive. Although the characters in the book fall into certain stereotypical categories (the wicked aunt, the kind and quirky grandparents), the story is not one that teaches intolerance.

Levoy returns at the end of the story to the neighborhood he so lovingly draws in his earlier work *The Witch of Fourth Street and Other Stories* (Harper, 1972). His style is respectful of his audience and of his characters. This book may be helpful, because its fantasy format is an unusual one in helping children sort out their feelings about an abusive situation, and their responsibility for extricating themselves from it.

599. MacLachlan, Patricia. *Sarah, Plain and Tall.* New York: Harper, 1985, hb and pap. 58 pp. Fiction.

Interest level: Age 8+ Reading level: Grade 3

This 1986 Newbery Award winner can be read at many different levels by readers from 8 to 80. It deals with the feelings of two children whose mother has died; it alludes to the loneliness of life on the prairie; it palpably presents the feelings of displacement caused by leaving home.

Sarah is a mail-order bride. She becomes very important to Papa, Caleb, and Anna, who fear that she will never recover from her longing for the ocean of her native Maine. Sarah's recovery takes a while; she manages to bring some of the sea to the prairie by her colored-pencil drawings and by using the simile of the grain looking like the ocean. She will probably never totally lose her sadness over having to leave her home, but she has added a set of people and things that she loves here in her new home.

Anna, the oldest child, is capable and sensitive. She harbors a secret pain whenever she sees her brother, Caleb. After all, it was as a result of Caleb's birth that her mother died. But she loves Caleb, and she never lets him know that she blames him for their mother's death. All the characters convey a depth of emotion that readers resonate to.

The language, though simple, is passionate. For example, when Sarah returns from a shopping trip, much to Caleb's relief, "Caleb burst into tears. 'Seal [the cat] was very worried!' he cried. Sarah put her arms around him and he wailed into her dress. 'And the house is too small, we thought! And I am loud and pesky!' " The child's anguish over the thought that Sarah might leave the family is communicated in his outburst, and the reader and Sarah understand that he needs to be reassured.

The book is a small gem that will be treasured by all who are fortunate enough to read it.

600. Miller-Lachmann, Lyn. *Hiding Places.* Madison, Wis.: Stamp Out Sheep Press, 1987, pap. 208 pp. Fiction.

Interest level: Ages 12–16 Reading level: Grade 6

Seventeen-year-old Mark Lambert has seen too much: his parents' divorce, the drug-induced automobile crash death of his physician father, school failure, ulcers, physically abusive treatment from his perfectionistic stepfather, a suicide attempt, and retreat from his timid mother, who can't seem to protect him. Now his stepfather wants him to get discipline at military school. "No way," Mark insists, and runs off to New York's East Village shortly after he's been released from the hospital after near death from drinking.

There, after his widowed stepmother can't help him, he lands at Harbor House, a home for runaways, but can't make good use of the counseling offered there. Always a poet, and a capable student when he wants to be, Mark enrolls in the local high school and eventually gets his own apartment and supports himself with a free-lance typing business.

This gritty novel from an alternate press is highly readable and in spite of its surface subject matter, rather tame, sweet, and clean-cut. It is blessed with smooth writing, action, and believability, as Mark establishes himself as a young adult, making friends, meeting a girl, and finding adults he can trust. A central character, Dr. Sam, an administrator in the New York high school, becomes a guiding figure, and when he dies of a heart attack right after an argument that he and Mark have, Mark's guilt over his own father is reawakened and reinforced. Over the course of the novel, Mark becomes able to take responsibility for what is his (for example, his poetry, his aspirations) and leave behind responsibility for events beyond his control.

601. Paulsen, Gary. *The Crossing.* New York: Orchard, 1987. 114 pp. Fiction.

Interest level: Age 13+ Reading level: Grade 7

Manny is an orphan struggling to survive on the streets of Juarez, Mexico. Robert is a sergeant, a veteran of the Vietnam War, an alcoholic, and a hard man, stationed just across the border at Fort Bliss, Texas. The two meet several times and touch each other's lives in a significant way. At the end of the story the boy who could not ask for favors asks for one, and the man who could not grant favors, grants one, and there is hope for them both as a result. The story is told dramatically, and Paulsen's use of the border as a symbol of a spiritual as well as physical crossing works well.

602. Pfeffer, Susan Beth. *The Year Without Michael.* New York: Bantam, 1987. 164 pp. Fiction.

Interest level: Age 12+ Reading level: Grades 6–7

One day, Michael, who is almost 14 years old, disappears. There seems to be no apparent reason for him to have run away, but there is also no evidence of foul play. His family is frantic, and his absence affects every one of them for an entire year. His parents snap at and blame each other; his sisters put their own lives on hold until his hoped-for return; his grandparents hire a private detective; his older sister, Jody, goes off for a couple of days to search for him. All is to no avail, and the family looks as if it will fall apart until, at the end of a full year of this agony, they decide to go into family therapy in order to learn how to deal with Michael's loss and with each other.

The author masterfully builds the suspense and the anguish of the family of the missing boy. We never find out what happened to him, and we are given no hope that he will ever return. The uncertainty is one of the most difficult things for the reader as well as the family to bear. There is, however, hope that the family will learn to live with their loss, despite the pain that exists because of Michael's absence.

603. Springstubb, Tricia. *Which Way to the Nearest Wilderness?* Boston: Little, 1984; Dell, pap. 166 pp. Fiction.

Interest level: Ages 9–12 Reading level: Grade 5

Eunice gets a knot in her stomach every time her parents argue, and they argue more and more, and with increasing hostility. Eunice's younger brother is a disturbed child; her older sister seems to be totally preoccupied with her current boyfriend, but she, too, is frightened about the prospect of her parents possibly getting a divorce. Eunice is a very bright child, whose mother overly relies on her and calls her "my sensible child."

The story is about running away, but not in a conventional sense. Although it is Eunice who plans throughout the course of the book to emulate Thoreau and create her own Walden, it is Eunice's mother who runs away for a while. The family is jolted into the reality of life without their mother. Surprisingly, they manage very well, but equally surprising to them is that they miss her very much, even with all the fighting that their parents did.

When the mother, at last, returns, the author wisely does not provide a facile reconciliation and elimination of all the family's problems. It becomes clear that everyone will have to compromise a little, and that each person must bear the burden of anxiety about what will happen to the family. There are no guarantees, but there is hope.

604. Steiner, Connie Colker. *On Eagles' Wings and Other Things.* Illus. by the author. New York: Jewish Publication Society, 1988. 32 pp. Nonfiction.

Interest level: Ages 5–9 Reading level: Grade 2

The title is matched by poetic, heartfelt sentiment within, as the author-illustrator tells of the mass influx of immigrants Israel experienced at her birth. Four composite representative stories are told simultaneously: There is Avraham, a young Yemenite whose voyage in Operation Magic Carpet suddenly transports him and his family into mid-century technology; Eli, who left discrimination in Tunisia; Mira, who was left orphaned in the Holocaust and arrives with a group of supervised children; and Adrena, whose family left America for ideological reasons and who joins other Zionist relatives. The narrative is busy, but the emotions of each child and family as they pack, travel, and arrive are individually right on target. For Mira, whose life has held terror within, there is fear; for Avraham's airplane trip there is the "miracle" alluded to in the Bible: "Is it not written that we will return to our land on the wings of eagles?" In their new home, everyone "knew he was needed and—even better—wanted."

In the five years between 1948 and 1952, Israel's population more than doubled with groups and individuals arriving from all over the world. Israel's varied people have not always enjoyed peace with one another and their neighbors, but this is a book about the vibrant hopes as they truly existed at that time.

605. Sweeney, Joyce. *Center Line.* New York: Delacorte, 1984; Dell, pap. 246 pp. Fiction.

Interest level: Age 13+ Reading level: Grades 7–8

The five Culligan brothers range in age from 14 to 18. Shawn, the eldest, has devised a plan for all five to run away from home, in order to escape from their abusive alcoholic father. The boys are regularly beaten by their father, and it is possible that one day he might kill one of them.

The boys have many mishaps and narrow escapes on their journey. Four of them (Steve gets married along the way) settle for a while in Florida. Rick, next to the youngest of the brothers, has always been a problem. He has felt unloved and unwanted and has been particularly disturbed since his mother died. His mother had gone on a shopping trip and jokingly threatened that she would not return if Rick hit his baby brother, Mark. But he did hit him, and then she was killed in an automobile accident and did not, indeed, return. Rick thinks that he was to blame for her death.

When Rick accuses Shawn of being a bad brother, Shawn, in a rage, beats Rick, whereupon Rick reports his brothers to the police. It is ironic that for the first time the brothers are financially and situationally secure, and now they are threatened with being separated or sent back to their father. The probation officer and judge are sympathetic to Shawn and his brothers. They permit the young men to remain together.

Rick leaves his brothers, knowing that Shawn will always permit him to return whenever he wants to, but Rick vows never to return. The reader has very little hope for Rick's survival. But Shawn and his brothers will persevere and flourish.

The book is a painful saga of the ugly consequences of alcoholism and abuse. It is miraculous that childen can survive the conditions that some of them are subjected to. The author uses many profanities, and the gratuitous sex is out of place and dangerously cavalier. No young reader can afford to buy into that attitude in today's climate of danger. The judge is somewhat preachy, but makes a wise decision. The author makes the father disappear without explanation, so that it seems as if she couldn't find anything to do with his character. He is, at best, a stick figure, even at the beginning of the story.

Although the characterization is weak, and the characters' motivation and qualities are shadowy, the story serves to point up the dramatic and desperate situation of many runaways. It also illustrates again how lives can be destroyed by alcohol.

606. Thomas, Jane Resh. *Courage at Indian Deep.* New York: Clarion, 1984. 108 pp. Fiction.

Interest level: Ages 9–12 Reading level: Grade 4

Cass is angry at his family for having to move to the wilderness of the Lake Superior shore. He misses their home and his friends in the city. He does not make friends here; as a matter of fact, he has enemies. He stays more and more by himself and frequently goes to a cave where he has hidden some food and supplies. When an incident happens at school that causes Cass to fear his father's anger and punishment, he runs away. A storm arises and he is almost killed, but he and his former enemy manage to save most of the crew of a boat that was in danger of being wrecked by the storm. In the end Cass and his family are reunited in more ways than one. They have developed a new awareness of each other's feelings and needs.

Although Cass feels that he has to run away in order to solve his problems, and although the running away does seem to be the catalyst for the resolution of all his trouble, the author makes the reader aware of the danger of this act, and of the anguish that the family feels at the loss of their son. Young readers might benefit from trying to invent other ways that Cass could have behaved.

PART III

Selected Reading for Adult Guides

9

Separation and Loss

Books and Chapters in Books

Abramson, Jane B. *Mothermania: A Psychological Study of Mother-Daughter Conflict.* Lexington, Mass.: Lexington Books, 1986.

Adamec, Christine. *There Are Babies to Adopt: A Resource Guide for Prospective Parents.* Emeryville, Calif.: Publishers Group West, 1987.

Adler, Robert. *Sharing the Children: How to Resolve Custody Problems and Get on with Your Life.* New York: Adler and Adler, 1988.

Ahrons, Constance R., and Rodgers, Roy H. *Divorced Families: A Multidisciplinary Developmental View.* New York: Norton, 1987.

Alexander, Sherry. *The Home Day-Care Handbook.* New York: Human Sciences, 1987.

Amos, William, Jr. *When AIDS Comes to the Church.* Philadelphia: Westminster, 1988.

Andre, Pierre. *Drug Addiction: Learn About It Before Your Kids Do.* Pompano Beach, Fla.: Health Communications, 1987.

Arnold, L. Eugene, and Estreicher, Donna. *Parent-Child Group Therapy: Building Self-Esteem in a Cognitive-Behavior.* Lexington, Mass.: Lexington Books, 1985.

Atwater, P. M. *Coming Back to Life: The Aftermath of the Near-Death Experience.* New York: Dodd, 1988.

Balaban, Nancy. *Learning to Say Goodbye: Starting School and Other Early Childhood Separation.* New York: Plume, 1987.

———. *Starting School: From Separation to Independence—a Guide for Early Childhood Teachers.* New York: Teachers College, 1985.

Barun, Ken, and Bashe, Philip. *How to Keep the Children You Love Off Drugs.* Boston: Atlantic, 1988.

Battle, Stanley F., ed. *The Black Adolescent Parent.* New York: Haworth, 1987.

Baucom, John Q. *Bonding and Breaking Free: What Good Parents Should Know.* Grand Rapids, Mich.: Zondervan, 1988.

Belovitch, Jeanne. *Making Remarriage Work.* Lexington, Mass.: Lexington Books, 1987.

Benjamin, Harold, and Trubo, Richard. *From Victim to Victor: The Wellness Community Guide to a Fulfilling Life for Cancer Patients and Their Families.* Los Angeles: Tarcher, 1987.

Berg-Cross, Linda. *Basic Concepts in Family Therapy.* New York: Haworth, 1987.

Bernstein, Norman, et al., eds. *Coping Strategies for Burn Survivors and Their Families.* Westport, Conn.: Praeger, 1988.

Beschner, George M., and Friedman, Alfred S. *Teen Drug Use.* Lexington, Mass.: Lexington Books, 1986.

Bienfeld, Florence. *Helping Your Child Succeed After Divorce.* Claremont, Calif.: Hunter House, 1987.

Bodenhamer, Gregory. *Drug Free: The Back in Control Program for Keeping Your Kids Off Drugs.* Englewood Cliffs, N.J.: Prentice-Hall, 1988.

Bolton, Iris, and Mitchell, Curtis. *My Son, My Son: Healing After a Suicide.* Augusta, Ga.: Bolton Press, 1983.

Borg, Susan, and Lasker, Judith. *When Pregnancy Fails: Families Coping with Miscarriage, Stillbirth, and Infant Death.* Boston: Beacon, 1981.

Bradshaw, John. *Bradshaw On the Family: A Revolutionary Way of Self-Discovery.* Pompano Beach, Fla.: Health Communications, 1988.

Brazelton, T. Berry. *Working and Caring.* Reading, Mass.: Addison-Wesley, 1985.

Brenner, Avis. *Helping Children Cope with Stress.* Lexington, Mass.: Lexington Books, 1984.

Brondino, Jeanne, et al. *Raising Each Other: A Book for Parents and Teens.* Claremont, Calif.: Hunter House, 1987.

Brook, Judith, et al., eds. *Alcohol and Substance Abuse in Adolescence.* New York: Haworth, 1985.

Bross, Donald, et al. *The New Child Protection Team Handbook.* New York: Garland, 1987.

Brown, Barbara. *Between Health and Illness.* Boston: Houghton Mifflin, 1984.

Bruch, Hilde, et al., eds. *Conversations with Anorexics.* New York: Basic Books, 1988.

Burgess, Jane. *The Single-Again Man.* Lexington, Mass.: Lexington Books, 1988.

Byrne, Katherine. *A Parent's Guide to Anorexia and Bulimia.* New York: Schocken, 1987.

Cargas, Harry. *Face to Face: A Book about the Holocaust for the Christian Reader.* Bryn Mawr, Pa.: Seth Press, 1988.

Carpenter, Cheryl, et al. *Kids, Drugs and Crime.* Lexington, Mass.: Lexington Books, 1987.

Ciborowski, Paul J. *The Changing Family I.* Port Chester, N.Y.: Stratmar Educational Systems, 1984.

———. *The Changing Family II.* Port Chester, N.Y.: Stratmar Educational Systems, 1986.

Colligan, John, and Colligan, Kathleen. *The Healing Power of Love: Creating Peace in Marriage and Family Life.* Mahwah, N.J.: Paulist Press, 1988.

Corless, Inge, and Pittman-Lindeman, Mary. *AIDS: Principles, Practices, and Politics.* New York: Hemisphere, 1987.

Couburn, Karen, and Treeger, Madge. *Letting Go: A Parents' Guide to Today's College Experience.* New York: Adler and Adler, 1988.

Cowan, Paul, and Cowan, Rachel. *Mixed Blessings: Jews, Christians, and Intermarriage*. New York: Doubleday, 1987.
Curran, David. *Adolescent Suicidal Behavior*. New York: Hemisphere, 1987.
Cusack, Odean, ed. *Pets and Mental Health*. New York: Haworth, 1988.
Daley, Denis. *Surviving Addiction: A Guide for Alcoholics, Drug Addicts, and Their Families*. New York: Gardner, 1988.
Dalton, Harlon, Burris, Scott, and the Yale AIDS Law Project. *AIDS and the Law*. New Haven, Conn.: Yale University Press, 1987.
Danne, Edward J., et al., eds. *Suicide and Its Aftermath: Understanding and Counseling the Survivors*. New York: Norton, 1987.
Daro, Deborah. *Confronting Child Abuse: Research for Effective Program Design*. New York: Free Press, 1988.
Davidson, Christine. *Staying Home Instead: How to Quit the Working-Mom Rat Race and Survive Financially*. Lexington, Mass.: Lexington Books, 1986.
Davis, Samuel M., and Schwartz, Mortimer D. *Children's Rights and the Law*. Lexington, Mass.: Lexington Books, 1987.
DeFrain, John, et al. *On Our Own: A Single Parent's Survival Guide*. Lexington, Mass.: Lexington Books, 1987.
———. *Stillborn: The Invisible Death*. Lexington, Mass.: Lexington Books, 1986.
DeHartog, Jan. *Adopted Children*. New York: Adama, 1987.
Dobson, James. *Parenting Isn't for Cowards*. Waco, Texas: Word Books, 1987.
Donnelly, Katherine F. *Recovering from the Loss of a Child*. New York: Dodd, 1982.
———. *Recovering from the Loss of a Sibling*. New York: Dodd, 1988.
Droege, Thomas. *Guided Grief Imagery*. Mahwah, N.J.: Paulist Press, 1987.
Duda, Deborah. *Coming Home: A Guide to Dying at Home with Dignity*. York Beach, Maine: Samuel Weiser, 1987.
Ehrensaft, Diane. *Parenting Together: Men and Women Sharing the Care of Their Children*. New York: Free Press, 1987.
Elkind, David. *Miseducation: Preschoolers at Risk*. New York: Knopf, 1987.
Erickson, Patricia G., et al. *Steel Drug: Cocaine in Perspective*. Lexington, Mass.: Lexington Books, 1987.
Everett, Craig A. *Divorce Mediation: Perspectives on the Field*. New York: Haworth, 1985.
———, ed. *The Divorce Process: A Handbook for Clinicians*. New York: Haworth, 1987.
Faller, Kathleen. *Child Sexual Abuse: An Interdisciplinary Manual for Diagnosis, Case Management, and Treatment*. New York: Columbia University Press, 1987.
Fisher, Esther, ed. *Impact of Divorce on the Extended Family*. New York: Haworth, 1982.
Fishman, H. Charles. *Treating Troubled Adolescents: A Family Therapy Approach*. New York: Basic Books, 1988.
Fitzgerald, Kathleen. *Alcoholism*. New York: Doubleday, 1988.
Foos-Graber, Anya. *Deathing: An Intelligent Alternative for the Final Moments of Life*. York Beach, Maine: Samuel Weiser, 1987.
Forman, Susan G., and Maher, Charles A., eds. *School-Based Affective and Social Interaction*. New York: Haworth, 1987.

Fox, Sandra Sutherland. *Good Grief: Helping Groups of Children When a Friend Dies.* Mt. Rainier, Md.: Gryphon House, 1985.

Francke, Linda Bird. *Growing Up Divorced.* New York: Simon & Schuster, 1983.

Frank, Mary, ed. *Primary Prevention for Children and Families.* New York: Haworth, 1982.

Freeman, Arthur, and Epstein, Norman, eds. *Depression in the Family.* New York: Haworth, 1986.

Friel, John. *Adult Children: The Secrets of Dysfunctional Families.* Pompano Beach, Fla.: Health Communications, 1988.

Gaffney, Donna A. *The Seasons of Grief: Helping Your Children Grow Through Loss.* New York: New American Library, 1988.

Gardiner, Muriel. *The Deadly Innocents: Portraits of Children Who Kill.* New Haven, Conn.: Yale University Press, 1985.

Garner, David, and Garfinkel, Paul. *Handbook of Psychotherapy for Anorexia Nervosa and Bulimia.* New York: Guilford Press, 1985.

Gaskin, Ina May. *Babies, Breastfeeding, and Bonding.* Chicago: Independent Publishers Group, 1987.

Genevie, Louis, and Margolies, Eva. *The Motherhood Report.* New York: Macmillan, 1987.

Gold, Mark S., et al., eds. *Cocaine: Pharmacology, Addiction, and Therapy.* New York: Haworth, 1987.

Goldberg, Susan, and Divitto, Barbara. *Born Too Soon: Preterm Birth and Early Development.* New York: Freeman, 1983.

Golden, Susan. *Nursing a Loved One at Home: A Caregiver's Guide.* Philadelphia: Running Press, 1988.

Goldstein, Sonja, and Solnit, Albert J. *Divorce and Your Child: Practical Suggestions for Parents.* New Haven, Conn.: Yale University Press, 1984.

Greeley, Andrew M. *When Life Hurts: Healing Themes from the Gospel.* Chicago: Thomas More Association, 1988.

Greenwald, David S., and Zeitlin, Steven J. *No Reason to Talk About It: Families Confront the Nuclear Taboo.* New York: Norton, 1987.

Greif, Geoffrey, and Pabst, Mary S. *Mothers Without Custody.* Lexington, Mass.: Lexington Books, 1988.

Gullo, Stephen V., et al., eds. *Death and Children: A Guide for Educators, Parents, and Caregivers.* Dobbs Ferry, N.Y.: Tappan Press, 1985.

Hagen, Frank E., and Sussman, Marvin B., eds. *Deviance and the Family.* New York: Haworth, 1987.

Hart, Louise. *The Winning Family: Increasing Self-Esteem in Your Children and Yourself.* New York: Dodd, 1987.

Haugaard, Jeffrey, and Reppucci, N. Dickon. *The Sexual Abuse of Children: A Comprehensive Guide to Current Knowledge and Intervention Strategies.* San Francisco: Jossey-Bass, 1988.

Haynes, John M. *Divorce Mediation.* New York: Springer, 1981.

Hechler, David. *The Battle and the Backlash: The Child Sexual Abuse War.* Lexington, Mass.: Lexington Books, 1987.

Hodges, William. *Interventions for Children of Divorce: Custody, Access and Psychotherapy.* New York: Wiley, 1986.

Hooyman, Nancy, and Lustbader, Wendy. *Taking Care of Your Aging Family Members*. New York: Free Press, 1988.
Hope, Marjorie, and Young, James. *The Faces of Homelessness*. Lexington, Mass.: Lexington Books, 1986.
Hughes, J., and Oomura, Y. *Cancer and Emotion*. New York: Wiley, 1987.
Humphrey, Penny. *Stepmothers Try Harder*. New York: Evans, 1987.
Hutchings, Nancy, ed. *The Violent Family: Victimization of Women, Children and Elders*. New York: Human Sciences, 1988.
Hyvrard, Jeanne. *Mother Death*. Lincoln: University of Nebraska Press, 1988.
Irwin, Stephanie. *We, the Homeless: Portraits of America's Displaced People*. New York: Philosophical Library, 1987.
Jan, J. E., et al. *Does Your Child Have Epilepsy?* Baltimore: University Park Press, 1983.
Janus, Mark-David, et al. *Adolescent Runaways: Causes and Consequences*. Lexington, Mass.: Lexington Books, 1987.
Joan, Polly. *Preventing Teenage Suicide: The Living Alternative Handbook*. New York: Human Sciences, 1987.
Jones, Billy E., ed. *Treating the Homeless: Urban Psychiatry's Challenge*. Washington, D.C.: American Psychiatric Press, 1986.
Kagan, Sharon L., et al. *America's Family Support Programs: Perspectives and Prospects*. New Haven, Conn.: Yale University Press, 1987.
Kane, Elizabeth. *Birth Mother: America's First Legal Surrogate Mother Tells the Story of Her Change of Heart*. San Diego, Calif.: Harcourt, 1988.
Kaplan, Helen Singer. *The Real Truth About Women and AIDS*. New York: Simon & Schuster, 1987.
Kauffman, Danette G. *Surviving Cancer*. Washington, D.C.: Acropolis, 1987.
Kennedy, D. James. *Your Prodigal Child*. Nashville: Nelson, 1988.
Ketterman, Grace. *Depression Hits Every Family*. Nashville: Nelson, 1988.
Klein, Josephine. *Our Need for Others and Its Roots in Infancy*. New York: Tavistock, 1987.
Kozol, Jonathan. *Rachel and Her Children: Homeless Families in America*. New York: Crown, 1987.
Kramer, Rita. *At a Tender Age: Violent Youth and Juvenile Justice*. New York: Henry Holt, 1988.
Kranitz, Martin. *Getting Apart Together: The Couple's Guide to a Fair Divorce or Separation*. San Luis Obispo, Calif.: Impact, 1987.
Kressel, Kenneth. *The Process of Divorce*. New York: Basic Books, 1985.
Krieger, Dolores. *Living the Therapeutic Touch*. New York: Dodd, 1987.
Krystal, Henry. *Integration and Self Healing*. Hillsdale, N.J.: Analytic Press, 1987.
Kupfersmid, Joel, and Monkman, Roberta, eds. *Assaultive Youth: Responding to Physical Assaultiveness in Residential Community and Health Care Settings*. New York: Haworth, 1988.
Lang, Denise V. *The Phantom Spouse: A Family Survival Guide for Business Travelers*. New York: Dodd, 1988.
Laufer, Moses, and Laufer, M. Egle. *Adolescence and Developmental Breakdown: A Psychoanalytic View*. New Haven, Conn.: Yale University Press, 1984.

Lechtenberg, Richard. *Epilepsy and the Family.* Cambridge, Mass.: Harvard University Press, 1984.

Lemmon, John Allen. *Family Mediation Practice.* New York: Free Press, 1985.

Leuner, Hanscar, et al. *Guided Affective Imagery with Children and Adolescents.* New York: Plenum, 1983.

Levy, Sandra M. *Behavior and Cancer.* San Francisco: Jossey-Bass, 1985.

Lewis, Robert A., and Sussman, Marvin B. *Men's Changing Roles in the Family.* New York: Haworth, 1986.

Lingle, Virginia, and Wood, M. Sandra. *How to Locate Scientific Information About AIDS.* New York: Haworth, 1987.

Linzer, Norman, ed. *Suicide.* New York: Human Sciences, 1984.

Locke, Steven, and Hornig-Rohan, Mady. *Mind and Immunity: Behavioral Immunology.* New York: Praeger, 1983.

Lukas, Christopher, and Seiden, Henry. *Silent Grief: Living in the Wake of Suicide.* New York: Scribner, 1987.

McDermott, John. *The Complete Book on Sibling Rivalry.* New York: Perigee, 1987.

McKaughan, Molly. *The Biological Clock: Reconciling Careers and Motherhood in the 1980s.* New York: Doubleday, 1987.

McKillop, Tom. *What's Happening to My Life? A Teenage Journey.* Mahwah, N.J.: Paulist Press, 1987.

Maltz, Wendy, and Holman, Beverly. *Incest and Sexuality: A Guide to Understanding and Healing.* Lexington, Mass.: Lexington Books, 1986.

Marlin, Emily. *Hope: New Choices and Recovery Strategies for Adult Children of Alcoholics.* New York: Harper & Row, 1987.

Marrus, Michael. *The Holocaust in History.* Hanover, N.H.: University Press of New England, 1987.

Martin, Cynthia. *Beating the Adoption Game.* Rev. ed. San Diego: Harcourt, 1988.

Maurer, Daphne, and Maurer, Charles. *The World of the Newborn.* New York: Basic Books, 1987.

Miller, Derek. *Attack on the Self: Adolescent Behavioral Disturbances and Their Treatment.* Northvale, N.J.: Jason Aronson, 1986.

Mintz, Steven, and Kellogg, Susan. *Domestic Revolutions: A Social History of American Family Life.* New York: Free Press, 1988.

Mizel, Steven B., and Jaret, Peter. *The Human Immune System: The New Frontier in Medicine.* New York: Simon & Schuster, 1986.

Montgomery, Jason, and Fewer, Willard. *Family Systems and Beyond.* New York: Human Sciences, 1988.

Morris, Monica. *Last Chance Children: Growing Up with Older Parents.* New York: Columbia University Press, 1988.

Murphey, Cecil. *Day to Day: Spiritual Help When Someone You Love Has Alzheimer's.* Philadelphia: Westminster, 1988.

Neumann, Hans, and Simmons, Sylvia. *Dr. Neumann's Guide to the New Sexually Transmitted Diseases.* Washington, D.C.: Acropolis, 1987.

O'Gorman, Patricia, and Oliver-Diaz, Philip. *Breaking the Cycle of Addiction: A Parents' Guide to Raising Healthy Kids.* Pompano Beach, Fla.: Health Communications, 1987.

Okimoto, Jean, and Stegall, Phyllis. *Boomerang Kids: How to Live with Adult Children Who Return Home.* Boston: Little, Brown, 1987.

Orbach, Israel. *Children Who Don't Want to Live.* San Francisco: Jossey-Bass, 1988.

Ornstein, Robert, and Sobel, David. *The Healing Brain.* New York: Simon & Schuster, 1987.

Osborne, Judy. *Stepfamilies: The Restructuring Process.* Brookline, Mass.: EmiJo Publications, 1983.

Osherson, Samuel. *Finding Our Fathers: How a Man's Life Is Shaped by His Relationship with His Father.* New York: Fawcett, 1987.

Overvold, Amy. *Surrogate Parenting.* New York: Pharos, 1988.

Paradis, Lenora, ed. *Stress and Burnout Among Providers: Caring for the Terminally Ill and Their Families.* New York: Haworth, 1987.

Parkes, Colin M., and Weiss, Robert S. *Recovery from Bereavement.* New York: Basic Books, 1983.

Parry, Ruth. *Custody Disputes: Evaluation and Intervention.* Lexington, Mass.: Lexington Books, 1986.

Petti, Theodore A., ed. *Childhood Depression.* New York: Haworth, 1983.

Plaut, Thomas. *Children with Asthma: A Manual for Parents.* Rev. ed. Amherst, Mass.: Pedipress, 1984.

Polovchak, Walter, with Klose, Kevin. *Freedom's Child: A Teenager's Courageous True Story of Fleeing His Parents and the Soviet Union—to Live in the United States.* New York: Random House, 1988.

Puiia, Nicholas. *Rules for the Traditional Family.* Augusta, Maine: Lance Tapley, 1987.

Quay, Herbert, ed. *Handbook of Juvenile Delinquency.* New York: John Wiley, 1987.

Quinn, Phil. *Spare the Rod: Breaking the Cycle of Child Abuse.* Nashville: Abingdon, 1988.

Quinnett, Paul. *Suicide: The Forever Decision.* New York: Continuum, 1987.

Rando, Therese A. *Grieving: How to Go On Living When Someone You Love Dies.* Lexington, Mass.: Lexington Books, 1988.

———, ed. *Loss and Anticipatory Grief.* Lexington, Mass.: Lexington Books, 1986.

Reed, Bobbie. *Single Mothers Raising Sons.* Nashville: Nelson, 1988.

Register, Cheri. *Living with Chronic Illness: Days of Patience and Passion.* New York: Free Press, 1987.

Richardson, Diane. *Women and AIDS.* New York: Methuen, 1987.

Robinson, Bryan E., Rowland, Bobbie H., and Coleman, Mick. *Latchkey Kids: Unlocking Doors for Children and Their Families.* Lexington, Mass.: Lexington Books, 1983.

Rosen, Helen. *Unspoken Grief: Coping with Childhood Sibling Loss.* Lexington, Mass.: Lexington Books, 1985.

Rosenstock, Harvey A., and Rosenstock, Judith. *Journey through Divorce.* New York: Human Sciences, 1988.

Rosewater, Lynne Bravo. *Changing through Therapy.* New York: Dodd, 1988.

Rubenstein, Richard L., and Roth, John. *Approaches to Auschwitz: The Holocaust and Its Legacy.* Atlanta: John Knox, 1987.

Rubin, Jeffrey, and Rubin, Carol. *When Families Fight: How to Handle Conflict with Those You Love.* New York: Arbor House, 1988.

Sadava, Stanley, and Segal, Bernard, eds. *Drug Use and Psychological Theory.* New York: Haworth, 1987.

Sandberg, David N. *Chronic Acting-Out Students and Child Abuse: A Handbook for Intervention.* Lexington, Mass.: Lexington Books, 1987.

Savina, Lydia. *Help for the Battered Woman.* South Plainfield, N.J.: Bridge Publishing, 1988.

Scarr, Sandra. *Mother Care/Other Care.* New York: Basic Books, 1984.

Schachter, Frances F., and Stone, Richard K., eds. *Practical Concerns About Siblings: Bridging the Research-Practice Gap.* New York: Haworth, 1988.

Schacter, Robert. *Why Your Child Is Afraid.* New York: Simon & Schuster, 1988.

Schaefer, Dan, and Lyons, Christine. *How Do We Tell the Children? A Parents' Guide to Helping Children Understand and Cope When Someone Dies.* New York: Newmarket, 1986.

Schlesinger, Stephen E., and Horberg, Lawrence K. *Taking Charge: How Families Can Climb Out of the Chaos of Addiction . . . and Flourish.* New York: Simon & Schuster, 1988.

Schneider, Joseph W., and Conrad, Peter. *Having Epilepsy: The Experience and Control of Illness.* Philadelphia: Temple University Press, 1983.

Schroeder, Bob. *Help Kids Say No to Drugs and Drinking: A Practical Prevention Guide for Parents.* Minneapolis: CompCare, 1987.

Segal, Marilyn. *In Time and with Love: Caring for the Special Needs Baby.* New York: Newmarket, 1988.

Shelp, Earl, and Sunderland, Ronald. *AIDS and the Church.* Philadelphia: Westminster, 1987.

Simpson, Eileen. *Orphans: Real and Imaginary.* New York: Weidenfeld and Nicolson, 1987.

Smith, Ann. *Grandchildren of Alcoholics: Another Generation of Co-Dependency.* Pompano Beach, Fla.: Health Communications, 1988.

Sprenkle, Douglas H., ed. *Divorce Therapy.* New York: Haworth, 1985.

Stearns, Ann K. *Coming Back: Rebuilding Lives after Crisis and Loss.* New York: Random House, 1988.

Steinglass, Peter, et al. *The Alcoholic Family.* New York: Basic Books, 1987.

Stepansky, Paul, comp. *The Memoirs of Margeret Mahler.* New York: Free Press, 1988.

Stimmel, Barry, ed. *Alcohol and Substance Abuse in Women and Children.* New York: Haworth, 1986.

———. *Children of Alcoholics.* New York: Haworth, 1987.

Straus, Martha, ed. *Abuse and Victimization Across the Life Span.* Baltimore: Johns Hopkins University Press, 1988.

Strean, Herbert, and Freeman, Lucy. *Raising Cain: How to Help Your Child toward a Happy Sibling Relationship*. New York: Facts on File, 1988.

Streib, Victor. *Death Penalty for Juveniles*. Bloomington: Indiana University Press, 1987.

Strongman, K. T. *The Psychology of Emotion*. 3rd ed. New York: Wiley, 1987.

Sunderland, Ronald, and Shelp, Earl. *AIDS: A Manual for Pastoral Care*. Philadelphia: Westminster, 1987.

Toder, Francine. *When Your Child Is Gone: Learning to Live Again*. New York: Fawcett Crest, 1987.

Trad, Paul V. *Infant and Childhood Depression: Developmental Factors*. New York: Wiley, 1987.

———. *Infant Depression: Paradigms and Paradoxes*. New York: Springer-Verlag, 1986.

Treat, Stephen. *Remarriage and Blended Families*. New York: Pilgrim Press, 1988.

Trepper, Terry S., and Barrett, Mary Jo, eds. *Treating Incest: A Multimodel Systems Perspective*. New York: Haworth, 1986.

Tronick, Edward Z., and Field, Tiffany, eds. *Maternal Depression and Infant Disturbance*. San Francisco: Jossey-Bass, 1986.

Van Pelt, Rich. *Intensive Care: Counseling Teenagers in Crisis*. Grand Rapids, Mich.: Zondervan, 1988.

Wald, Michael, et al. *Protecting Abused and Neglected Children*. Stanford, Calif.: Stanford University Press, 1988.

Wallerstein, Judith, and Kelly, Joan. *Surviving the Break Up*. New York: Basic Books, 1982.

Wallerstein, Judith, and Blakeslee, Sandra. *Second Chance: Men, Women and Children a Decade after Divorce*. New York: Ticknor & Fields, 1988.

Walsh, Froma, and Anderson, Carol, eds. *Chronic Disorders and the Family*. New York: Haworth, 1988.

Wartman, William. *Life without Father: Influences of an Unknown Man*. New York: Watts, 1988.

Wayman, Anne. *Successful Single Parenting*. Deephaven, Minn.: Meadowbrook, 1987.

Weisberg, D. Kelly. *Children of the Night: A Study of Adolescent Prostitution*. Lexington, Mass.: Lexington Books, 1984.

Weitzman, Lenore J. *The Divorce Revolution: The Unexpected Social and Economic Consequences for Women and Children in America*. New York: Free Press, 1985.

Weller, Elizabeth, ed. *Current Perspectives on Major Depressive Disorders in Children*. Washington, D.C.: American Psychiatric Press, 1984.

Whitmore, George. *Someone Was Here: Profiles in the AIDS Epidemic*. New York: New American Library, 1988.

Willenson, Kim, with correspondents of *Newsweek*. *The Bad War: An Oral History of the Vietnam War*. New York: New American Library, 1987.

Woititz, Janet. *Adult Children of Alcoholics*. Pompano Beach, Fla.: Health Communications, 1983.

Yeiser, Lin. *Nannies, Au Pairs, Mothers' Helpers–Caregivers: The Complete Guide to Home Child Care.* New York: Vintage, 1987.

Youngs, Bettie B. *Helping Your Teenager Deal with Stress.* Los Angeles: Tarcher, 1988.

Articles in Periodicals

Arena, Corinne, et al. "Helping Children Deal with the Death of a Classmate: A Crisis Intervention Model." *Elementary School Guidance and Counseling* 19, no. 2 (1984): 107–115.

Balk, David. "Effects of Sibling Death on Teenagers." *Journal of School Health* 53, no. 1 (1983): 14–18.

———. "How Teenagers Cope with Sibling Death: Some Implications for School Counselors." *School Counselor* 31, no. 2 (1983): 150–158.

Baron, D. A. "Emotional Aspects of Chronic Disease." *Journal of the American Osteopathic Association* 87, no. 6 (1987): 437–439.

Bergmann, M. S. "Reflections on the Psychological and Social Function of Remembering the Holocaust." *Psychoanalytic Inquiry* 5, no. 1 (1985): 9–20.

Berman, Lauren C., and Bufferd, Rhea K. "Family Treatment to Address Loss in Adoptive Families." *Social Casework* 67, no. 1 (1986): 3–11.

Bertman, Sandra. "Helping Children Cope with Death." *Family Therapy Collections* 8 (1984): 48–60.

Bertrand, Jeanne A. "What Might Have Been—What Could Be: Working with the Grief of Children in Long-Term Care." *Journal of Social Work Practice* 1, no. 3 (1984): 23–41.

Bonchek, Rita M. "A Study of the Effect of Sibling Death on the Surviving Child: A Developmental and Family Perspective." *Dissertation Abstracts International* 44, no. 4-A (1983):1024.

Burnell, George M., and Burnell, Adrienne L. "The Compassionate Friends: A Support Group for Bereaved Parents." *Journal of Family Practice* 22, no. 3 (1986): 295–296.

Calhoun, L. G., et al. "The Rules of Bereavement." *Journal of Community Psychology* 14, no. 2 (1986): 213–218.

———. "Suicidal Death: Social Reactions to Bereaved Survivors." *Journal of Psychology* 116-2nd half, no. 4 (1984): 255–261.

Camper, Frances A. "Children's Reactions to the Death of a Parent: Maintaining the Inner World." *Smith College Studies in Social Work* 53, no. 3 (1983): 188–202.

Connor, Terry, et al. "Making a Life Story Book." *Adoption and Fostering* 9, no. 2 (1985): 32–35, 46.

Cook, Judith A. "A Death in the Family: Parental Bereavement in the First Year." *Suicide and Life-Threatening Behavior* 31, no. 1 (Spring 1983): 42–61.

Danieli, Y. "Psychotherapists' Participation in the Conspiracy of Silence About the Holocaust." *Psychoanalytic Psychology* 1 (1984): 23–42.

Field, Tiffany. "Separation Stress of Young Children Transferring to New Schools." *Developmental Psychology* 20, no. 5 (1984): 786–792.

Fox, Sandra. "Children's Anniversary Reactions to the Death of a Family Member." *Omega: Journal of Death and Dying* 15, no. 4 (1984–85): 291–305.

French, Glenda. "Intercountry Adoption: Helping a Young Child Deal with Loss." *Child Welfare* 65, no. 3 (1986): 272–279.

Furman, Edna. "Studies in Childhood Bereavement." *Canadian Journal of Psychiatry* 28, no. 4 (1983): 241–247.

Garber, Benjamin. "Mourning in Adolescence: Normal and Pathological." *Adolescent Psychology* 12 (1985): 371–387.

Gross, Alan M., et al. "The Effect of Mother-Child Separation on the Behavior of Children Experiencing a Medical Procedure." *Journal of Consulting and Clinical Psychology* 51, no. 5 (1983): 783–785.

Gunnar, Megan R., et al. "Peer Presence and the Exploratory Behavior of Eighteen- and Thirty-Month-Old Children." *Child Development* 55, no. 3 (1984): 1103–1109.

Haley, John A. "Death: What Do I Tell My Child." *PTA Today* 10, no. 3 (1984–85): 23–24.

Johnson, Sherry. "Sexual Intimacy and Replacement Children after the Death of a Child." *Omega: Journal of Death and Dying* 15, no. 2 (1984–85): 109–118.

Klass, Dennis. "Bereaved Parents and the Compassionate Friends: Affiliation and Healing." *Omega: Journal of Death and Dying* 15, no. 4 (1984–85): 353–373.

———. "Marriage and Divorce Among Bereaved Parents in a Self-Help Group." *Omega: Journal of Death and Dying* 17, no. 3 (1986–87): 237–249.

Lampl, Jeanne De Groot. "On the Process of Mourning." *Psychoanalytic Study of the Child* 38 (1983): 9–13.

Lehman, Darrin R.; Wortman, Camille B.; and Williams, Allan F. "Long-Term Effects of Losing a Spouse or Child in a Motor Vehicle Crash." *Journal of Personality & Social Psychology* 52, no. 1 (1987): 218–231.

Leon, Irving G. "The Invisible Loss: The Impact of Perinatal Death on Siblings." *Journal of Psychosomatic Obstetrics and Gynaecology* 5, no. 1 (1986): 1–14.

Lerman. L. G. "Elements and Standards for Criminal Justice Programs on Domestic Violence." *Response* 5 (1982): 12–14.

Lichtman, H. "Parental Communication of Holocaust Experiences and Personality Characteristics among Second Generation." *Journal of Clinical Psychology* 40, no. 4 (1984): 914–924.

Lindy, Joanne G. "Social and Psychological Influences on Children's Adaptation to the Death of a Parent." *Dissertation Abstracts International* 44, no. 5-B (1983): 1639.

Littlefield, Christine H. "When a Child Dies: A Sociobiological Perspective." *Dissertation Abstracts International* 45, no. 8-B (1985): 2734B.

McShane, C. "Community Services for Battered Women." *Social Work* 24 (1979): 34–39.

Miles, Margaret Shandor, and Demi, Alice Sterner. "Toward the Development of a Theory of Bereavement Guilt: Sources of Guilt in Bereaved Parents." *Omega: Journal of Death and Dying* 14, no. 4 (1984): 299–314.

Moore, DeWayne. "Pre-Adolescent Separation: Intrafamilial Perceptions and Difficulty Separating from Parents." *Personality and Social Psychology Bulletin* 10, no. 4 (1984): 611–619.

Mufson, Toni. "Issues Surrounding Sibling Death During Adolescence." *Child and Adolescent Social Work Journal* 2, no. 4 (Winter 1985): 204–218.

Murphy, Patricia Ann. "Parental Death in Childhood and Loneliness in Young Adults." *Omega: Journal of Death and Dying* 17, no. 3 (1987): 219–228.

Newman, Susan B. "The Home Environment and Fifth-Grade Students' Leisure Reading." *The Elementary School Journal* 86, no. 3 (1986): 335–343.

Noble, Barbara S. "Childhood Bereavement." *Dissertation Abstracts International* 43, no. 9-B (1983): 3037.

O'Brien, Shirley. "For Parents Particularly: Children Shouldn't Die—But They Do." *Childhood Education* 63, no. 2 (1986): 112–114.

Pynoos, Robert S., and Eth, Spencer. "The Child as Witness to Homicide." *Journal of Social Issues* 40, no. 2 (1984): 87–108.

Rando, Therese A. "Bereaved Parents." *Social Work* 30, no. 1 (1985): 19–23.

Ronald, P. "Divorce—Through the Eyes of the Victim." *Dissertation Abstracts International* 47, no. 2-A (1986): 469.

Rosen, Helen. "Prohibitions Against Mourning in Childhood Sibling Loss." *Omega: Journal of Death and Dying* 15, no. 4 (1985): 307–316.

Rosenheim, Eliyahu, and Reicher, Rivka. "Children in Anticipatory Grief: The Lonely Predicament." *Journal of Clinical Child Psychology* 15, no. 2 (1986): 115–119.

Rudestam, K. E., and Imbroll, D. "Societal Reactions to a Child's Death by Suicide." *Journal of Consulting and Clinical Psychology* 51, no. 3 (1983): 461–462.

Scanlon, M. Kathleen. "A Chronically Ill Child's Progression through the Separation-Individuation Process." *Maternal-Child Nursing Journal* 14 (Summer 1985): 91–102.

Scheier, M. F., et al. "Coping with Stress: Divergent Strategies of Optimists and Pessimists." *Journal of Personality and Social Psychology* 51 (1986): 1257–1264.

Schumacher, J. Donald. "Helping Children Cope with a Sibling's Death." *Family Therapy Collections* 8 (1984): 82–94.

Sekaer, Christina, and Kate, Sheri. "On the Concept of Mourning in Childhood." *Psychoanalytic Study of the Child* 41 (1986): 287–314.

Sheskin, A., and Wallace, S. E. "Differing Bereavements: Suicide, Natural and Accidental Death." *Omega: Journal of Death and Dying* 1, no. 3 (1976): 229–242.

Soricelli, Barbara A., and Utech, Carolyn Lorenz. "Mourning the Death of a Child: The Family and Group Process." *Social Work* 30, no. 5 (1985): 429–434.

Varela, Lynn Millikin. "The Relationship between the Hospitalized Child's Separation Anxiety and Maternal Separation Anxiety." *Dissertation Abstracts International* 43, no. 9-B (1983): 3048.

Wolfson, Orna. "Adolescent Separation from Home: An Ethnic Perspective." *Dissertation Abstracts International* 46, no. 12-B, pt. 1 (1986): 4416.

Ziegler, Patricia. "Saying Good-Bye to Preschool." *Young Children* 40, no. 3 (1985): 11–15.

10
Bibliotherapy

Books and Chapters in Books

Adams, Jeff. *The Conspiracy of the Text: The Place of Narrative in the Development of Thought.* London, England: Verso, 1987.

Brown, Eleanor Frances. *Bibliotherapy and Its Widening Applications.* Metuchen, N.J.: Scarecrow, 1975.

Griffin, Barbara K. *Special Needs Bibliotherapy—Current Books for/about Children and Young Adults Regarding Social Concerns, Emotional Concerns and the Exceptional Child.* DeWitt, N.Y.: The Griffin, 1984.

Pardeck, Jean A., and Pardeck, John T. *Young People with Problems: A Guide to Bibliotherapy.* Westport, Conn.: Greenwood, 1984.

Rubin, Rhea J. *Using Bibliotherapy.* Phoenix: Oryx, 1978.

Rudman, Masha K. *Children's Literature: An Issues Approach.* 2nd ed. New York: Longman, 1984.

Rustin, Margeret, and Rustin, Michael. *Narratives of Love and Loss: Studies in Modern Children's Fiction.* London, England: Verso, 1987.

Weiner, Pamela J., and Stein, Ruth M., eds. *Adolescents, Literature and Work with Youth.* New York: Haworth, 1985.

Zaccaraia, Joseph S., and Moses, Harold A. *Facilitating Human Development through Reading: The Use of Bibliotherapy in Teaching and Counseling.* Champaign, Ill.: Stipes Publishing, 1968.

Articles in Periodicals

Anderson, Marcella. "Children and Books in Pediatric Hospitals." *Horn Book* 62, no. 6 (1986): 787–788.

Angelotti, Michael. "Uses of Poetry and Adolescent Literature in Therapy for Adolescents." *Child and Youth Services* 7, nos. 1–2 (Spring 1985): 27–35.

Axelrod, Herman, and Teti, Thomas R. "An Alternative to Bibliotherapy: Audiovisiotherapy." *Educational Technology* 16 (1976): 36–38.

Bohning, Gerry. "Bibliotherapy: Fitting the Resources Together." *Elementary School Journal* 82 (1981): 166–170.

Brisbane, Frances L. "Using Contemporary Fiction with Black Children and Adolescents in Alcoholism Treatment." *Alcoholism Treatment Quarterly* 2, nos. 3–4 (Fall–Winter 1985–86): 179–197.

Bunting, Kenneth P. "The Use and Effect of Puppetry and Bibliotherapy in Group Counseling with Children of Divorced Parents." *Dissertation Abstracts International* 45, no. 10-A (1985): 3094.

Clarke, Barbara K. "Bibliotherapy through Puppetry: Socializing the Young Child Can Be Fun." *Early Child Development and Care* 19, no. 4 (1985): 338–344.

Coleman, Marilyn, and Ganong, Lawrence. "An Evaluation of the Stepfamily Self-Help Literature for Children and Adolescents." *Family Relations* 36, no. 1 (1987): 61–65.

Coleman, Marilyn, et al. "Beyond Cinderella: Relevant Reading for Young Adolescents about Stepfamilies." *Adolescence* 21, no. 83 (Fall 1986): 553–560.

Davison, Maureen M. "Classroom Bibliotherapy: Why and How." *Reading World* 23 (1984): 103–107.

Edwards, Patricia A., and Simpson, Linda. "Bibliotherapy: A Strategy for Communication between Parents and Their Children." *Journal of Reading* 30, no. 2 (1986): 110–118.

Forber, Susan L. "Divorce Discussion Groups for Elementary-Age Children: A Curriculum Plan." *Dissertation Abstracts International* 46, no. 11-A (1986): 3252.

Garrett, Jerry E. "The Effects of Bibliotherapy on Self-Concepts and Children and Youth in an Institutional Setting." *Dissertation Abstracts International* 45, no. 9-A (1985): 2757.

Heath, Charles P. "Understanding Death." *Techniques* 2, no. 1 (1986): 88–92.

Hipple, Theodore W., et al. "Twenty Adolescent Novels (and More) That Counselors Should Know About." *School Counselor* 32, no. 2 (1984): 142–148.

Jalongo, Mary Renck. "Bibliotherapy: Literature to Promote Socioemotional Growth." *The Reading Teacher* 36 (1983): 796–803.

———. "Using Crisis-Oriented Books with Young Children." *Young Children* 38, no. 5 (1983): 29–36.

———, and Renck, Melissa. "Children's Literature and the Child's Adjustment to School." *The Reading Teacher* 40 (1987): 616–621.

Martin, Maggie; Martin, Don; and Porter, Judy. "Bibliotherapy: Children of Divorce." *School Counselor* 30, no. 4 (1983): 796–803.

Mikulas, William L., et al. "Uses of Poetry and Adolescent Literature in Therapy for Adolescents." *Child and Youth Services* 7, no. 3 (Fall 1985): 1–7.

Morris, Artie. "The Efficacy of Bibliotherapy on the Mental Health of Elementary Students Who Have Experienced a Loss Precipitated by Parental Unemployment, Divorce, Marital Separation or Death." *Dissertation Abstracts International* 44, no. 3-A (1983): 676.

Nelms, Beth, et al. "Broken Circles: Adolescents on Their Own." *English Journal* 74, no. 5 (1985): 84–85.

Newhouse, Robert C. "Generalized Fear Reduction in Second-Grade Children." *Psychology in the Schools* 24, no. 1 (1987): 48–50.

———, and Loker, Suzanne. "Does Bibliotherapy Reduce Fear Among Second-Grade Children?" *Reading Psychology* 4 (1983): 25–27.

O'Bruba, William S.; Camplese, Donald A.; and Sanford, Mary D. "The Use of Teletherapy in the Mainstreaming Era." *Reading Horizons* 24 (Spring 1984): 158–160.

Pardeck, Jean A., and Pardeck, John T. "Bibliotherapy Using a Neo-Freudian Approach for Children of Divorced Parents." *School Counselor* 32, no. 4 (1985): 313–318.

Pardeck, John T., and Pardeck, Jean A. "Treating Abused Children through Bibliotherapy." *Early Childhood Development and Care* 16, nos. 3–4 (1984): 195–203.

Sargent, Karin L. "Helping Children Cope with Parental Mental Illness through use of Children's Literature." *Child Welfare* 64, no. 6 (1985): 617–628.

Sheridan, John T.; Baker, Stanley B.; de-Lissovoy, Vladimir. "Structured Group Counseling and Explicit Bibliotherapy as In-School Strategies for Preventing Problems in Youth of Changing Families." *School Counselor* 32, no. 2 (1984): 134–141.

Storey, Dee. "Reading Role Models: Fictional Readers in Children's Books." *Reading Horizons* 26 (1986): 140–148.

Swantic, Frances. "An Investigation of the Effectiveness of Bibliotherapy on Middle-Grade Students Who Repeatedly Display Inappropriate Behavior in the School Setting." *Dissertation Abstracts International* 47, no. 3 (1986): 843.

Tillman, Chester E. "Bibliotherapy for Adolescents: An Updated Research Review." *Journal of Reading* 27, no. 8 (1984): 713–719.

Wahlstrom, Wanda L. "Developing Self-Concept through Bibliotherapy." *Dissertation Abstracts International* 44, no. 3-A (1983): 669–670.

Weiner, J. Pamela, and Stein, Ruth M., eds. "Adolescents, Literature, and Work with Youth." *Child and Youth Services* 7, nos. 1–2 (Spring 1985): v–137.

William, L., et al. "Behavioral Bibliotherapy and Games for Testing Fear of the Dark." *Child and Family Behavioral Therapy* 7, no. 3 (1985): 1–7.

Wilson, Laura W. "Helping Adolescents Understand Death and Dying through Literature." *English Journal* 73, no. 7 (1984): 78–82.

Winfield, Evelyn T. "Relevant Reading for Adolescents: Literature and Divorce." *Journal of Reading* 26, no. 5 (1983): 408–411.

Yellin, Michael. "Bibliotherapy: A Comparison of the Effect of the Traditional Folk Fairy Tale and 'Issues Specific' Imaginative Literature on Self-Esteem, Hostile Attitudes, and the Behavior of Children." *Dissertation Abstracts International* 43, no. 8-A (1983): 2614.

Zimet, Sara Goodman. "Teaching Children to Detect Social Bias in Books." *The Reading Teacher* 36 (1983): 418–421.

Unpublished Work

Fox, Barbara J., and Collier, Helen S. *Skilled Focused Bibliotherapy.* Unpublished manuscript, North Carolina State University, 1983.

Appendix: Directory of Organizations

This directory provides addresses and telephone numbers for self-help groups and professional and voluntary organizations that offer support services to children undergoing loss experiences and to their adult guides. Many organizations provide free or low-cost literature as well as services such as discussion groups and referrals.

Addictions

Alcohol

Al-Anon Family Group Headquarters
1372 Broadway
New York, NY 10018
212-302-7240
This organization helps families of alcoholics. Alateen is the adolescent discussion group affiliated with Al-Anon.

Alcohol Education for Youth and Community
362 State St.
Albany, NY 12210
518-436-9319
Workshops and educational materials are provided.

Alcoholics Anonymous World Services
Box 459, Grand Central Station
New York, NY 10163
212-686-1100
International fellowship of men and women sharing experiences, strength, and hope with an aim toward recovery.

American Council on Alcoholism
8501 LaSalle Rd.
Suite 301
Towson, MD 21204
301-296-5555
Coalition of local, state, and national groups working to end alcohol abuse.

Children of Alcoholics Foundation
200 Park Ave.
31st floor
New York, NY 10166
212-949-1404
Seeks to educate the public and promote open discussion on problems of children of alcoholics.

National Association for Children of Alcoholics
31706 Coast Hwy.
Suite 201
South Laguna, CA 92677
714-499-3889

Resource to increase public awareness and to protect rights of children of alcoholics to live in a safe environment.

Other Drugs

Drug-Anon Focus
Box 9108
Long Island City, NY 11103
718-361-2169

This organization offers help to abusers of mood-altering drugs and to their families.

Drugs Anonymous
Box 473, Ansonia Station
New York, NY 10023
212-874-0700

Application of the Alcoholics Anonymous approach to persons addicted to all types of drugs including prescription drugs.

Families Anonymous
Box 528
Van Nuys, CA 91408
818-989-7841

Help for drug-abusing people and their families; patterned after Alcoholics Anonymous in format.

Just Say No Clubs
3101-A Sacramento
Berkeley, CA 94702
415-848-0845; 800-258-2766

Promotes formation of clubs in schools to give students a supportive peer group to resist drugs.

Narcotics Anonymous
Box 9999
Van Nuys, CA 91409
818-780-3951

Self-help and information for drug abuse; aims toward rehabilitation.

National Association on Drug Abuse Problems
355 Lexington Ave.
New York, NY 10017
212-986-1170

Information and referrals.

National Federation of Parents for Drug-Free Youth
8730 Georgia Ave.
Suite 200
Silver Spring, MD 20910
301-585-5437; 800-544-KIDS

Network of parent groups; promotes education; speakers' bureau.

National Parents' Resource Institute for Drug Education
100 Edgewood Ave.
Suite 1002
Atlanta, GA 30303
404-658-2548; 800-241-7946

Up-to-date research information and formation of community action groups; speakers' bureau.

Other Addictions

Gam-Anon International Service Office
Box 967, Radio City Station
New York, NY 10101
212-391-0911

Modeled on Alcoholics Anonymous, this group works with addictive gamblers and their families.

Gamblers Anonymous
3255 Wilshire Blvd.
No. 610
Los Angeles, CA 90010
213-386-8789

Gamblers seek support here; aims toward rehabilitation.

National Council on Compulsive Gambling
444 W. 56 St.
Room 3207S
New York, NY 10019
212-765-3833
Information and referrals.

Adoption

Adoptees' Liberty Movement Association
Box 154, Washington Bridge Station
New York, NY 10033
212-581-1568
This organization maintains a data bank and offers advice on searching for adoptive parents and children.

Committee for Single Adoptive Parents
Box 15084
Chevy Chase, MD 20815
202-966-6367
Information and lobbying for legislative reform.

Concerned United Birthparents
2000 Walker St.
Des Moines, IA 50317
515-262-9120
Aims to open birth records for adoptees and birthparents.

Independent Search Consultants
Box 10192
Costa Mesa, CA 92627
Assists individuals in searches for birth families separated by adoption.

International Concerns Committee for Children
911 Cypress Dr.
Boulder, CO 80303
303-494-8333
Adoption of children from foreign countries.

Latin America Parents Association
Box 72
Seaford, NY 11783
516-795-7427
Aids people adopting or seeking to adopt children from Latin America.

National Adoption Exchange
1218 Chestnut St.
2nd floor
Philadelphia, PA 19107
215-925-0200
Referral for adoptive parents seeking children with special needs—older, handicapped, minority, siblings seeking same placement.

National Committee for Adoption
1930 17 St., N.W.
Washington, D.C. 20009
202-638-0466
Resource and lobbying organization.

North American Council on Adoptable Children
1821 University Ave.
St. Paul, MN 55104
612-644-3036
Information about adoption and local parent groups in chapters.

Origins
Box 444
East Brunswick, NJ 08816
201-251-5411
Support for women who have given up their children for adoption.

Orphan Voyage
2141 Rd. 2300
Cedaridge, CA 81413
303-856-3937
Tries to open lines of communication, encouraging open attitudes in the non-adoptive population.

OURS, Inc.
3307 Highway 100 North
Suite 203
Minneapolis, MN 55422
612-535-4829

Support groups and information for adoptive parents.

Aging

Aging in America
1500 Pelham Parkway S.
Bronx, NY 10461
212-824-4004
Research and service organization for professionals in gerontology.

American Aging Family Services, Inc.
62 Pierrepont St.
Brooklyn, NY 11201
718-852-7124; 800-63-UNITE
Helps families care for aging relatives who live at a distance by arranging for social workers, doctors, and other helpers.

American Association of Retired Persons
1909 K St., N.W.
Washington, D.C. 20049
202-872-4700
Information, insurance, lobbying.

American Society on Aging
833 Market St.
Suite 512
San Francisco, CA 94103
415-543-2617
Works to foster unity among those working with the elderly.

Center for the Study of Aging
706 Madison Ave.
Albany, NY 12208
518-465-6927
Promotes education, research, training, and leadership.

Gray Panthers
311 South Juniper St.
Suite 601
Philadelphia, PA 19107
215-545-6555
Activist group to combat discrimination.

National Alliance of Senior Citizens
2525 Wilson Blvd.
Arlington, VA 22201
703-241-1533
Informs of needs of senior citizens.

National Association for the Advancement of the Black Aged
150 Michigan Ave.
4th floor
Detroit, MI 48226
313-224-4966
Seeks to advocate rights of all people, not only blacks and senior citizens.

National Council on the Aging
600 Maryland Ave., S.W.
W. Wing 100
Washington, D.C. 20024
202-479-1200
Information and consultation center; cooperates with other organizations.

Burn Victims

American Burn Association
c/o Shriners Burn Institute
202 Goodman St.
Cincinnati, OH 45219
Professionals interested in treatment of burn patients.

International Society for Burn Injuries
c/o John A. Boswick, Jr.
2005 Franklin St.
Suite 660
Denver, CO 80205
303-839-1694
Professionals engaged in care and research; promotes prevention.

Phoenix Society
c/o National Organization for Burn Victims
11 Rust Hill Rd.
Levittown, PA 19056
215-946-4788

Self-help service association that discourages concealment of disfigurement, which society believes compounds adjustment difficulties.

Child Abuse

Adults Molested as Children United
Box 952
San Jose, CA 95108
408-280-5055
Support and therapy.

Batterers Anonymous
1269 N.E. St.
San Bernardino, CA 92405
714-383-2972
Families of battered spouses benefit from discussion groups.

Child Abuse Listening Mediation, Inc.
Box 718
Santa Barbara, CA 93102
805-682-1366
Aims at prevention of child abuse.

Children's Rights of America
12551 Indian Rocks Rd.
Suite 11
Largo, FL 33544
813-593-0090
Aids families of missing or exploited children.

Committee for Children
172 20 Ave.
Seattle, WA 98122
206-322-5050
Develops curricula to prevent sexual abuse.

Daughters and Sons United
c/o Institute for Community as Extended Family
Box 952
San Jose, CA 95108
408-280-5055
An information exchange and support system for sexually abused children and their families.

Incest Survivors Resource Network, International
Box 911
Hicksville, NY 11802
516-935-3031
Resource program for primary prevention.

National Committee for the Prevention of Child Abuse
332 S. Michigan Ave.
Suite 950
Chicago, IL 60604
312-663-3520
Information, referrals, and legislative lobbying.

National Organization for Victim Assistance
717 D St., N.W.
2nd fl.
Washington, D.C. 20531
202-393-6682
Aims to assist crime victims in their claims.

Parents Anonymous
6733 S. Sepulveda
Los Angeles, CA 90045
213-410-9732; 800-462-6406
Aims to prevent child abuse and offers immediate support through its hotline.

Parents United
Box 952
San Jose, CA 95108
408-280-5055
Support groups for sexual molestation and drug abuse problems.

Death

Bereavement

Bereaved Children's Program
Westchester Jewish Community Services

141 N. Central Ave.
Hartsdale, NY 10530
914-949-6761

This therapy-discussion group has served as a model nationwide for those who have lost a family member.

The Compassionate Friends
Box 3696
Oak Brook, IL 60522
312-990-0010

Parents who grieve for their dead children find support groups here; parents of dying children also seek help within this organization.

First Sunday
c/o Pope John XXIII Hospitality House
3977 Second Ave.
Detroit, MI 48201
313-832-4357

Counseling and self-help groups for parents who have lost a child; holds liturgy for families on first Sunday of each month.

Inter-National Association for Widowed People
Box 3564
Springfield, IL 62708
217-787-0886

Promotes interests and understanding of widows' and widowers' special needs.

Orphan Foundation
Box 14261
1500 Massachusetts Ave., N.W.
Suite 448
Washington, D.C. 20044
202-861-0762

Assists orphans and foster-care youth by providing guidance, support, and emergency help.

Parents of Murdered Children
100 E. Eighth St.
B-41
Cincinnati, OH 45202
513-721-5683

Support services for survivors of murdered children and its aftermath.

Widowed Person Service
1909 K St., N.W.
Washington, D.C. 20049
202-748-4370

Referrals and information for support.

Death Education

Association for Death Education and Counseling
2211 Arthur Ave.
Lakewood, OH 44107
216-228-0334

Goal is to upgrade quality of death education and patient care.

Center for Death Education and Research
University of Minnesota
1167 Social Science Bldg.
267 19th Ave., S.
Minneapolis, MN 55455
612-624-1895

Many scholarly and nontechnical publications are available here.

Center for Thanatology Research and Education
391 Atlantic Ave.
Brooklyn, NY 11217
718-858-3026

Books, journals, and media; referrals to organizations, institutions, and counselors; research library.

Continental Association of Funeral and Memorial Societies
2001 S St., N.W.
Suite 630
Washington, D.C. 20009
202-462-8888

Information concerning the conduct and cost of funerals.

Foundation of Thanatology
630 W. 168 St.
New York, NY 10032
212-928-2066
Conferences and publications about bereavement and care for the dying are aimed at both general audiences and professionals.

Grief Education Institute
2422 S. Dowing
Denver, CO 80210
303-777-9234
Publications, conferences, and support groups concerning bereavement.

National Funeral Directors Association
11121 W. Oklahoma Ave.
Milwaukee, WI 53227
414-541-2500
Educational materials concerning funeral planning and problems of bereavement.

Euthanasia

Concern for Dying
250 W. 57 St.
New York, NY 10107
212-246-6962
Workshops, study groups, conferences, speakers' bureau; distributes Living Will (allows individuals to express in writing their wishes in case of terminal illness).

Hospices

Children's Hospice International
1101 King St.
Suite 131
Alexandria, VA 22314
703-684-0330
Aims to promote hospice support through pediatric care facilities; encourages inclusion of children in existing and developing hospices and home care.

Hospice Education Institute
Box 713, Five Essex Sq.
Essex, CT 06426
203-767-1620; 800-331-1620
Educational programs on hospices, bereavement, and dying.

National Hospice Organization
1901 N. Fort Myer Dr.
Suite 307
Arlington, VA 22209
703-243-5900
British concept of a homelike hospital where one goes to die peacefully has spread to America.

Suicide

American Association of Suicidology
2459 S. Ash
Denver, CO 80222
303-692-0985
Dedicated to research and the prevention of unnecessary deaths, this organization offers information and counseling referrals.

International Association for Suicide Prevention
c/o Suicide Prevention and Crisis Center
1811 Trousdale Dr.
Burlingham, CA 94010
415-877-5604
Information and counseling referrals.

National Committee on Youth Suicide Prevention
825 Washington St.
Norwood, MA 02026
617-769-5686

Network of parents, professionals, and government officials who publicize the warning signals of suicide and establish referral systems.

Samaritans
500 Commonwealth Ave.
Kenmore Sq.
Boston, MA 02215
617-247-0220
Suicide prevention service and information.

Seasons (Suicide Bereavement)
1358 Sunset Dr.
Salt Lake City, UT 84116
801-596-2341
Support groups; educational materials; library.

Yad Tikvah Foundation
c/o Union of American Hebrew Congregations
838 Fifth Ave.
New York, NY 10011
212-249-0100
Seeks to educate parents and synagogue professionals about symptoms and prevention of suicide; also known as Task Force on Youth Suicide.

Youth Suicide National Center
1811 Trousdale Dr.
Burlingame, CA 94010
415-692-6662
Educational materials; reviews current educational programs.

Emotional Health and Illness

American Anorexia/Bulimia Association
133 Cedar Lane
Teaneck, NJ 07666
201-836-1800
Information and referral.

American Association for Marriage and Family Therapy
1717 K St., N.W.
No. 407
Washington, D.C. 20006
202-429-1825
Training for therapists; information exchange.

American Association of Psychiatric Services for Children
1133 15 St., N.W.
Suite 1000
Washington, D.C. 20005
202-429-9713
Information and research.

American Family Therapy Association
1255 23 St., N.W.
Washington, D.C. 20037
202-659-7666
Information dissemination to scientists and the public about the family therapy systems approach.

American Orthopsychiatric Association
19 W. 44 St.
No. 1616
New York, NY 10036
212-354-5770
Interested in a wide range of problems, this organization is a good source for scholarly, technical information.

American Psychological Association
1200 17 St., N.W.
Washington, D.C. 20036
202-955-7600
Scientific and professional society of psychologists.

American Schizophrenia Association
900 N. Federal Hwy.
No. 330
Boca Raton, FL 33432
305-393-6167
Research on biochemical and genetic causes of schizophrenia.

Anorexia Nervosa and Related Eating Disorders
Box 5102
Eugene, OR 97405
503-344-1144
Information and research.

Autism Society of America
1234 Massachusetts Ave., N.W.
Washington, D.C. 20005
202-783-0125
Research, information, and referrals.

The Bridge, Inc.
325 W. 85 St.
New York, NY 10024
212-724-1200
This organization focuses on rehabilitation of the mentally ill.

Council for Children with Behavioral Disorders
c/o Council for Exceptional Children
1920 Association Dr.
Reston, VA 22091
703-620-3660
A division of the Council for Exceptional Children, this organization promotes the welfare of children with serious emotional disturbances.

Emotions Anonymous
Box 4245
St. Paul, MN 55104
612-647-9712
Sets up local discussion groups to promote emotional health; a self-help atmosphere.

Family Service America
11700 W. Lake Park Dr.
Milwaukee, WI 53224
414-359-2111
An organization geared to directly helping families under emotional stress.

International Association of Psychosocial Rehabilitation Services
Box 278
McLean, VA 22101
703-237-9385
Serves groups and provides information on residential and day centers nationwide.

Mental Health Law Project
2021 L St., N.W.
Suite 800
Washington, D.C. 20036
202-467-5730
A public service legal firm specializing in the rights of mental patients.

National Alliance for the Mentally Ill
1901 N. Fort Myer Dr.
Suite 500
Arlington, VA 22209
703-524-7600
An umbrella organization for self-help and advocacy groups.

National Anorexic Aid Society
5796 Karl Rd.
Columbus, OH 43229
614-436-1112
Aids patients and families.

National Association of Psychiatric Treatment Centers for Children
2000 L St., N.W.
Washington, D.C. 20036
202-955-3828
Information about accredited residential centers.

Neurotics Anonymous International Liaison
Box 4866, Cleveland Park Station
Washington, D.C. 20008
202-232-0414
Promotes local discussion group formation; adapts techniques from Alcoholics Anonymous as they apply to emotional illness.

Family Relationships

Divorce, Single-Parent Families, and Stepfamilies

Divorce Anonymous
Box 5313
Chicago, IL 60680
312-448-2598
Discussion groups and support.

Fathers Are Forever
Box 4804
Panorama City, CA 91412
800-248-3237; 800-255-3237 (in California)
Lobbies for joint custody laws concerning child visitation; favors mediation.

Mothers Without Custody
Box 56762
Houston, TX 77256
713-840-1622
Advice and information for mothers who for any reason live apart from their children and who have lost custody of their children or fear losing custody of their children.

North American Conference of Separated and Divorced Catholics
1100 S. Goodman St.
Rochester, NY 14620
716-271-1320
Support and information.

Parents Without Partners
8807 Colesville Rd.
Silver Spring, MD 20910
301-588-9354; 800-638-8078
Aims to alleviate problems of single parents; social networks and referrals for child support enforcement and fathers' rights assistance.

Remarried Parents, Inc.
102-20 67 Dr.
Forest Hills, NY 11375
718-459-2011
The problems of the reconstituted family are examined in support groups; information dissemination.

Second Wives Association of North America
58 Walker Ave.
Toronto, ON, Canada M4V 1G2
416-968-1647
Brings attention to unique problems of second marriages, for example, lack of societal support and financial difficulties.

Single Mothers by Choice
Box 1642, Gracie Sq. Station
New York, NY 10028
212-988-0993
Single women deciding to have or adopt children outside marriage can find information and support here.

Single Parent Resource Center
1165 Broadway
Room 504
New York, NY 10001
212-213-0047
Tries to organize a network of local single-parent groups for collective political action.

Sisterhood of Black Single Mothers
1360 Fulton St.
Suite 423
Brooklyn, NY 11216
718-638-0413
This organization promotes solidarity and mutual self-help.

Stepfamily Association of America
602 E. Joppa Rd.
Baltimore, MD 21204
301-823-7570
Support network and advocacy group.

Stepfamily Foundation, Inc.
333 West End Ave.
New York, NY 10023
212-877-3244
Information, workshops, and counseling.

Homeless, Missing, and Kidnapped Children

Child Find of America
Box 277
New Paltz, NY 12561
914-255-1848; 800-431-5005
Parents of missing children can attempt contact with their youngsters through this organization.

Child Welfare League of America
440 First St., N.W.
Washington, D.C. 20001
202-638-2952
Particularly interested in children in distress, this organization publishes many materials for professionals and interested parents.

Children of the Night
1800 N. Highland Ave.
No. 128
Hollywood, CA 90028
213-461-3160
Provides protection and support for young people involved with pornography or prostitution.

Citizen's Committee to Amend Title 18
Box 936
Newhall, CA 91321
805-259-4435
Aims to change penal code exempting parents of minors of kidnapping charges.

Find the Children
11811 W. Olympic Blvd.
Los Angeles, CA 90064
213-477-6721
Clearinghouse for groups searching for missing children.

Friends Disaster Service
241 Keenan Rd.
Peninsula, OH 44264
216-650-4975
Restoration services to communities devastated by natural disasters; volunteers in Quaker ethic.

Hands Across America
6151 W. Century Blvd.
12th floor
Los Angeles, CA 90045
213-670-2700
Seeks to feed the homeless and hungry in the United States.

National Coalition for the Homeless
105 E. 22 St.
New York, NY 10010
212-460-8110
Resources and referrals; seeks expansion of low-income housing.

National Network of Runaway and Youth Services
905 Sixth St., S.W.
Suite 411
Washington, D.C. 20024
202-488-0739
Coalition to develop responsive local services and act as a clearinghouse.

National Runaway Switchboard
3080 N. Lincoln Ave.
Chicago, IL 60614
800-621-4000
Parents and children can call this number to make contact and leave messages.

Runaway Hotline
Governor's Office
Box 12428
Austin, TX 78711
512-463-1980
Runaway switchboard.

Toughlove
Box 1069
Doylestown, PA 18901
215-348-7090
Basing its approach on discipline as well as understanding and forgiveness, Toughlove offers support groups for parents and problem teens so that families can continue to live together through crises.

Infertility and Pregnancy Loss

American Fertility Society
2140 11th Ave., S.
Suite 200
Birmingham, AL 35205
205-933-8494
Research and information.

DES Action, U.S.A.
Long Island Jewish Medical Center
New Hyde Park, NY 11040
516-775-3450
A national clearinghouse for information and referrals.

Endometriosis Association
Box 92187
Milwaukee, WI 53202
414-962-8792
Information and research.

HERS (Hysterectomy Educational Resources and Services)
422 Bryn Mawr Ave.
Bala-Cynwyd, PA 19004
215-667-7757
Education and counseling.

Loving Arms (Pregnancy and Infant Loss Center)
1415 E. Wayzata Blvd.
Wayzata, MN 55391
612-473-9372
Educational materials.

Resolve
5 Water St.
Arlington, MA 02174
617-643-2424
Resources, counseling, and support groups for infertile couples.

SHARE
St. Elizabeth's Hospital
211 S. Third St.
Belleville, IL 62222
618-234-2120
Support groups for miscarriage, ectopic pregnancy, stillbirth, and infant death.

Other Family Concerns

Big Brothers/Big Sisters of America
117 S. 17 St.
Philadelphia, PA 19103
215-567-2748
Provides children from single-parent families with adult friends who can offer understanding, acceptance, and guidance.

Fatherhood Project
c/o Bank Street College of Education
610 W. 112 St.
New York, NY 10025
212-663-7200
Encourages development of new options for male involvement in childrearing; clearinghouse on participation programs for fathers.

Foster Grandparents Program
806 Connecticut Ave., N.W.
Room M-1006
Washington, D.C. 20525
800-424-8580
Fosters volunteer work in schools, hospitals, and day care.

International Soundex Reunion Registry
Box 2312
Carson City, NV 89702
702-882-6270

A reunion registry for people age 18 and over who were foster children, orphans, adopted, or wards of the state, and their blood relatives.

National Association for Family Day Care
815 15 St., N.W.
Suite 928
Washington, D.C. 20005
202-347-3356
Advocates and providers of family day care.

National Coalition for Campus Child Care
c/o University of Wisconsin-Milwaukee Day Care Center
University of Wisconsin-Milwaukee
Milwaukee, WI 53201
414-229-5384
Promotes child-care services on college campuses; information for organizing and operating such centers.

National Coalition to End Racism in America's Child Care System
22075 Koths
Taylor, MI 48180
313-295-0257
Encourages recruitment of foster and adoptive homes for all races and cultures; believes while race and culture should be a factor, no child should be denied service because of race.

National Council for Family Reconciliation
4200 Wisconsin Ave.
Suite 106
Washington, D.C. 20016
202-898-0870
Helps families deal with crises of teen pregnancy and drug abuse.

National Council on Family Relations
1910 W. Country Rd. B
Suite 147
St. Paul, MN 55113
612-663-6933
Families under stress can find referrals and information here; maintains a file of family-oriented groups, particularly single-parent family organizations, for all parts of the country.

National Foster Parent Association
226 Kitts Dr.
Houston, TX 77024
713-467-1850
Advocacy and information.

Prison Families Anonymous
353 Fulton Ave.
Hempstead, NY 11550
516-538-6065
A local organization offering support that may be able to help other local groups get started.

Illness

AIDS

AIDS Action Council
Federation of AIDS-Related Organizations
729 Eighth St., S.E.
Suite 200
Washington, D.C. 20003
202-547-3101
Provides information about AIDS.

American Foundation for AIDS Research
5900 Wilshire Blvd.
2nd floor
Los Angeles, CA 90036
213-857-5900
Raises funds to support research.

American Red Cross AIDS Educational Office
1730 D St., N.W.
Washington, D.C. 20006
202-737-8300
Provides information and referrals.

Gay Men's Health Crisis
Box 274
132 W. 24 St.
New York, NY 10011
212-807-7035
Social service agency providing support and therapy groups; legal, financial, and health-care advocacy.

International AIDS Prospective Epidemiology Network
c/o David G. Ostrow
155 N. Harbor Dr.
No. 5103
Chicago, IL 60601
312-565-2103
Public health workers and other professionals; organizations interested in sharing data and information.

Mothers of AIDS Patients
3403 E St.
San Diego, CA 92102
619-293-3985
Provides support groups and information.

National AIDS Network
1012 14 St., N.W.
Suite 601
Washington, D.C. 20005
202-347-0390
Provides information about AIDS.

National Council of Churches/AIDS Task Force
475 Riverside Dr.
New York, NY 10115
212-879-2421
AIDS action and support.

National Gay and Lesbian Task Force Hot Line
1517 U St., N.W.
Washington, D.C. 20009
202-332-6483; 800-221-7044
Emotional, financial, and social support.

People with AIDS Coalition
263A W. 19 St.
No. 125
New York, NY 10011
212-627-1810
Local support networks; public forums; chapters around the country.

San Francisco AIDS Foundation
333 Valencia St.
4th floor
San Francisco, CA 94103
415-864-4376
Educates public on prevention; social services for people with AIDS.

World Health Organization Collaborating Center on AIDS
c/o Centers for Disease Control
1600 Clifton Rd., N.E.
Atlanta, GA 30333
404-329-3311
Research and public health training programs; compiles statistics; speakers' bureau.

Blood Conditions

Center for Sickle Cell Disease
Howard University
2121 Georgia Ave., N.W.
Washington, D.C. 20059
202-636-7930
Information and referrals.

Children's Blood Foundation
464 E. 62 St.
Room 1045
New York, NY 10021
212-644-5790
Research and clinics to help children with rare blood conditions or chronic diseases affecting the blood.

Cooley's Anemia Foundation
105 E. 22 St.
Suite 911
New York, NY 10010
212-598-0911

Reading materials, referrals, and medical assistance.

National Association for Sickle Cell Disease
4221 Wilshire Blvd.
Suite 360
Los Angeles, CA 90010
213-936-7205
Promotes research and provides assistance to families.

National Hemophilia Foundation
110 Greene St.
Room 406
New York, NY 10012
212-219-8180
Families can find support and information here.

Cancer

American Cancer Society
261 Madison Ave.
New York, NY 10016
212-599-3600
Educational brochures, prevention programs, and counseling.

Association for Research of Childhood Cancer
Box 251
Buffalo, NY 14225
716-681-4433
Seeks to fund research; support to parents.

Cancer Care
1180 Ave. of the Americas
New York, NY 10036
212-221-3300
Educational programs, counseling, financial support, and research.

Cancer Connection
H & R Block Bldg.
4410 Main
Kansas City, MO 64111
816-932-8453
Sponsors a hotline matching victims with volunteers who have been cured, are in remission, or have been treated for the same type of cancer.

Candlelighters Childhood Cancer Foundation
1901 Pennsylvania Ave., N.W.
Suite 1001
Washington, D.C. 20006
202-659-5136
Groups of parents whose children have or have had cancer; emotional support and research.

Cansurmount
c/o Dr. Morton Bard
90 Park Ave.
New York, NY 10016
212-599-3600
Trained volunteers help patients better understand cancer; liaison with doctors.

Leukemia Society of America
733 Third Ave.
New York, NY 10017
212-573-8484
Raises funds; aids needy patients and their families.

Make Today Count
101½ S. Union St.
Alexandria, VA 22314
703-548-9674
Aims to discuss openly false implications and actual realities of cancer.

Heart Disease

American Heart Association
7320 Greenville Ave.
Dallas, TX 75231
214-373-6300
Consultation and information; a subsidiary, Mended Hearts, offers encouragement to patients who have

heart disease or have undergone heart surgery, including children.

Hospitalization

Association for the Care of Children's Health
3615 Wisconsin Ave.
Washington, D.C. 20016
202-244-1801
Fosters child-life centers in hospitals for play, education, and good adjustment to a trying situation.

Children in Hospitals
31 Wilshire Pk.
Needham, MA 02192
617-482-2915
Parents, educators, and health professionals who seek to minimize trauma of a child's hospitalization; encourages live-in accommodations and flexible visiting policies.

Neurological Conditions

Alzheimer's Disease and Related Disorders Association
70 E. Lake St.
Suite 600
Chicago, IL 60601
312-853-3060
Family members of Alzheimer's disease are organized to promote research and provide educational programs.

Alzheimer's Disease International
70 E. Lake St.
Suite 600
Chicago, IL 60601
312-853-3060
Professionals concerned with finding a cure.

American Epilepsy Society
c/o Priscilla S. Bourgeois
179 Allyn St.
No. 304
Hartford, CT 06103
203-246-6566
Fosters research and treatment.

American Spinal Injury Association
250 East Superior
Room 619
Chicago, IL 60611
312-908-3425
Aims to develop knowledge and exchange of ideas.

Child Neurology Society
Box 486
420 Delaware St., S.E.
Minneapolis, MN 55455
612-625-7466
Scientific forum for information exchange.

Epilepsy Concern Service Group
1282 Wynnewood Dr.
West Palm Beach, FL 33409
305-586-4804
Starts and maintains self-help groups of epileptics, relatives, and friends.

Epilepsy Foundation of America
4351 Garden City Dr.
Landover, MD 20785
301-459-3700
Voluntary agency concerned with controlling epilepsy and improving the lives of those who have it.

Muscular Dystrophy Association
810 Seventh Ave.
New York, NY 10019
212-586-0808
Research into causes and cures for neuromuscular diseases.

National Head Injury Foundation
333 Turnpike Rd.
Southborough, MA 01772
617-485-9950
Research, information, and referrals.

National Multiple Sclerosis Society
205 E. 42 St.
New York, NY 10017
212-986-3240
Research and support for families.

Other Conditions

American Digestive Disease Society
7720 Wisconsin Ave.
Bethesda, MD 20814
301-652-9293
Public information exchange.

American Juvenile Arthritis Organization
1314 Spring St.
Atlanta, GA 30309
404-872-7100
Patients, families, and professionals interested in the problems of juvenile arthritis; advocacy unit.

American Lupus Society
23751 Madison St.
Torrance, CA 90505
213-373-1335
Aims to increase public awareness and conduct research.

Children's Liver Foundation
76 S. Orange Ave.
Suite 202
South Orange, NJ 07079
201-761-1111
Parents and friends raising research funds and offering support.

Children's Transplant Association
Box 2106
Laurinburg, NC 28352
919-276-7171
Support for families; purchases air tickets to evaluation and treatment sites; assists with lodging.

Cystic Fibrosis Foundation
6931 Arlington Rd.
No. 200
Bethesda, MD 20814
301-951-4422
Medical programs, professional education, and support services for young adults.

Lupus Erythematosus Support Club
8039 Nova Ct.
North Charleston, SC 29418
Support and self-help education.

Make-a-Wish Foundation of America
Box 78236
Phoenix, AZ 85062
602-240-6600
Grants a wish for a terminally ill child.

National Foundation for Asthma
Box 30069
Tucson, AZ 85751
602-323-6046
Medical and rehabilitative care.

National Foundation for Ileitis and Colitis
444 Park Ave. South
New York, NY 10016
212-685-3440
Information, research, and support groups.

National Kidney Foundation
2 Park Ave.
New York, NY 10003
212-889-2210
Research and patient services.

National Sudden Infant Death Syndrome Clearinghouse
8201 Greensboro Dr.
Suite 600
McLean, VA 22102
703-821-8955
Information exchange.

National Sudden Infant Death Syndrome Foundation
8200 Professional Plaza
Suite 104

Landover, MD 20785
301-459-3388; 800-221-SIDS
Phone service on hotline; information exchange; research.

St. Francis Center
5417 Sherier Place, N.W.
Washington, D.C. 20016
202-363-8500
Nondenominational group providing information and counseling to individuals affected by life-threatening illnesses, impairments, or other emotional difficulties associated with death.

Starlight Foundation
101000 Santa Monica Blvd.
Suite 785
Los Angeles, CA 90067
213-557-1414
Helps fulfill wishes of terminally and chronically ill children.

Sunshine Foundation
4010 Levick St.
Philadelphia, PA 19135
215-335-2622
Fulfills wishes of chronically ill or terminally ill children.

Self-Help Clearinghouses

American Conference of Therapeutic Selfhelp/Selfhealth/Social Action Clubs
Ross Towers, Apt. B 1104
710 Lodi St.
Syracuse, NY 13203
315-471-4644
Information and materials.

National Self-Help Clearinghouse
Graduate School and University Center
City University of New York
33 W. 42 St.
New York, NY 10036
212-840-1259
Information and referral for every condition and concern imaginable.

ODPHP National Health Information Center
U.S. Department of Health and Human Services
Box 1133
Washington, D.C. 20013
301-565-4167; 800-336-4797
General information and referral.

Self-Help Center
1600 Dodge Ave.
Evanston, IL 60201
312-328-0470
A clearinghouse for referral.

War

Group Project for Holocaust Survivors and Their Children
60 Riverside Dr., Apt. 3F
New York, NY 10023
212-724-2161
Preventive and reparative therapeutic work with Holocaust survivors and children.

International Network of Children of Jewish Holocaust Survivors
c/o World Jewish Congress
One Park Ave.
Suite 418
New York, NY 10016
212-755-5770
Liaison among organizations.

Veterans Education Project
Box 42130
Washington, D.C. 20015
202-686-2599
Promotes the rights of veterans.

Vietnam Veterans Agent Orange Victims
205 Main St.
Stamford, CT 06901
203-323-7478
Promotes research, legal rights, and improvement of conditions for those suffering from consequences of exposure during the Vietnam War.

Author Index

Numerals refer to annotation numbers in Part II. Numerals in parentheses refer to page numbers in Part I.

Title Index

Numerals refer to annotation numbers in Part II. Numerals in parentheses refer to page numbers in Part I.

Subject Index

Annotations are listed in this index under one or more subjects corresponding to both the key loss experience faced by the main character in the book and other loss experiences having a direct influence on the main character's life. Numerals refer to annotation numbers in Part II. Numerals in parentheses refer to page numbers in Part I.

Interest Level Index

Annotations are listed in this index only once, in the category that corresponds with the key loss experience faced by the main character in the book. The categories are the same, for the most part, as those in the book, with the exception of several that have been divided into smaller groupings for easier reference. In each category annotations have been arranged by age in ascending levels of maturity. The numerals refer to annotation numbers.

Reading Level Index

Annotations are listed in this index only once, in the category that corresponds with the key loss experience faced by the main character in the book. The categories are the same for the most part, as those in the book, with the exception of several that have been divided into smaller goupings for easier reference. In each category annotations have been arranged by grades in ascending levels of reading difficulty. The numerals refer to annotation numbers.